ARCHBISHOP LAUD

By the same author

HISTORICAL ESSAYS

THE LAST DAYS OF HITLER

WILLIAM LAUD, ARCHBISHOP OF CANTERBURY, IN 1635

ARCHBISHOP LAUD

1573—1645

BY

H. R. TREVOR-ROPER

Second Edition

MACMILLAN
London · Melbourne · Toronto

ST MARTIN'S PRESS
New York
1965

First Edition 1940
Second Edition 1962
Reprinted 1963, 1965

PRINTED IN GREAT BRITAIN

ACKNOWLEDGMENTS

WHILE writing this book I have received help from many quarters. My thanks are especially due to the Warden and Fellows of Merton College, who provided me with the leisure for its preparation : to Enid, Countess of Chesterfield, whose information led to the discovery of the Scudamore papers : to the Librarian of St. John's College (the Rev. S. L. Greenslade), the Keeper of the Muniments of Westminster Abbey (Mr Lawrence E. Tanner), and Mr. Arthur Oswald, who gave assistance on several points : to the staff of the Public Record Office and of Lambeth Palace Library : to Miss C. V. Wedgwood and Mr. David Ogg, who read the proofs and made many helpful suggestions and corrections : and to Mr. Gilbert Ryle, who, like Eve in Paradise, ranged through the whole wilderness, weeding out the solecisms, trimming the luxuriant phrases, and unmixing the metaphors.

PREFACE TO NEW EDITION

This book is now twenty-one years old. In these days of continuous research and changing historical fashions, twenty-one years is a long time: a time in which much may happen to a subject, much also to a book and its author. Any author must therefore feel pleasure if his first-born offspring survives to attain its majority. But his pleasure is likely to be tinged with some regret. As he re-reads his old work he finds so much that, if he were to write it now for the first time, he would write very differently, but which, once written, he cannot change. For unless a book is a mere compilation, its date is an essential part of it. A book expresses the author's mind at the date of writing, and that expression cannot, by mere verbal changes, be brought "up-to-date"—that is, up to another date, at which it was not written. After twenty-one years a book can only be either superficially adjusted or totally rewritten: anything between is mere deformation.

In republishing this book I have, of course, made some superficial adjustments. Such errors of fact as have come to my notice I have corrected. They are small and few and I shall not trouble to specify them. The greater changes which I would make if I were rewriting the book are of an altogether different kind. They represent a pervasive change of emphasis, the response of a historian's mind to a wider and deeper knowledge, not necessarily of the facts which he presumed to recount, but of the background which makes those facts significant in the context of history. As I am not writing a new book but republishing an old, I do not seek to effect this change: I merely, in self-defence, point it out. I ask the reader to remember that the book was written between 1936 and 1939, and not to expect me now, so long afterwards, to die in the ditch on behalf of every expression or judgment in it.

What, in fact, is this difference? A juvenile book, seen in retrospect by its author, tends to have certain standard features.

It tends to be too confident in its judgments, too clear in its definitions, and insufficiently sensitive to the complex background of politics. This book has all these features. I do not now believe that the past is basically identical with the present, though I still regard it as very similar. I do not accept, as firmly as I did, Max Weber's identification of Calvinism with capitalism, or certain other crude social equations whose periodic emergence will doubtless irritate the perceptive reader of this book. And no doubt there are other sharp phrases that I would now, in a new work, seek to blunt, and summary verdicts that I would prefer to attenuate. I like to think that, today, I would show more sympathy for Laud as a person. Perhaps I would show less sympathy for his ideals.

Basically, what I would like to add to this book is a dimension, or rather, I would like to deepen a dimension which here I have only sketched. Archbishop Laud, and those who thought with him, had a conception of society: a conception of which, I think —thanks to the shift in historical emphasis in this century—I was more conscious than his earlier biographers. But this conception was opposed by the majority of Englishmen then and would, I hope, be opposed still. In this book, as I re-read it now, I do not think that I have grossly over-simplified Laud's conception, for Laud himself had a crude, narrow mind and himself over-simplified the problems of humanity. But I think I have over-simplified the opposition to him. For in this book Laud's opponents appear as somewhat shadowy figures ranged in the dark behind leaders who are described, too often, simply as "puritans" or "Calvinists". But, in fact, behind that "puritan", "Calvinist" leadership (and how narrow, how inaccurate, these adjectives are, even if applied only to the leadership), there was a busy, substantial world whose rejection of Laudianism, both in religion and in society, was more complex than I may have suggested: the world of the inarticulate but not unsophisticated English laity who were not yet "puritan" and would only very temporarily, and in times of great crisis, accept "Calvinist" leadership. I wish that, in this book, I had more positively emphasised the role of that large and significant body of Englishmen who rejected Laud and Prynne alike (though it may have used one against the other), that elusive, still neglected force in our religious history: the English laity.

If I had done that, I would inevitably have been led further. In this book I have mentioned and illustrated the local impact of Laudianism: the struggle in every parish between the new claims of the clergy, suddenly supported and driven on from above, and the hitherto latent strength of the laity, who sought not only to defend material gains but also to realise, in their own way, and more effectively than Laud could do, a positive social religion not always different from his. If only Laud had co-operated with the laity in the pursuit of those aims which they shared, instead of driving them, by frontal attack, into temporary alliance with an opposite clericalism, how much might have been achieved, how much misfortune avoided! Instead, this frontal opposition created universal tension and imposed, for a time, an artificial simplicity on a naturally complex pattern. I wish that I had revealed this complex substructure and documented this multiple struggle more amply than I have done, though I could not have hoped to do it, then or now, as brilliantly as it has since been done by Mr. Christopher Hill in his profound and illuminating book, *Economic Problems of the Church*.

If I had given more sympathetic attention to the laity I would also necessarily have dealt more carefully with another still neglected subject: the real religious leaders of the laity. These were not, of course, the shrill " Calvinist " clergy or the eccentric separatists, who too often caught and still catch the eye, but those " moderate Anglicans " whom first Laudianism, then revolution, squeezed out and whose survivors sometimes, without real inconsistency, became " Independents ". For between anti-Laudian Anglicanism and anti-Presbyterian Independency there is a more direct connexion than is generally admitted: they were different phases in one movement, the episcopal and non-episcopal phase of an English protestantism which respected the religious claims of the laity. It was not without reason that Oliver Cromwell, in the days of Independency, gave a state-funeral to the leader of the old " moderate Anglicans ", Archbishop Ussher; or that educated, modern-minded clergy like John Wilkins and John Pell would return, under Charles II, to an Anglicanism which at last could accommodate them. Had I examined this group of men and their positive ideas more carefully, I would surely have pronounced a more favourable opinion on that opportunist episcopal politician whom so few men trusted (and one can never discount the personal distrust of contemporaries), but in all whose views and actions we can detect an enlightened sympathy with lay claims: Laud's great enemy, John Williams.

So much for Laud's adversaries; but on Laud's own side there is also, in one area at least, a complexity which deserves attention if a portrait of that strange man is to be complete. In this book I have not ignored, but perhaps I have insufficiently emphasised, the intellectual liberalism which contrasts so strongly with Laud's illiberal policies. For in his dislike of controversy Laud was perhaps not merely the martinet, more concerned with order than with truth: he was also the man who, for all his schoolman's outlook, allowed that some parts of doctrine were genuinely " indifferent ", and who, to that extent, has a foothold, however tenuous, in the noble tradition of " rational theology ". " Arminianism ", in England as in Holland, was intellectually a liberal movement: it joined hands with the " Socinianism " which it officially repudiated; and once it was separated from Laudian clericalism, it was attacked as an " Independent ", " sectarian " heresy. We should not forget that Laud and the Laudians were attacked from the Right as well as from the Left. They were attacked under that all-embracing charge of " Socinianism ". The crypto-papist Bishop Goodman accused Laud of favouring bishops Howson, Montague, Curll, Mainwaring and others " whom I suspected to be Socinians "; and the same charge of Socinianism was made against others whom we can praise him for patronising: William Chillingworth, John Hales, Jeremy Taylor.

These gaps, this missing, or rather foreshortened dimension in my book, cannot now be supplied within its old framework. They cannot even be supplied in a preface. They can only be adumbrated. But I can take this opportunity to mention some of the works, since published, which help to fill them. Apart from Mr. Christopher Hill's book, already mentioned, which sheds direct light on the tensions between Laudianism and the laity, the social attitudes of the laity, or some of them, are indirectly shown in Mr. W. K. Jordan's great work, *Philanthropy in England* 1480-1660. The puritan work of evangelisation, which Laud so mistakenly resisted, is not only illustrated in a particularly interesting passage in Mr. Jordan's second volume, *The Charities of London*; one particular episode in it, the work of the Feoffees for Impropriations, has been specially studied. Miss Isabel M. Calder has described it in detail in her article " A Seventeenth-Century Attempt to Purify the Anglican Church " (*American Historical Review*, 1947-8), and has documented it in her book, *Activities of the Puritan Faction of the Church of England* 1625-33 (1957). If Laud's " moderate Anglican " critics, Williams, Ussher, Prideaux, are still relatively neglected, his " Anglo-Catholic " colleagues have had some attention. Mr. Paul Welsby's life of Lancelot Andrewes (1958) is pleasantly unhagiographical, and there is Mr. G. Soden's biography of Godfrey Goodman (1953). The parallel introduction of " Laudianism " in Neile's province of York is illustrated in Mr. R. A. Marchant's *The Puritans and the Church Courts in the Diocese of York* 1560-1642 (1960). The incompleteness of Laud's control over lay studies in the universities is shown in Mr. Mark Curtis' illuminating work *Oxford and Cambridge in Transition* (Oxford 1959). The history of " Laud's Liturgy " in Scotland has been fully documented in Mr. Gordon Donaldson's *The Making of the Scottish Prayer Book of* 1637 (Edinburgh 1954), and the nature of the brief clerical reconquest in Ireland emerges from two excellent works: Mr. Hugh Kearney's *Strafford in Ireland* (Manchester 1959) and Mr. Terence Ranger's forthcoming study of Richard Boyle, first Earl of Cork; to which I would also add Mr. Ranger's article on Strafford in *Past and Present* 1961. Finally, though it deals explicitly with the period after Laud's death, I cannot omit Mr. R. S. Bosher's *The Making of the Restoration Settlement, The Influence of the Laudians* 1649-1662 (1951): a work which incidentally illuminates far more than it professes to describe, and is the essential complement to any study of Laud.

Such are the criticisms which, after twenty-one years, I make of this early book. I make them without undue humility, first, because the book is my own and I would not republish it if I did not, all deductions made, still think it worth publication, and secondly, because the criticisms are also my own: none of my public critics, when the book first appeared, thought of making them. Indeed, the criticisms they made were of an entirely different kind. I was reproached by some reviewers for relying only on " partisan Anglo-Catholic sources ", by others for showing an improper partiality for Dissent. These theological criticisms, though they have sometimes surprised me by their ferocity, I find that I can bear. I bear them the more easily because this book won me the public praise and private encouragement of the Anglican clergyman whom I would most have wished to please and whose name it is a pleasure to recall: Herbert Hensley Henson.

H. R. Trevor-Roper

Chiefswood
Melrose
August 1961

CONTENTS

CONTENTS

ILLUSTRATIONS

CHAPTER ONE

INTRODUCTION

THERE are certain periods of history in which, on a superficial view, the actions of men appear to have followed rules entirely different from those with which the modern world is familiar. Between the sceptical observer of the twentieth and the religious material of the seventeenth century the gulf seems at first sight so great that the common residuum of humanity appears by comparison almost negligible, and we hesitate to study characters with whom we cannot hope to sympathise. Reading of " Wars of Religion ", in which the combatants, heroically determined to establish the Kingdom of Heaven in Heaven, showed more solicitude for the posthumous condition of their neighbours' souls than for the immediate comfort of their own or their neighbours' bodies, we might pardonably conclude that all analogy between the past and the present is superfluous, since the rules of human behaviour have plainly been revised in the interim.

To some people, — to those sentimental persons who find in the past not a variation of the present but an escape from it, — this interpretation is perfectly satisfactory. But it cannot easily satisfy those who seek in history not romance but instruction, and who believe, as an historical axiom, that human nature does not change from generation to generation except in the forms of its expression and the instruments at its disposal. How can we hope to understand the actions of men whom we believe to have been actuated by passions from which we feel ourselves immune ? To suppose that grave, learned, well-intentioned divines tortured and executed less conventional believers solely to please God, or that enthusiastic philosophers sprang to arms

> To prove their doctrine orthodox
> By apostolic blows and knocks,

is to people the past with fools and bigots ; and although we know that fools and bigots, like saints and visionaries, did exist, yet we can be equally sure that it was not such as they who provided the material and the makers of history. Then, as now, they remained on the fringe of political movements, sometimes uplifted into brief eminence on the crest of a wave, sometimes waiting in obscurity for the leisure of later historians to discover them. It was not they, with their purely intellectual and spiritual ideas, who worked great changes: and the more we analyse the "Wars of Religion", the less of religion, properly so called, do we find in them. Indeed, it would be as easy to believe that the nations of Europe fought for four years over the death of an inconvenient Archduke, as that they ever fought for a hundred over the attributes of an unproven God.

What then was all the fighting about? If religion be merely a doctrine about the origins of the world and the destiny of the soul, certainly it was not about religion, as neither one nor the other of these things could be altered by revolution. But if religion be the ideal expression of a particular social and political organisation as well (and observation shows us that men prefer to idealise their political ambitions for the purpose of defending them), then we can understand why men were once prepared to fight for "religion" in a way that they will not fight for it now, when most religions have shed their political implications. The Roman religion, it is true, has not thus divorced itself from politics; and it remains a dynamic force today.

Religion, in fact, was also an aspect of politics, — the outward symbol, the shibboleth, by which parties were known: and the fact that it was also believed to be absolutely true by those who regarded its political content as convenient will surprise no one who has observed human nature. "Predestination", "No Bishops" or "A Godly Ministry" were good battle-cries, whatever they meant: and the actual requirements of those who used them so freely could not be directly expressed with such terseness. But it was not for these shibboleths that men fought and intrigued, but for the realities of which they were the superficial evidence. This point, however, should not need much labouring: for we have evidence of the same general condition on the Continent today, although the forms assumed are not now those of religious denominations. And if we wonder now how it was that men could fight so passionately over the question of bowing in church, or the position of the communion-table, our descendants will perhaps find it equally incomprehensible that among their ancestors — apparently rational creatures like themselves — the colour of a shirt, or the form of a salute, or the chalking of a symbol on a wall, should have aroused passions, led to violence, and even resulted in war. The great heresiarchs of the sixteenth and seventeenth centuries, had they legislated for the soul of man only, would have passed from the European stage as unnoticed as the great poets. But they did not legislate for the soul only, — although, like all political theorists, they began with the nature of man before proceeding to the organisation of men. " It is not wholly fanciful to say ", says Professor Tawney, " that, on a narrower stage, but with not less formidable weapons, Calvin did for the bourgeoisie of the sixteenth century what Marx did for the proletariat of the nineteenth." [1]

This is not, of course, to say that there was any hypocrisy in the behaviour of those who fought political campaigns under denominational colours, or that religion is nothing more than a political programme idealised. Religion is a complex thing, in which many human instincts are sublimated and harmonised : and political ambition is only one among these, although in politics it is naturally by far the most potent. Nor would it be suggested that the men of the seventeenth century did not believe with all their heart and soul in the doctrines which they evolved with such ingenuity, held with such tenacity, and defended with such ferocity. Being themselves inside the movements, they had not the objective outlook towards them which critical analysis requires ; and forms of expression, when the substance beneath them is alive, assume a vitality of their own. Only when the material basis is disturbed do they drop away, like flowers without roots, and the convictions of one generation become the joke of the next.

Once this postulate is admitted, other difficulties which might have hindered the understanding of those times rapidly become explicable. Take the principle of religious toleration. To us who have rendered religion impotent by dissociating it, at any rate temporarily, from politics, religious intolerance is merely inexplicable; and sympathetic biographers of the churchmen of old, when they come across the burning of a heretic in 1612 by the gentle Bishop Andrewes and the charitable Bishop Neile, or find that Neile, twenty-seven years later, recommended that a

[1] *Religion and the Rise of Capitalism* (Pelican Books), p. 111.

similar course be taken with a Dover stonemason who disapproved of episcopacy, pass it off as a sad reminder of the errors of that age, from which even its most enlightened spiritual teachers were, unhappily, not exempt. But this is surely an unwarrantable assumption of superiority in our own age, which has merely transferred its credulity to other things, attributing to pills and mixtures the miraculous properties which it denies to relics, and accepting from the advertisement hoardings dogmatic assurances which would come unheeded from the pulpit. Except by a few gentle spirits like Erasmus and Montaigne, religious toleration was considered a shocking error in the sixteenth century. The Pope officially condemned it, and did not even claim it, as a principle, for Catholic minorities. It was better, he told them, to be persecuted than tolerated : and asked whether they expected to live among thorns without being pricked.[1] Later, even Cromwell, who avowed the principle, took care to limit its practical application to those who were either sufficiently weak or sufficiently orthodox not to threaten his government. Those who were neither were outside the pale. And even those arm-chair idealists whose principles were unmodified by the necessity of applying them, while advocating toleration, were careful to distinguish between tolerable and intolerable opinions. To us, on the other hand, religious toleration is an accepted axiom. We may even go further, and say, with Tom Paine, that toleration is not enough, for toleration implies a right not to tolerate ; and that if intolerance is the Pope armed with fire and faggot, toleration is the Pope selling or granting indulgences. Must we then assume that the age of Grotius and Descartes, Hobbes and Pascal, Rubens and Harvey, was so dull and crass as not to see the obvious futility of religious persecution and the obvious necessity of toleration ? This is surely not so. Surely it was because religion was not merely a set of personal beliefs about the economy of Heaven, but the outward sign of a social and political theory, that it was enforced and persecuted by Church and State. To deny the government any control over the religious beliefs of its subjects was then equivalent to denying it any right to interfere in social and political matters. We can see well enough in our own day that governments, uncertain of their security, attempting to impose

[1] A. O. Meyer, *England and the Catholic Church under Elizabeth* (Engl. transl. 1916), p. 445.

or consolidate a new social order, cannot afford to tolerate social and political heresies in their midst.

It must be added that these facts were not unrealised at the time, though subsequent writers have tended to forget them. No one then pretended that religion was the private concern of God and the individual soul, outside the jurisdiction of the government. Religion, it was generally admitted, was the propaganda of political parties, and no one supposed that it ought to withdraw to the cloister and busy itself exclusively about theological niceties. " Religion it is that keeps the subject in obedience ", declared Sir John Eliot in 1625, and the parliament of 1628–9 voted that " whosoever shall bring in innovation in religion, or . . . seek to extend or introduce Popery or Arminianism, or any other opinion disagreeing from the true and orthodox Church, shall be reputed a capital enemy to this kingdom and commonwealth ". So it was not the religious heresy of Prynne, Burton, and Bastwick that was their chief fault or the sole reason for their persecution. " These men ", Wentworth wrote to Laud, " do but begin with the Church that they might have free access to the State ",[1] and Laud replied that it was only too true, and that he wished that more people realised it.[2] When Lord Saye and Sele accused Laud of too seldom preaching, Laud made it clear that his Church was a political instrument. " You must not measure preaching ", he replied, " by a formal going up into the pulpit. For a bishop may preach the Gospel more publicly, and to far greater edification, in a court of judicature, or at a council table, where great men are met together to draw things to an issue, than many preachers in their several charges can." [3] To accuse Laud and his bishops of interfering in social and political affairs is ridiculous : for social and political affairs were their business. It was only later, after the struggles of the century were over, that the Church of England, looking back upon them, and seeing what disasters had attended her when she backed the wrong horse in politics, decided in future to prefer safety to influence, and never to back any horse in politics again. So she withdrew, like the monarchy, from the rough-and-tumble of political life, and remained an unmolested cypher, neither loved nor hated, and approached with the decent, if meaningless, reverence allowed to the dead. Churchmen sometimes looked

[1] *Strafford Letters*, ii. 101. [2] Laud, *Works*, vi. 500. [3] *Ibid.* vi. 188.

wistfully back to her great days and, drawing a mistaken inference, said that the world had been religious then, when really it was that religion had been secular ; and laymen, judging the religion of the past from that of the present, thought it incomprehensible that men could once have been driven to revolution in defence of a set of unplausible conjectures.

So much has been said by way of preface to a life of Archbishop Laud, because Laud has so often been judged from such a point of view. Extracted from the social conditions in which he lived and with which his policy was identified, he has been regarded as a theologian whose views, independent of his age, may be judged by the eternal standard of Divine Truth, and his failure ascribed either to the wrongness of his opinions or the wickedness of the world, according to the religious denomination of the judge. To Macaulay he was " a ridiculous old bigot ": to Newman, less succinctly, " a character cast in a mould of proportions that are much above our own, and of a stature akin to the elder days of the Church "; and as his biographers and commentators have generally been either high Anglican clergymen concerned to puff, or doughty dissenters determined to slang him, these two opposite judgments have been regularly, if less eloquently confirmed. Professor David Masson undoubtedly enjoyed the picture which he gave of a red-faced little bishop trotting obediently at his master's tail :[1] a Mr. Henry Bell, a retired Indian Civil Servant and lawyer, who is not above emending his text to serve his brief, launched a furious broadside in order to counter high Anglican propaganda :[2] and Laud's clerical biographers, since they approach him on their knees, are naturally unable to see very far. Only Gardiner, who treated him not as a churchman, but as a protagonist in English history, was able to look upon Laud in that secular spirit from which alone an impartial view can come.

We must therefore regard Laud here not as a theologian who must stand or fall by the accuracy of his theological opinions, but

[1] *Drummond of Hawthornden*, p. 203.

[2] *Archbishop Laud and Priestly Government*, 1905.

The author's interpolation of the words " my Lord Keeper " in the passage quoted from Laud's speech at the trial of Sherfield (p. 122), which alters the whole purport of the passage in Laud's disfavour, is an almost incredible instance of intellectual dishonesty.

as a politician whose material was English society in the early seventeenth century. As for his divinity,

> Il n'appartient a moy, pecheur :
> Aux theologiens le remetz,
> Car c'est l'office de prescheur.

For our purposes, the state of English society in his time is more important than the intricacies of the Will of God.

The life of William Laud coincided with the period in England when the social changes initiated by Henry VIII were reaching their climax. These changes had been neither revolutionary nor violent except in the manner of their beginning, but after seventy years they had radically, if gradually, changed the whole structure of society. A pious Catholic, the hammer of Luther, decorated by the Pope, Henry VIII, with that political genius which consists in knowing the right moment at which to make a bold move, had suddenly taken the predominant class in the nation into partnership, had withdrawn his allegiance from Rome, and had assumed to himself the revenues which had previously financed the dubious politics of the Pope. There was nothing revolutionary about the programme except the thoroughness of its execution. Almost every Act which Henry secured from his obedient parliament had precedents in English history, and Henry merely re-enacted them all together. Monasteries had been dissolved by the Catholic prelates, Cardinals Morton and Wolsey. Henry V, that pillar of orthodoxy, who reasoned with heretics with apostolic conviction before sending them to the stake, had stopped payments to religious authorities abroad. Edward III had legislated against appeals to Rome. It has been said that Henry VIII did but dine off Church property, while Henry V had breakfasted. And after dinner the old king died professing himself a true believer in the Catholic faith. Had he not founded six new bishoprics out of the spoils of the monasteries ? And did not Cardinal Pole himself admit that the Ten Articles of religion which the King had issued contained " nothing much at variance with the Catholic standard except that their authorship is ascribed to the king in the text " ? Certainly Henry, in dining off Church property, had no intention of introducing heresy, — a heresy, moreover, which struck at the roots of monarchy, of which he was so thorough and successful an exponent. If he seemed to humour heretics at times, that was no more than Charles VIII had done, who found Savonarola useful, or Charles V, who kept Luther in reserve to use him against the Pope. Henry had hardly expected to go even so far as he did, — it seemed obvious to him, as to many good Catholic bishops, that the Pope would allow him the dispensation for which he applied. But his hand had been forced. As Mr. Chesterton says, " he sought to lean upon the cushion of Leo, and found he had struck his arm upon the rock of Peter ", — although it would be more accurate to say that he found the Emperor had been there first and had filched the cushion.

But if the religious changes initiated by Henry VIII were in reality slight, the economic consequences were not. It was not merely exasperation at the attitude of Clement VII, nor the stings of his own conscience, which had suggested the breach with Rome. The temptation offered by the vast estates of the Church was not to be resisted. Preserved from the attacks of Wycliffe and his followers, undiminished by the attainders and confiscations which followed the Wars of the Roses, the lands of the Church, on the eve of the Reformation, comprised one-fifth of the lands in England. For a rich institution to be arrogant and discredited is bad policy : and the Church in England was both. It was therefore without any great danger that Henry VIII launched his attack upon it to strengthen his own position. It appeared to a harassed government like some rich new market, ripe for exploitation. If Charles V had Mexico and Peru, Henry had abbeys and monasteries and rich bishoprics. The six new bishoprics which he founded were but a sop to the Almighty, to whom he had promised eighteen : and he never properly endowed even the six. Provided the economic redistribution went unchallenged, few cared to dispute the religious. Ejected abbots stepped quietly into the new bishoprics and deaneries : and, with the honourable exception of Mary's Catholic bishops, those already in possession took each new oath and used each new service-book, with the serene immobility of the vicar of Bray. Like the Marquis of Winchester, who retained his secular offices through the same changes, they could explain that they were sprung not from the oak, but from the willow. Meanwhile the inroads upon Church property, once begun, continued merrily. During the anarchy of Edward VI's minority, the pace quickened :

under Mary, Parliament willingly reintroduced all the paraphernalia of Popery so long as no attempt was made to recover Church lands: nor was there any great hankering after a purer form of religion, until England was made an appanage of Spain, — and then it was not Protestantism that protested: for Spain was using English resources to fight the Pope.

Such was the situation which Elizabeth sought to stabilise in the first year of her reign. The religion of the State, after the vertiginous changes which it had recently undergone, needed to be regulated to suit the altered circumstances. Popery was impossible. The English never had any love for the Bishop of Rome, and the Bishop of Rome had declared Elizabeth to be a bastard and a usurper. Protestantism, on the other hand, was equally unsatisfactory. By now Luther had been succeeded by Calvin: and although Calvin himself, while he had hopes of the favour of princes, disclaimed republican ideals, his followers, who found little support from kings, were less considerate and allowed the full consequences of their doctrines to emerge. Already at Elizabeth's accession, John Knox, who had sat at Calvin's feet in Geneva, had blown three separate blasts of the trumpet against the monstrous regiment of women: and before long trumpets were to be blown against the monstrous regiment of anyone at all. The great heresiarch wrote hastily from Geneva assuring Elizabeth that he had banned the republican works of Knox and Goodman in his capital, and offered to dedicate to her his commentary on the Book of Job: but she declined the dubious honour. Soon afterwards the revolt of the Netherlands against Spanish centralisation emphasised the republican tincture of Calvinism. Thirty years before James I made his aphorism "No bishop, no king", the English Puritan Thomas Cartwright, as a corollary to his statement that archbishops had come out of the bottomless pit of Hell, added that, in secular government, monarchy was equally superfluous, and that Calvin himself, having frequently been chosen moderator at Geneva, "misliked that that small preheminence should remain so long with one, as which in time might breed inconvenience".[1] By the end of the century the identification of Calvinism with republicanism was common.

Faced with this dilemma, the government of Elizabeth chose

[1] *Reply to Whitgift's Answer*, 1573.

neither one horn nor the other, but, with a knack, which never deserted it, of making the best of both worlds, devised the Elizabethan compromise. Elizabeth's church, like Elizabeth's policy, was so comprehensive that it was capable of any inconsistency without exceeding the limits of its definition. In her prayer-book the completely contradictory words of Zwingli and the Mass Book on the sacrament were neatly compressed into a single ambiguous sentence. The thirty-nine articles managed to sanction almost every known doctrine. And in policy the same latitude was observed. The government encouraged the Dutch against Spain, while refusing to countenance rebels against their sovereign. Her very choice of ministers reflected her dexterous balancing of the two parties whose aims grew ever farther apart. The Puritans Leicester and Walsingham were set off by the cautious politique Burghley: and when Walsingham died in 1590 the difficulty of finding a successor who would maintain the same delicate equilibrium caused his office to remain vacant for six years. Elizabeth guarded her prerogative carefully, — "this chiefest flower in her garden, the principal and head-pearl in her crown and diadem": but she exercised it in the direction required by the Commons. She appointed bishops, — but they were what would now be called low church bishops. A few doctrinaires might attack from left or right: but the Queen and her government remained safely in the middle, merely oscillating a little. There were no English heresiarchs to raise the banner of religious revolution, though the leaven of Protestant doctrine was imported by exiles returning from Switzerland, whither they had fled from the Marian terror. England was not seriously interested in religion, or in political theory. The one work of political theory published in England during the reign of Elizabeth, while the Continent buzzed with new heresies, was a slim volume by Sir Thomas Smith, complacently justifying the *status quo*.

The genius of the Elizabethan government was its practicality. In a world unbalanced by a multitude of theories, it paid regard to none, and prospered by refusing to yoke itself to any body of doctrine. Committed to no positive policy, it preserved its independence and its liberty, a brilliant freelance among a crowd of cumbrous combines. Meanwhile the practice of despoiling the Church went on as before. Bishoprics were no longer the great dignities which they had been in the days of Morton and Wolsey, and the new class of men who occupied them were only too glad to purchase them at the government's price, which was generally the alienation of part of their revenues. They had the less hesitation because they could always recoup themselves at the expense of their successors. So Dr. Bennet, the Master of the great Hospital of St. Cross at Winchester, despoiled the hospital in order to buy himself the deanery of Windsor. For the see of Winchester, Bishop Bilson paid £400 a year to the Queen. Drs. Coldwell and Cotton allowed Sherborne Park and Castle to be detached from the see of Salisbury for Sir Walter Raleigh as the price of securing the rest of the bishopric. The rich coal-mines of Whickham and Gateshead were easily extorted from the weak hand of the Bishop of Durham, and yielded fabulous wealth to their new and more energetic owners; and Bishops Cox and Heton made hay with the endowments of the see of Ely. The conscientious Lancelot Andrewes was considered eccentric for refusing two sees in succession on condition of alienating part of their revenues to the Queen; and the Queen herself kept the diocese of Ely vacant for 19 years in order to appropriate the revenues, that of Bristol for 30, and that of Oxford for 41. Left thus, unprotected by the government and without strength of its own, it was no wonder that the Church suffered. While Queen and courtiers picked slices off the bishoprics, country squires and speculators encroached less noticeably on glebes or charitable foundations. Nor was the Church the only sufferer, for the interests of the Church and the poor were frequently bound up together. Hospitals and almshouses maintained by the Church served the poor also: those who enclosed Church lands enclosed common lands too: and even writers who have no sympathy with the pretensions of the Church admit that the old ecclesiastical landlords were not rack-renters.[1] The new landlords, often speculators who never visited their purchases, but merely bought to resell at a profit as soon as possible, certainly were.

[1] *E.g.* Thomas Wilson, *State of England, 1600* (Camden Soc., 1936), p. 22. The causes were, of course, less personal than contemporary sufferers assumed. It was not *because* the new landlords were unscrupulous laymen that rents rose, but as the lower rents were associated with the old period when the landlords had, incidentally, been clerical, the personal connexion was easily made. In fact, American silver and the increasing profits of agriculture were more decisive than the supposed difference between lay and clerical tempers, and there is plenty of evidence that enclosure, engrossing, and rent-raising were practised by abbots of the less apathetic sort.

So the reign of Elizabeth drew to its close. It had been a splendid epoch in achievement, and no government could have handled more brilliantly a situation so full of difficulties. While ideologies hardened on the Continent, crushing out the humanism with which the century had begun, and lowering all the standards which it had once promised to maintain, England had emerged from civil war to independence and freedom, both political and intellectual, by a policy of inspired opportunism. The economic changes in society had been carried through, for better or worse, without the terrible series of wars and revolutions which had overwhelmed the Continent. Between the Scylla of a hostile Roman Church, preaching the righteousness of assassination and the right to depose offensive sovereigns, and the Charybdis of Genevan doctrine, threatening to subvert all government, Elizabeth and her obedient bishops cruised with agility and success. Whether the communion-table was or was not an altar, whether the sacraments were or were not the body and blood of Christ, — these were questions about which they did not greatly care : and their ambiguous and evasive answers were to be a source of some embarrassment to their successors, who did.

The death of Elizabeth marked the end of an age. The great figures of her reign had for the most part gone before her, and those who survived lingered uneasily in the next generation like ghosts after sunrise. The versatile soldiers, scholars, and diplomats, — Sir Walter Raleigh, Sir Henry Wotton, Sir Henry Savile, Sir Thomas Bodley, Sir Thomas Roe, — are irrelevant ornaments rather than protagonists in the early seventeenth century, whose great characters are of a less subtle mould, — Strafford, Laud, Pym, Cromwell, Milton, and Hobbes. The reign of James I is like morning twilight, behind which the great and decisive events of the next reign are slowly awakening.

Many causes conspired to produce this result. First of all, the agrarian revolution had run its course. Throughout the reign of Elizabeth, the progressive classes, the improving landlords, the shrewd speculators, the manufacturers, traders, and colonists, who consecrated their individualism by the profession of a strenuous Protestantism, had set the pace to the government : and the government, apprehending the consequences of both their practice and their professions, had kept them at bay by sanctioning the plunder of the Church. By 1600 this process could hardly go further. The poverty and discredit into which that once splendid institution had fallen since the government first withdrew its protection was obvious to all. " It is not long ", wrote one observer, " since you should not ride or go through country or town but you should meet such troops of these priests' retinue as exceeded 100 or 200 of these caterpillars, neither fit for war nor other service, attending upon this pontifical crew, furnished and appointed in the best manner that might be " : but now, " to say the truth, their wings are well clipped of late by courtiers and noblemen, and some quite cut away, both feather, flesh, and bone " : and he added that England had prospered accordingly.[1] The natural stoppage of this process, however, entailed a further change. Those who had profited by the boom and had made their fortunes were now settling down into the comfortable estates which they had secured : while those whose appetites had only been whetted, not satisfied, had to look around for fresh outlets. One such outlet was in the West Indies : but King James' peace with Spain soon stopped that too, and they had to look nearer home. The Church had been a wealthy corporation defended not by its own activity but by privilege. So were the monopolists, — the courtiers to whom the Queen gave lucrative patents, thus robbing the enterprising merchant of his legitimate market. Would not the government withdraw its protection from them too ? So, when the ecclesiastical scapegoat was dead, government and enterprising subjects found themselves face to face : and one of the last actions of Elizabeth was the use of her prerogative to renounce monopolies.

There was another side, too, to the picture. The removal of the danger from abroad, followed by the peace with Spain, had concentrated the attention of Englishmen on England : and there it was obvious that individual initiative, though it alone can achieve progress, is bound, if widespread and unchecked, to lead to social dislocation. The government of Elizabeth had done something to regulate the new social conditions, but it had not kept pace with the change; and from the end of the century observers became uneasily conscious of the existing malaise. With the victory of the enterprising had gone the decline of the

[1] Thomas Wilson, *State of England*, 1600 (Camden Miscellany, xvi., Camden Soc., 1936), pp. 38, 23.

weak, — of the Church and of the poor; and although the Church by itself could excite little sympathy, it might attract the attention of the charitably-disposed by association with the poor, whom it could claim to have protected because it was theoretically supposed to have protected them. So in the religiously-inclined and the socially-conscious arose a crop of queasy doubts. Was it not time now to regulate private appetites in the name of social solidarity? Had the spoliation of the Church been altogether a good thing? And if not, was not this perhaps the divine punishment for the sin of sacrilege? What of the old monasteries, too, — were they as black as they had been painted by those who were anxious to buy up their property? Had they not performed a vital service to society, — a service now unhappily neglected? The answer was, of course, that in practice they had not. In practice we know that monastic charity was the exception rather than the rule, and that the scraps which should have gone to the poor were frequently kept to feed the monastic packs of hounds. But the idealists did not look back to the practice, but to the theory which it failed to fulfil.

One of those whose conscience was thus perplexed was a learned antiquary, Sir Henry Spelman, who, in 1594, had cheerfully bought the leases of a couple of disestablished abbeys. It was not a profitable bargain, for the antiquary was not a good business-man, and he found himself involved in a series of expensive lawsuits, whereby "he first discovered the infelicity of meddling with consecrated places". Thereupon he set himself to investigate the question which he had raised. His tithes he returned to the Church, and in 1613 he published the result of his research under the title *De Non Temerandis Ecclesiis*, — a book which, though mainly nonsense, exercised some influence on his devouter contemporaries. The rest of his life was spent in the preparation of an amply documented *History of Sacrilege* from the earliest times. As for the monasteries, — the convivial and gossipy John Aubrey thought it was a pity they had been destroyed: but that was because he would so have liked to travel from monastery to monastery in search of good wine and tittle-tattle, as he travelled from country house to country house. The more unpractical side of that movement was exemplified by the eccentric family of Ferrar, whose establishment at Little Gidding, with its finicky devotions and studied odour of sanctity, contrasts comically with the frank worldliness and open jobbery of the undissolved monasteries.

This difference in social theory, and the religious colouring appropriate to it, was further emphasised both by the growing self-expression of the middle classes in England, and by the example of the Continent. As long as the attack on the English Church had been carried out by the Crown and the nobility, its character, like its purpose, was purely secular. No one need regard Henry VIII's Duke of Norfolk, who thanked God that he had never read the Scripture, and declared that it was merry England before all this New Learning came in, as a religious crank. Neither the calculated spoliation under Henry VIII, nor the frank and systematic orgy of speculation under Edward VI, was inspired by any doctrinal enthusiasm. But later, as the Norfolks and Northumberlands were followed by new and smaller men, — the middle classes now pushing their way to prominence and eager to salve their consciences by the profession of a suitable superstition, — the proceedings inevitably assumed a religious tinge. For while it is a general axiom that scepticism spreads from the upper classes downwards, it is equally true that religion, as St. Paul says, begins from beneath. While the English aristocracy fleeced a discredited institution without humbug or sanctimony, in Germany and Switzerland the theorists of the Reformation gathered like locusts in the fat middle-class trading cities; and the reign of Elizabeth saw English bishoprics, whose diminished splendour and dwindling revenues had ceased to tempt the aristocracy, in the hands of bourgeois clergymen who had spent the winter of Mary's reign in Switzerland, — Jewel, Cox, Grindal, Pilkington. From these sources, and among these classes, the Puritan religion spread to hallow and consecrate the Puritan outlook of the business man. If the Queen sought to keep it out of her own chapel, she suffered it to grow in the Universities and the country: for she could not stop it, and, temporarily at least, it was better than Rome. When her old servant, Sir Walter Mildmay, founded Emmanuel College, Cambridge, in 1584, on the site of an old Dominican house, to disseminate his own Protestant notions, the Queen granted a charter to the work of charity and edification, but she did not conceal her misgivings. "I hear, Sir Walter", she said, "that you have been erecting a

Puritan foundation": and Sir Walter modestly replied that he had but planted an acorn, "which, when it become an oak, God alone knows what will be the fruit thereof". The fruit, however, did not belie the seed, and Emmanuel College became such a notorious hotbed of Puritanism in the next generation that any member of it was automatically suspect.[1] In 1603 its unconsecrated chapel, its unorthodox doctrines, and its irregular services, aroused official complaint.[2] In 1615, when James I visited Cambridge, the rest of the University broke out into demonstrations of colourful orthodoxy:

> But the pure House of Emmanuel
> Would not be like proud Jezebel,
> Nor show herself before the King
> An hypocrite or painted thing:
> But, that the ways might all prove fair,
> Conceiv'd a tedious mile of prayer.[3]

Later, the unregenerate ways of the college were to distress Archbishop Laud. Among the prominent Puritans of his time, Yates, Stoughton, Hooker, Bastwick, Bridges, Burroughes, Cotton, and the second Earl of Warwick were all old Emmanuel men; and when Bishop Corbett looked for a seminary to which to attribute the crazy visions of his "Distracted Puritan", it could only be "the House of pure Emmanuel".[4]

The Calvinism of Cambridge University was emphasised in the last twenty years of the sixteenth century by the activities of one William Perkins, of Christ's College. Known in his undergraduate days as "Drunken Perkins" he had suffered a spiritual regeneration, and now, as a fellow, he drew crowds to his lectures, eager to hear the difficult doctrines of Calvin expounded in moral terms, and the undoubted damnation of others illustrated with terrifying detail, — for we are told that "he would pronounce the word 'Damn' with such an emphasis as left a doleful echo in his auditors' ears a good while after".[5] Peter Baro, the Lady Margaret professor of divinity at Cambridge, a Frenchman who

[1] Cf. Brent's report of his visitation in 1635, in which he says that at Warwick he found "a Mr. Roe, an Emmanuel man, who is much suspected. I could not fasten anything upon him, though I charged him with many things." (*S.P. Dom. Car. I.* 293, no. 128.)

[2] B.M. Add. MS. 32093, p.175.

[3] *Poems of Corbett* (ed. Gilchrist, 1807), p. 14.

[4] *Ibid.* p. 243.

[5] Fuller, *Holy State* 1652, p. 80.

had learnt Calvinism from Calvin himself, but had later deviated from the strict orthodoxy of his master, was forced to flee from the University to escape expulsion after a difference with Perkins: and when Perkins was safely coffined, the great Arminius wrote an answer to one of his works. These works had gone through fifteen editions at the time of his death, and continued best-sellers for many years. They were translated into Latin, Dutch, and Spanish: they penetrated to Wales, where Perkins' graphic comparison of the pains of Hell with those of toothache converted Vavasour Powell, who suffered from the latter, to his austere gospel rather than face the former; and thirty years after his death, Laud's visitors found Perkins' books commoner than the Prayer Book in Puritan districts.

Such was the state of Cambridge: and even Oxford, which had never been so ardent in the cause of reform as her sister University, was at this time little better. Under the chancellorship of the Puritan Leicester, "the face of the University", according to Wood, "was so much altered, that there was little to be seen of the Church of England according to the principles and positions upon which it had been reformed". The University was described as "a colony from Geneva", and the chair of divinity was held by a long succession of Calvinists, — Humphrey, Holland, Robert Abbot, Benefield, Prideaux.

About the turn of the century, when the minds of men were exercised in this fashion about social and religious questions, it was natural that they should again look to the Continent, from which all doctrinal novelties had hitherto come. The Continent, too, invited inspection. For there, while England had prospered by a hand-to-mouth policy comparatively free from positive doctrines, the rival ideologies, sharpened by definition and made realistic by practice, had crystallised into their final form. The states of Europe had made their choice: and the doctrines of Geneva and Trent, with all their implications, faced each other from their established thrones, offering to still hesitant governments no choice but one of them.

First there was the Roman system, impressive in its antiquity, tried by experience, and confirmed by success. To the static society of the Roman Empire it had been loosely applied: and even after the impact of new forces at the Reformation it remained, and remains, fitted to an agricultural community. Designed to secure order and stability, it postulated the existence of a strong central government to regulate the conflicting appetites of the subjects : and such a strong government, its champions could urge, could not be relied upon regularly and noiselessly to emerge from the shifting balance of power among struggling parties. It must be imposed from above, not emerge from beneath. The law administered by this government, similarly, must not depend upon the success now of this group of interests, now of that. It must be something objective, imposed from outside upon all alike as a guarantee of justice and security. If government is made the prize of a victorious interest, who knows what selfish legislation may not ensue ? It might indeed be said that individual conscience would restrain the victor from exploiting his victory at the expense of the defeated : but individual consciences show a remarkable tendency, without conscious hypocrisy, to

> Compound for those sins they're inclined to
> By damning those they have no mind to.

Would it not be better to entrust this task of restraint to a corporate conscience which will take cognisance of all the inclinations of its members, — a Church, paid to know good and evil, and so to direct the government that it shall eschew evil and pursue good in the performance of its tasks ? There must be a discretionary power somewhere ; would it not be better to establish one, to give it an official position and the unquestioned prestige which is attached to traditional authority, even when it is not (as in this case it is) founded by the explicit injunction of God, rather than to leave it to chance, to human whims, perhaps to force, with Chaos umpire ? The same regulation would, of course, have to apply to intellectual as to material speculation. As individual initiative in the sphere of action would be subject to the surveillance of the government, acting in the interest of the community as decided by the Church out of Holy Scripture, so a like censorship would control individual discoveries or ideas which might lead to individual action or undermine the philosophic basis of the perfect society. People who made irrelevant objections (such as, that there was no warrant for all this in the Gospels, or that in fact the earth is not the centre of the universe) were just as dangerous to the delicate and elaborate structure of politics as those who sought to shift the balance of power in society by an excessive insistence on their own economic interests. In the name of justice, a certain amount of regimentation is essential.

There is, of course, a possible objection, — that the people who live under this perfect system might not be content with its limitations. Well-fed people like to express themselves in some external sphere. Full of life and health, they like to impose themselves upon the world around them. They have ambitions which, if thwarted, might be dangerous. They might not be content to have their government run by officials, their religion controlled by priests, their intellectual food handed out from above, licensed by the government. This danger was not overlooked by the architects of the Roman system. The layman, if originality in some spheres was denied to him, was compensated in others. The Church, however austere her priests might be, was not going to foster the dangers of repression in healthy worldlings. If they were natural introverts, they would be sent to a monastery where they would be kept orthodox: otherwise they were encouraged to express themselves in innocent recreations. Eschewing the austere morality of Tertullian, the Church came to the practical decision that beer is better than heresy, and that the duty of the layman, as Mgr. Talbot put it, is to hunt, to shoot, and to entertain, and to leave doctrine to his priests. So, in the Catholic states, holidays, beanfeasts, carnivals, processions, local pageants, commemorations, pagan rites, folk-dances, and every form of junketing, were discreetly blessed by the Church for the occupation of the layman on those occasions when his obedience was not required.

Such, briefly and in its ideal form, was the Catholic system, — a system in which a government placed above the community applied administrative law throughout a carefully regulated society, ensuring that administrative efficiency which, after all, is as much as most people require of a government. Except for the fact that the Church, according to the Jesuit theory, was placed on an altogether higher plane than the State so that, in the case of a refractory monarch, it could use the people as its secular arm to dethrone him, this was the old Roman system, — the Pax Romana of the Empire as well as of the Church. It represented the triumph of justice, order, and stability over the acquisitive appetites and anti-social discoveries of individuals, — a vast ant-heap so perfectly regulated that it needs no modification,— "the Bee-hive of the Roman Church" as Marnix of St. Aldegonde called it,—a system of impressive permanence and solidity, for which there is undoubtedly much to be said, so long as man lives by bread and faith alone. The gravest objection is that man is not always content with bread, but has frequently an invincible hankering after cake, and that some few men are not content with faith in revelation, but find themselves impelled to seek truth by enquiry.

Those who seek truth by enquiry will ultimately resent the restrictive dogmas of any revealed religion: but for those who preferred cake for some to bread for all, Calvinism was undoubtedly the most comfortable spiritual assurance. Admittedly it could offer nothing so complete as the Roman system: but as it was not, like the Roman system, adapted to a static society, it did not require finality. It was moreover the attacking power, and was never so securely entrenched as its adversary was. It could rely partly upon non-Calvinist but anti-Catholic support, and had allies in every sect which repudiated the authority of Rome. It was a doctrine for the mercantile classes who, having acquired wealth, looked for power, and found power denied to them under the Roman system. As a natural result, aided by the intellectuals who would never follow them to their positive conclusions, they found all kinds of defects in the Catholic interpretation of Scripture, and undertook to interpret it anew. Come unto me, said Calvin, and you shall find that you have been chosen by God. Labour with this conviction, and you shall be rewarded: your camels and concubines and all the beasts of your field shall increase: you shall gather in honours with your right hand and more substantial profits with your left, though the right hand know not what the left hand doeth. No self-appointed authority shall restrict your legitimate enterprises by its undeserved privileges, but the race shall be to the swift and the battle to the strong. Laws shall not be made for you,—you shall make them. Government shall not be let down upon you from the clouds, relying upon an army of specialists and a system of hieratic mumbo-jumbo, but shall be carried out by the industrious and chosen majority, making wars and statutes for the furtherance of the glory of God and the interests of His Elect.

Calvinist theology was indeed stark and rigid. Like Roman theology, it appealed to the wavering soul by its imposing completeness, its categorical answer to every question, its firm denial of the possibility of any doubt. For if there is one thing upon which people insist, especially in matters, like religion, upon which there can be no possibility of certainty, it is certainty. A revealed religion, stating dogmatically that 2 = 3, will be accepted by thousands, while the most persuasive system of philosophy is rarely believed implicitly even by its founder; and advertisers win far more converts to their patent foods by asserting that they are infallible than philosophers to their theories by proving that they are right. Politically, however, Calvinism drew greater strength from the very fact of its opposition to Rome. As a constructive theory, history has shown its inadequacy: but as a temporary expedient for changing the basis of society, thanks to its bold assumption of the weapons of revolution and to the uncompromising challenge of its manifesto, it was hailed as the leader of all those weaker and less determined sects which, in their different ways, opposed the despotic hierarchy of Rome. And in predominantly mercantile and manufacturing countries it triumphed.

Such were the two systems between which the government of James I in England was invited to choose. Across the Channel each party exhibited the excellence of its finished wares: and nowhere was the antithesis more marked than in the country with which the English people had long been most intimate, — the Netherlands. Six years after the death of Elizabeth, a truce between Spain and the Netherlands fixed the boundary between the reconquered and the free provinces roughly where it has since remained, and while the North continued the practice of the Calvinism which, in the course of the struggle, it had adopted, in the South the Catholic system was imposed *à merveille*. The reconquered provinces were governed by officials who received their policy ready-made from the Escorial. A Spanish court set the fashion in taste. A Dominican confessor sat at the ear of the Archduke. In Louvain the political doctrines of the Roman Empire, that the Sovereign is the State, and the religious doctrines of the Jesuits, that the Pope is the Church, were blandly repeated, and in the rest of the country either applauded or ignored, but not disputed.

The Counter-Reformation enjoyed its triumph by teaching its recovered subjects to forget it in bread and games blessed by Church and State. The trade of the Southern Netherlands was ruined by the policy of Spain : but there was no discontent, no resistance. Unity and Uniformity, the platform of the Counter-Reformation, were accepted as a boon which ensured peace and security and did not prevent the enjoyment of colourful pageantry, popular festivals, and the other safety-valves of autocracy. The intellectual life which accompanied and reflected this form of rule was, of course, non-political. There was a cosmopolitan culture, and connoisseurs of it. To admire what had already been pronounced admirable was orthodox and safe. The intellectual product of a self-conscious Catholicism was as negligible here as elsewhere. Its peculiar contribution to the arts has always been in correct magnificence rather than in bold ideas : and the gorgeous colours and rich exuberance of Rubens are the pictorial counterpart of the categorical splendour of Bossuet.

In the North it was far otherwise. The history of Belgium proves, by its absence, the success of the Catholic government : for to the Catholic there is no history, merely the regular working of the divinely ordained machinery, varied only by changes in the official personnel. But in Holland the seventeenth century is a period of intellectual ferment, political experiments, and economic expansion. Not indeed because Calvinism triumphed there, — for Calvinism was itself, had it ever been perfectly realised, as exclusive, as levelling, as tyrannical, as the Catholicism of the Counter-Reformation could ever be, — but because, through the cracks of an imperfectly established Calvinist discipline there was room for individual ideas to emerge. There we can see the struggle of ideas between Calvinists and Remonstrants : the continual resistance of local particularism to attempts at coercion by the States-General : the duel between the House of Orange and the mercantile oligarchy : the series of revolutions, which must have convinced the Southerners of the superiority of their form of government, which enabled them, like the saints in St. Augustine's Heaven, to derive half their bliss from watching the agonies of tormented sinners : the expansion of trade in the Baltic, in Africa, in America, and in the East Indies : and a ferment of ideas liberated by the speculations of free minds, in contrast to the safe sterility of a disciplined state.

What compromise could there possibly be between two such systems? The sixteenth century, it seemed, had evolved two possible worlds between which agreement appeared impossible, and the seventeenth century had to choose whether it would commit itself to one or to the other. On the whole, after years of struggle, decision had gone by states. France had chosen the Catholic, Spain the Catholic, Holland the Calvinist world. Which would England choose?

Of course it was too much to hope that opinions should be absolutely determined by political frontiers. The complete regimentation of the twentieth century was not possible when communications were bad and central control far from complete, and fresh cracks were continually breaking out within national frontiers. In Catholic France the Jansenists were soon to revolt from Jesuit doctrines, and, like all the more intolerant heretics, appealed to St. Augustine, — a saint whose orthodoxy was so unimpeachable, and whose authority was so great, that both Calvin and Loyola claimed him for their own. And all Europe watched with interest while the same rift opened in Calvinist Holland, where Arminius raised his voice against the relentless rigidity of the orthodox dogma, from which, he said, it could only result "that God is the author of sin: nor this alone, but that God really sins: nay, that only God sins". He was at once accused of falling into the error of Pelagius, — an amiable heretic who had opposed St. Augustine on the question of free will, and had scandalised that oracle of orthodoxy by suggesting that such academic differences should not be taken seriously. Augustine and Pelagius lived again in the early seventeenth century, and the true meaning of St. Augustine was the object of as much unprofitable speculation as has ever been expended on the equally inscrutable mind of God. An obscure predestinarian of the ninth century, one Gottschalk, more successful as a poet than a theologian (he was the author of "O quid jubes pusiole"), was also unearthed: and those who found themselves abused by the unco guid as Pelagians learned to use the name of Gottschalk as a retaliatory insult. There were even a few separatists who appealed from St. Augustine to Christ: but they were sharply condemned by all denominations. These complications only added to the difficulties of the still uncommitted English government. But sanguine observers might at least remind themselves that the new King was known as a man of great erudition, who could doubtless understand these perplexing questions.

James I, having been educated in the school of Scottish politics, was well trained in the art of political lying and prevarication. Having made his initial errors in his northern kingdom, he ascended the English throne a cautious man, merely thanking God that he could now let himself go in the matter of expenditure ; and throughout a reign of twenty-two years he managed to avoid committing himself to any definite decision on any subject. He expressed himself, it is true, with some warmth on the subject of prerogative : but prerogative was a fragile and precious thing, exhibited frequently to impress the beholder, but unable to stand the strain of actual use. And his theological learning was similarly a collector's piece, less for the solution of enigmas than for spectacular display, that the world might be dazzled by the sight of the British Solomon shining in controversy with cardinals and professors. In actual practice he wished only for peace : and as controversy is not the mother of peace, he was soon obliged to make it a royal monopoly, and rely upon a series of ingenious dodges rather than a consistent policy in order to postpone the dilemma of a choice made all the more difficult by postponement. All around him, rival forces struggled for mastery. James kept out of the struggle, and theorised his inactivity into a doctrine of *laisser faire*, a policy of letting sleeping dogs lie and not noticing when they woke up. Abroad the Counter-Reformation, nerved by the work of the Jesuits and the Propaganda, was gaining ground. Arminius in Leyden was splitting the doctrinal unity of the Netherlands. The political dispute between Venice and the Pope threatened to lead to the apostasy of the Republic. James I liked to play with fire. He had a finger in all these pies. He admonished the government of the Netherlands to preserve unsullied the primitive purity of its Calvinism. He recommended the Venetians to come to no terms with Rome. He favoured the project of a Protestant seminary in the Valtelline as an advance-guard of the Reformed religion, a counterpart to the Catholic seminary at Douai. He even contemplated a school for Protestant controversialists — King James' College at Chelsea — that the English Church might have her Jesuits, and actually got as far as the nomination of the first members. But he had no intention of committing himself in any of these dangerous projects. He only meant to use Protestantism, of whose subversive implications he was well aware, not to extend its influence ; and in fact every one of these plans came safely to nothing. For while Solomon owed his reputation for wisdom to the decisions which he made, the British Solomon owed his to the skill with which he avoided making decisions. " It is true ", he told his parliament at the end of his reign, " a skilful horseman doth not always use the spur, but must sometimes use the bridle and sometimes the spur. So a king that governs evenly is not bound to carry a rigorous hand over his subjects upon all occasions, but may sometimes slacken the bridle, yet so as his hands be not off the reins." Thus King James jogged along, using now the spur and now the bridle : and when his past actions were brought up against him, he had conveniently forgotten them. To improve his prospects of succeeding to the English crown, he had written to the Pope, hinting at the chance of an impressive convert, should the English Catholics be instructed to vote aright. Later, relations with the Holy See were badly damaged by the Gunpowder Plot, and the Roman court published the letter. But James found a compliant secretary to take the blame, condemned him to death, reprieved him, and restored him to favour. When Puritan pressure grew at home, James became a crusader for the Protestant faith,—abroad. In 1611, when Vorstius, the disciple of Arminius, was appointed to fill his master's chair at Leyden, James, as the champion of true Calvinism, wrote to the States-General protesting against the advancement of " that wretched heretique, or rather atheist ", and threatening, if the States-General " suffered hereafter such pestilent heretiques to nestle among them ", to summon a General Council of the Reformed Churches " to extinguish and remand to Hell these abominable heresies " : and secretary Winwood instructed the English ambassador at the Hague to declare the religious ties between the two countries broken. Later, James wrote in a more tolerant mood, saying that he had studied the points of difference involved, and had reached the conclusion that both doctrines were compatible with salvation. But in 1618, partly to be avenged on Oldenbarnevelt, who had redeemed the cautionary towns from the impecunious monarch at a bargain price, he sent official delegates to the Synod of Dordt, and expressed his satisfaction at the discomfiture and condemnation of the Arminians.

To justify this policy, James, with his usual combination of intellectual shrewdness and blindness to important issues, advocated the principle of toleration. "I did ever hold persecution as one of the infallible notes of a false Church", he wrote to the Earl of Salisbury:[1] in which case he must have been hard put to it to find a true Church in his day. Good Puritans were agog at such a doctrine which, they assured him, would but establish "the damnable and heretical doctrine of the Church of Rome, the Whore of Babylon"; and they were right. For toleration is a virtue which depends both on the unimportance of the issues involved and reciprocal toleration from the other party, and in this case neither of these conditions was fulfilled. At Rome, England was still regarded as the head of the Reformed Church, whose defeat would entail the collapse of heresy in Europe: and though the idea of a military conquest had perforce been abandoned, there were other weapons in the armoury of Antichrist. A policy of friendly intercourse had been adopted, and the Pope, like the wolf in the fable, took to sucking lozenges and speaking with a honeyed tongue. Cardinal Allen, in his last days, had greeted English Protestants in Rome and showed them round the sights of the Holy City with ingratiating charm, while his bellicose rival, Fr. Parsons, kicked his idle heels in Valladolid. To many observers, like Sir Henry Wotton, this friendly dalliance between England and Rome seemed more dangerous than open enmity: and in fact, a single year of James' unilateral toleration gave to Rome 10,000 proselytes, including 200 students from Oxford which, during the whole reign of Elizabeth, had only lost two or three converts to Popery.

James I has always cut rather a ridiculous figure in English history: and that largely because he was immune from the destructive enthusiasms of his contemporaries. His shrewdness and perception cannot be denied. Pressed on either side by the clamours of rival zealots, he exhibited the cold common sense of Gallio and the unheeded prevision of Cassandra, ridiculous only because no one minded him. Did he not warn his son that he

[1] *Correspondence of Robert Cecil* (Camden Soc., 1860), p. 37.

would live to have his bellyful of parliaments? Did he not tell Buckingham that, by reviving impeachment, he was making a rod with which he would one day be scourged himself? Did he not insist that Laud would drive Puritans to revolution if in power? And did he not say that it was an ill-fangled platform to make the stubborn Kirk of Scotland stoop to an English pattern? And yet all this wisdom in the details of politics was wasted, for he never took any steps to make it practical. Instead of coping with these questions at their material roots, he studied them only in their intellectual blooms, subjecting to his judgment as an idea what might more profitably have been tackled by his statecraft as a task. As a result, the individualism in society which had begun to cause doubts at the beginning of his reign continued unchecked, except when it actually came into conflict with the prerogative of the King. Promoting each side equally, James I relied on holding the balance himself in order to evade such a conflict; and then he found that he was not permitted to do so, but remained an omniscient umpire whom no one consulted. By refusing to theorise, and by the exercise of day-to-day dexterity, Elizabeth had succeeded in manipulating both parties and comprising both definitions within one elastic frame. By the time of James I, however, the two parties had outgrown such tutelage, and the King, seeking to continue the tactics of his predecessor, found that he could do no more than manipulate himself so as to avoid kidnap at the hands of one or the other. Meanwhile, on each side, men of more determination and less wisdom were waiting to raise the issue which he was so carefully deferring.

Throughout the reign of James I the adherents of that party had been gaining ground which, for social or doctrinal reasons, regretted the thoroughness of the Reformation. The papal connexion appealed, of course, to very few: it had never been popular, and could no longer be useful. And few went so far as to contemplate the revival of the obsolete monastic system, except one or two incorrigible romantics. But the Roman system, with its great ideals of responsibility, order, and justice, had an appeal of its own, quite apart from the usurper who had appropriated them, or the temporary accretions which it had assumed and could deposit: and this appeal was especially strong to those who were conscious of a growing social anarchy. Besides this social aspect, to which it owed its political power, the Roman system had, too, a variety of personal appeals whereby individuals were drawn to its support, — its traditional antiquity, its aesthetic perfection, its comfortable philosophy. By these attractions many eloquent and influential men were predisposed to favour it, like Sir Thomas Browne, who refused to regard the Church of England as a creation of Henry VIII, and loved to lose himself in an *O Altitudo*. Then there were the theologians who looked for a body of doctrine intellectually more complete than that of the Bible only, less radical than that of the Reformers. They declined to disown the Early Fathers, and claimed for the English Church the continuance of the apostolic tradition which had been usurped and corrupted by medieval Rome. After all, Henry VIII had never broken with Catholic doctrine, — he had merely purified it of some expensive abuses. But Henry VIII had been responsible for the economic ruin of the Church to which the social injustice which had followed could be attributed : so there were others who approached it from this side. The power of the Church, whereby it had been able to enforce social justice, these men could say, had been due to its economic position. It had been a great estate of the realm, had attracted the best men to its service, and was thereby able both to defend itself and enforce its decisions. " Bishops ", said Selden, " were formerly one of these two conditions : either men bred canonists and civilians, sent up and down ambassadors to Rome and other parts, and so by their merit came to that greatness ; or else great noblemen's sons, brothers, and nephews, and so born to govern the state. Now they are of a low condition, their education nothing of that way : — he gets a living, and then a greater living, and then a greater than that, and so comes to govern." [1] So these men saw that the restoration of the influence of the Church depended upon the restoration of its economic preponderance, and — whether by scruples of conscience, like Spelman, or by the realisation of a great mission, like Montague — came to demand not simply a reversion to the doctrines of Henry VIII, but a restoration of the wealth of which Henry and his successors had deprived the Church. From all these causes, and for all these purposes, a group of men came together in the

[1] *Table Talk* (" Bishops in the Parliament ").

slack days of James I to advocate positive doctrines. They could claim good English antecedents : for ever since the Reformation their views had been represented in some quarters, — by Hooker, who preached an apostolic English Church, even by Whitgift, who chose to redeem rather than to alienate the lands of his sees, and by Bancroft who repudiated parliamentary control of the Church ; but their contemporaries, preoccupied with the acute doctrinal differences of the Continent, called them Arminians after the " Pelagian " heretic of Leyden. It is true that their doctrines were in many ways dissimilar from his, but we may nevertheless call them, without misunderstanding, by the name which their contemporaries used. For their contemporaries were not principally interested in their doctrines : and one of them, being asked, in the reign of Charles I, what the Arminians held, merely replied that they held the best bishoprics and deaneries in England.

In the days of James I, only one of the leaders of this party held high office, and to him all the others, who languished unpreferred in the wilderness, looked as to their leader. This was Lancelot Andrewes.

Lancelot Andrewes had been educated at Cambridge, where the Puritan party, observing his great learning, sought to enrol him among them. But Andrewes, who had surprised these strict sabbatarians playing bowls one Sunday on a private green, was unimpressed by their sincerity and gave them no satisfaction. After taking his degree, he rose through the usual series of university fellowships, chaplaincies, and livings, and soon attracted the attention of Queen Elizabeth, who liked scholarship and herself possessed it, by the euphuistic elegance of his preaching. She offered him the bishopric of Salisbury : but he refused to share the revenues with her, and it went to a more compliant clergyman. She offered him Ely, on similar terms : but again he declined. And when King James made him Bishop of Chichester in 1605, he could congratulate himself on reaching eminence without simony. From Chichester he was translated to Ely, from Ely to Winchester, and there he died, having surprised many by failing to obtain Canterbury when it was vacant. From his episcopal throne he defined the doctrine of the apostolic English Church in controversy with the Jesuit Cardinal Bellarmine, preached sermons of unreadable preciosity, assisted in the translation of the Bible, and instilled into the faithful the necessity of good works as well as faith. His learning, his munificence, and his eloquence made him universally admired : and his refusal to take any part in politics, though a Privy Councillor, rendered him quite safe. " The world wanted learning to know how learned this man was ", wrote Fuller, " so skilled in all, especially Oriental, languages, that some conceive he might (if then living) have served as an interpreter-general at the Confusion of Tongues." He corresponded with the most eminent scholars of his time. He was consulted by Bacon concerning his philosophical works. His munificence was famous. Since the Reformation, English bishops had been so consistently engaged in pillaging the Church that it was remarkable when one of them set the example of enriching it. " To do good and distribute forget not, for with such sacrifices God is well pleased ", was the text of the funeral sermon preached for him by Bishop Buckeridge. Confident in his own unimpeachable orthodoxy, he asserted the divine right of episcopacy and the necessity of Anglican orders, suggesting to James I that the new Scots bishops be first ordained priests ; but in correspondence with Dumoulin, the French Protestant, he graciously forgave the Huguenots for their lack of bishops owing to the political circumstances of their reformation. For Andrewes was a professor rather than a churchman, and politics he regarded as outside the Church, whose doctrines only he expounded and annotated. At the council-table he refused to give an opinion except upon ecclesiastical matters. When the King asked him and Bishop Neile whether he might not tax his subjects without their consent, Neile at once replied that His Majesty was the breath of their nostrils and undoubtedly possessed that right : but Andrewes discreetly said no more than, " I think Your Majesty may take my brother Neile's money, since he offers it ". Entirely unpolitical, he was entirely unobjectionable. The poet Crashaw, who became a Roman Catholic, admired him. To the high-church firebrand Richard Montague he was " Gamaliel noster ". Laud and Buckeridge edited his works. The low-church Fuller dilated in his praises. And when he died, with all the apparatus of sanctity, his soul was escorted to Heaven in elegant Latin elegiacs by the young Puritan Milton.

Andrewes was a man after James' own heart : one who, in

the serene detachment of an assured position and a clear conscience, displayed his learning and advanced his theories without disturbing the world by any dangerous attempt to apply them : one who, when the Church which he represented fulfilled a vital function in a dynamic society, preferred to regard it as an aesthetic thing, and, as a modern admirer has said of him,

contemplando gustò di quella pace.

While James I advanced his uncompromising views on the divinity of Kings, the errors of Popes, and the duty of subjects, he succeeded in divorcing these academic theories from the practice of government, which he conducted like a skilful horseman, using now the bit and now the spur. And while Andrewes pronounced the English Church to be apostolic, bishops to rule by divine right, and good works to be necessary to salvation, Archbishop Abbot continued to give official support to the Puritans in doctrine, and in ecclesiastical politics to let what would be be.

Meanwhile his more determined disciples, since the government would pay no attention to them, drawing together into a coterie, waited their turn. None of them had the intellectual appeal of the master whom they all venerated : it was not their task to formulate a policy, or to consecrate it by doctrinal exegesis, but to carry it out, — to achieve that great revolution which lies between laying and hatching. For they were practical men, prepared to endure the dust and heat, the opposition and the hatred, which attends those who seek to realise the ideal which the sage, from the comfort of his study, has outlined to an admiring world.

One of these disciples was William Laud.

CHAPTER TWO

OPPOSITION AND INTRIGUE

> "'*Suddenly advanced*'! What does my Lord call 'suddenly'? I was eleven years His Majesty's Chaplain in Ordinary before I was made a bishop. I was a bishop twelve years before I was preferred to be Archbishop of Canterbury, that highest place my Lord mentions. When I was made Archbishop, I was full threescore years of age, within less than one month."
>
> LAUD, Answer to Lord Saye's speech touching the Liturgy (*Works*, vi. 91).

WILLIAM LAUD was born at Reading in 1573, the only son of a Reading clothier, but the tenth child of his mother, who had married twice. As his birth was not high, so he was particularly sensitive to the charges, frequently made by his enemies, that it was low; and we learn from his indignant rejoinders that his family was regarded as very respectable, that his father was a conscientious citizen and bore all offices in the town except the mayoralty, and that his house (which Prynne had described as a cottage) was rented at £33 a year.

Throughout his life, Laud remembered Reading, and was its benefactor, as it had been his: for it was the accident of his birth there that sent him to St. John's College, Oxford, where his active career began. St. John's College had been founded in 1555 by another Reading man, also a clothier's son, Sir Thomas White, who had, in addition, endowed two scholarships there for boys from Reading Grammar School. From Reading Grammar School Laud proceeded to St. John's, matriculating as a commoner, in 1589. It is said that it was the generosity of a Mrs. Burningham that enabled him to do this: but at the next election he was appointed to receive one of Sir Thomas White's scholarships. For the next twenty years his life was bound up with St. John's College, of which he was first a scholar, then a fellow: and when he gave up his fellowship in 1610, it was only to return, seven months later, as President.

Nevertheless we know practically nothing about Laud's life at Oxford. He was himself uncommunicative: and if others came across him, it was generally as enemies rather than as friends. Throughout his life he had patrons, allies, and agents: but we seek in vain through his voluminous correspondence for evidence of any personal intimacy. We know, indeed, that he shared rooms as an undergraduate with one John Jones: but we only know it from the enemies of Laud, who pointed it out when John Jones returned to England as a papal agent under the more impressive name of Dom Leander a Sancto Martino. We know also that one Michael Boyle was one of his contemporaries and acquaintances at St. John's: but all that we learn from him of Michael Boyle, who became Bishop of Waterford, was that "he would have done anything, or sold anyone; for sixpence profit", and that in 1633 he still owed the college £35.[1] A later acquaintance was Francis Windebank, who came up to St. John's ten years after Laud, and knew him as a fellow. They got on well enough together, and Laud was a frequent visitor at Windebank's house at Haines Hill, near Reading. But this friendship was to come to a dramatic end thirty-five years later as the result of a difference of opinion on a matter of soap. For Laud was never a man of wide personal interests. "Few excellent men have ever had fewer friends to their persons", wrote one of the small number who remembered him with affection. Such personal relations as he maintained were dependent entirely upon principles, and when principles were found to differ, friendships were unable to survive.

Even the intellectual development which led to the adoption of these principles is unknown to us. We cannot follow in Laud the growth of those ideas which he held so strongly, or ascribe dates and causes. As far as we can say, the first views which he uttered were identical with the last. But it is a reasonable conjecture that it was during his early days at Oxford that he was inspired with that passion for order, that hatred of Puritan doctrines and Puritan freedom, which characterised the whole of his life. For Oxford, at the time of his arrival there, was conspicuous for both Puritanism and disorder, such as may well have revolted a conscientious and meticulous young man. In addition, it was intellectually bankrupt. The rule of the Puritan Leicester had ended in the year before Laud's admission, and throughout the 1580's the government, oppressed by fear of

[1] Laud, *Works*, vi. 352, 308.

Spain, had connived at the activities of the fervently anti-Spanish, anti-Roman party. Shortly before Laud's arrival, Giordano Bruno had visited Oxford, and described the university as " a constellation of ignorant, obstinate pedants : a herd of donkeys and swine " ; and in the year of Laud's matriculation Archbishop Whitgift wrote to Burghley that in Oxford professors were underpaid, lectures unattended, statutes ignored, and discipline despised.[1] All this may well have had its effect on Laud's opinions.

St. John's College itself, however, represented a more liberal tradition. Its founder had been a Catholic, and many Catholics, including Edmund Campion, had been educated there. Laud's tutor, Dr. Buckeridge, was one of the Arminian group which looked to Andrewes for inspiration. And another member of the college, Sir William Paddy, who became physician to King James, both accepted his views and followed his precepts, — for he was a generous benefactor to his college. The college was also, during Laud's early days there, distinguished for its enthusiasm in the production of dramatic pieces. In 1603 *Narcissus*, an Ovidian burlesque, was enacted, and from October 1607 till March 1608 we possess a chronicle of comedies produced under the auspices of Thomas Tucker, appointed master of the ceremonies, and written up by Griffin Higgs, who later became chaplain to the Queen of Bohemia at the Hague.[2] As a young fellow, Laud contributed ten shillings towards the cost of the latter performances, but, as he afterwards said, " I was never play-hunter ", and it is unlikely that he took any more direct interest.

For it is impossible to associate Laud with any ordinary humane interests. He was neither an agreeable nor a convivial character : and the violence of the opinions which have been formed about him must be ascribed to the lack of any common humanity upon which his judges may be agreed, even if they differ about his ideals. The opinions and public actions of men may arouse the extremes of hatred and admiration : but their pastimes and recreations show us a less controversial side of their character, enabling us to modify the extravagance of our praise or the severity of our censure. We may hate Strafford the politician : but Strafford in his leisure hours, surrounded by

[1] Strype, *Whitgift*, i. 610.

[2] MS. in St. John's College, no. lii.

his family, his horses, and his dogs, is not a politician but a man, with whom we can sympathise regardless of political differences. Hampden the Puritan malcontent may be an idol or he may be anathema : but Hampden the Buckinghamshire squire can be neither. With Laud, however, it is different. Like Chatham, he was one of those public figures without private lives. While his predecessor at Lambeth, Abbot, and his successor, Juxon, were both devotees of the chase, Laud had neither time nor inclination for any such activity. Recreation he had none : and for exercise he relied on the jolting of his carriage from London House to Whitehall, or, dreariest of all, physical jerks, swinging a book in his room, until he ruptured himself by that exertion.[1] And if he never relaxed in recreation, equally he never enjoyed the epicurean pleasures of idleness and good company which reconcile us to so many Popes and Cardinals. When staying with his friends, his head was always " full of my business ": and the splendid banquet to which he later entertained the Court was to him a tedious business, chiefly satisfactory because none of the spoons were filched. If this absence of any humane interests renders Laud's later life, which was so crowded, somewhat admirable, so that we feel incapable of judging a man devoted with such fervour to a single ideal of duty, it makes his early days at Oxford, which are so sparsely documented, somewhat repellent in their barrenness. We are advertised of a series of academic squabbles caused by his opinions, and in the intervals we cannot say what he was doing, but can be fairly sure that it was nothing either interesting or amiable. He remained at St. John's, taking degrees, securing his fellowship, being ordained, studying patristic divinity under Buckeridge, who educated him " upon the noble foundations of the Fathers, Councils, and the ecclesiastical historians ", and serving as Proctor in 1603.[2] At the end of that year, finding his prospects of promotion in the University slight, he accepted the offer of a chaplaincy in the household of the Earl of Devonshire at Wanstead in Essex.

Charles Blount, Earl of Devonshire, had much to recommend

[1] Laud, *Works*, vi. 311 ; iii. 209.

[2] The only detail of Laud's proctorial activity comes from Wood (*Life and Times*, ed. Clark, ii. 234 n.) : " 'Thou little morsel of justice, prithee let me alone and be at rest ', quoth a drunken fellow, sleeping on Penniless Bench, Oxon, to Laud of St. John's Coll., then Proctor of the University ".

him as a patron to an aspiring young clergyman. He had just returned from Ireland with the reputation of a general, the favour of the government, and the title of an Earl. Unfortunately his domestic affairs were not yet completely regulated, and when Laud accepted a position in his household, he was living in adultery with Penelope Devereux, the divorced wife of Lord Rich. A marriage between the two had been projected some time ago: but the lady's relatives, regarding a second son with a limited estate as too poor a match for the daughter of an Earl, passed over his claims and married her, against her will, to Lord Rich. The marriage had not been successful: and when Lord Devonshire returned to England, enriched by the death of his elder brother as well as by his own exploits, he found that Lady Rich had been divorced for adultery with himself, and determined to marry her. He therefore applied to his new chaplain to perform the ceremony, and Laud performed it. The state of the ecclesiastical law on this, as on many other subjects since the Reformation, was ambiguous, so that both Laud and the Earl could have made a case for themselves when the King expressed his strong disapproval: and the Earl did. He produced a tract in which he sought to prove the legality of his marriage. But the King was unmoved, and Laud chose the wiser course of saying nothing at all about it until the Earl was dead. Then he decided that it was better to agree with a living King than with a dead Earl, and wrote a short paper refuting the logic of his former patron.[1]

This affair of the Earl of Devonshire's marriage was a disastrous episode in Laud's career. It was not only that he had sacrificed his moral views to his chances of preferment,—for he admits himself that "my conscience cried out against it" and that he did it "serving my own ambition and the sins of others",—but, as it turned out, it proved as impolitic as immoral, for his chances of preferment were seriously damaged by it. No one, of course, could be expected to speculate with any confidence upon what King James' views on any question would be at any given moment: and in fact he shortly changed his mind on this, as on other subjects. But the unfavourable opinion which he conceived of Laud remained with him, and Laud's own remorse was redoubled by the disfavour in which

[1] Laud, *Works*, vii. 614.

he found himself. Every year, on the anniversary of the unfortunate wedding, he remembered it with abject contrition in his devotions. He confessed it to Buckingham as a thing that weighed heavily upon his mind. King James made it an objection against his elevation to a bishopric. And anonymous opponents reminded King Charles, at the beginning of his reign, that his chosen counsellor had once committed an indiscretion of the kind which the austere monarch was least likely to forgive.[1]

Meanwhile, as a fellow of St. John's, Laud had been advancing the uncompromising views which he was always to hold. In 1603 he showed himself a strenuous opponent of the Millenary Petition presented to the new King by his Puritan subjects;[2] and in the same year he had his first recorded quarrel with the future Archbishop, Abbot.

As a fellow of Balliol, George Abbot had attracted the favour of the Puritan Chancellor, Lord Buckhurst, later the Earl of Dorset, "a special maintainer of the true religion", by his pronounced Protestant views. The Chancellor had made him his chaplain in 1592, and, thanks to this patronage, Abbot became Master of University College in 1597, Dean of Winchester in 1600, and, in the same year, Vice-chancellor of the University, — an office to which he was reappointed in 1603, and again in 1605. In all these capacities Abbot was conspicuous for his Puritan sympathies, his hatred of Romanism, or anything which seemed to him to savour of it, and his harsh discipline. Religious pictures, which he considered incentives to popish idolatry, were burnt in the market-place of Oxford by his orders: and in 1600, when Bancroft, as Bishop of London, ordered the re-erection of a stone cross which had fallen down in Cheapside, and the Puritan Londoners objected, appeal was made to Abbot, who expressed his decided but ineffectual condemnation of the renewal.

Such doctrines were, of course, repugnant to Laud, and the characters of the two men were not such as to make agreement easy. In 1603, when Abbot was Vice-chancellor and Laud Proctor, the first of many wrangles between them took place. In the preceding year, probably in the course of the divinity lecture which he was appointed to read in St. John's, Laud had

[1] Laud, *Works*, iii. 157, 160; Hacket, *Scrinia Reserata*, i. 64.

[2] Hacket, i. 64.

scandalised the Puritans by maintaining the perpetual visibility of the Church of Christ, continued from the Apostles by the Church of Rome until the Reformation.[1] To the Puritans the Church of Christ was not visible, and they would not admit that any good had come out of the Church of Rome, even before the Reformation. Next year Abbot took up the challenge and drew up a summary of the correct Puritan view, which was widely circulated in manuscript. Twenty years later, Laud was able to turn this to his advantage, when an enthusiastic supporter of Abbot published the work, and Laud used it to disparage the Archbishop to the King.[2]

In 1606 Laud offended another Vice-chancellor by another sermon. This was Dr. Airay, the Provost of Queen's College, who cited him to appear before him for expressing such unorthodox views. But the case was not allowed to remain there. Laud had an influential ally in Sir William Paddy, who has been mentioned as a generous old St. John's man of high-church views : and he interposed his offices with the Chancellor, assuring him that Laud was " an excellent learned man of very honest and good conversation ", who had no intention of accepting the Vice-chancellor's decision, but would make appeal to the Chancellor, thus causing grave scandal. The Chancellor thereupon wrote to Airay taking cognisance of the affair, which he resolved to determine himself, with the aid of some of the bishops. The Vice-chancellor, however, succeeded in satisfying him of the justice of his action, and Dorset wrote back leaving the whole affair in his hands. Nothing was done after this, but Laud had made himself very unpopular by his action, and, although he avoided the public recantation in Convocation which most of the Heads of Houses had intended for him, he found himself cut in the streets of Oxford as " a busy and pragmatical person . . . at least very popishly inclined ".[3]

In 1608 Laud, who had meanwhile been presented by Sir Thomas Cave to the living of Stanford in Northamptonshire in 1607, and had obtained the advowson of North Kilworth in Leicestershire next year, proceeded Doctor of Divinity, and advanced such unseasonable views at his examination for that

[1] Heylin, *Cyprianus Anglicus*, p. 49.

[2] Laud, *Works*, iii. 145.

[3] *Ibid.* iii. 133 ; Wood, *Annals*, ed. Gutch, ii. 288ff. MS. Rawlinson, A. 289, p. 80.

degree [1] that Dr. Holland, the divinity professor, "publicly checked and turned him out of the schools with disgrace as a sower of discord between brethren, — to wit, the Church of England and other Reformed Churches". Such at least is Prynne's story, although the Archbishop denied the truth of it. We can conclude at any rate that he advanced these views, and that they were not popular.

But if Laud was unpopular with the University authorities, he was gradually associating with himself a growing movement of which St. John's College was to be the Oxford headquarters. Besides Sir William Paddy, who was useful because of his outside influence, and John Buckeridge, Laud's tutor, there was also William Juxon, who came to the college in 1602 and, for the rest of Laud's life, may be regarded as his understudy. Buckeridge, Laud, and Juxon formed a group which spread high-church doctrines first in St. John's, then in Oxford, and ultimately throughout England: and when Buckeridge became President of St. John's in 1605, the college was to be under the successive rule of these three for the next thirty years. Besides this, by the regular iteration of his unpopular convictions Laud secured the notice of a patron who was to prove more helpful to his career than the Earl of Devonshire had been, — Richard Neile.

The practical leader of the Arminians during the reign of James I, Richard Neile formed the complete antithesis to his spiritual counterpart Lancelot Andrewes. A man of humble origin (his father, it is said, was a tallow-chandler), as devoid of spiritual feeling as of humane learning, he had sound practical instincts, an agreeable sympathy with ignorance, and a charitable disposition: and he knew well which side his bread was buttered on. We have seen how, while Andrewes stood discreetly aside, he assured King James that he might tax his subjects at will: and in 1614 his opinions on this subject brought him into collision with Parliament. In the course of a speech urging the Lords not to confer with the Commons upon a bill to abolish the new impositions, Neile, then Bishop of Lincoln, after enlarging upon the subversive implications of such a suggestion, added "that the Lower House was known to be composed of such turbulent and

[1] Or this may have been when he took his B.D. in 1604. Prynne, *Breviate*, p. 2; *Canterburie's Doome*, ed. 1646, p. 389.

factious spirits as, if they should give way to a communication or treaty with them, they (the Lords) were like to hear such mutinous speeches as were not fit for those honourable personages to lend their hearing to ". The Commons naturally resented such language, and Neile was forced to make a tearful apology at the bar, protesting that he had the highest opinion of the honourable House of Commons and would never have thought of disparaging them. Even so, only a timely dissolution saved him from further humiliation.

This incident had not yet occurred when Neile first took Laud into his service : but it indicates well enough the character of the man to whom Laud became chaplain in 1608. Neile was then Bishop of Rochester : so in 1609 Laud gave up his Leicestershire living and took instead that of West Tilbury in Essex, in order to be nearer his new patron, who also presented him to the living of Cuckstone in Kent : and in 1610 he gave up his fellowship at St. John's in order to devote himself more stedfastly, not, as his recent panegyrists declare, to parish work, but (as his earliest admirer states) to " the service of his lord and patron, whose fortunes he resolved to follow till God should please to provide otherwise for him ".[1] His parish, indeed, only saw him for six months : for he caught " a Kentish ague " in it, and exchanged it for another.

At this point occurred a series of changes in the personnel of the Church, which had a great influence on Laud's career. In November 1610 Archbishop Bancroft died, a man who had shown himself more determined than his predecessors to restore the Church to wealth and independence, and there was a great deal of speculation about his successor. Lancelot Andrewes seemed the most obvious candidate, and he was widely tipped : but George Abbot had not been idle since his last encounter with Laud. The patron to whom he had owed his Oxford appointments had died : but in the Earl of Dunbar, the King's Commissioner and High Treasurer of Scotland, he had found another more serviceable for the great world. Thanks to this happy connexion, Abbot had entered Scottish politics just at that moment when Scottish politics were occupying the attention of the government. He had prepared the way for the introduction of episcopacy at the General Assembly of Linlithgow in 1608,

[1] Heylin, p. 55.

and, by an opportune pamphlet on the Gowrie Conspiracy, in which King James was compared to his advantage with the good kings of Israel and the Christian emperors of Rome, he had appeased some of the suspicions of the Scots, who regarded the plot as little more than an excuse for political executions. For these services Abbot had been rewarded with the bishoprics of Lichfield and London in rapid succession, and now, on the death of Bancroft, his hopes of the highest position in the Church were only dashed by the inopportune death of his patron two months after that of the primate. Providence, however, was determined that he should not fail. Although Abbot himself did not know it, the King had found time between the two deaths to consult his commissioner: Dunbar had recommended Abbot as Bancroft's successor: and "by a strong north wind coming out of Scotland, Abbot was blown over the Thames to Lambeth".

The appointment of Abbot to Canterbury was important in many ways. It was typical of King James, who thus avoided the dangers of either action or consistency. For the new Archbishop, while acceptable to Parliament as a Puritan, was too ineffective to harm the King, and, though a Calvinist in doctrine, somehow managed to reconcile this with a belief in the necessity of such a superintendent episcopacy as he had helped the King to introduce into Scotland. Thus, if he preached Puritan doctrines, that did not matter much: for the danger of Puritanism lay in its implications, which he rejected. It seemed that both parties would be satisfied by his appointment, and a crisis averted, or at any rate postponed.

In fact, however, Abbot's elevation was welcomed by neither party. He was a disciplinarian, who extended the claims of the prerogative courts in order to enforce Calvinist doctrine, and he was therefore opposed by the Puritan lawyers, whose hatred of prerogative courts was stronger than their love of doctrinal purity. He had never held any ecclesiastical preferment with a cure of souls, and therefore had little acquaintance or sympathy with the difficulties of the smaller clergy. Above all, though he might be courageous in expressing his views, and showed far more independence in his relations with the King than Laud ever did, he was incapable of effective action. Heylin compared his reign to that of Nectarius, Bishop of Constantinople, to whom St. Gregory of Nazianzus wrote describing the widespread dissensions in the Early Church, " the cause of which disorders he ascribeth to Nectarius only ; a man (as the historian saith of him) of an exceeding fair and plausible demeanour, and very gracious with the people : one that chose rather (as it seems) to give free way to all men's fancies, and suffer every man's proceedings, than draw upon him the envy of a stubborn clergy and a factious multitude . . . a pregnant evidence that possibly there could not be a greater misfortune in a church of God than a popular prelate ".[1]

The result was that the problem of an ecclesiastical policy, which was now realised to be pressing, was deferred for more than ten years, while Abbot's rule was not strong enough to prevent the two parties from becoming more antagonistic by opposition. Abbot himself undermined his own power by his fitful opposition to the king, and his disastrous introduction of George Villiers to the court. He became a bigot and a martinet in theory, and in practice merely an inconveniently long-lived occupant of a throne for which more determined claimants were competing. Another result was that Laud, whom Abbot had learnt to hate at Oxford, was systematically kept down for another ten years, becoming more intransigent than ever in opposition, and, at the end of ten years, rising all the more suddenly to cope all the more impetuously with problems which had become all the more acute.

Nevertheless, Laud secured some pickings out of Abbot's success : for, in the episcopal general post which followed, Neile was translated from Rochester to Lichfield and Coventry, and Buckeridge succeeded him at Rochester. This left the Presidency of St. John's open, and Buckeridge proposed Laud as his successor in it. Abbot was alarmed at this prospect, and at once made objections to the Lord Chancellor, Lord Ellesmere, who was also Chancellor of the University, representing the disastrous consequences which such an appointment would entail in Church and State. Ellesmere passed these objections on to the King : but on the other side Neile defended Laud and reminded the King of Abbot's personal prejudices. As a result the King decided to leave the matter entirely to the electors, — the fellows of the college. This, however, did not settle the matter. There was

[1] Heylin, p. 161.

another candidate, Dr. Rawlinson: and party feeling ran high, as it did wherever Laud was involved. The vice-president of the college, who supported Laud, refused to allow the undergraduate fellows to vote, although by the statutes entitled to do so: and when this manœuvre was successful in securing Laud's election, one of Laud's opponents, Richard Baylie, seized the voting-papers from the altar and tore them in pieces. The defeated candidate then appealed to the visitor, Thomas Bilson, Bishop of Winchester, who, though he had bought his bishopric by bribing Queen Elizabeth, was scandalised by the impropriety of mere college stratagems. "I received the manner of their election", the Bishop reported to the King, "in a public instrument subscribed by a notary and brought to me by Dr. Laud himself; . . . upon the reading whereof (I confess to your sacred Majesty) I marvelled to see them swerve and vary so much from the true intent and plain and grammatical sense of their statute in so many material points. For where the founder in manifest words appointeth all and every of the fellows to take the same oath . . ., and every fellow to give his voice to the scrutators, in the same order that he was first admitted into the College, . . . I found that in the late election of Dr. Laud they had neither sworn the fellows that were not graduates, nor suffered them to give voices in their scrutiny with the rest, nor so much as to be present when the scrutiny was made."[1] After three months the case was brought before the King at Tichborne, and, after a three hours' session, King James decided to leave things as they were. "It was apparent", he declared, "that there had been practice and corruption on both sides, but yet of such a kind as we think in this time no election in any college, corporation, or company is free from it." So Laud's election was confirmed, and St. John's College remained the stronghold of Arminianism in Oxford.

In November of the year in which he became President of St. John's, Neile's influence secured Laud's appointment as one of the King's chaplains. Next year, when Neile was engaged in examining and finally burning a recalcitrant fanatic called Wightman at Lichfield, Laud was with him, taking part in the proceedings from beginning to end.[2] In 1613 we come across him in the unexpected capacity of a poet, and in the unexpected

[1] *S.P. Dom. Jac. I.* 64, no. 35.

[2] *S.P. Dom. Car. I.* 427, no. 78.

company, among others, of John Prideaux, John Hampden, and Robert Burton, the anatomist of melancholy, on the occasion of the marriage of the princess Elizabeth with the Elector Palatine, — a marriage which evoked such enthusiasm at the time, and led to such misfortunes in the sequel.[1] In 1614 Neile became Bishop of Lincoln, and again Laud received his portion in the Arminian advance, in the form of a prebend of the cathedral, to which, next year, he added the archdeaconry of Huntingdon. At the same time he came into conflict again with the Abbots, — this time with the Archbishop's elder brother Robert, the Master of Balliol and Regius Professor of Divinity. In a sermon on Shrove Tuesday, Laud had again exasperated the Puritan party, and had been understood to make personal reflections upon Dr. Abbot. Abbot, who was Vice-chancellor at the time, retaliated from the University pulpit on Easter day, no less personally: and Laud, who was not present at this sermon, was persuaded to appear in person on the following Sunday when, according to custom, it was repeated. There, he said, "I was fain to sit patiently and hear myself abused almost an hour together, being pointed at as I sat", while Abbot demanded whether he was Romish or English, Papist or Protestant, "or a mongrel compound of both".[2] It seems that Laud was forced to retire from Oxford for a time after this quarrel, for the King later gave him permission to return, Abbot having apologised.[3] By the end of the year peace had been restored, and Abbot was removed as bishop to Salisbury, his chair of theology being conferred on John Prideaux, one of the most influential Calvinists inside the Church, who remained in Oxford throughout Laud's tenure of power, the single obstacle to his influence there as Chancellor and Archbishop.

Next year, in his capacity of royal chaplain, Laud preached for the first time before the King, his sermon being on Miriam's leprosy, "as a warning to detractors of government". This was a familiar topic among high-church preachers, and, considering the audience to which it was addressed, it is not surprising that it was much applauded, — the same arguments, when preached to the parliaments of Charles I, were less relished. The style of

[1] *Epithalamia, sive Lusus Palatini*, etc., 4to, Oxon, 1613. Latin Verses by Laud are also included in *Justa Funebria Thomae Bodleii*, 1613; and other Oxford compilations.

[2] Heylin, p. 61; Laud, *Works*, vii. 3.

[3] *S.P. Dom. Jac. I.* 80, no. 124.

Laud's sermons was commented upon at the time as being based on those of Andrewes, which were unaccountably popular among his contemporaries. These were an intellectual exercise both for the preacher and the audience, being endlessly subdivided according to fixed rules, and expressed almost entirely through elaborate verbal conceits, principally in dead languages : and it is most charitable to agree with Laud and Buckeridge, who edited them, that " they could not live with all that elegancy which they had upon his tongue ". The analytical method of Andrewes is certainly noticeable in Laud's sermons, but Laud possessed no elegancy with either tongue or pen : and from the laboured style of all his literary efforts it is fair to suppose that it was the subject rather than the manner of his preaching which appealed to a King who liked to consider himself an autocrat. Meanwhile his ascent continued to be gradual but slow. In 1616 he accepted the Deanery of Gloucester, accompanied the King, as Neile's chaplain, to Scotland, and secured royal instructions for the regulation of studies at Oxford. In Oxford, Gloucester, and Scotland trouble immediately ensued.

The Bishop of Gloucester was the learned Orientalist and translator of the Bible, Dr. Miles Smith : and either his conservatism or his Puritanism was outraged when the new dean signalised his arrival by having the communion-table removed from its place in the body of the church and fixed altarwise in the chancel, and by ordering those who entered the church to bow to it. To the Puritan the communion-table was only a table, and the communion a commemorative meal : to set the table up in the east, bedizened with trappings, was to convert it into an altar, as the Papists did, and to show it reverence was idolatry. To the high churchman, however, the table was an altar, the communion a magic function : the sacraments were the body and blood of Christ, transmuted by the divine power delegated to the priest ; and no reverence, no ceremonies, were superfluous in the presence of so important and formidable a mystery. This difference of practice thus entailed a difference of doctrine, and the difference of doctrine involved the fundamental political difference between those to whom a priest was an official invested with authority from above, without regard to merit or capacity, and those to whom he was a minister appointed by the community to assist them in the realisation of their own powers. On so ticklish a question Queen Elizabeth had declined to make any definite ruling: and as, in doctrine, she dexterously enshrined both opinions in a single formula, so, in practice, she discreetly avoided committing herself, and left the whole question as a mere matter of procedure, "in the ordering whereof, saving for an uniformity, there seemeth no matter of great moment, so the sacrament be duly and reverently administered".[1] She therefore recommended that the table be kept in the east end, when not in use, and moved down at the time of service. She had appealed throughout from principle to convenience, — to the practical advantages of uniformity, audibility, and accessibility. But the question which Queen Elizabeth had shelved the Dean of Gloucester undertook to determine: and the Puritan inhabitants of Gloucester and the peaceable old Bishop of Gloucester were scandalised. Laud wrote with some asperity to the bishop, justifying his action by declaring that the King had instructed him to reform the state of affairs in Gloucester, and that "there was scarce ever a church in England so ill governed and so much out of order"; and at the same time he wrote to Neile to secure his support. The injured bishop never entered his cathedral after the outrage which he conceived it to have suffered, and the parishioners took their revenge by putting libels in the pulpit, — a form of revenge to which Laud was particularly susceptible.

The Gloucester affair was in February 1617. Next month the King set out for Scotland, taking with him Bishops Montague of Winchester, Andrewes, and Neile: and with Neile went Laud. The object of the journey was to complete the work which, with the aid of Abbot, had already been begun, of bringing the ecclesiastical constitution of Scotland into conformity with that of England. James had already secured the subservience of the lay estates of Scotland by allowing them to plunder the Church lands; but the wealth which at first bound its possessors to the throne might afterwards, when gratitude and hope of more had vanished, become a stepping-stone to independence. He therefore resolved, while the estates were still on his side, to use their concurrence to reorganise the remains of the Church into an

[1] The Queen's Injunctions, 1559 (Prothero, *Statutes and Const. Documents*, p. 190).

institution which could in future be a stone about their necks, should they attempt to outstep the condition of subjects. " Presbytery ", he had said, " agreeth as well with a monarchy as God with the Devil."

The first steps had been taken in 1606, when the Linlithgow Assembly, thanks partly to the influence of Abbot, who had reconciled a supervisory episcopate with Calvinist theology in his own brain and hoped to reconcile them in Scotland as well, agreed to the establishment of " constant moderators " over each of the fifty-three presbyteries into which the Scots Kirk was divided. From that time the process had been continued gradually. In 1609 the Scottish Parliament at Perth had increased the powers of these new bishops. In 1610, while the English Parliament was protesting against the independent jurisdiction of the High Commission court in England, two courts of High Commission were erected in Scotland, each under the presidency of an archbishop. In the same year the arrangement was confirmed by a General Assembly at Glasgow, judiciously packed and bribed for the purpose, and three of the new prelates came to England for consecration. Two years later the Acts of the Glasgow Assembly were ratified by the Scottish Parliament, and the change in the Scottish Church became the law of the land. The bishops, nevertheless, remained in a dubious position. They were not, as in England, part of the structure of the Church. Archbishop Abbot intended them to be supervisors of the clergy : but the lower clergy and the laity found that they could manage perfectly well without such supervisors, and the bishops remained little more than the ambassadors of a foreign power, dependent entirely on the English government. " For the Lords spiritual ", wrote Sir Anthony Weldon, " they may well be termed so indeed, for they are neither fish nor flesh, but what it will please their earthly God the King to make them." [1]

The King's intention in 1617 was to initiate a change in the Scottish Church far more radical than the mere superimposition of bishops. The presence of bishops without coercive powers affected few : the imposition of a new form of service, or new ceremonies, was a change in which everyone would have to participate. And yet this is what James meant to introduce. " His Majesty ", secretary Luke wrote to Bacon from Edinburgh

[1] Description of Scotland (Nichols, *Progresses of James I*, iii. 338).

after the arrival of the royal party, " is in consultation by way of preparation for his ends, — that is, to procure better maintenance for the ministry, and some conformity between this church and ours in England in the public service." Holyrood Chapel was rigged up for Anglican services. " A pair of organs ", reported the news-writer Chamberlain, " costing £400 had been sent to Edinburgh, besides all manner of furniture for a chapel, which Inigo Jones tells me he has charge of, with pictures of the apostles, Faith, Hope, and Charity, and such other religious representations, which how welcome they will be thither, God knows." [1] It was not long before others besides God knew how welcome they were, including Chamberlain. " Our churchmen and ceremonies ", he wrote, " are not so well allowed of " : and he described how one of the royal guards, who had died during the visit, had been buried with Anglican rites. This had proved so unpopular that the Dean of St. Paul's had to make a public recantation for recommending the dead man's soul to God. " Another exception was made to Dr. Laud's putting on a surplice when the corpse was to be laid in the ground. So that it seems they are very averse from our customs, insomuch that one of the bishops, Dean of the Chapel there to the King, refused to receive the communion with him kneeling." [2] Next month James required the Estates to pass a bill leaving external matters of ecclesiastical policy entirely in the hands of himself and the bishops. This was too much for the Scots. Even the bishops boggled at it, and insisted on the inclusion of " a competent number of the ministry " in the deliberative council of the Church. The ministers, when the news of the proposal leaked out, were indignant, and fifty-five of them drew up a protest against it. James yielded to this opposition, and finally withdrew the measure. Meanwhile a clerical convention at St. Andrews had declined to take the responsibility of passing the articles subsequently known as the Five Articles of Perth, which enjoined kneeling at communion, private communion if necessary, private baptism, observance of fasts and feasts, and confirmation by bishops. James had already envisaged these innovations at the close of the Assembly held at Aberdeen in 1616, and Archbishop Spottiswood had warned him against them. Now the Convention at St. Andrews protested

[1] Chamberlain to Carleton, in Birch, *Court and Times of James I*, i. 446.
[2] Chamberlain to Carleton, in Nichols, *Progresses of James I*, iii. 344.

that only a General Assembly could deal with changes so fundamental, and James withdrew from Scotland with none of his projects effected and the opposition of the people to religious changes apparent. After his departure, the Five Articles were safely piloted through both a General Assembly and a parliament : but they were fiercely resisted in the country, and were nowhere successfully enforced.

The alterations which were introduced at the same time in Oxford tended in the same direction, and were mainly the work of Laud. They were embodied in an order which substituted the study of the Early Fathers, the Councils, and the Schoolmen, for the Protestant abridgements in use at the time. In other words, the Catholic instead of the Protestant documents were introduced into the University where the clergy received their theological training. For to the true Protestant the Bible alone was sufficient for salvation, and Protestant theologians spent most of their study in commenting on the Old and New Testaments. To them the works of the Fathers and Schoolmen were the insidious interpretations of Scripture which had made it possible for the political organisation of the Roman Church to claim affinity with the teaching of Christ, and in which, obviously, there must be some tremendous fallacy. This order, therefore, was naturally greeted with opposition from the Calvinist party in the University. The Vice-chancellor, the Dean of Christ Church, and the two professors of divinity, Drs. Prideaux and Benefield, all objected to it. But by this time the power of Calvinism in Oxford was on the wane. The leaven which had spread from St. John's had leavened the whole University, and opposition was unavailing.

It was not only in Oxford that Laud seemed at last to be rising superior to the adversaries who had so long kept him down. Hitherto neither his patrons nor his pushfulness had been able to make much headway for him against the systematic opposition of Abbot and the distrust of the King ; but now two causes were operative which depressed the fortunes of Abbot and exalted those of Laud.

First, Abbot's influence with the King, and therefore his power to harm Laud, were on the wane. For a few years Abbot had directed the ecclesiastical policy of the government. He had persuaded the King to champion the cause of the Dutch Calvinists: and when Grotius himself had come to England to plead the Arminian cause, Abbot had warned secretary Winwood against paying any attention to an interfering busybody whose conversation was "tedious and full of tittle-tattle". He had dealt roundly with high churchmen and such as did not denounce Arminianism frequently and vigorously. He insisted on the regular extortion of the statutory fines from Catholic recusants. But the King was growing tired of him. His doctrines, useful enough for reconciling the Scots to an ineffective episcopacy, were embarrassing in England, and his behaviour was often far from complaisant. When Thomas Sutton left his dubiously acquired wealth to found the Charterhouse, James lodged a claim to the estate, and Abbot opposed it. When James, who had changed his views on divorce since the case of Lord Devonshire, supported the efforts of the Countess of Essex to disembarrass herself of one husband and secure another, Abbot again opposed him. And in 1618, when the King, on his return from Scotland, observed the dismal evidence of Puritan sabbatarianism in Lancashire, and issued the Book of Sports, whereby dancing and maypoles were pronounced to be legitimate forms of amusement, Abbot refused to allow it to be read in church. The failure of the King's Scottish visit may have contributed to Abbot's eclipse, but even before that, in 1616, Abbot's support had failed to prevent the condemnation and public burning of a book by his chaplain Dr. Mocket, Warden of All Souls College. This was a book *De Politia Ecclesiae Anglicanae*, which ascribed to the Archbishop of Canterbury a higher position in the government than the government found convenient or than the event proved to be true. The author did not long survive the disgrace of its burning, and was callously known thereafter as "the roasted Warden": while Abbot regarded the condemnation as a deliberate blow to himself, and was "off the hooks" for some time afterwards.[1]

But the depression of Abbot was not enough by itself to advance the prospects of Laud: for the King still distrusted him and would not suffer him to profit by the discomfiture of his rival. There was a second reason, more potent than the first, for the improvement in Laud's fortunes. Both Abbot and the King were being eclipsed by the rising of a new star.

[1] Heylin, p. 75.

When individuals seek to make history dependent on their personal inclinations, history frequently takes her revenge by examples of irony: and it was one of such ironies that the man who was to overthrow the pacific policy of the King, and to be instrumental in humiliating the Archbishop, was introduced to the Court by the Archbishop, and elevated to power by the King. This was George Villiers, first Duke of Buckingham, whose meteoric career was to hasten and accentuate all the troubles which James I had so dexterously evaded, and which were to crowd so thickly into the reign of his son. Equipped with no greater recommendation than his good looks, a cavalier manner, and an alternation of insolence and servility which fascinated the old King, he rose by an ascent "so quick that it seemed rather a flight than a growth" through all the titles of the peerage to that position of King's favourite which was part of the constitution under James I. But whereas Montgomery, the first holder of the title, had "pretended to no other qualification than to understand horses and dogs very well", and Somerset, who succeeded him, had offended merely by his personal arrogance, Buckingham had a political megalomania which was a political disaster. At first, indeed, this was not apparent. To those who sponsored his introduction at Court, he seemed a complaisant instrument, not an overbearing minister. He was pleasant and affable to all, easy of access, bountiful of the King's graces. Whether he was competent, or, as Lord Admiral and Warden of the Cinque Ports, did anything to rescue the navy from the disrepute into which his predecessors had allowed it to sink, — this was nothing to those who clambered about him for favours. To them he was sole minister for places and pensions, and all differences of political principles were forgotten by the motley crowd of courtiers, nobles, and clergy, who tumbled head-over-heels to buy a title, or beg a lucrative office, or solicit the hand of one of the many Villiers relatives whom he had ennobled and enriched. "The King was the fountain of honour indeed", says the Rev. Dr. Hacket, "but there was one pre-eminent pipe through which all graces flowing from him were derived": [1] and Clarendon that "he was of a most flowing courtesy and affability to all men who made any address to him, and so desirous to oblige them that he did not enough consider the value of the obligation, or the merit of the person he chose

[1] *Scrinia Reserata*, i. 39.

to oblige; from which much of his misfortune resulted ".[1] An ill-assorted company found themselves competitors for his favour. The Puritan lawyer Sir Edward Coke bullied and starved his daughter into a marriage with the favourite's brother. Coke's rival Bacon was an assiduous courtier of Buckingham. The poetical Dr. Corbett, the place-hunting Dr. Field, the Romanising Dr. Goodman, the political Dr. Williams, all grew up into bishops under the same shade. Sir John Coke, the conscientious Secretary of State; Sir Richard Weston, who was to reverse the Duke's adventurous policy; Sir John Eliot, who led the attack on him in parliament, launching his demagogic invective against the new Sejanus; Sir Edward Dering, who moved the wholesale extirpation of the ecclesiastical hierarchy in the Long Parliament; — all these owed their first advancement to Buckingham; and William Laud was not behindhand in the great gold-rush. His earliest patron, the Earl of Devonshire, had been an unhappy choice. Neile had been unable, in the face of the opposition of Abbot and the King, to secure more than a few titbits and scrapings for his chaplain. But the favour of Buckingham opened the door to the highest positions in Church and State, and once Laud had secured it, in the words of Clarendon, " he prospered at the rate of his own wishes ".

He was not a minute too early. Already among those who were pledging themselves to live and die in the service of the favourite was one who was to be Laud's greatest rival and most powerful enemy for the next twenty years, — Dr. John Williams.[2]

It would be hard to find two more opposite characters than these two, now for the first time thrust together. In the days when Laud's enemies were triumphing, it was a commonplace among Puritan pamphleteers to compare the fallen Archbishop to Cardinal Wolsey. The shade of the Cardinal was made to visit Laud in the Tower: *A True Relation, or rather Parallel, between Cardinal Wolsey, Archbishop of York, and William Laud, Archbishop of Canterbury* was published in 1641: and it was in 1641 that Thomas Cavendish's *Life of Wolsey*, after nearly a century in manuscript, was first printed for William Sheares, the

[1] *History of the Rebellion*, i. 65.

[2] For a modern biography of Williams see B. Dew Roberts, *Mitre and Musket*, 1938.

text suitably garbled to point the obvious parallel. But save that they were both hated Princes of the Church, that both built in stone, and both taught " the law of the Star Chamber ", there was little in common between Wolsey, the politician in orders, and Laud, the clergyman in politics: and Laud was as bad an example to politicians as Wolsey was to the clergy. Williams, not Laud, was the true disciple of the Cardinal: and his first patron, Lord Ellesmere, told him so in as many words. Personal ambition counted for nothing with Laud. If he sought power, it was not because he loved it for itself or any of its privileges, but because he wished to impose his ideal in church government, — an ideal to which all else was with him subservient. Wealth and splendour meant nothing to him. He had no cultured tastes, no delight in lavish pomp: austerity was the only beauty which he appreciated. Personal extravagance he hated, and he checked it in the manners of others as rigorously as in himself. He wore his hair very close, and insisted that fellows and undergraduates at Oxford, and the clergy everywhere, should do the same. Fuller makes a deliberate antithesis between Laud and Wolsey in their attitude to personal finery: " as Cardinal Wolsey is reported the first prelate who made silks and satins fashionable among clergymen, so this Archbishop first retrenched the usual wearing thereof ".[1] Nor did he share Wolsey's arrogance. " There need be no fear of pride in him ", Stephen Goffe wrote to Vossius when Laud was at the zenith of his power, " for he is not the man to write ' Ego et Rex meus '."[2] Even the writer of the *Parallel* admits that, while Wolsey lived in the princely state and ostentation of a Renaissance monarch, " I answer in behalf of our Canterbury that he never had that means or employment by which he might make so vainglorious a show of his pontificality or archiepiscopal dignity ". It was not the means and employment that Laud lacked, but the desire. While Wolsey revelled in the magnificence of his equipage and the lavishness of his banquets, Laud found a royal progress " very tedious, and how I shall be able to bear it God knows: but well or ill it must be borne "; and when his great banquet to the King and Queen at Oxford was over, the Archbishop merely sighed with relief and meticulously counted the spoons.

[1] *Church History* (ed. Brewer), vi. 301.
[2] *Epistolae Ecclesiasticae et Theologicae* (Amsterdam 1684), no. 539.

In all these things Williams was the antithesis of Laud, the imitator of the Cardinal. If Laud was a fit minister for the austere pietist Charles I, Williams was the ideal servant for the astute, evasive James I: a politician of the type of Bacon, who imitated Nature and did nothing in vain. He had none of Laud's minute scruples, none of his austerity, none of his single-mindedness, none of his superstition. At his episcopal house at Buckden he "lived like a magnifico": and the interests of the Church were nothing to him when weighed in the balance against his own advancement or the humiliation of a rival. He was a politician with a taste for splendour, who had taken orders as medieval noblemen took them, to be a step to power and feudal dignity,—a far cry from the humdrum, middle-class bishops around him, who had "got a living, and then a greater living, and then a greater than that, and so come to govern". Proudly indifferent to the ideas and convictions held by more earnest churchmen, he behaved throughout his career as if no differences in religious principles existed. At Cambridge he had offended Anglicans by attending the lectures of Perkins, and Puritans by insisting on ceremonies, and to the end of his life he retained the same independence. Laud he despised as an unpolitical enthusiast and hated as a successful rival: and Laud returned the hatred. For five years they competed desperately, each watching the other with fear and suspicion,—for it was for no mean prize that they struggled, but for the priceless conscience of the King's favourite. While they were both attached to his household, neither dared to leave the other alone with their patron. In his very dreams Laud saw the sinister figure of Williams undermining his influence with Buckingham: and had Williams recorded his dreams as superstitiously as Laud catalogued his, the content would probably be found to have been similar.

Williams had a short start in time. In 1620, already "a diocese in himself", such was his pluralism, he came to the conclusion that Buckingham, contrary to his original expectations, had come to stay. Hitherto, says his biographer, he had "crept far, as I may say, for ground-ivy: but he must clasp on this tree or none to trail and climb":[1] so he insinuated himself into the minister's favour by converting Lady Catherine Manners from Rome to Canterbury, and thus removing the King's objections to her marriage with the

[1] Hacket, i. 40.

JOHN WILLIAMS, BISHOP OF LINCOLN
AND ARCHBISHOP OF YORK

favourite. As his reward Williams secured the deanery of Westminster, where Laud was already junior prebendary; and thus the Abbey close witnessed the beginnings of a quarrel which was soon to divide the entire Church of England.[1] Next year Williams showed himself still more valuable. Parliament, summoned for the first time since the Addled Parliament of 1614, which had made things so uncomfortable for Dr. Neile, was crying for the blood of its old enemies the monopolists : and since he was himself the patron and chief of monopolists, " Mormo's and ill-shaped jealousies . . . robbed my Lord of Buckingham of all peace of mind, till the Dean of Westminster, his good genius, conjured them down ".[2] Williams' method of exorcising these spirits was to recommend Buckingham to detach himself from the party of the monopolists and forestall the opposition by joining the hue and cry against them. The advice was followed : the favourite emerged unscathed : the blow fell instead upon Lord Keeper Bacon, who was impeached and deprived of office : and the position thus opportunely vacated was conferred upon the expectant Williams.

There remained, however, one difficulty. It had been customary for the Lord Keeper to maintain his state not solely out of his official revenues, but also out of unofficial or semi-official perquisites. But since it was the taking of perquisites which had been the technical reason for Bacon's downfall, it was necessary for his successor, especially as he was a churchman, to derive these indispensable emoluments from some other less questionable source. The difficulty was, however, solved to the satisfaction of all. The largest diocese in England, that of Lincoln, was at the time unoccupied. It was given to Williams as a consolation for the pretended loss of his perquisites. He kept his deanery of Westminster *in commendam*, and his other sources of revenue, — his parsonage at Walgrave, where he chiefly resided, and his rectory at Grafton Underwood in Northamptonshire, his prebend and chantry at Lincoln, his choral places at Peterborough, Hereford, and St. David's. All these, together with his private fortune and the considerable income which he derived from the wardship of his young relatives, served to keep him in that state and splendour which he so affected.

[1] For details of Laud's life as prebendary of Westminster, see J. Armitage Robinson, " Westminster Abbey in the early part of the 17th century " (*Proceedings of the Royal Institution*, vol. xvii. pp. 519 ff.).

[2] Hacket, i. 49.

Only a nimble and resourceful mind, free alike from scruples and enthusiasms, could keep the evasive conscience of James I: and Williams was certainly a worthy successor to Francis Bacon's post. He never lacked arguments to prove his master right. His religion was a mere parergon to his politics, — a spare-time job designed to secure his income while he devoted himself to more serious activities. When instructing the judges to drop cases impending against Roman Catholics, he very sensibly appealed from the Word of God to the convenience of the government, and while conceding that toleration was contrary to the former, pointed out that it was temporarily necessary to the latter. And when Charles I was placed in the dilemma of either sacrificing his most faithful servant or precipitating a constitutional crisis, it was Williams who, after fourteen years of disgrace and three of imprisonment, returned unchanged to political life with the suggestion of a neat and sophistical distinction between public and private conscience which would enable him to satisfy both.

Meanwhile the fortunes of Laud were ripening, though less rapidly, in the same sun. Since his return from Scotland, the progress of the Arminian movement had been illustrated by the opening of new headquarters in London. In 1617 Neile was promoted to the see of Durham, and for the next few years his London residence, Durham House in the Strand, became the party headquarters. Among those for whom permanent rooms were kept there, were Richard Montague, the assertor of Catholic doctrine and the divine right of tithes, who was soon to set Parliament by the ears, Buckeridge of Rochester, Augustine Lindsell, whose scholastic abilities Laud was to reward with a bishopric, John Cosin, who outdid them all in ritualism, and Laud himself, many of whose early letters are written from that address. In January 1620 he received his prebend at Westminster, and about the same time, although the exact occasion is not known, he became one of those whose fortunes were dependent on Buckingham. Buckingham urged James to consent to his advancement, but the old king was still suspicious. " He hath a restless spirit ", he said, " and cannot see when matters are well, but loves to toss and change and bring things to a pitch of reformation floating in his own brain "; his resistance, however, was feeble, and the demands of Buckingham were supported by Williams, who was afraid that, if Laud did not get a bishopric, he would get the deanery of Westminster.[1] Finally James acquiesced with a bad grace. " Take him to you ", he said, " but on my soul, you will repent it." On June 3rd, 1621, he indicated his acquiescence by a gracious speech to Laud, remarking on his long service, and saying that hitherto he had given him nothing but Gloucester, which he knew was a shell without a kernel.[2] A fortnight later Laud was selected to preach before the King at Wanstead on the occasion of his birthday ; and at the end of the month he was nominated Bishop of St. David's, Williams, who had thus preserved his deanery of Westminster, receiving a living worth £120 a year in Laud's diocese as the broker's fee.

It was open to Laud to increase his revenue by the accumulation of offices too. The King would have allowed him to keep his presidency of St. John's : but the college statutes would not, and Laud declined the offer, and handed the college on to the guidance of Juxon, who could be trusted to continue his policy. His own rule had been uneventful,[3] and the absence of such disturbances at the election of his successor as had accompanied his own confirms his claim that " I made all quiet in the college, and for all the [*sc.* alleged] narrowness of my comprehensions, I governed that college in peace, without so much as a show of a faction, all my time, which was near on eleven years ".[4] One of his achievements was the winning over of Richard Baylie, the young fellow who, on Laud's election, had torn up the voting-papers. Baylie became one of Laud's most devoted disciples in Oxford, and ultimately succeeded Juxon as President, in order to

[1] Cf. Laud's diary (*Works*, iii. 136) : " The general expectation in court was that I should then have been made Dean of Westminster, and not Bishop of St. David's ". Writing to Stuteville on June 23rd, Meade reports a rumour that Laud had actually been made Dean of Westminster (Birch, *Court and Times of James I*, ii. 260).

[2] Laud, *Works*, iii. 136.

[3] Owing to his other appointments it is likely that Laud was very frequently absent from his college, although he does not appear thereby to have neglected his duties. A manuscript volume of Oxford poems chiefly composed at this time (MS. Douce, f. 5.), contains an epigram " On a non-resident President ", which most probably refers to either Laud or Juxon :

" St. John's is governed only by a P,
For there's no resident as we can see.
If vice rule then there, take it not amiss :
The vice in President's room by statute is."

[4] Laud, *Works*, vi, 89.

carry on the Laudian tradition for another decade. The college, too, had prospered under Laud's rule. The numbers had been maintained, and the buildings extended : and Sir William Paddy had enriched it by his benefactions. The only charge which his opponents could bring against Laud at his retirement was that, in contravention of the statutes, but at the request of Sir William Paddy, he had lent the college copy of the Venerable Bede's *De Temporibus* to the antiquary Sir Robert Cotton, who had not returned it. Laud wrote to Cotton in 1623, begging for its return, but when it was finally returned, several pages had been torn out by the borrower. Laud, however, made amends by presenting a copy of Bede's works to the College himself.[1]

So Williams and Laud, both rivals for Buckingham's favour, both raised, by that favour, to bishoprics together, awaited consecration at the hands of Archbishop Abbot. At the moment, Williams appeared to possess the lead : but events soon showed that he was losing it. For in July the Bishop of London, John King, died, and Williams saw his chance of still greater honours. "It hath pleased God to call the Bishop of London", he wrote to Buckingham, and suggested his own elevation to that see, adding that he would like, if nominated, to keep all his lesser pluralities, and also his present profits for the first year, as the late bishop had just survived pay-day.[2] But no sooner had he written this letter than the prospect of a yet greater dignity suddenly presented itself. Archbishop Abbot had been out hunting in Bramshill Park, as the guest of Lord Zouche, and while aiming at a deer had accidentally killed a keeper. The Archbishop was greatly concerned at this misadventure, but all exonerated him from any blame in the matter. The man had been warned to keep out of the way, said Lord Zouche : and the King, who was exceptionally fond of the chase, said that an angel might have miscarried in that sort, — in fact, he had nearly done so himself. Abbot settled an annuity of £20 on the keeper's widow, "which soon procured her another husband" : and the King at once excused him all the penalties of forfeiture demanded by the law of the land.

The law of the Church, however, was less easily disposed of.

[1] Laud, *Works*, vi. 242. Cf. Neil Ker in *British Museum Quarterly*, 1938, article 58 (Membra Disjecta). The missing pages are now among the Cotton MSS. in the British Museum.

[2] *Cabala*, p. 54.

Many non-hunting clergy shook their heads gravely and pronounced that, in such a case, they would have retired from the world for the remainder of their days, only begging His Majesty for a slender pension to keep body and soul together till it should please God to take them.[1] Such conscientious scruples perplexed the mind of Williams. The day after writing to regret the passing of the Bishop of London, and without waiting for a reply to his request for that diocese, he wrote off to Buckingham to sympathise with the misfortune of the Archbishop. " Nevertheless ", he added, after his perfunctory condolences, " for the King to leave *virum sanguineum*, a man of blood, Primate and Patriarch of all his churches, is a thing that sounds very harsh in the old Councils and Canons of the Church." And he reminded his patron, in words which his industrious panegyrist somehow omitted to transcribe, that " His Majesty hath promised me, upon my relinquishing the Great Seal, or before, one of the best places in this Church ".[2]

Neither of these applications bore fruit, and Williams, disappointed of both London and Canterbury, could merely emphasise his conscientious scruples by seeking consecration as Bishop of Lincoln not from Abbot, but from the commission of bishops who performed his functions while the exact status of the Archbishop was under consideration. Laud too was consecrated at the same time and by the same bishops. His scruples were probably more genuine, for he was a great stickler for the Canons and Councils of the Church : but he was doubtless glad to avoid consecration by his old enemy Abbot, and anyway, with Williams so close a rival, it would be unwise to run the risk of being subsequently regarded as an irregular bishop. In November, Abbot was reinstated in all his functions by a formal pardon or dispensation.

Next year Laud further strengthened his position in Buckingham's favour. The favourite's mother, created Countess of Buckingham in her own right, was turning in her old age to the consolations of the Roman Church, and Buckingham himself was beginning to waver in the same direction. He was still pursuing a Spanish match for Prince Charles, and working hand-in-glove

[1] Hacket, i. 65.

[2] *Cabala*, p. 56. A rumour that either Andrewes or Williams was to replace Abbot as Archbishop at this time is reported by Meade to Stuteville (Birch, *Court and Times of James I*, ii. 275-6).

with the Spanish ambassador Gondomar, using the supple conscience of Williams to provide reasons for favouring the English Catholics as part of the bargain, and it is not strange that he should have been influenced by the views of those with whom he was working. Nor was the austere and somewhat cantankerous Puritanism of Abbot congenial to one of such splendid tastes and princely extravagance. From the danger of conversion, however, he was saved by Laud, whom King James had appointed to see if he could not be as successful with the favourite as Williams had been with his bride. The instrument of Rome who had convinced the Countess and was persuading her son was a Jesuit whose real name was Piercey, but who had assumed the title of Father Fisher and had obtained a great reputation for the subtlety of his propaganda: but in a conference with him, in the presence of the King and Prince of Wales, Laud so expounded the teaching of his master Andrewes that, although the old Countess was past recovery, the favourite himself was " settled in the true Protestant religion ". After this triumph Laud was thanked by King James, and his ascendancy over the mind of Buckingham was complete. A fortnight after the conference he recorded in his diary that " My Lord Marquis Buckingham was pleased to enter upon a near respect to me ", and added, " the particulars are not for paper ".[1] He became Buckingham's chaplain and stood to him in that relation which has often set confessors above kings in Catholic countries. Next year when Buckingham was in Spain with Prince Charles, he maintained a continual correspondence with Laud.[2] In England Laud drafted speeches for him and compiled memoranda for him. He was frequently closeted alone with him, and knew his secrets. He relied on him for promotion, and every vacancy in the episcopal bench saw him promoted. His fellow Arminians recognised him as their leader, while Andrewes remained in scholarly seclusion, " content with the enjoying without the enjoining ",[3] and Neile, under whose wing Laud had

[1] Laud, *Works*, iii. 139.

[2] Laud recorded in his diary on Feb. 17, 1622–3 (*Works*, iii. 141), that " the Prince and the Marquis Buckingham set forward very secretly for Spain ": and his knowledge of this supposedly strictly secret departure was afterwards charged against him by Prynne. It is an interesting sidelight on Laud's position, at the time of the Spanish journey, that the private letters between Buckingham and the King on that occasion were afterwards found in Laud's study.

[3] Fuller, *Church History*, vi. 40.

first risen, contented himself with a back seat. King James, who had consistently shown his distrust of Laud, was in eclipse. Discredited by the failure of the Spanish match and the policy of recovering the Palatinate without recourse to war, he was taking a back seat also. So was Williams. The divergence of policy between the King and the favourite caused a difficult dilemma for the ingenious bishop, and, thinking he saw signs of Buckingham's impending fall, he committed himself to the pacific policy of the King which was also more congenial to himself.[1] But Buckingham did not fall, and Williams was left committed to the losing side, while Laud pressed home his advantage and undermined his rival. It was in vain that Williams sought to recover his position, in vain that he wrote to Buckingham rebutting all charges of being opposed to his interests in any way whatever.[2] The Countess of Buckingham told him " that St. David's was the man that did undermine him with her son, and would underwork any man in the world that himself might rise ".[3] The Lord Keeper was kept waiting in an antechamber for two hours on one occasion, and then dismissed without an interview, while Buckingham was closeted with the Puritan Dr. Preston, who was widely tipped as the next Lord Keeper, and was actually proposing a plan for the abolition of deans and chapters as " fat, lazy, and unprofitable drones ". For a time it seemed that this sinister character, who was tempting the favourite with the prospect of new power based on still further inroads upon the property of the Church, might actually supplant both Laud and Williams in his counsels ; but his ascendancy was short-lived, and he proved to be but " a court meteor for a while, raised to a sudden height of expectation : and having flashed and blazed a little, went out again and was as suddenly forgotten ".[4] Finally Williams sought to recover his influence by a typical manœuvre. The archdeacon of Cambrai warned King James that he was now no more than a tool in the hands of the Duke, and Williams, having discovered this indiscretion by pumping the archdeacon's mistress, reported it to Prince Charles in the hope of deserving his gratitude. But the Prince, however gratified he may have been at the detection, entertained prudish objections to the means employed. Williams

[1] Clarendon, *History of the Rebellion*, i. 19 ; cf. Heylin, p. 107.

[2] *Cabala*, p. 83 ; cf. Laud, *Works*, iii. 148.

[3] Hacket, ii. 19.

[4] Heylin, 149.

was ready with a justification. " In my studies of divinity ", he said, " I have gleaned up this maxim : it is lawful to make use of the sin of another. Though the Devil make her a sinner, I may make good use of her sin." As a means of recovering the favour of the Prince and Buckingham the experiment failed dismally, and, if anything, only served still further to alienate the sombre, strait-laced prince from a clergyman whose conscience was so adaptable.

In the midst of these necessary intrigues Laud had of course little time for his distant bishopric, which, as is clear from his disparaging references to it, he regarded as a very inadequate return for so many years of waiting. In December 1621 he was installed by proxy, and in the following summer made his first journey into Wales to visit it. He was there for just over a month, — just long enough to be installed in person, to reprimand the chapter for their disorderly keeping of the Church muniments, and to issue visitation orders requiring that services be performed with the orthodox rites and ceremonies. On August 15th he began his homeward journey, — which was not without misadventure : for his papers were nearly spoiled when his sumpter-horse fell into a Herefordshire bottom. On the way he also stayed with a friend who may here be conveniently introduced, — Sir John Scudamore of Holme Lacy in Herefordshire, afterwards the first Viscount Scudamore.

Sir John Scudamore came of an old Herefordshire family which had served the Tudor sovereigns in various capacities, and had received a proportionate reward out of the neighbouring Church lands. The Sir John Scudamore of Queen Elizabeth's reign had been typical of the cultured country gentlemen who were rising out of the ruins of an effete Church, and among those who enjoyed his hospitality at Holme Lacy, recently rebuilt and enlarged, were Sir Thomas Bodley, whose delightful letters testify to his appreciation of it, and the learned mathematician Dr. Thomas Allen, whose watch the Herefordshire servants threw into the moat, thinking that it was a devil.[1] His son, Sir James Scudamore, was also intimate with Bodley, and as " Sir Scudamour " represents in Spenser's *Faery Queen* the type and pattern of chivalry. But with the passage of a generation, and especially

[1] Aubrey, *Brief Lives* (Thomas Allen).

the generation of James I, the old carefree culture was replaced by something more introspective and austere, and young Sir John Scudamore, the son of Sir James, a man of frail health and studious disposition, was subject to a crop of religious doubts. Returning at the age of twenty from the Grand Tour, he was one of those who lost no time in worshipping the rising sun: and it was no doubt in the service of Buckingham that he first met Laud, whose earliest letter to him is dated 1621. Between the introspective pietism of the young baronet and the unhesitant churchmanship of the middle-aged bishop a natural alliance was possible, and Laud's relations with Scudamore, which resulted in a lifelong correspondence, were of much the same nature, though on a less prominent stage, as those which bound him to Buckingham. In his letters he fusses over Scudamore's health, both physical and spiritual, like an old family nursemaid, urging him to take precautions against the cold weather and resolving his minute religious doubts. Some of the results of this friendship will be seen later. At present it is sufficient to remark, if we may take Laud's bread-and-butter letter literally, that he found his entertainment at Holme Lacy "as full of respect as ever I found it of any friend": although it seems that he had been well teased by the ladies of the household.

On his return to court, Laud settled down again to the business of countering the real or imagined manœuvres of Williams, of maintaining his intimacy with Buckingham, and of advancing the Arminian cause. The controversy with Fisher was continued on paper; and at Christmas, in the course of three interviews with the King, Laud read over to him the answers which he had made to the Jesuit's charges. The King required him to print them, and this was done, pseudonymously, Laud using the initials of his chaplain Richard Baylie. As for Archbishop Abbot, he had already ceased to count. Continued disfavour, the affair of Lord Zouche's Keeper, and his failure to prevent the rise of Laud weighed on his mind, and he scarcely attempted to raise his voice in public any more. In 1624 Laud suggested to Buckingham that the subsidy voted by Convocation be paid in instalments as a concession to the lower clergy, whose lot he was genuinely concerned to improve. For this he was soundly rated by Abbot, who asked "what I had to do to make any suit for the Church, —

told me never any bishop attempted the like at any time, nor would any but myself have done it " ; but he defended himself, and went straight off to report the affair to Buckingham, " lest I might have ill offices done me for it to the King and the Prince ". At the end of the same year Abbot attempted to keep him out of the High Commission : but again Laud appealed to Buckingham, and secured his inclusion.[1]

Meanwhile the Arminian clergy, after many years in the wilderness, naturally looked to Laud for promotion. The letters of Richard Montague to John Cosin show the situation clearly.[2] Every episcopal death, or impending death, or reported death, drew from this busy champion of the Church hasty condolences followed by eager speculations about the succession. In October 1624 died Miles Smith, the Bishop of Gloucester, whom Laud had so offended seven years ago. " My Lord of St. David's must now, and in such cases ", wrote Montague, " put for the Church with the Duke, and use his great credit that we be not swallowed up with a puritan bishopricry " : and he added that Laud might do well at the same time to remind Buckingham of Montague's own claims to a mitre. Three months later we find him urging Cosin not to deliver a certain sermon until he knows whether Laud approves of it. Shortly afterwards, he has heard that the Bishop of Exeter is unlikely to recover. " My Lord of St. David's will have none of that, will he ? " he wrote ; " if not, he may do a friendly part to put his great friend in mind of his voluntary and large offerings unto me once." In the following July this indefatigable place-hunter (who professed that a bishopric would be a burden to him which only his duty would persuade him to shoulder) is writing to Neile : " at present I hear the Bishop of Worcester is very sick. . . . If my Lord of St. David's might succeed, and I him, I should be half-delivered." The Bishop of Worcester, however, had another sixteen years of life in him, and Montague had to wait. In 1626 it is, " Res ἐπὶ ξυρᾶς ἀκμῇ : but my Lord of St. David's (if yet St. David's) [3] must direct. Nobis ea jussa capessere fas est." Arminianism had at last become so fashionable that even the sycophants and toadies of the Church hastened to embrace what they had quite recently denounced as

[1] Laud, *Works*, iii. 151 ; vi. 243.
[2] *Correspondence of John Cosin* (Surtees Soc., 1868).
[3] Laud being then bishop designate of Bath and Wells.

heresy : nor was it only the clergy who saw in Laud a door leading to Buckingham and the loaves and fishes ; for two of Sir John Scudamore's female relatives descended upon him one day in an attempt to secure lucrative positions for their husbands. And in the meantime the last obstacle to the triumph of Charles and Buckingham and Laud had been removed. In March 1625 James I had died, attended by Williams, with all the circumstances of humbug inseparable from the deaths of kings and the ministrations of priests, professing his firm belief in the true Protestant faith, without any admixture of Romanism, and declaring his regret that he had not had an opportunity of suffering martyrdom for it, — James I, who "naturally loved not the sight of a soldier, nor of any valiant man" !

In Puritan circles there was immediate apprehension. One Henry Burton, who had been clerk of the closet to Charles as Prince of Wales, and who was disappointed at not being continued in the royal household under him as King, presented him with a paper in which he pointed out "how popishly affected were Dr. Neile and Dr. Laud, his continual advisers" : and someone communicated to the new King the unfortunate affair of Lord Devonshire's marriage, which so tormented the conscience of Laud. But these protests were unavailing. In April Buckingham applied to Laud for a list of such clergy as were eligible for promotion, and Laud supplied him with a list of names divided into two categories, headed respectively "O" for orthodox, or Arminian, and "P" for Puritan, or heterodox. And on the other side Williams, after seeing the old King to his grave, was excluded from the coronation of the new.

CHAPTER THREE

PARLIAMENT

"I have little hope of good success in Parliament till —

(1) they leave personal prosecution:
(2) meddling with the Church:
(3) sit less time, that they may not understand one another too well:
(4) remember that the law of God, which gives Kings aids and subsidies, may not be broken by them without heinous sin."

(Laud's analysis of political views, 1628. *S.P. Dom. Car. I.* 499, nos. 64-5)

AFTER lying in state on a catafalque supported by plaster caryatids, the work of Inigo Jones, James I was expensively buried, and all his ideas went with him. The ministers of his policy disappeared from the scene at the same time. The supple philosopher Bacon died in the same year: the olympian doctrinaire Andrewes was to follow in the next; and the ingenious Lord Keeper Williams, after preaching the funeral sermon on the death of Solomon (with the essential proviso that "Solomon's vices could be no blemish to King James, who resembled him only in his choicest virtues"),[1] was deprived of his office on the grounds that it involved a time-limit of three years, and succeeded by Lord Coventry, who held it for fifteen. He was ordered to withdraw to his diocese of Lincoln, forbidden to take part in the coronation of the new King, discouraged from officiating as Dean of Westminster, instructed not to attend the House of Lords, and deprived even of the pension which he had recently purchased. In Church and State, these men had sought to manage the opposition and avoid trouble: to keep idealism in its place and confine war to the Continent, until those who profited by the tranquillity of such a policy chafed at its ignominy. One disgruntled pamphleteer declared that the policy of the government — in contrast to the "peace with honour" of which later statesmen have boasted — was "discord at home and dishonour abroad", and protested to the King that

[1] Fuller, *Church History*, vi. 10.

his subjects had no inkling of the principles upon which he stood. " That you are head of the Church they do not doubt : but of what Church they would gladly know." Since it could not be the Church militant, and certainly was not the Church triumphant, " they conclude it must be the Church dormant or none ".[1] At least no one could say this of King James' successor.

For Charles I was the very antithesis of his father. James I had loved nothing so much as a good controversy, and had even founded a college to encourage it. He liked others to be wrong, that he might point out their errors. He had taught kingcraft to kings and defined theology to cardinals. And if, in his public utterances, he sometimes proclaimed grand and universal principles, they were like the vague and cloudy effusion behind which the octopus dodges his foes. All this was repellent to his son, who was unable to argue much owing to an impediment in his speech, and hated controversy with the hatred of one who already knows truth. His father, it was said, had destined him, while his elder brother Henry was alive, to be Archbishop of Canterbury : but he disliked disputation, and disapproved of King James' College at Chelsea, which he refused to revive in 1636. " Instead of studying controversies ", he told the papal emissary Panzani, " one should rather work for union " : and to Laud he said that he could never be a lawyer, for he could not defend a bad cause or yield in a good. After his return from the Spanish adventure in 1623, the Arminian churchmen, Andrewes, Neile, Wren, and Laud, met together, and Wren, who had accompanied the Prince abroad, was asked to report upon his spiritual condition. At first he was reluctant to speak, but, when pressed, he replied that " for upholding the doctrine and discipline and the right estate of the Church, I have more confidence of him than of his father, in whom they say (better than I can) is so much inconstancy in some particular cases " : whereupon Andrewes told Laud and Wren that they would " live to see that day that your master will be put to it upon his head and his crown, without he will forsake the support of the Church ".[2] Charles' obstinate devotion to certain fixed ideals needs no emphasis. Nothing was ever able to alter his affections, not treaties or acts of parliament or solemn engagements : and his enemies soon found that, though

[1] *Tom Tell Troath*, 1622 (?), pub. in *Harl. Miscellany*, ii. 419.

[2] MS. Dugdale, 10, p. 114.

they might bind his tongue, his words meant nothing, for his heart remained set on the same goal as before.

Charles' ideal was the Catholic ideal in both Church and State. His court was completely Catholic in interests, and increasingly Roman in religion. If the King hated ideas, he was a connoisseur of art. While disputation was silenced, the aesthetic pleasures which were divorced from politics were fostered and patronised. Poetry and drama came under his protection, — that is, such poetry and drama as dealt merely with the delights of love and the deaths of kings : not Milton, but D'Avenant and Waller, Suckling, Lovelace, Shirley, and Wat Montague. Gerhard Honthorst was attracted to England, and Antony Van Dyck and Peter Paul Rubens were knighted by him. The Earl of Arundel toured Europe on expensive embassies, with the King's Master of the Works, Inigo Jones, in his train and Wenceslas Hollar in his baggage, in search of masterpieces and antiquities for himself and his sovereign. Charles kept his ministers of state waiting in ante-rooms while he walked round his famous picture gallery, pointing out his treasures to the sympathetic papal Agent : and Cardinal Barberini sent Leonardos, Correggios, Andrea del Sartos, and Veroneses to hasten his conversion. The proceeds of justice were diverted to the beautification of churches. Such a court might have won the credit of posterity for a Renaissance Pope : but it failed to commend Charles I to Puritans who were also philistines.

In politics Charles appealed to that same Catholic ideal which his court superficially represented. There is little evidence, certainly, that the King was personally interested in the better side of that ideal, — its great sense of social responsibility, — or, if he was, it occupied in his mind a place subordinate to the political constitution which it entailed. The end of Charles' policy, if he may be said to have had a policy, was, if not to exercise, at least to possess sovereign rule. Details of policy, and the unpopularity excited by obedient execution of orders, these might be left to his ministers, so long as the King was recognised as the ruler, under God, of the kingdom. The constitutional crisis of the reign was caused, in the first place, by Parliament's refusal to finance an unpopular foreign policy : but when forced to make a choice, Charles showed that it was not the foreign policy, but the principle of his personal sovereignty, for which he really cared; for after the breach with Parliament he did not attempt to continue the foreign policy against which Parliament had protested, and by eleven years of precarious self-support he secured nothing except the absence of parliament. But it was enough. Had he been willing to accept the position of a Dutch Stadtholder, he might have done it, and perhaps have done something in it. He preferred to live like a Belgian Archduke or a Duke of Florence: and in order to do so he was prepared to be a helpless cypher in European affairs; to see his sister and her family driven from their inheritance, and merely to go, cap in hand, to her assailants, without the power to threaten or the means to bribe them; to be at loggerheads with his subjects; and to be no richer by it than if he had drawn his revenue from parliamentary sources.

The religion which he advocated was, of course, the religion which reflected and justified this political choice. That is, the Catholic religion, whose doctrinal exponent might be (as the Pope chose to consider) the Pope, or (as the Archbishop of Canterbury preferred) the Archbishop of Canterbury. King Charles, it is well known, died a martyr for the Anglican confession: but that does not mean that he had any fundamental objection to the claims of Rome. It was against Puritanism, not Romanism, that he was prepared to defend his Church to the end: and while he never seriously consented to negotiate with Puritanism, he was quite prepared, at one time, to admit the Roman religion, if only the Pope had been willing to give him some more substantial *quid pro quo* than was actually forthcoming. He had a sentimental hankering after unity, and, conscious of his own weakness, he sought some strong external prop upon which he might rest, in the assurance that it would not give way beneath him while he trifled with his unreal eminence. Such a prop Rome undertook to supply. Her doctrine was infallible, supernatural, splendid. With its roots in the heroic age, its branches extending over the whole world, it appealed to the aesthetic sense, fascinating as well as supporting. But to the acceptance of the Roman supremacy there were three objections which ultimately proved insurmountable. First, its head was at Rome, and it would be an unforgivable sacrifice of prestige for an English king to divest himself of the headship of the Church and bestow it upon an Italian prince, who might not be so indulgent to a faithful son as to a returning prodigal.

Then there were the Jesuits, who advanced a hideous doctrine that kings might lawfully be deposed by the Pope or assassinated by the people. The Jesuits, Charles said, were the Roman Puritans :[1] and but for the Puritans upon one side and the Jesuits on the other, the disastrous breach in the unity of the Church might be healed. And thirdly there was the Palatinate. Try though he would, — whatever concessions he might offer to the English Catholics, whatever prospect of his own conversion, — Charles could never persuade the Vatican to give any effective aid towards the recovery of the Palatinate for his sister. Fair words, honours, distinctions, pictures, and *objets d'art*, — these inessentials were showered upon him : but the things for which his heart really yearned, — a renunciation of the deposing power and assistance towards the recovery of the Palatinate — these were never offered. However skilfully the Vicar of Christ might gild his pill, he would not alter its ingredients. So Charles remained a devoted adherent of the Catholic ideal, — of its unity, uniformity, infallibility, external splendour, ceremonies, and hierarchical organisation, — only its head was not to be at Rome, with its Jesuits, its exclusive claims, its political independence, but at Canterbury, where there were none of these things. Nevertheless, he could not bring himself to hate Rome as he hated Geneva. Whatever its present or future policy might be, Rome at least would always support the theoretical basis upon which Charles meant to rule, while Puritanism was not only hostile to the government in matters of immediate policy, but subversive of all government in principle. So Charles' court continued to be crowded by Papists or crypto-Papists, while Puritans were treated with fear and distrust. And Protestant Englishmen, since they

[1] The most offensive characteristic shared by Jesuits and Presbyterians was their doctrine of the right of subjects to depose unsatisfactory kings. This was represented particularly by Buchanan's *De Jure Regni apud Scotos*, and Mariana's *Regis Institutione*, and later inspired a royalist rhyme :

" A Scot and Jesuit, hand in hand,
First taught the world to say,
That subjects ought to have command,
And monarchs to obey."

At the time of the Bishops' Wars, the disaffection of the Scots was frequently attributed to Jesuit propaganda, and in 1640 one John Corbet fabricated a document to prove it, — " The Epistle Congratulatorie of Lysimachus Nicanor, of the Society of Jesu, to the Covenanters in Scotland, wherein is paralleled our sweet harmony and correspondence in doctrine and practice ". Cf. also p. 395, *inf*.

hated an autocratic government under whatever name, called it by the worst name that they knew, — the name which conjured up the memory of Bloody Mary, the Spanish Armada, and the Powder Plot, — Popery. For then, as in Defoe's time, there were a hundred thousand men ready to rise in arms against Popery, without knowing whether Popery were a man or a horse.

Such was the court of which Laud was now a prominent member, such the ideals which he found it incumbent upon him to advance, even although he did not approve of all of them himself. He had no use, for instance, for the dilettanti who surrounded the King, on the look-out for pickings, for the Romanists who looked beyond Canterbury (or, at the moment, beyond St. David's) for instructions and salvation, or for the placemen who were mere passengers in the government, lacking his own serious mission and dissipating the resources of the kingdom in frivolous pleasures which were hateful to him. Still, he had to get on as best he could with them : for as yet he could not afford to pick and choose, and it was essential at all costs to preserve his influence with the King and Buckingham. Once robbed of court favour, he had no power of his own to fall back on. He might, like Williams, be packed off to his remote diocese : and a bishop of St. David's was a very insignificant creature, — a mere ecclesiastical squireen.

In attaching himself so closely to this court, therefore, Laud was also committing himself to the support of a policy. For Charles I had succeeded to a kingdom at war. He could not blame his predecessor for the war, which had in fact been forced upon James I by a combination of Prince Charles himself, Buckingham, and Parliament. The old King had yielded to this combined pressure with the observation that his son would live to have his bellyful of parliaments ; and this observation was soon proved to be true. The alliance was an expedient of the most temporary nature, and each party required the war for a different purpose. To Charles it was a war to restore his sister and her family, not indeed to the Crown of Bohemia, which they had rashly usurped, but to the Palatinate from which they had been expelled in consequence : and Buckingham threw himself into this military adventure, not merely to serve the dynastic ambitions of his master, but to exhibit the splendid strategical genius, with which he credited himself, in the welding and directing of European coalitions. But this was not at all what Parliament had intended. A war of religion had indeed been outlined, but it was to show a good financial profit as well, and this could hardly be expected from a campaign which included the subsidising of German and Transylvanian princes. A series of piratical and remunerative descents on Spain and the Indies seemed to them the best way of doing good in the sight of the Lord, and they had no intention of paying for ambitious and costly operations on the Continent. "Are we poor?" demanded Sir John Eliot. "Spain is rich! There are our Indies! Break with them, and we shall break our necessities together!" And Sir Francis Seymour said that he had heard "wars spoken of, and an army, but would be glad to hear where. The Palatinate was the place intended by His Majesty. This was never thought of, nor is it fit for the consideration of the House, in regard of the infinite charge."

So when Charles faced his first parliament in June 1625 the divergence between King and subjects in the matter of policy was already plain. The King was committed to a foreign policy which Parliament had already condemned, and now, what with the expenses of the war, the extravagance of the old King, and the costs of the new reign in funeral, pensions, and an impending coronation, he found himself "in such straits for money as is not to be spoken of", and was applying to Parliament to finance the policy of which it disapproved.

Parliament opened with a sermon from Laud, in which the completeness of the understanding which bound the Church, as far as he could claim to represent it, to whatever policy the government intended to pursue, was made clear.[1] The King, Laud said, was God's immediate vicegerent on earth, so that "one and the same action is God's by ordinance and the King's by execution", and the royal power "is not any assuming to himself, nor any gift from the people, but God's power". The law and the parliament, he continued, were mere agents of the King, dependent on him for their very existence, and without any authority of their own: "All judges and courts of justice, even this great congregation, this great council now ready to sit, receive influence and power from the King, and are dispensers of his

[1] Laud, *Works*, i. 94.

justice as well as their own, both in the laws they make and in the laws they execute, in the causes which they hear and in the sentences which they give ". The sole original function of Parliament, he said, was to provide the King with the money necessary for the support of his independent and absolute authority : " The King is the sun. He draws up some vapours, some supply, some support, from us. It is true he must do so : for if the sun draw up no vapours, it can pour down no rain." Any attempt by subordinate magistrates to show originality could only lead to chaos and confusion such as prevailed in Israel when " every man did what seemed good in his own eyes, and the punishment was great ". James I himself could not have gone further in his exaltation of the royal function and the royal authority.

This was not a conciliatory beginning to the session : and the parliamentary party emphasised its rejection of such doctrines at the earliest opportunity by an attack upon the high-church party, which advanced them, in the person of Richard Montague.

Of all the Arminian clergy of that time, Montague seemed to the layman to be the most dangerous. One of the Durham House party which acknowledged the leadership of Neile and Laud, he had controversial dexterity, which Neile and Laud had not : and the books which he hurled, like apples of discord, into an interested world, were weighted with massive learning, and pointed with a stinging wit, which Neile and Laud even more conspicuously lacked. " These his great parts ", says Fuller, " were attended with tartness of writing ; very sharp the nib of his pen, and much gall in his ink, against such as opposed him." [1] As evidence of his erudition, he had, while fellow of Eton, prepared for the press the famous edition of St. Chrysostom which the Provost, Sir Henry Savile, launched into the learned world of which he was the universal patron. He had also edited the two Invectives of St. Gregory of Nazianzus against the Emperor Julian, and Casaubon's posthumous commentary of the Roman chronicle of Baronius, — a work which had to wait till 1622 before it could evade the veto of the Puritan Archbishop. And lest these topics should appear remote and academic, he had also disputed the vexed question of tithes with the learned John Selden, who, however, declined to believe that he ought to pay tithes to anyone merely because Abraham paid them to Melchisedec.

[1] *Church History*, vi. 15.

Montague's immediate offence, however, arose from the apparently laudable activity of combating the missionaries of the Pope. In 1619, as rector of Stamford Rivers in Essex, he had discovered some of these " Romish rangers " seeking to pervert his flock, and had issued a challenge to them, offering to become a Papist himself if his rivals could prove him wrong in any of his assertions. But instead of proving the whole Roman doctrine fundamentally false, the Pope Antichrist and the horn of the Beast, and his Church a diabolical imposture from its very beginning, Montague had endeavoured to show that it was unnecessary to go as far as Rome for the most comfortable parts of her doctrine, as these were all provided, in a far purer form, by the orthodox Church of England. The result was an ecclesiastical scandal. Trailing his coat provocatively in the face of both Romanists and Calvinists, Montague was at once accused by each of belonging to the other. The Papists attacked first with *A Gag for a New Gospel*, and in 1624 Montague retorted with *A New Gag for an Old Goose*, in which he defined the differences between the doctrines of Rome and Canterbury, and, by defining them, reduced them, in the eyes of enthusiastic Protestants, to merely superficial divergences. The Puritans Yates and Ward protested to the last Parliament of James I: Parliament protested to Archbishop Abbot: and Archbishop Abbot protested to Montague. But Montague protested to the King, who declared, " if that is to be a Papist, so am I a Papist ", and Montague retired with the assurance that no harm could now befall him. Parliament might attack him, — Parliament always was attacking him, —

> Dulichii Samiique, et quos tulit alta Zacynthus
> In me turba ruunt

is one of his most frequent tags (for he had a ready commonplace-book): but the King, Buckingham, and Laud were among his champions, and

> παρ' ἐμοὶ δὲ καὶ ἄλλοι
> οἵ κέ με τιμήσουσι, μάλιστά τε μητιέτα Ζεύς

is another. In 1625 he exploited his victory by publishing another book, *Appello Caesarem*, in which he dealt roundly with the Calvinists and English Puritans who sought to intrude foreign doctrines into the English Church and establish " Popes in every parish ". " All is not Popery that Papists say ", he contended : some of it was even truth, and the Roman Church, if not a sound Church, was not fundamentally corrupt but superficially corrupted. These were exactly the views which Laud had expressed in his Oxford sermons, and, coming from Montague, they were no less offensive through being more trenchantly expressed. The manuscript had been submitted before publication to Neile and Cosin, to alter as they thought fit, and then Montague had applied to Abbot for the Archbishop's imprimatur. This was refused : but the Dean of Carlisle, Dr. White, supplied the necessary licence, and the book was published.

Immediately the outcry was renewed. Within a year, four books were written against it, — one by the Bishop of Chichester, one by the parliamentarian Rous, one by the Puritan apologist Yates, and one by the ex-courtier Burton. A fifth, *The Unmasking of a Massmonger*, by Matthew Sutcliffe, the projector of King James' College at Chelsea, was suppressed in proof ; and next year a new publicist came upon the scene, protesting that it was as irrational to question the infallibility of Calvinism merely because of Montague's book as to believe that the planets revolve round the sun merely because " one brainsick Copernicus, out of the sublimity of his quintessential transcendal speculations, hath more senselessly than metaphysically, more ridiculously than singularly, averred it ". This belated pamphlet was *The Perpetuity of a Regenerate Man's Estate*, the first of a great torrent of literature which was to flow from the pen of William Prynne.

In such circumstances it was obvious that Parliament too would take cognisance of the affair, and it was reported to Montague that Dr. Prideaux, the Regius Professor at Oxford, " hath threatened the first thing the Parliament shall be (for they are doubtless at his beck) to burn my book, and why not me ? " He was duly hailed before the Commons and bound over in £2000 : but the new King came to his rescue, appointing Montague as his chaplain, and ordering Parliament to desist from attacks on his personal servant. This good news was reported to Montague by Laud, as he went from the plague-stricken capital to stay in the country with his friend Francis Windebank.

After a thoroughly unsatisfactory session, the King adjourned a parliament which had attacked his religious views, refused the ordinary sources of revenue, and questioned the impositions levied by his father. When it reassembled in August, it was at Oxford, as London had been made unsafe by the plague ; and while Laud, Howson, and Buckeridge wrote to Buckingham testifying to the orthodoxy of Dr. Montague,[1] Dr. Montague was summoned to Westminster to defend himself in recognition of his bond. He replied that he was ill, and could not come : and although the Commons were naturally sceptical, he seems to have spoken truth ; for he wrote to Cosin at the same time that " if the Parliament send for me, they must send a litter for him that cannot go nor ride, after a sore sickness, six clysters, a strong purgation that gave me twenty-two stools ". Within a fortnight Parliament had been dissolved with nothing done, and the King was left to continue the war with a hopelessly inadequate grant of £127,000 and such meagre additions as he could scrape together from City loans, the Queen's dowry, the sale of Crown lands, and the fines of Roman recusants.

Meanwhile Laud was on his way to make a second visit to his Welsh diocese. He was there for three months, in the course of which he consecrated the chapel which he had caused to be built on to his episcopal house at Abergwili, preached, picnicked in the hills, and had a continual series of dreams about the Duke of Buckingham, the Duchess of Buckingham, and all the Villiers family. In one of his dreams he saw the Bishop of Worcester, who beckoned to him and urged him to come and live in Wales, " but not staying for my answer, he subjoined that he knew I could not live so meanly ".[2] Certainly it was not Laud's intention to spend the rest of his days in a poor Welsh diocese. His imagination, he admits, " ran altogether upon the Duke of Buckingham, his servants and family ",[3] and in November he started back for England, stopping on the way first with Sir John Scudamore at Holme Lacy, then with Francis Windebank at Haines Hill. There he learnt of the birth of Buckingham's son, and hastened to write a letter of congratulation.

Meanwhile preparations were afoot for the coronation of the King, which was to take place on February 2nd. As Dean of Westminster, Williams ought to have officiated, but the King would not allow him to attend, instructing him to name one of

[1] Laud, *Works*, vi. 244. [2] *Ibid.* iii. 174. [3] *Ibid.* iii. 172.

the prebendaries of the Abbey in his place. It was as good as an order to name Laud, but Williams avoided both the humiliation of naming Laud and the odium of not naming him. He merely submitted a complete list of the prebendaries, so that the King might make his own choice. The King chose Laud.

On the same day upon which he learnt of his appointment, Laud was present at a consultation held by the King's command to discuss the case of Montague. Andrewes, Neile, Buckeridge, Mountain the Bishop of London, and Laud were present; and after the conference they sent a letter under their hands to Buckingham, repeating their confidence in Montague's orthodoxy, and suggesting that in future for the peace of the Church, all controversy should be silenced by royal proclamation.[1]

It was thus with the knowledge that the government was as intransigent as ever that Charles I's second parliament met in February 1626, full of indignation against Buckingham for the failure of the Cadiz expedition, which they had declined to finance, and he had been incompetent to lead. Anticipating trouble, the government had taken pains to deprive Parliament of its sting. The most active members of the opposition had been pricked as sheriffs for their counties: Bishop Williams was instructed not to attend the House of Lords: the Earl of Arundel was put in the Tower on a frivolous charge to prevent his attendance: and the Earl of Bristol, who was able to produce damaging evidence against the Duke's behaviour during the Spanish journey, was confined to his house.

To a parliament thus deprived of its natural leaders, Laud addressed a premonitory sermon on the text, "Jerusalem is builded as a city that is at unity in itself", urging the duty of unanimous obedience. But it was ineffectual. "The preacher had done his part in it", says Heylin, "but the hearers did not." The case of Montague, which was still being busily disputed by high and low churchmen in two conferences at York House, was allowed to drop while the Commons flew at higher game. Buckingham was impeached. Eliot delivered a speech against the exclusion of members, which he condemned as a foolish and impotent manœuvre: for if the great were silenced, the lesser would speak up against tyranny and incompetence. He spoke up himself, and,

[1] Laud, *Works*, vi. 249.

in a great philippic, compared Buckingham to Sejanus, the minion of Tiberius. The King sought to save his minister, first by imprisoning offensive members, then by dissolving Parliament: and though the last method succeeded, it cost the King four subsidies, which Parliament had promised to vote once grievances had been redressed.

So Buckingham escaped, his power unimpaired. In the midst of his impeachment, as if in deliberate spite of Parliament, the University of Cambridge had elected him as their Chancellor,[1] and early next year Laud accompanied him thither, that he might be the first to receive a degree at his hands. Laud too was secure. In the course of the session, Arthur Lake, Bishop of Bath and Wells, died, and Laud applied for his diocese. He had hoped, indeed, for something bigger, but, as he wrote to Sir John Scudamore, " I had no reason but at that time to do as I did, and fasten upon any indifferent thing to get out of Wales " ; so on June 20th, five days after the dissolution of Parliament, he was promoted. Three months later, to his chagrin, Lancelot Andrewes died, and the see of Winchester and the deanery of the Chapel Royal were at the King's disposal. Had he but waited, Laud might have had Winchester: but having just taken Bath and Wells, he could not decently apply for a further promotion so soon, and chafed at the prospect of seeing another promoted over his head. This, however, was avoided. The King gave Laud the deanery of the Chapel Royal, and kept the bishopric vacant for a year, appropriating the revenue to his depleted treasury. This was a custom, as Heylin admits, " more old than commendable ", and one which neither Andrewes nor Laud could approve. But at present Laud was aiming at power through influence, and could not afford to object: for if he had principles, he was also a courtier. Besides, by postponing the episcopal transfers for a year, the King allowed a decent interval to elapse after Laud's appointment to Bath and Wells, and so, when those transfers came, Laud got his promotion after all. For the present, he took the deanery, and at once set about improving the services. It had been customary for the King to come into the chapel for the sermon only, and for the dean at once to interrupt the prayers at

[1] Parliament was so outraged by this election that it even summoned some of the doctors who had voted for Buckingham to come and account for their behaviour at Westminster: but the King interposed and forbade their attendance.

his entry and proceed to the pulpit. This was a frequent custom at the time, — in Bristol the same honour was given to the Mayor: but with Laud's appointment it ceased to have the support of the royal example.[1] A month after his appointment to this office, Laud received from the Duke of Buckingham the comfortable news of "what the King had further resolved concerning me, in case the Archbishop of Canterbury should die".[2]

Archbishop Abbot was an unconscionable time a-dying: but it made little difference. The fortunes of Laud were rising, — in April 1627 he and Neile were made Privy Councillors, — and in the other pan of the scales those of Williams were descending still further. In January 1627 he made another attempt at reconciliation with the Duke, and Laud had an alarming dream about him the same night: but it came to nothing. As the government became more and more embarrassed in its attempt to carry on a spirited foreign policy without either means or leadership, Laud committed himself still further in its support. In the gambler's hope of retrieving all by a lucky throw, Buckingham was plunging into another expensive expedition, and the King, disappointed of his four subsidies, resorted to a forced loan. Unfortunately those who had already refused to give in Parliament were equally reluctant to lend in the counties. It was not enough to imprison refractory gentlemen and dismiss refractory peers from their offices. Encouragement was needed, and Buckingham applied to Laud to give it. Laud drew up a paper in which he urged the clergy to encourage contributions to so pious an enterprise, again reminding them that "the Church and the State are so near united and knit together, that though they may seem two bodies, yet indeed in some relations they may be accounted as but one",[3] and composed prayers for the success of the fleet in which the religious object of the expedition was remembered; and the clergy — or at least such as saw which way the wind was blowing — responded readily. The Dean of Canterbury, Dr. Isaac Bargrave, an assertive hunting clergyman, who had been chaplain to Sir Henry Wotton in Venice, and was formerly a champion of popular rights, now preached an effective sermon on the necessity of

[1] Hist. MSS. Comm. iv. App. 143 (House of Lords MSS.); Laud, *Works*, iii. 197.

[2] *Ibid.* iii. 196.

[3] Wilkins, *Concilia*, iv. 471.

supplying the government:[1] Dr. Manwaring preached two sermons before the King, one on Religion, one on Allegiance, and both proving the duty of submission: and Dr. Sibthorpe, preaching on Apostolic Obedience at Northampton, was equally successful in making unparliamentary taxation square with the Word of God. Archbishop Abbot, indeed, had misgivings about Sibthorpe's sermon, and refused either to license it for the press or to be convinced by Laud's arguments that it was quite unobjectionable; but his opposition was unavailing. He was suspended from all his functions and superseded by a commission of more satisfactory bishops, — Neile, Laud, Buckeridge, Howson, and Mountain; and it is said that when the other bishops hesitated to sign the order for his suspension, Laud, though the junior of them all, demanded the pen and placed his signature first.[2] On instructions from Laud, Dr. Mountain, the easy-going Bishop of London, then licensed both Sibthorpe's and Manwaring's sermons, which appeared in print, the latter with the inscription "by His Majesty's special command".

Again, it proved, the preachers had done their part but the men of action had not done theirs. The expedition to the Isle of Rhé, which took place in the autumn of 1627, proved a colossal fiasco, "the greatest and shamefullest overthrow since the loss of Normandy". But before the third parliament of the reign could meet to voice its indignation at unconstitutional expedients, military incompetence, and religious heresy in high places, an accident occurred which may serve to introduce two new characters to this history. Laud strained a muscle in his leg, and in the six weeks of forced rest which followed, he had leisure for personal correspondence.

One of those who hastened to condole with him on this misadventure was the Dutch scholar Gerhard Johann Voss, better known as Vossius. "When I read in your Lordship's last letter of your misfortune", he wrote, "a deathly horror overcame me (totus expallui atque exhorrui)." We should not, however, interpret too literally the words of a poor scholar to his patron: for Latin is adulation's language, and the humanists of the Renaissance had accustomed it to excess. Vossius was typical of the seventeenth-

[1] Birch, *Court and Times of Charles I*, i. 214-15.
[2] Fuller, *Appeal of Injured Innocence*, 1659, iii. 10.

century Continental savant, with his servile manners, his massive erudition, and his prolific family: and the conscientious correspondence which Laud, even at his busiest,[1] contrived to keep up with him, although there was so little, except doctrinal views, in common between the omnivorous historian and the ecclesiastical disciplinarian, is one of his most admirable traits.

A lifelong friend of Hugo Grotius, and, like him, an Arminian in doctrine, Vossius had published in 1618 his *Historia Pelagiana*, which had evoked a counterblast from Archbishop Ussher, won the admiration of Laud, and lost the author his position as director of theological studies at Leyden University. The Synod of Dordt, which met in the same year, had driven both Vossius and Grotius into exile: but Vossius was allowed to return soon afterwards, after giving satisfactory assurances about his future conduct: he became professor of history first at Leyden, then at Amsterdam, and resisted the efforts both of Lord Brooke to entice him to Cambridge and Archbishop Ussher to bring him to Ireland; and in 1627 his friendship with Laud began.

He was not an easy correspondent to have. Like Erasmus, he corresponded with the great scholars and statesmen of Europe, but he could not carry his learning lightly, as Erasmus did. He did not write in praise of Folly, but of learning and the patronising rich. He was voluble, earnest, and erudite: and Laud was far too busy either to write or to study much, except in the way of practical business, as he indicated in his first letter to his new friend. "One thing I beg of you", he wrote then, "do not seek me too often in these hasty lines. I dwell elsewhere, the slave of actions, not words"; and later Stephen Goffe wrote to him begging him to remember that "our illustrious Archbishop greatly appreciates your letters, but would apparently prefer them to be shorter, describing your studies rather than your gratitude".[2] Vossius' gratitude, however, could not thus easily be restrained. Laud had recommended him to Buckingham, had secured him a stall in Canterbury cathedral, and had sent one of his sons to Cambridge for his education, — although unfortunately the young Vossius did not share his father's zeal for exact scholarship, and, becoming almost immediately entangled

[1] On Laud's side the correspondence was frequently dealt with directly by his secretary William Dell. After Laud's elevation to Canterbury, all his letters to Vossius are in Dell's hand. (Bodl. MSS. Rawl. letters, 83, 84 b, 84 f.)

[2] G. J. Vossii, *Epistolae*, ed. Colomesius (London, 1690), *ad Vossium*, no. cxcii.

with a Cambridge barmaid, had to be recalled and sent off to the Dutch Indies.[1] In return for these solid benefits, Vossius increased the length of his letters and became almost embarrassing in the fulsomeness of his adulation. He addressed his benefactor as " a man, — no, a hero, — so richly adorned with piety, genius, learning, and dignity that, in a word, you come near to Almighty God " : and he developed the troublesome habit of swelling his letters with enclosures. Nor was it only his own works which he sent. " I have received your letter ", Laud wrote on one occasion, " and the tragedies and other poems by Grotius dedicated to you. Many thanks. I have read a few of them, and wish I had time for more."[2] The hint is plain enough, but it was unavailing. Tragedies by Grotius were not the worst. Vossius had a younger son with a literary bent, and his juvenilia were also forwarded to the Archbishop, who was far too busy in England to read the early works of Denys Vossius. And in October 1640, on the eve of the Long Parliament, when Laud was overwhelmed with business and cares, he received a letter from Vossius lamenting that the early departure of his cousin had prevented him from enclosing " my voluminous work on God and Nature ".[3] Nevertheless, it was not only literature which Vossius sent to Laud. On one occasion at least he performed solid services. In 1632 he became professor of history at the Athenaeum at Amsterdam, and there we shall find him acting as Laud's agent in his campaign against the emigrant English Puritans.

Another with whom Laud became acquainted while laid up with a strained leg was Peter Heylin, a fellow of Magdalen College, Oxford, who was to become his chaplain, his most industrious henchman, and, later, his most enthusiastic panegyrist. The account of their meeting is best given in Heylin's own words, which provide also one of the few intimate portraits of Laud which we possess.

" Coming precisely at the time ", he says, " I heard of his mischance, and that he kept himself to his chamber : but order had been left among the servants that if I came he should be

[1] Laud, *Works*, vi. 304 ; Vossius, *Ep.*, no. cclxvi.
[2] *Ibid.* vi. 446.
[3] B.M. Add. MS. 32093, p. 198.

made acquainted with it. Which being done accordingly, I was brought into his chamber, where I found him sitting in a chair with his lame leg resting on a pillow. Commanding that nobody should come to interrupt him till he called for them, he caused me to sit down by him, enquired first into the course of my studies, which he well approved of, exhorting me to hold myself in that moderate course in which he found me. He fell afterwards to discourse of some passages in Oxon, in which I was specially concerned, and told me thereupon the story of such oppositions as had been made against him in that University by Archbishop Abbot and some others: encouraged me not to shrink if I had already, or should hereafter find the like. I was with him thus, *remotis arbitris*, almost two hours. It grew towards twelve of the clock, and then he knocked for his servants to come unto him. He dined that day in his ordinary dining-room, which was the first time he had done so since his mishap. He caused me to tarry dinner with him, and used me with no small respect, which was much noted by some gentlemen (Elphinstone, one of His Majesty's cup-bearers, being one of the company) who dined that day with him; — a passage, I confess, not pertinent to my present story, but such as I have a good precedent for from Philip de Commines, who telleth us as impertinently of the time (though he acquaint us not with the occasion) of his leaving the Duke of Burgundy's service to betake himself to the employments of King Louis XI." [1]

Laud's advice was not wasted on Heylin, if it was even needed. He proved himself as troublesome an assertor of extreme high-church doctrines as ever Laud had been: and it was to this habit that many attributed his misfortune in failing ultimately to net a bishopric.

On March 17th, 1628, in circumstances more ominous even than those of the previous assembly, Charles faced his third parliament. Laud himself felt the increase of general unpopularity: for when the news of the Duke's ill success came home, he heard it twice said that a scapegoat would be necessary, and that he would do as well as any;[2] and in the analysis which he drew up of the advantages and disadvantages of a parliament, the "fears", which considerably outbalanced the "hopes", included

[1] Heylin, p. 166. [2] Laud, *Works*, iii. 206.

one that " at least they will look to sacrifice somebody ". The King, however, had reassured him ; and now he emerged from his apartments to preach the usual introductory sermon. Interspersing his sermon with allusions to his recent misadventure, which still made it difficult for him to stand, he expounded the text, " Endeavouring to keep the unity of the spirit in the bond of peace " : and the King ended his speech from the throne with a pious, but, as it proved, vain hope that the Houses would follow the advice of the preacher.

The Houses had no such intention. Having at last come to grips with a government which had persisted in an unpopular policy, financed it by the most objectionable means, and obtained no results from it except debt, disaster, and an extension of the war, the members who assembled at Westminster were determined to prevent any such thing from happening again. Twenty-seven of them had suffered imprisonment for refusing the forced loan, and arrived in London more indignant at their imprisonment than grateful for their timely release. Resolutions were passed against unparliamentary taxation, arbitrary imprisonment, and the billeting of soldiers, and incorporated, on the suggestion of Sir Edward Coke, in a Petition of Right. And Manwaring and Sibthorpe were attacked for preaching propagandist sermons in support of the government.

Manwaring was sent to defend himself before the Lords, where he demanded that his doctrine be considered by the spiritual Lords only, as they only were competent to deal with such abstruse matters. But the spiritual Lords were a set of bishops who, with a few exceptions, obediently voted for the government : and the lay Lords would not admit their own incapacity to judge religious questions. They might not have read the Fathers, but they were quite capable of seeing the practical results of Manwaring's extravagant teaching. So he was sharply reprimanded by the Lord Keeper for seeking to divide his judges, and told that doctrine was the province of all the Lords conjointly. Then they came to his doctrine, and accused him of proving the necessity of submission out of the Jesuit Suarez. Dr. Manwaring thereupon promptly proved it out of Calvin. But the Lords did not want it proved at all, and silenced him as he was proving it out of the Psalms. When Manwaring was about to withdraw, he was recalled by Archbishop Abbot, who reminded him of the philosopher

Anacharsis " whom the King of Cyprus caused to be brayed in a brazen mortar for his base flattery, as a just reward for all flatterers of princes ". The unfortunate clergyman submitted, and sentence was pronounced. He was to suffer imprisonment, to pay a fine of £1000 to the King, to be suspended for three years, never to preach at Court again or to hold any secular office or ecclesiastical dignity, and his book was to be recalled and burnt. The King, who had commanded the book to be printed, was not greatly perturbed at the consequences to its author. " He that can preach more than he can prove ", he said, " let him suffer for it. I give him no thanks for giving me my due."

Parliament next enquired into the licensing of Manwaring's sermons, and discovered that the royal command had been sent to Mountain, Bishop of London, by the hand of Laud. When questioned, Laud admitted having written the letter at the King's instance: but the Earl of Montgomery, who was present at Woodstock at the time, attested that he had acceded to the royal command with great reluctance. This is thoroughly in keeping with Laud's character. He hated discussion, and only entered upon controversy unwillingly. The way to secure orthodoxy was not, he believed, to prove the true doctrine but to enforce it, and to silence all disputation which tended to reopen a closed question. So in 1622 he had " had a hand " in King James' declaration limiting freedom of religious discussion: and in 1625, together with Howson and Buckeridge, he had written to Buckingham in defence of Montague that " the Church of England would not be too busy with every particular school-point . . . because she could not be able to preserve any unity amongst Christians if men were forced to subscribe to curious particulars disputed in schools ".[1] In the following year, after the parliamentary attacks on Montague and Bishop Goodman of Gloucester, he had drawn up a royal declaration signifying the King's " utter dislike of those who, to show the subtilty of their wits, or to please their own humours, or vent their own passions, do or shall adventure to stir or move any new opinions ". Before long he was to silence controversy by a more notable declaration.

Nevertheless Laud was not saved from attack by this disclaimer. The Commons saw clearly enough that Montague and Sibthorpe and Manwaring could not have published their offensive

[1] Laud, *Works*, vi. 244.

doctrines without at least general support from higher ecclesiastics: and on June 11th a Remonstrance was drawn up calling for strict enforcement of the penal laws and the suppression of Arminian doctrines, and naming Neile and Laud as "justly suspected to be unsound in their opinions".

Meanwhile the practical details of arbitrary government were faring as ill as its theoretical doctrines. The Petition of Right was being pushed forward, and the attempts of a moderate party to add a saving clause which acknowledged a discretionary power resident in the Crown were overborne by Eliot and his radical followers. When the bill was sent up to the Lords, it provided the occasion for a notable defection. Bishop Williams had hitherto sought by every means in his power to recover his influence with Buckingham. Now he decided that there was no hope from that quarter, so he made a virtue of necessity and came out on the side of the Opposition. Champions of popular rights recorded with satisfaction the sudden conversion of this former minister of the Crown. "The Bishop of Lincoln", reported a news-writer, "was much commended for what he spoke on behalf of the subject, acknowledging he had once offended in the days of his late master in standing for the prerogative to the prejudice of the subjects' liberties: for which he now desired forgiveness, professing that neither hope of great preferments, nor fear of the loss of what he presently enjoyed, should make him do or speak against his conscience."[1] "On the free side", wrote the same writer five days later, "the Bishop of Lincoln used the greatest freedom, giving neither way nor respect to those of the opposite party, — no, not to the Duke himself. The King only he mentioned with humble reverence."[2]

The King might have rejected the Petition and dissolved Parliament: but that would mean again the sacrifice of supply. Even so, he might have saved his independence at home by withdrawing from a costly and ignominious war abroad. But the news of still further military disasters, — of Denbigh's retirement from Rochelle with nothing done, and Morgan's surrender of Stade — finally decided him to sacrifice everything for the means to wipe away this last blot on the reputation of his government. On June 7th he signed the Petition in return for a niggardly supply of £275,000, eked out in driblets, to meet an expenditure of well over

[1] Meade to Stuteville, April 28th, 1628, in Birch i. 347. [2] *Ibid.* 349.

a million. Then Parliament turned again on Buckingham, and drew up a Remonstrance praying for his immediate dismissal from all his offices. Once again the King prorogued Parliament to save his minister.

For Williams, yet another nail in his political coffin was the reward of his latest defection. The empty title of Privy Councillor was taken away from him, and when he asked Lord Holland for the reason, he was told that " he must expect worse than this, because he was such a champion of the Petition of Right ".[1] Never is the character of Charles I less attractive than when he chose openly to tread upon the fallen.

The only political scandal which escaped unscathed from this turbulent session was Buckingham : and in the recess he too was removed, by the hand of an assassin, as he prepared to sail from Portsmouth with a mutinous fleet to Rochelle. Rarely has a political assassination been hailed with more universal delight. It was not only greeted with enthusiasm by those whose indignation and hatred were aroused against the omnipotent and incompetent minister : it brought relief to those who were conscientiously seeking some way out of the impasse into which the affairs of the Kingdom had been brought by the King's refusal to sacrifice either the favourite or the policy which he embodied. Now at last, it seemed, peace between government and opposition was possible.

In the eyes of Laud, however, all other considerations were insignificant compared to the loss of his patron and friend. The news of the murder was first sent to him by Sir John Scudamore, now Viscount Scudamore, who, after defending the Duke in Parliament, had gone to Portsmouth to take part in the campaign, and reached him at Croydon, where he was assisting at the consecration of Richard Montague as Bishop of Chichester. Laud had never shown any sign of either approving or understanding Buckingham's foreign policy : but he had defended it. When Parliament had refused to finance it, he had called for public subscriptions ; and when Parliament had attacked its failure, he had drawn up a paper in which every mistake was extenuated, every incompetence excused, by a series of weak explanations.[2] It is apparent, too, that there existed between Laud and Buckingham a personal intimacy such as sometimes binds widely different

[1] Hacket, ii. 89. [2] Laud, *Works*, vii. 631.

characters together. The volatile favourite, like the later Rochester, had his streak of religiosity, and confided in his stolid and fussy confessor: and Laud, on his part, could not but be dazzled by the magnificence of the young minister who both raised him to a position of influence and listened to his advice. When two consecutive letters from Vossius made no mention of the calamity, Laud was scandalised at such apparent insensibility and ingratitude. " In the first letter ", he wrote, " I ascribed your silence to ignorance, assuming that the news of the bloody deed had not yet reached you; but when your son delivered the second, also mute, I was dumbfounded. How is this? Has Rumour grown so slow? Does she take longer now to cross the narrow sea between us? Are her wings clotted by the blood spilt by that cruel, impious hand? No, surely! for blood speeds her and cries out upon the way. There must be some other reason. You prefer, surely, not to mention a deed so savage, a man so famous, a doom so sudden. But enough, — or the fountains of my heart will burst their bounds and pour my life away. He is dead, our benefactor. . . . That damnable murderer, that blot upon his country and his religion, has robbed us both of our dearest friend, who (for all the calumnies of spiteful tongues) was rich with the gifts of both body and mind. He, doubtless, is in Heaven: we remain here, denizens of earth, from whom Astraea has departed."[1] In reply to these somewhat painful efforts at classical eloquence, Vossius replied that he had heard reports of the assassination, but had found it quite impossible to believe the truth of such a catastrophe: and Laud wrote again urging him to fulfil the promise which he had rhetorically made of immortalising his patron's name in literature " lest one devilish blow seem to have destroyed him for ever ".[2]

Such hysterics might well argue insincerity: but the quite unusual eloquence of Laud's letter to Scudamore on the same subject makes it clear that it is his latinity rather than his sentiments which are here at fault. There he expresses his sense of the loss which he has suffered and of the isolation in which it has left him —

" I purpose not to write these either to declaim in his commendations, which so few would believe, or to express my grief, which as few would pity: but only to let your lordship know that

[1] Laud, *Works*, vi. 255. [2] *Ibid.* vi. 259.

though I have passed a great deal of heaviness, yet I have cause to expect more to come "; and he goes on to declare that henceforth he will set less store upon the malice of the world, or the ambitions of court life, and more upon the fidelity of those friends who, like Scudamore, have stayed by him " in the times when friends fall off ". As for the court, since this bereavement it " seems new to me, and I mean to turn over a new leaf in it, for all those things that are changeable ".[1]

If further evidence were required of the genuineness of the affection which bound Laud to Buckingham, it is enough to record that all the surviving members of Buckingham's family were remembered in Laud's will.

Judged from a purely political standpoint, however, the death of Buckingham probably did Laud more good than harm. The constructive part of Laud's policy was essentially social, and could only be diverted, and perhaps frustrated, by an extravagant foreign policy such as that of Buckingham, which he was compelled to support. The death of Buckingham enabled the government to drop Buckingham's foreign policy, and the peace which followed allowed Laud leisure, and freedom from parliamentary interference, in which to realise, or attempt to realise, the programme in which he was really interested, and which only the resumption of hostilities, bringing the return of Parliament, ultimately thwarted. And besides, it is possible that, had Buckingham lived, his unpopularity would have resulted in a revolt which would have overthrown him and Laud together, before Laud had had an opportunity to try his hand at the task for which he was preparing himself.[2]

So one phase in Laud's ascent to power passed, and Buckingham was soon forgotten under the stress of further political developments. The King, overwhelmed with grief, ordered

[1] *Vide* Appendix, letter 18.

[2] Laud's dependence upon Buckingham is emphasised in one of the many poems written against the Duke at this time. Referring to Buckingham's failure at the Isle of Rhé, the writer asks :

> " Could not thy chaplain London's sacrifice
> Nor move nor suffocate thy destinies,
> That sends from the altar of his paunch more fumes
> Of smoke and vapour than Llandaff consumes."
>
> (Sloane MS. 826, p. 61).

Llandaff here is Theophilus Field, on whom see below, page 186.

preparations for a splendid funeral: but, as the Genoese Resident observed, "as there is no money to spare, it is doubtful whether any splendour is possible". The new lord treasurer, Sir Richard Weston, was initiating a policy of retrenchment all round after the late Duke's extravagances, and it is said that he prevented a lavish funeral by suggesting a monument as a more appropriate tribute: and then, when the Duke had been safely and cheaply buried, by saying that a monument would be improper, as there was no monument yet to King James, owing to lack of funds. At all events, the Genoese Agent wrote later that "a few days ago the Duke of Buckingham was buried in Westminster Abbey without pomp of any kind, in order to escape any demonstration of public fury".

The death of Buckingham was not the only conciliatory event which had occurred during the recess. Another was the restoration of Abbot to the exercise of his archiepiscopal functions, and the royal declaration, secured by Laud, and approved by the Privy Council and bishops, forbidding dogmatic discussion. The declaration was prefixed to a new issue of the Articles of the Church of England, and the faithful were required to believe the articles, not to dispute about them. "We will [it read] that all further curious search be laid aside . . . and that no man hereafter shall either print or preach to draw the article aside any way, but shall submit to it in the plain and full meaning thereof: and shall not put his own sense or comment to be the meaning of the article, but shall take it in the literal and grammatical sense."[1] Even the Universities, the natural homes of disputation, were forbidden to dispute; and it was noticed that a sentence was printed in the text of the articles which had been omitted from most of the printed copies and from the two manuscript copies signed by Convocation. The interpolated sentence ran, "The Church has the right to decree ceremonies, and authority to decide controversies of religion". It was a warning to the Puritans that the individual conscience was to have no status against the decisions of the Church.

It might appear, therefore, that there was nothing left for King and Parliament to quarrel about when they faced each other once more on January 1st, 1629. Buckingham was dead,

[1] Cardwell, *Documentary Annals*, p. 223.

religious controversy silenced, and political abuses condemned. But in fact all these renunciations were academic compared to other activities of the government, which showed clearly how little control Parliament had over the Church. The declaration against controversy had declared that the only judge of doctrine was the Church: but who was the Church? During the recess that question had been answered decisively by a series of promotions in the episcopal hierarchy. All the high churchmen whom Parliament found most objectionable had been promoted, and parliamentary disqualifications had been set aside by royal pardons. Bishop Carleton of Chichester, who had written against Montague, was dead, and Montague himself, as if to insult his memory, was installed in his throne. Dr. Manwaring, who had been forbidden by Parliament to hold any ecclesiastical preferment again, had been pardoned by the King and held the rectories of both St. Giles-in-the-Fields and Stamford Rivers in Essex, where his parishioners, having had Montague as their rector for fifteen years, were presumably prepared for anything. Cosin, too, who had offended the last Parliament by a ritualistic book of devotions, was pardoned and promoted. The bishopric of Winchester, after the Michaelmas rents had gone into the Exchequer, was conferred upon Neile, and the see of Durham, which he had vacated, was pressed upon the reluctant Bishop of London, George Mountain, who had no wish to exchange the genial atmosphere of the court, which he so loved, for exile in the north, and protested that he would die of cold in Durham. Before being put to the test, however, Mountain received the welcome news that Toby Matthew, the Archbishop of York, who "died yearly in report",[1] was at last dead in earnest. He had himself long hankered after York, where the northern climate had no terrors for him, and had in fact applied to Buckingham for it on the last rumour of Matthew's death; and now he was disappointed when the King, discussing the future archbishop in his presence, made no mention of his own name. At last he could bear it no longer. "If you had faith as a grain of mustard-seed", he told the King, "you would say unto this Mountain, Go and be removed into that see!" Charles appreciated the

[1] News-writers and aspiring clergy had reported the death of Dr. Matthew regularly during the past twenty years. It is said that the Archbishop himself circulated these reports, and derived a cynical amusement from the ecclesiastical scurry which followed them.

witticism and sent Mountain to York as his reward : but the new Archbishop "was scarce warm in his church before cold in his coffin ", and York was vacant again.[1] The chief object of Mountain's translation was, however, attained : for London was vacant and bestowed on Laud, who, what with Parliament, his duties at Court, and the necessity of attending a royal progress, had never had an opportunity to visit his recently acquired diocese of Bath and Wells.

This epidemic of convenient deaths gave control of half the episcopate at once to Laud and his party. The new Archbishop of York was Samuel Harsnet, "such a furious Hildebrand that, like Davus in the comedy, he perturbed all things wherever he came "[2], but who had independence enough to vote for the Petition of Right with Abbot and Williams against all the other bishops. Heylin magnifies Laud's impartiality in the distribution of bishoprics by pointing out that he sent Barnaby Potter, the Provost of Queen's College, Oxford, "a thorough-paced Calvinian ", to Carlisle. But Carlisle was an out-of-the-way diocese which mattered little,[3] and a Calvinist, even were he more thorough-paced than the amenable Dr. Potter, could probably do less harm there than as head of an Oxford College. Besides, his transfer meant that his predecessor, Dr. White, who had licensed Montague's book when Abbot had refused, had been elevated to the more influential throne of Norwich. White was particularly obnoxious to the Puritans as one who had previously dissembled his Arminian views to avoid unpopularity : but now the turn of the tide had induced him to come forward in his true colours in order to share in the spoils. "Qui color albus

[1] This amiable but unapostolic bishop is singled out by Milton, thirteen years after his death, as the type of worldly prelacy. "He that would mould a modern bishop into a primitive, must yield him to be elected by the popular voice, undiocesed, unrevenued, unlorded, and leave him nothing but brotherly equality, matchless temperance, frequent fasting, incessant prayer and preaching, continual watchings and labours in his ministry, — which what a rich booty it would be, what a plump endowment to the many-benefice-gaping mouth of a prelate, what a relish it would give to his Canary-sucking and swan-eating palate, let old bishop Mountain judge for me " (*Of Reformation in England*).

[2] Prynne, *Antipathie of the English Prelacie*, 1641, p. 221.

[3] Cf. Montague to Cosin on the appointment of Richard Senhouse to Carlisle in 1624 : "Honest John . . . I am sorry . . . that *Puritani rapiunt episcopatum* ; yet this is alleviated, that it is but one for another, and *in remotis*, whereby I hope we shall get rid of him " (*Cosin's Correspondence*, vol. i., Surtees Soc., 1868).

erat nunc est contrarius albo ", complained Sir Walter Earle in the debate on religion in February ; " Dr. White has sold his orthodox books and bought Jesuits' books.[1] Therefore let White go arm-in-arm with Montague."

Faced with these alarming changes, which seemed to show that all their successes in other departments meant nothing, the Commons on their reassembly started to deal seriously with the religious question. Rous moved that " first it may be considered what new paintings are laid on the old face of the whore of Babylon, to make her more lovely and draw more suitors to her ". Property and religion, he averred, were intimately connected, and an attack on one was an attack on the other, — " it was an old trick of the Devil : when he meant to take away Job's religion, he begins at his goods ". Seymour, who had advocated smash-and-grab raids on Spanish ports as the policy approved by God, now declared that the failure of the alternative policy had proved him right. " If God fight not for us in all our battles ", he said, " the help of man is in vain." Attacks were no longer wasted on such as Sibthorpe and Manwaring : the axe was laid to the root of the tree, and Montague in doctrine and Laud in practice were declared " the main and great roots of all those evils which have come upon us and our religion ". " That all men be not so free, sound, and orthodox in religion as they should be ", said Eliot, " witness the men complained of in the last remonstrance we exhibited, — Drs. Laud and Neile ; and you know what place they have. Witness likewise Montague, so newly now preferred. I reverence the order, though I honour not the man." A sub-committee was formed to discover the source of the pardons given to Montague, Cosin, Manwaring, and Sibthorpe, and it was found to have been Neile. Cromwell, in his maiden speech, attacked Neile as having instructed the clergy in his new diocese of Winchester to preach " flat Popery ". Montague's consecration was impugned as invalid. Cosin was assailed as denying the royal supremacy which Manwaring had too vigorously asserted, — " an incredible slander ", he complained to Laud, " spread by a son of Belial and solicitor of

[1] White was said to have sold his books to buy his bishopric (letter in Archbishop Ussher's correspondence, Feb. 13th, 1627-9). For White's dissimulation cf. Montague to Cosin, Dec. 1624 : " I know the Dean is *animitus* of our mind, but

δειδίαται Τρῶας καὶ Τρῳάδας ἑλκεσιπέπλους.

Mr. Smart's ".[1] Waller delivered a petition from the London booksellers and printers complaining that Laud and his chaplains had gained exclusive control over the licensing of the press. A list of heads of articles for religion was drawn up, assailing by name Laud, Neile, Montague, Goodman, White, Buckeridge, Cosin, and Wren.

All this came to nothing. Parliament might change the foreign policy of the government by withdrawing supplies : but it could not change its ecclesiastical policy, because the Church was not dependent on parliamentary supply. It could only agitate and protest, and the government, provided that it was confident of a working majority in the country, could afford to ignore its protests. On March 2nd, 1629, amid scenes of tumult and disorder, the Speaker being held forcibly in his chair, Parliament was adjourned. A week later it was dissolved. Soon afterwards peace was concluded, first with France, then with Spain. The Commons had triumphed over Buckingham : but not over Laud.

" The Parliament which was broken up this March 10th ", Laud recorded in his diary, " laboured my ruin, but (God be ever blessed for it) found nothing against me." A fortnight later he reported that libels threatening death to him were found in the Dean of St. Paul's garden. But he was not deterred. For although posterity has painted a halo around the Parliament of 1628, its fanaticism and its incompetence gave it no title to success. It had made no constructive effort, and the one statesman who had sought to achieve a reasonable and positive compromise by the exhibition of its strength was so revolted by its excesses that he shook its dust from his feet and entered the direct service of the King. Laud thought no better of it. Besides attacking the foreign policy of his patron, and thereby aggravating the resentment that led to his murder, it had made furious and impotent attacks upon the Church which he was determined to establish. " I have left no stone unturned (*omnem ego semper movi lapidem*) ", he wrote to Vossius, who had expressed apprehension at the dissensions, " in my efforts to prevent the public discussion of these intricate and thorny problems, lest, while pretending zeal for truth, we should offend against religion and charity. I have ever counselled moderation, lest turbulent spirits

[1] *Cal. S.P. Dom.* 1628–9, p. 390.

with no real care for religion should set the world at odds. . . . If these methods prove my ruin, leaving me helpless in the hands of the victors, my reward is in myself, and I shall look for no other consolation, save in God." [1] Laud had a natural antipathy to discussion, and his conviction that constructive work required complete freedom from distracting criticism can only have been confirmed by his experience of the first three parliaments of Charles I. Certainly from that time onwards Parliament was to him " that noise ", and only in its absence could he regard his task as possible.

That this work was constructive, and did not mean merely the enforcement of unpopular theological doctrines, is shown by a letter written by him two years earlier to Sir John Scudamore. Scudamore had found himself obliged to raise money to pay debts, and the prospect of selling land which his ancestors had derived mainly from the Church raised in his mind a crop of religious scruples, for which his previous study of Hooker and Spelman, and his intimacy with Laud, had prepared a fertile soil. Not only did the Scudamore property consist chiefly in Church lands, but Lady Scudamore had brought as her dowry the lands of Lanthony Priory, which she had inherited. These doubts once raised, Scudamore applied to Laud to resolve them : and Laud's reply, though expressed with polite qualifications, was unambiguous in its conclusions. The lands of the Church, he said, were sacrosanct, and to touch them was sacrilege. If Scudamore's ancestors had committed this sacrilege, then the best course was for Scudamore to restore the impropriations to the Church, not necessarily at once or all together, but at least by a gradual process spread over several generations, so that the Church might ultimately recover her heritage. He did not enter into the patristic subtleties of Montague, or the mythological fantasies of Spelman : for throughout his life, Laud was more concerned to achieve results than to prove a theory. To him the Church was a great social institution, designed to praise God with its voice, but with its hand to regulate the anti-social appetites of individuals by the imposition of external justice. For this purpose it required independent power, and for such independence it needed such a basis of material wealth as would make it an estate in the realm. The nationalisation of Church property under Henry VIII, which

[1] Laud, *Works*, vi. 265.

had destroyed the Church as an estate of the realm, had shown that the Church must protect her property by the erection of a wall of taboo, a myth of "sacrilege", since she lacked the necessary force. The purely mythical part of this programme of re-establishment, as we have seen, was provided by Spelman. Laud's part was the practical part. Throughout his administrative career we find him seeking to recover the alienated property of the Church and to secure it against a second dissolution by an emphatic declaration of its sacred character. Hence his superstitious insistence on the sin of sacrilege, illustrated in such trivial examples as his recording the ominous death of a prospector who had dug for saltpetre within the college church at Brecknock.[1] Hence, too, his enforcement of such ceremonies as the consecration of churches, which served as a public warning that this was the property of God.

With Scudamore, in spite of his vested interests, Laud's argument prevailed. The murder of Buckingham ended Scudamore's public appointments for a time, and he returned to Herefordshire, where he followed Laud's advice, and, in the intervals of his favourite pastime of fruit-growing, gradually disbursed himself of some £50,000 by restoring his impropriations to the Church.[2] But Scudamore was a rare exception, one pious enough to sacrifice his interests to his conscience. In most men the relation between these two forces is reversed: and Laud's efforts to achieve from them by compulsion and the old forms of law the results which had here followed so easily from persuasion were far less successful.

[1] Laud, *Works*, iii. 155.

[2] See Matthew Gibson, *A View of Door, Holme Lacy, and Hempsted, 1727*.

CHAPTER FOUR

LONDON

FOR his breach with Parliament in 1629 Charles I has had to bear a great deal of blame. But the position which confronted him was not an easy one, and even the choice which he made involved a heavy sacrifice. Parliament's demands had been very radical. Taking as their excuse the incompetence of Buckingham, they had demanded the surrender of the admitted prerogative of the Crown to deal with trade, religion, and foreign affairs : and no one, least of all one with so sensitive a consciousness of his regal dignity as Charles I, is prepared to renounce without a struggle his ancient rights. Nevertheless, although the dissolution spared the King this sacrifice, it involved the sacrifice of another ambition which always lay near his heart, — the cause of his sister and her family, for whose sake he had pushed his father into war, and differed with his subjects over its conduct. Now his sister was sacrificed to his sovereignty ; for without parliamentary aid there could be no war, and if he could not make peace with Eliot and Holles, he must make it with France and Spain. On March 10th, 1629, Parliament was dissolved. The Peace of Susa was signed on April 1st. It is true that Charles never finally abandoned his efforts on behalf of his sister, but he never intended to go to war again ; and since his adversaries were afraid of nothing short of war, the tortuous diplomacy of the following decade could only be futile and ignominious, as the Queen of Bohemia herself somewhat pathetically declared. To this futility and this ignominy Charles could not be blind, but he had chosen his course and had no alternative. He was prepared to be a cypher abroad, so that he might be a king at home.

So there followed a period of ten years in which the government could devote its energies and resources to social reconstruction at home, undistracted by war or parliament. The new Lord Treasurer, Sir Richard Weston, would husband the resources of the Kingdom. The new President of the Council of the North, Lord Wentworth, would impose order. The new

Bishop of London, Dr. Laud, would preach those doctrines that are, as it were, the immortal soul of responsible autocracy. It was a policy of deliberate reaction, — " Stare super antiquas vias " was a favourite tag of both Wentworth and Laud, — but it was reaction in the name of social stability and justice. By insistence upon ancient forms the old rights of the Crown, of the people, and of the Church were to be vindicated, and social harmony restored. And if, in effect, this stupendous task of reconstruction was a great failure : if it was frequently carried out in a narrow, intolerant spirit : if its execution was frustrated by weak members and strong enemies : if it attacked individual exploitation at the cost of suppressing individual thought : if it struck at oppressive magnates only to connive at a parasitic Court : if the reforming energies of the earlier years gradually gave way to a purely destructive conservatism ; nevertheless it is impossible not to admire the ideal which they strove so tirelessly to realise, even while the reality slipped further and further from it. Against them were arrayed the strongest forces in the country, — strong because they had made progress in the immediate past and were confident of increasing that progress in the future. There were pioneers in every field who by their energies had contributed to material civilisation and to their own prosperity, even though they had had to break through the old social structure and its doctrinal envelope in order to do so. There were the merchants and prospectors, the successors of the Elizabethan pirates, who, by spurning the old ways, had discovered new roads to wealth. There were the manufacturers whose new industries were springing up, and dislocating old social arrangements, in the City and in the Midlands. There were improving landlords, whose new methods of cultivation ruthlessly destroyed ancient rights, — the rights of the Church and the poor. And as the old social system, which sought to block the endeavours of these men, found its divine sanction in the doctrine of a visible Church of which the individual was a responsible member, so, as a battle-cry against that system, especially now that it was becoming dynamic once more, these men took to themselves Puritanism as an ideal sanctifying their aims : not indeed the rigorous, authoritarian Calvinism which had first summoned the middle class to revolution against a dominant feudalism, but an indistinct medley of doctrines, better suited to an unorganised and miscellaneous community, all proclaiming the necessity of faith and the truth of predestination, but leaving, in their diversity, loopholes for the practice of some of those profitable habits which the more complete system of Calvin had condemned. Industry and Puritanism flourished together, and wherever the first predominated, the second seemed to follow. New industrial towns in backward districts, like the " Genevas of Lancashire ", or where the genius of the Foley family was founding the heavy industry of the Midlands, were conspicuous for a Puritanism which contrasted with the Catholicism around them. The great adventurers who had exploited new opportunities under Elizabeth had been sturdy Protestants,—Drake, Grenville, Raleigh, and Leicester. The aristocratic leaders of Puritanism in the seventeenth century too, Lord Saye and Lord Brooke, were champions of colonial expansion : and the family of Warwick owned and directed a whole fleet of pirate ships. The piratical county of Cornwall, which had sent the Wentworths to trouble the parliaments of Elizabeth, sent Eliot and Francis Rous to those of Charles I. London itself, which, during the wars on the Continent, came to rival Antwerp as the exchange of Europe, was " the retreat and receptacle of the grandees of the Puritan faction ". East Anglia, the headquarters of a European cloth trade and the asylum of fugitive Protestants from abroad, fostered Puritan doctrines, publishing them from the University of Cambridge with the authoritative voice of learning. So, to a lesser extent, did Wiltshire, where a similar industry throve. In Buckinghamshire and the shires also, where the fine pastures tempted the enclosing landlord and speculator, the same doctrines were preached and found believers. The great days of maritime piracy, indeed, were over,—that trade, as Raleigh found to his cost, had been ruined by the peace with Spain. But the trading companies which supplied its place hatched the same doctrines, and James I had complained that the Virginia Company " was but a seminary to a seditious Parliament ", and that, in spite of the time and money absorbed by it, " yet it hath not produced any other effects than that smoky weed of tobacco ".

Thus these two *Weltanschauungen* faced each other in the reign of Charles I. On the one side a grand sense of social harmony and communal responsibility, even at the expense of material and intellectual progress; on the other a determination on the part of hundreds of enterprising men not to hide in a napkin the talent which God had bestowed upon them. The names of the latter are legion, — country squires like Hampden and the Asshetons, shrill pamphleteers like Prynne and Bastwick, pushing merchants like Chambers, spiritual pilgrims like Milton and Bunyan, projectors and speculators large and small who crop up whenever history has need of examples; and on the other side two names alone stand out like giants, Wentworth and Laud, determined to resist disruptive activities in every form, in their doctrinal credentials and in their social results, by propaganda and in administration. For Laud, at any rate, now that he had secured power independent of his patron, it was a great change since the days when all his activities were directed to maintaining his influence with a worthless favourite and defending a foreign policy which was indefensible. Since Buckingham's death, as he wrote at the time, he had resolved to turn over a new leaf: the constructive part of his life's work was ahead.

And yet there was a qualification to this confident outlook upon the future. It was not merely the strength of the opposition which faced him: it was the weakness of the allies upon whom he must rely. On Buckingham's death Laud had also declared that he had become a stranger to the court; but this could not be. Like Archimedes, he required somewhere to stand before he could move the world, and that somewhere, in his case, could only be the shifty soil of King Charles' court, where his aims were only half understood and only half supported. That Laud's doctrines gave the highest sanction to royal authority King Charles saw well enough: that they required justice and responsibility also he was less willing to see. And even when he seemed most devoted to his clerical adviser, he always had another ear open to a counsellor who had no understanding of any such conceptions, and whom Laud was powerless to influence, — his French queen. For Laud had no personal influence with women. He was not interested in personal topics such as appeal to them, but only in principles and those abstract conceptions which so rarely attract them. And so the King was never really a wholehearted ally to Laud and Wentworth in their stupendous task of raising order out of chaos. Though he gave them permission to embark upon their sublime failure, he gave them neither gratitude nor assistance: and though openly they worked entirely for him, in their private correspondence they did not hesitate to complain of the way in which he hindered all their efforts to serve him by his dilettantism, his selfishness, and his dependence on an irresponsible court.

Such were the ideals which Laud now felt himself equipped to enforce, and the society in which he was to enforce them. There remain the methods by which they were to be enforced.

Here it is necessary to emphasise the comparative unimportance of the constitutional issue involved. The Long Parliament attempted to make a constitutional case against both Laud and Strafford, but in both cases it had ultimately to drop the proceedings and resort to attainder. For a constitution is the formulation of a social system, and, since the Reformation, the whole policy of the government had been to avoid the dangers of such a formulation. As a result, though Laud might stretch the constitution, the constitution was itself too elastic to be broken. It was admitted, for instance, that the actual structure of the Church could only be changed by an Act of Parliament; but as the existing and legal structure included bishops, deans and chapters, archdeacons and their courts, together with a Court of High Commission and a Court of Delegates, there was no need to change it. As for doctrine and ceremonies, although Parliament asserted that only Parliament was entitled to dictate them, it had never made good its assertion. King Henry had declared himself Head of the Church, implying that the Crown could dictate doctrine: but Queen Elizabeth had changed the title to "Supreme Governor" implying that it could not[1]; and in fact the ecclesiastical forms which had been so loosely prescribed in her reign had been issued on the most indeterminate authority. The comprehensive solution of the altar-controversy had been enjoined by the Queen only. The advertisements which ordered the use of copes and surplices were enacted simply by the Queen and the Archbishop. The canons of 1597, and again of 1604, were the work of Convocation confirmed by the Sovereign.

[1] So Selden: "There's a great deal of difference between Head of the Church and Supreme Governor, as our canons call the King. Conceive it thus: there is in the kingdom of England a College of Physicians. The King is supreme governor of those but not head of them, nor President of the College, nor the best physician" (*Table Talk*, "King of England").

And Archbishop Whitgift had issued articles on his own authority alone. Parliament, it is true, had sometimes protested. It had sought to emend the book of articles in 1571, — " make you Popes who will ", exclaimed Peter Wentworth when the Archbishop had suggested that doctrine was an affair for the bishops only, " for we will make you none ". And in 1605 it had protested against the canons in whose compilation it had had no part. But these protests had been unavailing, and Parliament could not claim that any constitutional precedents were being broken by Laud when he proceeded to use and enforce the royal and episcopal authority.

Nor did Laud have to invent any new instruments for this work. The Protestant Reformation of the preceding century had taken place so quietly, without disturbing the existing ecclesiastical constitution, that it could, he hoped, be reversed with as little disturbance. The old machinery of episcopal courts had merely to be put into effective operation after a period of abeyance, a new spirit was to be infused into the whole administration from above, and the government to be rendered more effective by the literal interpretation of the old forms. For this purpose excellent instruments lay ready to hand, only in need of sharpening. There was the Star Chamber, an age-old institution whose powers, being undefined, were capable of indefinite expansion so long as they did not conflict with statute. There was the Council of the North, founded indeed by prerogative, but as yet undisputed. Under James I it had become negligent and discredited, its officials preferring to line their pockets rather than exercise their powers ; but in the hands of Wentworth it could become again an engine of efficient government in the north. There were similar courts in the Welsh Marches and elsewhere. And for purely ecclesiastical affairs there was the Court of High Commission, whose authority was the most surely founded of all, for it was based upon statute. During the last years of Elizabeth and the early reign of James it had been the object of a bitter attack by the Common lawyers, but that attack had spent itself in vain with the dismissal of its leader, Sir Edward Coke. A censorship of the press, too, was in existence, dating from a Star Chamber decree in 1586, and only required rigorous enforcement. It was lack of enforcement, not lack of instruments, which, in the eyes of Laud and Wentworth, had produced the social and ecclesiastical dislocation which they were determined to correct. " Before God ", Montague wrote to Cosin in November 1624, " it will never be well till we have our Inquisition." In a very short time he was to have it.

Against this policy of revivifying dead instruments the opposition, inarticulate by the dissolution of Parliament, could only proceed by sabotage ; and the great battle of rival creeds, dispersed from Westminster, resolved itself into a multitude of petty skirmishes throughout the country. Everywhere there were disputes, rendered more bitter by the appeal to rival principles, between bishops and their chancellors, their chapters, their neighbours, or their local corporations. Vicars were thwarted by their churchwardens or bullied by their patrons, and local and ecclesiastical authorities encroached upon each other's jurisdiction. To Laud all these petty differences were skirmishes in one great Armageddon. He was determined that the Powers of Light should win in them all, and constituted himself the court of appeal in all of them. And if the Common lawyers, jealous for their rights and their fees, tried to stay the business thus crowded into the prerogative courts by the issue of prohibitions — which frequently had no bearing on the immediate case but were served on the general principle of opposing all the activities of their hated rivals — Laud, who hated lawyers with their antiquarian restrictions upon his large policy, determined that " he would break the back of prohibitions, or they would break his ". He denounced them from the pulpit as a sin against God, who " would prohibit the entry into the kingdom of Heaven of all who granted prohibitions to the disturbance of the Church's right " ; and when a prohibition was threatened in a matrimonial case in the High Commission, he declared that, were it enforced, Abbot ought to excommunicate all the judges involved, adding that, if Abbot refused, he would do so himself.[1] And so effectively did he set his face against them that in 1640 the Londoners complained that " of later times the judges of the land are so awed with the power and greatness of the prelates . . . that neither prohibitions, Habeas Corpus, nor any other lawful remedy can be had ".[2]

It is true that the dissolution of Parliament did not immediately

[1] Meade to Stuteville in Birch, ii. 119.

[2] Gardiner, *Constitutional Documents of the Puritan Revolution*, p. 143.

set Laud in the place of highest authority: but the place was all that was lacking to him. Old Archbishop Abbot, though he had another four and a half years of life before him, was in complete eclipse. His efforts to stem the rising tide of Arminianism had only brought him disgrace and disillusionment. He disapproved of Laud's ideals, and had no part in Laud's demonic energy; and now he lived largely in retirement, either at his house at Ford, or at the hospital which he had founded and endowed in his native Guildford, or at Lambeth, where he was reported to turn midnight into noonday, receiving the nocturnal visits of "all the malcontents in Church and State".[1] He still attended the Star Chamber and High Commission: but the last word in those courts was always with Laud, not with him. When a Puritan preacher submitted to the High Commission, "the Archbishop of Canterbury then would only have imprisoned him and suspended him from his ministerial office: but it was moved by the Bishop of London that he might undergo the censure of the court, and that to be given in order, for that he and others were minded to degrade him".[2] On another occasion a misguided tailor admitted to the court that, through Jesus Christ, he believed himself to be perfect and to have no need to use the Lord's Prayer. The Dean of the Arches, Sir Henry Marten, suggested that he would feel less perfect after a term in Bridewell; to which Laud at once added that he deserved "*ultimam poenam*", and ought to "taste the severest discipline of Bridewell". And when a doctor of divinity, who had added a "scandalous table" to a translation of the Psalms, having admitted his error and submitted to the court, was dismissed by the Archbishop, he was called back by Laud to receive a severe lecture on the flamboyant cut of his clothes.

One of the first ways in which Laud exercised his new power was in the compilation, with Archbishop Harsnet of York, of a series of instructions to all the English bishops, which the King then ordered Abbot to send out. These instructions aimed at increasing the efficiency of the bishops by keeping them, sufficiently provided, in their dioceses, where they were to exercise themselves

[1] Heylin, p. 229.

[2] *Select Cases in the Star Chamber and High Commission* (Camden Soc., 1886), p. 184.

husbanding the attenuated resources of the Church and disorganising the Puritan ministry.

For this purpose the bishops were first required to live permanently in their dioceses, in the episcopal houses allotted to them. Unless they actually held court appointments, as Laud had done, they were not to hang about the Court, angling for preferment and neglecting their administrative duties. Nor, like Williams, were they to live away from their cathedrals on commendams which they found more comfortable. The difficulty, however, was that some of the poorer dioceses, — those, especially, which had been founded by Henry VIII at a time when the Church excited the cupidity rather than the benevolence of laymen, — were without episcopal houses. The Bishop of Oxford, for instance, had at first received Gloucester Hall in Oxford ; but this had soon been regranted to the Crown, which had granted it to St. John's College : and the bishop was unable to make good his claim although, in 1605, he invaded the Hall from the river by night and drove off the horses at pasture there. The Bishops of Peterborough, Bristol, Chester, and St. Asaph were similarly unprovided. For all of them, however, Laud in time secured palaces. In 1632 the new Bishop of Oxford, Dr. Bancroft, obtained the grant of the vicarage of Cuddesdon, then vacant, in perpetuity, and built there a palace for himself and his successors, Laud securing the transfer of Shotover and Stow Wood to the see also, to augment its revenues. Dr. Wright, Bishop of Bristol, was persuaded to provide his successors with a house in the same way, and was promoted to Lichfield and Coventry as his reward : and Dr. Pierce, who, by annexing the parsonage of Castor, had done the same at Peterborough, was rewarded with Bath and Wells, where he became one of Laud's most diligent henchmen. Thus the Elizabethan process was reversed ; for whereas Elizabethan bishops had secured promotion by renouncing part of their revenues, Laud's bishops secured it by increasing theirs. St. Asaph and Chester were similarly served.[1]

At the same time, as bishops were not to be absentee landlords so they were not to be bad landlords. The royal instructions required that no bishop, on his nomination to another see, should lease, or in any way reduce, the lands belonging to the diocese

[1] *S.P. Dom. Car. I.* 237, no. 38.

which he was leaving. If he did so, his translation would not receive royal confirmation, "for we think it a hateful thing that any man, leaving the bishopric, should almost undo the successor".

The rest of the instructions deal with the extension of episcopal control over lecturers, — supernumerary clergy who, possessing no benefice, were appointed to preach sermons in market-towns and other places on fixed days, and paid from a fund established for the purpose. The result was that once a man had received episcopal ordination the bishop had no further control over him. He was qualified to preach, and, if he held Puritan views, to preach them. When the lecturer was paid, as he frequently was, by a local corporation themselves holding Puritan views, his own convictions were fortified by the assurance of their protection; as he was not required to read divine service, but only to deliver a sermon, there was no guarantee that he even conformed to the Prayer Book; and as he held no ecclesiastical preferment, there was not the same means of exerting pressure upon him as upon the beneficed clergy. Selden compared the lecturers to the friars of the Roman Church. Had there been no friars, he said, Christendom might have continued undivided: and but for the lecturers the Church of England might have remained flourishing. The lecturers, he complained, secured for themselves "not only the affection but the bounty that should be bestowed on the minister".[1]

To check this movement the instructions of 1629 required bishops to suppress the afternoon sermons in their dioceses, replacing them by elementary and harmless catechisms in which there was no room for heterodoxy. The King's declaration against controversy was also to be enforced, and lecturers must give an earnest of their orthodoxy by reading divine service from the Prayer Book in hood and surplice. In addition, the wandering habits of the new friars were to be regulated by the establishment of a local tie which would keep them under the eye of their diocesan; for when a lecturer was appointed by an independent authority, such as a corporation, he was not to begin his career of preaching till he had undertaken to accept a living with a cure of souls in that district, so soon as one should be offered. When a lectureship was vested in a number of persons preaching in

[1] *Table Talk*, "Friars".

rotation, these persons were to be "grave and orthodox divines", resident in the district. Laud would have liked to eliminate lectures altogether and leave the spiritual needs of the country entirely to the ministrations of regular beneficed clergy: but the poverty of the Church rendered this impossible, for there were not enough benefices to go round. The difficulty was that the rich, who might have supplied this deficiency, were generally Puritan business-men who preferred to subsidise Puritan rather than Anglican preachers. So lecturers continued, *faute de mieux*, and Laud did what he could to secure their responsibility, dealing with individual cases through the ecclesiastical courts. In 1633 he went a step further and instructed bishops not to ordain any man except to a title, which would keep him under the control of the Church: and he even insisted that bishops who ordained men for whom they could not provide out of the livings of the Church should provide for them themselves.

Another loophole by which Puritans obtained the freedom to express their doctrines was by being appointed as private chaplains. The right to entertain a private chaplain was restricted by law to noblemen, judges, bishops, and certain other dignitaries: but this restriction was widely disregarded, for rich Puritans were glad enough to have an inspired voice in the house, assuring them that their actions, though disliked by the established Church, were pleasing in the sight of God. This loophole was also stopped (at least in theory) by the instructions. There remained, however, the more serious difficulty of lay patronage. Until this could be restored to the Church, the Church could not regard herself as independent, and Laud's ambition, which was only fulfilled in very small part, was to recover all lay-impropriations to the Church. For this purpose, however, injunctions were not enough. The method could only be by purchase: and purchase required money, of which at present there was very little available.

Unhappily, here again the greater wealth of his opponents was brought home to him. For before he had time to act the Puritans forestalled him in the very project which he had intended to carry out himself. A corporation styling itself "the Collectors of St. Antholin's", and consisting of four lawyers, four city men, and four ministers, making a total of twelve Puritans, under the chairmanship of a London alderman, advertised their intention of raising a subscription to buy in for the Church those impropriations still in lay hands. The excellence of the intention could not be denied, and the corporation exhibited a studied moderation, even offering to submit their plans to Laud for his approval ;[1] but Laud could not persuade himself that figs grew upon thistles, and determined to take no risks. His chaplain, the pragmatical Dr. Heylin, was soon on the track of the feoffees (as they were called), making enquiries to discover in what way they allowed their Puritanism to affect their charity.

He was soon able to report that they were not nearly so innocent as they pretended to be : " for if such public mischiefs be presaged by astrologers from the conjunction of Jupiter and Saturn (though the first of them be a planet of most sweet and gentle influence), what dangers, what calamities might not be feared from the conjunction of twelve such persons, of which there was not one that wished well to the present government ? " Impropriations had already been bought in, he discovered, in Hertford, Dunstable, Cirencester, and elsewhere : but the feoffees had no mind to relinquish their control to a Church whose present policy was so distasteful to them. They did not regard themselves as mere collectors of subscriptions, but also as judges in the distribution of rewards : and while Laud's Church was restricting preferment to high churchmen, the feoffees, by a natural antithesis, provided Puritans to the positions at their disposal. Heylin reserved his pronouncement for the time when it could be made with most effect : then, ascending the University pulpit at Oxford to preach the Act sermon on June 11th, 1630, he chose for his text the words, " But while men slept, the enemy came and sowed tares among the wheat ", and denounced the feoffees as agents of Darkness. That done, he had his sermon printed, bound neatly in vellum, and sent to Laud, who encouraged him to proceed in his investigations, and noted among his memoranda the resolve " to overthrow the feoffment, dangerous both to Church and State, going under the specious pretence of buying in impropriations ".

Soon he received from Heylin sufficient evidence to enable him to act. The impropriations, he was informed, were not being annexed to the parish church as an inalienable source of revenue to the orthodox incumbent. They were being used to support ministers whom the Church had silenced, and to maintain

[1] Fuller, *Church History*, vi. 87.

a Puritan lecture at St. Antholin's in the City. In fact, instead of being applied locally, they were being diverted to a central fund for the support of heterodoxy generally, and those preachers who benefited from them, instead of receiving a guaranteed income, were continually dependent on their paymasters, who might revoke their stipend in the event of doctrinal differences. In 1632, therefore, the feoffees found themselves called to the Exchequer Court, the Corporation was dissolved, and the impropriations, to the value of seven or eight thousand pounds, confiscated, Laud (according to his enemies) thanking God that he had destroyed the work.[1]

Thus the Puritan attempt to evade Laud's ecclesiastical monopoly had failed. Unfortunately Laud's effort to do himself the work which he would not allow them to do also came to little. He succeeded in recovering impropriations in Ireland, and intended to do it by a gradual process in England, once the repair of St. Paul's was completed.[2] But the repair never was completed, and the difficulties of lay patronage, and especially presentation by corporations, hindered his work to the end. About the same time as the case of the feoffees, however, he succeeded in increasing his control of presentation by a lucky coincidence. The right to present to benefices in the gift of the King's wards was then being disputed between the Lord Keeper, Lord Coventry, and the new Master of the Wards, Lord Cottington: and while these two ministers were engaged in controversy, Laud stepped in himself and secured the prize. He persuaded the King to assume the right of presentation to himself and to exercise it on the advice of Laud, thus at the same time resolving the dispute to the satisfaction of both litigants, and striking a shrewd blow both for God and himself. For "by this accession of power, as he increased the number of his dependents, so he gained the opportunity by it to supply the Church with regular and conformable men".[3]

Meanwhile the aftermath of Parliament had brought to the Star Chamber two cases which gave Laud a good deal of unfortunate publicity. The first concerned one Alexander Leighton, a fanatical Scotsman whom even the English congregation at

[1] Prynne, *Canterburie's Doome*, 388.

[2] Laud, *Works*, iii. 255; cf. *ibid.* iii. 188.

[3] Heylin, p. 213.

Utrecht had found too Puritan for their liking and had expelled from the ministry there. In 1624 Leighton had become notorious by his *Speculum Belli Sacri*, calling for a holy war against Spain, and now he had dedicated to the last parliament a book, *Sion's Plea against Prelacy*, in which fanaticism had risen to a baffled scream. Neither Church nor State was spared. Buckingham was denounced as Goliath, the Queen as Jezebel, and as for bishops, they were antichristian and satanical prelates, ravens and magpies preying upon the State, knobs and wens of bunchy popish flesh, whom the godly were exhorted to strike under the fifth rib. The government, unfortunately, did not regard hysteria as an excuse for libel, and in February 1630 Leighton was caught as he emerged from a Puritan sermon in London, and, after a spell of solitary confinement, faced his judges. The sentence which they imposed was heavy, — a fine of £10,000, degradation by the High Commission, the pillory and the lash at Westminster and at Cheapside, his ears to be cut off, his nose slit, and his cheeks branded. The prisoner was then sent before the High Commission and there degraded, refusing at the time to take his hat off: but the execution of the rest of his sentence was postponed by his escape from the Fleet. Puritans claimed that he had been miraculously delivered, like St. Peter, by an angel: but more reliable authorities attributed his escape to "a zealotical Scotsman", a tailor, called Livingstone, who had entered the prison with a companion in a grey suit, and left it with Leighton, also in a grey suit.[1] Leighton, however, did not get far. The King is reported to have remarked that, by escaping, he had saved him the trouble of banishing him: "but Dr. Laud, Bishop of London, not so satisfied, gat him discovered".[2] The hue and cry was raised, and Leighton was soon caught in Bedfordshire and brought back to receive the rest of his punishment which, but for his escape, might have been remitted. A fine of £500 apiece, and imprisonment during the King's pleasure, was also imposed upon his abettors.

The next case was that of Henry Sherfield, the recorder of Salisbury. He had made himself conspicuous during the last parliament by his attacks upon the pardons granted to Montague and Manwaring: and having obtained no satisfaction in a parlia-

[1] Meade to Stuteville, in Birch, ii. 83.

[2] *Diary of John Rous* (Camden Soc., 1856), p. 56.

mentary way, he had returned to his constituency and taken it by violence. In the church of St. Edmund in Salisbury there was a stained-glass window representing God the Father, in the semblance of an old man, making the world with a pair of compasses. The vestry, regarding this as blasphemous idolatry, voted for its removal: but the bishop, Dr. Davenant, whose views on Predestination had already got him into trouble with Laud, was taking no risks and forbade them to remove it. Thereupon Sherfield, who, although he knew of the bishop's prohibition, had received no official intimation of it, took the case into his own hands, and, entering the church, climbed up by a ladder to the offensive window and smashed it with his pikestaff. After which he slipped and fell, injuring himself on a pew beneath.

It was February 1633 when Sherfield came before the Star Chamber. The judges, though unanimous in their condemnation, differed over the sentence to be imposed. Laud, who almost always voted with the highest, would have had Sherfield fined £1000, dismissed from his office as recorder, and sentenced to make public acknowledgement of his fault: and he took the opportunity in his speech to express his dislike of vestries and lawyers in general. Neile agreed with him: but the two chief justices, Heath and Richardson, and the Lord Keeper Coventry, voted for a milder sentence, and Sherfield escaped with a fine of £500, acknowledgement of his fault, and the costs of repairing the window. His death intervened, however, and the financial part of his sentence fell upon his relatives. Sherfield's case served to increase Laud's distrust of the legal profession: and the difference of opinion which it occasioned between himself and the Lord Keeper is perhaps the reason for the statement made next month by the Venetian ambassador that Laud was intriguing to ruin Coventry and gain control of the Great Seal.

At the same time the Declaration against controversy did not pass undisputed. When Bishop Davenant of Salisbury, preaching before the King at Whitehall, allowed himself to express his views on Predestination, he found that even bishops were not immune from its restrictions. He was summoned before the Privy Council, and, after listening to a tirade from Archbishop Harsnet, submitted and was dismissed with a caution.[1] Nor

[1] Fuller, *Church History*, vi. 77.

was any greater liberty allowed to the Universities, which might fairly have claimed a certain measure of intellectual freedom, — although the University disputations, to judge from surviving accounts, seem to have been exhibitions of rival prejudices rather than any attempt at critical originality.[1] Archbishop Ussher of Armagh wrote to Dr. Prideaux, the Rector of Exeter College and Regius Professor of Divinity, suggesting that his forthcoming edition of the letters of Polycarp and Ignatius might be printed at Oxford, but Prideaux feared the Laudian veto. "I am loth to speak", he wrote, "but the truth is, our Oxford presses are not for pieces of that coin. We can print here Smiglecius the Jesuit's metaphysical logic, and old John Buridan's ploddings upon the *Ethics*: but matters that entrench nearer on the true divinity must be more strictly overseen."[2] Certainly the time at which the declaration was issued favoured the high-church party, nor was Laud quite impartial in its application, — for when the "Arminian" Mr. Page took up his pen to confute Prynne on the subject of bowing in church, and Abbot ordered him, in the name of the royal declaration, to desist, Laud encouraged him to ignore the Archbishop and proceed.[3] Nevertheless, Laud certainly hated controversy more than he loved truth, as over-zealous high churchmen soon discovered. A Mr. Rainsford of Wadham College, Oxford, who preached on Universal Grace and was caught up by Prideaux was ordered to submit, and a Mr. Tooker of Oriel, who "was not content only to justify the five articles commonly called Arminianism, but would needs lay an aspersion on the Synod of Dordt" was reproved. And when the Master of Trinity College, Cambridge, declared that, after fifteen years of lucubration, he had at last found the way out of the wood and wilderness in which the world had so long been lost, and offered, by the publication of his views on the knotty topic of Predestination, to silence Puritanism for ever, Laud replied firmly that Predestination was an unmasterable problem which the King did not wish to be ventilated. Dr. Brooke protested that it was a very important matter, that Predestination was the root of Puritanism, and Puritanism the root of all

[1] Cf. Robert Skinner's account of such an Act, sent to Laud in 1629 (Lambeth MS. 943, p. 133).

[2] Parr, *Life and Letters of Ussher*, p. 400.

[3] Laud, *Works*, v. 39, ff.

rebellion and disobedient intractableness in Parliament, and of all schism and sauciness in the country and the Church. It was the protest of a man who thought that he had found truth ; but Laud, like jesting Pilate, was more interested in keeping the peace, now that he had secured it on his own terms, and the book was not licensed.[1]

These academic squabbles were destined once more to impinge upon Laud's career, for at this time he was once more plunged into the midst of University politics. Since 1621, when he resigned the Presidency of St. John's, he had held no official position at Oxford : but he had by no means lost touch with it. In 1622 he had assisted in the compilation of King James' order against "airy novellisms" in the University. In 1626 he had drafted a statute for Wadham College, imposing fines upon absentee fellows, — for absentees are inefficient, and Laud hated inefficiency in fellows as much as in bishops. In 1628, after a particularly tumultuous proctorial election, he secured the royal assent to a new method of election by rotation, thus eliminating the competitive element which had caused the disorder. And at the same time he began that series of benefactions to the University which have secured his name more permanently there than anywhere else. At the end of 1628 he persuaded the Chancellor of the University, the Earl of Pembroke, to purchase the Baroccian collection of 242 Greek manuscripts, at a cost of £700, and present them to the Bodleian library : and shortly afterwards he forwarded a further collection of 28 Greek manuscripts sent by Sir Thomas Roe, souvenirs of the Oriental embassies of that brilliant and versatile diplomat. A year later, when the Chancellor Pembroke suddenly died of an apoplectic fit, Laud was obviously qualified to be a candidate for the succession.

He was not unopposed. For though he had gradually nursed the Arminian party at Oxford into a majority, a minority still gathered round the standard of Dr. John Prideaux, the learned professor of divinity, in whom the moderate Calvinist doctrines of Jewel and Ussher made their last determined stand. Succeeding Robert Abbot in 1615, Prideaux held his chair and his opinions throughout the period of Laud's ascendancy, maintaining his

[1] Heylin, p. 203 ; Laud, *Works*, v. 15 ; *Cal. S.P. Dom.* 1629–31, pp. 384, 396, 411.

independence as stubbornly as Williams, only with more dignity. He could look upon Laud's power as a mushroom growth, and he survived it, rising into a bishopric at the same time as Williams rose to an archbishopric, when Laud was in the Tower. Wood[1] gives a long list of the distinguished foreigners who went to Exeter College " purposely to improve themselves by his company, his instruction, and direction for course of studies ", adding that " some also of the English nobility, having been sent thereunto, have, by the principles that they have sucked in, proved no great friends either to the Church or State ". Among the latter were the Earl of Radnor, " a severe predestinarian and a promoter of the Grand Rebellion ", Lord Wharton, Anthony Ashley Cooper, and the fifth[2] Earl of Pembroke, who " lived and died little better than a Quaker ". Thanks to his European reputation and unassailable position in Oxford, Prideaux was the greatest obstacle to Laud's triumph there, and he is always mentioned with particular distaste by the minor prophets of Arminianism, — Montague, Heylin, Sheldon, and Skinner. Round him the broken rear of Oxford Calvinism rallied for its last effort to prevent the triumph of Laud.

The opposition candidate for the chancellorship was the late Chancellor's brother, the Earl of Montgomery : and it was not only champions of Puritanism, but all who, from whatever motive, opposed the growing power of Laud, that united in his support. There was Sir Nathaniel Brent, the Warden of Merton, who owed his position to the influence of Abbot, whose niece he had married and whose Vicar-General he had become. There was old Ralph Kettell, the President of Trinity, an immovable monument in the University, steadily opposed to any change of any kind whatsoever, whether Puritan or Arminian.[3] Professing no other scholastic ambition than to repress the " *juvenilis impetus* " of his scholars, he also survived Laud's ascendancy : and Laud respected his opposition enough to attempt to buy it off, — at least, that was the only construction which Kettell could place on a gift of venison which Laud insisted on his accepting, in spite of his plea that his stomach was too old and weak to digest it. Not least among Laud's opponents was Williams, who, as Bishop of

[1] *Athenae Oxonienses*, iii. 269.

[2] Not, as Wood says, the second.

[3] *Vide* Aubrey, *Brief Lives* (Ralph Kettell).

Lincoln, was visitor of Balliol, Oriel, Lincoln, and Brasenose Colleges, and exerted his influence there in the interests of Montgomery. For Montgomery, too, the Welsh party (who might also be expected to favour Williams) gave their voices, although the Principal of Jesus, Dr. Mansell, supported Laud.

Over all these, however, Laud triumphed, thanks to the devoted service of his followers. In Magdalen, which, twenty years ago, had been " a nest of puritans ", Heylin sang treble to the President's bass. The President, Dr. Accepted Frewen, was Vice-chancellor at the time, and rushed back from Andover, where he was on a college progress, as soon as he heard of Pembroke's death, in order to lend his support to Laud. Christopher Potter, the Provost of Queen's, though brought up a Calvinist, had already been converted to more profitable doctrines. Sheldon kept the Arminian flag flying at All Souls. There could be no doubt about the attitude of St. John's under Juxon. And Corpus Christi, Wadham, Jesus, Pembroke, and New College [1] came in on the same side.

With his election as Chancellor of Oxford, Laud had secured a notable personal triumph. It was in Oxford that his earliest humiliations had occurred, when he had been denounced from the pulpit and cut in the streets. Since then it was not he, but Oxford, that had changed, and the change had been effected by no one more than by himself. " Nothing is more impolitic ", wrote Bacon, " than to be continually bent upon one action." But whereas the political career of Bacon proved a failure, the ultimate success of Laud had justified another maxim, less old, but more reliable, that a hundred repetitions make one truth. Laud had persevered in his unpopular doctrines, until the institution which had first rejected them with such indignation signalised its conversion by choosing him as its head. But it was not this personal triumph which Laud regarded with the most satisfaction: for he was never interested in persons, not even in himself. By his election as Chancellor, he saw that he had secured a ministry of propaganda for the faith. Oxford was where future churchmen learned their doctrine, and, with himself in command,

[1] The Warden of New College, Dr. Pinke, later proved less successful in forwarding Laud's cause, and Laud attributed his failure to secure the election of his nominee as Warden of Winchester to Dr. Pinke's inactivity, for which he reproved him. (Laud, *Works*, vi. 289-90.)

he could make sure that they would learn the right doctrine. There he fostered the right learning and suppressed the wrong learning. He enriched the University with benefactions and adorned it with buildings. It was to be the headquarters of the Arminian faith in England, an institution of orthodoxy, decorous, disciplined, and correct. He spared himself no labour to secure this result, taking the most minute interest in all its affairs, and requiring a weekly report from the Vice-chancellor of its discipline and its doctrine. And the character which Laud imposed upon Oxford remained peculiar to it throughout the century.

This double blow to the Puritan propagandists, — first the declaration forbidding them to defend their position, and now the election of their grand enemy as Chancellor, was not at first quietly accepted. In a number of defiant sermons, Puritan Oxford raised its last protest for many years.[1] One Thomas Cook of Brasenose attacked the new orthodoxy in the pulpit and was forced to recant : so was William Hobbs of Trinity College for a like offence. But the most serious trouble occurred in 1631, when William Hodges of Exeter College, Thomas Ford of Magdalen Hall, and Giles Thorne of Balliol preached against Laud and his doctrines on such nicely-chosen texts as " Let us make a captain, and let us return to Egypt ", and " He cried against the altar in the word of the Lord and said, O Altar, Altar ! " Summoned before the Vice-chancellor, these three boldly appealed to Convocation, and the Proctors boldly admitted their appeal. The Vice-chancellor then appealed to the King, who held a meeting of the council at Woodstock to decide the matter. There, after a hearing that lasted six hours, the three preachers were sentenced to lose their fellowships and be expelled from the University, the Proctors were compelled to resign, two ex-Proctors who had acted a dubious rôle were made to submit, and the chance of administering a rebuff to Prideaux, who was accused of complicity, was not allowed to pass unused. We are told that Prideaux would have been deprived of his chair, but for the intercession of the Lord Chamberlain, Laud's defeated rival, Lord Montgomery.[2] As it was he was censured, together with Dr. Wilkinson, the Principal of Magdalen Hall.

These measures were effective, and we hear little more of

[1] Laud, *Works*, v. 49 ff.

[2] *Diary of Thomas Crosfield*, Aug. 23rd, 1631.

antagonism to Laud in Oxford, although Prideaux was kept under close supervision, and in 1632 there was an unfortunate incident when a young fellow read a commonplace attacking Laud in Laud's very holy of holies, — St. John's College chapel. He was a young man called Spinke, and in his intemperate zeal he denounced images, vestments, altars, and political bishops : but he soon regretted this rash outburst, and made a public recantation.[1] As for the three offenders of the previous year, — Hodges soon recanted. Later in the same year he wrote to Laud, submitting entirely and begging to be restored, as " a young man whom age may make wise ". His application was granted, and next New Year's day he was enjoined to preach in St. Mary's, this time on the less dangerous subject of obedience. Thorne too submitted, although he seems never to have been restored to his fellowship. Ford, however, refused to acknowledge his fault. He hoped to escape this humiliation by being elected lecturer in Plymouth : but here he was disappointed, for the trustees of the lecture were ordered not to elect him, under pain of incurring the royal displeasure, and they did not.

So the University accepted the impress of Laud's character, and exchanged the doubtful prospect of disorderly originality for the staid antiquarian learning of a rich clerical foundation. It became the University of Sheldon and Fell, that burnt *Leviathan*, expelled Locke, and censured Hearne's *Camden* and Wood's *Athenae*. It flourished, not as a hatchery of bold speculations and intellectual exuberance, but as a splendid academy whose fine ceremonies, orderly discipline, and respected pundits would be a credit to the country which it adorned. In the year of his election, Laud received a letter from Vossius describing the melancholy state of affairs in the University of Leyden. " Recently ", it lamented, " the students coming to the University from the neighbouring towns are younger and more ignorant than they used to be, and their morals deteriorate daily. Not only is there a regular cult of Bacchus and Venus, but the last six years have seen more murders committed than the previous thirty." " I was sorry to hear of the decay of discipline in your University ", Laud replied. " I am sure this is the cause of all our ills in Church and State, — that the places formerly dedicated to the education of the young in religion and the arts are now given

[1] Tanner MS. 303, p. 108 ff.

over to everything least worthy of a Christian. But to think that it should have come to murder, and that frequently!"[1] Such things were not to occur in Oxford. Oxford was not to be like Leyden, with its undisciplined brilliance, but like Louvain, with its ordered mediocrity. And in the limited field which he prescribed for himself, Laud was brilliantly successful. "Authority and the breath of Heaven" were set up and worshipped, not Venus and Bacchus. There was no luxury, no dissipation, no controversy, but grave and orthodox divines expounding their ample learning from well-endowed chairs. A rigid discipline was enforced: statutes, operative to-day, were promulgated: long hair, extravagant dress, and alehouses were regulated. Chairs were founded and enriched, new buildings raised, new treasures accumulated, new subjects expounded. And when the King came to Oxford in state, he looked at Laud's handiwork and saw that it was good, — the epitome of all that he wished to see in England. In the intellectual sphere Laud may have sacrificed something, but that was part of his success, — the price of it. What he set out to do he did, and did it splendidly.

Meanwhile, there was also his diocese of London to look after, and to this Laud was able to give more personal attention than St. David's or Bath and Wells had received. Here his most prominent activities were the suppression of lecturers whose views he disliked, and the State Papers for the period are full of petitions from parishes suddenly deprived of their Puritan ministers. The most famous case was that of Thomas Hooker, who deserves notice as having some personal claim to consideration besides the accident of the irritation which he caused to Laud. He was an Emmanuel College man, and had carried the Puritan gospel which he had there imbibed first to Esher and then to Chelmsford, gathering around him such a following, especially of younger ministers, to whom "he was an oracle and their principal library", that when Laud threatened him with the High Commission in 1629, observers thought that the peace was in danger. Hooker, however, whose behaviour was throughout moderate if his convictions were intense, offered to leave the country quietly provided that no proceedings were taken, and in May a correspondent wrote to Dr. Duck, Laud's chancellor, that,

[1] Vossii, *Ep.*, no. cxxxv; Laud, *Works*, vi. 294.

in view of Hooker's large following, this was far the best course.[1] Indeed, so great was the excitement raised by the report of the proceedings, that in East Anglia the major question of tonnage and poundage was relegated to the background, and in Cambridge the University disputed Hooker's case *pro* and *con*.[2] In November Laud heard that Hooker was still active in Essex: petitions and counter petitions flowed in to him from that district: and Hooker was reported to have opened a school.[3] Next year Laud took the step which he had so long deferred, and cited Hooker before the court of High Commission. Hooker thereupon fled to Holland: but even there he was not safe from supervision, and his Independent views brought him into conflict with the emigrant Presbyterians. From Holland, like other Independents, he fled still further to America, and there became the apostle of Connecticut.

Nevertheless Laud could not afford to be as rigid as he is sometimes represented to be in his treatment of lecturers. The insufficiency of orthodox and beneficed clergy could not be remedied all at once, and, like his own bishops later, he frequently had to sacrifice the orthodoxy which he preferred to the moderate Puritanism which was the most he could get. So a vague pledge of conformity was generally sufficient to secure the restitution of a suppressed lecturer.[4] Against any lay interference, however, he took a rigid stand; for he would never admit the right of lay patrons or corporations to prescribe the doctrine of the preachers whom they supported. During his London episcopate, he supervised the erection of a new chapel in the village of Hammersmith, for which he opened a subscription-list: but when the subscribers suggested that they might submit two names to Laud, of which he was to select one as the new minister, Laud replied categorically that the maintenance of the vicar must be settled in perpetuity, that popular nomination is utterly inadmissible, and that the bishop, in this particular case, being not only diocesan but also patron of the living, "no township shall, upon any pretence, make me give away the least hair of the inheritance of my bishopric".[5] Against churchwardens who

[1] *S.P. Dom. Car. I.* 142, no. 113.
[2] *Ibid.* 144, no. 36.
[3] *Ibid.* 151, nos. 12, 45; 152, no. 4.
[4] E.g. *S.P. Dom. Car. I.* 167, no. 34; 169, no. 23.
[5] Laud, *Works*, vii. 31.

attempted to dictate the form of church services he was equally severe. He found them dictating in this way to the vicar of St. Lawrence's, Old Jewry, and again in the case of Sherfield; and when the latter case gave him an opportunity of denouncing the abuse in a place of great authority, he did not omit to give publicity to the former also, and to remark how Archbishop Abbot had then intervened on the side of his opponents.[1]

At the same time ceremonies, which were the outward and visible expression of the deference due to the functions, the persons, and the property of the Church, were being more zealously enforced. Besides bowing, altars, and vestments, he was a great stickler for the consecration of churches which impressed upon the material fabric of the Church a magic seal as a deterrent to those who might otherwise be tempted to despoil it. The Puritans, who considered that a good conscience sufficiently consecrated any place in which it exercised itself, without the protection of supposedly miraculous properties, accused Laud of introducing this innovation; but like most of his "innovations", Laud merely made regular what had already been frequent. Andrewes, Mountain, and Abbot had all consecrated churches, and Williams, who rejected Laud's example in the altar-controversy, followed it in this. The form of service adopted by Laud was that drawn up by Andrewes, and Laud had first used it at the consecration of his new chapel at Abergwili in St. David's. In January 1630 he consecrated the church of St. Catherine Cree, which his predecessor had rebuilt, and so established a precedent for the ceremony which the Puritans found so offensive. Next Sunday he consecrated Manwaring's new church of St. Giles-in-the-Fields, and the next year another church which Sir John Wolstenholme, a farmer of the customs, had built out of the proceeds of that lucrative office at Stanmore Magna in Middlesex. In Oxford, in 1631, the new chapel of Lincoln College, built by Williams, was consecrated by the Bishop of Oxford, the poetical *bon viveur* Dr. Corbett. Williams himself was not present at the ceremony. His rival had triumphed too recently in Oxford, and he remained in contemptuous retirement at Buckden.

But the ceremony of consecration presupposed a fabric to consecrate and, by consecration, to preserve: and it was Laud's policy not only to conserve the existing, but to construct new

[1] Laud, *Works*, vi. 14.

church buildings. Since the days of Henry VIII, thanks mainly (in Laud's opinion) to the absence of a proper consciousness of sacrilege, church-buildings had repeatedly been suffered to decay, or converted to secular uses, while church lands had been transferred to more active hands. But a reaction had now begun to set in, and Laud determined to centralise this reaction in himself and to express it in his policy. The period of his ascendancy was to be a period of restoration, and he could not too frequently rub into the minds of his contemporaries the assurance that their ills were the natural result of their negligent attitude towards the property of God, —

> Delicta majorum immeritus lues,
> Romane, donec templa refeceris,
> Aedisque labentes deorum et
> Foeda nigro simulacra fumo.

As, however, such a movement must necessarily be inspired from the top, he resolved himself to give a splendid example by harnessing, utilising, and turning to constructive achievement the somewhat dilatory and tentative attempts of his contemporaries to remedy the dilapidated condition of his cathedral church, St. Paul's.

The recent history of St. Paul's [1] had been the history of innumerable churches and cathedrals throughout the country during the last hundred years. It had fallen into neglect and disrepair, and in 1561 further destruction had been caused by lightning, which brought down the spire. This last calamity had aroused the attention of the Queen, who ordered the Lord Mayor to see that it was repaired, and herself contributed a hundred marks in gold and a thousand loads of timber from the royal woods. By 1566 the wooden roofs were finished: but after that little was done, and it was not till the reign of James I that the continual agitation of a private person resulted in official notice again being directed to the state of the cathedral. By this time the fabric was almost ruinous, and the smoke from sea-coal added its effects to those of man's neglect and nature's vengeance.

This private person was one Henry Farley, who, like Spelman

[1] On this subject see generally Sir Wm. Dugdale, *History of St. Paul's Cathedral* (1658).

in another sphere, represented the awakening of conscience to some of the less admirable features of the Reformation. In 1616 he began his campaign of agitation by publishing a pamphlet entitled

> " The Complaint of Poule's
> To All Christian Souls :
> or
> An Humble Supplication
> To our good King and Nation
> For her speedy Reparation " ;

and he paid one John Gipkyn to execute a triptych depicting the solemn visit of the King to the cathedral which he hoped thereby to stimulate. In this he was successful, and on March 26th, 1620, the royal visit took place amid pageants, civic receptions, and banquets, with the object of advertising the repair of the church. Farley was there himself, and presented a petition in his own name, which was, however, carried off by the Master of Requests before the King had had time to see it. However, he brought out, and presented on the same day, another publication on the subject, a medley of prose and verse in which he dwelt at some length on the crying need for repair, adding that

> My love for Paul's is such
> That if I had an Angel's pen, I'd write ten times as much.

The result of all this publicity was the setting up of a commission for the repair of the cathedral, in which the whole Privy Council, some of the bishops, and a proportion of residentiaries, aldermen, and citizens were included. The Bishop of London was entrusted with the care of the body of the church, the Dean and Chapter with that of the choir, and all were encouraged to subscribe to the cost, Royalty and Privy Councillors heading the list.

Interest, however, soon lagged. All the money that came in was insufficient to keep the roof and other decayed parts of the building in repair, and the stone which Bishop Mountain had collected from Portland for the work of restoration was borrowed by Buckingham for his water-gate at York House. It was not until Laud became Bishop of London that sufficient enthusiasm was aroused to enable the work to proceed.

He found the cathedral again sunk in a state of neglect, if not contempt, caused, according to the report made in 1631 by Dr. Rives and Attorney-General Noy, by " the neglect and sufferance of the dean and chapter in times past ".[1] While divine service was being celebrated in the church, the west end was full of people walking and talking, children playing, and porters engaged in their business. " Paul's Walk ", as the west porch was called, was the general meeting-place where city men met their friends to expatiate on politics, business, or scandal, like the coffee-houses of the Commonwealth and afterwards. " The noise of it ", wrote Earle in his *Microcosmographie*, " is like that of bees, a strange humming or buzz mixed of walking tongues and feet ; it is a kind of still roar or loud whisper. It is the great exchange of all discourse, and no business whatsoever but is here stirring and afoot. It is the synod of all pates politic, jointed and laid together in most serious posture, and they are not half so busy at the Parliament. . . . It is the general mint of all famous lies, which are here, like the legends of Popery, first coined and stamped in the church. All inventions are emptied here, and not few pockets." [2] So little of the atmosphere of sanctity was there in the cathedral that one man, who was brought before the High Commission for having made water in it, was able to plead that he did not realise that the place was a church ! [3]

Such a state of affairs in his cathedral church shocked the punctilious propriety of Laud, and in 1631 a new commission was set up, consisting of himself and Neile, the dean and residentiaries of the cathedral, Privy Councillors, the Lord Chief Justices, the Lord Mayor of London, and some of the aldermen. The houses which were built up against the fabric of the church were demolished by order of the Privy Council on the ground that they had been built on Church property without authority, and the owners were compensated. A notice was posted forbidding walking and talking, or children's games, or carrying of burdens by porters, inside the church at time of divine service.[4] New efforts were made to raise subscriptions.

[1] *Documents relating to St. Paul's* (Camden Soc., 1880), p. 131.

[2] " Paul's Walk." Cf. Bishop Corbett's elegy upon Dr. Ravis, Bishop of London :

" When I past Paules, and travell'd in that walke
Where all our Brittaine sinners sweare and talk " ;

and " A Sixefold Politician ", 1609, quoted by Gilchrist *ad. loc.*

[3] *Select Cases in Star Chamber and High Commission*, p. 280.

[4] *Documents relating to St. Paul's* (Camden Soc., 1880), p. 133.

Where Abbot, in his applications, had made no difference between clergy and laity, Laud applied to each separately [1]: and the munificence of the clergy — who either considered the work an especial credit to their order, or regarded a prompt response as a means of catching the eye of the Bishop of London — was thus greatly increased. The response of the rest of the country was less satisfactory: but Laud circularised J.P.s and city officers, the King wrote to the Inns of Court for their offerings, and bishops and clergy preached on the godliness of church restoration with the same gusto with which they had recently advocated the necessity of obedience. The notorious Montague, now settled quietly in his see of Chichester, was particularly insistent in urging his clergy to contribute. Even Williams was not behindhand, " perfuming his visitation with the sweet gums of his eloquence ", and declaring that, divine service being once decently ordered and churches repaired, " the mouth of detraction is quite stopped, the priests and Jesuits are blank and silenced, the government in Church and State is generally approved, and (what is more considerable than all the rest) God Himself is magnified and glorified ".[2] Bishop Corbett of Norwich, in the same year, addressed his clergy in his usual brisk style. " St. Paul's Church! One word in behalf of St. Paul; he hath spoken many in ours. He hath raised our inward temples: let us help to requite him in his outward." [3] There were some Puritans who suggested " that it was more agreeable to the rules of piety to demolish such old monuments of superstition and idolatry than to keep them standing ", — was it not the rattle of Tetzel's money-box raising collections through Germany for the building of St. Peter's that had started the Reformation on its course? — and a fellow of Pembroke College, Oxford, had to recant in Convocation for declaring that he " would rather give ten shillings towards the pulling down of that church to build other churches where they want them, than five shillings towards the repairing of it ".[4] " Some petitions there are ", said Corbett, " for pulling down of such an aisle, or changing lead for thatch, — so far from reparation that our suit is to demolish. If to deny this be persecution, if to repair churches be innovation, I'll be of that religion too."

[1] Wilkins, *Concilia*, iv. 486.
[2] Hacket, ii. 59.
[3] Harl. MS. 750, p. 312 b, etc.
[4] Wood, *Hist. and Antiquities of Oxford* (ed. Gutch), ii. 393.

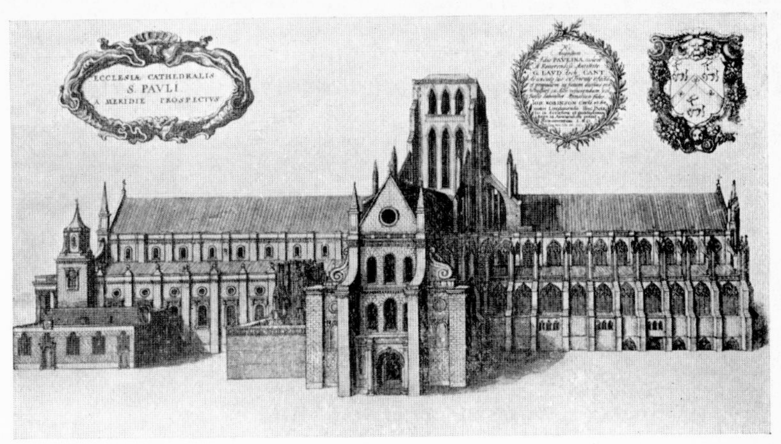

SOUTH FRONT

WEST FRONT

ST. PAUL'S CATHEDRAL, ACCORDING TO LAUD'S DESIGN:
SHOWING THE WEST PORTICO BY INIGO JONES

Corbett gave £400 to the work, and, in addition, gave money to poor clergymen in his diocese to give in their own names, in order to stimulate the generosity of others. Neile gave £500. Laud promised £100 a year, and gave more. The King promised £500 a year for ten years, which he later increased to an undertaking to repair the whole west end.[1] When the Lord Mayor and Aldermen gave only £10 apiece, Laud begged for more, pointing to the King's generosity, and adding that there were many well-disposed citizens who would have given more than they did, but had not liked to outbid their superiors.[2] Contributions came from the East India Company, and £1000 was sent out of the proceeds of a successful venture in the East by a merchant named Thomas Smethwick, — a gift which Laud remembered to his advantage later, when Smethwick wished to obtain some favour from Wentworth.[3] Sir Paul Pindar, a rich Turkey merchant who had been ambassador to the Porte and was one of the King's most generous supporters, gave contributions, amounting in all to £19,000, which included such decorations as black marble pillars and statues of Saxon kings on the west front, and wainscot carvings of cherubim within. When Lord Cromwell sought a position in the Irish government Laud wrote to Wentworth urging him to grant it to him, although he knew that the King disliked him, because " his respects to me have been outwardly very fair . . . and in the particular of St. Paul's he did more than many that have double his estate, and he did it in a very free and noble way with me ".[4] The King's master of the works, Inigo Jones, was given charge of the repairs, and the sailors engaged in importing the stone were given exemption from impressment for the navy. In April 1633 the work began for the east end, where the first four stones were laid by Laud, Windebank, Sir Henry Marten, and Inigo Jones, and proceeded by the south-east side to the west end, where a portico supported by Corinthian pillars, and intended by Laud to fulfil the functions of Paul's Walk, was constructed at the King's expense, adorned with statues of King Charles and King James.

The restoration of St. Paul's, — even if, considering the

[1] Stow, *Survey* (ed. Strype), iii. 151; Wood, *Athenae Oxonienses*, i. 601; *S.P. Dom. Car. I.* 327, no. 47; Wilkins, *Concilia*, iv. 492.

[2] *S.P. Dom. Car. I.* 259, no. 22.

[3] *S.P.* (East Indies), Dec. 17th, 1634; Laud to Wentworth, *Works*, vii. 497.

[4] Laud, *Works*, vii. 188. Cf. *ibid.* vii. 247.

design according to which it was to be restored, it cannot be called beautification — was a striking instance in the aesthetic sphere of that Catholic culture which Charles I and Laud were seeking to impose, as a stabilising mould, upon a society suffering from the disintegrating effects of change. The motives which inspired them were not identical, — for Laud looked upon the arts in a more utilitarian spirit, as the external forms by which men were drawn to the support of a given system, — but they operated in the same direction. The King had a genuine love of art, which all recognised who could understand it, and he indignantly repudiated the rumours that the money collected for the restoration of the cathedral were to be diverted to political purposes.[1] There was no surer way to interest him than to call his attention from politics to pictures, as the papal envoy soon discovered : in 1627 he had bought the entire collection of the Duke of Mantua, and later he used Arundel as his agent in Vienna for the purchase of works of art as well as the negotiation of treaties. In this direct aspect of the arts, however, Laud had no interest. He made no mention of Rubens when he came to England in 1630 as ambassador from the King of Spain and received from Charles a knighthood and a commission to decorate the banqueting-hall at Whitehall for £6000. Van Dyck, who came to England in 1632 and was also knighted by Charles, he regarded only as a court painter who charged exorbitant fees.[2] Laud encouraged the setting up of organs to swell the praises of God : but he admired them, as most Puritans hated them, less for their music than for their ceremonial effect. Not discrimination, but propriety, led him to order his portrait from Van Dyck and an anthem from Orlando Gibbons.[3] It was not because Laud himself had artistic tastes that he fostered some of the arts, nor because he was himself an Orientalist that he patronised Oriental studies : but, like the statesmen who found libraries and academies, he understood the social value of these things.

At the same time Laud was careful to maintain his position at Court. At the beginning of the reign he had been promised

[1] Wilkins, *Concilia*, iv. 492.

[2] Laud, *Works*, vii. 295.

[3] The original score of Gibbons' " Anthem for St. John the Baptist's day " has a note in Gibbons' autograph : " This anthem was made for Dr. Laud, President of St. John's, Oxford ". (Cf. *Orlando Gibbons' Sacred Compositions*, ed. Sir F. A. G. Ouseley, 1873, p. 73.)

the archbishopric of Canterbury on Abbot's death, and he still seemed in full possession of the royal favour. But he had seen Williams, apparently within reach of the highest positions in Church and State, suddenly, by the loss of favour at Court, stripped of his power and sent packing into the wilderness: and the example of Abbot, who, although nominally the highest ecclesiastical dignitary in the realm, had in fact been completely eclipsed by himself, could not but remind him that royal favour was both essential and uncertain. His hold over the King, indeed, seemed firm enough. He officiated at all court functions, usurping the places both of Abbot, as Archbishop of Canterbury, and of Williams, as Dean of Westminster. When the Queen, frightened by a dog-fight, had been delivered prematurely of her first child, who died almost immediately, Laud had buried him. When Prince Charles was born in 1630, Laud had christened him, "His Grace of Canterbury being infirm" and Williams being unasked, — although, by the marriage treaty, the child should have been baptized into the Roman faith. From other quarters at Court, however, there was a continual danger which involved him in continual intrigues.

First there was the Queen, whose influence on her husband was the more dangerous because it was exerted not at the council table but in the closet. Popish in religion, given to frivolity, completely unsympathetic to all the ideals of Laud, she was herself in turn influenced by a group of selfish and irresponsible courtiers whom Laud openly despised. Then there was the Lord Treasurer Weston, whose careful economy enabled the King to dispense with Parliament, but who, while restraining the royal bounty to everyone else, directed it in a steady stream towards himself, and whom only the Papists whom he fined so heavily did not believe to be a Papist. And there was Lord Cottington, the Chancellor of the Exchequer, with his breezy Spanish tastes and lively sense of humour, which he loved to exercise at the expense of the uncomprehending bishop. If the Queen surpassed him in influence with her husband, Weston and Cottington surpassed him in administrative and diplomatic ability: and Laud, who disliked them all for their refusal to apply themselves to the public service with the same impersonal devotion which inspired himself, was continually afraid that they were seeking to oust him from his favourable, but perhaps precarious, position. He therefore looked around for allies whom he could place at the King's ear to counteract any such sinister designs.

An opportunity for this presented itself in February 1632, on the death of Lord Dorchester, the Secretary of State. Four months elapsed before his successor was chosen, and during that time there was plenty of speculation as to who that successor should be. Among the candidates mentioned were Cottington himself; Lord Falkland, the sage of Great Tew, who assailed bishops so bitterly in the Long Parliament; Lord Holland, the Queen's favourite; and Sir Kenelm Digby; but well-informed opinion generally favoured the brilliant and cultured diplomat Sir Thomas Roe.

Roe had had a varied career as an explorer, a courtier, and a diplomat, and with his engaging character, his many friendships, and his wide interests, he reminds us of Sir Walter Raleigh, — a figure who would have been more at home in the brilliant court of Queen Elizabeth than he could be among the hatreds and intrigues which surrounded Charles I. In the early days of James I he had explored the Amazon. He had been on embassies to the Shah of Persia, the Great Mogul, and the Grand Turk. He had collected coins and manuscripts in the East for presentation to the Bodleian through Laud. Cyril Lucaris, the enlightened Patriarch of Constantinople, had been among his friends, and had presented the Codex Alexandrinus of the Greek Bible to the King through him. To the exiled Queen of Bohemia he acted as unofficial adviser. And another of his acquaintances was Laud. Apart from their common interest in Oriental studies, they had another connexion in Lady Roe, whom Laud had no doubt known in his youth: for her father, Sir Thomas Cave, had been the patron of his earliest living. Now Roe had just returned from successfully mediating between the Kings of Poland and Sweden, to the advancement of the Protestant cause on the Continent, and on his arrival in England had received a splendid welcome. King Charles had had a medal struck in his honour. King Gustavus Adolphus, who attributed to him the design of putting himself at the head of the Protestant powers of Europe, had rewarded him after the victory of Leipzig with a gift of £2500. With such credentials and the friendship of Laud, Roe might well feel confident of obtaining the post which had become vacant.

Laud, however, did not support his candidature. Roe was too independent a character to be ruled by anyone, and his Continental policy had too Protestant a tinge to appeal to one who wished at all events to keep out of the war, lest hostilities involved the summoning of Parliament. And so Roe found himself passed over when the vacant post was filled, and saw it filled by a hitherto unknown character, a clerk of the signet, Francis Windebank.

Roe could not conceal his disappointment, although from the start he had professed to have little hope. The English Court, he had said, was a labyrinth to which he had no clue : " the way to Heaven is strait and narrow, and in this only the court is like it : there is but one entrance ". He retired to a house which he bought himself in Northamptonshire, and compared himself, in language which shows the period in which his sympathies lay, to Drake's ship in dock at Deptford. In applying to the Lord Treasurer for the payment of debts owing to him from the Crown,[1] he begged him not to bruise a reed : and in urging upon Lord Holland the necessity of giving help to Sweden, he added : " the privacy of my life forbids me to meddle or to pry into the ark of His Majesty's secrets. Yet I am a member, and have an interest in the head. I shall be extremely joyed to hear from Your Lordship . . . that though I live out of the active world, I may know what it doth, and be kept among the living ; for ignorance is a civil death, nor can I so bury myself without a constant profession that if His Majesty at any time remember me, I can never decline his service. If he call, I answer 'Adsum, Domine!' I see many occasions : is there none for me ? Are all men thought and cared for, I only forgotten ? "[2]

His applications were in vain, and Roe had to wait several years before the government would entrust him with an appointment. Two years later, when he applied to Laud for some assistance to escape from the " civil death " to which he was consigned, Laud disingenuously pretended that he was quite without influence in the matter of Court appointments. " It may be ", he wrote, " because I had once the happiness to join in assistance to help my old acquaintance Mr. Secretary Windebank

[1] Roe was said to have spent £7000 of his own money on his recent embassy (Pory to Puckering in Birch, ii. 144).

[2] *S.P. Dom. Car. I.* 172, no. 10 ; 173, no. 49 ; 219, no. 51.

forward, you may conceive me able to do more than I am: but I would very willingly have you understand that if he had not had more powerful friends than myself, he had never been where he is. And therefore, I pray, build no more hopes upon me than I am able to answer." [1]

Who these "more powerful friends" were, Laud would have been hard put to it to explain, for in fact Windebank was quite unknown except to himself. His father had been clerk of the signet before him, and had occasionally done some minor administrative work under Burghley when the Secretaryship of State was vacant after Walsingham's death; and Francis Windebank had merely succeeded his father in an office which, but for Laud, he would have continued to occupy. Laud, as we have seen, knew him well at St. John's, and frequently stayed at his house in Berkshire: two years ago he had used his influence to secure a scholarship at Winchester for one of Windebank's sons; and now it was he who wrote to him, in the nearest approach to a jocular style of which he was capable, to inform him of his surprise appointment. And in his diary he recorded that on June 15th, 1632, "Mr. Francis Windebank, my old friend, was sworn Secretary of State: which place I obtained for him of my gracious master King Charles ".[2]

Laud thought that he had secured an ally at the King's ear: but in fact, as we shall see, Windebank was to prove a broken reed, and his activities in behalf of Roman priests, and his conversations with Roman emissaries, were gladly seized upon by Laud's enemies as proof of the treasonable and popish intentions of the prelate who had advanced him. "To what end this instrument was advanced to this place of trust by Canterbury", Prynne commented on the entry in Laud's diary, "and what good service he did to the priests, Jesuits, Nuncio, Papists, Pope, and his nuncios therein, will appear in the sequel of this narration." [3]

A month later Laud succeeded in placing another of his confidants at the King's side. This was William Juxon, his successor as President of St. John's. On July 10th, 1632, Laud wrote in his dairy that "Dr. Juxon, the Dean of Worcester, was at my suit sworn clerk of His Majesty's closet, that I might have

[1] Laud, *Works*, vii. 74. [2] *Ibid.* vii. 36, 43; iii. 215.
[3] *Hidden Works*, 1645, pp. 122-3.

one that I might trust near His Majesty, if I grow weak or infirm ".[1]

Windebank and Juxon availed Laud but little. Windebank joined his enemies, and Juxon was too unpolitical, too entirely dependent upon Laud, to exercise any independent influence in his support. But in the meantime Laud had made another ally of more enduring quality, one whose name is intimately connected with his throughout the period of his power until both fell together, and whose administrative genius made him Laud's secular arm,—Thomas Wentworth.

Efficiency was Wentworth's religion. He liked to see things done, and done well. Throughout the reign of James I nothing had been done, and apathy in the government had led to abuses in the country. In the days of Buckingham nothing had been done, and Wentworth, as member of Parliament for Yorkshire, had protested against this neglect. As a result he had been pricked sheriff for his county and so excluded from the next Parliament. When all that Buckingham would do was to continue an expensive war and seek to finance it by a forced loan, Wentworth refused to pay and was committed to the Marshalsea. But when Parliament, under the influence of Eliot, abandoned constructive efforts for an equally ineffective policy of radicalism, Wentworth had detached himself from the parliamentary cause and, in 1629, pursued by the philippics of Eliot, he went to govern the North in the King's name, as President of the Council at York. There his apathetic predecessors had left him plenty to do, and he set about doing it.

It has been suggested that Wentworth and Laud first came into contact at the trial of Leighton in the Star Chamber, and this may well be so. Certainly it was about that time; and two months after Leighton's case Laud mentions in his diary that he was closeted in his "little chamber at London House" with Wentworth, whom he had not mentioned before. But however their first meeting was brought about, it was the beginning of a long intimacy. There was a great deal of difference between the rich Yorkshire squire and the superstitious old bishop. There was a difference of twenty years in age to start with. Wentworth was a gentleman, born to a great estate, who had entered Parliament

[1] Laud, *Works*, iii. 215.

at twenty-one and had acquired wide experience by the time he was appointed President of the North at thirty-five. Laud had reached middle age before he was a bishop, and had never known any politics except those of a college. Wentworth had early forced himself upon the notice of the government by the skill and determination with which he had opposed its policy: Laud had gradually risen by anchoring himself to the very man whom Wentworth had assailed. Wentworth had suffered imprisonment for refusing to subscribe to the forced loan: Laud had instructed the clergy to preach the divine approval of the same forced loan. The opponents of "Thorough" feared Wentworth, and cried for his death because "stone dead hath no fellow" and they dared not leave him alive. He was "Black Tom Tyrant", who dispensed his ruthless justice to all alike and trembled before no man or combination of men; who was not frightened of parliaments because he knew that he could browbeat and manage them by sheer personal ascendancy and political skill. Laud had no such imposing stature. His adversaries hated him as a "little meddling hocus-pocus" who owed his position not to strength of character or political ability, but to patient, subterranean work. His presence inspired no awe, — he was "a little, low, red-faced man", — his manner was not despotic but rude, and he was ridiculously superstitious. Every trivial dream, every anonymous libel, every malicious rumour, every ominous coincidence, was a source of unconcealed anxiety to him. And yet once these two men, by ways so different, had risen to a place in the King's Council, their common devotion to the ideal of order and efficiency, their common contempt for the corruption and incompetence around them, their common impatience at the discontent and disorder in the country, due, as they were convinced, to lack of control by the government, established between them a bond which all the differences in their ages, experience, and temperaments were powerless to unfasten. In his personal religion, as far as he had any, Wentworth could be described as Puritan. But Puritanism covers a multitude of religions, and there is a great difference between the sectarian hysterics of Prynne and the proud, personal austerity of Wentworth. His Puritanism was a manner, not a theological or political system, and in some ways Laud shared it. Both hated disorder and extravagance. To both an imposing structure appealed more than exotic luxuriance. To those who regard Wentworth as a Puritan Laud must be a Puritan also.

It is possible that these very differences in their characters provided an additional bond between Laud and Wentworth. We have seen, in the cases of Scudamore and Buckingham, the attraction which was exercised upon Laud by men much younger and much more confident of their position than himself; and on Buckingham's death it may well be that Wentworth stepped opportunely into the breach, to which Laud's letter to Scudamore on that occasion so well testifies, offering that strong external support upon which he depended for his assurance. On the other hand, Wentworth's attraction to Laud was no doubt partly due to the same motives which led Laud to advance Windebank and Juxon. Wentworth had but lately joined the government, and to most of the Court he was more familiar as a dangerous enemy than as an ally; he was therefore conscious of his isolation, with his late allies attacking him for apostasy, and his new allies beneath his contempt. He was not so hostile to Weston and Cottington as Laud was, for he did not, like Laud, regard differences of principle as overriding all personal relations. Weston had persuaded the King to accept his services, and with Cottington he remained on friendly terms. But he did not trust them; and he trusted the Queen and her party less, who interposed themselves between the King and his most devoted counsellors and persuaded him to lavish on courtiers the revenues for lack of which the country was in disorder. His morose and austere temperament, moreover, and his frail health, upon which his restless mind imposed so severe a strain, emphasised his loneliness. To go off from a capital where he was either unknown or distrusted, with no assurance of continued favour from a fickle master, no agent to represent his interest and prevent the intrigues of his rivals, might well be the end of a career rather than the beginning of it. But Laud could be trusted to appreciate his work in reducing disorder, in enforcing "the law of the Star Chamber". Laud, like himself, was personally incorruptible and hated corruption. Laud had an immense capacity for business and regular access to the King. Laud was therefore an obvious ally at Court, whether Wentworth was stationed at York, or even further afield in Ireland: and the great magnates whom Wentworth punished in the provinces, when they appealed from him through their friends at Court, found that Wentworth too had a friend at Court, far more watchful and devoted than theirs. So the alliance was cemented, and when Windebank fell away, Wentworth became still more indispensable to Laud. To him alone he communicated his opinion about the ministers with whom he had to work, and about the King under whom he had to work. But for the extensive correspondence between these two, and the fortunate omission by Wentworth to burn the secret side-papers which accompanied Laud's letters, we should know even less about Laud's personal relations than we do.

Thus by the end of 1632 Laud was well established in position. There had been no Parliament for four years, and during those years peace and the non-committal policy of the Lord Treasurer had enabled the King to reign and Laud to enforce his policy without organised opposition. Voices were raised against him among Puritan circles, but on the whole there was little articulate resentment, and on Christmas day 1632 he preached a conciliatory sermon to the royal household, attacking Popery and Arminianism, and even quoting Calvin with respect. It had its effect. Philip Burlamachi, the government's financial agent, when he heard of it, said that it was a good julep against a parliament, and an Oxford don reported that it gave great content and confuted the opinion of the vulgar.[1] It might also have made his imminent translation to Canterbury less offensive: for Archbishop Abbot had been seriously ill in the summer, and the high-church party had seen the juiciest plum in the hierarchy ready to drop into their mouths. They were disappointed, however, for the Archbishop had recovered, and in September a newswriter reported that "His Grace by his diet hath so moderated his gout as it is now rather an infirmity than a pain. He looks fresh and enjoys his health, and hath his wits and intellectuals about him. So that if any other prelate do gape after his benefice, His Grace perhaps (according to that old and homely proverb) may eat of the goose which shall graze upon his grave."[2] So Laud was kept from Lambeth for another year, and in the interim had the occasion still further to exasperate the Puritans by another of his unfortunate irruptions into Scotland.

[1] Pory to Puckering, Jan. 3rd, 1632–3, in Birch, ii. 213; *Diary of Thomas Crosfield*, Feb. 1st, 1632–3.

[2] Pory to Puckering, Sept. 1632, Birch ii. 177.

In May 1633, seeing his southern kingdom at last settled, King Charles decided to go in state to Scotland for his coronation as King of Scotland. At the same time he intended to hold a parliament to ratify the measures which he had adopted to settle an uneasy situation there.

James I had established bishops in Scotland: but their influence remained small. He had secured the passage of the Articles of Perth through a General Assembly, but they were resisted in the country. He had ordered the use of the English Prayer Book in the Chapel Royal at Holyrood, but it was neglected. Apparently the establishment of the Anglican Church in Scotland required more than Acts of Parliament, orders, and bishops. It must be made independent of the nobility, and draw its power from the sound basis of inalienable property; and it must be consecrated in the minds of the people by the regular use of Anglican formularies. It was Charles' purpose to continue the work of his father by the recovery of Church property for the Scottish episcopal Church and by the imposition of an appropriate form of worship: and as this was the policy which Laud was attempting to carry out in England, he could look with confidence for Laud's assistance, although in fact, even when he was Archbishop, Laud had no constitutional authority in Scotland except when he acted as the King of Scotland's secretary.

The King's first attempt to recover the property of the Church in Scotland had not been successful. He had proceeded simply by an Act of Revocation, summarily revoking all grants of Church lands which had been made by his father, on the ground of a technical flaw in the original grant. But as these lands, which had been granted mainly during the minority of James VI, had by now, to a large extent, passed into other hands, either by inheritance or purchase, the new owners raised an immediate protest, and the King was made to understand that to visit the sins of the fathers upon the children to the third and fourth generation, though it may be good religion, is bad politics. When the Roman Catholic Earl of Nithsdale was sent to Scotland with an explanatory proclamation, many of the holders of church property were resolved to "fall upon him and all his party in the old Scottish manner and knock them on the head": and the Earl, on his arrival at Berwick, learnt that the coach which had preceded him to Edinburgh had been hacked to pieces by the mob, who had killed the horses and " seemed only sorry that they could not do as much to the Lord himself ".[1]

Hereupon the King proceeded by a more conciliatory way. By the advice of his Solicitor-General in Scotland, he undertook to deal separately with the tithe-holders. Commissioners were appointed to enquire into the tenure of lands; and those who surrendered had their property confirmed by Parliament on condition of paying rent to the King and commuting the tithes (which were paid in kind) either by purchase or for a rent-payment from which the minister's stipend was to be taken. " In its final shape ", says Gardiner, " the arrangement thus made is worthy of memory as the one successful action of Charles' reign." It reduced the arbitrary power of the lords over their tenants, who had previously been unable to garner their own harvests till the lord had taken his tenth part, and it provided satisfactory maintenance for the ministers. The nobility welcomed it as an alternative to the drastic Act of Revocation, and, as they feared that the King might proceed to deprive them of their hereditary jurisdictions, they pressed him to come north for his coronation and have the compromise ratified as a final settlement. So the King set out from London on May 13th, 1633, accompanied, among others, by Laud.

As for the second part of the design, — the imposition of an Anglican liturgy, — that was not yet ready. In 1629, on the King's instructions, Laud had received one of the Edinburgh ministers of known Episcopalian views, John Maxwell, to discuss the project, but some divergence had shown itself in their views. Maxwell had submitted a draft of a liturgy drawn up by the Scottish bishops on the lines of the English Prayer Book, but incorporating passages from Knox's Book of Common Order which was in use throughout Scotland. Laud, however, had opposed this, telling him that he was " clear of opinion, that if His Majesty would have a liturgy settled there, it were best to take the English liturgy without any variation, that so the same service-book might be established in all His Majesty's dominions "[2] Maxwell and the Scottish bishops believed that this would offend Scottish sentiment, always suspicious of any appearance of English domination. But the King supported Laud's opinion. As yet, however, the time was not ripe for the development of this project.

[1] Burnet ii. 20; Heylin, p. 224.

[2] Laud, *Works*, iii. 427.

The journey to Scotland was a leisurely progress, lasting a month. " This whole progress ", says Clarendon, " was made, from the first setting out to the end of it, with the greatest magnificence imaginable, and the highest excess of feasting was then introduced, or at least carried up to a height it had never been before, and from whence it hardly declined afterwards, to the great damage and mischief of the nation in their estates and manners. All persons of quality and condition who lived within distance of the Northern Road received the great persons of the nobility with that hospitality which became them : in which all cost was employed to make their entertainment splendid, and their houses capable for those entertainments." [1] Nor was it only the nobility who received the royal attention *en route*. Passing through Huntingdonshire, the King turned aside to visit the semi-monastic institution, " the Protestant Nunnery ", which the eccentric Ferrar family had set up at Little Gidding.

The household at Little Gidding, which consisted of some thirty members of a single family (not all of them equally enthusiastic) living in an atmosphere of devotional exercises, is one of the most curious testimonies to the revulsion of feeling against the Reformation which had affected certain classes, and the romantic idealisation of rejected practices. The moving spirit of this community was Nicholas Ferrar, who, in the course of his travels in Germany and Italy, had made some study of Roman devotional works, and, on his return, decided to realise their teaching in England. Ordained by Laud, he had set up his " nunnery " in the diocese of Williams : and these two bishops, who agreed in so little besides, agreed to indulge the foundation. It was perhaps as a concession to Williams that the communion-table at Little Gidding was set table-wise, and not altar-wise according to the Laudian pattern : and Williams, when he visited the place, expressed his approval. As Williams, however, never set foot inside the cathedral of which he was bishop for twenty years, and never once, during his three years in the Tower, received the sacrament or even went to church, it is improbable that this approval was based upon any personal sympathy with uncomfortable religious observances.

The place was, in fact, a sort of ecclesiastical greenhouse, in which the pious practices associated with the better days of the

[1] *History of the Rebellion*, i. 167.

Church were somewhat artificially revived. These practices were quite harmless, for they did not impinge upon the outside world, and the outside world took a benevolent sightseer's interest in them. Among the visitors was a Puritan lawyer Edward Lenton who, though a trifle shocked at anything so obviously reminiscent of Popery,[1] sent a careful and fair-minded account of Little Gidding to his friend Sir Thomas Hetley ; and this account, falling into the hands of fanatical Puritans, was used as material for a violent attack in a pamphlet, *The Arminian Nunnery*, published in 1641. Ferrar was then dead : but the author describes an imaginary visit in which Ferrar, " a jolly, pragmatical, and priestlike fellow ", had conducted him round as he had conducted Lenton. " Oh, the stupid and blind devotion of these people," he exclaims, " for men and women in health, of able and active bodies and parts, to have no particular callings, or to quit their callings, and betake themselves to I know not what new form of fasting and prayer and a contemplative and idle life . . . as if diligence in our particular lawful callings were no part of our service to God ! "[2] And Laud and his bishops were attacked for having allowed the existence of such a foundation " so nearly complying with Popery ".

In fact, however, the most that could be charged against Laud was his toleration of the place. For though he had no objections to the principles set forth by the Ferrars, his was no cloistered religion, nor could he ever content his active spirit with the pleasures which some are alleged to derive from vigils, contemplation, and the painting of capital letters. To the King, however, this stained-glass pietism made a far greater appeal. He made a special journey to visit Little Gidding, and was met at the parish boundary by the Ferrar family who led him in procession to the church. There he was taken on a conducted tour

[1] He states, however, that Ferrar, when questioned, declared that " he did as verily believe the Pope to be Antichrist as any article of his faith " ; — which shows how little the papal claims had to do with English Catholic ideas. Lenton's letter is printed in *Papers Relating to Little Gidding, Transcribed and given to the Publisher by Mr. John Worthington* (Oxford, 1730).

[2] Weber, in his famous thesis, *Die Protestantische Ethik und der Geist des Kapitalismus*, emphasises particularly the antithesis between the contemplative ideal of the Middle Ages, represented by Dante, and the intensely practical spirit of Puritanism, illustrated particularly by the doctrine of the " calling ". A better illustration of this antithesis could hardly be desired than this extract from *The Arminian Nunnery*.

of inspection, and " enquired into, and was informed of, the particulars of their public and domestic economy " ; and next year, when he was at Apethorpe, not far distant, he sent again to Little Gidding for a copy of the Concordance made by the inmates, which he insisted on keeping.

After this the progress continued to Nottingham, where the Earl of Newcastle entertained the court at Welbeck " in such a wonderful manner, and in such excess of feasting, as had never before been known in England " : and so on, through York, Durham, and Berwick, to Edinburgh.

It is unlikely that Laud took much pleasure in the progress itself, — he looked on the last progress which he had attended as unmitigated boredom, — and he was not the man to derive any healthy secular enjoyment from the continual junketings which accompanied it. But he was not idle. Already in 1629 he had secured a royal order requiring bishops to repair churches and chapels in decay and to preserve them in good condition, making full use of the ecclesiastical courts for the purpose, and seeing " that the judges be required not to interrupt this good work by their too easy granting of prohibitions ".[1] Laud himself had set a great example in his own diocese, and now he had an excellent opportunity for seeing what others had done in theirs. In York he observed a number of houses and mean tenements built close to the minster wall, and wrote in the King's name to the dean and chapter ordering them to see to their demolition. He noticed too that there had been seats in the choir for the wives of the dean and canons, which had been temporarily removed for the King's visit, and ordered their removal to be permanent. Only the wife of the Lord President of the North was entitled to a seat in the choir. Similar instructions were sent to the Dean and Chapter of Durham, who had allowed similar abuses.[2] Then, on the 15th June, the royal party reached Edinburgh, and, on the same day, Laud was made a Privy Councillor of Scotland.

On the state of Edinburgh at this time all contemporary writers are agreed. It was the dirtiest and most unsavoury town in the British Isles. " The air might be wholesome ", said Sir

[1] Rushworth, *Collections*, ii. 28.

[2] King to Dean and Chapter of York, in writing of Laud's secretary, Wm. Dell, *S.P. Dom. Car. I.* 239, no. 56 ; 240, no. 10 ; 241, no. 7.

Anthony Weldon, "but for the stinking people that inhabit it"; and Sir William Brereton, who visited it in the year after the royal visit, though he approved of the Scots' religious practices, announced that "the sluttishness and nastiness of this people is such that I cannot omit the particularising thereof".[1] He found that their earth-closets consisted of "tubs or firkins placed upon the end, which they never empty until they be full, so as the scent thereof annoyeth and offendeth the whole house": the houses stank from afar, so that he could not approach his own lodging without holding his nose or squeezing a pomander: drains were unknown, — everything was deposited in the streets and left there; while "to come into their kitchen and see them dress their meat, and to behold the sink, (which is more offensive than any jakes), will be a sufficient supper, and will take off the edge of your stomach". For the royal visit, however, some effort was made to tidy up the city. Heads of malefactors were removed from the gates where they were impaled: a gallows, complete with corpse, was discreetly stowed out of sight: and a dustman was even temporarily engaged to clear the streets of promiscuous refuse. The King was then welcomed to his northern capital with pageants, processions, and other demonstrations of loyalty.

But if the King in his political capacity was everywhere greeted with affection, the ecclesiastical innovations which followed in his train (and these, of course, included Laud) were not. "The beauty of holiness" accorded ill with the unclean habits of the Scots, and when the King was crowned, three days after his arrival, it was with horror that they noticed "ane foure-nuikit taffill, maner of ane altar", chandlers, lighted candles, blind books, and a basin in the church. Behind the altar was a tapestry embroidered with a crucifix, "and as thir bishops who was in service passed by the crucifix, they were seen to bow the knie and beck, which, with their habit, was notit" — for they wore blue silk robes and white rochets with loops of gold — "and bred gryt feir of inbringing of poperie".[2] The Bishop of Brechin put the crown on the King's head, and Laud wanted the two Archbishops to stand on either side of the King during the ceremony. Archbishop Spottiswood, who had refused to wear a

[1] *Travels* (Chetham Soc., 1844), pp. 105-6.
[2] Spalding, *Memorials of the Trubles* (Aberdeen, 1850), i. 36.

surplice at King James' funeral, was prepared to wear one for King Charles' coronation: but the Archbishop of Glasgow, "being a moderate churchman", declined to follow suit and was pushed aside by Laud with the words, "Are you a churchman, and want the coat of your order?"[1] His place was supplied by the Bishop of Ross, in a surplice. Next Sunday, in St. Giles' Church, it was observed that Laud's agent, John Maxwell, came down from the royal loft and made the officiating minister withdraw, replacing him by two English chaplains in surplices. The Bishop of Moray, who preached the sermon, wore a rochet, "quhilk was never sein in St. Geillis Kirk sin the Reformatioun": and this was regarded as smelling particularly strongly of Popery, as the bishop had formerly been known as a Puritan. The Sunday after, Laud himself preached in Holyrood Chapel, "which scarcely any Englishman had ever done before in the King's presence, and principally upon the benefit of conformity and the reverent ceremonies of the Church, with all the marks of approbation and applause imaginable".[2] The next week was spent in sightseeing, — to St. Andrews, Dundee, Falkland, and, on the Sunday, to St. John's Town (now Perth), where Laud was made a burgess of the town, but avoided taking the usual oath to defend the "true, Protestant, Reformed religion" by saying that he was more accustomed to exact oaths than to take them. Next day, at Dunblane, he commented on the beauty of the church, and when one of those present replied, "Yes, my lord, this was a brave kirk before the Reformation", "What, fellow?" he interjected, "Deformation, not Reformation!"[3]

Most of these incidents are reported by hostile witnesses: but fundamentally they are probably true, for it was characteristic of Laud throughout his life to make enemies unnecessarily by the sharpness of his speech. Clarendon himself, his most sympathetic historian, has to admit that he was unfortunate in "a hasty, sharp way of expressing himself", and had to remonstrate with him about it personally. "He was observed", says Fuller, "... to infuse more vinegar than oil into his censures",[4] and it was not only the Scots who remembered these and similar discourtesies against him. Protesting Puritans, defendants in the

[1] Rushworth, ii. 182. [2] Clarendon, *History of the Rebellion*, i. 173.
[3] Row, *History of the Kirk of Scotland* (Wodrow Soc. 1842), p. 369.
[4] *Church History*, vi. 299.

Star Chamber and High Commission, humble petitioners, judges, magistrates, noblemen, and ambassadors of foreign powers, were all to experience and resent the offensive manner in which he dismissed them when their opinions differed.

On July 11th Laud began his return journey from Scotland, leaving behind him unpleasant personal reminiscences and many apprehensions for the future. These apprehensions were expressed when the Parliament showed great reluctance to pass two out of the thirty-one acts submitted to it, — one " anent His Majesty's prerogative and the apparel of Kirkmen ", and the other ratifying previous ecclesiastical enactments: and soon afterwards they received some confirmation. For in September the new diocese of Edinburgh was created, carved out of the metropolitan see of St. Andrews: and although the first bishop, William Forbes, was a benign and ineffectual clergyman, he only lasted three months, and was succeeded by David Lindsay, that Bishop of Brechin who had crowned Charles I and who was one of the four chief advocates of an Anglican liturgy. The Archbishop of Glasgow, who had refused to wear a surplice at the coronation, had also recently died, and the Bishop of Ross, Patrick Lindsay, who had replaced him at the ceremony, replaced him in his diocese. The vacant diocese of Ross was bestowed upon Laud's agent Maxwell, who, for some time (according to a hostile witness) had been " gaping for a bishopric ".[1] And in October 1633 a royal order imposed the English clerical dress and the English liturgy upon the Chapel Royal at Holyrood and the University of St. Andrews, the seat of Archbishop Spottiswood.

In England, too, there had been episcopal changes. The deaths of Harsnet, Howson, and Buckeridge had released the three great sees of York, Durham, and Ely. York went to Neile, as a reward for his early patronage of Laud, to whom he had now willingly accepted a second place. He was not learned, nor had he that large comprehension which he recognised in his colleague of envisaging a whole policy in all its details. Nor could he ever be a courtier: for he was at bottom a plain, uneducated man, whose style of language was sometimes comic in its simplicity. But he had many agreeable qualities besides his unselfish desire to promote a party which he knew that he could not lead. Many

[1] Robert Blair, *Autobiography*, p. 87.

stories are told of his charitable disposition and his own natural humility. He once reproved a schoolmaster for beating a stupid boy, explaining that he himself had never acquired much learning precisely because of the corporal punishment which had accompanied his instruction ; and when he was translated to York, and his ecclesiastical officers advised him to levy a tenth from his clergy, as his predecessor had done, he answered that " he would in no case attempt any such matter : for he was come to benefit, not to charge his clergy ". On another occasion he was passing through a town where there were many poor people, and his coachman whipped up the horses as if he meant to spare the Bishop's purse. But Neile reproved him, and made him stop his carriage " till such time as he had with his own hand freely distributed to them all ".[1] And five years later, when reporting the condition of his province to Laud, he remarked that " having been a bishop one and twenty years, he never deprived any man, but had endeavoured their reformation ".[2] Which must be allowed in part to mitigate the severity of his censure in the cases of Wightman and Trendall.

About Neile's successor in Winchester there was much speculation, and it was reported that Laud would take it, keeping the bishopric of London, but devoting all its revenues to the repair of St. Paul's.[3] Ultimately it was given to Walter Curle, who had previously succeeded Laud at Bath and Wells, — a man who once described a Puritan as " such an one as loves God with all his soul, but hates his neighbour with all his heart ",[4] — and Bath and Wells went to William Pierce as a reward for providing Peterborough with an episcopal house. To Peterborough in turn went Augustine Lindsell, a learned scholar who had been one of the Durham House party in the earlier days of the Arminian movement, but who did not live long enough to play a large part in its achievements. Buckeridge's see of Ely went to White, already notorious as a turncoat and the licenser of Montague's books : and Norwich, which he vacated, was conferred on Richard Corbett. In his early days at Oxford, Corbett had aroused the indignation of both the brothers Abbot by his anti-Calvinist

1 Pory to Puckering, Sept. 20th, 1632, in Birch, ii. 177.

2 *S.P. Dom. Car. I.* 345, no. 85, i.

3 Pory to Puckering, Sept. 20th, 1632, in Birch ii. 178.

4 *Manningham's Diary* (Camden Soc., 1868), p. 156.

opinions [1]: but he had attached himself to Buckingham and prospered in spite of them. By his promotion to Norwich, he left Oxford vacant for John Bancroft, who built the new episcopal palace at Cuddesdon. The only low-church bishop to profit by these removes was Thomas Morton. He had been Bishop of Lichfield and Coventry since 1619, and thus dated from the time before Laud's influence had begun to prevail. Now he succeeded Howson in Durham, after a year's revenues from the see had gone into the treasury. He was a pacific man who caused no trouble to Laud, although he gave testimonials to John Durie, the troublesome apostle of Protestant unity, and adorned the walls of his palace at Bishop Auckland with pictures of all the great Protestant reformers from Wyclif to Perkins.[2]

Laud had no need of the bishopric of Winchester which gossip had conferred upon him. When he reached London from Scotland on July 26th, Abbot was ill again, and this time he did not recover. On August 4th he died, and there was immediate apprehension among the Puritans. A preacher in London prayed God " not to send a Bonner or a persecutor of the Church among them ": [3] but it was too late for divine intervention, — the King had got in first. Two days after Abbot's death, Charles had greeted Laud with the words, " My Lord's Grace of Canterbury, you are very welcome ".

[1] Heylin, pp. 62-63.
[2] *Travels of Sir Wm. Brereton* (Chetham Soc.), p. 80.
[3] J. Paget to Tremyll, Aug. 22nd 1633, in Birch, ii. 227.

CHAPTER FIVE

CANTERBURY

"To the voice of persuasion the Archbishop was obliged to add the terrors of authority: and his ardour in the exercise of ecclesiastical jurisdiction was not always exempt from passion, nor was it always guided by prudence. Chrysostom was naturally of a choleric disposition. Although he struggled, according to the precepts of the Gospel, to love his private enemies, he indulged himself in the privilege of hating the enemies of God and of the Church; and his sentiments were sometimes delivered with too much energy of countenance and expression. . . . Conscious of the purity of his intentions, and perhaps of the superiority of his genius, the Archbishop of Constantinople extended the jurisdiction of the imperial city that he might enlarge the sphere of his pastoral labours; and the conduct which the profane imputed to an ambitious motive, appeared to Chrysostom himself in the light of a sacred and indispensable duty. In his visitation through the Asiatic provinces, he deposed thirteen Bishops of Lydia and Phrygia, and indiscreetly declared that a deep corruption of simony and licentiousness had infected the whole episcopal order."—GIBBON, *Decline and Fall*, ch. xxxii.

LAUD's promotion to Canterbury could have surprised no one: but it was accompanied by the usual crop of comments, rumours, and libels. Puritan letter-writers gave way to dismal forebodings: one Richard (alias Lodowick) Bowyer announced in Laud's native town of Reading that the new Archbishop was confined to his house under an armed guard for treasonable dealings with the Pope: and Lady Eleanor Davies, who, on the strength of a faulty anagram of her own name, claimed to embody the prophetic spirit of Daniel, predicted that he would not survive the fifth of November. Bowyer was savagely punished by the Star Chamber in November,[1] and in the Court of High Commission, where she

[1] At his trial, Cottington proposed that Bowyer should stand in the pillory at Westminster, Cheapside, and Reading, with a paper declaring his offence and his ears nailed; should pay a fine of £3000; and should undergo perpetual imprisonment. Lord Chief Justice Richardson suggested, "to be whipped, imprisonment in Bridewell, burning in the face R or L". The sentence was made to include both suggestions (*Cal. S.P. Dom.*, Nov. 13th, 1633; Rushworth, iii. 65).

was sentenced, Sir John Lambe produced from the name of Dame Eleanor Davies a more accurate anagram which disposed of her pretended powers of vaticination, — "Never so mad a ladie". Had he known it, Bowyer might have produced better evidence than mere divine inspiration in support of his statements; for on the very day of Abbot's death, and again a fortnight later, Laud was approached with a serious offer of a Cardinal's hat, would he but give his allegiance to Rome. But on each occasion he reported the suggestion to the King, replying to the offer that "something dwelt within me which would not suffer that, till Rome were other than it is".[1]

Among the letters of congratulation which reached him on his appointment, Laud received one from an unexpected source. Bishop Williams, after eight years' experience of the alleged pleasures of retirement, had decided to cut his losses, swallow his pride, and once again seek power by complaisance, since opposition had availed him nothing. He therefore wrote to the Archbishop protesting his desire to serve him, begging leave to attend his translation, and asking him to make peace for him with the King. As for his diocese, "God be praised for it, it is more free from unconformable ministers than it hath been these sixty years: and had been so many years ago, if I had been as fortunate as other bishops in the ability and faithfulness of those ecclesiastical officers which my predecessors' patents have pinned upon me".[2] To this olive-branch from the enemy whom he most feared and hated, Laud's reply was circumspect and evasive. He thanked Williams for his congratulations, but regretted that he had already appointed the bishops who were to take part in the ceremony of his translation. He had attempted to win the King over to Williams' side, but had been rebuked and told to desist from such intercession in future. And as for the diocese of Lincoln, — "whereas you add that you have not been fortunate in the ability and faithfulness of such ecclesiastical officers as have been left to you by the patents of your predecessors, that perhaps is not your lordship's case alone".[3] Laud was thinking of his own inheritance from Abbot, — his Vicar-General, Sir Nathaniel Brent, and his Dean of the Arches, Sir Henry Marten.

[1] Laud, *Works*, iii. 219.
[2] Williams to Laud, printed in Laud, *Works*, vi. 312.
[3] Laud, *Works*, vi. 314.

From Ireland, whither he had gone as Lord Deputy in July, Wentworth sent his less dubious congratulations, and to him Laud replied less guardedly, confessing his apprehensions of the huge responsibility which he had assumed. " I must desire your Lordship ", he wrote, " not to expect more at my hands than I shall be able to perform, either in Church or State ; and this suit of mine hath a great deal of reason in it, for you write that ordinary things are far beneath that which you cannot choose but promise yourself of me in both respects. For as for the Church, it is so bound up in the forms of the Common Law that it is not possible for me, or for any man, to do that good which he would or is bound to do. For your Lordship sees (no man clearer) that they which have gotten so much power in and over the Church will not let go their hold. They have indeed fangs with a witness — whatsoever I was once said in passion to have. And as for the State, indeed my lord, I am for Thorough : but I see that both thick and thin stays somebody where I conceive it should not, and it is impossible for me to go Thorough alone. Besides, private ends are such blocks in the public way, and lie so thick, that you may promise what you will, and I must perform what I can, and no more.

" Next, my Lord, I thank you heartily for your kind wishes to me, that God would send me many and happy days where I am to be. Amen, — I can do little for myself if I cannot say so. But truly, my Lord, I look for neither. Not for many, for I am in years, and have had a troublesome life ; not for happy, because I have no hope to do the good I desire. And besides, I doubt I shall never be able to hold my health there one year ; for instead of all the jolting which I had over the stones between London House and Whitehall, which was almost daily, I shall have now no exercise, but slide over in a barge to the court and Star Chamber. And in truth, my Lord, I speak seriously : I have had a heaviness hang upon me ever since I was nominated to this place, and can give myself no account of it, unless it proceeds from an apprehension that there is more expected from me than the craziness of these times will give me leave to do." [1]

Nevertheless, Laud set about his huge task with more determination than is usually shown by those who despair of success, and his health, in spite of his gloomy prognostics, was much

[1] Laud, *Works*, vi. 310.

stronger than that of Wentworth. Far different had been Abbot's last account of his province, which he had sent to the King at the beginning of the year. Abbot had known that his days were numbered, his hopes impossible of fulfilment, and a successor who would reverse his policy waiting to occupy his place. With languid unconcern he had reported that "it is enough to say that the bishops, for aught it appeareth to me, have lived at home": that "ordinations of ministers, for aught that I can learn, are canonically observed": "and so it may be said of the rest of the articles, that I find no noted transgression of them".

On September 19th Laud was translated and moved over to Lambeth with his household, his fortune of £3100, and his two pets, — the tortoise which survived him by more than a century before it was accidentally killed by a careless gardener in 1753,[1] and the cat from Smyrna recently presented to him by Lady Roe. His first visit to his new palace was not auspicious, for the ferry was overladen and his coach and horses sank in the Thames, — an omen remembered by the superstitious when it occurred twenty-two years later to Oliver Cromwell,[2] — "but, I praise God for it", he recorded, "I lost neither man nor horse". A more important consequence of his translation was yet another vacancy in the episcopal bench. As his successor in London he appointed Juxon, who had just been appointed to Hereford, also vacant. Now Hereford was conferred upon Augustine Lindsell instead, and the new Bishop of Peterborough was Francis Dee, a harmless man "of pious life and conversation, and of very affable behaviour", whose sermon before the Court, being in praise of virginity, was considered tactless.

Laud lost no time in his new position. In October a royal letter was secured forbidding the bishops to ordain ministers except to a specified title, in order to stop the supply of unbeneficed lecturers. In December a quarrel between the Societies of the Temple and their Master, Dr. Micklethwaite, gave him the opportunity to interpose the royal authority, and, while disclaiming any intention of encroaching upon their privileges, to require

[1] For Laud's tortoise, whose shell was exhibited at the Laud centenary celebrations, *vide* W. E. Collins (ed.), *Lectures on Laud*, 1895, p. 287, and authorities there quoted.

[2] Duke of Sutherland's MSS., H.M.C. Report V. 148.

their ministers to wear and use the badges of orthodoxy.[1] And at the same time further measures were being taken to preserve ecclesiastical property from the gradual diminution to which it had recently been subject.

The instructions of 1629, as has been observed, had forbidden bishops to make leases of the property of the sees which they were leaving, or to waste the woods belonging to them. Later these requirements were amplified, and in 1632 the King had commanded Abbot to find out what advowsons, which had been in the gift of the Crown in the thirteenth year of Elizabeth, had since been usurped by local magnates.[2] In 1633 Laud had resolved to forbid altogether the leasing of Church lands by lives,[3] and in the following June this intention was conveyed in two royal letters, one to deans and chapters, the other to bishops and archbishops.[4] " We know ", ran the former, " the statute makes it alike lawful for a dean and chapter to let their leases for the term of one and twenty years or three lives : but time and experience have made it apparent that there is a great deal of difference between them, especially in Church leases." In future, therefore, no Church property was to be leased for a longer period than twenty-one years ; and in forwarding these instructions to the bishops of his province, Laud commanded them also to make a thorough survey and inventory of all the lands belonging to their sees at present in the hands of tenants, and to report, before next Michaelmas if possible, the acreage of these lands, the names and descriptions of the closes included in them, the time for which they had been in the hands of the tenants, the condition of the buildings, the rents, and the right by which the tenants collected them. " And though this course be taken, yet it is not intended that you shall be concluded thereby : but the end is to prevent the concealment of the Church's land, and to discover such as go about to conceal the same. And if you make it appear that any tenant of your Lordship doth hold more lands than he doth acknowledge upon this survey, I will inform His Majesty of him and his course against the Church, that such further order may be taken with him as shall appertain to justice." These

[1] *S.P. Dom. Car. I.* 254, no. 49.

[2] Wilkins, *Concilia*, iv. 478.

[3] Laud's intention of stopping all leases by lives is mentioned in the royal letter to the Bishop of Bristol, March 28th, 1633 (Lambeth MS. 943, p. 329), requiring him not to lease the manor of Abbot's Cromhall in Gloucestershire.

[4] Wilkins, *Concilia*, iv. 493.

orders were not popular among ecclesiastical landlords whom either custom had encouraged or the depredations of their predecessors had compelled to profiteer out of their benefices, and means were found to evade them by deans who were empowered to lease lands without reference to their chapters, and who could therefore pretend that orders directed to deans and chapters conjointly did not concern them. A further order, however, was issued to stop this loophole ;[1] and when the royal instructions to Abbot were reissued early in 1635 to Laud, the revised form included a clause " that every bishop give his metropolitan a strict account yearly of their obedience to our late letters prohibiting them to change any leases from years into lives : and that they fail not to certify if they find that the dean, or dean and chapter, or any archdeacon or prebendary, etc., within their several dioceses, have at any time broken our commands in any particular contained in the aforesaid letters ". Those bishops, too, to whom benefices had been granted *in commendam* to increase the revenues of their sees, were required to give an annual assurance that these had not been alienated to their friends or relatives : and the Bishop of Oxford was to certify that he was keeping the new palace at Cuddesdon for his personal use. Unfortunately, even the most explicit orders were not always sufficient by themselves to prevent ecclesiastical profiteering, as the subsequent recriminations between the outgoing and incoming bishops of Bristol were to show.

Laud's instructions to his bishops are of more importance, though they are less conspicuous, than the Star Chamber cases which were to make him notorious ; for the bishops, as both parties realised, were the keystone to the Catholic system. They were the indispensable agents of centralisation in the provinces, nominated by the government, and responsible to it. Like the local magistrates, they were armed with legal powers, having their own courts, their own legal procedure, and their own legal officers : but unlike the local magnates they had no local ties or local particularism ; and the very process of the Reformation, which had so reduced their social standing that their enemies could refer to them as " equal commonly in birth to the meanest peasants ", and " tyrannising lordly prelates raised from the

[1] Wilkins, *Concilia*, iv. 494.

dunghill ",[1] made them more reliable than the old ecclesiastical princes with their baronial independence and great family connexions. To understand Laud's work it will be necessary to observe these bishops in their dioceses, and see how they carried out the orders and followed the example of their metropolitan. In the meantime, however, we must turn to the example which he set: for it was an essential part of his policy that it must be inspired, or enforced, from the top.

When Laud moved over to Lambeth, the beauty of holiness which he had imposed while at Fulham followed him thither. There he restored the stained-glass windows set in the chapel by Cardinal Morton, and moved the communion-table to the east end. It was the same change which he had introduced into the cathedral of Gloucester as Dean of Gloucester: and now, as Primate of all England, he was to impose it upon all England. The test case was that of St. Gregory's church, nestling under the wing of St. Paul's cathedral, and recently restored by the parishioners. But contributions of money, as Laud had already made clear, did not entitle the contributors to dictate doctrine or policy, and the dean and chapter of St. Paul's, under whose care the church was, ordered the removal of the communion-table to the east end. Thereupon five Puritan parishioners complained to the Court of the Arches.

The Dean of the Arches was Sir Henry Marten, one of the officials bequeathed to Laud by Abbot, a man whom his contemporaries regarded as the greatest civil lawyer of the time, but whose judicial independence rendered him an unfit instrument for any political party. Free from any such idealist theories as affected the decisions of Coke and Bacon, he sought only to interpret the law, not to make it, and found himself, in consequence, unpopular both with the Court and the Puritans. As judge of the Admiralty Court he vindicated that court against prohibitions from the King's Bench, and Buckingham had consulted him on questions of admiralty law: in Parliament, however, he had attacked Buckingham's policy, while urging moderation upon his other assailants. During the debate on the Petition of Right, he had opposed the clause which would have acknowledged in the King

[1] Prynne, *Looking-Glass for all Lordly Prelates*, pp. 71, 79; *News from Ipswich*, 1636, p. 7.

a power superior to the laws : but he refused to second the radical claims of Eliot, whom he accused of disloyalty. When Abbot was under suspicion of irregularity for his hunting accident, Marten had defended him : but he proved to the unwilling House of Commons that Montague was a regular and legal bishop. So zealous an assertor of law at the expense of politics was not allowed to judge the case of St. Gregory's church, where his decision could only have been in support of the Elizabethan compromise which the government, by this case, was determined to reverse. The King therefore stopped the proceedings and called the case before the Privy Council, where it was discussed in his presence. There Marten opposed and Laud supported the removal of the table to the east end : and the King pronounced in favour of Laud.

The importance of the case of St. Gregory's is that it was a test case, and that in it the Head of the Church gave a legal and legitimate ruling that the old compromise had been torn up, and the old problem, which Elizabeth had shelved, had been solved. Once the royal decision had been made, even Sir Henry Marten could hardly have opposed it. For Queen Elizabeth's Injunctions, even if they were valid after her death (which was doubtful), could claim no greater authority than King Charles' decision, judged as a purely constitutional question. If Elizabeth, in virtue of the royal supremacy, could compromise, Charles, in virtue of the royal supremacy, could decide. The ultimate authority in ecclesiastical matters had been legally vested in the Crown, which thus had a discretionary power limited only by Acts of Parliament; and if the Puritans found that the Crown was using this power indiscreetly, they might complain that this was unsatisfactory, or impolitic, or impious : but they could not (unless the Crown had infringed an Act of Parliament) pretend that it was illegal.

So a new precedent was set and confirmed by a legal ruling, and a new Dean of the Arches replaced the inconvenient Sir Henry Marten. This was Sir John Lambe, — " a very orthodoxal gent ", as a high church petitioner acknowledged him to be, — a man who had already served Laud by turning against his former master and benefactor, Williams. He had been commissary of the peculiars to the Dean and Chapter of Lincoln, and had exercised a wide jurisdiction in that diocese. There his high-handed actions and extortionate methods had brought him into trouble with Parliament: but Williams had intervened and saved him, not only with a whole skin and purse, but with a doctorate and a knighthood. Two years later Williams made him commissary for the diocese: but in 1626, when the Church policy of the new reign was obvious, Lambe began to evince a zeal for Arminianism in his legal activities, and when Williams refused to countenance his inquisitorial proceedings against Leicestershire conventicles, he abandoned the sinking ship and gave information to the Privy Council against his former master, accusing him of favouring sectaries and of revealing to Lambe, at his own dinner-table, secrets entrusted to him as a Privy Councillor. Having thus secured the favour of the new rulers of the Church by betraying the old, Lambe now bethought himself of his reward. In September 1632 he wrote to Laud protesting his desire to return, like an over-hunted hare, to live a quiet and retired life at Oxford: and next year he suggested himself as a candidate for the vacant mastership of St. John's College, Cambridge.[1] But Laud had other uses for so thorough-going an agent, and at the end of 1633 he stepped into the place of Sir Henry Marten.

Having established the precedent and secured the decision confirming it, Laud set about following up his victory and setting up altars throughout the Kingdom. Some bishops tempered zeal with discretion or apathy: but one went further in his resistance. Williams, in his great diocese, had already issued directions in the matter, on his own authority, six years ago, when vicar and magistrate had come to blows over the position of the communion-table in Grantham. Then he had restated the Elizabethan compromise: and now, when King Charles and Laud declared the Elizabethan compromise superannuated, Williams paid no attention. Like a medieval baron fortifying his liberty against the encroachments of the Crown, he asserted his independence by a stubborn rejection of all authority but his own. Elsewhere, however, Laud had more obedient supporters. He had not filled the episcopate with his followers for nothing, and although many of them evaded his orders when it meant sacrificing an easy perquisite, they were ready enough to enforce them when they merely concerned communion-tables, vestments, and Sunday games. When Puritanism raised its head in Somerset it found

[1] Cf. Laud, *Works*, vii. 44; *S.P. Dom. Car. I.* 241, no. 75.

that it had to deal with a bishop as determined and as thorough as Laud himself, William Pierce, the new Bishop of Bath and Wells. As Vice-chancellor of Oxford from 1621 to 1624, Pierce had carried on the Laudian tradition when Laud had ceased to hold office in the University. When a fellow of Pembroke College had glossed the indispensable text " Let every soul be subject to the higher powers " with the interpretation " that the inferior magistrate had a lawful power to order and correct the King, if he did amiss ", Pierce had referred the case to Laud : and when the offender attributed his offensive doctrines to the Heidelberg divine David Waengler, alias Pareus, the commentary of Pareus was promptly burnt at Oxford, Cambridge, and Paul's Cross. Another who felt the authority of Pierce at Oxford was Bishop Corbett's bottle-companion, Dr. Lushington, who was forced to read a recantation for allowing a tone of frivolity to creep into his preaching. And as Bishop of Peterborough Pierce had shown his sympathy with the constructive part of Laudianism by providing his successors with a palace at Castor. In his new diocese he was equally thorough-going,[1] encouraging church-decoration and organ-building and silencing Puritans, until he could boast that " thank God, he had not one lecture left in his diocese ".

On hearing of the decision reached in the case of St. Gregory's, Pierce at once proceeded to order the same uniformity in his own diocese,[2] and supported his order by a set of seven adequate reasons for the removal of the table to the east end. He referred to Queen Elizabeth's Injunctions, which, if they did not enjoin that the table should be fixed in the east end, equally required that it should not be fixed in the nave. The Lord's house, he added, ought to differ from the houses of men. It was unseemly (as even Abbot had agreed) that people should sit above the Lord's Table in church. Railed off in the east end, the table was also free from those profanations to which it was otherwise sometimes subjected, and was more commodious for practical purposes. And finally " it is fit the daughters should be like their mother, the parochial churches should be like the cathedral churches, that so there may be an uniformity in this respect in every church."

[1] Cf. Pierce to Laud, 1637, in Lambeth MS. 943, p. 563.

[2] *Vide* documents in " the Beckington Case " (*Proceedings of the Somerset Record Soc.*, vol. 43, 1928).

Neither the authority of the Bishop's command nor the cogency of his arguments, however, could satisfy the churchwardens of Beckington, Messrs. Wheeler and Fry: and when the incumbent attempted to carry out the order, they successfully obstructed him. They were therefore cited to the Bishop's court and ordered to drop their tactics: but they refused, and were excommunicated. Then they appealed to the Dean of the Arches, and were allowed further time for compliance. Again they refused, and again they were excommunicated. So they petitioned the Archbishop; but Laud had had enough trouble from churchwardens, and ultimately the petitioners found themselves arrested under a writ *de excommunicato capiendo* and put in prison. Then at last they submitted, and uniformity reigned in the parish of Beckington. The Beckington case was made one of the charges against Bishop Pierce when he was impeached by the Long Parliament: but there came a voice from the Tower from one whom, if no opposition could instruct, no perils could terrify. Laud, with characteristic boldness, announced from his prison that he alone had been responsible for the persecution of the recalcitrant churchwardens of Beckington.

In Somerset, at the same time, another case was also in process. This concerned the ales or wakes traditionally held in the district: and here again the case is in itself trivial, important only as symbolic of a far more important issue. For whereas Churchman and Puritan alike were agreed that the Church should be an ascetic and austere body, they differed in their definition of the Church. To the high churchman it was a separate, visible body represented by the clergy, a class quite distinct from the laity whom it guided and directed: but to the Puritan the Church was no such exclusive possession, nor was the minister separated from the congregation by any more mysterious difference than that which separates the plumber from his customers. The asceticism, therefore, which the Anglican and the Catholic confined to the clergy, was, by the Puritan, demanded of all the godly, whatever their profession: and the right of the clergy to permit indulgence to the laity was as hotly contested as its right to regulate their appetites in virtue of a divine commission. The whole conception of a specialised Church which can relieve the laity of their spiritual exercises, while leaving them the free enjoyment of their secular pleasures, is repellent to the Puritan, with his insistence upon individual personal effort.

Such was the profound difference which raised the question of the Somerset wakes from a matter of village propriety to one of religious, and thereby social, principles. It was the difference between the Catholic who likes to see the festivals, pageants, and carnivals of the people blessed by the Church, and the Puritan who relegates maypoles, Christmas, and mince-pies to the Devil. No one could accuse Laud of self-indulgence. He admitted that he had rarely seen a play, he found entertainments tedious, and attacked finery and long hair in the clergy as censoriously as Prynne attacked it in anyone. But cakes and ale were a matter of principle: and when unauthorised persons attempted to regulate matters of principle, that was another matter of principle, — an attack on the right of the Church to interpret and declare principles. Such attacks Laud resisted vigorously. As Bishop of London he had had a dispute with one Lord Mayor for publishing an order against sabbath-breaking under his own nose, in his own diocese, and had soundly rated another for forbidding a poor woman to sell apples in St. Paul's churchyard on Sunday;[1] and as Archbishop, when the affair of the Somerset wakes brought the matter to a head, he intervened decisively, making it a test case for parish festivities, as he had made the affair of St. Gregory's a test case for the position of the communion-table.

The Somerset wakes were parochial beanfeasts in honour of the saint to whom the parish church was dedicated: and if they began as religious celebrations they sometimes ended in what Dr. Gardiner somewhat circuitously describes as "indulgence of the lower passions". This gave the Puritans their chance. While the Anglican approved the principle, and sought to curb the excess, the Puritan saw in the excess the opportunity to attack the principle. In 1632 the local Justices of the Peace petitioned against the custom, and Lord Chief Justice Richardson, who happened to be judge of the western circuit at the time, reissued an earlier order forbidding its continuance. Then, outstepping the limits of his proper jurisdiction, he instructed the clergy to publish the orders in their churches.

Here was Laud's opportunity to intervene in defence of the

[1] Rushworth, ii. 22; Heylin, p. 242.

principle and the independence of the Church. To Richardson, no principle was involved. He was no Puritan, as his severity in Prynne's case was to show, and he acted solely as a lawyer. But his order, by implication, was an attack on both the doctrine and the function of the Church, and by opposing that order Laud could defend both. Richardson, moreover, was not a formidable opponent, for he was both weak and unpopular. " Never sat there a judge in that court that was less respected ", wrote a news-writer later, describing his unattended funeral. And Laud had an additional reason for disliking him, as an opponent of the severe sentence which he had demanded in the case of Sherfield.

The first to complain against Richardson's action was Sir Robert Phelips, one of the Somerset magistrates, who, though an active member of the parliamentary opposition, had recently changed sides. He wrote to Laud in protest, and Laud reported his protest to the King. Charles then wrote to the Somerset magistrates for a certificate of Richardson's order, while Laud wrote to Bishop Pierce outlining his views on the subject of wakes. Disorders, he said, were not an adequate reason for the suppression of the festivals at which they occurred : if they did occur, that was the fault, not of the custom, but of the magistrates who had failed to prevent their occurrence. He instructed Pierce to find out, by application to " some of the gravest of your clergy, and such as stand best affected to the Church and government in the several parts of your diocese ", exactly how much disorder there had been.[1] Pierce replied that he had applied to seventy-two of " the better sort of the clergy ", and had learnt that the wakes were orderly enough. " The true cause of the outcry against them ", he said, " was sabbatarianism ", and " if people should not have their honest and lawful recreations upon Sundays after evening prayers, they would gather into tippling-houses, and there on their ale-benches talk of matters of Church and State, or else into conventicles." Besides, " by church-ales many poor parishes have cast their bells, repaired their towers, beautified their churches, and raised stock for the poor ".

Pierce's letter hardly had an opportunity to influence the attitude of the government, for it had not yet arrived when the government acted. Indeed, it was superfluous, for Laud already held the views which Pierce was advancing, and the King agreed

[1] Laud, *Works*, vi. 319.

with him. So while Charles reissued his father's *Book of Sports* denouncing sabbatarianism and commending such innocent recreations as dancing, maypoles, ales, and archery, Laud sent for Richardson and required him to rescind his order. Richardson at first ignored this demand : but when it was repeated by the the King, he complied reluctantly, at the same time justifying his former action by proving from the local records that no other course had been open to him as a judge. The King was indignant at such independence, and summoned both Richardson and Phelips before a committee of the Council : and there Laud dealt so rudely with the unfortunate judge that he left the room in tears, complaining that he had been almost choked with a pair of lawn sleeves. Richardson soon forgot his animosity against Phelips, but reconciliation was not in the nature of either Laud or the King : and although he applied to Cottington to intercede for him with Charles, the King would never allow him to ride the western circuit again.[1]

The incident of the Somerset wakes is interesting in many ways. It illustrates Laud's determination to proclaim his principles, even when at first no principle seemed to be involved, and it shows that he was still ready to cause trouble in order to set an example, even in a trivial matter. His enemies, of course, saw other motives. It is said by Prynne that the seventy-two clergy " of the better sort " to whom Pierce applied were " the deboystest and worst in the diocese ". But it is scarcely necessary to refute this charge, or to pretend that a difference of principle implied any difference in morals. Laud's attitude towards wakes is best shown by his treatment of a petition from the inhabitants of Clungunford in Shropshire in 1637, where no controversy arose to obscure the issue. The petitioners asked for the renewal of the annual snack of bread and cheese at the parson's expense which had formerly been held after evensong on Easter Day ; and they explained that it used to take place inside the church until fifty years ago, when the then Archbishop of Canterbury transferred it to the parsonage. This year, however, it had not taken place at all. " I shall not go about to break this custom ", Laud replied, " so it be done in a neighbourly and decent way : but I cannot approve of the continuance of it in the church, and if ever I shall hear it be so done again, I will not fail to call the

[1] *S.P. Dom. Car. I.* 269, no. 55.

offenders into the High Commission Court." [1] Indeed, in many ways his punctiliousness was almost puritanical. When that great exponent of the theory and practice of horsemanship, William Cavendish, later Duke of Newcastle, had a fall and broke his horse's neck on Good Friday, Laud recorded the incident in his diary with the comment, " Should not this day have other employment ? " [2]

The Somerset wakes and the reissue of the *Book of Sports* were not alone in affirming the official attitude towards those recreations which Puritans found so impious. In 1633 also occurred the first *cause célèbre* of William Prynne.[3]

This voluminous author was already well known when his *Histriomastix* brought him before the Star Chamber and made him famous. He was a man of immense learning and no judgment whatever, and when he died in 1669, a respectable pensioner of the Restoration government, receiving his visitors " with old-fashioned compliments such as were used in the reign of King James I ", he had enriched, or burdened, English literature with nearly 200 books, mostly seditious and all unreadable. His complete works were kept in the library of Lincoln's Inn, of which he was a member : but another member remarked that it might equally well contain the equally voluminous works of the literary bargee, John Taylor ; and at the end of the century Thomas Hearne found that his books had been so extensively used as waste-paper that they were now prized by collectors as rarities. A certain pious Puritan lady, indeed, bequeathed a sum of money to the recently founded Sion College for the purchase of Prynne's complete works : but that was before Prynne had written much.

He came of an old Shropshire family, and was born at Swainswick, near Bath, the son of a gentleman farmer. From Bath Grammar School he went to Oriel College, Oxford, where he could witness the spread of those high-church doctrines encouraged by the President of St. John's, and thence to Lincoln's Inn, the Puritanism of whose members was reflected in the names of their preachers. For, with the exception of John Donne, they were a

[1] *S.P. Dom. Car. I.* 362, no. 57. [2] Laud, *Works*, iii. 150.

[3] On Prynne, see generally Ethyn W. Kirby, *William Prynne*, (Cambridge, Mass., 1931) ; *Documents relating to Wm. Prynne* (Camden Soc., 1877).

series of distinguished Puritans, from the Elizabethan Field, whose memory smelt in the nostrils of the faithful " like a field which the Lord hath blest ", to Dr. Preston, " the greatest pulpil-monger in England in man's memory ", — that Court meteor who had nearly caught the soul of Buckingham for God and the Great Seal for himself. Dr. Preston found a suitable employment as Master of Emmanuel College : and as preacher of Lincoln's Inn he found an apt pupil in William Prynne, who soon discovered his vocation as learned counsel for persecuted sectaries.

Of his learning there can be no doubt. Even in a century of intellectual omnivores he was acknowledged a prodigy. When Laud looked at *Histriomastix*, he accused the author of having accomplices, as even a man of sixty could not possibly have read all the authors quoted in it. But Prynne indignantly protested that, though only thirty-three, he had nevertheless read them all. The journalist Marchamont Needham described him as " one of the greatest paper-worms that ever crept into a closet or library " : but the works into which he distilled this vast and promiscuous learning, according to Wood, " by the generality of scholars are looked upon to be rather rhapsodical and confused than in any way polite or concise ". Certainly no one who looked at the accumulated scurrility of *Histriomastix* could call it polite, or its thousand pages concise. His appearance and habits corresponded to his activities. " He was of a strange, saturnine complexion ", says Aubrey,[1] — " Sir Christopher Wren said once that he had the countenance of a witch " ; and he adds, " his manner of study was thus : he wore a long quilt cap which came two or three at least inches over his eyes, which served him as an umbrella to defend his eyes from the light. About every three hours, his man was to bring him a roll and a pot of ale to refocillate his wasted spirits. . . . So he studied and drank and munched some bread, and this maintained him till night, and then he made a good supper."

The first result of this concentrated study was *The Perpetuity of a Regenerate Man's Estate*, a delayed addition to the already numerous attacks upon Montague, published in 1627. Laud dropped on him at once for this, but Prynne's fellow lawyers came to his rescue and saved him by a prohibition. Next year, when the complaints of Parliament showed that his first work

[1] *Brief Lives* (Wm. Prynne).

had been inadequate to stem the rising tide of Arminianism, Prynne returned to the attack with *A Brief Survey of Mr. Cosin his cozening Devotions*; and from that time onwards the spate of works never ceased to flow. Laud's censorship was powerless against him. By various ingenious shifts and dodges, the works of Prynne were circulated and distributed throughout the country, passing under the eyes of officials disguised as white paper, or in boxes labelled "Orthodox": and all that the government could do was to descend upon the author and the printers, since it was too slow to descend on the book. The drinking of toasts was attacked in *Health's Sickness*, long hair in *The Unloveliness of Lovelocks*, the practice of bowing in *Lame Giles his Halting*, which even Abbot found scurrilous, and bishops generally in *The Church of England's old Antithesis to the New Arminianism*, which was burnt twice within a year of publication. We have no record of his appearance, but Prynne says[1] that he was several times before the High Commission, and his printer Sparkes was certainly there after the publication of both *Lame Giles* and the *Antithesis*. In 1631 Prynne was in the Star Chamber, defending Suffolk church-rioters, and received an incidental rebuke to himself from Laud. In 1632 the High Commission was considering the case of three sectaries who held that "to the believer all things are pure, and that David, when he committed adultery, pleased God as well as when he danced before the Ark", and other quaint notions; and Laud, in ordering them to prison, added, "and let Mr. Prynne be articled against for the same. We must not sit here to punish poor snakes, and let him go scot free."[2]

Laud did not have to wait long. Four months later, Prynne, having at last secured from Abbot's chaplain, Dr. Buckner, the imprimatur which two more cautious clergymen had refused, was putting the finishing touches to his *Histriomastix*, a work of over a thousand pages, which would prove, by innumerable quotations from ancient and modern authors, interlarded with spicy reflexions by Prynne, that stage-plays were mortal sin. The knowledge that the Queen, who was known to be particularly fond of the drama and of dancing, was going to take part in a production of Wat Montague's *Shepherd's Pastoral* at Somerset House, no doubt suggested some of those touches, at the end of the book, and in

[1] *A New Discovery of the Prelate's Tyranny*, p. 7.

[2] *Select Cases*, pp. 72-3, 270-71.

the index, which were afterwards declared to be directed at Majesty, although Prynne could plead that his book had appeared before the play had actually taken place.

Prynne was quickly put in the Tower, and the Inns of Court, whose religious services were already feeling the pressure of the new orthodoxy, hastened to disown such a member, emphasising their disapprobation by producing a play — Shirley's *Triumph of Peace*, with stage effects by Inigo Jones — before the King at Whitehall. Both the King and the Attorney-General, it is said, thought it unnecessary to proceed against Prynne in the Star Chamber : but Laud, who had been on the look-out against him for so long, was not going to miss his opportunity; and the busy and obsequious Heylin was commissioned to select from the massive volume the most objectionable passages, to serve as evidence at the trial.

It was in February 1634 that the trial began. The prisoner was brought out of the Tower, where he had been for a year, and Privy Councillors boggled as they listened to Heylin's tantalising excerpts. For the purposes of indiscriminate attack, bay windows, new-year gifts, may games, dancing, organs, and pictures in church, were all classed as plays. The Devil was declared the author of dancing, which was proved by examples to make young men rakes and young women whores, and was repudiated by Virgil, Cicero, and Ovid (!). Plays were said to be condemned by Fathers of the Church and enjoyed only by such monarchs as Elagabalus, Caligula, and Nero, the last of whom was rightly assassinated for such perversity. The Presbyterian Prynne commended the Jesuit Mariana for his disapproval of plays, and complained that, such was the degeneracy of the times, Shakespeare was better printed than the Bible and more widely read than the choicest sermons. In the index, compiled when the Queen's intention was already known, were such entries as " women actors notorious whores ", and " delight and skill in dancing a badge of lewd lascivious women and strumpets ". And the Attorney-General complained that large parts of the book were irrelevant, and that for seven or eight pages the author " taketh a great deal of pains to no purpose to prove that St. George, Bishop of Alexandria, was born in Cappadocia ". This was in fact a favourite argument of the Puritans, who, like Gibbon, sought to discredit the apostolic church by identifying the patron saint of half Europe with a Cappadocian pork-profiteer.[1]

The sentence was heavy and brutal, but few questioned it, for the book was libellous, seditious, and Puritan. None of the judges thought it excessive, and some would have made it harder. Windebank and three others would have doubled the fine imposed, — an academic severity, as the fine was never paid anyway. For the huge fines imposed in the prerogative courts were frequently merely the judges' method of expressing their horror at the crime, in case their command of contemptuous language was inadequate. They were seldom exacted in full, and in both Star Chamber and court of High Commission there were "days of mitigation" at the end of the month in which the fines imposed by the court were remitted, — that is, until they were needed for the repair of St. Paul's. Before pronouncing sentence, each judge gave his appropriate comments on the enormity of Prynne's offence, or the falsity of his arguments. Archbishop Neile pointed out that the Emperor to whom St. Peter and St. Paul had preached obedience was, in fact, that Nero whom Prynne had declared to have been rightly assassinated for theatre-going: and Laud, after warning him against falling into the errors of the Manichees as well as those of the Puritans, enumerated the Fathers of the Church, saints, and even Puritan apostles like Buchanan, who had composed edifying dramas. So, his errors corrected, Prynne was sentenced to a fine of £5000, imprisonment for life, the pillory, the loss of both ears, and degradation from his university degrees and his membership of the Bar.

No part of this savage corporal punishment was remitted in the execution of it. Prynne lost one ear at Westminster, the other at Cheapside: and if the executioner mercifully cropped only the tips of them, the rest was merely spared for a later occasion.[2]

[1] In 1633 Heylin had himself, as he claims (p. 296), "gained some reputation for his studies in the ancient writers by asserting the history of St. George, maliciously impugned by those of the Calvinian party upon all occasions". Aubrey, however, describes Heylin's *History of St. George* as "a very blind business". Aubrey also says that Daniel Featly, for declaring St. George to be mythical in his *Handmaid to Devotion*, was "brought upon his knees before William Laud, Archbishop of Canterbury". The controversy also engaged Selden and Sir Thomas Browne. (*Vide* Thom, *Anecdotes and Traditions*, Camden Soc., 1839, p. 103.) Cf. Gibbon, *Decline and Fall*, ch. xxiii.

[2] Prynne's enemies said that he had paid the executioner 10s. for this mercy, but he denied it (*A Speedie Hue and Crie*, London, 1647). After the loss of his ears, Prynne wore his hair long, necessity excusing the impiety which he had assailed in *The Unloveliness of Lovelocks, or a Gag for long-haired Rattleheads*, in 1628.

As he stood in the pillory, his book was burnt " under his nose, which had almost suffocated him ".[1] Oxford University and Lincoln's Inn hastened to disclaim the apostate. Even the general public showed little indignation at the punishment of so unsympathetic a character, so extreme a dogmatist: for, as Cottington had said, " the truth is, Mr. Prynne would have a new Church, new government, a new King: for he would make the people altogether offended with all things at present ". Such criticism as was uttered was directed not against the cruelty of his punishment but against the indignity offered to a lawyer and a gentleman. " Most men ", wrote Sir Simonds D'Ewes, " were affrighted to see that neither his academical nor barrister's gown could free him from the infamous loss of his ears ".[2] The Puritan Milton wrote *Comus* to dissociate himself from the Puritan Prynne, and Shirley dedicated to him, as being " the author of a tragedy ", his new play *The Bird in a Cage.* It required a longer taste of clerical government and another Star Chamber Prosecution before the crowds would cry " Hosanna ! " to William Prynne. At present they were quite willing to see him crucified.

Having imprisoned the author, the Council next set about impounding the book, of which over a thousand copies had been printed. Attorney-General Noy drew up a form of warrant for finding out into whose hands the books had come, and left the rest to Laud. Reference to the books of Sparkes, the printer, showed that forty stationers in London and nine in Oxford, besides persons in Salisbury, Exeter, Manchester, Dorchester, Norwich, and Ludlow had received copies for distribution by the various ingenious methods which necessity had invented; and these persons were required to return those which they still possessed, and report to the wardens of the Stationers' Company the names of those who had purchased the others.[3]

The first instalment of Prynne's revenge was taken almost immediately after the execution of his sentence. It was a letter to the Archbishop, which, if it did not satisfy Laud that Prynne was right, indicated plainly enough that he was unrepentant.[4] The letter was of great length, attacking each of Laud's arguments

[1] Garrarde to Wentworth, *Strafford Letters*, i. 261.

[2] *Autobiography*, ii. 105.

[3] *Documents relating to Wm. Prynne* (Camden Soc., 1877), p. 58.

[4] *Ibid.* pp. 32-56.

in turn, and accusing him of illegality in issuing a warrant for the seizure of the books which Prynne had sent to his tailor's house in Holborn for safety. Laud handed the document on to Noy, and Noy, sending for Prynne, handed him the letter asking him if it was his. Prynne embraced the opportunity thus offered to him. Taking the letter to the window, as if to scrutinise the handwriting by a better light, he suddenly tore it to shreds and flung them out of the window, saying, " That will never rise up in judgment against me ". It did rise, however, for Noy had the fragments collected and pieced together.

Next day Prynne was brought again to the Star Chamber, where he refused to give any answer except to a legal charge. In the end no further penalty seems to have been inflicted upon him, but Noy suggested that, as a precaution against the recurrence of such an incident, he should be denied access to pen, ink, paper, or church while in prison, and Richardson's only modification of this drastic suggestion was that he should be allowed Foxe's *Book of Martyrs*, " for the Puritans do account him a martyr ". But Laud spoke against such a revenge, lest Prynne, in his solitude, should fall into errors even worse than scurrility. " My Lords ", he said, " he hath undergone a heavy punishment. I am heartily sorry for him. And, Mr. Prynne, I pray God forgive you for what you have done amiss. I confess I do not know what it is to be close prisoner, and to want books, pen, ink, and company. Certainly a man alone in that case, who knoweth how he may be instigated ? And as Mr. Attorney saith he is past all grace and modesty, surely then he had need to be more free, and have books, and go to church, that he may become better. I shall therefore be an humble suitor to your Lordships that he may have the privilege to go to Church." Thereupon Prynne was heard to say in a low voice, " I humbly thank your Grace ".[1] When Prynne further asked for the return of the books which had been seized in his study, Laud protested that they were taken without his privity or direction, and undertook to redeliver them. Laud's sentences in the Star Chamber were invariably harsh. With monotonous regularity, whatever the nature of the case, whether it were for opposition to the agents of government, or duelling, or enclosures, or fraud, or libel, or extortion, he would either agree with the highest sentence proposed or outbid

[1] Rushworth, ii. 249.

it.[1] But if in general he had the severe outlook of the idealist, he was at least merciful in details, as even Prynne was to experience; and on another occasion, when sentence was being pronounced on a woman who, together with her husband, had libelled the Lord Keeper in a petition to the King, and Lord Chief Justice Finch, the two Secretaries of State, the Archbishop of York, and others, all agreed to supplement her fine by a whipping, Laud was one of the few who gave their voices against it.[2]

But it was not only false prophets whom Laud harried in the Star Chamber. As he said afterwards to Lord Saye, the Star Chamber was his pulpit: and the lessons which he preached there were not confined to doctrine and ceremonial, but concerned also the material welfare of the Church and the social relations of the people. For only by restoring the Church to a position of economic, and therefore political independence, could he make it an effective instrument for the enforcement of social morality; and the social morality which consisted in recovering for the poor the rights and the protection of which their more powerful neighbours had deprived them, had its natural counterpart in the restoration of those temporalities which the same powerful neighbours had obtained from the Church, when it was discredited. By defending the credit of the Church, the wealth of the Church, and the rights of the poor, therefore, Laud hoped to re-establish the ancient social harmony which seemed to have existed before all collapsed in the Reformation, with its victory of individual appetites over social solidarity. "If any man", he had said in the pulpit in 1621, "be so addicted to his private, that he neglect the common state, he is void of the sense of piety and wisheth peace and happiness to himself in vain. For whoever he be, he must live in the body of the Commonwealth and in the body of the Church."[3] And now that the Star Chamber had become his pulpit, he reiterated the same doctrines in the Star Chamber, with the added pungency, lacking to the pulpit, of imprisonment and fine.

[1] Cf. Fuller, *Church History*, vi. 299: "In the Star Chamber . . . he was observed always to concur with the severest side". Fuller's editor, Dr. Brewer, indignantly denies the truth of this assertion: but the State Papers prove its accuracy.

[2] Case of James and Alice Maxwell, *Cal. S.P. Dom.*, 1635, p. 31.

[3] Laud, *Works*, i. 28-9.

The social policy of the government of Charles I was never free from other less disinterested motives, and every action can be viewed in two aspects, — as a means of restoring social justice, and as a means of replenishing the treasury without recourse to Parliament. More often than not, too, the latter aspect is more apparent than the former, and the Privy Council was frequently more willing to accept a fine than to reverse an injustice. But this was not altogether without reason: for it must be remembered that the Crown also was one of those forces in the old constitution of society which had suffered by the Reformation. At first, indeed, it had prospered immensely out of it, and for a brief space of time it had wielded a complete despotism on the strength of its sudden access of wealth. But it had lived, as it were, on its capital, and that capital was now gone, leaving its position even worse than before. The policy of restoring the ancient estates of the realm therefore involved the recovery of Crown lands, alienated to courtiers in the heyday of despotism, as well as the recovery of Church lands for the Church and common lands for the poor. For all these purposes, the ancient law must be the justification, and the new prerogative courts the means of its enforcement.

If we wish to see this policy at its worst, we need not look far: for in its actual application it was both impolitic and unjust. As Professor Tawney says, the whole of Stuart social policy "was smeared with the trail of finance" which, towards the end of the eleven years of personal government, completely concealed it. But to Laud it appeared in another light. To him the policy was an honest attempt to prevent the dangers of social and political dislocation: and although he was as eager as any of his colleagues on the Privy Council to make the King independent of Parliament by the discovery of new financial supplies, he had nothing but contempt for those besides the Crown who derived pickings from its policy; and he insisted, to the best of his ability, that the profits thus collected by the Crown should be spent, not on courtiers or luxuries, but on government. His pronouncements in the Star Chamber on social questions will show what sort of a government it was which he demanded.

Towards the end of the reign of James I, farmers and landlords had been hard hit by the low price of corn, and the government had permitted them to recoup their losses by the repeal of the Tillage Acts and the suspension of action against enclosures. But in 1629 and the years following, the rise in the price of corn had led to discontent which alarmed the government into activity. Letters were sent from the Privy Council to the magistrates of the Midland counties, where corn was chiefly grown, and where the conversion of tillage to pasture had caused serious rioting in 1607, ordering the removal of all enclosures made during the past two years. Commissions were issued in 1632, 1635 and 1636, and special instructions were given to the Judges of Assize in 1633, who were also required to attend the Council and give a report of their proceedings. In the Star Chamber, enclosure was declared to be an offence against the Common Law, — since the statutes against it, having been repealed, could only be re-enacted by Parliament. Even here, however, the sinister motives of increasing the revenue rather than remedying abuses soon became obvious. In 1631 it was suggested that money for the restoration of St. Paul's could be obtained from fines for enclosures in the Midlands; in 1634 Sir Robert Osborne suggested that money should be raised by composition with enclosers at the rate of 20 shillings an acre for all land enclosed since 1619, — the date when the Council had begun to connive at such activities; — and for the next four years compositions were levied in the Midlands, and fines imposed on some 600 persons.

In all the judicial cases which resulted from this activity, Laud spoke with no uncertain voice. Although he had, as a rule, little use for the Common Law, from whose trammels he had determined to free the Church, he found it a good enough stick with which to beat enclosers and their like. When an Essex farmer came before the Star Chamber in 1631 on a charge of enhancing the price of corn by keeping it till a time of shortage, Laud declared him guilty of "a most foul offence, which the Prophet hath in a very energetical phrase, grinding the faces of the poor". "This last year's famine", he declared, "was made by man and not by God, solicited by the hard-heartedness of men": and he announced himself "glad to hear it declared to be an offence against the Common Law of this realm".[1] When Sir Anthony Roper faced a charge of having converted five

[1] Archer's case, *Select Cases in Star Chamber*, etc., p. 46.

farms, amounting to 700 acres, in Kent, from tillage to pasture, and various fines were proposed, from £1500 to £4000, as well as reconversion and rebuilding, Laud's sentence was "with the highest in all things".[1] Two Wiltshire landowners complained to the Long Parliament of the Archbishop's severity and his strong language towards them when they were accused of conversion[2]: and in the House of Lords one Mr. Talbot deposed upon oath "how the Archbishop did oppose the law in the business of enclosures and depopulations. How, when the law was desired to be pleaded for the right of land, he bid them, 'Go plead law in inferior courts: they should not plead it before him'; and that the Archbishop did fine him for that business £200 for using the property of freehold, and would not suffer the law to be pleaded".[3] In 1636 Lord Brudenell, one of the Queen's Court, complained that, for effecting "a most benign and charitable enclosure" on his estate at Houghton, Laud had fined him £1000 and told him "that he had devoured the people with a shepherd and a dog";[4] and two years later, when he heard from the Commissioners that All Souls College had been guilty of enclosing, and the Warden wrote requesting him to stay proceedings until he could be present in person, Laud replied, "One thing I must tell you: that though I did you this favour, to make stay of the hearing till your return, yet for the business itself I can show you none. Partly because I am a great hater of depopulations in any kind, as being one of the greatest mischiefs in this Kingdom, and of very ill example from a college or college tenant, and partly because it concerns me very deeply in the particular of my archbishopric", — and he went on to explain that the depopulation had reduced the value of the rectory which belonged to his see.[5] For the partnership of the Church and the poor in oppostion to acquisitive landlords was continually being demonstrated, and Laud, in defending one was defending the other.[6] Throughout his period of ascendancy, petitions continually

[1] *S.P. Dom. Car. I.* 275, no. 36.

[2] *S.P. Dom. Car. I.* 499, no. 10. These were perhaps the same two Wiltshire men whose harsh reception by Laud caused Edward Hyde to remonstrate with the Archbishop (Clarendon, *Life*, Oxford, 1759, p. 32).

[3] *Lords' Journals*, vi. 468b.

[4] *S.P. Dom. Car. I.* 319, no. 104.

[5] Laud, *Works*, vi. 520.

[6] Cf. Garrarde to Wentworth, *Strafford Letters*, i. 491: "Also monies come in apace for depopulations. The trespassers in that kind come in apace and compound at the Council Table, some for £1,000, some £500, some £300,

reached him from country vicars and rectors against the encroachments of local squires, and each petition received the Archbishop's personal attention, as the Assheton family were to discover. The Asshetons, to judge from the diary of one of their members, led an unobtrusive life in Lancashire, hunting and drinking. But in the lax days of Abbot they had secured profitable leases of the rectory of Whalley, which Abbot's more energetic successor forced them to disgorge, and allowed them to resume only at a considerable loss and for a period of 21 years instead of three lives. In all, Ralph Assheton complained, when the Archbishop's fall enabled him to secure a favourable hearing, he had lost £3000 by the transaction.[1]

It is noticeable that the many inconspicuous landowners who suddenly emerged into prominence at the time of the Long Parliament for the redress of their wrongs in this way appealed not against the purely secular ministers of Charles I's personal government, but against Laud and his ecclesiastical officers: and although his harsh treatment of defendants in the Star Chamber may have imprinted his censure upon their memories more durably than those of Cottington or Windebank, it is nevertheless certain that he was the most determined champion of the old social harmony, in which he saw, not profit, like so many of the Council, but only justice. Indeed, it was to his hatred of depopulation as much as anything else that Clarendon attributed the Archbishop's fall, for "the revenue of too many of the Court consisted principally in enclosures and improvements of that nature, which he still opposed passionately except they were founded on law: and then, if it would bring profit to the King, how old and obsolete soever the law was, he thought he might justly advise the prosecution. And so he did a little too much countenance the Commission for Depopulation, which brought much charge and trouble upon the people: which was likewise cast upon his account."[2]

But if, in the Star Chamber, Laud's influence was emphatic and effective, it was not everyone who could aspire to the publicity

and to set up so many farms again. My Lord of Canterbury hath great care of the Church in this business, for by turning arable into pasture Churchmen have had great loss. I hear of 700 trespassers in this kind, great and small."

[1] *S.P. Dom. Car. I.* 499, nos. 22, 50, 51.

[2] *History of the Rebellion*, i. 204.

of a trial in the Star Chamber, and we must turn to examine the bishops who were responsible for the execution of his policy in the provinces.

Besides the metropolitical sees of Canterbury and York, there were twenty-five bishoprics in England, including the four Welsh dioceses of St. Asaph, Bangor, Llandaff, and St. David's, and the diocese of Sodor and Man, which was in the gift of the Earl of Derby and whose bishop was not a member of the House of Lords. These last five were the Cinderellas of the hierarchy, and the bishops received but scant revenues from them, and but scant attention from the government. Politically their importance was negligible. We shall be more concerned here to enquire how far Laud and his bishops succeeded in establishing control over the centres of population and civilisation, and how far the orders which were issued from Lambeth were made effective in the Eastern and Midland counties, to which the very peace-policy of the government was bringing increasing prosperity, and, with it, increasing intolerance of government regulation in either secular or spiritual affairs.

Here we soon find that Laud's authority was very limited. The control of the Church in the provinces was far from exclusive, and could not be made exclusive for lack of money. Even in wealthy districts the wealth did not belong to the Church but, more frequently, to its adversaries : and the result of this poverty was that it was impossible to secure the learned, the ambitious, and the orthodox to serve as parish clergymen. In all the seven dioceses which Laud visited in 1634 he reported, " I find one great complaint, and very fit to be redressed. It is the general grievance of the poor vicars that their stipends are scarce able to feed and clothe them. And (which is worse) the vicars in great market towns, where the people are very many, are for the most part worse provided for." Bishops, in their annual accounts, regularly repeated the same complaint, — that they were forced to ordain very mean ministers " to supply cures as mean ". For this no remedy was available from the government, for the government, in the absence of Parliament, could scarcely feed and clothe itself, and the Puritans preferred to supply the deficiency by setting up lecturers who would preach against instead of for the Church. Laud himself, by direct intervention, was sometimes able to secure an increase in the stipend of a vicar here and there, but the results, except as irritants, were practically negligible, and even in his own diocese of Canterbury the poverty of many cures remained to be remarked upon during the Long Parliament. The same lack of means prevented him also from supplying an effective substitute for the Puritan lecturers: for although he entered, among the "things which I have projected to do, if God bless me in them," both the overthrow of the feoffees for impropriations and the collection of money to buy in impropriations for the Church, once the repair of St. Paul's was completed, it is significant that the work of destruction was soon achieved, but that the constructive project remained a project to the end. The only solution to the economic problem was good husbandry on the part of the bishops: but Laud found it hard enough to prevent his bishops from profiteering out of their depleted capital, without augmenting that of their parochial clergy. In the wealthy city of Norwich, the ministers were continually petitioning for a fixed stipend: but the purse was in the wrong hands, and when, in 1638, Laud's most efficient and trusted bishop, Matthew Wren, secured it for them by exacting a rate of 2s. in the £ from the citizens, it was made a charge against him by the Long Parliament. At the end of 1634 Laud himself wrote to the Dean and Chapter of Norwich to draw their attention to the poverty of the choir, and required them to see that suburban livings were given to the petty canons. "But I hear withal there is a purpose amongst some of you, without any regard to the honour and good of the Church, to bestow those livings, when they fall, upon their private friends, without any respect had to the choir; which, if it be, will utterly overthrow the choir service, and you will not be able to retain either voices or skill amongst you. I would be glad to hope this information were not true, but it is so constantly affirmed to me that I cannot distrust it altogether."[1] Thus Laud's idealistic energies were dissipated in the application; for the majority of the clergy, then as always, had taken orders to support themselves and their families, not to advance the glory of God.

It must be admitted that the bishops had frequently far less control over their dioceses than the Archbishop required them to exercise. Communications were bad: by the Archbishop's own orders they were confined to their dioceses: and in the

[1] Laud, *Works*, vi. 403.

absence of Parliament there was small prospect of their ever coming to the capital and facing their metropolitan. In their dioceses their relations with the neighbouring gentry were of more immediate importance to them than the approval of a remote archbishop, and they were generally unwilling, by an injudicious exercise of their judicial powers, to make themselves unpopular with their influential neighbours.

Such was Bishop Bridgeman of Chester, who reigned rather than ruled over a poor and unruly diocese. He was not one of Laud's nominees, having been appointed to his see in 1619: and he remained there throughout Laud's period of power. The Puritan minister of Blackley, Thomas Paget, testified that Bridgeman was mild with Nonconformists until the approaching visitation of the Archbishop of York impelled him to severity; but in 1630 he felt the pressure of Neile and Laud, and the Puritans of Chester were made aware of it. Paget himself was suspended in that year,[1] — not by the Bishop, but by the ecclesiastical commissioners at York — and the Puritan minister at Ringley, John Angier, after being twice inhibited, was summoned for an interview with the bishop. "Mr. Angier," said Bridgeman, "I have a good will to indulge you, but I cannot: for my Lord's Grace of Canterbury hath rebuked me for permitting two non-conforming ministers, the one within a mile on one hand, Mr. Horrocks of Deane, and the other yourself; and I am likely to come into disfavour on this behalf. As for Mr. Horrocks, my hands are bound, I cannot meddle with him. But as for you, Mr. Angier, you are a young man, and may doubtless get another place: and if you were anywhere at a little further distance, I could better look away from you. For I do study to do you a kindness, but cannot so long as you are thus near me."[2] So Mr. Angier moved to Denton, where he pursued his ministry for a time under the blind eye of the bishop. Nevertheless, the old comfortable days were gone, and during the next ten years he complained that he was subject to repeated persecutions.[3] The bishop had a thin time of it, being chivvied by Neile and Laud from above, and yet unable to control and unwilling to persecute his unruly flock: and at the beginning of 1633 he

[1] He fled to Holland in 1638, and there succeeded his brother, John Paget, as minister to the English Church at Amsterdam. Cf. *infra*, pp. 250-1.

[2] O. Heywood, *Life of John Angier* (Chetham Soc. 1937), p. 57.

[3] Angier, *An Help for Better Hearts*, 1647 (epistle dedicatory).

found himself called before the High Commission on charges of undue leniency in commutation of penances on one hand, and lucrative malpractices on the other. To remit the censures of the Church, and to derive personal profit from it, were offences equally hateful to Laud, and it was only after a year's cross-examination that Bridgeman escaped, in order to avert scandal. Thereafter, under the vigilant eyes of both Archbishops, he struggled at least to give the impression of efficiency in a diocese where poverty bred heresy, organs were banned from the churches, and the surplice was known as "the rags of Rome". Early in 1637 he reported to Neile that he had been thoroughly successful, that uniformity and decency were restored, and the laity had contributed with alacrity to the repair of churches,[1] — a complacent account somewhat belied a few months later, when the citizens and Corporation of Chester publicly fêted and feasted Prynne and Burton on their way from the Star Chamber, where they had been sentenced, to the prisons where they were to be confined.

Against these practical difficulties it was no sufficient remedy for Laud to require annual accounts of their dioceses from his bishops. It was simple enough for easy-going bishops to report "Omnia bene", and many did not trouble to send in reports at all. For four successive years the Bishop of Coventry and Lichfield avoided sending in any report, and all that Laud knew was that he was complained of for wasting such woods as remained to his diocese, and that he avoided enforcing the rule about altars, while his successor in the see of Bristol was discovering that he had made leases for lives right and left before leaving it.[2] Bishop Wright was making a considerable fortune out of these transactions, which he invested in land in many places, and was able to pay the large sum of £18,000 for the estate of Nuneham Courtenay in Oxfordshire alone.[3] It was not till 1638, in answer to a peremptory summons from the Archbishop, that he ultimately sent in a report of his diocese, airily dismissing his previous omissions as "but a slip of forgetfulness".

Another regular defaulter was Dr. Goodman, Bishop of Gloucester. Like Bridgeman, he was one of the few bishops who were not Laud's nominees, having been appointed in 1625

[1] *S.P. Dom. Car. I.* 345, no. 85, i.
[2] Laud, *Works*, v. 346 ; Heylin, p. 271 ; *S.P. Dom. Car. I.* 386, no. 2.
[3] Wood, *Athenae Oxonienses*, iv. 800.

through the influence of Buckingham. He was perpetually at loggerheads with Laud, whom he survived, dying in 1655, a member of the Roman Church. His Roman sympathies had long been suspected, and were known, among others, to Laud. It was probably to Goodman that Falkland referred in his speech against bishops in the Long Parliament when he spoke of some who have " found a way to reconcile the opinions of Rome to the preferments of England, and to be so absolutely, directly, and cordially Papists, that it is all that £1500 a year can do to keep them from confessing it ". Only in his will did Goodman openly confess the change in his spiritual allegiance : but he had been censured by Convocation, in the first year of his promotion, for preaching at Court on the Real Presence in a sermon which was " supposed to trench too near the borders of Popery", and in 1628 that notorious triumvirate, Prynne, Burton, and Bastwick, had petitioned against his supposed idolatry. His actual conversion was said to have been achieved early in 1636 by the Jesuit Hanmer, who was on intimate terms with him : and in the same year the papal emissary Panzani noted that " among those of the episcopal order who seemed to desire an union, none appeared more zealous than Dr. Goodman of Gloucester, who every day said the priest's office, and observed several other duties as practised in the Church of Rome ".[1] In 1640 he made his Romanism so obvious that Laud was forced to suspend him.

It was not only his Roman leanings and his refusal to account for himself that made Goodman objectionable to Laud. In 1633 there was a scandal about his application for the bishopric of Hereford. " Goodman of Gloucester", says Heylin, " having stayed in that diocese long enough to be as weary of them as they were of him, affected a remove to the see of Hereford, and had so far prevailed with some great officer of State, that his money was taken, his *congé d'élire* issued out, his election passed. But the Archbishop, coming opportunely to the knowledge of it, so laboured the business with the King, and the King so rattled up the bishop, that he was glad to make his peace, not only with the resignation of his election, but the loss of his bribe."[2] Whether

[1] *Memoirs of Gregorio Panzani* (trans. J. Berington, 1793), p. 248. Cf. Panzani's report on Goodman, quoted in G. Albion, *Charles I and the Court of Rome* (1935), p. 413 : " Celibe, moderatissimo, e vorebbe aver un sacerdote in casa cattolico ".

[2] Heylin, p. 248.

this is true, or whether, as a contemporary news-writer reported, he had merely offended the King by a request to hold the bishopric of Gloucester *in commendam* for a year with that of Hereford, we cannot be certain : but evidently Goodman was looking for personal profit out of the Church, and that alone was sufficient to discredit him in Laud's eyes, and render him a monster of vice in the eyes of Laud's chaplain. Nor did he ever do anything to recover the favour which he had thus lost. In January 1634 he applied for leave of absence from his diocese, but Laud ordered him back, threatening to accept his resignation if he offered it.[1] His report for that year was unsatisfactory : next year he merely complained of the wretched poverty of his diocese : for 1636 and 1637 he sent no reports : and in 1638 he again applied for leave of absence. This was refused by the King, but Goodman then turned to Windebank, protesting that he was suffering from the stone, and must go to Spa. Windebank, however, was not to be taken in. He replied that the Bishop's health looked excellent, and succeeded in eliciting the real reason for Goodman's request. The indignities to which he had been subjected, he explained, had rendered life in Gloucester intolerable : "he had been for many years a spectacle to the clergy, disgraced in everything and upon all occasions, and disesteemed and vilipended in his diocese". Windebank, however, refused to consider his application, on the grounds that, if he ventured abroad, the Church of Rome would "use the utmost of their endeavours to catch such a fish as a prelate of the Church of England", — an argument somewhat ironical when used by one crypto-Papist to another. Laud expressed his approval of Windebank's action, and when Wentworth wrote applying for a favour for Goodman, Laud replied, "I must heartily desire you not to press me in that kind, for His Majesty's exceptions are both just and great against him, of my certain knowledge. And at this present I am calling his Lordship into the High Commission for giving the justices leave to hold the quarter sessions in a church. And, to speak all at once, he wants little the honesty of the Bishop of Lincoln." [2] Goodman, however, was determined to avoid residence in his diocese, and at the beginning of 1640 he was rebuked by Windebank

[1] *S.P. Dom. Car. I.* 259, no. 49 ; Laud, *Works*, vii. 62, 88.

[2] Windebank to Laud, Sept. 22nd, 1638 (Baker MS. 33, 6, 6 : printed in *Communications to Camb. Antiq. Soc.*, ii. 128 ff., by J. E. B. Mayor, "Materials for a Life of Bishop Goodman") ; Laud, *Works*, vi. 539 ; vii. 421.

for disobeying the royal instructions and residing at Windsor.[1]

However strongly Laud might disapprove of Goodman, the Puritans held him responsible for the sins of his bishops: and Goodman was the prime mover in the persecution of one John Workman, to which Prynne gave great publicity, and which shows how thorough Laud's inquisition could be on an individual whom it had once selected. Workman was a Puritan lecturer at Gloucester who was prosecuted in the High Commission for preaching that "pictures were no more ornaments to a church than stews to a commonwealth", and other Puritan commonplaces. He was excommunicated, made to recant, and imprisoned: and the Corporation of Gloucester, who, in view of his fifteen years' service, had granted him an annuity of £20, was summoned to the High Commission for contempt of court, and the annuity stopped. His term of imprisonment over, Workman set up as a tutor, but was inhibited. Thereupon he turned to the practice of physic, and was again prohibited. The last we hear of him is in 1638, when Bishop Coke of Hereford found him living "without any cure or other known employment" at the house of a Mr. Kyrle of Wallford, and chased him out "God knows whither".[2] The responsibility for this persecution is apportioned in about equal measure by Prynne to Laud and Goodman, according as it suits his book at the time, and it is one of the few actions in which they were in agreement. Goodman had his good points as a man, — he was charitable to the poor, and provided Gloucester with a library.[3] Three travellers in 1634 make special mention of his liberality, which, like the river Severn, "doth stream and flow in a most bountiful manner to the poor valleys about him: for he maintains a head of thirty or forty kine, mostly for the sustenance of the poor":[4] and Fuller says, "to give Goodman his due, he was a harmless man, hurtful to none but himself, pitiful to the poor, hospitable to his neighbours, against the ruining of any of an opposite judgment, and gave the most he left to pious uses".[5] The censorious moralists of the Long Parliament, too, accused him of allowing undue conviviality in his household, which a later generation may allow to be to

[1] *Cal. S.P. Dom.* 1639–40, p. 351.

[2] Prynne, *Canterburie's Doom*, p. 103; Laud, *Works*, iv. 233; v. 357.

[3] Sloane MS. 1199, 92b.

[4] *A Short Survey of 26 Counties, etc. 1634* (ed. L. G. Wickham Legg, 1904), p. 84.

[5] Fuller, *Worthies*, iii. 532.

his credit.[1] But as a bishop he was a bad ally to Laud, and a bad advertisement for Laudianism.

Then there was Bishop Thornborough of Worcester, to whom Laud's power was a mushroom growth. He had been a bishop for forty years when Laud was promoted to Canterbury,[2] and he was still a bishop when Laud was removed to the Tower. He had occupied the see of Worcester since 1617, and was by now firmly entrenched there, with a small dynasty of relatives and dependants in possession of the benefices at his disposal; and it was three years before Laud could elicit from him any account of his diocese, for he was more concerned with his quarrel with the Dean and Chapter than with the welfare of souls or the requirements of the Archbishop. The Dean and Chapter, who professed sympathy with the reforming zeal of Laud, attempted to preserve "from the Bishop's profanation" the old chapel at the cathedral door, while the bishop insisted that, since the Dissolution, this had been the episcopal hay-loft, and should continue to be so. The Dean and Chapter further offended him by building houses in the churchyard, one of which even overlooked the palace, and by laying a doubtful claim to his bake-house, slaughter-house, coach-house, and other premises. Where such important issues were concerned, the Bishop finally broke silence and appealed to Laud. The Dean, Dr. Christopher Potter, one of Laud's supporters in Oxford, where he was Provost of Queen's College, followed suit, and accused the Bishop of unorthodox opinions. Already, in 1635, the previous dean, the notorious Dr. Manwaring, had reported to the Archbishop on the scandalous condition of the church services at Worcester, and his own excellent reforms. Now Dr. Potter accused the Bishop of factious opposition to the peace and orthodoxy of the Church, of favouring Puritan lecturers, and courting the support of the Puritan citizens by the most humiliating and heterodox condescensions. So the citizens were brought into the affair, and two months later they petitioned the Archbishop, with the Bishop's support, in favour of the lecturers, while the Dean and Chapter counter-petitioned against the lecturers and "their oracle and asylum, the old Bishop, who has indeed debauched the people . . . by his popular fawning and flattering of them in all their fancies". When the contest was

[1] Verney's *Notes of the Long Parliament* (Camden Soc., 1845), p. 14.

[2] He was made Bishop of Waterford in 1593 and died in 1641.

left undecided by the advent of the Troubles, the honours remained with the Bishop and his allies: for Laud was compelled to yield to their protests and restore the lecturers' pulpit, which he had caused to be removed to a less conspicuous part of the cathedral.[1]

The most fractious of all Laud's bishops, however, was his old rival and adversary Williams, whose diocese, the largest in the Kingdom, comprising the Puritan counties of the Midlands, and stretching as far south as Buckinghamshire, where it marched with the diocese of London, was practically closed to his metropolitan.

Williams needs no introduction. In an age of giant hypocrisies and self-deceptions, he kept, if not, like the seraph Abdiel, his loyalty, his love, and his zeal, at least his head. While men around him rushed to submerge their individualities in creeds and armies, Williams stands out as an ecclesiastical careerist whose calculated self-interest was obscured by no destructive idealism. Of good, if Welsh, family, of independent wealth and considerable political experience, he was completely different from the type of Laud's other bishops, and was quite unfit, by his pride and independence, to be an agent of Laud's bureaucracy. As for religious views, as far as he had any, he was a high churchman. As Dean of Westminster he had ordered the Abbey services with such splendid ceremonial that a visiting French abbot had congratulated him on their approximation to the true Roman pattern. With the Reformed Churches of the Continent he had no more sympathy than Laud, and Puritan pamphleteers accused him, like any other bishop, of downright Popery. When the harassed Protestants of Bohemia petitioned King James to be allowed to come to England with their families, their property, and their trades, offering to be subject in all things to the English government, the King had at first been tempted to admit such profitable refugees: but he was dissuaded by Williams, who is praised by his biographer for choosing rather "to keep the Church of England in its sabbath and holy rest, than to help the neighbour's ox that was fallen into the pit".[2] His munificence, too, was on a lavish scale, and was so directed that Laud could not but approve it, had it come from another than Williams. The chapel which he

[1] *S.P. Dom. Car. I.* 343, no. 77; 344, no. 107; 349, no. 103.
[2] Hacket, i. 96.

built at Lincoln College, Oxford, says a contemporary, " deserves a particular commendation, which is raised with cedar: the communion-table, pulpit, and an excellent fair screen, all of cedar, which gives such an odoriferous smell that holy water in the Romish churches doth not exceed it, let them use what they can to perfume it".[1] At Westminster he panelled the Jerusalem Chamber, also with cedar, repaired the Abbey, founded a library, and endowed four scholarships. At his old college, St. John's College, Cambridge, he founded two fellowships and a splendid library; and he built yet another library at Lincoln. As Bishop of Lincoln he spent over £1000 a year in charity, and even as a vicar in Suffolk he had left a permanent charity for the poor of the parish. He was also a patron of scholars, assisting Patrick Young with the production of his *Clemens Romanus*, and entertaining John Selden and the learned canon of Ely, Dr. John Boys, at Buckden. But though his actions were often such as were advocated by Laud, he was too independent to subscribe to any programme. Serenely individual in his opinions, completely opportunist in his alliances, he gave unconditional allegiance to no man, and was constant only in his personal opposition to the clergyman who had supplanted him as the adviser of the Crown. Like a medieval bishop, before the days of heresies and holy wars, he expected to live in his diocese as a territorial magnate, undisturbed by any central authority, a local prince of the Church. That a bishop had any sacred mission to perform or was a responsible agent, was a strange doctrine to him, as unnecessary and deplorable as the fantasies of Calvin and Arminius, which he ignored. A bishopric was to him as an earldom or a large farm, and its responsibilities were the responsibilities of a great landlord, tempered by the satisfaction of his personal tastes. When the electoral family was driven into exile, and King James had been worried by the problem of its future provision, Williams had suggested that the younger Princes, Rupert and Maurice, should be placed in the rich bishoprics of Durham and Winchester, when these should fall void: and " if that happen in their nonage, which is probable, appoint commendataries to discharge the duty for them for a laudable allowance, but gathering the fruits for the support of your grandchildren, till they come of virility to be consecrated ".[2]

[1] Garrarde to Conway, *S.P. Dom. Car. I.* 331, no. 14. [2] Hacket, i. 208.

Such a counsellor was about as ill-fitted to be the adviser of Charles I as was Prince Rupert to be Bishop of Durham: but although he could be disgraced and driven from office, it was impossible to deprive him of his spiritual preferments: and although he could be discouraged from officiating as Dean of Westminster, or from sitting in the House of Lords, or from appearing at Court at all, this could only be done by packing him off to his bishopric. In his bishopric he was supreme: and since it was the only office out of so many which he was still permitted to enjoy, Williams was determined to enjoy it to the full.

So Williams left Court and retired to his episcopal house at Buckden, like a great whig nobleman seceding into the country. There he lived in the grand style, for "though forced to part with the King's purse, he kept his own, and that well replenished". He lived, says Fuller, "in a public privacy . . . it being hard to say whether his table were more free and full in diet or discourse", and "one great prelate" told the King that "the Bishop of Lincoln lived in as much pomp and plenty as any cardinal in Rome, for diet, music, and attendance".[1] Buckden, like most episcopal houses, had been neglected by his predecessors since the time of the Reformation, and had been allowed to fall into a ruinous state. Williams repaired it. He planted woods, pulled down outhouses, enclosed his park, and stocked it with a herd of elegant deer. He constructed "gardens, arbours, orchards, pools for waterfowl and for fish of all variety". He had a raised walk built in the grounds, a mile in circumference. "All the nurseries about London for fair flowers and choice fruits were ransacked to furnish him. Alcinous, if he had lived at Buckden, could not have lived better."[2] It became a great country seat, such as Evelyn would have loved to study in, or Sir Thomas Browne to expatiate; and scholars did resort thither to the musical soirées and festivities held by the Bishop, who loved to exhibit his own fine singing voice, and whose lavish entertainment had been admired ever since he celebrated the attainment of his M.A. at Cambridge with a feast.

The proud independence of Williams was not made any better in Laud's eyes by the exasperating fact that his doctrines were so scrupulously correct. Laud could not accuse him of wasting woods, or suffering his episcopal house to decay, or neglecting

[1] Fuller, *Church History*, vi. 36.

[2] Hacket, ii. 29.

the beauty of holiness. As a steward of his diocese he was an example to his more obsequious but less liberal brethren, and bought lands worth three hundred pounds a year for his bishopric from neighbouring landlords, Messrs. Gouldsborough and Oliver Cromwell. But the bitterness engendered by that fierce struggle for the favour of Buckingham was only increased after the struggle had been lost and won. Williams was defeated, but he declined to accept defeat, and when his applications for a renewal of friendly relations had been rebuffed, he studied to appear indifferent to his failure.

> You put ill fortune in so good a dress
> That it outshone other men's happiness

wrote Cowley of Williams' Buckden days : and certainly Williams in his Olympian retirement showed a more successful affectation of triumph than Laud in his restless archbishopric.

One of the most infuriating manifestations of this pose of correctitude was Williams' ruling in the question of the altar controversy. Here, as we have seen, he had already given a decision before Laud's ruling was published, and now, although in his visitation articles he enjoined an altar-wise position, he refused to exalt the matter into a principle by openly reversing his former decision or enforcing the will of his metropolitan in a diocese so strongly infected with Puritanism. He thus left the way of retreat open, and was able, later, to use it, when, his alliance with the Queen's party having failed, he leagued himself with the Puritans and published his *Holy Table, Name and Thing* in justification of the Elizabethan compromise. The same refusal to commit himself to the inconvenience of a principle is shown in many of his actions ; and although he would not advise the admittance of the Protestant refugees from Bohemia, still, when it came to irritating Laud, he did not hesitate to open his diocese to the French Protestants fleeing from the persecuting hand of Archbishop Neile. With exasperating dexterity he kept on the windy side of the law, and long refused to offer the Archbishop any occasion to seize him. The ecclesiastical machinery which might have been put into operation against the Midland Puritans remained idle in Williams' hands. Rather than bully them in ecclesiastical courts, the Bishop would invite recalcitrant Nonconformists to dinner at the palace : and there, in opposition to Laud's insistence that bishops should be abstemious and censorious, he regaled them so splendidly that they " did melt into meekness and shook hands, the rather being reconciled in his buttery or his cellar ".[1]

Laud was not without agents in the diocese of Lincoln who were ready to detect the first error in the conduct of his rival: and it was at one of these convivial gatherings that the material for the first charge was collected. Sir John Lambe and the prophet of apostolic obedience, Dr. Sibthorpe, had been enjoying the hospitality of Buckden one day when Williams advised them to proceed gently with the Puritans as King James had it in mind to indulge their foibles for political reasons. The first part of this statement was plainly unacceptable to the high church party, and the second might be construed as the revelation of an official secret. So in 1629, when King James was dead, and Lambe and Sibthorpe had entered a more profitable service, it occurred to them thus to construe it. They therefore delated Williams to Laud as having once communicated the secrets of the Privy Council to themselves, and a Star Chamber prosecution, which was destined ultimately to overthrow the Bishop, gradually grew out of this inconsiderable seed. Later the manifest unpopularity of Williams encouraged others to prefer charges: and before long the pragmatical Heylin, together with three other prebendaries of Westminster, came forward to accuse the Dean of embezzling funds and evading his duties. To this Williams is said to have made the inadequate answer that " a bargain is a bargain ", but he accounted for his behaviour as best he could.[2] Sibthorpe, in the meanwhile, was preferring further charges against Williams of favouring Puritans in his diocese, and Puritans were accusing him of having had *A Midsummer-Night's Dream* performed in his house on a Sunday;[3] and all these charges together involved the Bishop in a running fight over many years. Williams attempted various forms of evasion and prevarication, at one time airily pretending that the charges concerned the Earl of Lincoln, not the Bishop; at another bringing counter-charges of

[1] Hacket, i. 36.

[2] Garrarde to Wentworth, *Strafford Letters*, i. 360; Rossingham to Puckering, Apr. 13th, 1636, Harl. MS. 7000, p. 191. The charges, and Williams' reply, are printed from the Abbey Muniments in Judge Ivor Bowen's " John Williams of Gloddaeth " (Cymmrodorion Soc. Trans. 1927-8).

[3] Lambeth MS. 1030, no. 5.

conspiracy against his assailants. As the proceedings went on, further revelations were made, and the ultimate fall of Williams, deferred by his political alliances, did not take place till 1637, and will be treated in its proper place. Meanwhile, he continued to enjoy his liberty, and to use it to exasperate Laud by making his whole diocese a great loophole in the Laudian system.

Williams, Goodman, Bridgeman, and Thornborough were the four bishops over whom Laud had no control, because they had been appointed before his rise to power, and remained irremovable till he had fallen from it. But there were others, like Wright of Lichfield and Coventry, whom Laud had himself promoted and found wanting. Wright had been promoted from the small, poor diocese of Bristol expressly as a reward for not renewing a lease and so supplying that see with an episcopal house : but we have seen that in fact he made havoc of the possessions of that see, and he even attempted to cover up his tracks on leaving it by taking the relevant documents away with him to Coventry, thus causing considerable trouble to his successor, Dr. Coke. Dr. Coke's sole recommendation for episcopal rank was his relationship with Sir John Coke, the aged Secretary of State, and the consequent protection of Buckingham : and there were others whose promotion was due rather to their friends than to their merits. Here Laud was reaping the results of Buckingham's lavish and indiscriminate patronage, which had brought to eminence not only himself but also Williams and Goodman and many more. Another was Richard Corbett, the amiable Bishop of Norwich, who had attracted attention at Oxford by his theological differences with the Abbots, as well as by his practical jokes, his symposia, and his epigrams on butlers and college servants. Austere high churchmen like Anthony Wood, whose predilection for stewed prunes does not argue a convivial or self-indulgent nature, disapproved of Corbett's frivolities, of which many tales are related : but about 1620 the Oxford wits detected a strain of servility in his Muse. Epigrams on college characters gave way to congratulatory epistles to the Duke of Buckingham, and Corbett became Dean of Christ Church. Thereafter, to make room for Duppa at Christ Church, he was promoted to the bishopric of Oxford, where he found a suitable chaplain in the University poet, William Strode; and although the death of Buckingham soon robbed him of his patron, he was well served by luck, for in 1632, Oxford being required for Bancroft, Corbett was promoted to Norwich. This was a diocese of great importance, and full of Puritans: but Corbett, who was "of a courteous carriage and no destructive nature to any who offended him, counting himself plentifully repaired with a jest",[1] chose rather to satirise nonconformity than to punish it. During his three years' tenure of the see he only sent in one account, and when he died in 1635 Laud's Vicar-General found the diocese "much out of order".[2] Two Puritan lecturers, Bridges and Ward, who were driven out of England by Corbett's successor, had both come into contact with Corbett, but both, after suspension, were restored by him; and Ward, whose sermon entitled "Woe to Drunkards!" might seem to reflect on the Bishop (since Corbett was accustomed to lock himself in the wine-cellar at Ludham Palace with his chaplain, Dr. Lushington, and the bottles), even received a congratulatory letter after his submission, assuring him of his diocesan's support in the future.[3]

It is impossible not to feel sympathetic towards Corbett: but Buckingham had promoted others who were mere parasites in the vineyard of Christ. Prominent among such was Roger Manwaring, who had received two rich benefices from the King as a reward for being debarred by Parliament from holding any ecclesiastical preferment. Unlike Montague, who reached his conclusions with the aid of learning and was prepared to publish them even before they were popular, Manwaring sought promotion through servility, and, like Montague, got it. In January 1633 he wrote to Laud eloquently describing his claims to preferment, and was shortly afterwards made Dean of Worcester, where the state of affairs under the indolent Bishop Thornborough invited his interference. In September 1635 he was able to write again enumerating his services to Worcester cathedral under seventeen heads.[4] These improvements secured him the attention of the Long Parliament five years later, when he was accused of unclerical joviality and popish innovations while at Worcester: but at the time they secured him a bishopric. "Though, with Sibthorpe, accounted a sycophant by the Puritans", says Wood,[5] "yet by the Royalists he was esteemed worthy of the function of a bishop." So he was installed in Laud's old bishopric of St.

[1] Fuller, *Worthies*, iii. 83.
[2] Laud, *Works*, v. 334.
[3] Harl. MS. 464, 13.
[4] *S.P. Dom. Car. I.* 298, no. 43.
[5] *Athenae Oxonienses*, ii. 1141.

David's, to succeed Theophilus Field, whom he most nearly resembled.

Laud certainly showed scant respect to his earliest bishopric: for even Sibthorpe must yield the palm of sycophancy to Theophilus Field. Field had first acquired prominence as chaplain to Sir Francis Bacon, and had acted " as a sort of broker to Bacon in his peculations ". On the rise of Buckingham he transferred his allegiance, and was rewarded with the bishopric of Llandaff in 1619: but his connexion with Bacon involved him in the Lord Keeper's fall, and in 1621 he was impeached for bribery and brocage in Parliament, and censured by Abbot in Convocation. He did not, however, lose the protection of Buckingham, and in writing to the Duke to thank him for his speech in Parliament, Field expatiated on the blow which his reputation had suffered, and which only a more lucrative bishopric could heal, such as London, now vacant through the death of Dr. King, or Hereford, also opportunely void, " the next see to mine, whither my predecessors have oft been removed ".[1] In spite of Field's touching references to his wife and six children, neither of these applications bore fruit: but five years later he tried again, and after a fulsome panegyric of the Duke's liberality in the creation of bishops and deans, peers and privy councillors, drew gradually to his point. " My Lord, I am grown an old man, and am like old household-stuff, apt to be broke upon often removing. I desire it therefore but once for all, be it Ely or Bath and Wells, and I will spend the remainder of my days in writing an history of your good deeds to me and others, wherein I may vindicate you from the envy and obloquy of this present wicked age wherein we live." [2] These particular applications were again unsuccessful. Even Buckingham could hardly regard Field as a worthy candidate for the important see of Ely, and Bath and Wells had been promised to Laud. But Laud's vacated see of St. David's was conferred upon him, and although Field never wrote the promised history, he declared himself ready, such was his gratitude, to enlist in the army and serve the Duke in the wars. His enthusiasm, however, was not enough to persuade him to visit his new diocese. In spite of the royal instructions he remained at Westminster, explaining, when the King demanded the reason, that St. David's was too unhealthy for actual residence. One short visit he contrived to make, and

[1] *Cabala*, 1691, p. 109.

[2] *Ibid.* p. 111.

extended his episcopal activity to whitewashing the cathedral, but in 1633 Abbot reported that he was again in London, pleading ill-health. In 1635 he at last achieved his ambition, and went to die in Hereford.

But if the promotion of Field and Manwaring discredited the Church, it serves also to remind us again of the conditions in the Church which made such promotions necessary. The poverty of Welsh and other remote bishoprics was such that no able or ambitious cleric could be persuaded to accept them except as a stirrup to something better, and residence there was so unusual [1] that, before the Reformation, the government had frequently made it impossible by appointing foreigners. Four Italians in succession, including Pope Clement VII, had been bishops of Worcester between 1479 and 1535: another had been Bishop of Hereford under Henry VIII, and the Bishop of Llandaff had been a Spaniard. After the Reformation this became impossible, and when the native bishops were required by Laud to reside in their dioceses, they might well boggle at the discomforts which such an innovation entailed. Bishop Field, who had accustomed himself to the agreeable atmosphere of the Court, had reason to stigmatise St. David's as "that desolate place, his diocese, where there is not so much as a leech to cure a sick horse", even though, in fact, he must have been relying on travellers' tales, having never, at the time, seen it himself: and yet St. David's was four times as rich as Llandaff, which he had just left. Laud himself had done well by his Welsh diocese by making two journeys thither, in spite of his preoccupations at court, and in order to secure residence by his successors he appointed chiefly Welshmen to those sees. Able Welshmen, however, like Williams, took the earliest opportunity of leaving their native country for the greener pastures of England and the Court.

The result of this neglect was that the Anglican Church never effectively penetrated into Wales, and the inhabitants were either benighted in popish superstition or perverted by Puritan missionaries. Of the latter, Vavasour Powell was afterwards a conspicuous example: but in Laud's time the most influential agent of

[1] Browne Willis (*Survey of the Cathedral of Bangor*, 1721, p. 103) observes that Bishop Bulkeley (1541–52) was the first Bishop of Bangor to reside in his diocese for over a hundred years.

Puritanism in Wales was the Bishop of Bangor, Dr. Lewis Bayly, who died in 1631. In the reign of James I Bayly had been in continual trouble through his incursions into the forbidden area of politics. He had accused the Council of Popery in 1612: received an official reprimand in 1619 for praying for the Prince and Princess Palatine as King and Queen of Bohemia: and in 1621 was imprisoned in the Fleet for denouncing the Spanish marriage. In the same year he had a "hot encounter" with the King over his sabbatarianism and his book. This book, entitled *The Practice of Piety*, became the most famous evangelical handbook of the century, till *The Whole Duty of Man* and Law's *Serious Call* supplanted it in popular favour. By the time of Bayly's death it had passed through twenty-five editions, and another thirty-five were published in the century following. It was translated into French and German, Polish and Welsh, even into Romansh and whatever tongue was spoken by the redskins of Massachusetts. One of its most distinguished converts was John Bunyan, who first saw the true Gospel in his wife's edition of *The Practice of Piety*. The bishop's own practice, however, seems to have differed from that which he inculcated into so wide a public: for in 1626 he was accused before the House of Commons on charges which, endorsed by Laud and "palpably proved" in Parliament, included every kind of misdemeanour, from licensing promiscuity in others to practising it himself.[1] And even ten years after his death, the Long Parliament, when discussing episcopal delinquencies, recalled with horror that the late Bishop Bayly had indulged in the apparently innocent practice of drinking a toast to the Bishop of Ely with the words, "Ely, Ely, lama sabachthani".[2]

If such were the conditions of the Welsh bishoprics, it goes without saying that the Isle of Man was even less tempting to clerical ambitions. When Bishop Philips of that see died in 1633 Laud wrote to Secretary Coke that "the last bishop filled those parts of the Church with many unlearned and unworthy ministers. My Lord's Grace of York complains of this, and desires remedy for the future. His Majesty is pleased that you write to the Earl of Derby, and his son the Lord Strange, that neither of them pass

[1] Charges in Camb. Univ. Lib. MS. Gg. IV, 13, p. 77. Cf. *Cal. S.P. Dom.* 1625–6, p. 355; Birch, *Charles I*, i. 96.

[2] Verney's *Notes of the Long Parliament* (Camden Soc., 1845), p. 14.

any grant of that bishop till they have acquainted His Majesty with their right to nominate. And then, if the right be theirs, as His Majesty will afford them all that is theirs, so he expects from them that they name no man but such as shall be worthy the preferment to such a place, nor until His Majesty be first made acquainted with it." [1] But in fact neither the Stanleys nor Dr. Philips could fairly be charged with unorthodoxy, and the bishop had deserved a better reputation, considering that he had translated the Prayer Book into Manx and had been continually in trouble with the Puritan governor of the island. It was poverty, not Puritanism, which had caused him to fill the livings at his disposal with unworthy ministers. The bishopric, we learn from a paper written next year,[2] was worth £140 a year, the archdeaconry £60, and nine or ten of the seventeen livings no more than £4. And two years later, Bishop Parr reported that the extreme cold and the ruinous condition of his episcopal house compelled him to winter in England, that the island was destitute of educated men, that it was as much as most of the ministers could do to read the service clearly, and that the grossest superstitions were practised in church.[3] Nevertheless Laud did not entirely neglect even these remote bishoprics, as his intervention in the Isle of Man shows: and in 1637 he promoted the archdeacon of Anglesey to the bishopric of Bangor for discovering concealed lands belonging to the Church there to the value of £1000.[4]

Confronted by all these obstructions in the way of efficient administration, it was only by continued vigilance and repeated personal intervention that Laud could hope to see the policy which he outlined at Lambeth and Whitehall applied in the provinces. In 1634, therefore, he prepared to visit his province metropolitically, and began by announcing his impending visitation of the diocese of Lincoln, suspending the bishop and the six archdeacons from the exercise of their functions, and requiring the ministers and churchwardens to present themselves at appointed times before his Vicar-General and ecclesiastical commissioners.

This was a challenge to Williams, and Williams accepted it

[1] H.M.C. Cowper, II.31.

[2] *S.P. Dom. Car. I.* 265, no. 45.

[3] *S.P. Dom. Car. I.* 345, no. 85, i. 1.

[4] Wood, *Athenae Oxonienses*, ii. 888.

at once. That his own ex-commissary, Sir John Lambe, should have been appointed to represent the Archbishop during the visitation was an additional spur to resistance, and there were historical grounds upon which Williams might at least attempt to vindicate the independence of his see. For Lincoln, still the largest diocese in England, had once been even greater, a province in itself, from which the later dioceses of Ely, Peterborough, and Oxford had been carved out. In a letter to Attorney-General Noy, written from " my poor house at Buckden ", Williams recalled the past greatness of Lincoln, which had once comprised the entire kingdom of Mercia, and was " no way subordinate to those other kingdoms where the archbishopric was then seated ". This independent sovereignty, he claimed, had never been abrogated, and when Robert Grosseteste was bishop, and an archiepiscopal visitation had been threatened, he had obtained papal bulls declaring all dioceses in the province exempt from such innovations. Later encroachments had similarly been resisted, and it was only to royal or legatine authority that the bishop had ever yielded. There had now been no visitation for a hundred years, the last being that of Cranmer, acting on royal authority, in 1534 : and the lapse of a hundred years invalidated the power which the Archbishop claimed to possess. And Williams further objected to the inhibition of his own jurisdiction during the visitation. He asked that, if Laud were to visit, he should visit not as Archbishop but as the King's representative acting under a royal order : that the visitation should not take place that year, being the year of his own triennial visitation, or, if so, that Williams should visit as well : and that his own episcopal jurisdiction should not be inhibited, as he would be too poor to live, let alone to pay his taxes, without the revenues derived from his procurations.[1]

Laud referred the legal decision to Noy. " I am resolved ", he wrote to him, " to maintain and defend the ancient rights of my archbishopric, as far as in me lieth, to the uttermost : and I doubt not but herein you will give me all just assistance."[2] On March 20th, 1634, the case was disputed at the Attorney-General's chambers at Lincoln's Inn, and the representatives of both parties appeared with their proofs and documents. To each of the Bishop's arguments for exemption the Archbishop's

[1] Wilkins, *Concilia*, iv. 487.

[2] *Ibid.* iv. 488.

counsel produced a contrary testimony: and after an examination which lasted two days, Williams lost on all points, the papal bulls which he had pleaded being "so well baited by the Archbishop and his counsel" (among whom the renegade Sir John Lambe played a conspicuous part) "that, not being able to hold any long play, they ran out of the field, leaving the bishop to shift for himself as well as he could".[1] If previous visitations had been resisted, Laud pointed out, that signified nothing: for they had been resisted in vain. To Williams' contention that the passage of 100 years caused the right of visitation to lapse, Laud replied that from Cranmer's visitation to his own was not 100 but 99 years: and when Williams pointed out that Archbishop Chichele's visitation of 1424 had taken place 110 years before that of Cranmer, Laud reminded him that that had not prevented Cranmer from exercising his right. "I was and am of opinion", declared the Attorney-General, "that the Lord Archbishop of Canterbury of right ought to visit metropolitically the said church and diocese of Lincoln, as he ought to do other churches and dioceses of his province." Procurations were to be paid to the Archbishop, for although a papal bull of 1254 had forbidden this in certain cases, papal bulls were only valid in England according as they had been received, and in practice this had never been received. Nor was Williams permitted to exercise concurrent jurisdiction during the visitation, for "regularly in the presence of the superior, the power of the inferior ceaseth: and, in our law, commissions in the several counties may not be executed if the King's Bench happen to be in that county"; and although Noy refused to give a legal ruling on the matter, he suggested that, for convenience, Williams should be inhibited from all independent jurisdiction, "that the visitation metropolitical may be entire, and that His Majesty may be fully informed of the state of the Church as well in this as in other dioceses". Williams, whose behaviour throughout the contest had been scrupulously correct, accepted his defeat and admitted the Archbishop's visitors: and when Noy died five months later Laud noted in his diary, "I have lost a dear friend of him, and the Church the greatest she had of his condition, since she needed any such". "Oh, how I miss Mr. Noy!" he exclaimed to Wentworth early next year, when he found the Crown lawyers less dependable in the affairs of the Church.[2]

[1] Heylin, p. 286.

[2] Laud, *Works*, iii. 221; vii. 107.

For three years Sir Nathaniel Brent and his officers went on tour, visiting every diocese in the province of Canterbury, beginning with the metropolitical see itself. But it is not necessary to deal in detail with Laud's visitation. His articles were not inquisitorial, and he could not fairly be charged with insisting upon innovations. Were the canons of the Church observed? was the fabric of the church kept in repair? were the clergy punctual and regular in the performance of their duties? were the King's instructions about lecturers and leases kept? did anyone make encroachments upon ecclesiastical property? — these were the questions which clergy and churchwardens were required to answer: and the answers were generally less informative than the personal observation of the visitors, and the information which reached them from private sources.[1] To questions about their own regularity, deans and canons of cathedrals had no hesitation in replying that they were industrious, conscientious, hospitable, and orthodox; it was from a private source, not from the replies of the dean and chapter, that the Vicar-General was informed that the canons of Salisbury — long known as a haunt of "wrangling residentiaries" — under the pretence of custom neglected the statutes and kept neither the hospitality required of them nor the canonical hours: that the church ornaments had been sold forty years ago, and that surplice and hood were "now scarce seen one a quarter": and that in most parishes in Wiltshire and Dorsetshire Puritans were chosen churchwardens along with "honest men", and frustrated all the endeavours of the latter to improve the fabric, services, and discipline of the Church. If the clergy were communicative, it was in reply to questions about encroachment upon their rights or perquisites, rather than to those about the neglect of their duties. Enclosures in the precincts of Canterbury, a cart-track through the close at Salisbury, a thoroughfare through the churchyard at Exeter, were promptly reported. A whipping-post in the churchyard at Bristol was ordered to be removed: and a canon of Rochester complained that his predecessor's daughter laid an unjust claim to his canonical garden-plot.

After Canterbury, Rochester, Salisbury, Bristol, Bath and Wells, and Exeter, Brent proceeded to Lincoln. There Laud had two industrious agents, notorious for their hostility to the

[1] House of Lords MSS. (H.M.C. Report IV App., pp. 127 ff.).

WILLIAM LAUD, ARCHBISHOP OF CANTERBURY

bishop and their complete dependence upon himself. One was Sir John Lambe, the other John Farmerie, the chancellor of the diocese, a man whose time was spent in irritating the Bishop and then running for protection to Lambe and Laud with terrible tales of intimidation and persecution. It was to these two, after episcopal, capitular, and archidiaconal jurisdiction had been inhibited in the diocese, that commissions were issued, under Brent, to visit the counties of Leicester, Buckingham, Bedford, Huntingdon, and Hertford, while Williams looked impotently on from Buckden. Farmerie, indeed, ventured with two intended collaborators to visit him there for an interview: but the interview (he said) was so stormy that the two collaborators fled to Cambridge at the mere noise of it, and declined to take any part in so dangerous a business.[1]

On August 9th the visitation of Lincoln began, and Brent interpreted the constitutions of the Church in the cathedral in which its own bishop had never set foot.[2] He dwelt on the necessity of proper vestments and the use of the Prayer-Book in full. The clergy were to see that only orthodox preachers received licences, and that afternoon services were turned to catechism. Church buildings, parsonages, and vicarages were to be kept in good repair, and preachers were "not to preach of controversies, but faith and repentance, and to preach obedience to His Majesty to their several congregations four several times the year at least". After this Brent proceeded to Louth, Boston, Grantham, Huntingdon, and so to Buckinghamshire, similar instruction being given at every session. His practical activities are shown by the orders which he gave in Boston, "a great nursery of inconformity", where John Cotton had preached for twenty years before sailing for Boston in New England. There, after a courteous reception by the Puritan mayor, the Vicar-General called the magistrates into the High Commission for favouring Nonconformists and gave detailed instructions for the repair of the church. The seats were to be removed and rebuilt "in a uniform manner, as they ought to be, leaving a fair, spacious alley in the middle of the church": the paving stones and gravestones were to be laid evenly, the gallery removed from the east to the north, the

[1] Farmerie to Lambe, Lambeth MS. 1030, no. 25.

[2] *Reg. Laud*, 128 ff. Cf. Brent's account in *S.P. Dom. Car. I.* 274, no. 12, summarised by Laud, *Works*, v. 326.

whole fabric repaired, whitewashed, and adorned with "devout and holy sentences of Scripture", and the Ten Commandments and the royal arms inscribed at the east end. At the same time the bells were to be repaired and rehung, and the churchyard well kept "with a strong and sufficient fence to keep out swine and other noisome creatures from digging and rooting by the same".[1] Brent also sent up to the High Commission various Puritan preachers at whose inconformity Williams had long connived, required the Dean and Chapter of the cathedral to repair both its fabric and its ornaments, and visited Eton College; while Farmerie found himself dealing with John Hampden, who was accused of attending the wrong church and of parading the local militia in Beaconsfield churchyard. On this occasion, however, Hampden did not exalt the issue into a principle of national importance, but secured the dismissal of the case by private settlement with Brent.[2]

Brent was a kinsman and dependant of the late Archbishop, and Laud, suspicious at first of his reliability, had imposed a colleague upon him in his visitation. But Brent soon showed that such supervision was unnecessary, and the supervisor was withdrawn. In a paper drawn up next year, the Vicar-General made a careful report of his progress and entertainment in the dioceses of Norwich, Peterborough, Lichfield and Coventry, Worcester, Gloucester, Winchester, and Chichester, describing the state of the country and the measures which he had taken to counter Puritanism and neglect.[3] But the impotence of such measures in a predominantly Puritan county is shown by the correspondence of an orthodox Buckinghamshire clergyman, Dr. John Andrewes, who had presented Hampden to the ecclesiastical officers. From this we see that Brent's visitation was like a passing wind and no more. Hampden might apologise to the Vicar-General, as did Sir Edmund Verney also, but that did not mean that they would turn over a new leaf once the Vicar-General had departed, and in fact Hampden merely encouraged the local gentry to persecute the informer. Wherever Brent went, he received entertainment, respect, and apparent obedience, from local authorities, clergy, and gentry: but on his departure, all reverted to their old ways, and the only difference was that here

[1] Reg. Laud, 129. [2] Brent to Farmerie, *S.P. Dom. Car. I.* 276, no. 35.
[3] *S.P. Dom. Car. I.* 293, no. 128.

or there a Puritan minister had been suspended, or a Puritan magnate rebuked. Andrewes reported that Brent's injunctions had been kept " even by the dreadful grandees of our parish " for a day or two, but that now they had resumed the habits of nonconformity which they had but temporarily dissembled. A man whom Andrewes met out riding even asked him whether the Vicar-General's orders were seriously intended, as neither clergyman nor layman would keep them, and they excited general ridicule. " Yourself ", he wrote to Sir John Lambe, " are banned and cursed to the pit of Hell for suspending Mr. Gladman of Chesham and Mr. Valentine of Chalfont-St. Giles ";[1] and Lambe's action in erecting an organ in the church at Waddesdon was remembered against him by the parishioners when the Long Parliament gave them an opportunity to be heard.

For there was one thing which no visitation and no amount of injunctions could cure, — the poverty of the Church. The irregularities consistently reported from country districts were due more frequently to poverty than to doctrinal perversity, and Puritanism, which despised ceremonies, was frequently identified with indigence, which was unacquainted with them. So we find that the vicar of Llanidloes in Montgomery drove the people away from Holy Communion, refused to use the Prayer Book, received money on the altar, cut the surplices up for use as towels, spoke against the *Book of Sports*, and allowed pigeon-shooting inside the church, — a curious compound of heresy and indifference. At Knotting in Bedfordshire, which Brent found " most tainted of any part of the diocese " of Lincoln, and which later provided John Bunyan with a numerous following, cock-fighting and betting in church were a regular Shrove Tuesday feature, while in the Isle of Man St. John the Baptist's Day was set aside for superstitious observances. The belief in witchcraft was common in Lancashire, where many women had been condemned as witches at the spring assizes of 1634, and in 1631 a prisoner in the High Commission was accused of " being professor of the art magic, and, in particular, charming of pigs ". At Stratford-on-Avon Brent suspended a minister " for grossly particularising in his sermons, and for suffering his poultry to roost and his hogs to lodge in the chancel "; and at Lincoln, where he found everything in disrepair and decay, the organs " old and naught ",

[1] *S.P. Dom. Car. I.* 286, no. 86; 287, no. 31.

and the copes and vestments embezzled, "some alehouses, hounds, and swine were kept in the churchyard, very offensively". As for the more material consequences of poverty, they were manifest everywhere. Wherever he went, the Vicar-General reported decaying churches and parsonages, and glebe-land embezzled. In Norwich the wealth of the merchants contrasted strongly with the poverty of the church, and Puritanism justified the contrast: "the cathedral church is much out of order. The hangings of the choir are naught, the pavement not good, the spire of the steeple is quite down, the copes are fair but want mending, the churchyard is very ill-kept". Round Fakenham "in these parts many parsonage-houses are ruinous". At Yarmouth "the roof of the church is very ruinous", and the churchyard "kept very undecently". Lichfield was no better: and at Shrewsbury, whose increasing prosperity was shortly to be indicated by the grant of a corporation, a chapel had been abandoned through decay. "Pity it were it should fall to utter ruin, but who is to repair it?" And so on. Laud's policy of restoring churches, increasing the value of livings, and resisting encroachments on ecclesiastical property was being frustrated at every turn by the lack of means and the refusal of the prosperous classes to contribute towards it as long as the Church was identified with a social system which restricted their independence, and he found sufficient difficulty in collecting contributions for the repair of St. Paul's without raising other collections for the similar works of reconstruction which it was intended to inspire. Bishop Corbett might preach on the godliness of contribution towards a work on which his hearers would probably never set eyes, but the decaying churches of his own diocese and the neglected cathedral in which he delivered his address, were a reminder that such charity might well begin at home; and one of the reasons which the collectors for St. Paul's gave for their scanty results was the necessity of contributing to the repair of local churches. In these circumstances Laud was compelled to aim at making the Church self-sufficient less through the support of the laity than by the careful husbanding of its attenuated resources and the vigorous use of the ecclesiastical courts. But Brent's visitation showed that such a policy presupposed a more unselfish clergy and a stronger organisation than was actually at his disposal.

The idea that any church, corporation, or district should be exempt from his jurisdiction was hateful to Laud, valuing as he did the idea of equality before the fact of individual liberties and privileges, and while Brent was carrying his policy into every diocese in his province, Laud was striking at another group which claimed to be independent of his authority, — the French and Dutch Protestants who had found a refuge in England from the triumph of the Counter-Reformation abroad, and who had settled there under their own ecclesiastical constitutions. With the Protestantism of the Continent Laud had no sympathy, and from his early days he had emphasised his dissociation from it. But equally he had no desire to interfere with it on the Continent; for his was a national policy, and he had no leisure to tilt at windmills in the name of Truth. So, as far as the foreign Protestants in Europe were concerned, he was prepared to associate himself with the English Puritans and raise subscriptions for the relief of the ejected ministers of the Palatinate, since the King's sister requested it. But when they settled in England, he required them to become subject in all things to the English government, and in religious matters to the English bishops, lest by their exemption they should provide a permanent example of independent ecclesiastical jurisdiction, and attract to their Puritan services all those local English Puritans who could understand their languages.[1] Ever since he had been made Bishop of London, Laud had contemplated the overthrow of this community, so small in numbers, but so significant in principle. In March 1633 he had raised the question at the Council Table, having persuaded his recent nominee Windebank to take the initiative which he could not decently assume himself. Now, as Archbishop, he set to work to effect his project.

In the province of Canterbury there were ten French and Dutch congregations. There were French and Walloon churches in London, Canterbury, Southampton, and Norwich, Dutch in London, Norwich, Yarmouth, Colchester, Maidstone, and Sandwich. According to one of their ministers, who published an account of their suppression when the fall of Laud made it safe to do so,[2] the total number of French and Dutch Protestants

[1] Cf. *S.P. Dom. Car. I.* 265, no. 81.

[2] J. B. (= John Bulteel), *A Relation of the Troubles of the 3 Foreign Churches in Kent, caused by the Injunctions of Wm. Laud, Archbishop of Canterbury* (1645).

in England was 5213, of whom 2240 lived in London, 1450 in Kent, 1487 in East Anglia, and 36 in Southampton. Their privileges, granted by Edward VI, had been confirmed by Elizabeth and James I; and in 1625 Charles I, on his accession, had automatically renewed them. They were mostly artisans, engaged in the cloth-trade: and although the newly arrived refugees were generally poor, having no more possessions than they were able to carry with them, those who had been settled in the country for a generation or two had become prosperous in trade and were the chief financial supporters of the independent churches. Some of these richer members sometimes wished to leave their native churches and become English citizens by a process of naturalisation, but this was discouraged by the English local authorities, who did not wish to see the foreign churches thus impoverished and thrown upon the rates for their support. So in 1621, when Denis l'Hermite, a wealthy Walloon who had become a freeman of the city of Norwich and a worshipper at the English church there, complained that the Walloon church was seeking to prevent his apostasy, both the Anglican bishop and the Mayor wrote to the Privy Council championing the rights of the Walloon church to keep its richer members, without whose support it would be unable to continue.[1] The result was that the Privy Council issued an order requiring all Walloons, even if born in England, to belong to the Walloon church: and in 1631 the Dutch churches received similar orders.

If such incidents showed how the foreign churches could be preserved, they also showed how they could be destroyed: for if the epigoni of the original refugees could be detached from the newcomers, the foreign churches, as independent bodies, would collapse for lack of sustenance; and the justification for such a measure could be found in the fact that the richer members, like Denis l'Hermite in 1621, had actually applied for freedom to leave their native, and join their adoptive church.

So in April 1634 Laud opened his campaign by addressing three questions to the French community in Canterbury and the Dutch in Sandwich and Maidstone. They were asked what liturgy they used: and they answered that they used their own, French and Dutch. They were asked how many of them were born subjects of the King of England: and they answered, about

[1] *Cal. S.P. Dom.*, 1619–21, p. 297.

a third. To the third question, whether those who were born subjects of the King would conform to the English Church, they discreetly returned no answer. However, before these replies could be despatched to the Archbishop, the congregations were advised by the Coetus, the central representative body of both French and Dutch Protestant churches in London, to withhold their answers and stand upon the exemption granted to them by Edward VI and confirmed by his successors.[1]

But if the foreign congregations relied entirely on privileges granted by the King, they were implicitly admitting the right of the King to withdraw as well as to grant those privileges : and Laud's next move was a summary order in December 1634, sent through Sir Nathaniel Brent, requiring :

(1) That all natives of the Dutch and Walloon congregation in His Grace's diocese are to repair to their several parishes where they inhabit, to hear divine service and sermons, and perform all duties and payments required in that behalf.

(2) That the ministers and all others of the Dutch and Walloon congregations which are not natives and born subjects to the King's Majesty, or any other strangers that shall come over to them, while they remain strangers, may have and use their own discipline, as formerly they have done ; yet it is thought fit that the English liturgy should be translated into French and Dutch, for the better settling of their children to the English government.[2]

It was the logical result of the policy of an exclusive national church. Foreigners who were not subject to the King of England were not subject to the Archbishop of Canterbury, but the sons of foreigners, born in England, being native subjects of King Charles, must accept the ecclesiastical consequences of their political allegiance, even if it meant that parents must have their children educated in a religious creed to which they themselves would not subscribe. There could be no division between Church and State. Unless naturalised English subjects accepted the doctrinal forms in which the English social system was expressed, there was no guarantee that they were reliable in their professions : for nonconformity was either foreign or disloyal. In his account of his province for the year 1634, Laud asked the King for royal support in his campaign to bring the foreign churches in Canter-

[1] *S.P. Dom. Car. I.* 266, no. 65.

[2] *Ibid.* 278, no. 63.

bury and Sandwich into conformity, as being " great nurseries of inconformity in those parts ", and the King wrote in the margin, " Put me in mind of this at some convenient time when I am at Council, and I shall redress it ".[1] And in his instructions to Sir Nathaniel Brent when the latter was preparing to carry the metropolitical visitation into East Anglia, Laud wrote, " the same course to be taken with the French and Dutch congregations in the diocese of Norwich as at Canterbury ".

The French and Dutch, however, did not take kindly to Laud's design. They had fled, or their ancestors had fled, in order to keep alive in England the faith which Philip II and Catherine de' Medici would not allow them to keep alive in the Netherlands and in France : and now Laud was refusing to let them keep it alive in England for more than a generation at most. Indeed, it was doubtful if they would be able to keep it alive at all. Robbed of their richer members, and thereby of the funds upon which all organisation depends, what chance of survival had an independent community of 3500 persons in the face of Laud's organised and uniform Church ? So the congregations proceeded by the only way open to them, — by petition. Those at Norwich petitioned Corbett, but in vain. A deputation waited on the Archbishop, but with no more success. " I know your doctrine, — parity of ministers, — hail, fellow, well met ! " said Laud, " and used discourteous words, and would hear no more of the speech." [2] Appeal was made to the King as a Protestant prince, the head of the English Church to which the Protestant churches of the Continent looked for leadership. " Especially at this time ", they wrote, " wherein the churches of Germany do even swim in their own natural blood, and the churches of France in their own tears, all of them being in the very midst of their own ruin, and burdened with the apprehension of a mighty desolation, they have no other but Your Majesty unto whom they may fix their eyes and hopes with any assurance." [3] They were appealing, as so many of Laud's victims were to appeal, to the conception of the unity of Protestantism : and the appeal was ignored, because Laud was not interested in the unity of Protestantism, but in a national Church. Doctrinaire Protestants on the Continent lent the support of their arguments to the losing cause. " About that time ", says John Bulteel, " J. B.

[1] Laud, *Works*, v. 323.
[2] J. B., *op. cit.* pp. 5-11.
[3] Wilkins, *Concilia*, iv. 49.

received divers letters from divers learned men beyond the seas, as from Master du Moulin, Master Polyander, Master Festus Hommius, Master Bugnet, and others, in French and Latin." [1] Support came from other sources too, less academic and disinterested. As in the case of Denis l'Hermite, local authorities were troubled by the thought that the poor foreigners, deprived of the relief supplied by their rich compatriots in the form of church rates, would be a burden upon the local rates. Such was the complaint of the Mayor and Corporation of Canterbury, who petitioned the Archbishop on behalf of the French church there ; and they added that the destruction of the immigrant communities might well entail the end of the prosperity which their industry had brought to the town.[2]

These petitions had some effect in modifying the details of the Archbishop's demands. Through the intervention of the Duc de Soubise with the King, it was conceded that the present ministers of the foreign churches, even if born subjects of the King, might continue to hold their positions till their deaths, although all future ministers must be foreigners only : and the representations of the local authorities secured the addition of a clause " that the natives should contribute to the maintenance of their ministry and the poor of their church, for the subsisting thereof : and that an order should be obtained from His Majesty, if it were desired, to maintain them in their manufactures against all such as should endeavour to molest them by informations ". Such was the limit of concession ; and then, in May 1635, the royal orders to the Judges of the Court of Record renewing the permission to the Dutch and French congregations to enjoy all privileges granted by the King's predecessors were cancelled.[3]

Further resistance was useless, and the foreign churches resigned themselves to their disruption. In Norwich the Walloon congregation had enjoyed the use of the bishop's house since 1619. It was a house which was not used by the bishop, and was described in 1638 as " a poor, deformed, ill-contrived house of stones, not capable of good management or reformation anywise ".[4] In December 1634, however, Bishop Corbett gave them notice to quit. " Your discipline, I know ", he wrote, " care not much for a consecrated place, and any other room in Norwich

[1] J. B., *op. cit.* p. 41.
[2] *S.P. Dom. Car. I.* 289, no. 5.
[3] *Ibid.* 291, no. 66.
[4] Lambeth MS. 943, p. 619.

that hath but length and breadth may serve your turn as well as the chapel. Wherefor I say unto you, without a miracle, '*Lazare, prodi foras* !'." In the following August Laud wrote to them rejecting, clause by clause, their petition against his injunctions, and assuring them that in the end they or their posterity "shall have cause to thank both the State and the Church for this care taken of you": and in September they replied, declaring that they had published the injunctions and acknowledging the two saving clauses. In December 1635 the congregation at Canterbury officially submitted, and its ministers undertook to write to those of Sandwich recommending the same course. Full submission was not immediately achieved: for in his annual account, sent in to the King shortly afterwards, Laud complained that in Kent, "albeit they made some show of conformity, yet I do not find they have yielded such obedience as is required . . . so that I fear I shall be driven to a quicker proceeding with them". Next year, however, he reported that "the Walloons and other strangers in my diocese do come orderly to their parish churches, and there receive the sacraments and marry, etc., according to my injunctions, with that limitation which Your Majesty allowed"; and by 1638 he could say that "the strangers at Canterbury do reasonably well obey my injunctions for coming to our churches, and I shall give them all encouragement, holding it fitting to keep a moderate hand with them".[1]

In the province of York the same problem was dealt with by Neile even more summarily, the foreigners there "having no such powerful solicitors as the Coetus of the London churches to take off his edge".[2] Here it was not persecuted refugees but imported artisans who were the cause of the trouble. For many years Sir Cornelius Vermuyden, a Dutch engineer, had been engaged in draining the marshy district of Hatfield Chace under a commission from the government. The operations were lengthy and complicated, and before long Vermuyden found himself in trouble with Wentworth who, as President of the Council at York, was determined to protect the rights of the inhabitants against some of the activities of the "participants". Scarcely rid of Wentworth, Vermuyden next found himself embroiled with Wentworth's *alter ego*, Laud. For, by employing only French and Dutch workmen for the undertaking, Vermuyden had introduced those

[1] Laud, *Works*, v. 332, 337, 355.

[2] Heylin, p. 264.

very foreign Protestants whom Laud was so carefully regulating, and by his contract he had secured for them the right to build their own places of worship. In 1636 Neile wrote to Laud that there was already a plantation of 200 families as a result of the draining operations, and that more were expected to arrive.[1] These immigrants had set up a French church in a barn belonging to another foreign speculator, Sir Philiberto Vernatti: and this barn, being conveniently situated just over the border of Lincolnshire, was in the diocese of Williams, who, gladly accepting the opportunity of annoying his rival, had given them oral permission to worship there unmolested. Although the immigrants were acting strictly within the limits of their contract, Neile asked for Laud's assistance in the task of reducing them to conformity, and the busy Dr. Farmerie was commissioned to counteract the influence of Williams in the diocese of Lincoln. In a short time the Dutch minister whom Williams had allowed to conduct their services found it convenient to withdraw to London, and thence abroad; and with the departure of the principal settler also to Amsterdam, Neile reported that things were much better. He asked the Primate to send a supply of Prayer Books in French and Dutch, so that the workmen and their families might be initiated into the mysteries of their new religion, and explained that, in the meanwhile, they were coming to the English Church and sitting through the services with great decorum, although most of them did not know a word of English. That, however, did not greatly matter: for in the eyes of Neile it was manifestly better to sit still while truth was unintelligible than not to hear it at all, or, worse still, hear heresy and understand it. This treatment was successful. By next January the foreigners had sold the material which they had collected for the construction of a Nonconformist chapel, and soon afterwards they bought a place in the Isle of Axholme in Lincolnshire, where, in spite of the support of Williams, Neile refused to give them a dispensation from attendance at the parish church, ordered them to use the Prayer Book unabridged and unaltered, and forbade them to exercise any independent jurisdiction. Meanwhile Dr. Farmerie sent an orthodox clergyman, Dr. Cursol, to preach the true word of God to them in properly consecrated churches.[2] So the last

[1] *S.P. Dom. Car. I.* 327, no. 47.

[2] *Ibid.* 310, no. 1. Farmerie's letter (undated) is ascribed in the *Calendar*

of the foreign congregations enjoyed the blessings of conformity: and in March 1638, when the Bishop of Norwich, Dr. Wren, wrote to the minister of the Walloon congregation there claiming compensation for damage done to the episcopal house during their tenancy of it, he especially commended the example of the community at Axholme. "I cannot but heartily wish", he wrote, "that you in your wisdom and true fidelity to the Church of England would lay before you the example of the French congregation in the Isle of Axholme; who, though but lately settled in this land, yet have already entertained the liturgy of the Church of England, as it is set forth in French, and with great alacrity do conform themselves to the rites of that church in the protection whereof they live. I speak unto wise men: God give you a right understanding of it."[1]

So, one by one, all independent jurisdictions were being brought under Laud's authority. When the Dean and Chapter of St. Paul's claimed exemption from his visitation in April 1636, showing their records to prove that they held their privileges immediately from the King, their claims were soon disposed of. "His Majesty approves well of the modesty of these petitioners", replied Secretary Coke, "but withal is resolved, for the settlement of peace and good order in the Church, that no place, without special grounds of privilege, shall be exempt from archiepiscopal visitation: and least of all this church of St. Paul, in regard it appears by their own suggestion that the rest of the diocese hath been visited, and, *de ordinario*, it is known that the Archbishop or Bishop ought to begin his visitation at the Cathedral." So, next month, Laud was able to record with satisfaction, "I visited the Dean and Chapter of St. Paul's, London".[2]

The last exempt jurisdiction to fall before the Archbishop's attack was that of the Universities. In Oxford, as Chancellor and benefactor, his authority was unquestioned and his influence paramount: but even so he was determined to establish the right

of State Papers to 1635? But as it refers to the departure of Bontemps, which had not taken place when Neile wrote in June 1636, as having taken place some two years before, it is apparently not earlier than January 1638, when Neile wrote that the foreigners had settled in the Isle of Axholme.

[1] *S.P Dom. Car. I.* 331, no. 71 (Neile to Laud); *S.P. Dom. Car. I.* 345, no. 85, i. 5 (Neile to Laud); Lambeth MS. 943, p. 559 (Neile to Laud); Tanner MS. lxviii, 72 (Wren to Delaune).

[2] Wilkins, *Concilia*, iv. 524; Laud, *Works*, iii. 226.

of visitation which it was scarcely necessary for him to exercise. With Cambridge, however, he had no official connexion except an honorary degree: and the moral and religious state of that University cried aloud for his intervention. It had always been more advanced than Oxford in its Protestantism. From the Puritan fen country around it, it inhaled the infection of false doctrine, and reissued it with the guarantee of a seat of learning. The very name of Emmanuel College caused apprehension to the faithful: and the most famous teacher whom Cambridge had produced since the Reformation was the Puritan apostle Perkins. To counteract these tendencies, Laud required some more authoritative status in the University than that of an incorporated doctor.

Laud was not without influence in Cambridge, but his influence was undefined, and depended hitherto upon his personal contacts with individual Heads of Houses, and his fortunate possession of the ear of the King. While Buckingham was Chancellor, Laud had intervened in the affairs of the University although only Bishop of Bath and Wells. In 1627 he had written to the University in the King's name requiring it to assist the revival of ancient discipline by sending copies of all orders and injunctions on that subject since the accession of Elizabeth:[1] the next year he was instrumental in the removal of one Dr. Dorislaus from the chair of history which Lord Brooke had just founded for him.[2] The chair had first been offered to Vossius, but Vossius had declined it, and Dorislaus, also a Leyden man, proved to be far less satisfactory: for in his lectures on Tacitus, instead of stressing the orthodox doctrine of the divine right of kings, he "placed the right of monarchy in the people's voluntary submission". For this heresy, the Vice-chancellor, Dr. Matthew Wren, refused to incorporate him, and reported the affair to Laud in order that Laud might in turn use his influence with the Duke of Buckingham. As a result Dorislaus was compelled to abandon his chair, although Lord Brooke continued his stipend. He did not, however, abandon his objectionable views: but translated them so far into practice that in 1650, when serving the Commonwealth as ambassador to the Hague, he was assassinated as a regicide by royalist *émigrés*.

[1] Patrick MSS. (Camb. Univ. Lib.), 22, 7.

[2] *Vide* Mullinger, *Hist. of Camb. University*, iii. 87-8.

With the death of Buckingham, Laud's direct influence in the University declined : for the new Chancellor, Lord Holland (the son of that Penelope Devereux whom Laud had so injudiciously married to Lord Devonshire), combined a Puritan upbringing at Emmanuel College with the favour of the Queen, and was obnoxious to Laud on both accounts. But Laud still kept a party in Cambridge, especially in Peterhouse, where orthodoxy throve under the successive masterships of Wren and Cosin. Under these two a new chapel was constructed which provided a rich crop of angels and cherubim for the parliamentary iconoclasts, and Cosin even introduced incense into the college services. It was to Peterhouse, under Wren, that Laud sent the young Vossius for his education, and, under Cosin, Richard Crashaw became a fellow of the college. In other colleges, too, the rise of Arminianism was noted, and several Laudian Heads were imposed by royal order, including Edward Martin, one of Laud's chaplains, who had asserted the new doctrines in a book which was particularly offensive to Puritans.[1] Puritans, however, still claimed to be the majority in the University, and were represented particularly by the introspective master of Sidney Sussex, Dr. Samuel Ward, a man who entertained the most minute scruples if he found himself guilty of over-eating, or of experiencing an impure dream, but who added benefice to benefice and canonry to canonry without the least twinge of his otherwise over-susceptible conscience.

It was in May 1635 that Laud notified the Universities of his intention to visit them metropolitically, as parts of the dioceses of Oxford and Ely respectively, unless they could show good reasons for exemption. The Universities at once demurred. When Laud asked Oxford to forward to him Robert Hare's two compilations of the Privileges and the Memorables of the University, the University declined to be the means of sacrificing its own privileges, and the antiquary Brian Twyne was commissioned to examine the archives and draw up a set of reasons against the visitation.[2] Archives were rummaged at Cambridge too, and a long correspondence was carried on between the

[1] *An Historical Narration . . . concerning God's Election and the Merits of Christ's Death*. Described by Prynne as " the greatest affront and imposture ever offered to, or put upon, the Church of England in any age, deserving the highest censure " (*Canterburie's Doome*, p. 168).

[2] Wood, *Annals* (ed. Gutch), ii. 403 ; Twyne MS. vii. pp. 5-12.

University, the Chancellor, and the Archbishop which produced so little result that at the end of the year the Vice-chancellor and Heads of Houses received a strongly worded letter from Laud. He complained that nearly a year had elapsed since he gave them notice of his intention, in order that they might have every opportunity of proving exemption if they claimed it. " Notwithstanding, all this respect of mine hath been able to gain nothing from you but delays. . . . If you think by these delays to make me forget or forego the business, you will find yourselves much deceived, for I do not intend to do myself or my see that prejudice. And surely if I had not shown you that respect I did, but sent down my inhibition without more ado, you must long before this time have showed me what you could, for all such right as you pretend against me. These are therefore once more to desire yourself and the Heads to make some end of this dilatory course, as shall be fitting."[1] In reply to this, the University sent an immediate and conciliatory letter : but as it showed no sign of yielding to the Archbishop's claim, Laud finally cut the knot by petitioning the King to appoint a time and place in which the case between himself and the two Universities might be heard. The King appointed Hampton Court on June 14th, 1636 : a week's delay intervened : and finally, on June 21st, both parties presented themselves before the King with learned counsel and documents, and the case was argued.

The case put forward by the Universities was substantially the same for both Oxford and Cambridge. The Universities, they said, were royal foundations, and, as such, visitable only by the King or his commissioners. By a series of papal bulls during the Middle Ages they had further been explicitly exempted from episcopal or archiepiscopal jurisdiction, and if any archbishop had in fact visited them, that was in virtue of a legatine or royal commission. At the Reformation, when the papal power ceased in England, that of the Archbishop of Canterbury received no increase thereby, but only that of the King. If the Archbishop cared to visit as a royal visitor commissioned by the King, then Lord Holland said that he would raise no objection : but Laud would not accept such a solution. " No", he said, " I desire to have my own power ", and he prepared to claim it.

To the argument that the Universities, being royal foundations,

[1] Laud, *Works*, v. 564.

were by common law subject to royal visitation only, the Archbishop's counsel replied that they were not direct royal foundations, in the sense that particular colleges were royal foundations, and that as bishoprics and archbishoprics in England were royal foundations, the visitation of bishops and archbishops was also valid by common law. As for the papal bulls, they were easily disposed of: for such bulls were only valid if received, and these bulls had been expressly rejected by the Crown of England. When Oxford University had claimed exemption from the jurisdiction of Archbishop Arundel by appeal to their papal bulls, the Archbishop had entered the University after a pitched battle, and a royal order had confirmed his authority so decisively that the University had soon afterwards submitted to a visitation even by the Bishop of Lincoln. Laud exclaimed too against the abuse inherent in all exempt powers, whatever their authority. Exemption led to such outrageous things as unconsecrated chapels in Cambridge colleges, and in the Middle Ages the purchase of exemptions from Rome had been, "next to Purgatory", the chief source of papal affluence and corruption. Finally Laud produced, as his *coup de grâce*, the instrument which had been sent to King Henry VIII, signed by the Vice-chancellor and Heads of Houses of Cambridge, in which they explicitly renounced all the rights and privileges which they had received from the Bishop of Rome.

This settled the matter, and the King in Council gave his judgment for the Archbishop against both Universities. No papal bulls, it was declared, could exempt them from metropolitical jurisdiction, and no charters did: nor could the long intermission of the exercise of that jurisdiction be any bar to its present legality. Laud had the decision of the Council drawn up under the Great Seal as a guarantee for future reference, and although it was conceded that the Universities should not be subject to episcopal or archidiaconal jurisdiction, the custom whereby an archbishop might visit once only in his lifetime was abrogated. The Archbishop might now visit as often as he wished, on showing adequate reason to the King: and the personal pride of the Chancellor Holland was spared by permission to be represented during the visitation by proxy.[1]

Laud's victory over the Universities was regarded as a great

[1] Wilkins, *Concilia*, iv. 525 ff.; Rushworth, ii. 325 ff.

triumph: for with the defeat of Cambridge the last obstacle to his universal authority was broken down. While University archivists complained bitterly that their learned counsel had not done sufficient justice to their cause, or used all the arguments which were available, the partisans of the Archbishop gave way to rejoicing. Stephen Goffe wrote to Vossius to report the glad tidings, and Vossius wrote to Laud to offer his congratulations. "It is not only human bodies that are fickle and fragile", he wrote, "but even the best of our institutions, if neglected, tend to decay. So, for the preservation of the great blessing of discipline, there could be nothing more acceptable to God and the King than the Archbishop's recovery of his ancient right, to restrain the decay of morality."[1] Laud, in his reply, agreed with the platitudes, and professed his ambition to labour for the promotion of learning, orthodoxy, and discipline in his new provinces. In Oxford, indeed, this was unnecessary: but already in September 1636 he drew up a paper of the "common disorders" which required his intervention at Cambridge.[2] There all the indiscipline and unorthodoxy which he had banished from Oxford seemed still to prevail. Fellows rarely attended chapel, choir boys could not sing, fasts were neglected, St. Mary's Church was used as a theatre, and the scholars of Christ's College lived in the Brazen George Inn. The undergraduates luxuriated in sartorial irregularities, — gowns of every colour, light and gay clothes, and "round, rustic caps", some with boots and spurs, others with fantastically coloured stockings. In three colleges, — Sidney Sussex, Christ's College, and Emmanuel, — the chapels had not been consecrated, and when Laud required the reason, the 102-years-old Dr. Chaderton, who, though no longer Master of Emmanuel, was still regarded as master in it, gave the unsatisfactory answer that "he hoped they were consecrated by Faith and good Conscience". In Emmanuel College and St. Mary's Church the communion-table was also wrongly placed.

In fact, however, Laud never visited either of the Universities as he had intended. Pressure of time, and the imminence of the Troubles, forced him to content himself with securing the authority without exercising the power; and although Heylin

[1] *Epistolae Ecclesiasticae et Theologicae* (Amsterdam, 1684), no. dxxxix.

[2] Add. MS. 32093, p. 175.

says that the mere report of an impending visitation sufficed to bring consecration to chapels and rails to altars, " before anything was done in it, the troubles in Scotland, and the disturbances at home, kept it off so long that a greater visitation fell upon the visitor than could have happened unto them ". For already, while Laud was still adding to the number of his apparent triumphs, the system of Thorough was beginning to crack under its own weight. Everywhere lack of supporters as single-minded as himself was driving Laud to assume every burden and every responsibility alone, and the mere task of assuming these powers absorbed the energies which might have been expended in exercising them.

> So spake the fervent Angel, but his zeal
> None seconded, as out of season judg'd
> Or singular and rash :

and as in this chapter we have seen him gradually extending his authority throughout the English Church, suppressing dissidents and over-riding exemptions, without, however, materially increasing his actual power, so in the next chapter we shall see him forced, by the same lack of co-operation, to undertake in the secular world more tasks than he was either at leisure or qualified to fulfil.

CHAPTER SIX

WHITEHALL

"We begin to live here in the Church triumphant."

HOWELL TO WENTWORTH. March 15th, 1636 (*Strafford Letters*, i. 522).

WE have seen the methods by which Laud sought to apply his policy in the country, and the obstacles which he encountered there. But if it was in the provinces that he hoped to make his policy effective, it was in Whitehall that it was originated, and on the security of Laud's position there that it depended for its authority. We must now turn to Whitehall to examine Laud's personal life at the seat of government, and the methods by which he sought both to maintain his own position and to inspire the whole administration with the ideals which he himself entertained.

This was not an easy task; for although Laud stood in no danger of losing the affections of King Charles, he was surrounded by rivals more adept than himself in the arts of the courtier, and animated by principles widely different from his own, — men who seemed to him to epitomise those private interests which, in his eyes, had upset the old social harmony, had converted Parliament into a faction, and were now seeking at every turn to thwart his own large policy of reconstruction.

First there was the Lord Treasurer Weston, now Earl of Portland, who had performed indispensable services in reversing the extravagant policy of Buckingham. Skilful in husbanding the King's resources, determined on a policy of inexpensive and unadventurous peace, humouring, without materially forwarding, his master's Continental ambitions, he provided the essential foundation upon which alone the work of Laud and Wentworth could proceed; but between the policy of Laud and Wentworth and that of Portland there was a huge gulf of principle, and Laud preferred to blind himself to the Lord Treasurer's political services than to ignore his personal ambitions. For Portland seemed to entertain no higher ambition than his own continued employment in a lucrative position, and he sought to achieve this by the exercise of a venal patronage. It was noticed, too, that while he effectively prevented the exercise of the royal bounty in all other directions, his own financial needs — which were many, for he had dynastic ambitions and splendid tastes — were regarded as a necessary department of State. Twice the King paid off his debts, to the amount of £44,000 : and while royal forests were being reclaimed from others, he received the gift of the forest of Chute in Hampshire. In more serious business he was at best cautious, at worst dilatory : and caution and procrastination were deadly sins in the eyes of Laud, who saw before himself an unlimited amount of work to be done in a limited time. To him Portland was "the Lady Mora", the type of Delay, and this name, transferred from the Lord Treasurer to his policy, was afterwards used to characterise the successors who continued that policy when its original exponent was dead.

Then there was Lord Cottington, the Chancellor of the Exchequer, also a man of unquestioned ability, but also infected with the vices of Portland. Between Laud and Wentworth on one hand, and Cottington on the other, there was also a wide difference of temperament ; for Cottington had an easy manner and affected both the political sympathies and the personal tastes of a dilettante Spanish grandee : and his ready wit was offensive to both Laud and Wentworth, neither of whom was conspicuous for a sense of humour. Laboured and elementary puns were the limit of Laud's pleasantries,[1] and Wentworth's appreciation of a joke was scarcely more refined. On one occasion, in a despatch from Ireland, he described his speech to the Irish Parliament, in which he had warned them "to look well about and to be wise by others' harms : they were not ignorant of the misfortunes these meetings had run in England in late years". From the architect of the

[1] So "All fowls a moulting-time" at the censure of Sir David Foulis. Cf. his remarks at the censure of Sir James Bagg, *infra*, p. 225. Lord Rich, Mr. South, and Bishop Boyle were the objects of similar witticisms : and the merchant Chambers complained to the Long Parliament that Laud, in the Star Chamber, "was very violent, fining him about £3000, and descanted upon his name Chambers".

Petition of Right this had a touch of irony in it, and when the passage was read at the Council Table, Cottington, unable to repress an apt quotation, interpolated "et quorum pars magna fui". "I hope", Laud wrote to Wentworth, "you will charge this home upon my Lord Cottington. He hath so many Spanish tricks that I cannot trust him for anything but making of legs to fair ladies"; and Wentworth seems seriously to have contemplated having "my Don with his whiskers" brought before the Star Chamber on a charge of spreading false news. The dilatoriness and selfishness of both Cottington and Portland, whom Laud readily accused of deliberate malice in all their actions, was a source of continual embarrassment to Laud and Wentworth. "The Lady Mora commends her to you, and tells you she would make more haste, did she not stay to accommodate private ends", Laud wrote: and Wentworth was in complete agreement. "In sadness I have wondered many times", he once remarked, "to observe how universally you and I agree in our judgment of persons, as most commonly we have done ever since I had the honour to know you."

In the face of such obstruction from within the government, Laud, who was protecting Wentworth's rear as well as his own, and whose personal relations with those of opposite principles were never easy, saw no alternative but to secure every vacant post for some dependable supporter. Unfortunately, as time was to show, there were few, either in Church or State, who shared his own unselfish devotion to business, his scrupulous integrity, and his large political ideals. He could not find enough among the clergy to be his bishops, nor among the laity to be his politicians. Only Wentworth seemed to answer such a description, and Wentworth was away in Ireland, providing Laud with an added responsibility rather than support at Whitehall. So Laud was compelled either to fill the places at his disposal with obedient nonentities, which did not relieve himself of the work, or to engross them in himself. So, as Bishop of London, he had advanced Windebank and Juxon to places of trust: and so, as Archbishop, he was to accumulate a plurality of offices for which neither his time nor his ability was sufficient.

On his elevation to Canterbury, Laud was already a Privy

Councillor for England and Scotland, and was shortly to become one for Ireland also. For the next year his political activities consisted largely in intrigue against "Lady Mora". He complained that Portland was wasting the revenue by selling royal forests unnecessarily cheap. In Ireland, Wentworth was at grips with the Earl of Cork, who had sacrilegiously erected a family mausoleum in St. Patrick's: and Laud discovered that Cork was being supported by Portland, whose second cousin was buried in the tomb. He later heard from disgruntled merchants that Portland compelled them, to their own and the private wharfingers' loss, to unlade their wares at the Customs House Quay only, in which he was financially interested.[1] In an attempt to get rid of the Lord Treasurer, Laud showed the King the letters in which Wentworth complained of his insufficiency.[2] But these manœuvres were unsuccessful, and when the Treasury at last fell vacant in March 1635, it was through Portland's death, not his removal. As the Treasurer lay dying, the Archbishop sent to offer his spiritual services: but they were refused, and Portland died, as many had suspected him of living, a Roman Catholic, leaving his office to be disputed between the parties of Lady Mora and Thorough.

The strength of Laud's influence in the bestowal of political office at this time had just been indicated by another appointment which can only have been due to him. On the assassination of Buckingham, the active career of Laud's friend, Viscount Scudamore, had come to an end. He had associated himself entirely with the fortunes of Buckingham, had supplied him with cavalry for the expedition to Rochelle, had defended him in Parliament,[3] and had himself been at Portsmouth to attend the Duke on his campaign when the hand of Felton frustrated the design. Since then Scudamore had lived in retirement in Herefordshire, engaging himself in local affairs, following Laud's advice by restoring Church property, and (what is more attractive to posterity than orthodoxy) practising his favourite pursuit of fruit-growing, which led to his discovery of the redstreak cyder apple and the conversion of Herefordshire into the orchard

[1] Clarendon, *Life*, Oxford, 1759, p. 12.
[2] *Cal. Ven.* xxiii. 226, June 2nd, 1634.
[3] Lonsdale MSS. (H.M.C. Report XIII, pt. vii, p. 46).

of England.[1] From these activities he was called once more to take part in politics at the beginning of 1635, and it is impossible not to attribute to Laud, who had professed himself ever ready to serve Scudamore when Buckingham's death had removed his other patron, the appointment of Scudamore as ambassador to Paris, where, as we shall see, he became an agent of the Archbishop's policy. It seems, however, that Scudamore's orthodoxy was superior to his diplomatic ability: for next year another ambassador was sent out to accompany him, and this colleague, the Earl of Leicester, was an experienced diplomat, even if he was a Puritan in doctrine and an enemy of the Archbishop.[2]

It was thus apparent that the Archbishop would have considerable influence in the choice of a successor to Portland, and his known antipathy to Portland's policy made it certain that he would exercise this influence. The difficulty was that the party of Thorough had no candidate. Wentworth was indispensable in Ireland, Laud inexperienced as a politician: and the party of Thorough, it was increasingly obvious, consisted of these two alone. On the other side, Cottington was both ready and able to succeed Portland: and since he was unwilling to take the position himself, Laud's sole ambition now became to prevent it falling into the hands of Cottington. In this he was, at any rate temporarily, successful. The final appointment was shelved, and the Treasury was put into commission. Both Cottington

[1] Cf. John Philips, *Cyder* (ed. 1708), p. 31:

> " Yet let her [the musk apple] to the redstreak yield, that once
> Was of the sylvan kind, uncivilis'd,
> Of no regard, till Scudamore's skilful hand
> Improv'd her, and by courtly discipline
> Taught her the savage nature to forget:
> Hence styl'd the Scudamorean plant. . . ."

Edmund Smith, *A Poem on the Death of Mr. John Philips*:

> " Redstreak he quaffs beneath the Chianti vine,
> Gives Tuscan yearly for thy Scudamore's wine."

Evelyn, in the preface to *Pomona*, remarks that " by the noble example of my Lord Scudamore, and of some other public-spirited gentlemen in those parts, all Herefordshire is become, in a manner, one entire orchard ". Evelyn also calls the redstreak by the name of Scudamore's crab. Scudamore's services to agriculture and forestry are praised by Beale in a letter to Samuel Hartlib of May 3rd, 1656 (in *Herefordshire Orchards a Pattern for all England*, 1724, p. 22). In the reign of Charles II he also introduced the breed of Herefordshire cattle from the Netherlands.

[2] *Vide infra*, p. 375.

and Laud were among the Commissioners, who also included the two Secretaries of State, Coke and Windebank, and the Earl of Manchester; but the head of the Commission was the Archbishop: and since Laud soon afterwards increased his predominance in the King's counsels by his appointment as first of the Junto for Foreign Affairs, and was already head of the Commission for the Plantations, observers might well regard him as a royal favourite no less powerful than Buckingham had once been.

Among these observers was Sir Thomas Roe, who had never been deceived by Laud's protestations of impotence at Court: and now this great diplomat, since, among his other amiable qualities, he was incapable of bearing malice for his recent disappointment, urged the Queen of Bohemia to court the rising sun. Already at the end of 1634 he had urged her to cultivate him. "My Lord of Canterbury", he wrote, "is an excellent man, and if Your Majesty have no relation to him, I wish you would be pleased to make it: for he is very just, incorrupt, and, above all, mistaken by the erring world." "For my Lord of Canterbury", Queen Elizabeth answered, "I am glad you commend him so much, for there are but few that do it. I have been willing enough to enter into correspondence with him since he was Archbishop, but you know I do not love to begin. He hath indeed sent me sometimes a cold compliment, and I have answered it in the same kind. I have now written to him . . . in behalf of the poor preachers of the Palatinate, by this honest man, one of them, who will deliver this letter. . . . I will see how he takes it, and either end or continue my correspondence as he will answer me." Laud's reply proved satisfactory. He had already encouraged collections in aid of the exiled ministers of the Palatinate, Calvinists though they were, — for outside England he had no animosity against Calvinism, just as he had no sympathy with it.[1] It was noticed, however, that in the circulars which were sent out to encourage subscriptions to the charitable fund, he secured the erasure, after the patent had passed the Great Seal, of certain unnecessarily Protestant passages which declared the religion of the Palatinate to be identical with that of England,

[1] He had written to Dr. Dove, Bishop of Peterborough, urging him to encourage such contributions, in 1629 (*Works*, vii. 22). A letter from Laud to the bishops of his province for the same purpose in May 1635 is printed in *Works*, vi. 417, and was perhaps the result of this application of the Queen of Bohemia.

and referred to the "anti-Christian yoke" of the Roman doctrine.[1]

Thus encouraged, the Queen of Bohemia was disposed to continue her correspondence with Laud, and now, upon Laud's further elevation, her counsellor again urged her to cultivate his acquaintance. "This is the great man", he wrote, "made now of the Commission of the Treasury and the first of the Junto of Foreign Affairs, and in the greatest esteem with His Majesty of any in my observance; and I hope (whatever the world hath sinistrously conceived) that he will prove a happy instrument of the public, both at home and abroad." He begged the Queen not to confine her requests to small particulars in behalf of others, such as the poor ministers, but to engage his support for her cause in European politics, since "small requests, repeated, and for others, do abate the finest edge, and his nature had rather do you one great service than twenty trifles. For upon less than great actions he is not set, and being now so great he cannot be eminent and show it to the world by treading in beaten paths and the exploded steps of others; and this only hath made the Cardinal Richelieu so glorious. Therefore Your Majesty may expect a change, and, if not, yet you ought to attempt it, and to show him the way to make himself the Richelieu of England."[2]

The poor Queen took her counsellor's advice. She wrote to Laud again, congratulating him on the favour which he enjoyed with her brother, and, pleased with his apparent willingness to serve her, she begged Roe to treat with him about the affairs of Central Europe.[3] But nothing came of it. Roe was mistaken in both the character and the aims of the Archbishop, who had already dissociated himself from the affairs of Central Europe when he prevented the appointment of Roe as Secretary of State in 1632. Laud could give nothing but advice, and his political advice was not worth having. He was not, and could not be, an English Richelieu. His greatness in politics was thrust upon him, and he had no qualifications for it. He was an old man, without experience, and the sole reason for his assumption of the burden of foreign affairs was the fear that otherwise Cottington would control them, and so increase his influence on the Council. Six months later Roe, disappointed in the Archbishop for a second time, wrote to Queen Elizabeth that "I do not doubt my Lord of

[1] Rushworth, i. 34. [2] *S.P. Dom. Car. I.* 286, no. 34.
[3] *Cal. S.P. Dom.*, 1635, p. 35; cf. p. 2; *ibid.* pp. 241-2.

Canterbury hath good inclinations, and as much credit as ever any servant had : but he is not versed in foreign affairs, and he is fearful to engage himself and his master in new ways and of doubtful event, wherein himself is not grounded sufficiently to maintain and carry along his counsels. Neither is he without opposition and concurrency of power with those whose affections are contrary." Two months later the Venetian ambassador gave the same verdict when he reported that the Palatine ambassadors had been courting the Archbishop, " who, with his scant knowledge of the interests of State, which he has only approached in his old age, is very anxious to direct the affairs of the realm ". We may doubt, however, whether Laud was really anxious to direct English foreign policy. He recognised too well the magnitude of the task which he had set himself in the Church, without voluntarily adding to it a burden to which he was so obviously unequal : and his relations with the Queen of Bohemia soon resumed their normal tenor, — the granting of favours to individuals, the securing of degrees for the young Princes, or the interchange of presents and compliments. Roe was really wrong when he said that Laud would rather do one great service than twenty trifles.

It will be unnecessary to refer again to Laud's relations with foreign powers in any but an ecclesiastical capacity : but they do include one incident which is typical enough to be of interest. It occurred in 1636, when the King of Poland sent an ambassador to Charles I to arrange a marriage with one of his nieces. By insisting that the Princess must change her religion, the ambassador, Zawadski, nettled the King's pride, and, after a thoroughly unsatisfactory interview, he applied to the Archbishop, whose influence with the King was known, and whose support of Catholicism was reported. " But where he expected to find more mildness ", says the Venetian ambassador, reporting the incident, " he only encountered greater severity." Laud accused him of using dishonourable shifts to recommend a distasteful project to the King, and assured him that his methods were both dangerous and stupid, since protestations and violence might impress base and servile spirits, but were beneath the contempt of princes. " He went on with this harangue and these biting remarks, never giving the ambassador a chance to put in a word in defence of his cause, showing very scant respect for him personally, and finally dismissing him full of resentment." [1] In his passion for equality Laud was no respecter of persons. Servants of the Crown, in his eyes, were no more entitled to perquisites than small officials, and representatives of foreign Kings fared no better at his hands than Puritans convicted in the Star Chamber. Nor were they any more likely to forget it.

Meanwhile the Commission for the Treasury was proving daily more unworkable. It was the scene of perpetual differences between its two most prominent members, Cottington and Laud. Laud was president of the Commission, but Cottington was far more competent: and although the Archbishop sought conscientiously to repair his ignorance by interviews with experts, such as David Harvey, a rich merchant whose country house was not far from his own at Croydon,[2] he was never able to master the intricacies of finance with which Cottington had long been familiar. Besides, the breach which separated the principles of the two was made irreparable by the utter incompatibility of their temperaments. Laud's rigid mind was apt to interpret every difference of opinion as inspired by deliberate malice, and he was perpetually accusing Cottington of interested motives. Cottington, on the other side, was quite unperturbed by these displays of heat, and merely baited Laud the more in order to enjoy a laugh at his expense. "No man", says Clarendon, "so willingly made use of all those occasions as the Lord Cottington, who, being a master of temper, and of the most profound dissimulation, knew too well how to lead him into a mistake, and then drive him into choler, and then expose him upon the matter and the manner to the judgment of the company. And he chose to do this most when the King was present; and then he would dine with him the next day." [3]

One such incident concerned the King's intention to enclose Oatlands Park, between Richmond and Hampton Court, in order to stock it with red and fallow deer for hunting. This was an undertaking which Laud opposed on every count. First, it would be very expensive: for not only did the park include many private

[1] *Cal. Ven.* xxiv. 12. Dr. W. K. Jordan, in the second part of his *Development of Religious Toleration*, 1937, quotes this passage as referring to an interview between Laud and Panzani: but the Venetian ambassador makes it quite plain that the victim was Zawadski.

[2] Clarendon, *Life*, p. 10 ff.

[3] *History of the Rebellion*, i. 207.

estates which would have to be bought from the owners at their own price, but the King also projected the building of a brick wall some ten or twelve miles in circumference round part of the preserve; and Laud knew well enough that the experiment of government without Parliament was absolutely dependent on economy. Furthermore, the district which the King intended to enclose contained common lands, and Laud, who was "a great hater of depopulations in any kind", could not decently deal so harshly with enclosing gentlemen and farmers if he were seen to connive at the activities of an enclosing King. And there was also some opposition among those who owned land in the district. For although the majority of landowners were ready to sell to the King at a remunerative rate, there was a stubborn minority who refused, and, when pressed, raised the alarm that the King was attempting to claim a right over his subjects' property.

Cottington was fully aware of these objections, and used every opportunity to dissuade the King from the project. But the King was not to be dissuaded, and ultimately he resigned himself to acquiescence. Thereupon the work went forward: a beginning was made of building the wall before the reluctant landlords had yet agreed to part with their estates: and the murmurs of the people grew audible. Laud became alarmed at this and approached Cottington to suggest that they dissuade the King from so impolitic a design; but Cottington, who knew that dissuasion was useless, only saw in the Archbishop's suggestion the material for a joke at his expense. He shook his head gravely and said that he saw no objection to the enclosure, adding that hunting was excellent exercise, and necessary for the King's health, upon which all other considerations must wait. Full of righteous indignation, Laud retorted that Cottington was undermining the throne of his master and sowing dissension between Crown and people, and that he would himself let the King know how he was being deceived and ruined by unfaithful ministers. Cottington, still with the greatest composure, defended the project, and assured Laud that to oppose the King's exercise was to oppose his health, and might well be construed as high treason. Laud redoubled his recriminations and went off to the King, to whom he denounced Cottington as a pernicious minister who was encouraging him in projects dangerous to his throne. But after a warm attack the Archbishop suddenly found the wind taken from his sails by the King's calm admission that in fact Cottington had been opposed to the scheme from the start, and had consistently but vainly attempted to dissuade him from it. Humbled and ridiculous, Laud went away full of resentment against the irresponsible colleague whose bland and smiling face he would so soon have to see again at the Council Table and at the meetings of the Commission upon which they were expected to collaborate.[1]

Another and more serious difference between the chief commissioners was caused by the competition between two rival companies of soap-boilers. In this matter no question of principle was involved. It was merely a question of price and favour. The original chartered company of soap-boilers had been established in 1632 through the favour of Portland, of whose Roman Catholic friends it chiefly consisted, and who had received £2000 for himself as a rake-off. In return for a duty of £4 to the Treasury for every ton of soap sold, the company was allowed to test the quality of all independently manufactured soap, to pronounce upon its value, and, if it considered it unsatisfactory, to prohibit its sale. Such supervision by their rivals was not relished by the independent manufacturers, and when a group of them refused to submit to the test, and were faced with a prosecution in the Star Chamber in consequence, a lively controversy began. The Star Chamber prosecution was dropped, and instead an impartial tribunal, consisting of the Lord Mayor of London, the Lieutenant of the Tower, and other dignitaries, was set up to decide the respective merits of the two brands of soap. Before this tribunal two washerwomen, one using company's soap, the other independent soap, washed for all they were worth, and, when they had finished, showed their results to the judges. The judges declared in favour of the company, and their verdict was supported by a testimonial in its favour signed by over eighty persons, including peeresses and laundresses. The Privy Council then circularised the Justices of the Peace, advertising the excellence of the company's soap, and recommending its use to all.

The soap company profited little by all this official recognition. It was obvious that the Council was really more interested in the duty, which was bringing £20,000 a year into the Treasury, than

[1] Clarendon, *History of the Rebellion*, i. 208 ff.; *Cal. Ven.* xxiii. 436 (Aug. 6th/16th, 1635).

in the cleansing properties of the manufacture. In September 1634 there were Soap Riots in London, and the useful circumstance that the officially recognised company consisted largely of Portland's Roman Catholic friends enabled the advocates of independent soap to employ the stirring slogan of "No Popery!" in defence of their product. Soon afterwards the death of Portland occurred, and hope burgeoned anew in the breasts of the independent manufacturers. This time they did not attempt to raise an outcry against monopolies or cloud the commercial issue by the invocation of religious principles. They applied quietly to the Commissioners of the Treasury, and offered to double the duty, provided that the monopoly which Portland had secured for their rivals was now transferred to them.

Laud rose at once to the offer. He had no interest in soap, but he was determined to avail himself of every means of bringing money into the Treasury, and thereby establishing the independence of the Crown. Besides, the old company was a creation of Portland, whom he hated, and who had made personal profit out of its monopoly. It therefore forfeited all claim to favourable consideration from him except as a financial expedient: and since, as a financial expedient, the independent manufacturers promised to be more profitable, it was folly, in his eyes, not to accept their terms. "A greasy business it is", he wrote to Wentworth, "but *lucrum ex re qualibet*."[1] Such was the limit of his interest or principles in the matter. Cottington, however, took a different view. The mantle of Portland had fallen upon him, and the opposition of Laud confirmed him in his position as Portland's representative. He therefore supported Portland's company. And he urged, as a matter of principle, that, if the testimonials given by the government were to be regarded as anything other than ludicrous hypocrisy, an accredited company should not be deprived of its charter merely because another company, whose produce had been declared inferior, offered a higher bribe to the government. Laud, however, for all his hatred of bribery among persons, could not appreciate the immorality of a government receiving bribes: and Cottington's opposition in this matter merely convinced him still further of his deliberate malice.

[1] Laud, *Works*, vii. 105. Cf. *ibid.* 114: "And though the commodity stink excellently, yet *dulcis odor lucri*, etc."

Nevertheless, in this tragi-comedy, the unkindest cut of all was not the opposition of Cottington, which was only to be expected, but the defection of Windebank, who joined forces with him to oppose his benefactor. With no other qualifications for the office than the training of a Civil Servant and the friendship of Laud, Windebank had been raised to high office by Laud's means to serve Laud's ends: and now, yielding to the persuasions of the Devil and the tempting offers of Lady Mora, he deserted Laud and went with Cottington. In fact, Windebank's association with Cottington's policy had begun earlier, and the soap affair was merely an incident in it, for in May 1634 Laud wrote to Wentworth that "your Spaniard, and the gravity which he learnt there while he went to buy pigeons, hath tempted my old friend the Secretary from me, and he is become his man";[1] but the soap business brought the defection out in high relief at a time when Laud most needed allies, and made it especially conspicuous because, in the end, Cottington and Windebank carried the day, and the Company's charter was confirmed, although the duty which was paid to the Treasury was raised. To Laud it was inconceivable that a politician might differ from him on grounds of policy: it could only be devilish malice and base treachery. Windebank was henceforward included with Cottington under the name of Lady Mora, and Cottington was now not only a dilettante, a Spaniard, a humorist, and a rival, but a seducer. "You shall not need to bid me not trust Cottington", Laud wrote to Wentworth, "for I assure you the business of the soap hath washed off all that from me."[2] Windebank, he complained, though in private he behaved as usual, in public now always went with Cottington. That he should behave as usual in private after such treachery was of course only an additional insult, and Laud was particularly indignant that neither Cottington nor Windebank was sufficiently conscious of their meanness, or seemed at all ashamed of it. "And a pretty thing it is", he wrote, "both of them carry it towards me as if neither of them had done me wrong!"[3] A year later Windebank sought a reconciliation with the Archbishop through Juxon: but it was in vain. That friendship was over for ever.

Another case which illustrated the divergence between Laud

[1] Laud, *Works*, vi. 372. [2] *Ibid.* vii. 163. [3] *Idid.* vii. 209.

and Cottington occurred in November 1635, when the case of Pell *v.* Bagg came before the Star Chamber. Sir Anthony Pell, keeper of the King's hawks, was owed some £6000 by the Crown, but had been quite unable to obtain this sum from the late Lord Treasurer. In his difficulties he met a certain Sir James Bagg, who offered, through his intimacy with Portland, to recover the debt, provided that Pell supplied a bribe of £500 wherewith to attract the Lord Treasurer's attention. For the Lord Treasurer, said Bagg, was quite inaccessible except through such a preliminary gratuity, — in fact, Bagg himself claimed to have laid many thousands of pounds on Portland's table or under his bed for such purposes. Pell, who was in financial straits, borrowed the £500 and handed it over to Bagg: but next year Bagg reported that the Lord Treasurer had raised the price of his ear and demanded another £2000. So the unfortunate Pell borrowed another £2000 at interest, and gave it too to Bagg. Still he could not recover his debt: and ultimately, upon Portland's death, finding that he had merely thrown good money after bad, he sued Bagg in the Star Chamber for gross deceit and cozenage, and slander of the late Lord Treasurer. Bagg contended that he had paid the money to Portland, and was absolved from further responsibility in the matter.

This was a case particularly revolting to Laud, intent as he was to suppress corruption, and it was an unpleasant sidelight on the nature of the Court in which he was attempting to introduce these reforms. The Queen herself came to Whitehall, and watched the proceedings of the court from a window, in the hope of influencing the verdict in Bagg's favour. Laud, and those who, with him, voted against Bagg, contended that, even if Bagg had handed over the money to Portland, he was still guilty as a broker of bribery: and he was supported by the two Chief Justices, Finch and Bramston, and the Lord Keeper Coventry. On the other side were Cottington, Windebank, and others. When votes were counted, it was shown that each party had nine votes, and the sentence was finally given against Bagg by the casting vote of the Lord Keeper.

The defection of Windebank had already taken place, and his alliance with Cottington was to be taken for granted. So was Cottington's hostility to himself. But it must have been a heavy blow to Laud to see the court evenly divided on such a case, and to hear from Privy Councillors arguments which assumed that political society was necessarily built upon a foundation of jobbing and corruption ; and it must have been a surprise to him to find himself in agreement at last with the sentiments of the judges. " For the public ", said Lord Chief Justice Finch, " there is mothing more dangerous, or of less comfort to the commonwealth, than when there shall be panders and brokers about judges, for the administration of justice " ; and Laud was also less concerned with the case between Pell and Bagg than with the social consequences of such practices. " I will not look upon Pell, but the public ", he said : and he pointed out that if the relatives or dependants of ministers of State even appeared to be corrupt, the administration was necessarily suspected and discredited. When he turned from general principles to the immediate case, he merely quoted Bagg's letters to Pell, which ended, " James Bagg, your most real friend ", or, " your business will be better done if you leave it to your friend James Bagg ". " He was a most base fellow ", said Laud, " to say ' your most real friend ' and to serve Sir Anthony as he did. I have now done with that bottomless Bagg, and my censure " ; and he proceeded to suggest a huge fine, loss of office, and imprisonment during the King's pleasure. The King, however, refused to punish Bagg at all.

If the allotment of the office of Lord Treasurer was too difficult for solution on Portland's death, when these violent animosities between the parties of Lady Mora and Thorough were submerged, it was even more difficult when the Commission had run for a year and had made them evident. Manifestly the Commission could only be a temporary expedient ; and, concurrently with the wrangles which resulted from it, the problem of its ultimate successor exercised the minds of politicians and observers.

From the beginning Cottington was favourite, for he was so obviously better equipped for the post. But there were others besides Laud and Wentworth who opposed him. The Queen of Bohemia and the Protestant party generally had no desire to see a pro-Spanish minister engrossing the great offices of state in England. " God keep it from Cottington ", she wrote to Sir Thomas Roe in April 1635, " who has places enough already ! " [1]

[1] *S.P. Dom. Car. I.* 286, no. 2. Cottington had recently succeeded Sir Robert Naunton as Master of the Wards.

The difficulty was to find an alternative to Cottington. At first Wentworth himself was proposed and was widely favoured: but he could not be spared from Ireland, and he made it clear that he did not wish for the office.[1] Laud was already overburdened with political offices, as even his supporters realised,—"The Archbishop's ability and integrity both make him capable of as much employment as may be for his honour", wrote one of them, on hearing of Portland's death; "but to manage all can be no more than a glorious burden"[2]; and anyway, as the Commission showed, he lacked the necessary experience. Cottington, on the other hand, was strong in the King's favour, which was increased by the affair of Richmond New Park: and in August the Venetian ambassador, reporting that the quarrels between the six Commissioners had now become so acute that the King could no longer postpone his decision, added that that decision could only be for Cottington.[3] In every letter to Wentworth, Laud bemoaned the certainty of Cottington's appointment: but Cottington himself was less certain. He protested that the King would as soon make Wentworth Archbishop of Canterbury as himself Lord Treasurer.[4] Laud and Wentworth, he said, were the only candidates in the running: and he begged the Lord Deputy, with whom at least he had no personal differences, to "come and take the white staff, which will be a great help".[5] The knowledge that Wentworth was coming to England next year made many people think that he was coming to solve the dilemma by taking the post. Only at the very last moment did the Venetian ambassador report a rumour that the Bishop of London might be appointed Lord Treasurer; but he added that the rumour did not disturb Cottington.[6]

The rumour proved correct. After Christmas Cottington had been laid up by a bad attack of gout, and during this time Laud had increased his influence with the King, spending several hours a day in his presence, unembarrassed by his rival.[7] It was no doubt during this period of lucky ascendancy that he was able

[1] *Strafford Letters*, i. 420.

[2] Matthew Nicholas to Edward Nicholas, *S.P. Dom. Car. I.* 285, no. 11.

[3] *Cal. Ven.* xxiii. 436.

[4] *Strafford Letters*, i. 449.

[5] *Ibid.* i. 439.

[6] *Cal. Ven.* xxiii. 527.

[7] "Mi vien detto che adesso che stà male il Cotintone, il Cantuariense si vale dell' occasione, e va ogni giorno al Rè e tratta seco per molte hore" (Panzani's report, Jan. 23rd, 1636, in Add. MS. 15389, p. 127).

to persuade his master to cut the Gordian knot by appointing a dependable outsider; and, a week after the Venetian ambassador had reported the rumour, the King nominated Juxon as Lord Treasurer.

Surprise and indignation everywhere greeted the appointment.[1] The Church, it was said, had become "a gulf ready to swallow all the great offices". Complaints were heard "that the most conspicuous offices and the greatest authority in the royal Council are falling by degrees into the hands of ecclesiastics, to the prejudice of the nobility and governing houses".[2] "The clergy are so high here since the joining of the white sleeves with the white staff", wrote one news-writer, "that there is much talk of having a Secretary a Bishop, Dr. Wren, Bishop of Norwich: and a Chancellor of the Exchequer, Dr. Bancroft, Bishop of Oxford. But this comes only from the young fry of the clergy. But it is observed they swarm mightily about the court."[3] Laud did not conceal his triumph. "No churchman had it since Henry VII's time",[4] he wrote in his diary. "I pray God bless him to carry it so that the Church may have honour and the King and State contentment by it. And now if the Church will not hold up themselves under God, I can do no more."[5]

Laud was of course accused of seeking to establish ecclesiastical control over secular government: but it is obvious that his real desire was only to keep the Treasury out of the hands of Cottington. Cottington, he was convinced, would merely continue the policy of Portland. He would be dilatory and corrupt; and besides, during their uneasy partnership on the Commission, they had become bitter enemies. Unfortunately, there was no one whom Laud could support as a rival to Cottington among the existing politicians, for it was one of the weaknesses of the policy of Thorough that no one except Laud and Wentworth believed

[1] For the surprise, cf. Garrarde's letter to Wentworth, March 15th, 1636: "For my part I did believe, and do, that your Lordship or my Lord Cottington would have done the business of that place best, for the good of His Majesty and this kingdom; and many, I assure myself, concurred in that opinion. But we were all deceived in the expectation of the man" (*Strafford Letters*, i. 523. Cf. Howell to Garrarde, *ibid.* 522). Nevertheless, Garrarde had himself mentioned Juxon as a reported candidate, even before Portland's death (*ibid.* 388), although he seems later to have dropped out of the running until his actual appointment.

[2] *Cal. Ven.* xxiii. 531.

[3] Garrarde to Strafford, *Strafford Letters*, ii. 2.

[4] Presumably he meant Henry VI, in whose time William Grey, Bishop of Ely, was made Lord Treasurer.

[5] Laud, *Works*, iii. 226.

in it sufficiently strongly to be willing to practice it. In these circumstances, all that Laud could do was to keep the Treasury from Cottington as he had kept the Secretariat of State from him, by filling it with a dependable nonentity. Windebank had proved unsatisfactory : but he hoped that Juxon would be more reliable ; and no doubt he reflected that a clerical Lord Treasurer would be more likely than Portland to spare funds for the work of the Church.[1] At any rate he could be sure of Juxon's integrity. For whereas Portland had used the Treasury as a means of raising up a great family, and enriching himself and his dependants, Juxon was unmarried and scrupulously honest. " No hands ", says Fuller, " having so much money passing through them, had their fingers less soiled therewith." The Venetian ambassador, after an interview with him, reported that " he is certainly a man of integrity, not fanatical for any party : which is a valuable characteristic, unusual in anyone nowadays ". " He is devoted to hunting ", wrote the papal agent Panzani, ". . . and is completely dependent on the Archbishop. . . . He is little versed in politics, and professes no other ambition than the King's advantage, and to administer the Treasury with clean hands, as he told the King on accepting office. He is very moderate in his views, and far removed from any kind of pride or ambition."[2] The appointment certainly caused universal surprise and widespread indignation : but rarely has there been such unanimity on the character of one suddenly elevated to so invidious a position. " He was much delighted with hunting ", says Whitelocke, " and kept a pack of good hounds, and had them so well ordered and hunted, and chiefly by his own skill and direction, that they exceeded all other hounds in England for the pleasure and orderly hunting of them. He was a person of great parts and temper, and had as much command of his temper as of his hounds. He was full of ingenuity and meekness, not apt to give offence to any, and willing to do good to all."[3] To him, " in true admiration of his Christian simplicity and contempt of earthly power ", Sir Henry Wotton thought it appropriate to bequeath a picture

[1] Cf. Portland's unwillingness to pay the debts owed to Heriot's hospital in Edinburgh (*infra*, p. 340).

[2] Quoted in Albion, *op. cit.* p. 412. " Moderate " in Panzani's language means favourably disposed towards Roman doctrine. Cf. his remarks on Laud (*ibid.*) : " è d' animo moderato e non alieno dalla Religione Cattolica ", and on Goodman (quoted above, p. 175 n.).

[3] *Memorials*, i. 24.

of Heraclitus bewailing and Democritus laughing at the world: and after the meeting of the Long Parliament, when the whole episcopal order was attacked and threatened, Juxon alone, who alone, except Laud, had combined high political office with a great diocese, was exempted, particularly and by name, from the general condemnation. "Even now", said Lord Falkland in his tirade against the episcopate, "in the greatest defection of that order, there are yet some who have conduced in nothing to our late innovations but in their silence: some who, in unexpected place and power, have expressed an equal moderation and humility, being neither ambitious before, nor proud after, either the crozier's staff or the white staff." Even Prynne himself, in the midst of his scurrilous onslaught upon every bishop in turn, when he came to the name of Juxon, stayed for a moment the tide of his vituperation and wrote "his disposition and carriage as a man have been amiable and commendable".[1]

If Laud, in advancing Juxon, was impelled by the same motives which had inspired the elevation of Windebank, he certainly made a happier choice. Juxon never fell into the sin of Windebank. He never allied himself with Lady Mora against Thorough;[2] and in the matter of the soap company he helped to secure the final victory for Laud. For in the year after his appointment the company was bought out and the independent manufacturers, incorporated in a company just as exclusive, reigned in their stead, paying to the government which protected them a duty of £8 per ton of soap sold. In 1640, when Windebank fled to France, Juxon had no need of such an escape. Unmolested through the Civil Wars, he remained in England, attended King Charles on the scaffold, and then retired to his house at Little Compton in Warwickshire to hunt his hounds, in which alone he was enthusiastic. On one occasion, indeed, there was a scandal,— when his hounds followed a fast scent through Chipping Norton churchyard and scattered a meeting of devout Puritans, assembled there to "seek the Lord". The outraged votaries appealed to the Lord Protector: but Cromwell dismissed their complaints

[1] *The Antipathy of the English lordly Prelacy both to Regal Monarchy and Civil Unity* (1641), p. 240.

[2] In the case of Bagg, however, Juxon had voted with Cottington and Windebank against Laud and the judges (Rushworth, ii. 303). So had Neile.

as frivolous, declaring that so long as the bishop did not disturb his government he was free to enjoy his hunting.[1] So Juxon remained at Little Compton, performing Anglican services at Chastleton Manor, and declining all rewards which were offered for his good works, except once, when he found himself unable to refuse the gift of a good hound. On the Restoration, he again succeeded Laud, this time as Archbishop of Canterbury. A man who lived in such prominent positions in Church and State, and yet remained unassailed and unassailable through the personal government of Charles I, the rule of the Long Parliament, the Civil Wars, the Commonwealth, the Protectorate, and the Restoration, deserves to be remembered as a unique instance; and certainly we cannot suspect Laud of any sinister designs when he prevented the Treasury from falling into the hands of Cottington by the elevation of so unexceptionable a competitor.

With the appointment of Juxon, Laud could feel that his position in the administration was at last secure. The defection of Windebank had been counterbalanced, and his ascendancy with the King had been proved to be as strong as ever. As far as authority went, his position seemed impregnable. And at the same time the same process had been at work, enhancing the political and ecclesiastical authority of the Archbishop in the other kingdoms and dependencies of the British Crown.

[1] W. Marah, *Memorials of Archbishop Juxon*, p. 77.

CHAPTER SEVEN

THE CHURCH ABROAD

" For your divinity you are very right : it was John of Constantinople that would have been Universal Bishop ; but I never heard till now that he made choice of an Irishman to be his Vicar-General."—LAUD TO WENTWORTH, Dec. 2nd, 1633.

" I was fain to write nine letters yesterday into Scotland. I think you have a plot to see whether I will be *universalis episcopus* ".—LAUD TO WENTWORTH, July 3rd, 1634.

THE advocates of " pure religion " have made two serious objections to Laud's policy. They have objected to the Erastian methods which he used, and to his indifference to the fortunes of the faith in other countries. But if we understand Laud's aims aright we see that he was not primarily interested in " pure religion ", but in the practical application of a social policy to given conditions which seemed to him to require it. And while the missionaries of an universal gospel may ignore political frontiers, and the champions of a purely spiritual faith may reject political methods, the practical man, whose faith is the reflection of a political and social system, will naturally confine his activity within the limits of his authority, and employ whatever methods seem to promise success. These limitations Laud accepted : but within them he exerted his authority to the full. As a minister of the English government he prescribed remedies for all the subjects of his master, and sought, by the exercise of his authority, to enforce them. Outside the dominions of Charles I he had no interest, — he was a politician, not a missionary. Where Louis XIII or Philip IV or the Emperor ruled, Urban might be Pope : and in the principalities of Germany, for all he cared, the spirits of Luther and Calvin might linger on, so long as they stayed there. But inside those dominions, wherever Charles I was King, Laud was determined to act as Archbishop ; and in this chapter we shall examine his efforts to spread his authority in Scotland and Ireland, and over the English subjects resident as merchants or colonists abroad.

The rule was simple. Unfortunately its application was much harder. Laud's acquaintance with the world was not wide : his was not a mind that could appreciate the advantages, or the innocence, of diversity : and he had no more sympathy with local loyalties than with individual appetites. He was resolved that over all the provinces of his master a single rule should prevail : and yet how diverse were those provinces, how tenacious of their particular liberties, he could not understand. With that haste which is implicit in the policy of Thorough, he set out to reduce them to uniformity without understanding the reasons which wedded them to their diversity. There was Scotland, which owed allegiance to King Charles, but pretended devotion to Knox. There was Ireland, where the English Church had been introduced without any of the safeguards of government, like a rich traveller walking unarmed into a nest of highwaymen. There were English regiments and English merchant companies exposed to all the dangers of intercourse with the irreligious Dutch. And there were colonists in the American Plantations of whom Laud knew little except that they were English and ought to be Anglican. Up to these limits he determined to extend the discipline of his Church : further than these he had no intention of going, and was not even concerned to look.

Of all these outlying provinces, Scotland alone had had the privilege of Laud's personal presence and the opportunity to instruct him in its local peculiarities. But such differences as had resulted from those two visits of 1616 and 1633 had been to Scotland, not to Laud. We have dealt with the immediate consequences of those two visits, and their ultimate results, since they were the proximate cause of Laud's fall, must be dealt with more fully later ; here it will suffice to say that the innovations then introduced continued to operate, not indeed with the marks of obvious success, but without apparent setback. The Scottish bishops, who had formerly been like the gods of Epicurus, mere spectators of the lay world beneath them, assumed their new task of regulation and inquisition with varying degrees of enthusiasm ; and deaths in the episcopal bench gave opportunities for the promotion of those who showed themselves most in sympathy with the new ideas. As in England, the clerical estate was being recreated: and in England Laud was kept informed, if not of the state of affairs in Scotland, at least of the opinions and requirements of his most ardent supporters there. Prominent among these was John Maxwell, whom he had recently elevated to the bishopric of Ross.

The character of John Maxwell, Laud's most thorough-going agent in the north, is difficult justly to appreciate, for it has been interpreted almost entirely by clergymen. A constant assertor of the divine institution of episcopacy, he passed his life at the mercy of the storms which he raised about him: and having been forced to flee for his life from the fury of the Scottish Presbyterians, and stripped and wounded and left for dead by the Irish Catholics, he ended it as Archbishop of Tuam, and was discovered dead upon his knees on the report of King Charles' failure. Such a career, if it argues sincerity in the convictions which he entertained, and fearlessness in the expression of them, does not suggest tact in their application: and Maxwell seems to have been of a proud and aspiring nature which was not softened by success. His motto, says a hostile critic, might well have been

Asperius nihil est humili dum surgit in altum:

and now, confident that the favour of the government gave him all the political support which he required, he proceeded to carry out the policy of Laud with brutal determination, outraging pious Calvinists by his ostentatious heterodoxy and proud feudatories by his arrogant usurpations.

He had first become intimate with Laud in 1629, when the two of them, as Bishop of London and an Edinburgh minister, had discussed the project of an Anglican liturgy for Scotland; and soon afterwards both Scotland and Ireland felt the influence of this new rising star. In 1631, a disgruntled Scottish Calvinist reported, he preached two sermons demonstrating episcopacy to be *juris divini et apostolici*: but "his arguments by all unprejudiced hearers were counted stark naught" [1]; and next year two immigrant Scottish ministers in the diocese of Down in Ireland, Messrs. Blair and Livingstone, found that the Edinburgh minister wielded more authority there than the Primate of Ireland. Suspended by the Bishop of Down, they had been

[1] Row, *History of the Kirk of Scotland* (Wodrow Soc., 1842), p. 354.

restored by Ussher: but Maxwell reported to the King that they were stirring up the people to unbecoming exhibitions of religious enthusiasm. It was true, one of them admits, that some of their neighbours, by the affectation of sustained panting during the sermon, simulated a peculiar intimacy with the Holy Spirit: but they themselves disclaimed any responsibility in the matter. Nevertheless, the Archbishop's indulgence was overruled, and the two ministers were again suspended.[1] The royal visit to Scotland in 1633 brought Maxwell into still greater prominence: and before the year was over he had been rewarded with the diocese of Ross.

As Laud eclipsed Abbot, and Bramhall Ussher, so Maxwell gradually ousted old Archbishop Spottiswood from the management, under Laud, of the episcopal Church in Scotland: and Spottiswood, who had neither the redeeming courage of Abbot nor the scholarship of Ussher, went, as he had always gone, with the wind, expressing just enough reluctance to salve his conscience, but not enough to imperil his position. In January 1635 the anti-clerical Lord Chancellor, the Earl of Kinnoul, died, and, as if to provide a precedent for the elevation of Juxon in England next year, Spottiswood was appointed as his successor, to the apprehension of good Presbyterians, who feared that it was but to prepare the way for Maxwell. At the same time seven of the new bishops had become Privy Councillors, and a project to restore the old abbey lands to the Church was only prevented by the Earl of Traquair, who enlarged on the loss of revenue to the Crown which would ensue. "In this kingdom", commented an English visitor early in 1635, "the clergy of late extend their authority and revenues. Archbishop of St. Andrews is Lord Chancellor of Scotland and Regent here; and I was informed by some intelligent gentlemen it is here thought and conceived that they will recover so much of that land and revenues belonging formerly to the abbeys as that they will in a short time possess themselves of a third part of the kingdom."[2] Next year, when Traquair was appointed High Treasurer, the disappointed bishops were indignant. Maxwell, it is said, "vowed that either Traquair should break his neck or he his"; he accused the new

[1] Blair, *Autobiography* (Wodrow Soc., 1848), p. 90; *Life of John Livingstone*, by himself (Edinburgh, 1848), pp. 81-3.

[2] *Travels of Sir Wm. Brereton* (Chetham Soc., 1844), p. 100.

Treasurer of being "cold in the King's service" and of managing the Treasury deceitfully; and the intervention of the King was necessary to effect a temporary reconciliation.[1]

Meanwhile the probability of more thoroughgoing measures to enforce the Anglican discipline was kept continually before the eyes of the Scots, and the wide gulf which separated Charles from his northern subjects was emphasised by the affair of Lord Balmerino. Lord Balmerino was the son of that complaisant secretary who had assumed the responsibility for James I's correspondence with the Pope, and he was one of several of the Scottish nobility who had prepared a supplication to the King against certain of the acts of the last parliament. This supplication was never presented, for the framers learnt in advance that its reception would not be cordial: but Balmerino had kept a copy of it in his library at Barnton, near Edinburgh, where it was transcribed, without his knowledge, by a friend, John Dunmure of Dundee. Dunmure's copy, in turn, was copied by a friend of the English government, Peter Hay of Naughton, and presented to Spottiswood: and thus the contents of the unpublished document reached the eyes of Charles' ministers. The result was a commission sent to Spottiswood and six others of the nobility and bishops in June 1634, empowering them to examine all who were implicated in the supplication: and since the author of the draft escaped abroad, and Lord Rothes, who had proposed its submission to the King, cleared himself satisfactorily, the government fastened upon Balmerino, who, after nine months of close confinement in Edinburgh Castle, was tried under a statute of James VI for being in possession of a libel against the administration. The case became a *cause célèbre*: demonstrations in the prisoner's favour were held in the streets and could not be prevented by the government: and when the jury considered the case, they were equally divided, and only the casting vote of Traquair pronounced Balmerino guilty. Ultimately, however, he was discharged; and it is to Laud's credit that it was chiefly through his influence that the King undertook to remit the sentence.

His intercession on behalf of Balmerino did nothing to endear Laud to the Scots, who already identified his name with other things than justice. It was not the voice of Justice, they said,

[1] Burnet, *History of his Own Times*, ii. 26.

to which the government had yielded, but the fear of trouble: nor did they trust the government any further because of its tardy dismissal of a case which had already gone too far. Their thoughts were fully occupied by the visible growth of the clerical estate, and the resurgence of that clerical authority and splendour which had not been seen since Cardinal Beaton. It was unlikely that the bishops, having been so blatantly exalted, would allow their new powers to lie unused: but their use, in view of its large consequences, must be reserved for a later chapter. Meanwhile we shall turn to a less serious subject, — the Church in Ireland.

The English Church in Ireland has always been a comic, indeed a pathetic, institution: but then the English have never been very successful in any of their Irish enterprises. Without hope, or much effort, to convert the popish inhabitants, and powerless to prevent the immigration of Scottish Presbyterians, it was an institution imported to console the English settlers; and the chief consolation which the English settlers derived from it was the knowledge that, although never rich, it could always be plucked.

For Ireland existed under the blind eye of the English government. Throughout the reign of James I there had been negligent government in England: but in Ireland there had been none. And the Irish had easily adapted themselves to such conditions. The interest which the English Crown took in its third kingdom was that which an absentee landlord takes of a distant estate left in the hands of rapacious agents. It was merely a source of revenue: and so long as the revenue was not held up by overt rebellion, the estate could be left to the agents, even if rapacious. Meanwhile, undesirables might be sent thither to bury their reputations, and pensions might be derived thence to satisfy courtiers. In such circumstances the race was to the swift and the battle to the strong, and speculators throve and prospered. The plunderer of seventeen villages was appointed a Justice of the Peace: a Lord Chief Justice and a sheriff condemned an innocent man to death to divide his lands between them: a junto of the most successful speculators engrossed the offices of State in order to perpetuate and increase their acquisitions: and the weaker parties, seeing no justice to protect them, compounded with their plunderers for such sums as they were lucky enough to get.

Among the weaker parties was the unfortunate English Church, which, for its very existence, had to depend on the same settlers who pillaged it. English bishops, who had surreptitiously leased a small parcel of Church lands to a neighbour on terms more profitable to themselves than to their sees, could fold their hands in complacency, or raise them in horror, at the sight of their Irish brethren signing away whole dioceses for a retaining fee; and country clergymen in the remoter parts of Lancashire, with livings of £4 a year, could look with pity, or condescension, on the Bishop of Aghadoe with his diocese of £2, or the Bishop of Cloyne with his five marks. The Irish speculators, after all, had done no more than imitate the English, only more successfully, because there was no one to restrain them; and the Irish Church had suffered like the English, only more severely, because there was no one to protect it. It made little difference that James I endowed it with £76,000, for the endowments soon left the Church; or that he forbade leases of more than twenty-one years, when there was no one to enforce his veto.

From the poverty of the Church the rest followed naturally. An Irish bishopric was an unremunerative exile among barbarians, unless the recipient could accumulate a dozen or so preferments at a time, and avoid residing on any of them. "I hope we shall not long stay in Ireland", wrote a Mrs. Montgomery, reporting her husband's promotion to three Irish dioceses, of which she could only remember the name of one, "but once he must needs go". On the other hand, for those who were skilful enough to imitate the methods of their plunderers, even an Irish bishopric could be made lucrative. Such was the case of Miler Magrath, the converted Franciscan friar, who for nine years held a popish bishopric and a Protestant archbishopric together. Deprived of the former by the Pope, he amassed four Anglican bishoprics and seventy other spiritual preferments, and did handsomely out of them. When the government ordered a prosecution Dr. Magrath effectually silenced it by threatening to rejoin the Roman Church, to which the Vatican hastened to promise him a cordial reception; and so he lived on unmolested, drinking away the revenues of his accumulated sees, into his hundredth year. In such conditions Church buildings were naturally ruinous, ecclesiastical discipline naturally imperceptible, clerical morality naturally non-existent. Everything which Laud most abominated in England flourished tenfold in Ireland: and conscientious English clergymen like Bedell, Bramhall, and Jeremy Taylor who set out to take possession of Irish dioceses soon discovered with horror and disillusionment the giant task which awaited them.

Laud never went to Ireland, nor acquainted himself with the full details of the spoliation and disrepute of the Irish Church. But as soon as he was established in power he made contact with the Archbishop of Armagh in order that Ireland too might feel the benefits of reform.

The Archbishop of Armagh and Primate of all Ireland was James Ussher, a man of austere Calvinism and copious scholarship, lacking indeed in missionary zeal, but painstaking in theological research. He was as harmless as Juxon, though less amiable: and though a royalist in the Civil Wars, Cromwell honoured him at his death with a State funeral. To Laud a man who was neither an administrator nor a high churchman, and who rated the Lord Deputy for allowing the production of plays in his house, could hardly be sympathetic: but as Laud ruled the English Church, and Ussher was meant to rule the Irish, some correspondence between the two was necessary, and for eighteen months, from the beginning of 1629, it was kept up. Laud disposed of Irish benefices, suggested such well-meaning but impracticable reforms as that no deaneries be held *in commendam*, urged the Primate to encourage church restoration, and in short "there was scarce anything of moment concluded on, or any considerable preferment bestowed by His Majesty in the Church of Ireland, without his advice and approbation";[1] while Ussher on his side urged Laud to purchase for Oxford University a collection of old coins available at bargain price, and sought to persuade Vossius to accept the deanery of Armagh in the interests of scholarship. In 1631 the differences between the two were made more apparent by Ussher's publication of his *History of Gottschalk*, of which Laud expressed his disapproval, at the same time ordering Ussher to suppress the Bishop of Down's work on Perseverance, as a hint that the Archbishop's own opinions were not strictly orthodox. Meanwhile Prideaux was warning Ussher that it was no good hoping to get his edition

[1] Parr, *Life of Ussher*, 1686, p. 40.

of Polycarp printed at Oxford, where such scholarship was discouraged by the new Chancellor: and Laud instructed his new Irish agent to keep an eye on the Irish press, in order to prevent the issue of such works in the future.[1]

This new agent was William Bedell, Bishop of Kilmore and Ardagh. In spite of an education at Emmanuel College, Bedell had retained a respect for the beauty of holiness, and his amiable and simple character made him generally admired. Even in the midst of one of his differences with him, Laud wrote to Wentworth asking him "to use that bishop very kindly: for either I understand nothing, or else (setting my Lord Primate aside) he is worth more than half the bishops there". For three years Bedell had been chaplain to Sir Henry Wotton in Venice, and it was on the recommendation of Wotton, Abbot, and Ussher,— none of whom could be described as high churchmen,— that he was nominated Provost of Trinity College, Dublin. Already at this time he must have been known to Laud: for when he was promoted to the bishopric of Kilmore and Ardagh, and the Fellows of Trinity College sought to maintain their right to elect his successor against the King's claim to nominate him, it was Bedell who gave them an ineffectual letter of introduction to Laud.

In his diocese Bedell's task was not easy: but he set to work conscientiously. To the disapproval of Ussher, he sought to establish friendly relations with the neighbouring popish bishop, and he encouraged the translation of the Prayer Book and the preaching of sermons in the vernacular. But he soon found himself overwhelmed with difficulties. His own chancellor, irremovable from office, devastated his diocese so thoroughly that the inhabitants called him Puck, because "they fear him like the Fiend of Hell", and a thousand of them fled from the country in a year. The Roman Catholics around him also remained hostile: and Bedell was attacked by his co-religionists on both sides for his toleration. Though Laud continued to respect Bedell for his work in his own diocese, he soon found that he could not rely on him to regulate the whole Church of Ireland: and, in fact, in 1632 Bedell found even two dioceses too much for himself to manage, and resigned that of Ardagh. So Laud had to look elsewhere for an agent,— one who would be not a scholar

[1] Heylin, p. 204.

only like Ussher, nor a saint like Bedell, but an administrator. He did not have to look far. In 1633 Wentworth succeeded the ineffectual Falkland as Lord Deputy of Ireland, and brought with him as his chaplain John Bramhall.

Two more valuable confederates Laud could not have wished to discover. Indeed, they were more than confederates. They took the work out of Laud's hands, and merely left him to applaud the *fait accompli*. Wentworth determined at once that what Ireland needed was government : and he set out to undo the work of the last forty years, when no government had been, — to restore to the Church and the Crown and the small landowners what had been filched from all alike by the great landlords and speculators, and to preserve what he had recovered by the establishment of the vigorous rule of law. So he could attain this object, he was unscrupulous as to the means by which it was attained. His adversaries, after all, had not been more scrupulous in the pursuit of their less unselfish ends. They had extorted from the King a charter, " the Graces ", by which sixty years of tenure was recognised as legal possession. Wentworth repudiated the Graces as shamelessly as they had been extorted. In England Laud was relying on the methods of bureaucracy to oppose the encroachments of individuals upon the rights and patrimony of the Church. He sat at Lambeth or Whitehall, sending out orders or officers, avoiding personal contact ; and when, in the last resort, his victims faced him in the Star Chamber or High Commission, they found not an impressive and commanding figure, but a little rude old man. Wentworth's methods were far more splendid than these. He was not a bureaucrat, but a born tyrant, inspiring both fear and love. His argument was the argument of force, and he was afraid of no force that could be opposed to his. Conscious that he was acting for the ends of justice, he dispensed imperiously with the forms of law, intimidating intimidators and bullying bullies. He went out of his way to overbear his opponents by his commanding presence. He did not need to worm himself into a position of influence by intrigue as Laud had done : he openly overthrew the junto which thought to rule him, one by one, and installed in their places trusted supporters of his own, — Mainwaring, Wandesford, Radcliffe. While Laud trembled at the prospect of a parliament, Wentworth delighted in it. He summoned it,

THOMAS WENTWORTH, 1ST EARL OF STRAFFORD

browbeat it, managed it, and used it to endorse his own programme. Laud sent instructions, orders, reprimands to his disobedient bishops, or employed agents to report upon them, and still they contrived to evade his demands. Like the headmaster who boasted that he had flogged the entire episcopal bench, Wentworth never enjoyed himself so much as when he was, in his own expression, "trouncing a bishop or two in the Castle Chamber"; and soon the Irish bishops dreaded the very thought of disobedience. It was not a system productive of lasting success, — but then neither was Laud's.

In his dealings with the Irish Church Wentworth was ably assisted by his chaplain, Bramhall. Bramhall had been promoted in the English Church through Wentworth's friend, Christopher Wandesford, and Archbishop Neile, and had come into contact with Wentworth as subdean of Ripon and a prebendary of York Minster while Wentworth was President of the Council of the North. On Wandesford's suggestion, he followed Wentworth to Ireland, where he soon became Bishop of Derry, and, at Laud's insistence, was compelled to give up his English prebend.[1] He was a hard and bigoted character, not unlike Laud, of mean presence and sharp tongue: but he was a tireless administrator of relentless efficiency, far better qualified to carry out Laud's policy in a backward country than Ussher or Bedell. It was not for nothing that Cromwell called him "the Irish Canterbury", and the Irish Presbyterians hated him as "Bishop Bramble".

Soon after his arrival Bramhall wrote a melancholy letter to Laud describing the decayed state of the Church in Ireland. "It is hard to say whether the churches be more ruinous and sordid or the people irreverent", he said: and he described one church converted into the Lord Deputy's stable, another a nobleman's dwelling-house, a third a tennis-court, kept by the vicar. Christ Church, the principal church in Ireland, fulfilled the functions of a place of worship and a public-house at the same time. The Earl of Cork, the most successful speculator in Ireland, had built

[1] Vesey, in his life of Bramhall, says that, before going to Ireland, Bramhall "resigned all his Church preferments in England"; but this is untrue, for in May 1634 Laud wrote to Wentworth, "What Dr. Bramhall holds in England he must leave. The bishopric [of Derry] being good needs no *commendam*. If it did, it must be helped there. For I foresee marvellous great inconveniences, and very little less than mischief, if a way be given to bishops there to hold *commendams* here" (*Works*, vi. 376).

a family tomb in the place where the altar should be in St. Patrick's. Neither the canons nor the articles of the English Church were accepted, which Bramhall regarded as a great inconvenience. Poverty and ignorance were the chief distinction of the lower clergy, pluralism and non-residence of the upper. Compositions with the invaders of Church property were regular, and incumbents received a wage of one-tenth of their rents as a reward for handing nine-tenths over to their patrons. "The Earl of Cork holds the whole bishopric of Lismore at the rent of forty shillings or five marks by the year." So the monotonous catalogue of abuses continues, only mitigated by one consolation: "It is some comfort", concludes Bramhall, "to see the Romish ecclesiastics cannot laugh at us, who come behind none in point of disunion and scandal".[1]

The methods by which this state of affairs was partially and temporarily remedied belongs to the history of Wentworth, not of Laud: and that history has been well and fully described elsewhere.[2] Laud merely protected Wentworth's rear when his victims appealed for protection to the Queen or Lady Mora, while Wentworth and Bramhall went ahead, restoring churches, establishing a court of High Commission, recovering alienations, harrying bishops. Wentworth secured Laud's appointment as Chancellor of Dublin University. Laud said that he would prefer Wentworth to take the position himself, but if he must have it, he must have a commission under the Great Seal to alter the statutes at will.[3] Within a month he had the commission, and within three years Dublin University had new statutes. Otherwise he left Wentworth a free hand, knowing that he could be trusted and was far better acquainted with the conditions in Ireland than he himself could be. It was no use Laud's writing to suggest that no clergyman should hold more than two benefices. Laud knew nothing about Ireland, and Wentworth replied that it took six Irish benefices to find a minister clothes. It was without any reference to Laud that Wentworth forced the Irish Convocation to accept the English Thirty-Nine Articles, thus implicitly repealing the Calvinist Irish Articles of 1613, and promoted the dissentient Dean of Limerick to the worst diocese in Ireland in

[1] *Works of John Bramhall* (ed. 1842), vol. i. pp. lxxix-lxxxii.

[2] *Vide* Lady Burghclere, *Strafford*, 1931; C. V. Wedgwood, *Strafford*, 1935.

[3] Laud, *Works*, vi. 352.

revenge. Afterwards he reported the act to Laud, and undertook to make the next Convocation revert to the old Calvinist articles if Laud disapproved of the change : but there was no danger of Laud's disapproval. In spite of the protestations of Ussher that it was an ornament to the church, and far better than the partition of boards and lime which it had replaced, Wentworth compelled Lord Cork to demolish his family tomb in St. Patrick's : for boards and lime, in Laud's eyes, were better than sacrilege. In spite of his attempt to evade restitution by conferring it upon his son, who had married Wentworth's niece, Wentworth made Cork disgorge the college of Youghal, together with a large fine: while Laud merely had to prevent the King from listening to the appeals of Cork's friends at Court.

Those who had compounded with the invader, whether for profit or through weakness, received no mercy. The best way to restore the credit of the Church, Wentworth believed, was to chastise the bishops. A former Bishop of Killaloe had alienated 99 per cent of the endowments of his see, and his successor, finding it hard to keep much state on the remaining 1 per cent, appealed successfully to the Deputy. But the present bishop merely required restitution in order that he might himself alienate : and when Wentworth found that he had accepted a composition of £26 for lands worth £500 leased to one Sir Daniel O'Brien, he sent for him, told him roundly that he had betrayed his bishopric and " deserved to have his rochet pulled over his ears and to be turned to a stipend of four nobles a year : and so warmed his old sides as I made him break the agreement, crave pardon, and promise to follow the cause with all diligence ". " You did very nobly to harrow him as you did ", Laud replied with satisfaction, when he heard of this treatment.[1] The unfortunate old bishop was in his ninety-second year : but he lived to be a hundred and four in spite of his salutary harrowing.[2] Bishop Michael Boyle of Waterford, and Bishop Richard Boyle of Cork, were both made to tremble when the inquisition into the doings of their great cousin, the Earl of Cork, brought their own sins to light. The Archbishop of Cashell vainly pleaded sciatica to avoid revealing the sixteen vicarages which he had

[1] *Strafford Letters*, i. 172 ; Laud, *Works*, vii. 58.

[2] Laud calls him Bishop of Killala, but Killaloe is evidently meant, as he afterwards refers to him by the name of Jones, and Lewis Jones was Bishop of Killaloe, not Killala.

swallowed; "I will roundly prepare him for a purge so soon as I see him", wrote the Lord Deputy.[1] With every letter Wentworth reported some new and unscrupulous exercise of power in the interest of the Church. When a certain Loftus left an annuity of £80 to the Catholic bishopric of Limerick, Wentworth unhesitatingly declared that the Anglican bishop was the Catholic bishop, and diverted the legacy to him. "You have excellently stretched the donor's meaning into the right sense", exclaimed Laud gleefully, and added that he had shown the letter to the King, who had laughed heartily.[2] Bramhall, in the meantime, was assiduous in the task of recovering impropriations for the Church: and in this he was certainly more successful than Laud in England, for in four years he is said to have regained thirty or forty thousand pounds a year, and in 1638 he reported that, in addition, he had recovered lands worth between fourteen and fifteen thousand pounds yearly from the encroachers.[3] In 1634 Laud also prevailed on the King, in spite of the dissuasions of the Queen and her Treasurer, to hand over to the Church all the Irish impropriations in the gift of the Crown, retaining only an annual rent. It was a work of construction which might be held to counterbalance the overthrow of the feoffees for impropriations in England: but, as Fuller remarks, "those conceived to have done hurt at home will hardly make reparations with other good deeds at distance".[4]

Thus in Ireland the Church raised her head again, — or at least Wentworth held it up for a space, — and all that Laud needed to do was to admire the results of authority enforced. But Ireland was a special case, — a backward country so unused to law that it was prepared for tyranny. With the English settlers in the Netherlands the problem was far different, and we must revert from the bold assertion of power to the busy operations of intrigue.

The ties which bound England and Holland together in the sixteenth and seventeenth centuries were many and intimate. Together they had opened a breach in the world empire of Spain, in whose pretended preserves they had conspired to poach;

[1] *Strafford Letters*, ii. 42.
[2] *Ibid.* i. 171; Laud, *Works*, vii. 58.
[3] Lambeth MS. 943, p. 535.
[4] *Church History*, vi. 104.

and an intimacy dictated by geography and commerce was increased by rivalry. Every political event in the Netherlands had its repercussions in England, and English affairs were eagerly followed in the Netherlands. After the truce between the States-General and Spain in 1609 the English ambassador continued to sit on the Dutch Council of State, and Brill and Flushing remained in English hands as a pledge for the repayment of war debts. The controversy between Arminius and Gomar invited the attention of King James, and English representatives were sent to the Synod of Dordt. Continual disputes over fishing rights and the cloth trade entailed continual embassies, one of which brought Grotius to England. English merchants had their headquarters in Dutch towns, and Dutch engineers built docks and drained fens in England. When the Thirty Years' War broke out, the daughter of James I and her family, driven from Bohemia and the Palatinate, established a miniature Court at the Hague, and English and Scots volunteers, with the permission of the government, were recruited for the service of the States-General. Four English and two Scots regiments were stationed in the Netherlands: and it was they who made the heroic defence of Bergen-op-Zoom against the forces of Spinola.

It was therefore singularly unfortunate, in the eyes of the English government, that these intimate neighbours both professed Calvinism and tolerated anything. There was no guarantee that English merchants and soldiers might not become tainted with the most unwholesome doctrines: and as the regiments employed on the Continent were the only English forces who obtained any practice in the art of warfare, it was most undesirable that they should imbibe the wrong opinions. In fact, when war did break out in England it was the trained soldiers who had served the Protestant cause under Leslie and Gustavus Adolphus who first defeated the orthodox armies of King Charles. Besides, merchants and soldiers had souls, and therefore required clergy. If they tolerated Puritanism among themselves, they would attract from England all the ministers whom Laud was seeking to convert: with ministers would go parishioners, until the eastern counties were depopulated: and depopulation by emigration was as unwelcome to the English government as depopulation by enclosure. The toleration practised by the Dutch had other unfortunate consequences. What availed it that Laud was establishing a rigorous censorship of books in England if English libels merely transferred their place of origin from London to Amsterdam ? With the two countries so closely connected, what was spoken on one side of the Channel was soon heard on the other. The works of Prynne, the speeches of Laud, the proceedings of Parliament were quickly translated into Dutch. The prophecies of Lady Eleanor Davies issued simultaneously from England and Holland. And, at a more exalted level, Grotius and Selden, like Milton and Salmasius, wrote in Latin that all Europe might give ear to their controversies.

Such conditions cried aloud for intervention, and Laud was prepared to intervene, — not, of course, in the internal affairs of Holland, which would be intolerable, but in the economy of the English subjects resident there, which would be perfectly legitimate, if it were practicable.

Certainly it would not be easy, for Puritanism in the English churches of Holland was hydra-headed and many-tongued. There was the Company of the Merchant Adventurers at Delft, who maintained their own preachers. Each of the four English regiments had its chaplain. There were garrisons in twelve Dutch towns, and each garrison employed a minister. And there were English congregations in Amsterdam, Rotterdam, Flushing, Middelburg, Leyden, Arnhem, and the Hague. Some of these ministers were orthodox enough, — Stephen Goffe, for instance, the chaplain to Lord Vere of Tilbury's regiment, a communicative and pragmatical person who upheld the pure doctrine of Canterbury among the heathen Nonconformists, and had dared to use the Prayer Book in 1632. The Dutch Council of State had protested, but it had been snubbed by Sir William Boswell, the English ambassador at the Hague. With the rise of Laudianism, Goffe was to acquire some fame and notoriety as the Archbishop's agent, before the collapse of the English Church led him to find a more durable comfort in the bosom of Rome. At Wesel, too, the English services were conducted by an orthodox young Dutchman called Grimm, who gained a reputation for erudition by proving the existence of Pope Joan.[1] But these were solitary apostles : and among their colleagues were to be found some of the most notorious Puritans of the time. The ministers in the towns were particularly

[1] *Boswell Papers*, Add. MS. 6394, p. 134.

independent of the English government, for they received their allowances from the States-General. At Rotterdam the Independent gospel was preached in a converted playhouse by the notorious Hugh Peters, afterwards Cromwell's chaplain. In Amsterdam sat an officious Presbyterian, John Paget, expelled from his Cheshire ministry nearly thirty years before. Goodyer, who officiated in Leyden, was also a distinguished Presbyterian. And for ten years the chair of theology at Franeker was occupied by an English Puritan, — Dr. William Ames, known to the learned world as Amesius, the author of works against ceremonies and in defence of the individual conscience, whom the Bishop of London had silenced in 1610.[1] Even more notorious as a centre of Nonconformity was Delft. For there the Merchant Adventurers had their headquarters, living in splendid style, "accommodated with all necessaries and invested with many privileges, — their houses rent-free, their victuals excise-free, a stately room to dine in, a dainty bowling-alley within the court, a pair of butts, accommodated with fair convenient lodgings";[2] and the Merchant Adventurers, with the obstinacy which characterised prosperous merchants, adhered to that form of religion which seemed most to promote, or at least to accompany, worldly success. Their minister was a Scotsman, John Forbes, whose sentence of death had been commuted to banishment by James I. He had selected Holland as his place of exile, and there, according to an orthodox commentator, "wound himself into familiarity with young men of the Company beyond the seas, and so got himself to be entertained for their preacher: whereby he hath corrupted them exceedingly with his Presbyterian doctrine and discipline, and is now become the oracle of all refractory preachers in the Low Countries".[3] Forbes set up an English classis in 1621, which his colleagues, however, were reluctant to join, and exercised a wide influence over the English residents. The deputy-governor of the English merchants at Hamburg was said to be his creature: and at Hamburg a visiting chaplain was howled down for using the Prayer Book. He also withstood the King's

1 Ames' *De Conscientia* is discussed by Tawney, *Religion and the Rise of Capitalism* (Pelican Books), pp. 195-6. His *Medulla Theologica* was the starting-point of Milton's doctrinal beliefs. (Cf. A. Sewell in *Essays and Studies of the English Association*, vol. xix 1933.)

2 *Travels of Sir Wm. Brereton* (Chetham Soc.), p. 19.

3 Memorandum of Misselden, *S.P. Holland*, July 16th, 1633.

orthodox ambassador at the Hague, and deposed the Company's orthodox deputy at Delft: and when a Puritan preacher at Schonehoven was deprived by authority, Forbes promptly got him installed with the garrison at Bergen-op-Zoom, where he proved his worth by persuading the Dutch ministers to protest at the use of the English liturgy on an English ship.[1] In 1630, when Thomas Hooker fled from the Laudian persecution in Essex, he found congenial employment for a time as Forbes' assistant at Delft.

Laud's first attempt to regulate this situation was in 1627, when he was still Bishop of Bath and Wells. Then he received a letter from Lord Carleton, the ambassador at the Hague, warning him of a new liturgy, a hybrid of the Dutch and English services, which the English churches in Holland were adopting,— a business which Carleton referred to Laud, "conceiving that a churchman would most fully understand it, and most feelingly take care to prevent it". Laud at once wrote to the Secretary of State, Lord Conway, requesting him to instruct Carleton in the right sense; and the result was a set of six articles which Carleton published and against which the ministers appealed to the King. The appeal was in vain: but that mattered little, for so were the articles. Hybrid liturgies continued to flourish in their Dutch recesses: and the saints of God, persecuted in England, looked with increasing envy at the felicity enjoyed by their brethren in Holland.

At the beginning of 1633, therefore, Laud returned to the task, and submitted to the Privy Council a formidable document embodying ten proposals for the introduction of orthodoxy into the English communities in the Low Countries.[2] It was not immediately acted upon, but the ensuing events were sufficient to convince Laud of its necessity. For about the same time Sir William Boswell, who had succeeded Carleton as ambassador at the Hague, was reporting upon the disordered state of the English Church at Delft. Its form of government, he said, was entirely Presbyterian: no proper ceremonies were observed: and there was continual friction between the orthodox deputy-governor of the Merchant Adventurers, Edward Misselden, and the Calvinist preacher Forbes.[3] In reply to this despatch, the

[1] *S.P. Holland*, July 16th, 1633; *Boswell Papers*, Add. MS. 6394, p. 175.

[2] Heylin, pp. 219-20.

[3] *S.P. Dom. Car. I.* 234, no. 8.

King wrote to Boswell insisting upon the necessity of conformity and giving his support to Misselden; and Misselden, thus encouraged, assumed the rôle of government agent and informer in the Company, — a rôle which, like so many of Laud's agents, he performed with rather more zeal than discretion. In a memorandum of July 16th, 1633, he described the character and antecedents of Forbes in no very complimentary style, and complained that the royal order had had little effect, as Forbes had at once secured an order from the States-General requiring conformity with the Dutch Church: and he suggested that the whole affair be examined in London, away from these pernicious influences, and that the headquarters of the Company be removed from Delft to London, thus necessitating a new charter in which appropriate conditions might be interpolated. Next week he wrote to Windebank suggesting that, on the return of Laud from his Scottish progress, a conforming minister be sent out, armed with a Prayer Book, to supersede Forbes.[1]

These sudden activities on the part of Misselden were not altogether to the liking of Boswell, who saw himself being replaced as the official adviser to the government by an officious underling, and he wrote to Secretary Coke explaining that, although Misselden had reported him as complaining of the Nonconformity of the English settlers, "I take leave to appeal to my letters in your Honour's and the Lords' hands: for I cannot remember ever to have said or signified any such thing". However, Boswell soon saw which way the wind was blowing, and decided to throw in his lot decisively with Laud. In November he wrote to Coke, thanking him for having excused him to the King and, more particularly, to Laud, and expressing his regret "if Mr. Misselden or other man, by calling upon my name to make his case considerable, hath unhappily left any spot upon the same, or question of my judgment or zeal in the advancement of our Church service and orders for His Majesty's content".

In the meantime Laud had returned from Scotland and had been translated to Canterbury; and on October 1st he implemented his memorandum of six months earlier by securing an Order in Council which required that all ministers received by the Merchant Adventurers be first approved by the King, that the use of the Prayer Book be compulsory, and that the Company

[1] *S.P. Holland*, July 16th, 1633; *S.P. Dom. Car. I.* 243, no. 29.

be under the ecclesiastical jurisdiction of the Bishop of London. The results of this order were not immediate: for the personnel of the Company was at the moment somewhat disorganised, Misselden having been ousted from his position as deputy by Forbes, and Forbes having gone to England to defend himself to the King. Before any action could be taken in the affairs of the Merchant Adventurers at Delft, the attention of the Archbishop and his supporters was diverted to the case of John Davenport at Amsterdam.

Coming at this crucial time, the case of John Davenport assumed a disproportionate interest in the eyes of contemporaries, for it was a test case which the government was determined to win. As vicar of St. Stephen's Church in Coleman Street, Davenport had already excited the disfavour of Laud as one of the original feoffees for impropriations: and now, in December 1633, fearing a prosecution in the High Commission, he did not wait for trouble to descend upon him, but packed up his belongings and slipped over to Holland "disguised in a grey suit and an overgrown beard".[1] There he accepted an invitation to be co-pastor with John Paget of the English church at Amsterdam, sent to England for testimonials from his congregation, and sought to prejudice the Dutch authorities in his favour by spreading rumours that Laud intended "to contrive an episcopal jurisdiction not only over the English, but also over the Reformed Belgic churches themselves in these parts".[2]

The agents of orthodoxy at once bestirred themselves. Boswell satisfied himself that he had "by secret friends so shuffled the cards at Amsterdam" that Davenport would not easily be admitted. These secret friends of course included Goffe; and Goffe in turn impressed the services of another familiar character, no other than Vossius, who had recently moved from Leyden to Amsterdam. Vossius had already given a foretaste of his potential usefulness in other than theological controversy by justifying the policy of Laud to his compatriots on his return from England in 1630: and now Goffe approached him both directly and indirectly. In a letter sent direct to the professor he pointed out that Davenport was an Independent, "equally

[1] *S.P. Dom. Car. I.* 252, no. 55.

[2] Boswell to Coke, *S.P. Holland*, Jan. 2nd/12th, 1633–4; Goffe to Boswell, Add. MS. 6394, p. 176.

hostile to our hierarchy and your classis", and that he had fled from England without any reason, in defiance of Acts of State, leaving his congregation to languish without a pastor. To another friend he wrote suggesting that other letters of encouragement be sent to Vossius "as a zealous excellent instrument for the Church of England".[1]

Vossius showed himself quite willing to co-operate: but he was alarmed by the rumours which Davenport was spreading about Laud's designs. In view of their wide circulation, he said, Davenport's chances were generally considered good, provided that he could prove his departure from England to be entirely due to religious grounds, and that the English secular government had no charge against him.[2] Goffe hastened to reassure both Vossius and the magistrates that "he was never so much as called in question for ceremonies and discipline", but had abandoned the kingdom contrary to law, and had proved his fear of the English government by avoiding an interview with Boswell although he spent two days at the Hague. Laud also sent a belated letter to Vossius to rebut the charge of seeking to extend his jurisdiction over the Dutch Church. "It is an absolute figment", he declared. "The English bishops never dreamed of such a thing. If the poetaster Davenport says that they did, he lies."[3]

It was not only the orthodox who joined in the intrigue to defeat Davenport. It happened that the differences which divided Davenport from Goffe were slight compared to the fierce divergence of opinion which separated him from his Presbyterian colleague Paget on the thorny question of infant baptism; and Paget, who had already driven Hooker to America rather than tolerate an Independent in the vicinity, and who soon sent Peters to join him, was quite ready to join the Anglicans in order to be rid of Davenport. So between all these intrigues and alliances Davenport was defeated. Vossius convinced the Dutch magistrates that he was *desertor ecclesiae* and an enemy of the English government, adding that, since his arrival in the Netherlands, he had attacked the Dutch government for allowing freedom of

[1] Goffe to Brough, *S.P. Dom. Car. I.* 252, no. 55.

[2] *Vossii Ep.*, no. cclxxv.

[3] Goffe to Boswell (Add. MS. 6394, p. 176); Goffe to Vossius, *Ep. ad Vossium*, no. cxcv. Cf. Davenport's letter to Boswell, I. M. Calder, *Letters of John Davenport* (New Haven, 1937), p. 40; Laud, *Works*, vi. 37.

preaching to the Remonstrants: Goffe declared that Davenport would now, with any luck, follow Hooker to America: felicitations were exchanged by all the orthodox agents in turn: and Davenport, deterred from returning to England by Laud's "reproachful invectives and bitter menaces" against him in the High Commission,[1] spent a year of uneasy residence in Holland, engaging in paper-warfare with Paget on the topic of infant baptism, and then departed, as Goffe had prophesied, to America.

In the midst of these activities Goffe received news of an appointment which gave him but little pleasure. The zeal with which he had served the cause of orthodoxy in the Davenport affair had marked him out as one eminently suited to restore conformity to Delft. After an unsatisfactory interview with the King, Forbes had been relieved of his ministry, and Goffe received the news that he had been appointed in his stead. This, however, was not at all what he wanted, and he wrote in anguished terms to Boswell, protesting that he much preferred the retired life of a scholar, which by nature he was far better fitted to adorn. If the report of his appointment were true, he said, "then no more study, everlasting jealousies and contentions, a Hell rather than a life. They have threatened in my hearing that he that comes after Forbes shall have but a poor life and being of it, and particularly their judgment and condemnation of me is such that I shall but come to the stake."[2] When the report was confirmed, Goffe spent nearly a month at the Hague seeking to escape through the mediation of Boswell, and ultimately he seems to have been successful. For after four months in his new ministry, it was conferred on a new preacher, one Beaumont, "a man learned, sober, and conformable", who arrived in June with a letter of recommendation from the Archbishop, and a Prayer Book, which from that time onwards was regularly used by the Company.

Thus Laud signalised his triumph even in the Netherlands, and, on the other side, the spirits of the Puritan party drooped. Forbes had returned in January: and when he wrote to one of his Puritan friends in England three months later, it was as a disillusioned man. The expulsion of Davenport, he said, had been the greatest possible blow to the Puritan cause, and the power

[1] Davenport to Boswell, *loc. cit.* Cf. *Boswell Papers*, Add. MS. 6394, p. 196.

[2] Add. MS. 6394, p. 180.

of godliness was so much upon the wane in Delft that he could only suppose that God had withdrawn His Gospel from those parts because the Puritans there were insufficiently puritanical. At the same time Griffin Higgs, the Queen of Bohemia's chaplain at the Hague, who had been an undergraduate at St. John's College with Laud, informed Boswell that the Dutch authorities were developing a dislike of English Nonconformists, and would not continue to pay stipends to any English minister who came over contrary to the King of England's pleasure.[1] Next year saw the exodus of Davenport and Peters to America. And in 1637 the independence of the Merchant Adventurers was still further limited by the withdrawal from them and from other companies of the right to elect their officers by ballot, — a right which they had abused by declining to elect the orthodox but unpopular Misselden as their deputy.[2] Laud indeed seemed to have triumphed, and Heylin records with pride how "the like course was also prescribed for our factories in Hamburg and those farther off, — that is to say, in Turkey,[3] in the Mogul's dominions, the Indian islands, the plantations in Virginia, the Barbadoes, and all other places where the English had any standing residence in the way of trade", as well as for ambassadors' households and the regiments in the Low Countries, "the surinspection of which last was referred to Boswell, His Majesty's Resident at the Hague, and his successors in that place".[4] Even the court of the Queen of Bohemia was not regarded as exempt, for later her English chaplain, Dr. Samson Johnson, found himself rated by the Archbishop for alleged Socinian leanings, and had to clear himself: and in Paris Lord Scudamore, readily

[1] Add. MS. 6394, pp. 200-1.

[2] *S.P. Dom. Car. I.* 367, no. 85.

[3] Here Heylin seems to overreach himself. There were English chaplains in Smyrna, Constantinople, and Aleppo in the Near East: but in none of the appointments there does Laud appear to have interfered. The appointment of Pococke to Aleppo in 1630, to succeed the Puritan Charles Robson, might be attributed to Laud's influence, were it not known that Laud first became acquainted with Pococke after his appointment. The first chaplain at Smyrna was appointed in 1637, when Laud's influence was at its zenith: but the chaplain was a Puritan appointed by the Levant Company on the recommendation of the Master of Emmanuel College. In 1639 he absconded from his post, and recommended another Puritan as his successor, — Jeremiah Burroughes, whom Wren had suspended from his ministry in 1636. Sir Sackville Crowe, appointed ambassador to the Porte in 1636, was a friend of Laud: but his official instructions contain nothing relevant to ecclesiastical discipline.

[4] Heylin, p. 260.

obeying his instructions not to attend the Huguenot services at Charenton, as his predecessors had done, was " careful to publish upon all occasions, by himself and those who had the nearest relation to him, that the Church of England looked not on the Huguenots as a part of their communion ".[1]

The exercise of his authority in the United Provinces, and especially his imposition of conformity upon the Merchant Adventurers, was very satisfying to Laud : but to establish there an effective censorship of the press was less easy, for it depended on the willingness of the Dutch authorities to co-operate ; and while Richelieu in France, the Catholic Church in Spain and the Empire, and Laud in England were taking every step in their power to establish unity of thought, or at least of expression, the Dutch authorities, almost alone in Europe, seemed actually to encourage diversity. Owing to the proximity of England and Holland, and the intimate relations between them, this Dutch toleration opened a continual breach in Laud's otherwise closed system, and the Puritan books which were printed in Holland and smuggled into England, and whose circulation neither Boswell nor the English coastal authorities could prevent, were a source of endless embarrassment to him. All that the Archbishop could do was to find out the authors, if he could, and fine them if he could catch them. In October 1633 Lady Eleanor Davies was fined and imprisoned for having her comminatory prophecies printed at Amsterdam : but the example deterred no one, and at the same time Boswell was reporting that one Mr. Puckle was selling the works of Dr. Ames at the Hague to passengers bound for England. Three or four hundred copies, he wrote, had already been sent to a London stationer, disguised as white paper, and the second part was expected to follow. Two impressions of the English Bible, with the Geneva commentary, had also been sent to England under the name of white paper.[2] Early next year Goffe reported to Boswell that he was looking out for a book called *The Crown of Christian Martyrdom*, but had not yet been able to find a copy, and that Mr. Widdowes, the English minister at Husden, was said to have a Puritan book in the press, " which I must enquire after ".[3] But again Boswell

[1] Clarendon, *History of the Rebellion*, vi. 184.
[2] *S.P. Dom. Car. I.* 246, no. 66. Cf. Laud, *Works*, iv. 263.
[3] *Boswell Papers*, Add. MS. 6394, p. 179.

was too late : for when he wrote to the Secretary of State soon afterwards it was to inform him that " a most peevish pamphlet against our ecclesiastical constitutions and order," called *The Crown of a Christian Martyr*, had already been printed, and most of the impression smuggled across to London in English ships lying ready at Rotterdam and Delfshaven.[1] All that Boswell could do in these circumstances was to send for Davenport, who was suspected of being the author of the work : but Davenport declared that he had published nothing since his arrival in the Low Countries.[2]

Later Laud secured an order requiring that a catalogue of all books imported from abroad be submitted either to himself or to Juxon before sale, and forbidding the printing of English books abroad ; but since he was unable to prevent the printing of works by Ames and Festus Hommius in Oxford, it was plain that such orders would be useless in Holland. Theophilus Brabourne's *Defence of the Sabbath Day*, Robinson's *Treatise of Separation*, and books by Bastwick and others, were all imported from the Dutch presses. In 1637 Socinian books also began to reach England from the same source. Boswell's nephew, Thomas Raymond, relates that these works were very rare in the Low Countries until some busybody undertook to confute the errors of Socinus, and so caused a boom in the heretical books. " The Archbishop", he says, " was very careful to suppress this growing damnable heresy in the Dutch churches. To that end the Resident had orders from him, in the King's name, to importune the States-General for the seizing and suppressing Socinus his works or books containing these devilish errors . . . which books, through the importunity of the Resident, were by the States-General called in and seized upon " ;[3] and Laud enjoyed the dubious honour of being thanked by a Jesuit for his intervention. In the same year the works of Prynne, Burton,

[1] *S.P. Holland*, Feb. 4th/14th, 1633–4.

[2] Calder, *op. cit.* p. 42. Miss Calder states that " no copy of this pamphlet has been found " ; but although not mentioned in the *Short Title Catalogue*, or in *Halkett and Laing*, a copy is preserved in the Library of Merton College, Oxford. It is called " *The Crowne of a Christian Martyr* . . . published by John Richards ", and is dated 1634. No place of origin is given, but it appears to have been printed at Delft, and, since it was presented to the library by Griffin Higgs, was no doubt procured by him during his residence in Holland as Chaplain to the Queen of Bohemia at the Hague.

[3] Raymond, *Autobiography* (Camden Soc., 1917), p. 32.

and Bastwick were seized in the Netherlands : but in the following winter an English traveller found that Bastwick's works were still being printed in Delft and Rotterdam, while Prynne's works, already available in Dutch, were being translated into French also, "to make the bishops' cruelty known to all nations".[1] It was probably as an attempt at counter-propaganda that Laud sent copies of his speech against Prynne, Burton, and Bastwick both to Boswell at the Hague and Scudamore in Paris. Among other books discovered in Holland by the same traveller were the works of Sibbes and Preston, Robinson's *Treatise of Separation*, and pamphlets with such obviously Puritan titles as *The Saint's Spiritual Strength*, *The Poor Doubting Christian*, *The Soul's Humiliation*, and *A Guide to Sion*. The trouble in Scotland, too, had its echo in the Netherlands, where a Scottish attack on "Anglo-popish ceremonies" was on the bookstalls, and a copy of the Solemn League and Covenant in the press. All shipmasters, continued the writer, were engaged in the trade of smuggling books into England. Their method was to strike on the sands of Queenborough, send their passengers ashore, and then deliver the prohibited goods in small boats. Having thus evaded the customs officials in the ports, they brought their ships off the sands without danger, and returned to the Dutch ports for further consignments. Next year John Lilburne faced the Star Chamber on a charge of having subversive works printed at Rotterdam, and a letter from Laud to Boswell shows that it had proved impossible to control either the emigration of Puritans from England to Holland, or the return of their opinions from Holland to England. "I am sorry", he wrote, "to hear that such swarms of wasps (for bees they are not) are flown over to those parts, and with such clamours against our Church affairs,—for which (God be thanked) there is no cause. Nor hath the Church of England suffered of late any way so much as by their base and libellous both tongues and pens. For which God forgive them."[2]

But indeed, considering that Laud proved unable to eliminate Puritan doctrines in England, where no rival jurisdiction was allowed, no principle of toleration admitted, we can hardly be surprised at the failure of his attempts to do so in the Netherlands,

[1] Relation of Matthew Symonds, *S.P. Dom. Car. I.* 387, no. 79.

[2] Laud, *Works*, vi. 528.

where his authority was so limited, and had to be exercised with such discretion. The rejection of Davenport and the calling in of Socinian books had been effected through the co-operation of the Dutch authorities: but when the Dutch refused to act as Laud's police, the efforts of Boswell or Goffe, or any other English agent, could avail but little. The English in the Netherlands might be included, on paper, in the diocese of London: but the bishop's court could not reach them. Laud might forbid the importation of Puritan books: but such a veto merely increased smuggling. So the Archbishop's activities were confined to punitive raids, which might result in a small success somewhere, but could never lead to conquest. In Amsterdam alone, thanks to the toleration of the authorities, Sir William Brereton found French, Dutch, and English Protestant churches; in addition, he reported, there were three congregations of Brownists, three Jewish synagogues, and over thirty sects of Anabaptists; and "Bapists, Arians, Socinians, and Familists of Love have also their public meetings in houses turned into churches, and that without control".[1] Among such swarms of refugees a few conscientious agents of uniformity could achieve but little, and that little depended as much upon the intolerance of rival sects as upon their own efforts. In fact, when Goffe drove Hugh Peters from Rotterdam, it was not an orthodox Anglican who succeeded him, but William Bridges, sometime lecturer in Norwich, who had fled from the persecution of Bishop Wren. At the same time Rotterdam also afforded an asylum for Samuel Ward, another victim of the same bishop. So Laud's agents had only driven out one devil in order to make room for two.

When Laud learnt that the objectionable Davenport had finally left the Low Countries and gone to New England, he

[1] *Travels* (Chetham Soc.), pp. 64-5. For the multiplicity of sects at Amsterdam, cf. Marvell, "The Character of Holland" (*Marvell's Poems and Letters*, ed. Margoliouth, i. 97):

> "Sure, when Religion did itself embark,
> And from the East would westward steer its Ark,
> It struck, and splitting on this unknown ground,
> Each one thence pillaged the first piece he found.
> Hence Amsterdam, Turk-Christian-Pagan-Jew,
> Staple of sects and Mint of Schism grew;
> That Bank of Conscience, where not one so strange
> Opinion but finds Credit and Exchange."

boasted that his arm should reach him even there. At least, so his enemies alleged : and Laud, although he professed not to remember having made such a boast, admitted that he considered the sentiment unexceptionable.[1] We must therefore turn for a moment to look at America, and discover there the brief effort to impose unity and uniformity upon the colonists who, as often as not, had left England in order to be free from such restrictions.

Until the advent of Laud to power the English government had taken little interest in the souls of American colonists, many of whom were such characters as it was only too glad to be rid of without imposing conditions. Official documents sometimes paid lip-service to the Church of England, or, more vaguely, the Christian religion : but the Virginia Company's charters made no reference to religious orthodoxy, and when the *Mayflower* pilgrims applied for leave to settle, the authorities discreetly avoided enquiring into their religious professions. Even in 1629, when the Massachusetts Bay Company received its charter, no insistence upon religious conformity was included in it : and four years later, when the Company was accused before the Privy Council of political and religious separatism, the Council made it clear that it entertained no designs of imposing true religion upon profitable manufacturers. After all, the Plantations were so far away that they were unlikely to infect the mother country with heresy, and they might be regarded as a valuable safety-valve for the discharge of dangerous humours.

So politic a view did not long survive the rise of Laud. " New England ", says Heylin, " like the spleen in the natural body, by drawing to it so many sullen, sad, and offensive humours, was not unuseful and unserviceable to the general health. But when the spleen is grown once too full, and emptieth itself into the stomach, it both corrupts the blood and disturbs the head, and leaves the whole man wearisome to himself and others." So Laud determined that America too should know the benefits of conformity, and proposed to send a bishop across the Atlantic, " and back him with some forces to compel, if he were not otherwise able to persuade obedience ".[2] Fortunately for the bishop, this was one of those projects which were prevented of fulfilment by the outbreak of the Troubles.

It was not solely a bigoted craving for uniformity which im-

[1] Laud, *Works*, iv. 260.

[2] Heylin, p. 347.

pelled Laud to an ambition which seems ridiculous to us, although such a craving no doubt influenced his actions. There was also a serious social problem, which seemed to him to demand such a remedy. In the previous reign it had not been easy to supply the new colonies with settlers, and we read of discouraging massacres in Virginia, and forcible impressment of colonists in England. But with the increasing prosperity of the colonies, to which the founding of new companies and the granting of new charters bears witness, emigration lost its terrors, and those who had previously been transported to Virginia as punishment now went thither voluntarily to avoid it. Further, when Laud's ecclesiastical tyranny added heretics to debtors and speculators, emigration received a sanctifying halo, and emigrants became martyrs and pilgrims, facing unknown perils, as well as the prospect of lucrative careers, for conscience' sake. Many a shady character, as he embarked surreptitiously for an interesting and profitable voyage, enjoyed the temporary consideration due to a saint of God: and English poets invested their adventures with a romance which could never be associated with Laud's meticulous beauty of holiness. The English government, however, saw no reason to wax lyrical over the Elect

> Safe from the storm's and Prelate's rage

in their American Paradise, or the prospect of Religion standing

> on tip-toe in our land,
> Ready to fly to the American strand;

for it was not only religion and the religious that were leaving the country. The spectre of depopulation, so real in those days, was again causing sleepless nights; and the romantic associations which were settling round this disquieting exodus only added to the government's embarrassment by raising depopulation into the realm of ideals and giving publicity to the wrong side. How effective this publicity was is shown by the fact that the last quotation is from an Anglican clergyman, George Herbert: and Nicholas Ferrar, whom Puritans attacked as an Arminian even unto Popery, struggled to pilot the offensive lines past the censorship.

A large proportion of this evil could be traced to the founding of the colony of Massachusetts, which had by now emancipated itself from royal control by the removal of the governing company to America, and was giving continual evidence of an established and exclusive Puritanism. Once the Company had withdrawn itself from England, and so from the effective influence of the government, prominent English Puritans saw their chance and followed it. John Winthrop, a doubting, introspective Calvinist, just deprived of his attorneyship in the Court of Wards, was one of the first to go, taking his brother-in-law, Emmanuel Downing, with him. Puritanism was made a condition of admittance to the governing body of the colony : toleration was expressly rejected : and two brothers, detected in the surreptitious use of a Prayer Book, were promptly shipped back to England.

The value of this exception to the general rule of orthodoxy was made apparent when Laud became Archbishop of Canterbury. Till then it had attracted but little notice, and the charges preferred against it had been dismissed by the Privy Council. In 1633, however, seven hundred refugees left England. From the ports of Puritan East Anglia, the departure of ships for New England was frequently reported. In February 1634 Dade, the commissary for Suffolk, wrote to Laud that two ships were ready to sail in a week's time, each with a hundred and twenty emigrants, mostly sectaries and bankrupts, and that another six hundred were soon to follow them.[1] This exodus he attributed to the contagious preaching of one Samuel Ward, whom he hoped to hale before the High Commission when a favourable opportunity presented itself, as it shortly did. Laud replied with an Order in Council stopping the voyage : but a week later it was allowed to proceed, on condition that the Prayer Book was used throughout the crossing of the Atlantic. Only when actually in America might the Puritans taste the full freedom which they were seeking.

In 1634, when Laud was accumulating offices in every department of State, he still found time to keep his eye on America, and, for the express purpose of dealing with New England Puritanism, two commissions were almost simultaneously created under his presidency. The first was the Commission for New England, a revival of the commission which had been erected under Archbishop Harsnet to deal with the charges brought against the Massachusetts Bay Company by Gorges and Mason,

[1] *Cal. S.P. Colonial*, i. 174.

and which was now made permanent under Laud. The second, which was in fact a committee of the Privy Council, and which was identical in personnel with the Commission for New England, was known as the Commission for Foreign Plantations. On paper these two commissions, which for practical purposes are indistinguishable, were powerful engines of the central government for the control of the colonies. Consisting of the two Archbishops, Laud and Neile, the Lord Keeper Coventry, the Lord Treasurer Portland, Lord Cottington, and the two Secretaries of State, Coke and Windebank, as well as other Privy Councillors, they were authorised to legislate for the colonies, to punish and imprison ecclesiastical offenders, to remove and examine governors, judges, and magistrates, to set up courts both civil and ecclesiastical, to hear and determine complaints, and to regulate charters and patents.

In fact, however, the establishment of the commissions showed the intentions rather than the powers of the government; and although, on paper, Laud had now absolute control of the ecclesiastical organisation of the English in the British Isles, the Netherlands, and America, in reality this control was imperfect in England, slender in Holland, and in America naturally ridiculous. The wide powers suddenly conferred upon the government for obvious use against the Puritan colony caused some alarm in Massachusetts, where the provincial legislature adopted measures for the fortification of the colony and set up a committee for the management of the war, should that be necessary. But it was not necessary; the government had no notion so fantastic as a transatlantic war. It merely continued to legislate against emigration, — in 1634 it forbade emigration without permission from Laud's Commission or a certificate of conformity from the parish minister, — and in 1635, under a writ of *quo warranto*, proceedings were taken against the Massachusetts Bay Company in the King's Bench. The Council of New England was persuaded to surrender its powers to the Crown in order that the Crown might recover authority over Massachusetts: and two years later the Massachusetts Bay Company was declared to have forfeited its charter by disregarding its limitations, and Sir Ferdinando Gorges was nominated governor of New England with authority to impose ecclesiastical discipline on the inhabitants.

In other colonies, too, the government showed the same interest in the spiritual condition of the settlers. In 1635, when Captain Roger North, whose previous ventures on the Amazon had been terminated by the intervention of Count Gondomar, received a new patent for colonisation in South America, it included a new condition by which he and his Company were required to submit to ecclesiastical and civil government; [1] in 1639, when Sir Ferdinando Gorges received a charter for the colonisation of Maine and Hampshire, a similar clause was inserted, declaring that the powers conferred on Gorges "for and concerning the government both ecclesiastical and civil in the said provinces and premises shall be subordinate and subject to the power and reglement of the Lords and other Commissioners here for Foreign Plantations for the time being"; and in the same year we find Laud writing to the Bermuda Company to complain of alleged unorthodoxy in the Islands.[2]

The effective result of this intervention was, however, negligible. The Troubles which nipped so many of Laud's projects in the bud, prevented any further action in the Massachusetts affair. Emigration, instead of being restricted, seemed only to be increased by repeated proclamations against it, and in 1638 it reached alarming proportions. Nor did the English Church in the colonies receive much benefit from the Archbishop's efforts in its behalf. The governor of Newfoundland might write assuring him of the superiority of his island over New England in point of doctrine: [3] but in Barbados, where one orthodox clergyman had already abandoned his post in despair and gone to Tobago, an informant told Laud that the clergy were entirely dependent on the governor and were taxed out of existence: [4] and in Bermuda the only result of Laud's complaints was that the Company indignantly protested their scrupulous orthodoxy in all things, and then discovered and suspended the informer who had denied it.[5]

What may be termed Laud's ecclesiastical foreign policy was probably the most odious, as it was the least successful, branch of his comprehensive activity. Only in Ireland can it be regarded as anything but offensive: and in Ireland it was taken out of his

[1] *Cal. S.P. Col.* i. 200. [2] *Ibid.* i. 303. [3] *Ibid.* i. 304.
[4] *Ibid.* i. 258-9. [5] *Ibid.* i. 302, 303, 304.

hands by a more competent ally. There he was seeking to raise a disreputable, and indeed comic, institution to a position of respect, and no ideas were at stake to exalt the conflict into a crusade, or give his adversaries the title of martyrs. But in Scotland he was seeking to obtrude a new religion upon a people already fortified by an old, and his methods were never such as recommended imported goods. In Holland toleration defeated him: in America distance. The only result of his multifarious activities was that he was constitutionally empowered to impose uniformity on all the subjects of the English Crown, — if he could do it.

It was by a natural corollary to this determination to impose uniformity throughout the dominions of the British Crown, that Laud showed himself completely uninterested in ecclesiastical affairs beyond those limits. Although he might sometimes shed a formal tear for persecuted Protestants abroad, he never entertained any idea of giving them practical aid: nor, on the other hand, did he show them any hostility for the deep tincture of their Protestantism. He was simply unconcerned with them; and although, in the odd company of such prominent Puritans as Sibbes, Gouge, and Davenport, he advocated relief for the ejected Calvinist ministers of the Palatinate, merely altering the document where it appeared to indicate any community of ideas with them, he had the greatest distaste for direct intervention, and neither as a politician nor as Primate of England could he lend any support to the policy of Sir Thomas Roe, who thought of raising a Protestant combination against the power of the Empire. Peace and no parliaments were more important to Laud than any crusade, and he refused to divert his attention from social and ecclesiastical reconstruction at home by unprofitable ideological ventures abroad. Similarly, when Buckingham was leading his expedition to the relief of the Huguenots of Rochelle, Laud was prepared to dwell upon the pious aim of the adventure, being the succour of true religion grievously oppressed; but when politics had ceased to require such intervention, true religion abroad looked for succour in vain, and Laud ostentatiously dissociated himself from it.

In these circumstances it was embarrassing to Laud when he was solicited by an earnest apostle of Protestant unity, who, having considerable support from the well-meaning, insisted upon seeking to convert the Archbishop to his grandiose but quixotic schemes of a general Protestant reunion based on a general confession of faith, — and that although Laud had already had the works of the most distinguished reunionist of the time, David Waengler, called Pareus, of Heidelberg, publicly burnt in three places.[1]

This new apostle, John Durie, was an idealist who based the activities of a lifetime upon the mistaken assumption that people really care about religious doctrines, and, though continually disappointed, never despaired. A Scotsman by birth, he had been educated in England and the Netherlands, and had subsequently served as a chaplain to English merchant companies in Germany and Sweden: and now he conceived the splendid design of uniting in a single Protestant Church all the national Churches of which he had thus gained experience. In the hope of making influential converts, he was destined to spend his days on a continual pilgrimage among the antechambers of princes and statesmen, bishops and theologians, who treated him as might be expected. The statesmen listened to him with respect, and sometimes with interest, when they thought that his schemes might favour their political designs. The theologians, however, who throve upon the metaphysical subtleties which disunity engenders, had less use for him, and turned him out of doors. One firm friend he had among the great: but he too was unwanted by his generation, — Sir Thomas Roe.

Attracted by his obvious sincerity, many well-intentioned persons gave Durie their benediction. The English low church bishops, Davenant, Morton, and Hall, gave him testimonials: so did also Archbishop Spottiswood: and Bedell provided him with a small annual pension. Sir William Boswell at the Hague, though he thought the project somewhat fanciful, conceded that Durie was the fittest instrument to be used in it.[2] Axel Oxenstjerna, the Swedish chancellor, who saw in a Protestant union the means of cementing the northern powers in their attack upon the Empire, supported him. And Sir Thomas Roe, intent upon the recovery of the Palatinate for his mistress, threw himself into the scheme and supplied Durie with money and encouragement.

[1] *Vide supra*, p. 139. [2] *S.P. Holland*, Nov. 4th, 1633.

Thus armed, Durie began his preparations in 1630, and in February 1631 wrote to Laud to interest him in the project.[1] Two years of preparation and propaganda followed, during which the way was prepared in Germany, and in January 1633 the pastors of the Church of Cassel wrote to Laud deploring the want of unity in the Protestant world and suggesting a conference of divines to remedy it. Laud had himself occasionally deplored the want of unity in the Church — " Death were easier to me ", he once professed, " than it is to see and consider the face of the Church of Christ scratched and torn till it bleeds in every part, as it doth this day, and the coat of Christ, which was spared by the soldiers because it was seamless, rent every way " [2] — but it was the Church of England, not the Church Universal, whose disunity he was really bewailing : and he had no love for assemblies of any sort, least of all assemblies of acrimonious divines. In July, however, he received another letter, this time from Sir Thomas Roe, in support of Durie and his project, which, he was assured, was widely favoured on the Continent, especially in Sweden, and now only required the support of England to be practicable : thus the names of Luther and Calvin might be buried, and ecclesiastical peace established as a foundation upon which temporal peace might be built. Roe enclosed a letter from Durie to Laud, informing him that, since the death of Gustavus Adolphus, the German churches looked to Canterbury for leadership and mediation, and giving an impressive list of the churches and statesmen who had given their blessing to the enterprise. All that was now required was the official support of the English Church, in order that Durie might negotiate as an Anglican plenipotentiary, instead of in the less impressive status of a mere wandering scholar.

Thus beset upon all sides, Laud could not but reply. He wrote therefore to the divines now met in conference at Sedan informing them that he had referred their letter to the King, who had replied that as yet he considered the plan premature, but that a confession of faith based on the fundamental tenets upon which all were already agreed might profitably be drawn up. This was not warm encouragement : and it was a further discouragement when Durie interviewed the Archbishop in person, and found him unwilling to do anything, either in his own or the

[1] House of Lords MSS. (H.M.C. Report IV, pp. 159 ff.).

[2] Laud, *Works*, i. 165.

King's name, without an express order from the King, — an order which he could have had for the asking, but which he was plainly not minded to ask.[1] In January 1634 Roe wrote to Bishop Morton of Durham that he had misgivings about the success of the mission because of the Archbishop's coldness: and a few days later Durie reported a further interview, at which Laud had listened to his plans, but had refused to give any advice or instructions.[2] The one material result of the audience was that the Archbishop offered Durie an English benefice, with permission of non-residence, to support him during his mission; so Durie set off to take possession of the living of Northlowe in Devonshire, in the diocese of the sympathetic Bishop Hall, while Roe wrote to the Archbishop again, pointing out the danger of a Franco-Dutch combination, which would dominate the Continent unless the Protestant powers stood together.[3]

All this badgering of the Archbishop produced little result. He wrote to Durie in February, giving him vague encouragement. He would do all that he could, he said, for a work so acceptable to the Anglican Church, but publicly nothing could be done in a country so remote from the scene of action. And he prepared two letters, one for the Calvinists, one for the Lutherans, of Germany, explaining that he had been overwhelmed with delight (*perfusus sum gaudio*) on hearing of the pious project: that his prayers for its success were continually besieging God: but that he was rather too far away to do anything about it, and was, at the moment, particularly busy with other things.[4] Meanwhile the unfortunate Durie had met with another disappointment. On arriving in Devonshire to take possession of his benefice, he had been greeted by the incumbent, who, so far from being dead, was enjoying excellent health and showed no intention of relinquishing his comfortable cure. Durie toiled back to London and interviewed the Archbishop again: but although Laud indemnified him for his fruitless journey, gave him the two letters for the Lutherans and Calvinists, and provided him liberally with praise for his past, and encouragement for his future work, when Durie suggested that he was in need of maintenance, the Archbishop at once changed his tone. He could not pay for every-

[1] *S.P. Dom. Car. I.* 259, no. 23. [2] *S.P. Dom. Car. I.* 259, no. 66.
[3] House of Lords MSS. (H.M.C. Report IV, p. 160).
[4] Laud, *Works*, vi. 410; vii. 112.

one's good works, he said. It was not his fault if the vicar in Devonshire was still alive. It would have been different for old Archbishop Abbot, who had been at Lambeth for twenty-two years when he died, and had been able to accumulate a tidy fortune in that time: but he himself had only just been promoted and was still comparatively poor. When Durie pointed out that he had spent all his own means and had neglected the chance of seeking preferment elsewhere, and was now in debt and could not possibly go abroad without a penny in his pocket, the Archbishop became impatient. "Let those who have set you awork", he said, "provide maintenance for you." [1]

Rather than abandon his mission, Durie turned to Roe, who gave him the money which the Archbishop had refused. In the hope of moving the King, he also wrote to Windebank and the Marquis Hamilton, to whom he poured out his complaints of the Archbishop's callousness. He sent to Ussher and the other Irish bishops for their advice and encouragement. He was a crusader, he said, who would never give over, but where he could not ride he would go on foot, and where he could not walk he would creep on all fours rather than abandon his project of bringing religious peace to the world. So he set out alone to Frankfurt, writing to Roe in April that he was desperately in need of £10 for his travelling expenses, and that the Archbishop showed no beneficence at all.[2]

So Durie pursued his ineffectual mission, unsupported by the Archbishop. Two years later he was in Holland, in great poverty, but not in despair, selling the remainder of his father's library to buy bread and beer for his support. There, while attending a synod at Utrecht, he received an invitation to the Diet at Stockholm, and went immediately to Sweden, where his hopes were raised again by his favourable reception. He received tokens of esteem from Oxenstjerna, and expounded his views enthusiastically to bishops and politicians. Again he hoped for official recognition, and once more he wrote optimistically to Laud, giving an account of his progress. But again he was doomed to disappointment. It was not religious unity for its own sake that Oxenstjerna desired (although Grotius declared that he was

[1] Durie to Roe, *S.P. Dom. Car. I.* 262, no. 84.

[2] *Cal. S.P. Dom.*, 1633–4, p. 439; Hamilton MSS. (H.M.C. Hamilton), p. 87; *Cal. S.P. Dom.*, 1633–4, pp. 525, 554.

a great student of divinity and had closeted himself for three or four days with Durie in his country house), but a fighting alliance which religious unity should cement and consecrate: and soon he had to admit that he saw no hope of such an alliance from the England of Charles I. Meanwhile the Swedish theologians had resolved to rid themselves of the intruder, and imposed impossible conditions upon him. The clerical estate declared that the names of Luther and Calvin, which Roe had hoped to bury, were irreconcilable: the bishops demanded the expulsion of the peacemaker, to which the Chancellor reluctantly assented: and in England the Troubles rendered all such negotiations academic, even if they had not been academic from the start. Even Sir Thomas Roe was made to suffer for his championship of the troublesome apostle of peace; for in October 1636 we find him writing to Laud, as one who had been censured to the King as a busybody in affairs which were above him, and pleading in self-defence that when Durie applied to him as one well-versed in the affairs of Europe, common charity required him to offer his support.[1] After all this, it is certainly rather a surprise to find that Laud, at his trial, claimed credit for assisting Durie in his mission. "As for his encouraging of Master Durie in his designs of reconciling the Calvinists and Lutherans," replied Prynne, "Mr. Durie undertook this work without his privity or advice, and found so small encouragement from him that he oft complained thereof to his friends."[2]

It took more than ten years of failure, the hostility of the authorities, and the defection of a few supporters, however, to discourage Durie.[3] He remained devoted to his impracticable ideal: and with the triumph of Cromwell he set to work again. In 1650 his former champion, Prynne, recognised in him the hated spirit of Independency, and turned against him with a pamphlet, *The Timeserving Proteus and Ambidexter Divine Uncased to the World*; but when Cromwell assumed the mantle of Gustavus Adolphus and proclaimed the Holy War against Rome on every front, Durie went forth again as the apostle of united Protestantism, seconding John Pell in Switzerland, and being rewarded with a knighthood from the Protector. With the Restoration he and his

[1] *S.P. Dom. Car. I.* 333, no. 20.

[2] *Canterburie's Doome*, p. 541.

[3] For the later career of Durie see K. Brauer, *Die Unionstätigkeit John Duries unter dem Protektorat Cromwells* (Marburg, 1907).

cause sank together, this time for good : but Durie lived on to a good age, and in 1677 William Penn recorded that, in Cassel, he met one John Durie, who " for his approaches towards an inward principle, is reproachfully saluted by some with the title of Quaker ".

Another champion of Protestant unity who received a cool reception from Laud was less troublesome, because less energetic, than Durie. This was Hugo Grotius, who, exiled from his native land for opinions too closely resembling those of Laud, was now at Paris as the ambassador of Queen Christina of Sweden to the Court of France. There is no evidence that Grotius, during his short visit to England in 1613, ever came into personal contact with Laud, but on two occasions he wrote to him, without receiving any direct reply,[1] and Laud was kept informed of his movements by Vossius, the friend of Grotius, and Scudamore, his colleague at the French court. Through the medium of Scudamore, Laud and Grotius exchanged protestations of mutual friendship and respect. " The next time that I see ambassador Grotius ", Scudamore wrote to the Archbishop on one occasion, " I will not fail to perform your commandments concerning him. Truly, my Lord, I am persuaded that he doth unfeignedly and highly love and reverence your person and proceedings. Body and soul he professeth himself to be for the Church of England, and gives his judgment of it, that it is the likeliest to last of any Church this day in being."[2] When Grotius thought of retiring to end his days in England, — a project which was ultimately prevented by the outbreak of the Civil War, — Scudamore made representations to the King and the Archbishop, and reported to Grotius that both would be glad to welcome him thither. " The King ", he said, " answered that it was a very fair proposition : and my Lord Archbishop of Canterbury, understanding all this, said to me that he would husband this to your advantage as occasion should be."

With Grotius' somewhat vague aspirations after a general

[1] *Grotii Epistolae* (ed. P. and I. Blaeu, Amsterdam, 1787), nos. 372, 402. Cf. Laud to Vossius, *Works*, vi. 297, " Attulit secum [*sc.* Franciscus Junius] literas ab amplissimo viro Hugone Grotio ad me datas. Gratissimae illae . . . sed rescribendi otium non datur." Also *ibid.* 446.

[2] Scudamore to Laud, in M. Gibson, *A View of the Church of Door, etc.*, pp. 77 ff.

Protestant reconciliation, however, Laud entertained less sympathy. Inspired by the missionary activities of Durie in his own adoptive country, Grotius too began to project an ideal Church, in which Protestants should forget their divisions, and which should bear the impress of his own rather more Arminian views. Membership of this Utopian institution was to be confined to the English Church of Laud and to the Lutherans of Sweden and Denmark. The French, at a pinch, might also be admitted, if they renounced all ultramontane loyalties: but the Calvinists, whom Grotius had good reasons for disliking, were to be excluded altogether. In many an interview Grotius spun out these rarefied fantasies to his diplomatic colleague, and Scudamore repeated them at length to Laud. But the Archbishop had little attention to waste upon them, and when his lukewarm replies were reported to Grotius, the philosopher "seemed to be surprised, and quailed much in his hopes", resigning himself ultimately to the consoling reflection that at least "it is a contentment to be and to live and die in the wishes of so great a good". Grotius was not, like Durie, a crusader: and after Durie's first failure he abandoned his professorial projects. He was anyway an old man, disappointed by a long exile, and looking for a peaceful retirement. Soon the English rebellion shattered those hopes, and he died after living just long enough to pronounce an epitaph upon Laud.

CHAPTER EIGHT

OXFORD

"Then was the University exceedingly regular, under the exact discipline of William Laud, Archbishop of Canterbury, then Chancellor." — JOHN EVELYN, *Diary*, May 10th, 1637.

IN spite of the weaknesses revealed by a retrospective survey, it might well appear to Laud, in the summer of 1636, that his policy had triumphed wherever it had been applied. The elevation of Juxon to the Treasury in March symbolised his political supremacy. In June Wentworth visited England, and it was observed that "since his coming, his addresses were wholly to the Archbishop". In ecclesiastical affairs he had established his claims to jurisdiction over every person, every institution, which disputed them. Throughout the world the subjects of the King were declared subject to his spiritual rule, by law if not in fact. He possessed the complete confidence of the King, who readily complied with all his requests, even though the Queen sometimes urged him otherwise. The clerical voice possessed a commanding influence in the administrative law-courts.[1] Such opposition as manifested itself was confined, it seemed, to a small number of unimportant extremists. Since the stormy dissolution of the last parliament seven years ago, there had been no wide demand for another. The country was at peace and prosperous: and peace and prosperity apparently reconciled it to the institutions which seemed to secure them.

All observers are agreed upon the completeness of this triumph. They looked back afterwards upon that time as the halcyon period of the restored English Church, and could only attribute its subsequent downfall to the agency of malignant characters actuated by personal spite. While all the nations of the Continent

[1] While Elizabeth had never allowed more than one bishop at a time to sit as a judge in the Star Chamber, in the period of Laud's ascendancy there were three, — Laud, Neile, and Juxon, — all of whom were constant in their attendance (H. E. I. Phillips, "The Last Years of the Court of the Star Chamber, 1630–1641", in *Trans. Royal Hist. Soc.*, 1939, p. 114).

languished under a long and ruinous war, Clarendon expatiated on the happier state of England, with the Court in plenty, the country rich, trade booming, the navy strong, "the Church flourishing with learned and extraordinary men, and (what other good times lacked) supplied with oil to feed those lamps: and the Protestant Religion more advanced against the Church of Rome by writing, especially (without prejudice to other useful and godly labours) by those two books of the late lord Archbishop of Canterbury his Grace and of Mr. Chillingworth, than it had been since the Reformation". To the obsequious Heylin it seemed as if a millennium had arrived, as he catalogued the glories of the Golden Age of the Church. The prelates were orthodox, the clergy obedient, ceremonies observed, and the material wealth of the Church properly husbanded: and he added, with the complacent *snobisme* of the successful chaplain, the satisfactory statement that "the gentry thought none of their daughters to be better disposed of than such as they had lodged in the arms of a churchman".[1] It was but reasonable, therefore, that Laud, surveying his extensive handiwork and finding it good, should choose a convenient time and place to celebrate it in a worthy and conspicuous fashion. If there was an appropriate time, it was surely now: if an appropriate place, it could only be Oxford.

For Oxford was the one place where Laud's triumph was never embittered by any admixture of gall. No place which had any connexion with him had ever cause to regret it: but no place had a closer connexion with him than Oxford, and his reward to it was memorable. From the time when he entered St. John's College as an undergraduate to the day when he wrote from the Tower to resign the chancellorship of the University, there was only a brief interval of eight years when he was not bound to Oxford by the tie of some official position. There, too, his triumph had been more personal than elsewhere: for it had been effected not through the strength of his position but by the force of his personality. And if it was a more intimate triumph, it was also a longer one. Oxford, almost alone, showed no signs of rejoicing at his fall, but rather recapitulated the benefits which it had received from him; and after his death, when he had already seen the demolition of most of his labours, and the rest were soon to be undone, his work at Oxford was to survive for

[1] Heylin, p. 237.

centuries. Even the new cathedral of St. Paul's, which he planned as his most enduring monument, was in fact but short-lived and never completed, and it was his quadrangle at Oxford, less pretentious indeed, but infinitely more beautiful, which was to preserve his name in stone to future generations. Indeed, his success at Oxford was such that sceptical writers have expressed the opinion that it would have been better had he never exchanged the life of a don for that of a Prince of the Church.

When we last dealt with Laud's activities at Oxford he was consolidating his victory after his election as Chancellor by the rigorous suppression of dissentient voices. This done, he could proceed at once to constructive work: and the history of his chancellorship for the next seven years is a record of constructive work so extensive and so thorough that it is hard to realise that it was but an item in his vast programme for the reconstruction of the whole basis of secular and ecclesiastical government.

Even before his chancellorship, Laud had directed the benefactions of others to the University, and could claim his share of its gratitude towards the Earl of Pembroke and Sir Thomas Roe. As Chancellor he continued these laudable activities, for which another opportunity arose in 1632 on the death of Dr. Thomas Allen, Master of Gloucester Hall, "the very soul and sun of all the mathematicians of his time", whom neither Polish princes, nor English peers, nor the prospect of a bishopric, could lure away from his crucibles and his alleged dabblings in the magic art. This old man bequeathed his fine library to his favourite pupil, Sir Kenelm Digby, that splendid dilettante, to whom he had already transmitted some of his more fantastic notions: and Digby, having had the books handsomely bound and engraved with his own arms, presented them, after consultation with Laud and Sir Robert Cotton, to the Bodleian Library. The collection thus acquired included 238 manuscripts in vellum: and at the end of 1634 Laud received the thanks of the University for his share in the transaction which had secured them. Nor was this the only occasion on which Laud utilised the munificence of Digby. At another time Digby mentioned to the King that he had made a collection of Arabic books which he intended for his old University, and Laud, who was present, begged him to send them to St. John's College, whither he was himself despatching a similar collection. Digby agreed, and put the books at Laud's disposal, with the result that they are now in the library of St. John's College, together with the Archbishop's own gifts.[1]

Laud's interest in Oriental studies was illustrated in many ways in his dealings with the University. He had not himself, as Andrewes had, any acquaintance with the Eastern tongues: but he was determined to patronise and encourage those who had. In February 1634 he procured a royal letter to the Turkey Company requiring that each of their ships returning from the East should bring one Persian or Arabic manuscript, — not a Koran, of which sufficient copies were already available in England, — and the number of Oriental manuscripts which he was able to present to the Bodleian or to his old college is witness to the results which he secured.[2]

For other branches of learning he was equally solicitous. In 1631, when the King's printers, Messrs. Barker and Lucas, produced a Bible in which their employees had introduced some indecent emendations, such as a direct command to commit adultery in the Decalogue, they were heavily fined in the High Commission, and received a sharp homily from Laud, who criticised not only their corrupt text but their inferior paper and exorbitant price. Their punishment, however, was afterwards altered in a characteristic way. Patrick Young, the King's librarian, a man whose reputation for scholarship stood second only to that of Selden in his day, and who had probably come into contact with Laud when he was appointed to catalogue the Barocci manuscripts, had recently published a fine edition of Clemens Romanus in Greek and Latin. This edition came to the notice of Laud, himself a great champion of patristic studies, and, fired by its excellence, Laud offered to commute the fine which he had imposed upon Barker and Lucas if they would undertake to procure a Greek fount in order to issue one learned book a year, at the dictation of Patrick Young, or Augustine Lindsell, or some other qualified person.[3] The printers agreed with alacrity, and thus Laud realised one of his ambitions, — "to set up a Greek press in London for the printing of the library manuscripts". No effort was spared to make the

[1] Digby to Langbaine, Nov. 7th, 1654, in *Letters written by Eminent Persons* (1813), i. 1.

[2] *S.P. Dom. Car. I.* 260, no. 116.

[3] Laud, *Works*, vi. 342.

new venture successful. The London printer John Haviland was sent to Brussels to negotiate the purchase of the best possible types and matrices, and when the Antwerp printer was reluctant to part with his types the English Resident at Brussels, Balthazar Gerbier, enlisted the support of the painter Rubens, and went to Antwerp in person to secure them.[1] In 1636 the first volume from the new press was published — the late Augustine Lindsell's edition of Theophylact: and next year it was followed by Nicetas of Heraclea's *Catena*, or collection of Greek commentaries on the book of Job, — a work which won for Laud the congratulations of Archbishop Ussher. Included in the *Catena* was the text of Job reprinted from the *Codex Alexandrinus* of the Greek Scriptures which the Patriarch Cyril Lucaris of Constantinople had presented, through Sir Thomas Roe, to the King; and Laud had an off-print of this text made and separately bound in gilded vellum for presentation to the Patriarch. Before the gift could be sent, however, the news of the Patriarch's assassination reached England, and the presentation copy went to the Bodleian instead. In it is a Greek inscription by Laud, which shows that he intended in time to have the whole text of the *Codex Alexandrinus* printed by the same press.[2] This, however, was not done: for Patrick Young's edition of Gilbert Foliot's exposition on the Song of Songs, which appeared in 1638, was the last work to be issued by the press under Laud's direction. When the Long Parliament declared the Court of High Commission to be unconstitutional, the penalty imposed upon Barker and Lucas was reversed, and the good work which it had occasioned came automatically to an end.

Laud's parallel ambition to provide Oxford also with a Greek press remained unrealised, but the official University press there received his attention. The printer maintained by the University had, at the time of Laud's accession to the chancellorship, no warrant in the University charter: but in 1633 Laud secured letters patent regularising his status. Agreement was reached with

[1] *Vide* W. N. Sainsbury, *Original Unpublished Papers illustrative of the Life of Rubens* (1859), p. 187.

[2] In the inscription Laud declares that he is sending the volume to the Patriarch—

ὡς πρόδρομον ἐπίδειγμα τῶν λοιπῶν τῆς παλαιᾶς διαθήκης βιβλίων . . . ἐν βραχεῖ σὺν Θεῷ εἰς φῶς καὶ ἡμέραν ἐκδοθησομένων.

(Cf. A. D. Macray, in *The Bibliographer*, i. 121.)

the Stationers' Hall Company whereby the University printer, on undertaking not to print Bibles or certain other remunerative works for a space of three years, was to receive a sum of £200 a year to be devoted to the purchase of stock: the paper, types, and other material were required to be the best available: and for the printing of Oriental works a skilled compositor was imported from Leyden, where the works of the Dutch Orientalist Erpenius had been printed. By a charter of 1636 the rights of the new University press were extended: but in spite of all these efforts we find the Vice-chancellor complaining to the Archbishop in January 1637 that the University printer refused to advance a learned press at Oxford, or to print an edition of John of Antioch, as was required, but would only produce more profitable almanacs and textbooks; and early in 1640 Laud protested to the Vice-chancellor against the publication of the works of Ames and Festus Hommius, both "professed friends to the presbyterial government", by the University printers. "I pray speak with the printers", he wrote, "and let them know from me that I will not allow them to print any book, though it hath been printed before, without new leave from the Vice-chancellor for the time being; and that if they do print anything without such leave, I will utterly suppress them." [1] Private enterprise, it was everywhere proved, was slow to second Laud's altruistic designs, and printers, even those whom Laud had himself advanced, preferred their own profit to the cold satisfaction of advancing learning.

Yet another example of Laud's use of the beneficence of others is provided by his presentation of coins to the University. On June 16th, 1636, Laud wrote to the University cataloguing a further list of donations which he had secured for it. First was a collection of manuscripts, procured at his own expense, during the last year, "eighteen Hebrew, fourteen Persian, fifty Arabic, one Armenian, two Aethiopic, one Chinese, four French, and two Irish". Next came an Arabian astrolabe, the gift of John Selden, whose zeal for learning made him a friend of the Archbishop in spite of their wide disagreement on the subjects of religion and the constitution. Then there was the statue of King Charles which Laud had had executed for his new quadrangle by Hubert le Sueur. A West Indian and an Egyptian idol were

[1] Laud, *Works*, v. 254-5.

added as curiosities ; and finally there were five cabinets of coins, carefully arranged and distributed according to their dates and origins.[1] These coins had been collected by a learned antiquary and numismatist, Dr. John Barcham, Dean of Bocking and a fellow of Corpus Christi, who had presented them to Laud. We shall see that Laud also procured Oriental coins through his protégé Edward Pococke : and it was no doubt a result of his influence that Sir Thomas Roe presented a further collection of 244 coins in the summer of 1644, although at that time Laud, a prisoner in the Tower, was no longer Chancellor. The University, on receipt of these handsome donations, expressed its gratitude in fulsome and obsequious terms, acclaiming the Chancellor as a reservoir of divine munificence, receiving the wealth brought by innumerable pipes, and discharging it into the Church and the University : and when Convocation somewhat overreached itself by calling him " our father, leader, angel, archangel ", the blasphemous words were, rather unfairly, charged against the Archbishop at his trial.

But if a University is a repository of learning and culture, it is also a place of government and discipline : and if Laud, as Chancellor, was a patron of learning and a zealous assertor of orthodoxy, he was also a meticulous administrator and a restless martinet. Immediately after his election he had written to the Vice-chancellor urging the careful observance of " formalities which are in a sort the outward and visible face of the University " : and the result had been seen on the following degree-day, when the long-neglected statutes concerning academical dress were scrupulously enforced. On every detail of University life Laud kept a vigilant eye, requiring full and frequent accounts from his subordinates, and allowing no irregularity to pass unnoticed. Undergraduates were ordered to desist from poaching His Majesty's game in the royal preserves of Stow Wood and Shotover. For both undergraduates and fellows boots and spurs beneath academical dress were absolutely forbidden, long hair explicitly discountenanced : and on one occasion the Vice-chancellor reported to the heads of their colleges all those who came before him for matriculation with long hair.[2] Drinking in taverns, too, which had been on the increase since King James' courtiers, attending

[1] Laud, *Works*, v. 135.

[2] Crosfield, *Diary*, Nov. 11th, 1632.

their master to Oxford in 1606, had set the example, was now restricted, and the licensed alehouses were reduced from three hundred to a hundred. These, however, were details, and Laud was more ambitious than to content himself with the regulation of details. For everything which he did, distrusting mere opportunist policy, he sought the support of an authoritative decision recorded in an indisputable document. The neglect of details in University life was evidence that the old statutes were superannuated, and therefore regarded with indifference. New statutes were therefore necessary, — indeed, they had long been contemplated : and Laud, who was not the man to set his hand to the plough and then turn back, saw them formulated and published.

The three most outstanding results of Laud's chancellorship at Oxford, — the Laudian statutes, the Laudian chair of Arabic, and the building of Canterbury Quadrangle in St. John's College, — were all completed in the same summer of 1636, in which his political career seemed also to have achieved its zenith. For the statutes it would be unjust to give the credit entirely to Laud. The idea had originated under his predecessor, and he was at that time placed on the delegacy to which the work was entrusted. Later, when Laud himself succeeded to the chancellorship, the delegacy remained charged with the task, and devolved it in turn upon a subdelegacy of four men, who were chiefly responsible for the details of the new statutes. These were Thomas James, Bodley's librarian ; Richard Zouche, the Regius professor of civil law ; Peter Turner, the professor of geometry, a zealous Laudian ; and Brian Twyne, an indefatigable antiquary, whose prominent part in the formulation of the statutes was rewarded by his appointment to the new post of keeper of the University archives. Nevertheless it was Laud's dynamic energy that forced through a project whose necessity was apparent to all, but which, like many other necessary projects, might otherwise have had to wait a century or two for its fulfilment. Laud watched the preparation of the statutes with great interest, and during the period of their gestation he hurried the delegacy on, even hoping to see the work completed within a year. This was impossible : but in August 1633, the month of his elevation to Canterbury, the draft was complete, and, having been accepted unanimously by Convocation, was passed on to the Chancellor for his revision. Next July Laud sent down printed copies, incorporating his amendments, for the University, colleges, and halls: the statutes were given a year's probation, from which they emerged with credit: on June 2nd, 1636, they received the signature of the Archbishop, on the next day that of the King: and on June 22nd a Convocation was held to confirm them as the written constitution of the University. Whether the University was exercising a sovereign right in confirming the statutes, or was merely accepting a set of rules imposed upon it by the royal authority, was a question which did not occur to the Vice-chancellor and Heads of Houses at the time, although it became a hotly contested point more than a century later, and was only finally settled by the University Commissioners in 1850. At present the University was only concerned to accept with gratitude the first comprehensive embodiment of its rules. Letters were read from the King and the Archbishop: the usual speeches of gratitude were delivered: and the statutes were received.

Apart from the obvious importance of their mere compilation, the chief change which they introduced into the life of the University was the substitution of examination for degrees, which has since developed into so universal a system, for the old method whereby candidates were required to listen for two years to Latin debates, to participate in them for a further two years, and to submit theses, declamations, and testimonials, — undoubtedly a salutary change, although at the time there was a regular flight of students to Cambridge to avoid its operation. Among the other rules incorporated in the statutes were three separate innovations which owed their inclusion not to the lucubrations of Brian Twyne but to the interposition of the King. These were known as the Statuta Carolina, and in the text of the statutes their authority is expressly attributed to the royal command. One of these was the order establishing a fixed proctorial cycle, to prevent the disturbances incidental to election, which had been imposed in 1628, and was partly due to the efforts of Laud as the King's unofficial adviser.

The importance of the Laudian statutes is undoubted, even as a mere act of compilation. It took more than a century for the University to discover that they provided no certain machinery for their own alteration. This problem probably never occurred to Laud: for we may safely assume that he intended the statutes to be received by the University as royal legislation. Throughout his career he acted on the general principle that all authority ought to come from above, from a government which he regarded as impersonal, conscientious, and efficient, while election and representation merely gave authoritative expression to obstructive personal interests. It is to this principle that some of the most objectionable of Laud's actions must be attributed: for in his substitution of devolved for elected authority in every department of administration he paid but little attention to the claims of statute, charter, or tradition; and whether it was the provision of a vicar for a parish, a schoolmaster, or a member of Parliament for a borough, a deputy-governor for a commercial company, or a provost for a college, we find him invariably convinced that the members themselves were incapable of choosing a more efficient candidate than he could impose upon them, — and if incapable in fact, then he regarded them as incapable in law also, whatever their customs or privileges might maintain. Even in Oxford he was guilty of the same usurpations, as a notable case in the autumn of 1635 had shown.

It concerned the election to a vacant fellowship at All Souls, Laud had written to the Warden and Fellows requesting them to elect his nominee, — a proceeding so frequent as not to be regarded as improper. But this nominee was a Cambridge man, and although Laud had had him incorporated at Oxford three days before he wrote, in order to qualify him for the position, and although the majority of the Fellows of the college were prepared to elect him, the Warden, Dr. Astley[1], was not. He wrote to the Archbishop objecting that, according to the college statutes, a candidate must have been a member of the University for three years, not three days. This objection, however, Laud would not admit. He insisted upon the claims of his candidate, whom the Fellows supported: and then, when the dispute between Warden and Fellows caused the matter to be referred to the Visitor, the Visitor, being the Archbishop himself, nominated his own candidate by his own authority. The whole affair shows the contemptuous way in which Laud used his authority to override local privileges, however well-founded, which hindered the fulfilment of his designs; but at the same time the name of his candidate shows the conscientious purposes for which he exercised these questionable powers, — for it was Jeremy Taylor. If Laud imposed his

[1] Not, as has been regularly assumed, Gilbert Sheldon.

nominees on bodies which were entitled to choose their representatives, at least his nominees did not owe their advantage to nepotism or favour.

A more exclusively personal achievement of the Archbishop, which was brought to fulfilment at the same time as the statutes, was the foundation at Oxford of a lectureship in Arabic, and the securing for it of the services of Edward Pococke. By a decree of the Council of Vienne in 1511 Pope Clement V had required all *studia generalia*, as the larger universities were called, to possess the faculties of Greek, Hebrew, Syriac, and Arabic. The response, however, was slow in coming: and when it came, it was due less to the authority of the Pope than to the efforts of humanist scholars. Cardinal Wolsey, to some extent, realised the educational aims of the Church by the foundation and endowment of chairs of Greek and Hebrew at Oxford, which Henry VIII confirmed: but Arabic, in spite of the fillip that it received from the enthusiasm of Scaliger and the work of Erpenius abroad, and the example of Lancelot Andrewes in England, remained still unendowed at Oxford when Laud succeeded Pembroke as Chancellor. By this time the deficiency was obvious, for Arabic studies were now being taken seriously in England. In 1625 Matthias Pasor, an Orientalist from Heidelberg, was giving lectures in the language at Oxford, and one William Bedwell was credited with greater attainments than Erpenius himself, had his slowness not deprived him of his just portion of fame: while in Cambridge a rich London alderman had founded an Arabic lectureship for Abraham Wheelocke in 1631. The deficiency at Oxford, made more conspicuous by this interest elsewhere, provided Laud with an opportunity especially adapted to his tastes. The patronage of right learning was in the tradition of the great Princes of the Church, and his own interest in the propagation of Oriental studies had already been signally illustrated. In addition to his many donations, he had enriched the already existing chair of Hebrew at Oxford by annexing to it a canonry at Christ Church, as he had done also to the office of Public Orator. The endowment of new chairs had received prominence, too, from the munificence of Sir Henry Savile, who had provided chairs of astronomy and geometry. Everything pointed to the early recognition of Arabic studies, and to their recognition by Laud. The immediate incentive, however, was probably Laud's desire to secure the services of Edward Pococke, which might otherwise have been diverted to the Netherlands, or wasted in the desert.

Edward Pococke [1] had studied Arabic under Pasor in Oxford, and had later received instruction from Bedwell. In 1628 he produced an edition of four hitherto unprinted epistles from the Syriac New Testament: and this work, being shown to Vossius when he visited Oxford in that year, so excited his admiration that he had it printed by Erpenius' press at Leyden. Then, in 1630, Pococke was selected by the Levant Company to act as chaplain to their factory at Aleppo.

There is no evidence of any connexion between Laud and Pococke before Pococke left England in 1630, and in Laud's first letter to him, written in the following year, in which he requests Pococke to bring back any Greek or Oriental coins or manuscripts which he may find on his travels, he expressly states that his application was due to the recommendation of Bedwell.[2] Nearly three years later, however, when the Archbishop wrote to thank Pococke for forwarding to him some coins, he added a hope that Pococke would equip himself so as to be able to teach Arabic in England on his return, indicating that he had already designated him for the chair whose foundation he was contemplating. It may well be that it was the high opinion of Vossius which determined Laud to found a lectureship especially for a scholar whom he had never met, and of whose attainments he was himself unable to form an opinion; but however this may be, in 1635 Pococke left Aleppo, and in the following July presented himself at Oxford to assume the degree of Bachelor of Divinity. A month later, the Vice-chancellor, Richard Baylie, announced in Convocation that the Chancellor was augmenting his many gifts of Arabic books by the foundation of an Arabic lectureship, which he had endowed for the length of his own life with £40 a year, and that the first lecturer would be Edward Pococke, who was installed two days later and began his course of lectures on the Proverbs of Ali.

[1] See L. Twells, *Life of Edward Pococke*, 1816.

[2] That Laud was unacquainted with Pococke before Pococke left England is also shown by a letter of Pococke (quoted by Twells, p. 99) in which he refers to "his continuance at Aleppo, which first recommended him to the choice of the Archbishop".

In the interests of completeness, even if at the expense of chronology, we may here continue the catalogue of Laud's Oriental interests. In 1637 he permitted Pococke to return to the East in search of new material in the company of another Orientalist whom he patronised, one John Greaves, whose brother, Thomas Greaves, supplied Pococke's place in Oxford during his absence. Armed with the recommendations of the Archbishop, Pococke pursued his researches in Constantinople, enjoying the friendship and hospitality of successive English ambassadors and of the reforming Greek Patriarch, Cyril Lucaris. In 1638 Laud wrote to him, on the motion of Archbishop Ussher, urging him to procure a copy of the Ὑποτυπώσεις of Clement of Alexandria, if possible, from the Patriarch, and to continue his search for manuscripts in Anatolia and the monasteries of Mount Athos. In his reply, however, Pococke related the assassination of the Patriarch by the orders of the Sultan, thus preventing the despatch of Laud's presentation copy of the Book of Job as well as the fulfilment of Ussher's intentions. Meanwhile Greaves proceeded to Alexandria, and reported thence his indefatigable journeys in search of manuscripts. When Pococke returned to England it was to find his patron in the Tower, but to learn that his lectureship at Oxford was no longer dependent upon the Archbishop's now precarious life ; this interview, however, will be related later, in its proper place. Another Orientalist whom Laud befriended was Christianus Ravius, a German whom Vossius had recommended to him. Laud gave him letters of recommendation to the British ambassador at Constantinople, Sir Sackville Crow, who looked after him when he arrived there in a penniless condition, having fallen among thieves on the way. Yet another was a Cretan, Nathaniel Conopius, who had enjoyed a position in the service of the Patriarch Cyril till the assassination of his master compelled him to seek safety outside the dominions of the Sultan. He reached England with letters from Sir Peter Wych, Crow's predecessor at Constantinople, and was received at Oxford by Laud, who selected Balliol as his place of education and later provided him with a petty canon's place in Christ Church. He was evidently a man of some attainments, for he corresponded with Patrick Young, and the French scholar Claude Saumaise, better known as Salmasius, the discoverer of the Palatine Anthology and adversary of Milton, who was also a student of Arabic:[1] and another of his patrons was William Harvey, the discoverer of the circulation of the blood, and physician to King Charles.[2] Conopius was later expelled from Oxford by the parliamentary visitors, and, after appealing through Vossius to the States-General of the Netherlands to pay his fare home, he returned to the Levant and became bishop of Smyrna.[3] His sojourn at Oxford, however, was not entirely barren: for Evelyn and Wood both record that he was the first man to drink coffee in England.

A less conspicuous, but equally typical, example of Laud's patronage is provided by Thomas Lydiat, the ecclesiastical chronologer, whose name, but for the odd fancy of Dr. Johnson in coupling it with that of Galileo, would scarcely have been remembered, even by the curious. Lydiat had been imprisoned for debt, first in Bocardo and then in the King's Bench, — a confinement which providentially prevented the publication of his six hundred sermons on the Harmony of the Evangelists, — and Laud joined his influence and generosity with that of Ussher, Sir William Boswell, and the Warden of New College, in order to secure his release.

The third great achievement of the year 1636 was the completion of Canterbury Quadrangle at St. John's College, which Laud had begun, as a lasting memorial of his connexion with that college, five years previously. In November 1630 he had made a memorandum of his intention " to build at St. John's in Oxford, where I was bred up, for the good and safety of that college ", and the execution followed quickly upon the intention. When the Fellows of the college first learnt of their former President's design, they wrote to him, in the usual fulsome strain of university divines, that if their gratitude were mute, the very stones of their college would, like the statue of Memnon mentioned by Tacitus, give forth music to his glory. In April 1631 they passed a resolution accepting the plan, and one of their number, John Lufton, was appointed overseer of the operations: and on July 26th of the same year the first stone of the new building was laid. Apart

[1] See Kemke, *Patricius Junius* (Leipzig, 1898), pp. 104-5, 136-8.

[2] A Greek manuscript volume in the library of Trinity College, Cambridge (no. 1165), contains a Greek inscription indicating that it was presented by Conopius to Harvey, τῷ ἐμῷ προθυμοτάτῳ εὐεργετῇ.

[3] *Vossii Ep.*, no. 818; *Ep. ad Vossium*, no. 220.

from the timber which the King provided from the royal forests of Shotover and Stow Wood, the entire cost was borne by Laud; and in 1636 enthusiastic verses by the wits and poets of the University celebrated the completion of what is perhaps the most beautiful quadrangle in Oxford, and certainly the most lasting achievement of Laud.

Both the plan and the cost of the undertaking had grown in the course of its fulfilment. The south and west sides of the quadrangle were already supplied by the Old Library and the President's Lodgings respectively, both built about 1597, and Laud's original intention, in 1630, had been merely to add a new range of buildings on the north side, opposite the library, and to complete the design by a high "dead wall" joining them at the east. Both the new building and the library were to be adorned with battlements: two new rooms at the east and a bay-window at the west were to be added to the President's Lodgings: a cloister on pillars was to run along under the dead wall: and the total cost was estimated at £1055. But the scheme was soon considerably enlarged, and in 1632 we find that it had come to include the addition of a gallery, carried on a cloister, to the President's Lodgings, while the dead wall on the opposite side was to be replaced by a range of buildings, completing the quadrangle, and also carried on a cloister exactly matching its counterpart. This new east range was to contain a New Library, and, to complete the symmetry, the Old Library was to be "pieced out" by a distance of twenty feet. Laud had also decided on elaborately sculptured frontispieces; and these changes raised the estimated cost to £3200, — just over three times the original figure. Even this, however, was ultimately exceeded: for when the work was finished in April 1636 it had cost a total of £5087,[1] all of which was met by the Archbishop.

The style of the new quadrangle is composite, —classical decoration superimposed upon a general Gothic design. While the outer front of the New Library, which looks out over the college garden, was finished in a simple and austere style, the inner façade, overlooking the quadrangle, is varied with the ornaments of Renaissance architecture. Above the graceful

[1] W. H. Hutton (*St. John's College*, 1898, p. 128) says that the total cost was £3208 : 4 : 3; but this is merely the sum paid out to Lufton by Baylie, who succeeded Juxon as president in 1632, after the work was begun. Juxon had already paid Lufton £1878 : 6 : 8.

colonnades, built according to the suggestion and design of the Archbishop, two bronze statues of the King and Queen, executed for a fee of £400 by Hubert le Sueur, were placed in the centre of the east and west frontispieces respectively, with a series of busts on either side, representing, around the King, the seven Liberal Arts, and around the Queen, the four pagan and three Christian Virtues. Busts of Laud himself, also by le Sueur, were placed in the library and in the President's Lodgings ; and another gilt bust of King Charles was in the library. Most of the stone for the quadrangle had been quarried at Headington or at Taynton, near Burford ; but the marble for the pillars of the colonnades had been brought from Bletchingdon, — Bishop Juxon's peculiar contribution : for he had discovered it while hunting his hounds there.

As to the architect of this work, there is no certainty, and there has been much speculation. For a long time it was supposed to have been Inigo Jones : but there is no early authority for this tradition, and Jones is not known to have built anything at Oxford. Others have suggested that the master builder John Jackson, who was entrusted with the execution of the building, and afterwards did much work at Oxford, had a hand in the design also : but Jackson was only brought from London in 1634, when two previous masons had been discharged in turn, and the work was already half completed. The sculptor le Sueur has even been mentioned as a candidate : but there is neither evidence nor likelihood for this conjecture. The most recent suggestion [1] is that the architect was Nicholas Stone, the master mason to the King, who executed much of Inigo Jones' work.

[1] By Mr. A. Oswald, whose admirable article on Canterbury Quadrangle in *Country Life*, Nov. 9th, 1929, has been followed in this account. Mr. Oswald, however, has since informed me that he has revised his view, and now believes that the Inigo Jones tradition may well be right after all. "The difficulty", he writes, "of accepting the Nicholas Stone theory (which otherwise meets the case) is that so important a work would almost certainly have found a place in the list compiled by his nephew, Charles Stoakes. I think, too, I over-emphasised the Flemish character of the work." He therefore suggests that Laud asked Jones, to whom he would naturally apply, to sketch designs for the frontispiece, arcades, and doorways, and sent them down to the masons on the spot to work from, and that any coarseness in execution or over-elaboration of the sculpture can be explained by the fact that Jones did not supervise the work in person. "The more one examines the careers of Inigo Jones and Wren, the more evidence accumulates of their providing designs for buildings which other work prevented them from supervising ; and I am inclined to think that this is what happened at St. John's." Mr. J. Alfred Gotch (*Inigo Jones*, 1928) rejects the attribution to Jones.

CANTERBURY QUADRANGLE, ST. JOHN'S COLLEGE

Classical Frontispiece and Cloister of Laud's Library Range

Stone was engaged on the portico at the west end of St. Paul's, and would thus have come into contact with Laud, and he is known to have visited Oxford at least twice during the time when the quadrangle was being built: and this suggestion is further supported by the Flemish character of the work, and its resemblance to other works by Stone, who spent some years in youth studying under the architect Hendrik de Keyser in Holland, and by the fact that the two principal carvers employed on the St. John's building, Gore and Acres, are both known as regular assistants of Stone.

The universal triumph of Laud in Oxford, which these three great achievements, coming to completion at the same time, so aptly symbolised, was consecrated in the summer of 1636 by the visit which the King and Queen made to Oxford to inspect his handiwork. The visit was unsolicited, and the Archbishop made the most of it: for in a sense it was a visit of homage to himself. Windebank, impressed by such manifest proof of the Archbishop's supremacy, sought to make his peace with him, and offered the hospitality of his house at Haines Hill, which Laud had been accustomed to enjoy in his earlier days. The attempted reconciliation was made through Juxon, who protested to Laud that an old personal friendship ought not permanently to be dissolved because the parties held different views on the relative merits of two brands of soap.[1] But to Laud there was no such thing as a purely personal friendship. His associations were based solely on community of ideas, and in the matter of the soap companies Windebank had shown that this community of ideas no longer existed. So Juxon went empty away, and Laud reported with satisfaction to Wentworth that secretary Windebank was mightily troubled at his refusal, which would confirm the report of his unworthy carriage towards him.

Another who solicited the honour of entertaining the Archbishop on his triumphal progress from Croydon to the seat of his splendour at Oxford was Sir Thomas Roe, who, though he knew well enough that it was Laud who had excluded him from political life, differed from him in making his personal relations independent of political disappointments. This invitation was accepted, but with two conditions which, if they prove Laud's frugality and his diligence, remind us also of his lack of humanity:

[1] Juxon to Windebank, *S.P. Dom. Car. I.* 330, no. 33.

"the one, that you will let me come as to a private lodging, for ease, and not trouble yourself with chargeable entertainment; the other, that you will let me be gone betimes in the morning, without eating: for my thoughts will be full of my business, and will make me no good company for any of my friends".[1] To Laud everything was business; he could not enjoy even the celebration of his own triumph.

So, after setting out in a coach-and-six accompanied by fifty mounted attendants, Laud stayed the first night of his journey with Sir Thomas Roe at Cranford, and then proceeded towards Oxford, spending the second night at Cuddesdon, in the palace which he had persuaded Bishop Bancroft to erect for himself and his successors in that see. At noon on the third day he entered Oxford unattended, having sent his servants ahead on the previous day, and found the University busy with the preparations for the royal visit, now only four days off. The town was full of noblemen, courtiers, and sightseers: and the preparations, as we should expect wherever Laud was concerned, were minute and comprehensive. To ensure discipline among the undergraduates a proctor was allotted to each college, and the licentious, but apparently ineradicable, habit of cultivating long hair was ruthlessly dealt with. "The chiefest thing they will amend", young Edmund Verney wrote to his father from Magdalen Hall, "is the wearing of long hair. The Principal protested that after this day he would turn out of his house whomsoever he found with hair longer than the tips of his ears"; and he requested his father to summon him home for the duration of the King's visit in order to preserve his own hair from such mutilation.[2]

On August 29th the King and Queen were due to arrive from Woodstock, and University dignitaries collected at St. John's to attend the Archbishop, who was ultimately released by his barber and walked out to greet them. "Courteous he was to all," says an eye-witness, "but walked most and entertained longest my Lord Cottington", — having defeated him in the matter of the Treasury, Laud could now afford to show a studied courtesy to his old rival, — "showing him his new building, the rooms where he meant to entertain the King, and the hall where the play was to be." After a period of perambulation, inspection, and gossip, the University bell was rung at one o'clock,

[1] Laud, *Works*, vii. 265. [2] *Verney Papers* (Camden Soc., 1853), p. 188.

and the company reassembled around the Chancellor to escort him in procession along the Woodstock Road. There, about a mile from the city, they were met by the royal party, among whom were the two exiled Princes of the Palatinate, Charles Lewis and Rupert. Laud had already met and entertained the Elector, but he was not impressed by his fitness to recover a lost inheritance, and agreed with Wentworth that "he is of too gentle a spirit to bustle through this business". Rupert, however, had already shown signs of his more adventurous disposition, which was later to receive such scope in the Civil Wars, and his mother had recently been sending urgent appeals from the Hague to prevent him from undertaking a fantastic project, which she compared to Don Quixote's exploits among the windmills, of conquering for himself a new kingdom in Madagascar.

The royal party was welcomed with a speech from the Vice-chancellor, Richard Baylie, the President of St. John's, and then Laud, in the name of the University, gave presents all round. The King received a folio Bible with a velvet cover, richly embroidered with the royal arms and valued at £80, together with a pair of gloves; Camden's *History of Queen Elizabeth* was given to Henrietta Maria, also with a pair of gloves; Hooker's *Ecclesiastical Polity* went to the Prince Elector; and for Prince Rupert *Caesar's Commentaries* (in translation) were considered more appropriate. After the presentations a procession was formed, headed by sixty citizens in scarlet robes, mounted on horseback, with attendants, and followed by the mayor: then the University officials, the proctors and the doctors; then the Bishops of Winchester, Oxford, and Norwich, followed by Lord Treasurer Juxon, with mace-bearers and attendants. Juxon was followed by Laud, and behind Laud came the royal coach with the King and Queen and two Princes Palatine. Cottington, as Lord Chamberlain, with the guards, brought up the rear. The road was lined on each side by spectators. Outside Bocardo, the old prison, stood the four companies of the City, and from Bocardo to Christ Church, where the royal party was lodged, the undergraduates, Bachelors of Arts, Masters of Arts, and Bachelors of Law and Divinity were ranged in their formalities. At St. John's another speech was made, and at Christ Church a third, by William Strode, the poet and Public Orator. Then the royal party were free to seek their lodgings, and the tedious succession of speeches was followed by the tedious alternation of religious services and plays.

Dramatic performances had long been the accepted method of entertaining royalty at the Universities, and the cold reception which these performances generally received failed to discourage the authorities from continuing to provide them. In the early seventeenth century they were particularly popular among producers, and, at Oxford, Christ Church and St John's College contended for the dramatic crown. Soon after Laud's admittance to St. John's as an undergraduate, as we have seen, that college indulged in a whole series of such revels: and in 1606, when King James visited the University, the dramatists and actors at once made the most of their opportunity. A pastoral, "Alba", was enacted at Christ Church on the first night: but it was not a success. The Queen and the ladies greatly disliked, or professed to dislike, the introduction of "five or six men almost naked", and only the entreaties of the Chancellors of both Universities prevented the King from leaving "before half the comedy had been ended". Undeterred, the University presented on the following night a play which had already been countermanded by Queen Elizabeth forty years earlier. King James thought no more highly of it. We are informed that he "was very weary before he came thither, and much more wearied by it, and spoke many words of dislike".[1] On the third night he was condemned to see *Vertumnus, sive Annus Recurrens*, composed by a Fellow of St. John's and acted at Christ Church. He did not, however, see all of it, as he fell asleep in the middle. Even that loyal Oxonian Sir Thomas Bodley had to admit that "their tragedy and comedies were very clerkly penned, but not so well acted, and somewhat over-tedious". When Prince Charles and the Elector Frederick, his brother-in-law, visited Cambridge in 1613, they fared no better. The comedy which was there presented to them lasted no less than six hours, and the Elector slept through the greater part of it. And in 1621 Oxford was rash enough to produce before the King Barten Holiday's *Technogamia, or the Marriage of the Arts*, which had already proved a fiasco at Christ Church four years previously. The result was as might have been forecast. "It proved so tedious, as well for the matter as the action", reported the news-writer Chamberlain, "that the King endured

[1] Account printed in Leland, *Collectanea*, ed. 1770, ii. 637.

it with great impatience, whereupon the boys and children flouted it with a rhyme ". This rhyme was probably that which the Oxford wits produced for the occasion :

Christ Church the Arts' Marriage shew'd before the King :
And lest the match should want an offering,
The King himself did offer — what, I pray ?
— He offer'd twice or thrice to go away.

In spite of this melancholy record, Laud prepared to continue the custom : on the first night the King was to see a play in Christ Church, provided by the whole University, and on the second Laud himself provided another entirely at his own cost. With characteristic thoroughness he entered into every detail of the productions, even giving minute instructions about the preservation and disposal of the stage effects. His own ideas, too, were somewhat obviously obtruded in the first play, which was written for the occasion by William Strode, the Public Orator. It was called *Passions Calmed, or the Floating Island*, and was elaborately staged with mechanical billows, and music by Harry Lawes ; and it conveyed an appropriate moral lesson, representing the evil consequences of rebellion. King Prudentius is deposed from his throne as the result of a conspiracy hatched by Audax, Irato, and other undesirable characters, who thereupon proclaim Fancy queen, whose only law is, like that of Rabelais' monastery, " that each man use his proper humour, be it vice or virtue ". Discord, of course, ensues, and in the end King Prudentius is implored to resume his crown and restore the rule of ordered orthodoxy. To complete the allusion to contemporary politics, a parody of Prynne was introduced in the character of Malevolo, a play-hating Puritan.[1] In view of the unexceptionable

[1] The parody of Prynne is clear from such lines as :

" For my part, if I broach
Some biting libel, venomous word or book,
Against some prosp'rous object which I hate,
My ears are question'd. Locks which I have scorn'd
Must hide my ear-stumps " ; (11.148-52)

and

" This trick, Malevolo,
Was chiefly meant to you, because your pen
Hath scourg'd the stage." (11.196-8)

It is probable that other characters in the play were intended to represent living persons in opposition to the government. (Cf. the *Poems of William Strode*, ed. B. Dobell, 1907.)

sentiments expressed in the play, it was unfortunate that it was not received with greater satisfaction. Laud declared that it was " very well penned, but yet did not take the Court so well ". Lord Carnarvon was more explicit, saying that " it was the worst that ever he saw, but one that he saw at Cambridge ".

Next day a Convocation was held, and the two Princes were given honorary degrees, their names being entered in St. John's College as a compliment to the Archbishop. Prince Rupert was made a Master of Arts : but as the Elector was able to give degrees in his own University of Heidelberg, — or at least would be if ever he should recover his lost dominions, — so slight an honour was considered beneath his dignity, and it was agreed that whomsoever he recommended should be made Doctor of Divinity for his sake. Afterwards honorary degrees were showered upon courtiers and upon the two Cambridge bishops, and the party adjourned to St. John's to admire the new buildings there, and to sit down to the splendid feast which the Archbishop had provided for them.

If the Court disapproved of the edifying play, they were appeased by the prodigious feast. " No man went out of the gates, courtier or other, but content ", the Archbishop recorded with satisfaction. On so lavish a scale was everything ordered that men were reminded of the pre-Reformation Princes of the Church and their ceremonial junketings. In the New Library, which Laud had built, he sat at the High Table with the King and Queen and Prince Elector, and at another table in the body of the room sat Prince Rupert with all the lords and ladies. Thirteen other tables were set in different rooms throughout the college, and all present gorged abundantly. Clarendon records the great excess of feasting as a vice of that age, and makes particular mention of the famous banquet given to the King by the Earl of Newcastle in 1633 : but the garrulous letter-writer, George Garrarde, assured Lord Conway that Newcastle's feast could not rival this sumptuous entertainment given by the Archbishop. Laud's steward reported the total cost as £2266 : 1 : 7, — almost half the cost of the entire quadrangle — without counting the provisions which were sent as gifts by noblemen and friends of the Archbishop. These included a fat ox, twenty fat sheep, a brace of stags, and a brace of bucks from Sir Thomas Lucy, fifty fat sheep and twenty brace of pheasant from the Earl of

Newburgh, " a huge fat ox, besides fowl and extraordinary fish " from Sir Thomas Somerset, and numerous smaller consignments of game. " The baked meats ", says one observer, " were so contrived by the cook that there was first the forms of archbishops, then bishops, doctors, etc., seen in order, wherein the King and courtiers took much content ".[1] Laud certainly advertised his contempt for Puritan ideas in the lavishness of his entertainment: and the Puritans did not allow it to pass without comment. Next year, Henry Burton published his *Divine Judgment upon Sabbath-Breakers*, in which Laud was attacked " for feasting and profane plays at Oxford ".

The profane plays which followed the feast were, perhaps for that reason, better received by the Court than that of the previous day. They were *Love's Hospital*, by George Wilde, a fellow of St. John's College, acted at St. John's, and financed by Laud, and then, after another repast, Cartwright's *Royal Slave*, produced at Christ Church, with scenery by Inigo Jones and music by Harry Lawes. The latter was a great success, and the Queen afterwards borrowed the costumes in order to repeat the performance with her own company at Hampton Court. Laud, however, could not resist the observation that " by all men's confession, the players came short of the University actors ".

Thus when, amid the usual congratulatory speeches, the royal party took their departure next day, their entertainment at Oxford seemed to have been an unqualified success: and the general satisfaction in the University was increased when Laud entertained all the Heads of Houses and of halls, the doctors and the proctors, and some other friends, in the same room in which, on the previous day, he had given his great banquet to the royal visitors. He had good reason to be satisfied himself: for the celebration of his success had itself been a further success, and all now knew that, in his greatest triumph, he could still rely upon the complete favour of the King. Nevertheless it would not be correct to say that Laud enjoyed himself during those three days of sustained homage. His was not a nature that was capable of enjoyment. He treated the whole affair as an arduous but necessary ordeal of which every detail required his minute and personal supervision; and even when it had passed off with

[1] Crosfield, *Diary* (Sept. 3rd, 1636).

such general satisfaction, he did not look back upon it as a triumph, but rather as a nuisance safely disposed of. In his account of it, he records with satisfaction that, in spite of having to borrow all the King's and the Lord Chamberlain's plate, and to hire more from his goldsmith, only two spoons, and those his own, were afterwards found to be missing: and a week later he wrote to Wentworth, with every token of relief, " I am now come back to Croydon from my weary, expenseful business at Oxford ". " 'Tis most true, the matters are small in themselves," he wrote in another letter, " but to me they have been great, and I am most heartily glad they are over." [1]

[1] Laud, *Works*, v. 155 ; vii. 278 ; vi. 465.

CHAPTER NINE

OPPOSITION

" Yet it joys me, in the midst of my bounden compassion and anxiety, to see you continue unmoved and resolute to stand the storm to the utmost, and so to rush through your martyrdom (for such it is) to the crown of glory that is laid up for you."

LORD SCUDAMORE to Laud, January 8th, 1637–8.

IF moments of time may be allowed to represent historical turning-points, the autumn of 1636 may be regarded as the zenith of Laud's career. When he entertained the royal party at Oxford, he celebrated his victory in every sphere. He had monopolised power in Church and State, and had asserted and enforced the principle of moral authority in both. He had brought learning within his jurisdiction, had secured the blessing of the King upon his work, and had commemorated his success by lasting monuments in the political and intellectual capitals of England. As for the Puritan opposition, he had smitten it hip and thigh, and it was discomfited. Wherever it had sought to organise itself, he had overthrown it. Wherever it was articulate, he had silenced it. Now it lay leaderless and disjointed in the face of a Church raised once more to its old position of an estate of the realm.

And yet to us, who look back from the safe vantage-point of afterknowledge, it is obvious that this whole imposing fabric was precariously founded, and that its dissolution began almost before its triumph was celebrated. The utter collapse of the Laudian Church within five years of its most signal triumph invites a tragic interpretation. And yet there is nothing tragic in it. The central figure of it never rose to the grandeur of his design, nor sought to overstep the limitations of humanity. In the height of his power, Laud remained what he had always been, — an industrious and conscientious official, too busy for personal pleasures, too businesslike for megalomania, and by nature averse from that splendour and ostentation which would have made his own fall as spectacular as that of his Church. The reasons for the failure of his work were far more humdrum than any tragic Nemesis. They were the reasons for the opposition to him at the start, only exasperated by his methods and his partial success, and strengthened by the political errors of the party upon which his authority depended.

For Laud had both bitten off more than he could chew, and was devouring it faster than he could digest it. The very monopolisation of power, which proved his personal success, was proof also of his isolation. He laboured alone in a cause which few supported with the fervour necessary for lasting results. Wherever he looked for instruments, he found broken reeds ; and on the other side, though he might silence Puritanism, he could not convert it. For it was not in the ridiculous doctrines of a few hysterical pamphleteers that the strength of the opposition resided, but in the inarticulate refusal of the preponderant classes in the country to co-operate with a government intent on limiting their power. Laud and Prynne were the prophets of two incompatible interests : but the silencing of a prophet did not make the interests compatible. And Laud's constructive programme, besides having too often to wait upon his destructive programme, was not based on such reserves of power as were commanded by the opposition.

Thus it needed but a slight shock to reveal the inherent weakness of Laud's position ; and in the year of his outward triumph this shock came. It was not delivered with violent suddenness, and it would not be easy to assign it to a precise date. But it was delivered with deadly aim, for it struck at the very foundations of his power, — the government.

For whatever the virtues of Laud's policy may have been, — and it would be useless to deny that he had a constructive social policy, — it lacked the two important political virtues of self-sufficiency and self-defence. It was directed towards the preservation of ancient rights, to the maintenance of the supposed anti-Roman, national, Catholic Church of pre-Reformation days. But the preservation of ancient institutions, though it has a certain aesthetic appeal, is unjustifiable unless it be for some relevant advantage which they assure. These advantages were there, but they were not such as appealed to the political forces of the country. The poor, whose cause Laud championed, were unorganised and inarticulate, and could give him no support, even if they were sensible of his efforts. The moral standards which he hoped to enforce in government hardly recommended him to a government intent on multiplying perquisites. The honour of the Church appealed only to the Church: and even in the Church, the inferior clergy, in spite of Laud's efforts, remained wretchedly poor, and therefore, even if orthodox, had little influence in their parishes. To champion ancient institutions, justice, political morality, and the poor, may be a recommendation in the eyes of posterity, but it is a policy which requires external support if it is to be practicable: for it is certainly not self-supporting.

For this external support Laud looked to the established government. His power depended for its effectiveness not upon any intrinsic strength, but upon the authority which backed it; and this partly explains Laud's own insistence upon authority, and his pathetic reliance upon authorised certificates as final justification for every action. Moreover, as the personal government of Charles I proceeded, the Archbishop became more and more committed to it as his only source of power. He was intimately and personally associated with the dissolution of the last parliament, and having made such use of the non-parliamentary interval, he could not face another unchallenged. During this interval Cottington sometimes urged the King to call another parliament as a necessary political expedient. Wentworth was not afraid of one, — for he felt his own position secured not only by authority, but by his own manifest success as an administrator. But Laud would never advise such a remedy. He drew up a paper to show, from historical precedents, that parliaments were no independent part of the constitution, and that "the Great Charter had an obscure birth from usurpation, and was fostered and showed to the world by rebellion";[1] even the antiquary Sir Henry Spelman, whose opinions on tithes and sacrilege were so orthodox, fell into disfavour with the Archbishop for giving undue publicity to such historical curiosities as Magna Carta and Parliament:[2] and the opposition to the government reasonably regarded Laud as the evil genius who advised against all parliaments as a matter of principle. Only unquestioned rule by the sovereign who authorised his actions could provide the atmosphere in which Laud could thrive; and the more precarious this rule became, the more deeply was Laud

[1] *Works*, vii. 627. [2] Aubrey, *Brief Lives* (Sir Henry Spelman).

committed to its defence, even when it openly violated the principles which he was proclaiming. We must, therefore, turn for a moment from the application of Laud's own policy to the fortunes of the government upon whose stability that policy was founded.

From 1629 to 1635 the government of Charles I, like that of Pharaoh, was blessed with seven fat years, and Laud had thriven extraordinarily. By withdrawing, albeit unwillingly, from the Continental war, the King had reduced his expenditure: and by reviving and enforcing feudal rights so obsolete that King James had wished to sell them, had the Commons thought them worth purchasing, he had so increased his revenue that both ends not only met but overlapped. In 1636, in a burst of unexpected solvency, he was able to redeem the Crown Jewels, which had been pawned in Holland, and to pay off old debts contracted by his parents. Laud, too, fattened on the surplus which he laboured to husband and increase. With a solvent government protecting his rear, he could embark on the luxury of a constructive programme. His work was furthered by handsome contributions from the King, and — so secure was his position — he was even able to criticise and intrigue against the administration of which he was a member. While proclaiming the responsibilities of despotism, he lobbied busily against Portland, Cottington, Windebank, and others whom he accused of caring only for its pickings; and in collaboration with Wentworth in Ireland, he alternately undermined and defied the allies with whom he was supposed to work.

About 1636, however, all this was altered. The fat years of the government were at an end, and the lean were beginning. Public opinion is a cumbrous engine, and requires much moving: but by now it was operative. Six years of peace amid a Continental war had diverted the commerce of Europe to England, enriching merchants by trade and the King by impositions. But peace and prosperity bring their troubles, when men, released from more immediate and pressing needs, begin to examine and question fundamentals. Instead of thanking the government for the peace which enriched them, English merchants only saw the disproportion between the growth of their wealth and the reduction of their political power, and fretted at the impositions, while the revival of the feudal dues and forest fines joined the old aristocracy with the new plutocracy in opposition to the government. The Commissions for Depopulation had struck at mere country squires and provincial landowners who had encroached on Church or common lands; the new Forest Court, held by Lord Holland as Lord Forester, attacked a far greater class of offenders. Half England, it seemed, was suddenly discovered once to have been royal forest, and all who had encroached upon it and could not produce their title deeds were heavily fined. The new delimitation of the New Forest cost the Earl of Southampton £2000 a year. The Earl of Westmoreland was fined £19,000. In Essex alone, where Lord Holland first held his court, the fines exacted amounted to £300,000. Even the acceptance of a reward from a previous sovereign was construed as encroachment: and because Queen Elizabeth had bestowed Rockingham Forest on the first Earl of Salisbury, the second Earl of Salisbury had to pay £20,000 to Charles I. It was noticed, however, that the ministers who proposed these courses were themselves immune from their operation: and the economical Lord Treasurer Portland, to the indignation of Laud, himself received the royal forest of Chute from the King at a nominal rate.

Naturally there was resentment: and this resentment was increased by the exaction from 1634 onwards of ship-money. The importance of ship-money in itself has been greatly exaggerated. It was not an archaic device suddenly unearthed by an industrious bookworm. Writs had been issued during the last war in 1626 and 1627, and although the tax was resented, and the counties concerned protested their poverty, there was no suggestion that the government was acting unconstitutionally. Nor is it true, as Whig historians have suggested, that there was no state of emergency to justify the measure. The Privy Council had continually received letters complaining of the aggressions of Turkish pirates on the western coasts. By the careful stewardship of Portland, the country was being saved from war, but starved of glory, and the government needed to strike some blow for military prestige as a substitute for participation in a ruinous conflict. Moreover, — what was more important — a critical situation had arisen in foreign affairs.

For in spite of the necessity of peace in the interests of sovereignty at home, Charles I was loth to abandon altogether his sister's cause, and even those in England who profited most by the peace, resented the stigma of inactivity when the future of Protestantism seemed at stake. Charles could not afford to fight: but he could subsidise, encourage, bargain. After the conclusion of peace with Spain in 1630, English volunteers continued to fight under the Marquis Hamilton in Germany, and the meteoric career of Gustavus Adolphus saved England from the necessity of direct intervention. The King of Sweden fought for the cause of the King of England, and the King of England, by keeping out of the war, found himself rich enough to forward a small annual subsidy to his champion. But Charles was not committed to the attainment of his ends by one method only: and according as the fortunes of war varied, he sought the restitution of the Palatinate alternately by supporting the Protestant and haggling with the Catholic side. After the death of Gustavus, he knew not whither to turn with the greatest chance of success. He was represented at the Protestant Convention of Heilbronn, and pressed the Protestant cause: but was glad to escape without commitments. He allowed his sister's agent to canvass for contributions in England, — until he found that the proclamation hinted at the legality of parliaments, and withdrew the permission. At the same time he did not abandon hope of begging from the Catholic powers as a favour what he could not extort as a prize; and he even put out feelers in the direction of the Vatican to discover whether Urban VIII might not intervene with the Emperor in return for the vague prospect of the soul of an English King.

But while he thus hesitated, his mind was made up for him by the news of an alarming combination, — a Franco-Dutch alliance organised by Richelieu to dominate the Continent. Before such a portent, all religious considerations vanished, — was it not itself an unholy league between a Roman Cardinal and a Calvinist Republic? The Palatinate itself was a remote question compared to this combination of England's old maritime rivals, the Dutch, with the new naval power of France, which would isolate England, control the Channel, and give the law to Europe. Sir Thomas Roe urged the government to split the alliance by raising the religious issue and subsidising John Durie to preach Protestantism indivisible. His, however, was a voice crying in the wilderness. The control of English foreign policy was in the hands of Portland, Cottington, Windebank, and the King: and they turned to Spain to redress the balance of power by a Spanish alliance of which even the other Secretary of State, Sir John Coke, was kept in ignorance. With a Spanish alliance, it was thought, England need not fear the nightmare of a Franco-Dutch coalition; and with Spanish money the English fleet, discredited in the last war and neglected since, could be put to sea. Now was the time for vindication. The Dutch scholar Grotius had written a tract, *Mare Liberum*, claiming the freedom of the seas for all nations. In fact it was directed against the exclusive claims of the Portuguese in the East: but in England it was regarded as a challenge to English sovereignty in home waters, where Dutch poachers had caused trouble for decades. In 1618 Selden had replied with *Mare Clausum*; and now, — at Laud's instance, it is said — this book was for the first time published, and all the author's political misdemeanours forgiven. And the Spaniards promised two subsidies to equip the fleet.

The foreign policy of Charles I seems academic enough to us, since it achieved so little in foreign affairs. But in domestic affairs it achieved so much that this short digression is indispensable. For it led to both ship-money and the Roman Agency, of which the former discredited the government upon which Laud depended, the latter the Church which he represented. The English fleet was equipped: but the Spanish money never came, and English money was needed to cover the expense. One of the last acts of Attorney-General Noy, after awarding Laud his victory over Williams, was the suggestion that writs of ship-money be sent out.

The issue of the writs was thus a move in foreign policy only. They had constitutional precedent, and the returns which they secured were used to equip annual fleets. It is true that these fleets achieved nothing proportionate to the expense of their equipment; but the proceeds of the tax went to their equipment, not, as was widely suggested, to the ordinary expenses of avoiding parliaments. Nevertheless, these justifications are mainly irrelevant, for the importance of ship-money far transcends the mere constitutional legality of its exaction; and the judicial decisions which extended its application from coastal to inland towns, convicted Hampden, and adjudged the tax to be independent of parliamentary assent, were far more effective than the original writs in exciting hostility to it. In default of an efficient administrative machinery in the counties independent of the local magnates the government had to rely on active co-operation from the provinces. But the provinces, if they were not yet prepared to rebel, were prepared to paralyse the executive, and from 1636 onwards the country replied to the government by a programme of passive disobedience. In counties where the sheriff was loyal and efficient, and opposition to the government not strong, the quota was soon collected : but in the Puritan Midlands, in East Anglia, and in the South, the administration was paralysed by the refusal of officials to collect or inhabitants to contribute : and in some counties, where the goods of delinquents were distrained, neighbours showed their sympathies by an organised refusal to bid for them at the sale. Lord Saye and Sele in Oxfordshire, Denzil Holles in Wiltshire, John Hampden in Buckinghamshire, Sir William Brereton in Cheshire, led the opposition : and the opposition suddenly discovered, in the affair of ship-money, wherein its strength lay, and how great its strength was.

What was Laud's part in this business ? Of the circumstances that had induced the government to adopt the tax, he knew little. His brief incursion into foreign affairs had only proved his incompetence to deal with them, and the Spanish treaty was kept a strict secret between his rivals in the Privy Council. In communicating with the Court of Brussels the King had begged the Cardinal-Infante to trust no one in the matter except himself and Windebank. Wentworth, too, was probably ignorant of the details, since his dealings with the home government, apart from his private correspondence with Laud, were through Secretary Coke, who was also kept in the dark. Both Laud and Wentworth, moreover, were unsympathetic with the King's dynastic policy, supporting the cause of the Queen of Bohemia out of loyalty rather than conviction : for neither of them wished to see their constructive programme at home suspended in order to carry on an expensive foreign policy, and a foreign policy which envisaged the prospect of a war might lead to both the calling of Parliament and the suspension of their programme. When the Queen of Bohemia was reported to have said that it was all one to her whether the Palatinate was recovered by peaceful means or by war, Laud could not forbear to express indignation at such unchristian sentiments. It was only the English Church which was entitled to make war upon its enemies ; a war for the Palatinate would be an expensive diversion which he could not countenance.

It is thus obvious that we must not associate Laud closely with the policy of the government which led up to ship-money. But once the tax was exacted and its exaction was resisted, the issue immediately became a matter not of expediency but of principle : and on matters of principle the government must be supported at all costs. So we find both Laud and Wentworth loud in condemnation of those who resisted a tax which they could not themselves commend. Wentworth, with his cult of efficiency at all costs, could have nothing but contempt for those who obstructed the administration by pretending individual rights, and he recommended that Hampden and all such " be whipped home into their right wits ". As for Laud, — the close association of Church and State in the matter is shown by the instructions to sheriffs to give particular attention to the complaints of such clergy as had been assessed at too high a figure, while disputed cases were referred to the arbitration of the bishops.[1] The private correspondence between the two, however, bears witness to the lack of enthusiasm with which they looked forward to a possible war and its consequences for them. " Good my Lord," wrote Wentworth, " if it be not too late, use your best to divert us from this war ; for I see nothing in it but distractions to His Majesty's affairs, and mighty dangers for us that must be the ministers, although not the authors, of the counsel. It will necessarily put the King into all the highways possible, else he will not be able to subsist under the charge of it ; and if these fail, the next will be the sacrificing those that have been his ministers therein ", — advice which might have been followed with advantage three years later, when Laud advised war and got it.

This time there was no war, but the crisis hung fire for a long time. The Spanish treaty came to nothing, and the government reverted to the well-tried expedient of a direct approach to the Court of Vienna. The Earl of Arundel was sent on a magnificent embassy, with everything to ask and nothing to offer. It was a counsel of despair. " Although the experience of eighteen

[1] *Cal. S.P. Dom.*, 1636–7, pp. 31, 109, 185, 467, 522.

years showed that all means but force were vain," wrote the Venetian ambassador, " yet the difficulties involved in such a decision made them decide on the last embassy of the Earl of Arundel." Nor was the unfortunate Queen of Bohemia any less sanguine of the results. " For her dislike of the King's sending to the Emperor," she wrote to the Archbishop, " it was as much for his honour, and not that she distrusts his intentions. For the Emperor having deluded the King her father, and now him, these sixteen years, she thought the King had no cause to try his falsehood further, and that it was not much to his honour." [1] When Arundel's embassy ended only in rebuff, the situation was indeed ticklish. " The Earl Marshal being returned ", Laud wrote to Wentworth, " has made it appear to us that no aid for the Prince Elector can be hoped for from Spain. And now I verily believe it will in time grow into a war. God speed what must go on. But God be thanked, in all this troublesome business God hath exceedingly blessed His Majesty ; for this term the judges have all declared under their hands, unanimously, that if the Kingdom be in danger, the King may call for, and ought to have, supply for ship-money through the Kingdom, and that the King is sole judge when the Kingdom is in this danger. So that now the King, if he be put to it, may anger his enemies at sea, — and I hope no man shall persuade him to take land forces out of the Kingdom. I did fear everything till this point was gained. Now, by God's blessing, all may go well, though it should be war." [2] A few months later he wrote, " If the judges' hands had not been gotten to the shipping business when they were, we had now had a very dead horse to lift ; for the arrear this year is like to be very great : the sheriffs not forward to distrain : some shires out of quiet about the sheriff's rate : many men very backward : and (which is worst of all) there hath been a libel spread, not only against the legality of it, but with most mischievous and dangerous inferences. It hath been up and down in men's hands, 'tis said, above this half year, and many spread ere found out. I got first notice of it of any man that would make it known to the King." [3] Laud's lack of political imagination is here well illustrated. In regarding the whole question as safely settled by a certificate, and in considering an anonymous libel

[1] *Cal. S.P. Dom.*, 1635–6, p. 525.
[2] *Works*, vii. 319.
[3] *Ibid.* vii. 364.

of more importance than the disaffection of whole provinces, he showed the mentality of a village policeman. If, as Clarendon states, it was the legal decision rather than the tax itself which caused the opposition to ship-money, then there is a delightful irony in Laud's claim to have saved the situation by his personal efforts to secure a legal decision.[1] At any rate, the savagery with which he visited libellers will be more comprehensible when we realise that he regarded them as more dangerous than any other evidence of revolt. This particular libeller, though it was not known at the time, was William Prynne, who thus employed his leisure in the Tower, and the pen and paper which Laud had secured for him.

Laud's attitude towards the question of ship-money is sufficiently illustrative of his position once the government to which he owed his authority found itself on the defensive. Unsympathetic to the policy which it implied, he was nevertheless unable to take an independent line. Worse dangers than bad policy loomed ahead of the government, and a government in danger cannot afford to be divided. In spite of the successful intrigues by which he had kept Cottington out of the Treasury and secured his own admission to every department of state, Laud had not really won in the struggle with Lady Mora. In matters of policy Cottington and Windebank still ruled, and it was too late to oppose them now; all he could do now was to support whatever policy they forced upon the government even if he himself disapproved of it. The alternative of a divided Council faced with the threat of a parliament too closely resembled mariners quarrelling in a storm. In his private correspondence with Wentworth he might still complain of his rivals. Even the King did not escape his censures for the betrayal of his own cause. But his complaints are those of a man conscious of his own impotence. "And now I am grown almost as proud as you," he writes on one occasion, "for whereas you write that His Majesty must not always look to be served upon such terms, I shall say so too; and perhaps when I am gone, my saying shall be found true."[2] In public, however, Thorough and Lady Mora must sink or swim together. It was no time now to assert grand principles which experience had proved impossible of application. Hitherto Laud had proclaimed the principles of

[1] *Works*, vii. 333. [2] *Ibid.* vi. 512.

authoritarian government as it might be. He had found no converts : and now he must support it as in fact it was.

So from about this time we find an eclipse of his constructive policy. He is now fighting on the defensive to preserve what he had already won and ward off every attack upon the government thanks to which he has won it. Still he advances his old programme, — but on a diminished scale. Still benefices are being augmented, enclosures resisted, bishops chivvied, orthodoxy asserted ; but these are the least conspicuous of his activities. Still Puritans are haled before the prerogative courts ; but the sentences show the panic of the judges, their execution the sympathies of the populace. Still contributions for the repair of St. Paul's are solicited ; but the returns dwindle, and the needs of a harassed government claim first right to the subject's purse. Nor is a high standard of political morality so constantly inculcated, — the government needs both offices for sale and officers who will purchase them. And at the same time we read of projects which Laud devised but, owing to the advent of the Troubles, was never able to execute, — the visitation of the Universities and the Channel Islands, the compilation of statutes for all cathedrals,[1] and the despatch of a bishop to tend the erring souls of the New England Puritans.

The open favour accorded to Roman Catholics in high quarters was another sign of Laud's inability to control the Court for whose religion he was held responsible. His contemporary opponents continually, and often quite sincerely, attacked him as a Papist himself : and the charge, though we can see that it was untrue, was natural. Laud's opponents, unrepresented at Court, had no opportunities of personal investigation. They could only judge from the changes which they saw in their local churches, from the obvious growth in clerical influence, and from the rumours which multiply under any censorship. Nor was the subtle difference between the new high Anglicanism and the old Rome likely to be appreciated by ears attuned to Puritan hysterics and papal bombast, while Laud himself took but little care to define

[1] Laud drew up new statutes for the Cathedral of Canterbury, which were sent to the Dean and Chapter in January 1637 (*Works*, v. 506). In September 1635 he had secured a new charter for the collegiate church at Manchester, in consequence of abuses in its management (see S. Hibbert-Ware, *History of the Foundations of Manchester*, 1830, i. 148 ff.).

his position, — his was a practical, not an exegetical mind. Reserved and uncommunicative, he went about his business: and Roman Catholics at Court were as deceived as Puritans in the country. The Earl of Arundel, whose acceptance of the Anglican communion in 1616 had shown his desire to enter public life rather than his sudden discovery of the true means of salvation, thought Laud a fitting instrument for the advancement of the Roman faith. The Queen's Scottish confessor, writing to Windebank about the selection of Roman bishops for England, begged him to show the letter, before burning it, to no one except Laud, " of whose wisdom and moderation I am so confident that I am not afraid you tell him my name ". When Thomas Gage, the chronicler of the West Indies, went as a Franciscan friar to Rome, high officials of the Curia confided to him their hopes of the Archbishop's support. In 1633, soon after his elevation to Canterbury, Laud was twice offered a cardinalate. And next year a Roman cardinal, whose long diplomatic career and intimate knowledge of English affairs caused his services to be specially requisitioned by the Pope, stated that Laud was on the lookout for a red hat. Of course they were all wrong, — the Venetian ambassador was one of the very few foreigners who did not share their error — but Laud, moving with proud indifference in an unsympathetic Court, made no effort to correct them.

For the Court of Charles I, in which Laud somewhat incongruously moved, was the centre of Roman Catholicism in England. Queen Henrietta Maria, brought over from France at the age of fifteen, had been married under papal supervision: and before setting out she had listened to homilies from the French clergy upon her duties as a missionary of the faith. It is true that these duties were not taken too seriously either by the new Queen or by Cardinal Richelieu, who was too intent upon an alliance to let it founder on such details as religion, and the first few years of the marriage gave little satisfaction to its Catholic brokers. The King quarrelled with his wife about her French attendants, and finally expelled them from the country. The Queen's ideas of missionary activity were somewhat elementary, and consisted of breaking into an Anglican service in the royal household with a pack of beagles and interrupting the preacher with hunting noises.[1] And when Prince Charles was born the King sent word

[1] *Salvetti's News-letters*, p. 38.

to the Queen's Capuchins who, by the terms of the treaty, were to educate him in the Roman faith, that they need not trouble themselves about it, and the child was baptized by Laud.

However, the quarrels which had at first disturbed the marital relations of King and Queen soon passed over, and gave way to that long period of agreement to which so many disasters can be traced. Charles became devoted to his wife, and could refuse her nothing; and though his wife still seemed more addicted to dancing than to missionary zeal, she was a rallying-point for all the romanising elements at Court. She gave assurances that the Prince was receiving surreptitious instruction in the true faith. Her two chapels, at St. James' and Somerset House, were open to the public, who resorted thither in great numbers. It was the spread of Romanism in the Queen's household which led Cosin to issue his rival Devotions in 1627, and so to incur the fury of Prynne and Parliament; and after 1629, when neither Prynne nor Parliament had any power to check it, the resort to the Queen's chapel became open and customary. Inside the Council the Catholics could rely at least on the clandestine support of Portland, Cottington, and Windebank. All this was galling to Laud; but Laud was dependent on the King and could not afford to take a stand against the activities of the Queen and her party. All that he could do was to walk by on the other side, and that not too publicly.

In these circumstances the English Catholics took heart. They had been given an inch and they saw an opportunity to take an ell. The initiative did not come from the Queen, who was busied about other things, but from more earnest Papists who looked with misgiving upon the disorganisation of the Catholic Church in England, disrupted by King James' Oath of Allegiance. They represented to the Vatican the favourable opportunity for intervention supplied by the abeyance of Parliament, when the Queen was for them, the King not against them, the Council friendly, and the Archbishop, as it seemed to them, working for reunion. At the same time the English government, despairing of recovering the Palatinate by encouraging other powers to fight for it, was looking for a Spanish alliance in which papal mediation might be of service. One of the intermediaries in these negotiations was Laud's old room-mate at St. John's, John Jones, now the Benedictine prior of Douai, Dom Leander a Sancto Martino, who arrived in England under a royal permit in the autumn of 1633, and whose suggestions of a direct correspondence between King Charles and the Pope so frightened the Vatican, unprepared for such haste, that he never dared to return. At the same time the project of reunion was openly canvassed at the English Court, and another Catholic priest, the Franciscan Dom Franciscus a Sancta Clara, alias Christopher Davenport, the brother of the Puritan John Davenport whom Laud was chasing from pillar to post, published a treatise, *Deus, Natura, Gratia*, in which the differences between the Roman and Anglican communions were whittled down to a minimum. But this again was too precipitate for the Holy See, and Davenport also fell into disfavour.

Seeing this enthusiasm in England, Rome proceeded methodically, but with care. It was suspected that the English government was really more interested in the Palatinate than in salvation, and the Cardinal Secretary of State distrusted the glowing accounts of emigrant Catholics. In December 1634, however, the first decided step was taken when Gregorio Panzani was sent as an unofficial papal emissary to spy out the land and report to headquarters.

His reports were encouraging. Moving, as was inevitable, in a closed circle, he found only what he looked for, and all England seemed to him to be hovering on the brink of Rome. His interviews with Windebank were most satisfactory: and when Windebank said that the King regarded the Jesuits as the Roman Puritans who were the chief obstacle to reunion, Panzani gaily hinted that the Pope would be quite ready to throw over these offensive agents. Cottington too was encouraging, and the King was quite ready to allow a papal agent to be officially accredited to his wife. All talked optimistically of a return to the Roman embrace, and the Queen, who ought to have known better, even thought that she could buy the approval of the Archbishop of Canterbury by appointing one of his dependants to succeed the late Lord Savage as her chancellor.[1] Even Panzani soon understood the Archbishop better than this, and modified his earlier view. He reported that he was unable to move the King to admit a Roman bishop, " he being naturally both fearful and tenacious, and his chief favourite and counsellor, the Archbishop

[1] Panzani to Barberini, Jan. 23rd, 1636, Add. MS. 15389, 99.

of Canterbury, keeping him close to the point". After some experience of the society in which he was working, Panzani reported that the whole Privy Council could be bought for 20,000 crowns, except the Archbishop.

In the prime object of his mission, however, Panzani was successful; for the project of a reciprocal agency was accepted, and, for the first time since the Reformation, diplomatic intercourse was established between the English Court and the Roman Curia. In June 1636 Sir William Hamilton arrived in Rome, with particular instructions to seek papal aid in the matter of the Palatinate: and next month George Con, a Scotsman long in the service of the Vatican, arrived in England. His instructions did not mention the Palatinate. He was to concentrate on the salvation of souls.

In fact the papal Agency, which continued in existence till the days of the Long Parliament, secured none of the things for which it was instituted. It contributed nothing towards the ultimate recovery of the Palatinate. The establishment of a Catholic hierarchy in England had to wait for two centuries. And Charles I died an Anglican martyr. But its immediate effect on English domestic affairs was considerable: for the popularity of the Agent and the number and importance of his proselytes rendered the whole Court suspect, and seemed to confirm the suspicions of the Puritans. Con was a man of diplomatic ability and suave, almost oleaginous manners. Combining the narrow views of the *émigré* with the universal affability of the professional ambassador, he was the perfect type of the Englishman Italianate: and in the dilettante society of the English Court, accustomed to the uneasy presence and brusque manners of the Archbishop, his success was immediate. As long as he continued in England the King dabbled with the idea of reunion, discussing religious topics freely and sympathetically with the supple Agent. Con flattered his political aspirations, assuring him that in the eyes of Catholics he was above parliaments. He appealed to him also through his aesthetic susceptibilities, discussing art with him as no one else at Court, except the Earl of Arundel, was able. From Rome, too, came similar inducements. The King's collection was enriched by Leonardos, Veroneses, Andrea del Sartos, and many lesser masters sent as complimentary gifts by the Cardinal Secretary of State; while the Queen, whose tastes were less elevated, received bottled sweets and relics from the same source. The sculptor Bernini, who refused all other Protestant princes, and would not even oblige the Gallican Cardinal Richelieu, was permitted by the Pope to make an effigy of King Charles. The King delighted in Con's conversation and presence. The Agent was lionised by London society. He was invited everywhere to dinner, and was made to go hunting with the royal party and presented with the antlers after the kill. Even Bishop Juxon was among his hosts, — although this may have been officially, as Lord Treasurer, or unofficially, as another hunting man. And with women the Agent was such a success that foreign ambassadors were stimulated to facetious comment. Strong in support of King and Queen, of Cottington and Windebank, Con moved with perfect freedom in the Court in which the Archbishop was but an uneasy visitor: and the complaints of the Protestant Secretary of State, Sir John Coke, that ten or twelve masses a day were publicly said in the Agent's chapel, went unheeded. Coke had already been kept in the dark, and his correspondence intercepted, during the negotiations for the Spanish treaty. He was known to be the confidant and friend of Wentworth, and to have stout anti-papal sympathies. He was also very old. He could therefore be ignored by the now triumphant Lady Mora.

To Laud the arrival of Con was equally distasteful. The Agent possessed and exercised all the arts which the Archbishop most conspicuously lacked and which the Court most obviously appreciated. Tactful where Laud was brusque, sociable where Laud was reserved, versatile where Laud was narrow, superficially cultured where Laud merely patronised learning, agreeable to women whom Laud repelled, — in everything he was the Archbishop's antithesis, and the Archbishop resented him as a successful interloper. Unable to compete with him, unwilling to recognise him, sensible of the danger which he represented, Laud had no rejoinder to the Agent's success except formal politeness and studied reserve. He invited him to Oxford with the rest of the royal party, and Con came for a short visit to the Bodleian, — the one sphere of Laud's activity which he could without indecency recognise; but when Con suggested a conference, it was declined. Con repaid suspicion with suspicion. He could no more appreciate Laud than Laud could understand him. The Archbishop, he declared, was "timid, ambitious and inconstant, and incapable of great designs".[1] A more superficial verdict could hardly be pronounced on one whose enemies recognised him to be beyond fear and above personal ambition, and whose efforts were constantly directed towards the realisation of a great design which the closed mind of the papal Agent could never comprehend.

Some well-meaning efforts were made to bridge this great gulf: but they were in vain. When peacemakers suggested an opportunity for overtures, Con refused to make them. He was continually suspecting Laud of seeking to discredit him with the King, and the Venetian ambassador reported that Laud frequently implored the King to send him away.[2] Certainly Con intrigued with the Queen against Laud. The King tried to make peace between his two ecclesiastical favourites: but beneath the frigid correctness of their external relations the difference in both personality and principle was too great for any understanding; and the Roman flirtation of the Court, while it weakened Laud in the country by his apparent connexion with it, was evidence also that his efforts to inspire the administration had failed.

If ship-money turned public opinion against the government, and the Roman Agency weakened Laud's hold on the Court, there were other symptoms which showed that the policy of Thorough was failing in its direct relations with the Puritans also. That the whole system of uniformity which Laud sought to apply was defective we have already seen. Unwilling instruments, local differences, conflicting loyalties, and the impossibility of complete supervision prevented its application with the thoroughness claimed for it, and robbed it of its universal character. But hitherto where it had struck, it had struck effectively. Its failures had been in the weakness of the system, not in the strength of the opposition. But now that the government was embarrassed, and classes hitherto inarticulate had discovered both their strength and their leaders in the affair of ship-money, the opposition to the religious policy of the government took heart. Through all the cracks in the system of Thorough the voice of rebellious

[1] Con to Barberini, June 5th, 1637.

[2] *Ven. Cal.* xxiv. 384.

Puritanism rose and was heard. From 1636 onwards sectaries and conventicles occupy far more official attention than before. In 1637 libels against the Archbishop, which had previously appeared only sporadically on appropriate occasions, — as on the dissolution of the last parliament or his elevation to the primacy,— became epidemic, and every instance was chronicled with grave apprehension by their victim. In East Anglia, where Puritanism had never been subdued, it now became menacing. There the genial Bishop Corbett had died in 1635, with the name of his bottle-companion on his lips, and the Queen of Bohemia had written to Laud recommending one of her dependants, Dr. Hassall, as his successor. But Laud had refused. Norwich, he said, being as it were a missionary see in a schismatic land, was too important to be bestowed as a favour.[1] It needed the strong hand of a crusading bishop ; and it was reserved for Matthew Wren.

If ever Laud's methods could have eliminated Puritanism in England, Wren would have eliminated it. He was the Archbishop's most efficient disciple, a man of strong intellect and fearless determination. No single bishop of Laud's creation was so hateful to the Puritans : but he survived their howls for revenge, maintained the dignity and continued the functions of a Prince of the Church while in the Tower throughout the Civil War and the Interregnum, refused to buy his liberty by recognising the Protector, negotiated with the exiled Court for the restoration of the Church, and, on its restoration, returned triumphantly to his diocese to defy the intervention of Charles II. His was no monastic piety : and he was the more hated because he was not merely a bigot but a governor who knew his business and did it with terrifying determination. As Master of Peterhouse, as Bishop of Hereford, and as Dean of Windsor, he had accepted all the responsibilities as well as the doctrines and rewards of Thorough. At Cambridge, if Dr. Dorislaus had been driven from his lectureship in history by him, it was through his co-operation that Spelman had been able to found a lectureship in Anglo-Saxon. If the diocese of Hereford, which he now left, smarted from his inquisitorial visitation, it also gained by his careful stewardship of its lands — and that although his duties at Court prevented his personal supervision :[2] and if in Norwich

[1] *Works*, vii. 167.
[2] Wren, *Parentalia*, 1750, p. 31.

he seemed to Puritans to be "little Pope Regulus", and "a lecherous proud insolent Prelate", against whom whole volumes of abuse were directed, a persecutor who drove more than a thousand of the saints of God to take refuge overseas from his inquisitorial articles, he also advanced learning, raised the stipends of poor ministers,[1] and sought to enrich his plundered diocese. His arrival was a rude shock to East Anglican Puritans, who had become accustomed to the easy-going orthodoxy of Bishop Corbett, and one of the first to experience the change was Samuel Ward, so influential a preacher in those parts that Hugh Peters had wished to secure his services in Holland, and Laud's agents did not dare to prosecute him before the High Commission for fear of the popular reactions. To Ward's influence the exodus from East Anglia to New England was attributed; but when he was finally brought before the High Commission on various charges he declared that "he was not of so melancholy a spirit, nor looked through so black spectacles, as he that wrote that Religion stands on the tiptoe in this land, looking westward, nor feared their fear that feared an imminent departure of the Gospel". He was suspended and silenced by the new Bishop, who offered the inhabitants of Ipswich leave to appoint another lecturer in his place. But they answered that they would have Mr. Ward or none, and on his death in 1640 they showed their respect by continuing his salary as a pension to his widow and eldest son for their lives.

Wren went ahead in his new diocese with all the thoroughness that Laud could have desired: but protest or flight, as well as submission, followed his visitation of 1636. Before long, oppressed by his gigantic task, he was recommending the division of the diocese into two, with a new cathedral at Bury St. Edmunds or Sudbury, and a threefold increase in the rents of those episcopal lands which the Elizabethan bishops had leased for next to nothing: and in 1636, in spite of Laud's censorship, a virulent pamphlet against Wren ran through three editions. It was entitled *News from Ipswich*, and was published under the name of Matthew White; but its author was William Prynne.[2]

[1] *S.P. Dom. Car. I.* 351, no. 53.

[2] *News from Ipswich* was distributed by Rice Boye, a silenced minister in Coleman Street, at whose house a great bundle of copies was taken (Birch, ii. 273). Two copies sent to a stationer at Exeter were intercepted and sent to Laud by the Bishop (*Cal. S.P. Dom.*, 1636–7, p. 487). Others were sent to Norwich and Ipswich (*ibid.* p. 427). The words on the title-page, "Printed at

Since the misfortunes brought upon him by *Histriomastix*, Prynne had kept out of the news ; but now the growing opposition to the government gave him fresh courage. He took up his pen and paper, and the spate of works began again to flow. As a lawyer he produced his anonymous pamphlet against ship-money. As a Presbyterian prophet he published, in 1635, *A Breviate of the Bishops' Intolerable Usurpations and Encroachments upon the King's Prerogative and Subjects' Liberties*, which had reached a third edition in 1637. In 1636, besides *News from Ipswich*, appeared *The Unbishoping of Timothy and Titus*, *A Dialogue between A and B concerning the Sabbath and Pastimes*, reprinted immediately, *A Looking-Glass for all Lordly Prelates*, *Certain Queries propounded to the Bowers at the Name of Jesus*, and *A Divine Tragedy lately Enacted, or God's Judgment on Sabbath-Breakers*. It is needless to say more of these publications than that they were all abusive and had not even the engaging feature of a lively scurrility. Other writers too were finding that the censorship was in reality a weak instrument. The year 1636 saw the beginning of a veritable flood of libels issuing from the secret presses of England and Holland : and a noticeable feature was that the attack was now delivered against the whole institution of episcopacy. No longer did Puritans say, like the revolutionaries of the parliamentary days, " I reverence the order though I honour not the man". The whole order was threatened together with its exponents and its policy. One attack on its policy in the same year came from within the order itself. It was from Williams, who, harassed by Laud and disappointed of support from the Court, had turned to the Puritans for assistance and, in *The Holy Table, Name and Thing*, attacked the altar-wise position which Laud's visitors were enforcing throughout the country. Next year the shrill voice of Heylin came to the support of his master with *Antidotum Lincolniense*, and here and there other pamphlets came out in support of the establishment, such as Pocklington's *Altare Christianum*, Dow's *Innovations Unjustly Charged*, and Meade's *Chapel Determination*. But these thin protests were soon drowned by the torrents of polemical abuse

Ipswich ", are evidently a blind, as there were no printers at Ipswich at the time. MS. copies were probably sent to various towns and then printed simultaneously. The Rev. W. J. Couper (*Glasgow Bibliographical Soc. Records*, vol. vii. p. 18) shows that one impression was probably printed by George Anderson at Glasgow.

poured forth by their opponents, now thoroughly self-confident. To the literature of 1637 Prynne contributed *A Quench-Coal*, attacking Heylin, and *A Catalogue of such Testimonies as plainly prove Bishops and Presbyters to be Equal*, before his voice was stifled for another three years. And in the same year Milton, who had once bestowed a poetical halo upon Bishop Andrewes, and who a few years ago, in *Il Penseroso*, had shown his appreciation of the beauty of holiness, and had retorted to *Histriomastix* with *Comus*, published *Lycidas* with its sudden, irrelevant, and savage onslaught upon contemporary bishops :

such as for their bellies' sake
Creep and intrude and climb into the fold.
Of other care they little reck'ning make
Than how to scramble at the shearers feast
And shove away the worthy bidden guest ;
Blind mouths, that scarce themselves know how to hold
A sheep-hook, or have learn'd aught else the least
That to the faithful herdsman's art belongs !
What recks it them ? what need they ? they are sped ;
And when they list, their lean and flashy songs
Grate on their scrannel pipes of wretched straw.
The hungry sheep look up and are not fed.

It would be dangerous at any time to look to Milton for historical accuracy, and compared with his mature productions the wildest works of Prynne are but a schoolboy's exercise in the art of abuse ; but it happens that at this very time there was some slight justification for Milton's complaints against those whom he later described as " swan-eating and Canary-sucking " prelates. For Laud had but recently experienced the difficulty of finding bishops who would combine doctrinal orthodoxy with that unselfish devotion to the cause which he demanded. In 1636 the sees of Bristol and St. David's fell vacant. Neither of them was of much importance, but the bankruptcy of Thorough in a critical time was shown by the characters who were chosen to fill them. To Bristol went Robert Skinner, who had gained some notoriety as a servile assertor of Arminianism in Oxford. He celebrated his elevation with an orgy of Bristol Milk on a Sunday, as a calculated insult to the sabbatarian and abstemious Puritans, and we shall hear no more of him. To St. David's went Roger Manwaring, of whom we have already heard enough.

Such were the imperfections in the system of Thorough, such the powers ranged against it, which, in spite of its consistent application for eight years, still threatened to subvert it once a favourable opportunity was given. In 1637, when Laud was showing the extent of his designs by endeavouring the ecclesiastical conquest of Scotland, and when the opposition had been roused over the question of ship-money, this opportunity seemed to have arisen. In that year resentment came to a head in each of these various forms, and the constructive policy of the government stood almost still while Laud dealt with it in exemplary fashion. With terrifying ferocity the shrillest propagandists of Puritanism were crushed beneath what seemed a final sentence: the great *saboteur* of the episcopal system, after long and tortuous machinations, was finally and completely ruined: the censorship received the support of summary and thoroughgoing legislation: and the Archbishop was compelled to raise a protest even in the Court of his master against the spread of Popery fostered by the intruder from Rome.

The first of these heavy strokes was directed against William Prynne and his accomplices, and the immediate cause of it was his latest work of vituperation, *News from Ipswich*, which — possibly because, unlike most of Prynne's works, it was so short — had been sold in such numbers during the preceding year. At first the pamphlet was attributed not to Prynne but to Henry Burton, the disgruntled Puritan rector of St. Matthew's Church in Friday Street, who had been dismissed from his position at Court in 1625 and had raised intermittent protests against Laud ever since. Burton was anyway a marked man, for in November 1636 he preached two sermons attacking every form of the new orthodoxy, and soon afterwards published them under the title of *For God and the King*. The third of the notorious trinity was John Bastwick, a physician trebly tainted with heterodoxy by his East Anglian origin, his education at Emmanuel College, and his service in the Dutch army. Nine years before, Bastwick had joined Prynne and Burton in raising the cry of Popery against Bishop Goodman of Gloucester: and while Prynne was preparing his *Histriomastix* in England, the presses of Holland were coping with Bastwick's *Flagellum Pontificis*, which brought him too before the High Commission, and sent him thence to prison. The co-operation between Prynne and Bastwick continued, confirmed by their common sufferings. In 1635 Prynne issued an appendix, supplement, and epilogue to *Flagellum Pontificis*; and next year Bastwick again turned his command of Latin to religious controversy by producing *πράξεις τῶν ἐπισκόπων*, *sive Apologeticus ad Praesules Anglicanos*, being an attack on the Court of High Commission. Early in 1637 appeared his *Litany*.

If Prynne revolts by his tedious and accumulated abuse, and if Burton is a contemptible whiner, it is yet possible to entertain some sympathy for Bastwick, who laid about him with obvious relish, trouncing the whole hierarchy of the Church with brilliant scurrility and choice vocabulary. His previous works had been in Latin, and were directed, nominally, against the Roman Church alone. Now, he declared, he would admit no such restrictions to his vituperative powers. "If two or three drops of my Latial rhetoric, which I let fall only on the Beast, did so much displease them, what will they say or do, think you, when I open the cataracts of all my Greek and Roman oratory upon them?" As for the two Archbishops, he announced, "I will so slang them as I shall make it evident they never knew what it was". And slang them he did: they were described as little toes of Antichrist, fishmongers of the elect of Christ, whom they marketed as "the mundungus and garbage both of sea and land", grolls, and vermin. With magnificent exaggeration interspersed with engaging anecdotes he painted lurid, fantastic pictures of the pomp and pride, gluttony and lechery, of contemporary prelates. Laud was represented as making his progress to the Star Chamber through prostrate multitudes, with gentlemen and servants "carrying up his tail for the better breaking and venting of his wind and easing of his holy body (for it is full of holes)", while graphic accounts were given of the unfortunate costermongers and fishwomen, whose fruit and puddings, baskets and all, were thrust promiscuously into the Thames to make way for the Archbishop's attendants, raising their hands to Heaven and crying "Save my puddings!", "Save my codlings, for the Lord's sake!", — "the poor tripes and apples in the meantime swimming like frogs about the Thames, making way for His Grace to go home again". "From plague, pestilence, and famine", ran the Litany, "from bishops, priests, and deacons, Good Lord deliver us!"

Bastwick need hardly have been in any doubt as to what the grandees of the Church would say or do when he swamped them with this flood of " Greek and Roman oratory ". The Archbishop had already for some time, as Bastwick said, " been nibbling at his ears " ; and early in 1637 he was in possession of sufficient evidence to enable him to strike. In March information was laid by the Attorney-General, Sir John Bankes, to the Star Chamber, and Burton and Bastwick were sent to the Tower to join Prynne, while Laud made a careful and painstaking scrutiny of Burton's sermons to discover traces of Prynne's influence.

For it was Prynne who was regarded as the chief offender, whom confinement had failed to silence, whose influence prevailed upon others to express his own extremist doctrines, whose resourcefulness, even in prison, baffled the vigilance of the authorities and eluded the censorship. And Prynne was the most dangerous of the three : for he was trained in the law, that profession which the champions of Thorough not only hated but feared. Throughout the present case Prynne employed his knowledge of the law to obstruct the proceedings and exasperate his prosecutors, driving them still further into the position which they were now taking up of arbitrary administrative acts supported by certificates of legality secured from a judiciary dependent on the government.

For three months the three prisoners, following the lead of Prynne, kept their opponents at bay. First they refused to file the necessary answers to the bill of information exhibited against them until they were allowed to consult with counsel. This was granted to them, and they were escorted out of prison for consultation, after which they were required to produce their answers within a certain time or to be held *pro confessis*. Next month, hearing that Prynne's chamber in the Tower contained papers of dangerous import, the Privy Council had it searched under a warrant, and Prynne's servants were arrested and imprisoned. But nothing was found, and it was only a few weeks later, when Prynne's *Instructions to Churchwardens*, — a pamphlet suggesting the best ways and means of avoiding Conformity, — were published, that the Council was able to see the matter which Prynne had ingeniously contrived to prepare and publish in spite of all their efforts. At the same time the three defendants presented a cross-bill, drawn up by Prynne, in which they accused the archbishops and bishops of the Court of High Commission of "usurping on His Majesty's prerogative royal, and innovations in religion". The bishops were indignant, and a charge of treason was meditated: but the judges had to admit that the bill was presented according to law, and the bishops had to content themselves with securing a certificate from the judges that the Court of High Commission was legally entitled to issue processes in its own name.

On June 14th, the case came at last before the Star Chamber. The prisoners were held *pro confessis*, not having entered their answers in time, and Prynne's request that they should nevertheless be admitted was rejected. Prynne's and Bastwick's answers were anyway so violent that no lawyer would sign them, while Burton's, though signed by his counsel, was dismissed as irrelevant, and the papers of Oliver St. John, who was thought to have drawn it up, ransacked in vain for proof of his complicity. Prynne also sought to obstruct the proceedings by pleading that his cross-bill be reconsidered: but this was rejected. His other demand, that the bishops be removed from court, as being parties in the case, was adjudged libellous. Nevertheless, the bishops took no part in the sentence which was passed.

The sentence was proposed by Cottington. All three were to lose their ears in the pillory at Westminster, — it having been remarked during the trial that the ears of Prynne had not been entirely removed at the time of the last sentence, or (as some Puritans preferred) had since been miraculously restored. In addition, they were to pay a fine of £5000 each, and to suffer perpetual imprisonment, Prynne in Carnarvon Castle, Bastwick in Launceston, Burton in Lancaster. The suggestion of Lord Chief Justice Finch, whose name was soon to be a byword for savagery, that Prynne's cheeks should be branded with the letters S.L., for Seditious Libeller, was also unanimously adopted. Prynne, however, preferred to interpret the initials as *Stigmata Laudis*.

When sentence had been pronounced, the Archbishop, who had remained silent during the proceedings, rose to speak. He dilated on the evils of libel, especially against the Established Church. He pointed out that it was not merely an ecclesiastical question that had been raised, but an attack upon the whole social order which the Church represented and consecrated, and rightly insisted that the main crime of which he and his colleagues were

WILLIAM PRYNNE

held guilty was not any particular action or actions in their episcopal capacity, but the fact that they were bishops, the very existence of whose order was now considered an intrinsic obstacle to reform. He dealt shortly with the attempt of the libellers to pretend an incompatibility between the kingly and sacerdotal power; and then, one by one, he dealt with all the innovations, even the most ridiculous, which had been charged against him by Prynne and Burton, supporting his apologia by the testimony of such unimpeachable Protestant bishops as Jewel and Davenant, and defending his conception of the beauty of holiness by a moderate exposition of his personal attitude. In the course of his arguments he stoutly defended the King from any charge of favouring Popery, — a somewhat difficult task when Con was being fêted and making converts so conspicuously at Court, and was actually watching the proceedings from Lady Arundel's box, — and took the opportunity to deliver a deliberate attack on a certain book recently published by a minister in Lincolnshire and licensed by Bishop Williams. This was *The Holy Table, Name and Thing*, which, as Laud well knew, was in reality the work of Williams himself; and Laud's words upon it foreshadowed a day of reckoning for its author too. "For my own part", he said, "I am fully of opinion this book was thrust now to the press both to countenance these libellers and, as much as in him lay, to fire both Church and State. And though I wonder not at the minister, yet I should wonder at the bishop of the diocese (a man of learning and experience), that he should give testimony to such a business, and in such times as these." The Archbishop ended his speech by thanking the judges for their "just and honourable censure" on the prisoners, and for their "unanimous dislike of them and defence of the Church".[1]

If ever government was given a signal warning of the results of censorship, it was the government of Charles I. The public, starved of news, and forbidden to express, even in moderate form, opinions which were officially discountenanced, took its revenge in extremes once it had discovered that the administration was in fact powerless to enforce its programme. The punishment of three wretched fanatics aroused a universal publicity, and was made the occasion of hysterical demonstrations of sympathy. In the pillory at Westminster, Prynne, Burton, and Bastwick

[1] *Works*, vi. 41-70.

justified their martyrdom to a sympathetic mob, which readily agreed to their claims to resemble Christ on Calvary, strewing flowers in their way, and collecting blood from their mutilated ears in handkerchiefs. Fasts and special services were held for them, and even Lord Saye made himself conspicuous by attending a six-hour sermon at one of these dreary functions. Their journeys to their distant places of confinement were also turned into triumphal processions. At Barnet, St. Albans, Coventry, and Chester, Prynne was publicly welcomed and entertained by the townsmen. Even the remote castles where they were incarcerated, this time without the luxury of pen or paper or any book except those bearing the imprimatur of the Church, proved insufficiently isolated, and they were ultimately transferred to still more distant strongholds. Bastwick was removed from Cornwall to the Scilly Isles, Burton to Cornet Castle in Guernsey, Prynne to Mount Orgueil in Jersey, whence, for the next three years, they were unable to disturb the government by anything other than the universal memory of their sufferings. "Relegatio in insulas", — the incarceration of political opponents in islands — is a practice familiar enough from the example of ancient and modern Italian despots; English governments have but rarely resorted to it, and then only in extreme cases. Such treatment is a distinction which is shared by Prynne, Burton, Bastwick, and Napoleon.

Never in his whole career, even in the hour of his manifest failure, did it occur to Laud that he might have seriously erred even in his methods. The possibility that there might have been some alternative and less disastrous way of reaching his ends, and perhaps securing them, was inconceivable to him: nor, even in the leisure of his imprisonment, when he reviewed his whole career, could he discover a single action in it which he viewed with even qualified regret. Every detail was carefully examined and pronounced unassailable. It is hardly surprising, therefore, that the lesson of Prynne's triumph over captivity was completely wasted upon him. It only proved to him that the punishment of the three libellers had not been sufficiently severe. He wrote to Wentworth complaining petulantly that they ought to have been gagged in the pillory:[1] and his avenging hand descended on the cities which had entertained Prynne on his

[1] *Works*, vi. 497.

journey to Lancaster. Coventry only avoided the forfeit of its charter by the submission of its aldermen to a fine of £100 apiece. At Chester the reception had been on a larger and more general scale, and the principal promoters of it were notorious characters. They included an ex-mayor of the city, Calvin Bruen, and an alderman : also a lawyer who was known as a distributor of seditious literature, and a stationer who had visited Prynne in the Tower and thus enabled him to evade the censorship. When Laud turned to deal with this recalcitrant city, the frightened Bishop was driven to a ferocity that was alien to his temperament. He pleaded that he had been away in Lancashire at the time of the demonstrations, and had therefore been unable to prevent them : and he atoned for this remissness by a rigorous inquisition after the event. The proceedings against the Chester men, says Prynne, were " so fierce and formidable (the pursuivants ransacking and breaking up their houses) that two of their wives with the fright miscarried of their children ". The victims were packed off to the High Commission at York, where Archbishop Neile received instructions from Laud to remember, when imposing fines, that the proceeds went to St. Paul's,[1] which was badly in need of contributions, and there they were compelled to pronounce a solemn condemnation of Prynne in the cathedral and common hall of Chester. A thousand pictures of Prynne were also collected and burnt at the city cross ; and when a Puritan minister complained to Bishop Bridgeman that a papist woman in his district had pilloried her three cats, cut off their ears, branded them, and christened them Prynne, Burton, and Bastwick, the Bishop, in his haste to dissociate himself from the objector, so far overreached himself as to imitate the lady and call his crop-eared horse Prynne.[2] Prynne's servant Wickens, who had assisted his master to get *Instructions to Churchwardens* past the censorship, also atoned for his complicity by imprisonment ; and a Northamptonshire vicar who encouraged his parishioners to contribute to the relief of the three saints was fined £200 in the High Commission. It must be added, however, as an example of the personal humanity of Laud, which contrasts so strongly with his political cruelty, that, in spite of the pressing need of money for St. Paul's, he afterwards mitigated the fine

[1] Neile to Laud, Lambeth MS. 943, p. 559.

[2] Prynne, *New Discovery*, p. 108.

imposed upon the Chester men in view of their poverty. At the time of his trial, however, even this was not allowed to rank as indulgence. His enemies claimed that he had been bribed by a couple of pipes of sack.

Such was the publicity of the case of Prynne, Burton, and Bastwick, and such the hatred of the government to which this publicity bore witness, and which expressed itself in a spate of libels against the Archbishop circulated in the City or posted in Cheapside and on St. Paul's, that the government sought to retaliate by the publication of official propaganda. By royal command the Archbishop's speech in the Star Chamber was printed and published, and the interest evinced in the whole affair was such that, according to a news-writer, " this book is bought up so fast as they are not to be gotten ".[1] It was also translated almost immediately into both Dutch and French, in which languages Prynne's *News from Ipswich* was also already available, and copies were sent by Laud to Boswell and Scudamore as counter-propaganda. The censorship, too, according to the practice which the government was now making regular, was bolstered up by a judicial decree. In July, between the sentence of the libellers and their triumphal progress to prison, a decree of the Star Chamber was issued still further restricting the liberty of the press. The number of authorised London printers was reduced to twenty : all foreign books imported into the realm were to be handed by the customs officers to the bishops before allowing their entry : the printing of English books abroad was declared illegal : and even reissues of books already licensed were to be licensed again, lest any exceptionable matter should have crept in between the first and subsequent editions. Any unlicensed printer found guilty of setting up a press was liable to be pilloried and whipped through the City ; and the terrors of the Star Chamber and Court of High Commission were threatened against all who should infringe the above rules.[2]

The inefficacy of this decree so far as the importation of printed books from Holland is concerned has already been remarked : nor was the output of seditious literature in England noticeably decreased by it, although the incarceration of Prynne dammed up for a time an otherwise copious and unfailing source. At all events, the public demand for forbidden books was rather

[1] *S.P. Dom. Car. I.* 362, no. 76. [2] Rushworth, ii. 450.

stimulated than suppressed by the recent events; and if English printers were deterred from satisfying it by the fear of the pillory and the lash, the printers and smugglers of Holland, as Laud discovered, were only too ready to take their place and their profits. Five months later John Lilburne faced the Star Chamber on a charge of printing Puritan books at Rotterdam for the English market, and was duly visited with the pillory, the lash, and the Fleet. This time Laud had been warned: and when Lilburne attacked bishops in the pillory he was gagged.

In the course of the proceedings against Prynne, Burton, and Bastwick mention has been made of the objectionable literary venture of Bishop Williams, whom Laud accused of deliberately encouraging the libellers. "I cannot prove it", he wrote soon afterwards to Wentworth, "but I have strong conjecture that the Lord Bishop of Lincoln hath more hands than beseems him in this business, as if he meant to fire all because he himself is in danger."[1] It is unlikely that there was any direct connexion between Williams and Prynne: but certainly the Bishop was in danger, and was never fastidious in choosing his supporters. His book was an appeal to the moderate Puritans in justification of his own practice and in opposition to the Archbishop. But the Archbishop, who did not know the difference between one kind of Puritan and another, and who saw his own comprehensive policy continually thwarted by the Bishop, was now determined on his ruin. When attacks were being multiplied upon the Church from without there was no room for division within it. It did not occur to Laud that Williams, whose own orthodoxy was unquestionable, was adopting the only practical method of dealing with a large diocese, principally Puritan, over which the Bishop could not exercise complete control. Laud would not forgive a political concession. No bishop might claim to him that he could not control his diocese. And besides his political methods and his lack of thoroughness, Williams steadily resisted the centralising policy of the Archbishop, and, in the face of every metropolitical demand, exhibited a personal independence which would only yield to force. The quarrel which had begun eighteen years ago when both were rivals for the favours of Buckingham, and which was based on differences of both person-

[1] *Works*, vii. 355.

ality and principle, had become more and more bitter since Laud's elevation to supreme power. For in spite of every accession to his dignity and power, Laud was never able to force the rebellious and disgraced Bishop into an inferior place. What Williams lacked in authority, he possessed in the superiority of his political tactics. For years he had kept up a running fight in the law courts and still seemed no nearer defeat. Now, as soon as Prynne had been dealt with, Laud turned to deal with him: and for the next three years Williams was as completely ruined as Prynne.

The legal proceedings against Williams were long and tortuous, and were complicated by the intrusion of lesser charges and by the practices and stratagems of the Bishop. The original charge, as we have seen, was one of revealing secrets of the Privy Council in the reign of James I, and was manifestly frivolous. In reply Williams accused his accusers of conspiracy, because he had not allowed them to pillage his diocese under colour of suppressing Puritanism. A further charge of embezzlement was preferred against the Bishop by the chapter of Westminster: and others who had some grudge against Williams, or some hopes from Laud, added their complaints on various trivial scores. Williams, however, was politician enough to know that his best interest lay not in refuting the charges, but in dividing his accusers. While Laud pressed the attack, Williams turned to Lady Mora for support. Unlike Laud, he was always careful to provide himself with friends against all emergencies, — he had alliances with Puritans, parliamentarians, the Court, and the Catholics, — even (according to Panzani) with the Jesuits. He was also well acquainted with the ways of courts, and sufficiently rich to buy what he could not command. If he had no hope of favour from Laud, he had taken an early opportunity of insinuating himself into the Queen's party. Already, while a minister of King James, he had perfected himself in the Spanish language in order to establish his influence with the intended Princess of Wales: and when the failure of the Spanish match made that labour vain, and a bride was sought from France instead, the Bishop did not lose heart, but "endeavoured to make himself expert in that quaint and voluble language".[1] To secure the support of Cottington, Portland,

[1] Hacket, i. 209.

and Windebank no such intellectual feats were considered necessary. Opposition to the Archbishop and a long purse were thought adequate for that purpose.

The legal process thus became a race between Laud and Williams. Could Laud induce the Star Chamber to sentence Williams before Williams had persuaded the other members of the court to settle the matter by composition with the King, in which they too would receive a handsome share? In the efforts of either party to secure a victory a number of auxiliaries were pressed into the battle.

The prosecution had been begun by Attorney-General Noy, but was afterwards carried on by a more determined character, one Richard Kilvert. Of this man Fuller tells us that "like an English mastiff, he would fiercely fly upon any person or project, if set on with promise of profit: and having formerly made his breakfast on Sir John Bennet, he intended to dine and sup on the Bishop".[1] The charge of having revealed secrets of the Privy Council some dozen years ago was not very promising, and Kilvert found more hopeful material in the discovery that one of Williams' most necessary witnesses, one Pregion, the Registrar of Lincoln, was the father of a bastard. To this irrelevant fact he therefore diverted the attention of the judges: and the Bishop, perhaps purely to gain time until his project for direct composition had succeeded, committed himself to the defence of his witness from what was in fact a true charge. Finding, however, that he had placed himself in a position from which he could not extricate himself except by withdrawal, he proceeded to buy false witnesses in order to defend a false position.

Probably Williams regarded these unfortunate moves as no more than manœuvres to gain time. If so, they failed, for he did not gain sufficient time to secure himself from their consequences. A fresh charge of subornation of perjury was instituted, and the case for the prosecution assumed a more encouraging complexion. Williams therefore took the only steps from which he could hope for success. He redoubled his efforts to divide his judges, and by the end of 1635 he seemed to have succeeded. The principle of suspension was accepted, and the parties were left merely haggling about the price to be paid. At first £2000 was suggested as an adequate sum; but the appetites

[1] *Church History*, vi. 127.

of the court were stimulated by the prospect of satisfaction, and soon his deanery of Westminster, his parsonage of Walgrave, and his prebend at Lincoln were also required. The Bishop hesitated at such a sacrifice, and Cottington intervened with a compromise, suggesting £4000 cash, which Williams accepted.

Laud was appalled at the prospect of such a victory for Lady Mora and for Williams. He was well aware of the intrigues, and at the end of November he wrote to Wentworth in disgust, " 'Tis certain now that the Bishop of Lincoln is come quite off the Star Chamber by Cottington. He is suffered to hold all his *commendams*, Westminster and all. . . . Two things are worse in it, if they be as they are reported. I hope they are not. The one is that this is not only done without me, but against me, by Lord Cottington. The other that Windebank seconded Lord Cottington in this. And thus much can money and friends do against honour in moveable courts." [1] Williams on his side was proportionately elated and was indiscreet enough to boast of his success before it was quite assured.

For before Cottington's bargain had been accepted by the King, Laud had exerted his influence with his master against composition. At the same time there were others who had an interest in the success rather than the supersession of the prosecution. One was Dr. John Farmerie, chancellor of the diocese of Lincoln, who had been Laud's informer and agent against the Bishop during the metropolitical visitation. In December he wrote a frantic letter to his protector, Sir John Lambe, reporting a rumour that Williams had made his peace with the King by naming the Duke of York as his heir, and that Farmerie was either to be thrown to the Bishop as part of the bargain, or banished with his family to Ireland, or to pay £2000 of the Bishop's fine.[2] More important were the efforts of Sir John Monson, a Lincolnshire justice of the peace, who had opposed the Bishop in the case of Pregion's bastard child at Lincoln sessions, where it was disputed, and who claimed to have been libelled by him. He too did not relish the prospect of losing his damages, and did his best to discredit the Bishop in all circles. He petitioned the King against Williams' indirect practices ; he

[1] *Works*, vii. 214. Cf. Howell to Wentworth, 28 Nov. 1635 (*Strafford Letters*, i. 489 ; Garrade to Wentworth, Dec. 1635 (*ibid.* i. 490)).

[2] Lambeth MS. 1030, no. 44.

wrote to Secretary Coke reporting that Williams was threatening vengeance against opposing witnesses and currying favour with the opposition : and he wrote to Laud urging the justice of his case. As a result of this activity the case against Williams was resumed : Coke offered the protection of the law to witnesses intimidated by the Bishop ; and when Williams increased his offers to the King to £8000 and his deanery of Westminster, and the case between himself and Monson to be tried separately, Monson assured the King that so small a fine was out of all proportion to the enormity of the offence, and that anyway the Bishop would be giving as much again to the courtiers who had negotiated the deal, while if the King were to appoint commissioners to try and condemn him, he might secure the whole swag to himself.[1] These sordid reasons prevailed, the prosecution proceeded, and Williams, having failed to escape through the corruptible medium of the Court, appealed to the other party which opposed the Archbishop, — the Puritans. In December 1636 he added to his previous offences by entering into religious controversy, issuing his *Holy Table, Name and Thing* in answer to Heylin's *Coal from the Altar*.

The final trial of Williams was deferred first by one of the petty cases which were continually brought against him by those who saw his unpopularity and hoped for a share of the spoils, then by the case of Prynne, Burton, and Bastwick, which occupied the attention of the Council. The first case was brought by a disreputable drover called Shelley, who happened to be churchwarden at Buckden, and, deciding that the official assessment of the Bishop for ship-money was too low, caused another and heavier assessment to be drawn up. When the Bishop demurred he became the centre of a new local storm, Shelley joining forces with Kilvert and the other small fry of the prosecution, and the " better sort " of the inhabitants of Buckden petitioning the Council in support of the Bishop. This affair was ultimately liquidated, and Shelley discredited : and, two days after the Star Chamber had passed sentence on Prynne and his colleagues, Williams was finally summoned before it to answer the charge of subornation of perjury.

The charge of countenancing the libellers, at which Laud had hinted in his speech against Prynne, Burton, and Bastwick,

[1] Lambeth MS. 1030, nos. 47, 48.

Williams explicitly repudiated : but he had no defence against the principal accusations of wholesale tampering with witnesses by bribery and intimidation, and Cottington and Windebank had no alternative but to pronounce a heavy sentence on their former associate.[1] Cottington provided the judges with a lead, suggesting a fine of £10,000 to the King and a thousand marks to Sir John Monson, with imprisonment during the King's pleasure and suspension *ab officio et beneficio* by the court of High Commission ; and this lead was unanimously followed. Laud delivered a speech at the censure, in which, after a few perfunctory sighs that a man of such eminent parts and dignities should have involved himself in such dubious courses, he dwelt upon the Christian patience which the Bishop might have exhibited, but did not, under his afflictions : dilated upon the enormity of the offence, and the savage penalties which the ancients had held it to deserve : and concurred in the sentence.[2]

"If they have done this *ad correctionem*, not *ad ruinam*," wrote Sir Thomas Roe a fortnight later, "they have kept the bounds of their court."[3] But it was the general opinion that the sentence represented rather the revenge of the Archbishop than the course of justice. The attendance at the court was large throughout the trial, and the public showed its sympathy with the Bishop, rather because it hated Laud, and was prepared to use any stick with which to beat him, than because it had any affection for Williams. For Laud, of course, the fall of Williams was a great triumph. Not only had he removed the principal obstacle to his aims in the Church, but he had vindicated impersonal justice against the corrupt influences of the Court which he had seen triumph in the case of Sir James Bagg. Nevertheless, if we commend the latter source of satisfaction, the former must necessarily qualify our commendation. Laud sought to clear himself of the charge of any vindictive aims against the Bishop : and in the course of his speech he protested that he had been down upon his knees before the King several times in Williams' behalf, and had been the intermediary who had delivered Williams' petitions to Charles, — services, he complained, for which the Bishop had shown scant gratitude. This may well be true : but we must distinguish between the formal correctness of outward

[1] Rushworth, ii. 416 ff. [2] *Works*, vi. 71.
[3] *S.P. Dom. Car. I.* 364, no. 47.

behaviour and the personal feelings which it might clothe, but whose satisfaction it was not intended to frustrate. Laud's determination to break Williams was manifested by the first prosecution in the Star Chamber on a frivolous charge with which it was not considered necessary to proceed. It was only later that Williams started tampering with witnesses, and the case could be converted into one of the integrity of the law. Laud's letters to Wentworth also shed continual light on his determination to overthrow Williams as well as to champion justice ; and his claims to have pleaded with the King for mercy accord ill with his subsequent behaviour. For Williams, condemned to pay a huge fine, and deprived of the revenues from which he might have hoped to pay it, pleaded for time, since there was no hope of mitigation. The King's reply was written down by Laud. He required more money, to be paid at once, and insisted that Williams give up all his *commendams*, exchange his rich bishopric for a poor and unimportant see in Wales or Ireland, acknowledge his offences, and recant *The Holy Table, Name and Thing*. All this was to be done under his own hand, and the money was to be paid or secured in full before Williams would be allowed to leave the Tower.[1] At the same time Laud wrote to the Attorney-General bidding him see that the punishment of Williams was executed in full. " You know ", he explained, " that all the Lords agreed upon so little fine, because they took away all the rents and profits of his bishopric and deanery, else three times as much would have been laid upon him." [2]

To these harsh conditions Williams preferred the Tower, and remained there till the Long Parliament secured his release. But even in the Tower he remained an incalculable force, such were his political resources, so many his influential contacts. By his intrigues and prevarications he continued to alarm the Archbishop for another three years : and the Archbishop heartily wished that he would accept the King's offer of freedom on condition of his exchanging Lincoln for a Welsh or Irish bishopric. In view of what we know of Wentworth's treatment of Irish bishops, and Laud's intimacy with Wentworth, it is not surprising that Williams consistently preferred the Tower ; and he never

[1] Lambeth MS. 1030, 68ab.

[2] MSS. of R. Bankes, Esq. (H.M.C. Report VIII, i. 209).

evinced any sentimental hankering to return to his native Wales. Meanwhile the diocese of Lincoln was again at Laud's mercy, and Sir John Lambe was appointed to execute ecclesiastical jurisdiction there during the Bishop's suspension. Apart from his faithful service in opposing Williams, Lambe had earned the warm thanks of the Archbishop by his zeal in the business of ship-money; and he was now appointed, together with four other clergymen and justices of the peace, to hear the complaints of any clergymen in the diocese who thought themselves assessed at too high a figure.[1]

Bishop Williams had scarcely been disposed of before Laud found himself faced with difficulties in another quarter. A series of spectacular, though in themselves unimportant, conversions to the Roman faith made it clear to the world that Con had replaced the Archbishop as the most powerful religious influence at the Court. In 1636 Laud had heard from Scudamore that his friend Sir Kenelm Digby had been converted to Rome, and had written a long but ineffectual letter of remonstrance to Digby about it: at the beginning of next year a storm had been aroused by the discovery that the sons of a peer were being educated by a Jesuit; and soon afterwards the King had the children of the late Duke of Buckingham removed from their mother's care to safer tutelage. These precautions, however, did not stop the drift to Rome. Con had found an ardent disciple in Mrs. Endymion Porter: and this lady made the year 1637 memorable by the impressive list of her converts. First there was her old father, Lord Boteler, whose soul she managed to rescue just before it abandoned his body. Then came her brother-in-law, similarly captured in the nick of time. The Marchioness of Hamilton followed. She too was in a promising state of illness, and the rival Protestant efforts of her father and the Bishop of Carlisle could not prevent her from preferring the certain salvation offered by Mrs. Porter, although she never openly acknowledged her conversion. The last straw came in October, when Mrs. Porter fished into her net the soul of her sister, Lady Newport, but recently an ardent Protestant, who had sought in vain to recover her dying father from her missionary sister.

The prominent position enjoyed at court by the Earl of Newport, who was half-brother to Lord Holland, the series of similar

[1] Laud, *Works*, vii. 303; House of Lords MSS., Nov. 1637.

conversions which had preceded it, and the suddenness of Lady Newport's change from Puritanism to Popery, made it the occasion of considerable scandal ; and Lord Newport, himself a staunch Protestant, was filled with indignation. Con reported that the conversion had not only saved the Countess from damnation, but had worked a wonderful change in her domestic behaviour, turning her from a domineering termagant into a model and submissive spouse. But this alteration, if true, did not seem to the Earl to be an adequate *quid pro quo* for the loss of his wife's soul and his own reputation, and he went in some heat to the Archbishop, accusing Sir Toby Matthew and Wat Montague, two notable converts among the courtiers, of having conspired with the Agent to seduce his wife. Laud brought the matter up before the Privy Council next day,[1] denouncing the growth of the Roman party, the free resort to mass at the Queen's chapel, and the activities of the new apostles. He fell upon his knees, and begged the King to banish Wat Montague from the Court, and to allow him to proceed against Toby Matthew in the Court of High Commission. As for Con, " he knew not how he came hither, nor what he did here, and therefore he would say nothing of him ".[2]

For the time being at least, Laud won his point. So effectively did he plead that both Montague and Matthew kept carefully to themselves for some time afterwards, although in fact neither were directly concerned in the present case. In December, in spite of the efforts of Con, a royal proclamation was issued against " the withdrawing His Majesty's subjects from the Church of England and giving scandal in resorting to masses " ;[3] and a year later the government again resorted to official propaganda. By royal command Laud republished his account of his conference in 1622 with the Jesuit Fisher, when his arguments against the Church of Rome had prevailed with the hesitating Duke of Buckingham and entrenched Laud in the favour of the favourite.

But this victory for the Archbishop was necessarily won at a cost ; for it was a defeat for the Queen. The Queen was the champion of the Catholics, the patron of Con, the friend of Montague. Her relations with Laud were never agreeable. When negotiations with Rome had first been tentatively begun,

[1] *Works*, iii. 229. [2] Garrarde to Wentworth, *Strafford Letters*, ii. 128.
[3] Rymer, *Foedera*, xx. 180.

she had sought to win his support. She had promised him "that she would be my friend, and that I should have immediate access to her when I had occasion";[1] and she had thought of winning him to change his principles by favours. These errors can hardly have been entertained by her for long; now they were completely and finally dispelled. The Archbishop's behaviour in the Council Chamber was reported to her the same night, and she made no secret of her displeasure. For two months there was an open rupture between them: and although relations were resumed in December when Laud had a long conversation with her about Wat Montague, and they "parted fair", it was nevertheless obvious that the breach between the two was irreparable even if it was papered over. It was in vain that the King sought to effect a reconciliation. Henceforth the King himself owed a double allegiance which it was impossible to conceal, the party of Lady Mora, Bishop Williams, and the Queen was consolidated, and Laud, as he wrote to Wentworth, was "between two great factions, very like corn between two millstones".[2]

From the intrigues and revenges which hampered his activities at the height of his power the character of Laud certainly emerges in disagreeable colours. Granted that Prynne was intolerant and intolerable, Williams obstructive and unscrupulous, that Hampden was factious and Con a charlatan: granted that Laud's enmity was inspired by devotion to an ideal and exasperated by pressure of work; yet how harsh and unsympathetic was his attitude, how repellent his refusal to admit the validity of any canon but his own, or the legitimacy of any bond save that of a common principle. Nevertheless, once this is allowed, such a general judgment again requires modification. For when we turn to those whose opposition to him was based upon more rational differences, we shall find him ready, even if slow, to discover in one common interest the nucleus of a permanent personal friendship, capable of surviving in spite of wide disagreement in other spheres. Those who, like the Queen of Bohemia, were able to get past the first brusque rebuff or cold compliment, frequently found themselves rewarded by an acquaintance which they shared with only a few others.

One of the first to make this discovery was the young lawyer

[1] *Works*, iii. 222. [2] *Ibid.* vii. 378.

Edward Hyde, afterwards Earl of Clarendon, who, he tells us himself, " was wont to say, the greatest want the Archbishop had was of a true friend, who would seasonably have told him of his infirmities, and what people spake of him ", adding that, " he knew well that such a friend would have been very acceptable to him ". Now Hyde, as Sir Charles Firth has said, possessed a natural genius for friendship : and it is not surprising that he should seek to supply the want from which he perceived that Laud suffered, especially as he was yet a stranger in the Court, to whom a powerful acquaintance might be of great assistance. He therefore cultivated the acquaintance of the Archbishop, and the free access which he had to him is testified by his own story of how, coming up from the country at the beginning of one Michaelmas term, he went to call at Lambeth. Walking with him in the garden, Hyde freely told the Archbishop that the whole country was discontented, and that Laud was regarded as the source of all the trouble : and upon Laud's expostulation, he repeated the complaints of two Wiltshire gentlemen who, having cause to appear before the Council, were treated with respect by all the other Privy Councillors, but found that " he alone spake very sharply to them, and without anything of grace, at which they were much troubled, and one of them, supposing that somebody had done him ill-offices, went the next morning to Lambeth to present his service to him and to discover, if he could, what misrepresentation had been made of him : that after he had attended very long he was admitted to speak with His Grace, who, scarce hearing him, sharply answered him that ' he had no leisure for compliments ', and so hurried away : which put the other gentleman much out of countenance." Such complaints, Hyde added, were continually being made against him throughout the country.

To this tale the Archbishop listened patiently, and expressed great concern for the offence which, he said, he had not intended to give, but which must have been due to his naturally brusque manner and the pressure of business upon him ; and when Hyde remonstrated with him for allowing such damaging impressions to be given, he admitted the justice of the reproach, — without, it must be added, noticeably overcoming the defect. This free conversation, however, only served to cement a long and close friendship : and the most favourable portrait which we possess of

Laud from his contemporaries comes not from the obsequious clergy who throve for a while in his shade, but from the lawyer who pointed out his errors to his face.[1]

Another unexpected friend of the Archbishop was another lawyer, — the great John Selden : a man who, in every capacity save one, would seem to have been the very antithesis of Laud. For Selden was a lawyer : and Laud distrusted lawyers with their insistence on Common Law and ancient rights against the State ; and he was an antiquary : and Laud distrusted antiquaries, with their unhealthy interest in precedents and privileges and parliaments. Selden, too, was a champion of complete intellectual liberty, and his motto, περὶ παντὸς τὴν ἐλευθερίαν, accorded ill with Laud's rigorous censorship and harsh suppression of opinions which he did not share. As a member of Parliament Selden had been imprisoned for his constitutional doctrines : as an exponent of the law of tithes he had been forced to make submission before the High Commission : while, as for religion, he was a complete Erastian, and rarely enjoyed himself so much as when he was confounding the preposterous divinity of the clergy, Anglican and Puritan alike, by his well-documented common sense. At a time when pompous high church ecclesiastics and disordered Puritan sectaries reared their rickety metaphysical superstructures upon the unsteady basis of patristic pedantry and Hebrew bombast, nothing is more refreshing to the modern reader than the solvent scepticism with which Selden undermined those pretentious erections. The taboo of sacrilege, the divine right of bishops, justification by faith, — all the mumbo-jumbo of ecclesiasticism was exposed by the light of his sound, tolerant, secular learning. " Chain up the clergy on both sides ", was his practical advice : and in the intellectual world, where he was acknowledged master, he pointed out that all the best emendations in the Scriptures had been the work of laymen.

One would imagine that no common interest could have united two such different characters as Selden and Laud. But this was not so. Laud respected learning, and Selden possessed it : and the bond thus established between them led to a friendship which agreed to differ on all other topics. Selden dedicated some of his learned works to Laud in recognition of assistance in collecting the material : he sent gifts to the Bodleian through

[1] Clarendon, *Life*, Oxford, 1759, p. 32.

Laud :[1] and it was Laud who persuaded him to reissue, in 1636, his *Mare Clausum* against the maritime pretensions of the Dutch. Thereafter, we are told, Selden was " both a frequent and welcome guest at Lambeth House, where he was grown into such esteem with the Archbishop that he might have chosen his own preferment in the Court (as it was then generally believed) had he not undervalued all other employments in respect of his studies ".[2] So completely was this reconciliation effected that though Selden never became a courtier, nor abandoned his constitutional opinions, he was returned to the Long Parliament for Oxford University, which might be regarded as Laud's pocket-borough : and when Laud sought to anticipate disaster by renouncing the canons of 1640, it was to Selden that he applied to let them die quietly.

Another of Laud's personal friends was his godson, William Chillingworth, an earnest and disputatious student who, having allowed himself to be drugged by the assurances of the Jesuit Fisher, was only reclaimed from Romanism by Laud himself. Thereafter he became a champion of rational Protestantism, a member of Lord Falkland's literary and philosophical society at Great Tew, and showed his impartiality by declaring, during the Civil War, that all the scribes and pharisees were upon one side, and all the publicans and sinners upon the other. Another was " the incomparable John Hales of Eton ", also a member of Falkland's circle, who had been cured of his early affection for Calvinism by his attendance at the Synod of Dordt. There he " bade John Calvin good-night ", and thenceforth he devoted himself to undenominational studies : but being summoned before the Archbishop to clear himself of a charge of heresy in 1638, he found, instead of a censorious martinet, an interested disputant, and after spending most of the day walking in the garden at Lambeth discussing the points at issue between them, he found that he had established a new intimacy. On the way out Hales could not resist the temptation to pull the leg of the pompous Heylin, assuring him " that he found the Archbishop (whom he knew before for a nimble disputant) to be as well versed in books as business ; that he had been ferreted by him from one hole to another, till there was none left to afford him any further shelter ;

[1] A copy of Selden's *Marmora Arundelliana* (1629) in St. John's College Library, was presented by Laud, and was most probably a gift from the author.

[2] Heylin, p. 303.

that he was now resolved to be orthodox and to declare himself a true son of the Church of England, both for doctrine and discipline ". Neither Hales nor Chillingworth shared Laud's Arminian views, either before or after their intimacy with him: and this intimacy is at least evidence that Laud, in spite of his intolerant practice, professed a more tolerant theology than his adversaries, and was not disposed to persecute those whose convictions were intellectually held and rationally defended.

These intellectual friendships, however, are but an interlude, if a pleasant interlude, in Laud's methodical programme; and as time went on he had less and less leisure to indulge them. For although English Puritans, refractory bishops, and Roman missionaries made the year 1637 a difficult period for him, they were not the only, nor, as it afterwards proved, the worst of the evils which crowded upon him during that year. It was then, too, that the failure of his Scottish policy was first made manifest by a striking and significant incident.

The idea of securing the loyalty of the Scots by the imposition of an appropriate form of worship was, as we have seen, not new, nor first invented by Laud. It had been the intention of James I, who had already begun the process before he had allowed Laud to rise from obscurity. But James I had proceeded warily, playing the nobility against the Presbyterian ministers, and inserting episcopacy between the two by the skilful exercise of royal authority. His canny timidity had prevented him from imposing it with a flourish or proceeding with it too fast: and even so, the opposition which it aroused persuaded him to suspend the programme. When he died, he left the work a mere shadow, tentatively and uncertainly traced.

This shadow Charles I and Laud determined to fill in, and they set about it in a methodical if undiplomatic manner. In the years from 1635 to 1637 the programme of Thorough, which was being carried out with partial success in England, was being imposed as steadily in Scotland. All the features of Laud's policy in England are visible in Scotland also. There too the Church was being restored to its old position, its old constitution, its old doctrines, and, as far as possible, its old wealth. As Juxon was made Lord Treasurer of England, so Spottiswood became Lord Chancellor of Scotland. As English bishops became agents of the government, so in Scotland they were placed on the Privy Council. As, in England, the Beauty of Holiness was enforced from above, beginning in the cathedrals and being imposed on the parish churches, so in Scotland the example was set in Holyrood Chapel and the University of St. Andrews, the archiepiscopal see. The loaves and fishes were naturally distributed on the same principle as in England. When Adam Ballantyne, Bishop of Dunblane and Dean of the Chapel Royal at Holyrood, omitted to use the English liturgy during the King's absence, he was sharply reprimanded by Laud, and shortly afterwards removed to the bishopric of Aberdeen, with strict orders to reside there. Reluctantly he submitted the care of the royal chapel to James Wedderburn, whom Laud had known and beneficed in England. And when Ballantyne in Aberdeen connived at the sabbatarian practices of his neighbours, Laud wrote to Archbishop Spottiswood ordering sharp measures against such offences " contrary to the rules of Christianity and all the ancient canons of the Church ".[1] It is somewhat ironical that Aberdeen, where Laud lamented his lack of control, was the only district where the ministers refused stubbornly to sign the Covenant. It was true, of course, that Laud had no direct jurisdiction over the Scottish Church. The head of the Scottish Church was the King of Scotland. But the King of Scotland sat in London, and his chief ecclesiastical adviser was the Archbishop of Canterbury. He had no independent ecclesiastical adviser for Scotland ; and in practice Laud dictated the policy of the Scottish Church without any hesitation, as if it were part of the province of Canterbury.

At the same time, the other features of Laud's English policy were being enforced in Scotland. The cathedral of St. Andrews was restored as was St. Paul's in London. New churches were built, a new bishopric constructed. The wealth of the Church was increased as much as possible, and the fear that the abbey-lands seized by the nobility would be resumed for the Church persuaded some nobles to forestall such an event by exchanging the uncertain tenures for less disputable properties in England. In this way the abbeys of St. Andrews, Arbroath, and Kelso were recovered for the Church, and the Duke of Richmond and Lennox, the Marquis Hamilton, and the Earl of Roxburghe

[1] *Works*, vi. 443.

avoided both the stigma of sacrilege and the prospect of financial loss. Laud also agitated for the better payment of the Holyrood choirmen and the Edinburgh ministers,[1] as he did for their English colleagues : and in Scotland, as in England, he gave his support to charitable institutions. The chief of these was the hospital in Edinburgh for the maintenance and education of poor orphans, founded in 1624 by the will of a rich jeweller and money-lender, George Heriot. Work upon this foundation was held up by the difficulty of recovering large debts due to Heriot's estate from the Crown and the reluctance of Lord Treasurer Portland to disburse for charity what might be kept for current expenses or his own reward ; but Laud continually and effectually moved the King to forward the work, and was thanked by the Edinburgh Town Council for his intercession.[2]

But if Laud was merely doing in Scotland what he was doing in England and Ireland, there were conditions in Scotland which made the work there far more difficult, and of which Laud, in spite of two visits, was quite unaware. In England the machinery for the restoration of the Church already existed, and had only to be used. In Ireland religious convictions were a luxury which few claimed and fewer possessed. The stagnant Catholicism of the inhabitants was hardly stirred by the English settlers, and as it was not yet exasperated, it was not yet organised. At the same time the appetites of Irish politicians and Irish bishops alike were curbed and frustrated by the exorbitant power of the despotic Lord Deputy. So long as Wentworth governed Ireland, naked power made it an English province, and suffered the English Church to prosper as it could never prosper once that power was withdrawn.

In Scotland the English government had no such advantages. The Kirk was already organised there, the Episcopal Church existed on sufferance only, as a result of royal authority and political manœuvres, and the English government had no such direct control as could be exercised by an absolute governor of

[1] Laud to Ballantyne, *Works*, vi. 340 ; Laud to Lord Provost of Edinburgh, *English Historical Review*, Oct. 1892. By the new liturgy the proceeds of the offertory were to be divided between the poor and the minister, instead of going to the poor alone, as in England.

[2] Laud to Lord Provost of Edinburgh, *Works*, vi. 318 ; *English Historical Review*, Oct. 1892 ; *Works*, vi. 420. Cf. W. Steven, *History of Heriot's Hospital*.

a defeated province. This James I had recognised; and he had secured some part of his designs there not by enforcing his royal commands, but by dividing his adversaries. He had defeated the Kirk by buying the nobility. Charles I alienated the nobility at the outset of his reign, and then proceeded to attack the Kirk before he had recovered the support of the nobles.

Thus the only party upon which the English government could rely in Scotland was the newly established Episcopal Church, and this party was without effective power because its authority was based entirely upon the English government.[1] Laud sought indeed to give it power of its own, that it might stand upon its own feet; but, except on the backstairs, he was no politician. He failed to provide it with any ally while it was securing power, and as a result, its ambitions raised up determined enemies before it had secured it. The nobility resented the encroachments of the new bishops, who claimed an equal share in the administration, usurping the functions of privy councillors and the revenues of territorial magnates; and having already been injured by the King by the Act of Revocation, they joined hands with the otherwise leaderless Kirk to oppose the innovations which affected them both.

This resentment was not created by "Laud's Liturgy". It had existed from the beginning of the reign, and had manifested itself during the royal visit and later during the affair of Balmerino. But in 1637 the opposition was able to organise itself, and the alliance between disaffected nobility and disestablished Kirk was consolidated, because Laud, true to his pathetic faith in the ultimate authority of the written document, provided his opponents with the slogan which they needed against the English government, — a written document.

Not that the liturgy was a sudden, unconsidered innovation. Its publication and imposition were implicit in the government's Scottish policy ever since the restoration of episcopacy, and Laud himself had been engaged on the project since 1629. But

[1] Cf. Burnet, *History of His Own Times* (ed. Airy), p. 40: "The most unaccountable part of the King's proceedings was that all this while, when he was endeavouring to recover so great a part of the property of Scotland as the Church lands and tithes were from men that were not like to part from them willingly, and was going to change the whole constitution of that Church and kingdom, he raised no force to maintain what he was about to do, but trusted the whole management to the civil execution".

the interval had not been used to prepare opinion in Scotland for the reception of the liturgy, — indeed, Laud thought surprise essential to prevent counter-organisation;[1] it had been used solely to prepare the liturgy and to strengthen the machinery for its introduction.

The most conspicuous preparations for the new Prayer Book were two publications which were brought out in 1636. One was a reissue, with some modifications, of King James' metrical version of the Psalms, edited by the Earl of Stirling, who had a monopoly of the profits from its sale; the other was the Book of Canons for the Scottish Church.

These canons had been drawn up by the Scottish bishops in the year 1635, and they incorporated the idea of Church government advocated and imposed by Laud. Laud himself had supervised them closely from the start: for the new Scottish bishops had no ultimate authority to appeal to except the King, and the King's mind was interpreted by Laud alone. Laud, too, was the intermediary through whom correspondence between the Scottish bishops and the English government was maintained, and he used them as advisers and informers about Scottish affairs. When Bishop Ballantyne was reported as having allowed a fast in his diocese on Sundays, Laud wrote to Spottiswood requiring that a canon against such practices be inserted, and he was duly obeyed.[2] By another canon, remonstrance to the King was permitted, "forasmuch as no reformation in doctrine or discipline can be made perfect at once in any church":[3] and here too the mind of Laud may be seen at work. Referring to this passage, he wrote to his agent Maxwell: "I am very glad your canons are in so good a readiness, and that the true meaning of that one canon remains under the curtain. I hope you will take care that it may be fully printed and passed with the rest. 'Twill be of great use for the settling of that Church."[4] It was not without reason that the Scottish commissioners charged Laud at his trial that "this canon holds the door open to more innovations". When the canons were completed, they were submitted to Laud and Juxon for their amendments, and then, after approval by the Scottish bishops, published by the authority of the King.

[1] Cf. Laud to Traquair, *infra*, p. 344.

[2] *Works*, vi. 443; Canons, ch. xiv. (*Works*, v. 599).

[3] Canons, ch. viii. 3 (*Works*, v. 595).

[4] Laud, *Works*, vi. 434.

Throughout the procedure, the use of the royal authority in ecclesiastical affairs was almost indecently obvious, and has frequently been condemned. But the royal authority was the only authority by which the voice of Laud could speak effectively in Scotland. As Archbishop of Canterbury he had no legal authority over the Scottish Church. He therefore spoke through the mouth of the King of Scotland, and the Erastianism charged against the government of the Church of Scotland was little more than a politic and necessary disguise.

But historically the importance of the canons of 1636 consists chiefly in their anticipation of the liturgy of 1637, which they declared to be legal, and to which they enjoined obedience, even though the liturgy had not yet been seen by those who were commanded to declare its orthodoxy. The preparation of the new Prayer Book was long and careful. Laud, as we have seen, would have preferred the imposition of the English Prayer Book without alteration, in the sacred name of uniformity ; and through all the days of trouble which followed he insisted that his advice should have been followed. In practice, however, he was compelled to allow certain alterations out of deference to Scottish national prejudices, imperfectly represented by the new Scottish bishops. The point, however, is of no importance at all. However the new liturgy might differ in form from the English model — and in fact it differed in being slightly more explicit in its Catholic doctrine — it was obviously dictated from England. If it had been the unaided work of the Scottish bishops, it would still have been regarded, like them, as an English imposition. And the fact that it was submitted to Laud and Wren for their final alterations made no difference to its reception in Scotland, although it provided Laud's enemies with an additional charge against him. In October 1636 the King wrote to the Scottish Privy Council ordering the use of the new service-book : by a proclamation of December every parish in Scotland was ordered to obtain two copies of it by Easter : at Easter the book was still not available : and finally, in May, it reached Scotland, and the orders for its circulation were put into force.

The immediate result is well known, and need not be treated in detail. Laud, at Lambeth, was busied with other things, — with the prosecution of libellers, the restriction of printers, the punishment of Williams, and the numerous details of ecclesiastical bureaucracy. He left the work of reducing Scotland to complete conformity to his agents in Scotland. He had done all the preparatory work, had embodied it in authoritative documents, and was prepared only to applaud its success. It was a complete surprise to him, therefore, when his labours in England were interrupted by the news of failure in the north. On July 23rd, at the first reading of the Prayer Book in St. Giles' Cathedral, the famous riot occurred when Archbishop Spottiswood, Bishop Lindsay, the Dean of Edinburgh, and all the Beauty of Holiness were suddenly assailed with stones and cutty-stools and feminine abuse, and only the intervention and the numerous retinues of the nobility whom they had so offended preserved the ecclesiastical dignitaries from lynching.

The situation produced by this spectacular riot appeared in a somewhat different light to the King and the Archbishop who had caused it, and the Scottish Privy Council which had to cope with it. The latter body, to begin with, had no love for the newly established bishops, as it consisted chiefly of the noblemen whom they were displacing; and secondly, even if it had the will, it had not the means to act with decisive thoroughness. It therefore proceeded to pacify rather than to suppress. Archbishop Spottiswood himself ordered the suspension of both the old form of prayer and the new liturgy until the King's pleasure could be known, and the Council made a few arrests and assured the Edinburgh ministers of the protection of the law in the performance of their duties. In Laud's eyes, however, the situation called for far more drastic measures. He wrote to the Lord Treasurer of Scotland, the Earl of Traquair, complaining of the weakness of the Council. That a week's notice of the service should have been given, in which the disaffected could prepare to wreck it, seemed to him most reprehensible, and he expressed great dissatisfaction with the cowardice of the bishops, and the suspension of the use of the liturgy. To Spottiswood too he wrote urging him not to be deterred from severity by the representations of laymen, and advising him as to the courses he should have taken to prevent the riot from occurring.[1]

Remote and impotent in Lambeth, unaware of the deeper causes of the trouble, and of his own responsibility for its occurrence, there was little that the Archbishop could do except complain of

[1] Laud, *Works*, vi. 493.

the lack of thoroughness shown by his subordinates, as he considered the Scottish bishops and Privy Councillors to be. The Venetian ambassador reported him as " exceedingly afflicted and depressed " by the tumult, whose repercussions in England he could not but apprehend, and which might even result in the loss of the royal favour, upon which his whole position depended. If, at present, he did not advocate extreme courses with the offenders, that was in order that he might take his revenge fully once the general feeling in Scotland had been calmed by a temporary lenity : later, he hoped that " with the extinction or crushing of the leaders, the others will yield ".[1] The idea of putting his hand to the plough and then turning back was repellent to him, nor had there been any occasion in his career hitherto when he had done so. If the King inclined to concession, Laud nerved him to resistance. The Scottish Council might protest the inadequacy of their power to enforce the royal orders, but the King wrote back that they must be enforced; the suspension was to be withdrawn and the Prayer Book read, and all magistrates were required to support the new ecclesiastical regulations. This strong line taken in London, however, achieved nothing in Edinburgh, where the refusal of the new Provost to forward the petitions of the townsmen caused a second riot, and the King's answer to the petitions resulted in a third. Seeing their authority thus flouted, King and Archbishop both advertised their determination not to surrender. " I mean to be obeyed ", was Charles' answer to those who asked his intentions, and Laud, according to the Venetian ambassador, " says he will risk everything rather than yield a jot ".[2] In December the opponents of Scottish episcopacy, who had now formed themselves into four " Tables " or committees representing the four orders of nobles, lairds, burghers, and ministers, for more effective negotiation, took the offensive by presenting to the Council, which had now withdrawn by royal command to Dalkeith, a collective " Supplication " in which they designated the bishops as the authors of the evil, requiring that they should be removed from the Council on the ground that they ought not to be judges of a case to which they were parties, and should be put upon trial. Thus the year 1637 closed in Scotland.

When we consider the number and variety and importance

[1] *Ven. Cal.* xxiv. 282, 289.

[2] *Ibid.* xxiv. 336.

of the various attacks directed against Laud in this year, and remember also that it was in November of this year that the *cause célèbre* of John Hampden for refusing to pay ship-money took place, and that in this year the plague, which had been epidemic for seven years, now reached its worst, we can hardly be surprised at the slowing down of the Archbishop's constructive policy. The sudden fall in the contributions towards the repair of St. Paul's indicates the growing unpopularity of the government and the fresh claims upon the subject's purse. For the first five years of the work, the receipts had steadily risen, reaching, in 1635, a maximum of £16,000. In 1636 a total of £9342 was collected, of which the amount raised from the country, which had been over £7000 in the previous year, was only £1401. In 1637 the total was £10,444, and the country's share in this had sunk to a mere £259. The efforts of Laud and his agents were not relaxed. Fines were diverted to the work of repair, and Sir John Lambe, who did much to encourage donations and legacies, seems frequently to have had his eye fixed more steadily upon the needs of the cathedral than upon the enormity of the crime when dealing with ecclesiastical offenders. But excuses came in from all sides. For the fewness of the contributions from the large diocese of Lincoln, Williams pleaded the plague as an excuse.[1] Nor could this be attributed only to the unwillingness of the bishop, for next year his adversary, and Laud's obedient supporter, Sir John Monson, wrote that he was doing his best to stimulate the generosity of the inhabitants of Lincolnshire, " but not with very wished success ".[2] Wiltshire Laud had already found in 1634 to be " as backward, both clergy and laity, towards the repair of St. Paul's Church as any part of England that I have observed ", and, in spite of Edward Hyde's encouragement, Laud was forced to circularise the magistrates in the summer of 1637, pointing out that in the past year the whole county, in spite of its thriving cloth industry, had only contributed 8s. 10d. This appeal seems to have elicited some response, for in September the commissioners wrote to the sheriff and justices of the peace of the county congratulating them on " the exemplary bounty especially, of those of the better sort ".[3] Puritan East Anglia was less respon-

[1] Williams to Laud, Oct. 31st, 1636 (Lambeth MS. 1030, 51).
[2] *Cal. S.P. Dom.*, 1637, p. 512.
[3] Add. MS. 32324 ; *S.P. Dom. Car. I.* 368, no. 46.

sive. In the Colchester district it was complained that, owing to the influence of Puritan preachers, contributions were very slow in coming and small when they came. One great parish gave only 6d., and some nothing at all.[1] From Suffolk Laud was petitioned to stop the collections altogether, as, what with ship-money and plague-relief, the people there were sufficiently taxed already.[2] In poor districts like Wales the commissioners naturally found little response.[3] Bishop Wright of Lichfield, who exasperated Laud by never sending him accounts of his diocese in the ordinary way, nevertheless found time to report that it was too poor to subscribe to St. Paul's.[4]

In spite of these difficulties, Laud still busied himself with innumerable details of constructive policy throughout the year, as is shown by the number of petitions which poured in upon him from every side. These petitions were encouraged by him, and each received minute and personal attention, because they tended to increase the centralisation of the Church at which he aimed. When some local squire made enclosures which reduced the value of a vicarage, or sought to bring the vicar into dependence upon him, the vicar appealed to the Archbishop, and the Archbishop wrote to the offender in defence of the rights of the Church. By the same means information reached him of the misdemeanours of bishops and local magistrates, and a hundred parochial squabbles caused by a general unwillingness to contribute to the repair of village churches which Laud was demanding everywhere, in imitation of St. Paul's. Among the petitioners during this year were three of Laud's own less reputable bishops, Dr. Wright, Dr. Coke, and Dr. Skinner. The recent episcopal transfers had revealed various shady activities in the diocese of Bristol. The diocese was small and poor; and as a result Laud wished to enrich it, and had placed Wright, when he was there, under special instructions with regard to the renewal of leases and careful stewardship of revenues. The bishops, however, because of the poverty of the diocese, had preferred to make it still poorer in order to compensate themselves; and now each began to accuse his predecessor of waste and peculation, and of carrying away to his new bishopric the perquisites which legitimately belonged to

[1] *S.P. Dom. Car. I.* 276, no. 42.
[2] *Cal. S.P. Dom.*, 1637–8, p. 157.
[3] *S.P. Dom. Car. I.* 288, no. 87.
[4] *S.P. Dom. Car. I.* 402, no. 43.

his successor.[1] It was an unhappy commentary upon Laud's conception of the duties of a bishop, so peremptorily required by the instructions of 1629, but so difficult to enforce; and some of the difficulties which faced even a conscientious bishop in the management of his estate are shown by a letter which Laud received at this time from Walter Curle, Bishop of Winchester. He explained that it was impossible to prevent the waste of episcopal woods because the copyhold tenants pretended a customary right to fell as much as they needed, and because the leases contained a clause that houses and mills were to be repaired with timber from the Bishop's woods. Sir Daniel Norton, said the Bishop, had recently claimed eighty-three tons of timber for such purposes; and when the Bishop had refused to provide them, Sir Daniel had cut down forty oak trees in his woods just before the expiry of his lease. The Bishop, of course, being a comparative stranger, was defenceless against pretended customary rights, and it was partly to guard against such pretensions that he insisted upon the possession of written certificates. In the present case, Curle took care to omit the clause about repairs from leases on renewal, and asked the King for an explicit command to do so.[2]

In pursuance of his policy of establishing the personal government of Charles I and the independence of the Church of parliamentary control by judicial decisions, Laud drew up in this year a collection of all the Councils held in England, which he intended to publish with an introduction by himself, proving that all ecclesiastical affairs should be defined by councils of bishops without any parliamentary interference. It was finished in June, written on vellum, and is preserved in Lambeth Library; but it was never published.[3]

In the sphere of education, too, Laud was not idle this year. The Provost and Fellows of King's College, Cambridge, had petitioned three years previously against their colleagues of Eton College, because the latter, contrary to their statutes, did not choose Fellows of King's to be Fellows of Eton, and only maintained seven instead of ten fellowships. Laud deferred his decision until 1637,

[1] *Cal. S.P. Dom.*, 1636–7, 176; 1637, 156, etc.

[2] *S.P. Dom. Car. I.* 375, no. 87. The Bishop's measures seem to have been ineffectual, for he later petitioned the Long Parliament against the inhabitants, who broke tumultuously into Waltham Chace and carried off the wood (*Lords' Journals*, iv. 461).

[3] *Ven. Cal.* xxiv. 168; Laud, *Works*, iii. 228, 255; Lambeth MS. 323.

and now he settled the matter in both respects. In future, he insisted, five out of the seven fellows must always be Fellows of King's, according to the founder's intentions. As to the number of fellows, he was unable to make any change ; for here too he was faced with the same difficulty which he so often encountered, and tried with but little success to remedy. It was not the disobedience of the Provost and Fellows of Eton which had reduced the fellowships, but the spoliation of ecclesiastical and educational institutions by royal plunderers, Edward IV having dissolved the foundation of his predecessor, in order to refound it with diminished revenues and pocket the difference himself.[1]

More successful was Laud's design to impart orthodox learning to the Channel Islands : and here, once again, it was at Oxford that his success was shown. Until the Reformation, the Channel Islands had been in the diocese of Coutances ; but in 1565 they had secured from Queen Elizabeth the right to worship as Calvinists. They were divided for this purpose into two classes, of which the first embraced Jersey, the second Guernsey, Alderney, and Sark. Under James I, however, the island of Jersey was incorporated in the diocese of Winchester, possessing its own dean, and using the Prayer Book in a French translation : but Calvinism continued to flourish, because preachers were drawn chiefly from the Universities of Saumur and Geneva. To correct this, Laud determined that they should be drawn in future from the University of Oxford, of whose orthodoxy, so long as he was its Chancellor, he need have no doubt. Early in 1637, therefore, when the estate of a rich London alderman, Sir Miles Hubbard, dying intestate, escheated to the Crown, Laud secured it from the King for the purpose of founding three fellowships, at Jesus, Pembroke, and Exeter Colleges respectively, for boys from the Channel Islands, who, it was hoped, having imbibed the true learning in Oxford, would then return to preach it in their native islands. In April he received the public thanks of the Deputy-Governor and Jurats of Jersey, who recommended one Daniel Brevin as the first holder of the honour ; [2] and a few months later the Channel Islanders were given a second opportunity to admire the advantages of conformity when Prynne and Burton were brought to lie for three years in their dungeons.

[1] Wilkins, *Concilia*, iv. 496 ; Laud, *Works*, v. 497-8 ; *S.P. Dom. Car. I.* 355, no. 15.

[2] Harl. MS. 787, p. 96.

CHAPTER TEN

WAR

If the year 1637 had been a critical period for Laud, he had preserved his authority by following the advice of the tyrant Thrasybulus and cutting off the heads of the tallest corn-stalks in the field. He had also gone further, and declared it illegal for them to grow again. This exemplary treatment had its effect, and during the next two years, to outward appearance at any rate, they did not grow again. Indeed, England seemed to enjoy a period of halcyon calm. In his island prison, Prynne, deprived at last of pen and paper, discharged his busy spirits through the incongruous medium of contemplative verse. Williams was in the Tower, and Laud told the King roundly that if he ever let that fierce mastiff loose again, his most faithful ministers would have little heart to continue in his service.[1] Con and his troupe of female corybants piped in a lower key. In England at any rate the storm seemed to have passed, even though in his own diocese of Canterbury separatists congregated at Ashford, so poor that the law could not control them, and at Sittingbourne Lady Teynham fostered a nursery of Papists.

Meanwhile the work of collecting money for St. Paul's was pursued with renewed zeal. Some heavy fines in the ecclesiastical courts swelled the receipts, and the bounty of the rich was stimulated in many ways. When several letters to the sheriff and justices of the peace of Huntingdonshire had failed to evoke a sufficient response, the Council wrote that they were loth to attribute this backwardness to the disaffection of any of the gentlemen of that district, but rather to the want of some discreet agent to put the case convincingly before them, and a discreet agent was accordingly despatched.[2] Letters were also sent to the Middle Temple, the Inner Temple, Gray's Inn, and Lincoln's Inn. Nor was generosity denied its rewards. In return for the honour of being chosen as the first Mayor of Shrewsbury, a certain Thomas Jones, a man worth between £30,000 and £40,000,

[1] *Works*, vii. 370.

[2] *Cal. S.P. Dom.*, 1637–8, p. 459.

offered to give liberally to the cathedral, and to encourage his friends to do likewise.[1] From the profits of industry, too, St. Paul's received a percentage. The projectors of a London fire-brigade promised £200 a year out of their profits, if the government would authorise their project: by an annual payment of £10 to St. Paul's, certain stationers secured a licence to print accounts of foreign news for twenty-one years: and the corporation of Starchmakers, as part of the price of royal patronage, undertook to pay £100 a year for seven years to the same good work.[2] Among others who responded to the Archbishop's appeal was the Lord Deputy of Ireland; and in conveying his thanks Laud designated as a future project the restoration of Christ Church at Dublin also, — "if God spare my life, some of my money shall be in that mortar".[3] By such various methods, the receipts in 1638 boomed again with nearly £16,000; and though prior claims of the Scottish expedition naturally reduced them again in the following year, a rich Wiltshireman, Robert Jason, the new squire of Broad Somerford, bequeathed the princely sum of £600 a year to the work of restoration.[4]

Other symptoms, however, were less encouraging. To replace the temporal estates of the bishops on a sound footing, and to preserve such gains to the sees in perpetuity, had been an important and necessary part of Laud's programme, and he had made consistent efforts to achieve that purpose. Some progress was made by public-spirited or businesslike prelates, but in face of the natural hostility of local gentry who saw the ancient rights of the Church being vindicated at their expense, and the natural desire of bishops to keep their gains to themselves rather than to secure them for their successors, large results had not been achieved. In the last chapter we saw the poor diocese of Bristol the centre of an inter-episcopal wrangle, and saw the difficulties against which Bishop Curle had to contend in Winchester. Now the rich diocese of Norwich is revealed in no better estate. In 1638 Wren, having made his name during his two years' tenure of that diocese, was promoted to the still more important see of Ely, and reported thence a great waste of episcopal woods while his predecessor had been performing his necessary duties as the

[1] *Ibid.* p. 306.
[2] *Ibid.* p. 392; 1638–9, pp. 165, 182.
[3] *Works*, vii. 405.
[4] *Cal. S.P. Dom.*, 1639, p. 392.

King's almoner in London. To Norwich went Richard Montague, his reputation as a trumpeter of innovations somewhat cooled by ten years in the see of Chichester. His first report from his new bishopric was a melancholy document. " The bishopric of Norwich ", he wrote, " since the dissolution of the former bishopric by King Henry VIII, who stole the sheep and gave not so much as the trotters for God's sake, is a mean thing " : and he proceeded to catalogue the waste and dilapidations, long leases and demises, by which Tudor Kings and all the intervening bishops had pillaged it. One episcopal house was structurally hopeless, the other situated in an unhealthy swamp. A third, given by Edward VI so that the bishop might extend his pastoral care more easily over Ipswich, had been alienated by Bishop Scambler, " that *fundi nostri calamitas* ", and was irrecoverable. As for the revenues, though Henry VIII had annexed the lands of the dissolved abbey of Hulme to the see, he had contrived that the transfer should represent a financial loss, not gain, to the bishopric ; " the lands conveyed were some poor manors, parcels of lands, pensions, portions of tithes, marshes, fishings, and suchlike poor pittances, to the value of about £500 per annum, in lieu of lands taken away at this day worth £20,000 per annum ". Rugge, the last abbot of Hulme and first protestant bishop of Norwich, " made leases of all for 99 years, beggared himself, undid his successors, was forced to resign, reserving a pension of £200 per annum during life " : and his successor Scambler alienated more lands to Queen Elizabeth for the use of Sir Thomas Heneage, which were still irrecoverable in Montague's time. Nor was it only Tudor bishops who undid their successors. Laud's own nominees, White and Corbett, had continued the policy, with the connivance of the Dean and Chapter ; " and whereas it is said commonly the bishopric of Norwich, when Scambler's demise expires, will be worth £3000 per annum, it is ignorantly spoken. It will not be one penny better than it is, unless an honest, conscientious man be then bishop, who will increase the rents to succession, and not take all to himself by fines." So Montague urged Laud to secure an order from the King which would prevent future bishops of the diocese from continuing the work of impoverishment.[1]

From other dioceses came similar tales of neglect and dis-

[1] Lambeth MS. 943, p. 619.

obedience. The Deans and Chapters of both Exeter and Chester received severe reprimands for their consistent evasion of the royal orders concerning leases: and from Bangor the Bishop reported that he could not execute the express instructions which he had received, since "everything is let for lives by his predecessors, down to the very mill that grinds his corn".[1] Nor had Laud's efforts to improve episcopal accommodation been uniformly successful. A few years earlier a traveller had been struck by the extreme decrepitude of Neile's episcopal house at York, — "the poorest and least capacious house which I have found in England belonging to any bishopric: a very little poor hall, and no fair rooms in the whole house". The parish church was equally disreputable and ill-served; but in this case it was at least some consolation that "the bishop's cellar here was well furnished with 32 hogsheads of good, strong beer and eight pipes of the same, — we tasted of it".[2]

Laud's failure in this respect was not, of course, entirely the fault of the bishops. He was attempting to undo in his own primacy the damage which it had taken a century to do, and which the passage of time had confirmed. In this same year, however, he was presented with a scandal which could not be attributed to such impersonal causes; and it was a scandal which touched him nearly. For it was in the very stronghold of his power, in Oxford, in Merton College, of which, as Archbishop, he was Visitor; and the offending Warden was his own Vicar-General, Sir Nathaniel Brent.

Brent, as we have seen, rose to high office in the days of Abbot, thanks to his judicious marriage with Abbot's niece: and Laud, on becoming Archbishop, looked with natural distrust upon the Vicar-General whose services he was compelled to accept as a legacy from his rival and predecessor. It has therefore been said that Brent's later activities — his attack upon Laud before the Long Parliament and his support of the parliamentary cause in Oxford — were occasioned by his firm adhesion to the constitutional principles which he had always maintained, but which, during Laud's ascendancy, he was compelled to dissemble. It is unfortunately impossible to credit Brent with such consistency, or to suppose any continuity between his early con-

[1] *Works*, vii. 497; Lambeth MS. 943, p. 471; *Works*, v. 359.
[2] Brereton's *Travels*, pp. 71-2.

nexion with Abbot and his later hostility to Laud. Laud himself was at first doubtful of his Vicar-General's loyalty, and, during his metropolitical visitation, burdened him with a colleague and supervisor: but later, when Brent made it clear that his former allegiance had passed away and that it was his intention to carry out the visitation in the spirit of his new master, Laud withdrew the colleague whom he had imposed upon him, and was not disappointed. As Warden of Merton, too, although during Abbot's lifetime he had upheld the principles of his uncle and had opposed Laud's election as Chancellor, he later fell in with the ideas of the new Chancellor, and insisted upon the observation of all the forms and ceremonies enjoined by him. It was not any revival of religious scruples or old loyalties which converted him, in 1640, from one of Laud's officials into one of his enemies; it was Laud's discovery of Brent's career of corrupt self-enrichment, carried on in the very centre of Laud's authority by a cynical disregard of Laud's principles under a mask of complete obedience to the outward forms prescribed by Laud.

In the reign of James I, Merton had prospered exceedingly under the wardenship of Sir Henry Savile, who kept alive in the seventeenth century the great traditions of an earlier age. A magnificent patron, he lived in ostentatious splendour, drawing the greatest scholars of the age into dependence upon him for the increase of their labours and his own glory. He founded chairs in Oxford, added a new quadrangle to his college, and by his long rule made Merton College famous in England. When the influence of Abbot promoted Brent to rule in his stead, the glory of Merton dwindled: but the fortunes of Brent began to increase most satisfactorily. Brent, according to Wood, who came to Merton during the last years of his rule, was one who "minded wealth and the settling of a family more than generous actions": and consequently the college "did nothing near so well flourish as under the government of Sir Henry".[1] He made the college bear the costs of his personal extravagances, juggled unscrupulously with the college estates, bribed the fellows into connivance with his practices, kept the college accounts secret, and secured the regular annual election of one Fisher, a reliable supporter, as his subwarden, to live "like another head of a college" during his own frequent absences.

[1] *Athenae Oxonienses*, ii. 316.

Laud, however, had his agents in the college, of whom the most industrious was Peter Turner, the professor of geometry, chiefly responsible for the proctorial cycle of 1628, and partly concerned with the Laudian statutes of 1636; and in August 1637 a correspondent informed Turner of some of the college secrets. The writer was bound by the statutes, he professed, to denounce the Warden to the Visitor if his offences and dilapidations deserved expulsion: and in his eyes, the offences of Brent certainly did require such punishment. Brent had borrowed college money for his own purposes and, after fourteen years, had still not repaid it. He had charged the college £300 for a London house for himself, which he did not use. He had lost college money in lawsuits, failed to recover college debts, and contracted bad debts in its name: and he had allowed rents to remain unpaid until they were irrecoverable.[1] At the same time a case of dissension between two of the fellows occurred, and the mild punishment which Brent inflicted upon one of them caused the other to appeal to Laud. As yet, however, Laud took no action. Out of deference to Brent, he said, he would not subject the college to a visitation: and Brent, in acknowledging this concession, added with virtuous boldness, "howsoever, I do so carry myself in my place that I dare and shall be a suitor for a visitation, that the secret informers against others are themselves the worst members of the college".[2]

Early next year, however, a visitation was decided on. Five commissioners were appointed, all strong supporters of the Archbishop, — Bancroft, Bishop of Oxford, Richard Baylie, the President of St. John's, Gilbert Sheldon, Warden of All Souls (of which also Laud was Visitor), Sir John Lambe, and the vicar-general of the Bishop of London, Dr. Duck, — and on March 29th, 1638, they arrived, a series of articles was drawn up, and the visitation began.

The commissioners sat in the hall of Merton College, taking examinations and answers by candle-light until eight o'clock in the evening, while the enormities of Warden and Fellows were slowly dragged into the light. Study and the college accounts had both been neglected, postmasterships [3] had been awarded by graft and bribery, the subwarden had sold college woods to a

[1] *Cal. S.P. Dom.*, 1637, p. 349. [2] *S.P. Dom. Car. I.* 366, no. 14.

[3] Postmasterships = scholarships at Merton College.

relative for less than half their value, and a whole catalogue of offences was substantiated against the Warden. He had spent nearly £1000 in building and furnishing houses for himself in London and Oxford: he had charged the college between £50 and £60 a year for his fuel: and he had sought to conceal his mismanagement of college properties by misrepresenting the college accounts and taking the fellows into partnership in the profits. "The Warden is left to your mercy, whereof he will have great need", Sheldon wrote to Laud a few days later, adding virtuously, "if I were conscious of so much carelessness of the main affairs of this college, or of such practising upon the company, to the wasting of the common stock and my own advantage, I should not have the face to endure a visitation, but should lay the key under the door and be gone".[1]

Presented with such accusations, which were swollen by the arrival of fresh petitions of individual fellows against the Warden and subwarden, Laud decided not to leave the matter in the hands of subordinates. At the moment he was in considerable difficulty over Scottish affairs; so he adjourned the visitation to his own hearing at Lambeth on October 2nd, and Brent took advantage of the interval to look around for stratagems whereby to lighten the inevitable blow. It was in vain. Laud refused to agree that three old fellows, including the subwarden, all selected by Brent, would be more reliable informants than three who had already complained against him: he insisted on a new subwarden being chosen before the hearing: and Brent's admission of the existence of a number of scandals which he had been unable to correct (all in discipline, none in the financial management of the college), did not divert the attention of the Archbishop. In October Laud devoted three days to an examination of the state of the college, — "the Warden", he wrote in his diary, "appeared very foul",[2] — and then, owing to the pressure of other business, adjourned it again. Faced as he was by more pressing calls upon his time, he had not the leisure to deal with mere college scandals: and yet this was a college scandal which concerned him intimately, and he was determined to deal with it himself. It was not till July 1640 that his detailed and inquisitorial injunctions were sent down to Merton,[3] and still the visitation continued by

[1] *S.P. Dom. Car. I.* 387, nos. 8, 23.

[2] *Works*, iii. 230.

[3] *Ibid.* v. 546.

successive adjournments, Laud professing that he would be Warden of Merton himself for seven years if necessary, until the Long Parliament cut it short after three and a half.[1] Even so it had taken longer than the visitation of the whole province of Canterbury, and the fellows hailed its termination as the end of an ordeal more oppressive and scarcely shorter than the siege of Troy.

Meanwhile another old enemy was continuing to cause Laud sleepless nights. It was a spirit which he could never feel that he had laid, — Bishop Williams. "That fierce mastiff", even when caged, remained dangerous, such were his political resources, his happy freedom from all scruples of conscience, his powerful friends. Already in September 1637 it was reported that he was in correspondence with Prynne,[2] and next year commissioners were twice sent to the Tower to obtain his answers to a charge of doctrinal heterodoxy in his book, *The Holy Table, Name and Thing*. They went empty away. "I do not know any positive doctrine in that book", said Williams, "which I would recant to save my life":[3] and he played for time while he intrigued with the Queen through Lord Dorset. That Williams would escape again through the Queen's influence was a nightmare from which Laud was never free. "It is most certain", he wrote on one occasion to Wentworth, "that the Queen hath not only been very earnest with the King for the Bishop of Lincoln, but hath prevailed too",[4] and he longed to see him safely despatched to a poor bishopric in Ireland, out of harm's way. But all attempts at negotiation were doomed to founder on the Bishop's absolute refusal to go to Ireland and deliver himself over bound into the hands of the terrible Wentworth. "Beggars must not be choosers", Laud insisted, "therefore he must go into Ireland or the Star Chamber."[5] Williams preferred the Star Chamber: and in February 1639 he was there again.

The charges for the second Star Chamber prosecution of Williams were furnished by some letters discovered at Buckden and addressed to Williams five years ago by a Westminster schoolmaster, Lambert Osbaldiston. In these letters the Bishop was

[1] Petition of fellows of Merton, Harl. MS. 1769, p. 7.
[2] H.M.C. de la Warr MSS., p. 293.
[3] Lambeth MS., 1030, p. 90.
[4] *Works*, vii. 481.
[5] Lambeth MS., 1030, p. 97.

urged to take advantage of a desperate struggle now alleged to be in progress between "the great Leviathan" on the one hand, and "the little urchin", alias "the little meddling hocus-pocus", on the other; and lest these names should be too enigmatic, one of the letters concluded with the words, "Your Lordship will hear that the Lord's Grace of Canterbury is come to lodge in Court: so is the Lord Treasurer. Your Lordship, I hope, will pick out my meaning." [1]

The meaning was indeed obvious: and the quarrel between Portland and Laud at the time when the letters were written was sufficiently well known not to need explanatory glosses. But it was no part of Williams' policy to facilitate the task of his accusers by admitting the obvious. Osbaldiston assured them that what they chose to regard as a malicious libel was in fact no more than an innocent and ingenious conundrum, and he explained the objectionable passages by identifying the little urchin with one Dr. Spicer, who was safely unknown, and the great Leviathan with Lord Chief Justice Richardson, who was safely dead. Williams agreed that this was a cypher frequently used between them to designate these two characters, and, to make doubly sure, added that he had never received the letters in question. The judges, however, were not convinced. They adjudged the Bishop guilty of *scandalum magnatum*, and fined him £5000 to the King and £3000 to the Archbishop, — Finch and Windebank would have made it more, — before restoring him to the Tower and his intrigues. As for Osbaldiston, he was condemned to the pillory, loss of his living, and a fine of £5000; but he chose the better part of valour and made his escape, leaving a note for his pursuers that "if the Archbishop enquire after me, tell him I am gone beyond Canterbury". Laud had messengers sent to the seaports to apprehend him, but Osbaldiston had not taken that route. He was lying low with friends in Drury Lane, and remained there till the summoning of the Long Parliament made it safe for him to emerge. To Wentworth Laud reported a rumour that he had gone to Scotland to teach General Leslie to read and write, "for certain it is he can do neither". [2]

With the Puritans, Laud's relations during the last two years of his power were less spectacular than they had been. The

[1] Rushworth, iii. 803.

[2] *Works*, vii. 530.

major prophets had been silenced, and the others, who had no desire to share the glory of martyrdom with Prynne, Burton, and Bastwick, hid their diminished heads in obscurity. But the discontent, if less defiantly voiced, was ineradicable, and all observers noticed its increase in volume, if not in intensity, after the suppression of its leaders. In spite of the guarantee of the legality of the ecclesiastical courts which he had secured after the challenge of Prynne, prisoners insisted on disputing the right of the Court of High Commission to impose oaths, and in 1637 Neile complained to Laud of the encroachments of the civil and common lawyers. In February 1638, therefore, two further documents were secured to bolster up the authority of the ecclesiastical courts. One consisted of letters patent from the King authorising the High Commissioners to exact oaths and to hold *pro confessis* those who refused to give them : the other forbade the judges of the common and civil law to interfere in the ecclesiastical courts without the permission of the Archbishop.[1] Even so, the power of the ecclesiastical courts was too limited to secure the results desired, and at the end of the year Laud protested that he could do nothing without more active support from the judges,[2] — support which the King promised to exact. A year later the Archbishop admitted that nothing but licensed emigration would be of any avail.[3]

Indeed, this course had already occurred to the separatists themselves, now that resistance had proved to be so disastrous. In spite of all proclamations, the growth of Puritan emigration to New England and the Bermudas reached alarming proportions in 1638. In East Anglia, Bishop Wren acquired the reputation of a crusader, like his predecessor Bishop Spencer, who had smitten the Lollards there : and Laud was continually hearing of the departure, or projected departure, of ship-loads of Puritans for America. From Essex he was told in March that large numbers of prosperous cloth merchants were preparing to sail to New England, and that parishes were being impoverished and corn made scarce by the daily departure of " incredible numbers " of wealthy citizens who had sold their lands. Fourteen ships were said to be lying in the Thames ready to sail by Easter.[4] Next month, thanks to a diligent agent, he was able to prevent the

[1] *S.P. Dom. Car. I.* 381, no. 29 ; 383, no. 49.
[2] Laud, *Works*, v. 355.
[3] *Ibid.* v. 361.
[4] *Cal. S.P. Col.* ix. 88.

departure of an expedition from the Isle of Wight:[1] and in May an Order in Council was issued to stop eight ships in the Thames from sailing to New England, while a proclamation at the same time forbade clergymen to leave for the Bermudas without leave from Laud or Juxon, and required that those who had already departed be brought back. "I am sorry to read in your letters," the Archbishop wrote to Wentworth, who was busy with the plantation of Ormonde and Clare, "that you should want men in Ireland, and that the while there should be here such an universal running to New England, and God knows whither." The repetition of these orders and proclamations throughout the year is sufficient indication of their inefficacy, and Laud, exasperated by the increasing exodus of refugees to New England, declared in the Star Chamber, "This hand shall pull and root them there and thence". "But," the Puritan chronicler records with complacency, "his head dropped off ere he did it."[2]

As for the spread of Romanism at court, the immediate crisis was past. Nothing so spectacular as Con's great haul of souls in 1637 was to recur, and the activities of the Agent were now less obtrusive, while his supporters in the Queen's party were less interested in proselytising than in unsuccessful efforts to persuade the reluctant Pope to grant a red hat to their favourite. One incident, indeed, caused considerable uneasiness to Laud. It was the arrival, in October 1638, of the Queen-Mother of France, Marie de' Medici, mother of Queen Henrietta Maria. Exiled from France by Richelieu, unwanted in Brussels and in the Hague, this lady "for many years had not lived out of the smell of powder and a guard of muskets at her door . . . so that most men were able to presage a tempest, as mariners by the appearing of some fish, or the flying of some birds about their ship, can foresee a storm".[3] She was beheld, says another writer, "as some meteor of ill signification",[4] and desperate, but ineffectual, efforts were made through Boswell at the Hague to prevent her coming. Her mind, however, was made up. "Nothing but everlasting foul weather at sea and a perpetual cross-wind could have kept her there," and when she arrived at Harwich there was nothing to

[1] *Cal. S.P. Col.* ix. 101.
[2] Woodcock Papers, *Camden Misc.* xi. (Camden Soc., 1907), pp. 53-4.
[3] Heylin, p. 359.
[4] Rushworth, ii. 725.

do but receive her as a welcome guest and accommodate her in St. James's Palace. Her enmity to Richelieu, her intriguing nature, and her ostentatious familiarity with Con aroused suspicions that a new attempt at co-operation with Spain and Rome was afoot: and these suspicions were confirmed by the news of the decisive defeat of the Prince Elector at Vlotho, which made any hope of recovering the Palatinate except by such negotiations ridiculous. "For my part", Laud wrote to Wentworth, when he heard of her imminent arrival, "I hold this as a miserable accident, as times and occasions are here"; and he confided the same fears to his diary.[1] But in fact Marie de' Medici caused little besides apprehensions and expense. France and Spain had by now ceased to regard English foreign policy as a serious business: and with the abandonment of hope in the matter of the Palatinate, the papal Agency also lost the reason for its existence.

Thus in England the experimental system of government which had been begun in 1629 continued to work, not indeed with great efficiency, nor with any great popular support, but with no obvious threat of danger from within. Since its inception, the success with which it had continued to work had made it less self-conscious: the reforming activity of the earlier years had died down; and the most strenuous exertions of the government were directed towards maintaining its own continued existence by the exercise of economy and a submissive judicature. "Government enterprise" there was none, for its chief exponents had been gradually extruded from the control of the government,—Wentworth to Ireland, Laud to the barren region of theological forms. Neither the vigorous reforms which Wentworth carried through in Ireland, nor the tyranny which they were held to justify, were for England; and the social policy of Laud, which, however imperfectly thought out and unwisely applied, may be allowed to justify his ecclesiastical rigidity, was also a failure. With every apparent victory he had in fact been more surely removed from the control of policy, and was left with nothing in his hands but a damning certificate of unreal power. The first few years of the personal government of Charles I may have allowed some play to the forces of Thorough: but with Wentworth absent and Laud easily outmanœuvred in Court and

[1] *Works*, vii. 494; *ibid.* iii. 230.

Council, the ultimate victory was with Lady Mora. Politics had become petrified, and the initiative of the administration dead. By the promotion of dependable judges to issue decisions justifying the actions of the government, and by the restriction of commerce through monopolies, a static system was secured : and all whose interests or ambitions were frustrated by this system, seeking, as men naturally seek, an ideal region in which to proclaim their dissatisfaction, directed their attack upon the religious institutions which seemed to justify the system.

> Reader, here you'll plainly see
> Judgment perverted by these three, —
> A Priest, a Judge, a Patentee,

ran a libel at the time of the Long Parliament, joining in an execrable trinity the types held to represent the recent government of Charles I. The priest, we can see, did but unwillingly associate himself with that government, which represented the corrupt form of his own ideal ; but necessity forced him to identify himself with it, and his surrender was shown when the office of Master of the Rolls was put up for auction, and the highest bidder, Sir Charles Caesar, " a man unthought of, and a very ass ", borrowed £10,000 towards the cost of his promotion from the money earmarked for the repair of St. Paul's.[1]

How long this system of government could have lasted if left to itself is a question impossible to answer and futile to ask. We can neither assume that it would have remained unchanged, nor account for the modifications which it might have undergone in order to survive. We can postulate neither the existence nor the default of an English Mazarin or an English Colbert. And equally we cannot supply the shocks to which it might have been subjected, had it avoided the shock to which it actually was subjected. We must deal with the shock to which it was subjected, and which provided the starting-point for its dissolution : and to do so we must revert to the affairs of Scotland, which we left at the end of 1637.

It is unnecessary to deal in detail with the affairs of Scotland, for Laud's connexion with them, besides being unofficial, was

[1] *S.P. Dom. Car. I.* 415, no. 65, Garrarde to Conway, March 28th, 1639, Rossingham to Conway, April 1st, 1639 ; *ibid.* 417, no. 3.

limited both by his ignorance of them and his lack of control over them. He sat in Lambeth, in Whitehall, or in the King's closet, like an amateur magician surprised and frightened by the demon which he had conjured up, and at a loss for a formula by which to conjure it down again. "I think as you do", he wrote to Wentworth during the Scottish troubles, "Scotland is the veriest devil that is out of Hell."[1] But to think thus brought him no nearer to understanding it.

Throughout 1638 Scotland remained menacing revolt, while the concessions tentatively offered by the King were so small that they did but stimulate the appetite they were designed to satisfy. On Laud's advice, Traquair was summoned to England in February; but his assurance that the Scots would accept no orders suspected of proceeding from Canterbury, and that the liturgy could not be enforced except by an army of 40,000 men, was given in vain. A royal proclamation read in Stirling only provoked a new protestation: the Four Tables were further organised as a representative and authoritative body: and at the end of the month the Solemn League and Covenant, in defence of "the true Reformed Religion, and of our liberties, laws, and estates" was drawn up and circulated. Nobility, gentry, clergy, and people hastened to subscribe: and those who showed any reluctance to do so were easily intimidated by the majority. "Now all that we have been doing these thirty years past is thrown down at once," exclaimed Spottiswood, when he heard of the eager signature of the document, and fled to the comparative safety of England. At the same time a party of Presbyterians broke into Maxwell's cathedral at Fortrose and carried off the Prayer Books to destruction. Maxwell paid a last visit to his cathedral, preached a short sermon without service-books, and then, after a conversation with the Bishop of Moray and the Marquis Hamilton, disguised himself and took horse for England, and "durst not for feir of his lyf return to Scotland again". Bishop Whitford of Brechin, driven from his cathedral by an angry congregation, also sought safety in flight: and the same course was adopted by the Bishops of Edinburgh, Galloway, and Dunblane. In face of such a movement, Traquair, Spottiswood, and the whole Scottish Council urged moderation; for only by concession could the King hope to recover control.

[1] *Works*, vii. 482.

Concession, however, was still repugnant to Charles and Laud. It was not merely of Scotland that they were thinking, but of England, where the Puritans were taking heart again, and John Lilburne, so persistent an enemy of every form of government that it was said of him " that if there were none living but himself, John would be against Lilburne and Lilburne against John ", was vociferous though in the Tower. Another who chose this inopportune moment to speak his mind was also singled out for exemplary treatment.

This was Archy, the King's fool, who had now enjoyed the favour of the Court for longer than any other of its members. Beginning life, it is said, as a sheep-stealer in the Eskdale of Cumberland (a profession in which he had shown a remarkable dexterity), he had attracted the attention of King James while still King of Scotland only : and having accompanied his master in his official capacity to London, he there (in the intervals of being tossed in a blanket) amassed by favour and intimidation, and preserved by avarice, a handsome fortune. Freely trading upon his prerogative of fool, he made many powerful enemies, but he was proof against them all, and was even permitted to rejoice openly on the death of Buckingham. When Prince Charles and the Duke went upon their Spanish adventure, Archy was one of their few attendants, and in Madrid his elementary witticisms won him gifts from Olivarez and a pension from the King. When a son was born to him, he was christened Philip after the King of Spain, and ministers of state and peeresses were impressed as godparents.

To Laud, destitute of humour and devoid of tolerance, this outspoken buffoon could hardly be a congenial character, and there was no love between them. On one occasion, when Archy had been permitted to pronounce grace in Laud's presence at Whitehall, he had said, " Great praise be to God, and little laud to the Devil " :[1] and the Archbishop, though indignant, had been unable to obtain any redress. Now, when the news came from Stirling of the rejection of the King's declaration, Archy happened to meet Laud on his way to the Privy Council and asked him, " Whea's feule now ? Doth not Your Grace hear the news from

[1] A similar pun had been made in 1603, when Laud's unpopular colleague was said to have been " proctor *cum parva Laude* " (Wood, *Life and Times*, ii. 234).

Striveling about the liturgy ?"[1] This time he did not escape. Laud brought the matter up before the Council, and a solemn order was secured "that Archibald Armstrong, the King's fool, for certain scandalous words of a high nature spoken by him against the Lord Archbishop of Canterbury His Grace, and proved to be uttered by him by two witnesses, shall have his coat pulled over his head, and be discharged of the King's service, and banished the Court". It is said that only the influence of the Queen saved Archy from the Star Chamber: but it is also said that only the intervention of Laud saved him from a whipping. At all events, Archy was expelled, and a new and more cautious fool installed in his place. Archy remained for a while in London, disguised in the black habit of a clergyman, — a costume, he explained, in which he could be as scandalous as he pleased with impunity, — and then retired to set up as a landowner in his native Eskdale. This was not, however, his last encounter with Laud. On his expulsion, he at once set about harrying his debtors, among whom was the Dean of York, whom he sued for a debt of £200, and on whose behalf the Archbishop intervened. And later, when Laud was safely in the Tower, the court fool emeritus published a choice anthology of the Archbishop's enormities entitled *Archy's Dreams*.

Archy, of course, became a popular hero to those who did not owe him money, and the unpopularity of Laud was increased. Already he was regarded as the sole author of the government's policy in Scotland, and it was not easy for him to rebut the charge, since the advice of the Scottish Privy Council was disregarded and the English Privy Council had not yet been officially informed. With Laud, however, the King sat in frequent and private consultation, and so closely was he identified with Scottish policy that people were heard to complain that there was no Felton to rise up and assassinate him.[2] Laud himself evidently became alarmed at the danger. There was, he reported at this time, "a great aim to destroy me in the King's opinion": and at the same time the King made an angry speech in the Privy Council, exonerating Laud from the sole responsibility for his policy. On

[1] This is the version given by Rushworth, ii. 470. Garrarde, writing to Wentworth at the time, says that Archy began to abuse the Archbishop when drunk in an inn at Westminster (*Strafford Letters*, ii. 154). The new fool was called Muckle John (*ibid.*).

[2] *Ven. Cal.* xxiv. 421.

Scottish affairs, he said, he had never taken the advice of any Englishman.[1] Nevertheless, he was singularly reluctant to accept the advice of the Scots, and, in spite of even Spottiswood's protests, he insisted on the revocation of the Covenant as a necessary preliminary to any settlement.

In May it was decided to send the Marquis Hamilton, the King's Scottish favourite, as High Commissioner on a mediatory mission to Scotland, and a conference was held in London shortly before his departure, at which were present the King, the Marquis, Spottiswood, and three of Laud's strongest supporters among the fugitive Scottish bishops, Sydserf of Galloway, Whitford of Brechin, and Maxwell of Ross. Laud, too, was present, and, evidently still uneasy about the prominent part which he was playing in Scottish affairs, he asked the King in what capacity he had been invited to attend. "To hear and bear witness what passed," he was told, "and because he was acquainted with the proceeding of the business hitherto, he should not be ignorant of what passed hereafter." Thus authorised, Laud "expressed himself to the full and well", and when the Scots bishops complained of their impotence, and indicated clearly that they would prefer to stay safely in England, the King and Laud insisted that they must go back to maintain the faith and the liturgy in their uncomfortable dioceses.[2]

Next month Hamilton arrived in Scotland, and sent a gloomy report to the King prophesying war. The King read it alone, and then closeted himself with Laud in a room at Greenwich.[3] Afterwards he repeated that no concession must be made, no parliament or general assembly called, until the Covenant had been disavowed. Laud remained the King's sole adviser in his relations with Hamilton, and was kept very busy. "Very crazy I was last week", he wrote at this time to Wentworth, "and my frequent letters to my Lord Marquis Hamilton by His Majesty's command lie heavy upon me."[4]

Not the least of his troubles was the obvious failure of his attempts to subdue the press. "All the Scotch horrid business is daily printed at Amsterdam", he wailed to Wentworth, "besides what they print here"; and he wrote ineffectually

[1] Laud, *Works*, iii. 230; *Ven. Cal.* xxiv. 423.

[2] Burnet, *Memoirs of the Hamiltons*, *1677*, p. 42; *Hamilton Papers* (Camden Soc.), p. 1.

[3] *Ven. Cal.* xxiv. 460.

[4] *Works*, vii. 456.

to Boswell about the presses in Holland which he had neither the authority to license nor the power to control.[1]

By the end of June the King had decided at least to prepare for war. The English Privy Council was at last informed: and Lord Treasurer Juxon, on being asked whether the Treasury could spare £200,000 to finance an expedition, promised that the money should be available. A modern historian has detected a "delicious irony" in the possibility that Juxon's honest efficiency, by producing such a surplus, involved the monarchy and the Church in a ruin which could never have been financed by "Cottington's ineptitude and corruption".[2] To Laud the whole situation was simply proof that the coercion of the Scots had not been sufficiently thorough. "The want of Thorough in a time of opportunity is cause of all", he wrote to Wentworth: and he saw the whole business as an English plot to secure a parliament and ruin everything.[3] From Ireland Wentworth wrote recommending strong measures as alone promising success.

Nevertheless the English government continued to negotiate in order to gain time for preparation. In August Hamilton was back again in Scotland, while the English government waited impatiently for news which did not come, and the Archbishop, according to the new Venetian ambassador, "does not now enjoy the customary abundance of the royal favours, with the fear that, if the trouble persists, he may lose them entirely".[4] All that Hamilton could obtain was a breathing-space which the government did not know how to use, and when he returned for a third time in September, bringing the "King's Covenant" as a rival version of the Scottish document, he found the demands of the Scots still higher. They insisted that a General Assembly was the highest ecclesiastical authority in the Kingdom, and demanded that one be summoned immediately: and although the bishops, fully aware of the consequences of such an action, urged him not to comply, Hamilton felt too weak to refuse. He suggested to the King that an Assembly be called and required to accept a modified form of episcopacy. If it refused, it could be dissolved. Its refusal was, however, a foregone conclusion. Already in October it was announced that it would cite the bishops as defendants before it, and when it met in Glasgow in November,

[1] *Works*, vii. 453. [2] F. C. Dietz, *English Public Finance, 1558–1641*, p. 278. [3] *Works*, vi. 469. [4] *Ven. Cal.* xxiv. 499.

it proceeded to do so. The bishops refused to comply, and Hamilton declared the Assembly dissolved. It continued to sit, however, for another month, and did for Scotland what the Long Parliament was later to do for England, passing what Laud could only describe as " many strange acts ", declaring the abolition of bishops, canons, liturgy, the Five Articles of Perth, the Court of High Commission, — all the ecclesiastical machinery which James I by policy and Laud by edict had attempted to set up. " I am sorry to hear it ", Laud had written to Wentworth a few days before the Assembly met, " but I doubt it is too true, that most of the nation dote upon their abominable traitorous Covenant. I marvel where they learnt this divinity, which was never taught in any Christian Church till schism and sacrilege joined hands to spoil it. . . . The greatest fear is want of money, and minds of men are mightily alienated and divided. And I fear you will see the King brought upon his knees to a parliament, — and then farewell to Church and ship-money, and no help but too late." [1] Laud saw clearly enough the consequences of a war for England, unless it could be short, cheap, and successful ; but after he had been attempting to impose episcopacy upon them for ten years, it was rather late to discover for the first time in November 1638 that the Scots had a strong predilection for Calvinism.

The acts of the Glasgow Assembly were a declaration of war from Scotland, and Laud's control over Scottish affairs, never complete, was now utterly lost. Already, on Hamilton's ineffectual dissolution of the Assembly, he had urged the King to hasten preparations for the inevitable war, and now, in the early months of 1638, while the preparations were going ahead, there was little for the Archbishop to do but encourage and complain. His complaints were full, frequent, and various, and were expressed chiefly to his confidant in Ireland. All the trouble, he reiterated, was due to lack of Thorough. It was a plot engineered in England to secure a parliament. The Bishop of Lincoln undoubtedly had a finger in it. The military appointments in England clearly showed the predominance of Lady Mora in the King's counsels, and as for Leslie, the brilliant *condottiere* newly returned from the Swedish service to command the Scottish army, he was quite illiterate, the bastard son of a

[1] *Works*, vii. 512.

housemaid. The loyalty of Hamilton, too, was not free from suspicion, and Cottington was demanding a parliament, — manifestly a trick to get rid of Laud and Juxon and secure the Treasury for himself. Not the least of Laud's troubles was the wide sympathy which the Scots received everywhere abroad. The complicity of Richelieu, the Pope, and the Jesuits was suspected. In Sweden, he heard, all the Scots had sworn the Covenant. In Holland, an informant assured him, " the defence of that unchristian business is in the mouths of all Dutch and most English ",[1] and he had to persuade the King once again to remonstrate with the States-General.[2] From Switzerland a number of Protestant ministers wrote to him, and having first, in the manner of all interferers, disclaimed any intention of interfering, protested against this division in the Reformed Church, which would only lead to a Roman triumph. Laud replied at length and conscientiously, explaining that it was all the fault of the Scots, and wrote in the same strain to reassure Vossius.[3] In Ireland, too, the Scots were getting restive, and while Wentworth circulated a counter-covenant for subscription, Laud ordered the publication, in Latin, of a refutation of the Covenant delivered by the Bishop of Down during his visitation at Lisnegarvy.[4] Meanwhile military preparations were hindered by lack of money. Apprehensions of war had had a paralysing effect on commerce, and the City was unwilling to lend; ship-money was in arrears, and the government only dared ask for a third of the sum previously required; the £200,000 promised by Juxon was not forthcoming; and the Duchess of Chevreuse and the Queen Mother of France were unwanted and expensive guests.

In the matter of finance at least Laud was able to do something positive. The impending campaign was to be a holy war: the whole existence of the Church was at stake: and the name of " Bishops' War " by which it has since been designated was not imposed by contemptuous Puritans but claimed by a crusading bishop. It was natural, therefore, that the clergy should be asked to support it generously: and in January 1639 an Order in Council required Laud and Neile to write to the bishops in

1 *S.P. Dom. Car. I.* 417, no. 78.

2 *Ibid.* 418, no. 49; Laud to Wentworth, *Works*, vii. 526.

3 *Works*, vi. 562, 563.

4 Laud to Wentworth, *Works*, vii. 573.

their provinces, ordering them to convene their clergy and press for speedy contributions. Laud urged his bishops to apply the greatest possible pressure. Every dean and chapter was assessed at 200 marks : the beneficed clergy were to give at least 3s. 10d. in the pound on the value of their livings : the names of those who refused were to be reported : and the bishops, though left to voluntary contribution, were to certify the amount that they had given.[1] Laud himself provided £300 ; and he also wrote to Sir John Lambe to circularise the ecclesiastical lawyers for the same purpose. " You shall not need ", he added, " to call Sir Henry Marten " — the former Dean of the Arches, ousted by Lambe himself, — " for His Majesty will send to him himself, and looks for a greater sum than in an ordinary way."

Amid the general reluctance to subscribe, the clergy, thanks to their intimate connexion with the cause, and the pressure to which they could be subjected, were conspicuous for their comparative generosity, providing a total of £24,395, — three times as much as the total contribution of the laity. The ecclesiastical lawyers, however, were less willing contributors. Dr. Duck reported that he had no money at all, Sir Charles Caesar protested that he was as poor ; and as for Sir Henry Marten, of whom such great expectations were entertained, he replied that he had two spendthrift sons, and that, in view of his good works and hospitality, he marvelled that anyone should have thought it worth while to apply to him.[2] £671 : 13 : 4 was the total sum raised from these sources. The sale of the Mastership of the Rolls, however, brought £15,000 from Sir Charles Caesar, who, a few days previously, had pronounced himself penniless ; and another welcome addition was a loan of £100,000 from Sir Paul Pindar, already conspicuous as a princely benefactor of St. Paul's. " This Sir Paul ", wrote an admiring news-writer, " never fails the King when he has most need." [3]

And yet even this activity had unfortunate implications for Laud : for it associated him again, and conspicuously, with the Roman Catholic party which he had been trying so ostentatiously to repudiate. At this very time, his Conference with Fisher was again in print as an earnest of his Protestantism, and he was

[1] Laud, *Works*, vi. 558. Cf. Smith to Pennington, *Cal. S.P. Dom.*, 1638–9, p. 465 ; Rossingham to Conway, *S.P. Dom. Car. I.* 417, no. 3 ; *Works*, vi. 360.

[2] Lambe to Laud, *S.P. Dom. Car. I.* 415, no. 4.

[3] Rossingham to Conway, *S.P. Dom. Car. I.* 417, no. 3.

promising a Latin translation of it to Vossius, as soon as it should be ready ;[1] but the necessities of the Scottish war were apparent also to Catholics, who had no more reason than Laud to look forward to a parliament. The Queen ordered her co-religionists to fast on Saturdays as a contribution to the military success of her husband, and, lest this should prove inadequate, urged them to contribute in cash also. The Catholics were more willing to aid the King spiritually than materially ; but by midsummer a sum of £10,000 was collected for his support. Thus Laud and the Queen again found themselves forced to work together; and in March, just before the King's departure for York, Laud reported that he " settled a great business for the Queen ", for which the Queen thanked him effusively. Next month he had another highly successful interview ; and in May he wrote to Wentworth that the Queen and himself were " growing to be on some good and free terms ". Another indication of this *détente* with the English Catholics is given in the same month by a letter from Bishop Montague to Secretary Windebank, in which the Bishop strenuously rebuts a charge of having proceeded against Roman Catholics. There is some irony in the protestations of this former political firebrand and anti-papal polemist when he says, " you never knew me a meddler in state business out of my element, nor such a zealot against Roman Catholics ".[2] Oppressed by these various cares, it is not surprising to find that in March Laud was unwell, " feverish and indisposed ".[3]

For three months the King remained in the north with an inadequate and undisciplined army, while the scant supplies of money ran out and all his elaborate plans for the subjugation of Scotland fell through. Before his arrival in York, the Scots had taken the offensive. The royal castles of Edinburgh and Dumbarton were seized, and Traquair escaped from the back door of his palace at Dalkeith while the Covenanters entered by the front. The resistance of Huntly in the north collapsed before Hamilton could arrive to support it. Wentworth could not spare forces from Ireland. Another attempt by Aboyne to rally the north was crushed by Montrose. And the activities of the royal

[1] This translation was made, but Laud suppressed it in proof as giving an inaccurate representation of his position (Laud to Vossius, *Works*, vi. 583).

[2] *Cal. S.P. Dom.*, 1639, p. 261.

[3] Garrarde to Conway, *Cal. S.P. Dom.*, 1638–9, p. 621.

army were confined to a brief raid on Duns by Arundel, a tentative reconnaissance and immediate withdrawal by Holland, and piratical activities by Hamilton in the Firth of Forth. Meanwhile the Archbishop remained in London. His anticipation that the reappearance of a nightingale in the walks at Lambeth meant the return of mirth and music and better times was not to be realised. Libels continued to be directed against him. Again there were demands for a second Felton. Lilburne, from the Tower, urged the London apprentices to rise against him, and rumours were circulated that the King had agreed to throw him to the Scots. Whether or not it was to defend him against personal attacks such as were frequently threatened, we hear that during the King's absence all the Archbishop's attendants went about armed with swords.[1] He was kept continually posted with news of the affairs in the north : but when he heard of the Pacification of Berwick of June 18th, it gave him little satisfaction. By it, in return for the restitution of the royal castles, the dissolution of the Tables, and the invalidation of the Acts of the Glasgow Assembly, the King had to promise a complete pardon to the Scots and allow the summoning of a General Assembly and a parliament for August. " Faction and ignorance will govern the Assembly ", Laud complained to Sir Thomas Roe, now ambassador in Hamburg, " and faction and somewhat else that I list not to name the parliament. For they will utterly cast off episcopal government, and introduce a worse regulated parity than is anywhere else that I know." " How this will stand with monarchy ", he added, " future times will discover." [2]

The failure of the Scottish expedition, the symptoms of unrest in England, and the prospect of their increase now that the weakness of the government had been demonstrated, produced in Charles' advisers a state of nervous panic, signally illustrated by the case, in July, of John Trendall.

This Dover stonemason was a separatist, — one of the great multitude of obscure dissidents who, more by their number than any individual brilliance, obstructed the programme of ecclesiastical uniformity. Conspicuous among them only by the accident of his arrest, Trendall could be accused only of having refused the Oath of Supremacy, and of having preached unorthodox

[1] Garrarde to Conway, *Cal. S.P. Dom.*, 1638–9, p. 621.

[2] *Works*, vii. 584.

opinions in his own house. On examination, he stoutly denied all charges except that of a general antipathy to bishops ; but witnesses attested that he had preached illegally against set prayers and the divine institution of the Church of England.

The Council nevertheless determined, it seems, to make of Trendall a terrible example, and they applied for assistance to Archbishop Neile as one well acquainted with the extremer forms of Church censure. Neile thereupon furnished them with a detailed account, written in an objective style, of the examination and burning of Wightman in 1611, — an operation which he had himself directed, with the assistance of his chaplain Laud. For any further information he referred them to Laud, and added his own opinion that Wightman's execution " did a great deal of good in this Church ", and that " the present times do require a like exemplary punishment, which I refer to your grave consideration ". Luckily, his advice was not followed, or the opposition would have had a yet more terrible stick than Prynne wherewith to beat the ecclesiastical establishment. Trendall's case was referred to the High Commission, and the Church hesitated to assume the sole responsibility for so drastic a course. So the heresy-hunt petered out with two years of custody and an apparent recantation.

In Scotland, too, Laud's gloomy prognostications were soon justified. For the Scots to admit the invalidity of the Acts of the Glasgow Assembly was no concession, since the new Assembly at Edinburgh promptly re-enacted them. The King was forced to acquiesce in the abolition of Scottish episcopacy, and could only show by the reservations which he made and the instructions which he issued that he intended to seek a favourable opportunity to restore it. The loss of the bishops furthermore left the King without a party in Parliament, for they had been the nucleus and the nominators of the Lords of the Articles who controlled parliamentary procedure. Meanwhile Hamilton had resigned his unsuccessful commission, and was suspected of using the King's favour to facilitate his intrigues with the Covenanters. The new High Commissioner was Traquair, who was now required to extricate the government from the crisis against which he had warned it in vain. By the time that the Scottish parliament was adjourned on the last day of October, having ratified the Acts of the Assembly and devised a system for the future selection of the Lords of the Articles which would entirely remove the influence of the King, the English government had already decided that another attempt at coercion would be necessary. Court intrigues and administrative incompetence had caused the first attempt to fail: for the second, more thorough precautions would be taken. On September 22nd, in answer to the urgent invitation of the King, Wentworth arrived in England. The Scottish commissioners, the Earls of Loudoun and Dunfermline, who arrived in London early in November, were shortly afterwards dismissed; and Scottish affairs were entrusted instead to a committee of eight, — Wentworth, Laud, Juxon, Cottington, Windebank, Vane, Hamilton, and Northumberland.

The arrival of Wentworth and his enthusiastic reception were signs that the English government was in earnest. For no other reason could it have appealed to one who was a stranger both to England and Scotland, and whose talent lay rather in reducing conquered provinces to order than in negotiation with an independent kingdom. Nor were these the only implications of the step. In order to acquire his ruthless efficiency, Charles turned against the government all the personal enemies of Wentworth, — great magnates of the north whom he had alienated as Lord President, but who, as long as he was in Ireland, reserved their hatred for the absent President rather than for the administration which had despatched him thither. In Ireland, too, his adversaries looked up, and began intrigues with the enemies of the English government; and the Irish Church, which had been purged by his discipline and had flourished under his protection, was exposed again to the dangers from which he had temporarily rescued it. Unhappily, by his presence in London we are deprived of one valuable source of information, — Laud's letters to him, and the side-papers, largely written in cypher, which Wentworth, in spite of Laud's frequent warnings, providentially failed to burn.

Nevertheless, though Wentworth was summoned to direct the energies of the English government, he could not, returning after a long absence, control the intrigues of its personnel. One sign of the divided counsels which still prevailed, and which ultimately prevented decided action, was provided by the dismissal and supersession of Secretary Coke.

Sir John Coke had long been superseded in fact, although not in name, by his colleague Windebank. The business of his department was frequently carried on by his colleagues without his knowledge, and ambassadors complained that he gave insufficient attention to their reports. His age too (for he was nearly eighty) disqualified him for dealing with a crisis and suggested him as an appropriate scapegoat to be sacrificed for the failure of the first Bishops' War. Even Wentworth, who had a personal affection for the old man, and to whom he had been useful, was prepared, for reasons of state, to see him succeeded by some more energetic counsellor, and suggested that the secretariat be given instead to the Earl of Leicester, the ambassador to Paris, who was doubly recommended to him by his own personal friendship and the advocacy of Lady Carlisle. Leicester came of a strong Protestant family: but his religion was rather the expression of his personal character than of his political views, and in this he was little different from Wentworth himself, whose austere self-confidence and contempt of ceremony were sometimes designated by the same name. Nor need Protestant sympathies have disqualified him to succeed Sir John Coke, who was also regarded as a Puritan by high-churchmen, in an office already beginning to be concerned principally with the northern and Protestant powers. Wentworth therefore urged his suit to the King, and found himself seconded by an even more influential advocate, — the Queen.

To the narrow comprehensions of Laud, however, these considerations had little value. To him, neither the advantages of conciliating an offended nobility, nor the prospect of securing an experienced diplomatist, nor even the necessity of supporting his firmest friend, could outweigh the fatal obstacle of doctrinal divergence. Leicester's Protestantism had naturally been emphasised in the Archbishop's eyes by its contrast with the high-church piety of Lord Scudamore, who had been his colleague in Paris: and throughout the period of his embassy Laud had looked upon him with disfavour, even urging that the debts owed to him from the Crown, for which Lady Leicester begged him to intercede with the King, should not be paid. As recently as May 1639 he had assured Wentworth that the ambassador was "a most dangerous practising Puritan, none like him in the Kingdom"; and it seems almost certain that it was the result of Laud's representations that neither Wentworth nor the Queen could prevail upon Charles to accept his services.[1] Certainly

[1] Laud to Wentworth, *Works*, vii. 248, 568.

Laud had another candidate, — he was now seeking to atone for his previous behaviour by recommending Sir Thomas Roe, whom he had succeeded in excluding in favour of Windebank in 1632, — and in condoling with the defeated candidate, the Earl of Northumberland had no doubt where to lay the blame for his failure. " To think well of the Reformed Religion ", he wrote, " is enough to make the Archbishop one's enemy." [1]

At all events, the result was disastrous : for the Queen, having failed to secure the vacant position for Leicester, put forward as her new candidate the Treasurer of the Household, Sir Henry Vane, — a man whose doctrinal orthodoxy could scarcely atone for his lack alike of scruples, experience, and efficiency. He was known also to be entirely dependent upon the Queen and her party, and a personal enemy of Wentworth, who was at this moment gratuitously insulting him by securing for himself a territorial title to which Vane pretended a claim. Rather than see Vane appointed, Wentworth urged that Coke should be continued in office : but he urged unsuccessfully. The subsequent career of Vane confirmed his worst apprehensions ; and Laud must bear the responsibility of having twice secured the exclusion of a qualified applicant, and twice permitted the appointment as Secretary of State of a candidate who subsequently contributed to his own ruin.

About the same time the reputation of the government was further damaged by another appointment. On January 14th, 1640, Lord Keeper Coventry died, and the Great Seal — again through the Queen's influence — was bestowed upon Lord Chief Justice Finch, a man whose political career not even the indulgence of posterity nor the ingenuity of historians has been able to praise. By parliamentarians he was remembered as the Speaker of their last assembly, who had been forcibly held in his chair, weeping and expostulating, while they protested against its dissolution. Lawyers were unlikely to forget the circumstances of his elevation to the Common Pleas in 1635. His judgment at the trial of Hampden and the large deductions which he drew in that case made him odious to all who opposed the tax. And defendants in the Star Chamber knew him as the most savage and ferocious of their judges. His sole ambition in his new office, he announced, would be to give immediate legal sanction to every order of the executive:

[1] Collins, *Sidney Papers*, 1746, I.623.

and before he had held it for a month, Sir Thomas Roe heard from his brother-in-law that he was as unpopular in Chancery as he had ever been in the Common Pleas. To Clarendon it seemed that Coventry, had he lived, might have directed the deliberations of the impending parliament to a satisfactory conclusion, thanks to his long experience and great reputation: but from Finch, who possessed neither of these assets, such a feat could hardly be expected.

For at last Parliament was to be called again. The prospects of a pacific settlement in the north had been abandoned in all but name, the peaceful professions of both sides were known to be equally disingenuous, and the immediate necessity was to discover the sinews of war. All the surplus in the Treasury, and much anticipated revenue, all that the City would lend or the Roman Catholics give, had been spent on the first Bishops' War. For the second, at a meeting of the Council held in November, Wentworth suggested that a parliament be summoned. He was too well accustomed to managing parliaments to entertain any fear of them, and he promised to summon an Irish parliament first, in order that it might give to its English counterpart an edifying example of obedience, unanimity, and generosity. The proposal was seconded by Laud and Hamilton; and at the same time, lest, as Laud put it, "the parliament should prove peevish, and refuse", the Council undertook to raise among themselves a loan of £300,000, Wentworth heading the list with £20,000. In March he set out for Dublin. On Laud's intercession the King had expressed his gratitude and confidence in him by the grant of the earldom of Strafford: the Queen's coach, as a token of her favour, carried him out of London; and he promised that, having shown what an Irish parliament could do, he would return at Easter to require an English parliament to imitate it.

CHAPTER ELEVEN

PARLIAMENT

> "Annus occupatissimus fuit, in quo vix libere spirare — nedum scribere — potui."
>
> LAUD to Vossius, August 31st, 1640

WITH the arrival of Wentworth in England in September 1639, Laud's political influence may be said to have reached an end. For six years he had been fighting a losing battle, seeking by the exercise of despotic authority and backstairs influence to establish a form of responsible autocracy: and he had failed. The opposition was too strong: his own methods were too impolitic: and his plans had been sabotaged from within by those who understood better than he did the secrets of the art politic. After the fiasco of the first Bishops' War it was beyond the wit of Laud to devise a way out of the impasse to which he had arrived, and for which he was himself largely responsible. If the principles of Thorough were to be vindicated in their darkest hour, it was by their most practical and ruthless exponent: and when Wentworth answered to the appeal, Laud tacitly conceded to him the leadership which he knew himself unable to exercise. From that time until the fall of both a year later, there is no political measure (except perhaps the exclusion of Leicester from office) for which Laud can be held personally responsible. Neither in the summoning nor in the dissolution of the Short Parliament, nor in the continuation of Convocation, nor in the second Bishops' War, was the initiative his, whatever might be alleged by the enemies who were unable to dissociate him from the measures which they disapproved.

This attitude of resignation, natural enough for political reasons, may be explained also on personal grounds. Laud was now an old man. He had been an old man of sixty when he was first advanced to Canterbury six years ago: and since then he had never spared himself a moment from any kind of business. In Church and State, in foreign and domestic policy, in the courts of justice and the seats of learning, he had assumed to himself all the arduous labours of responsibility for no other reward than the hope of achieving an ideal. He had advised the King on social policy, and had undertaken, at an advanced age and in his scanty intervals of leisure, to study the intricacies of finance and commerce, in order to take an active part on the Treasury Board. In every country vicarage the pressure of his finger was felt, and country clergymen in the remotest parts had been encouraged to appeal to him against local injustices. At the same time his influence was exerted in Scotland and Ireland and all the dominions of the British Crown. His correspondence was immense: and while he was legislating for Church, State, and University, he was always protecting the rear of his friend in Ireland from the intrigues of rivals at home, and was jockeying for influence and audience at Court with papal emissaries and factious politicians.

The contrast of these huge efforts, and the grandeur of the ideal to which they were devoted, with the slender results which they had achieved, must have been made more noticeable to Laud now that everything was in danger of reversal and he himself was an old man who could not hope to live much longer to defend the little that the resistance of his enemies and the treachery of his allies had allowed him to win. It is hardly surprising, therefore, if his letters now assume a despondent and melancholy tone, and if we find him ready to resign the defence of what he had achieved into the hands of those who seemed more confident of preserving it.

To one department of his activities, however, such qualifications do not apply. If his more grandiose ambitions were threatened with ruin by the train lit in Scotland, his lesser activities, which were independent of the rise and fall of governments, proceeded without check even when overshadowed by more spectacular actions. In 1639, while the attention of political observers was concentrated upon Scottish affairs, Laud, besides encouraging Bishop Hall to resume his pen in defence of episcopacy, investigating charges of Socinianism brought against the Queen of Bohemia's new chaplain, and again pressing for a more careful supervision of English printing-presses in Holland,[1] was still busy rehabilitating the Church as a local institution

[1] Laud to Roe, *Works*, vii. 589.

and endowing the seats of learning. Innumerable petitions continued to receive his personal attention : the policy of restoring vicars' glebes to their ancient boundaries was implemented in country districts sometimes by appeal to law, sometimes by composition, sometimes by convincing a pious patron of the perils of sacrilege. The Archbishop interested himself in a plan to augment the value of livings in Shrewsbury : he suggested improvements in estate management whereby the Dean and Chapter of Bristol might increase their revenues and provide accommodation for the choirmen :[1] he urged and contributed to the repair of country churches : and when the robbery of Church property forty years before was detected, reparation was demanded from the heirs of the original profiteer, and the aid of the King and Cottington enlisted to enforce it.[2] His interest in benefactions to Oxford was continued. In his letters to Sir Thomas Roe in Hamburg he reminded him " if you do light upon any manuscripts, forget me not " ;[3] and in Paris Lord Scudamore was evidently encouraged in the same way. " No good manuscript shall escape me loosely," he assured the Archbishop ; " I am unfortunate, not unmindful of your commands " ; and soon afterwards he enquired, " Has Your Grace employed Mr. Greaves to Constantinople for manuscripts ? 'Tis absolutely the best course." In June Laud presented to the University a further collection of 576 miscellaneous manuscripts, some Oriental, some modern, some classical, of which many had been picked up by the Earl of Arundel during his otherwise unprofitable mission to Vienna. In addition he sent a printed book on the liberties of the Gallican Church, which showed how a Church could be Catholic in doctrine while independent of papal jurisdiction : and another copy of the same book was presented simultaneously, with maps, manuscripts, and a Wiltshire living, to St. John's College. About this time, too, Laud settled in perpetuity the Arabic chair in Oxford which he had at first endowed for his lifetime only, by conveying to the trustees a parcel of lands

[1] *Works*, vi. 601.

[2] *Ibid.* v. 367. Willis' statement that he had seen an order by Laud requiring legal action against the executors of Dean Latimer of Peterborough (who had died in 1583) for his having sold the cathedral bell, is another example of Laud's determination to establish every claim, however ancient or trivial, which concerned the right of the Church (Willis, *Survey of Cathedrals*, iii. 511).

[3] Laud, *Works*, vi. 588.

called Budd's Pastures, in the parish of Bray, which he had recently purchased.[1]

Another important part of Laud's less conspicuous constructive policy was the endowment and support of charitable institutions and his interest in securing employment for the poor, especially in the cloth trade, in which his father had been engaged. One of the first foundations to benefit by his intercession was Sutton's Hospital, an institution founded in 1611 for the relief and education of the poor by Thomas Sutton, an Elizabethan land-speculator and usurer, said in his lifetime to be the richest commoner in England. The methods by which Sutton made his fortune were devious—it is pleasantly ironical that it was largely derived from the spoliation of the Church [2] — and Aubrey tells us that he was the original of Ben Jonson's *Volpone*: but his disposal of it was unexceptionable, except in the eyes of those who fancied themselves able to expend it better. One of the latter was King James, who, before Sutton's death, urged him in vain to make the Duke of York, later Charles I, his heir in exchange for a peerage: and after Sutton's death, Lord Chancellor Bacon suggested the diversion of his estate from pious to profitable uses. In 1624 the government again cast envious eyes upon so rich a booty, and Buckingham, needing money to finance his grandiose foreign policy, suggested that a standing army of ten or twelve thousand men might be maintained by the dissolution of the hospital, in which abuses could conveniently be detected. He mentioned this proposal to Laud: but Laud could not support it. Three weeks later he submitted to the Duke a written answer enumerating several reasons against the dissolution, both of principle and expediency.[3] His representations were successful: and Sutton's Hospital, better known as the Charterhouse, was spared to grow into a famous public school. Fifteen years later, when individuals and corporations were being fined for encroachment on the royal forests, Laud secured the remission of the fine imposed upon Sutton's Hospital.[4]

[1] *Works*, vi. 578.

[2] For the methods by which Sutton secured "the Grand Lease" of the rich collieries of Whickham and Gateshead from the Bishop of Durham, so founding his vast fortune, and the extent of the loss which this entailed to the Church in the seventeenth century, see J. U. Nef, *Rise of the British Coal Industry*, 1932, i. 148-56.

[3] *Works*, iii. 154-5.

[4] *Ibid*. vii. 601.

Another charitable foundation which owed something to the Archbishop was the Hospital of St. Cross at Winchester, an ancient institution for the relief of the poor, which, like many such institutions, had lost much of its property since the Reformation. In 1627 Laud secured the appointment of Dr. Lewis, late Provost of Oriel, to be Master of the hospital: and the change of policy implicit in this nomination was shown a few years later by the replies given to Laud's visitation articles. Both the woods belonging to the hospital had been leased by a former Master, all leases had been converted into three lives, and everything had been left in a condition of extreme dilapidation. But under Lewis the whole fabric had been extensively repaired, the property of the hospital had been carefully husbanded, and the new Master had spent £1000 of his private fortune on improvements. Of Heriot's Hospital in Edinburgh, and Laud's efforts to secure the debts owing to it from the Crown, mention has already been made: and in 1639 we find the Archbishop active to preserve the revenues of a small hospital in Sevenoaks.[1]

Laud's social policy, as far as enclosures and common rights are concerned, has already been outlined. Another aspect of it is shown by his efforts to foster regular employment by charitable endowments. Even in his treatment of the French and Dutch communities, this hankering for communal responsibility may be detected: for, as Neile complained, the foreigners settled in England and living in independent communities, were able to underbid English labour and so cause social dislocation,[2] while Laud objected against their refusal to employ Englishmen or teach them their methods. So, in 1634, Laud entertained a project for setting the poor of Oxford to work in the cloth-trade "much after the fashion that the Dutch and Walloons use at Canterbury, Norwich, and other places": and although "in the end such difficulties appeared in the business that the whole project suddenly vanished and came to nothing",[3] he was more successful elsewhere. At Reading especially, the place of his birth, he was anxious to imitate Abbot and perpetuate his name by an appropriate charity.

"When you are a little great man", his schoolmaster is reported

[1] *Cal. S.P. Dom.*, 1638–9, pp. 118, 493; 1639, p. 358.

[2] Neile to Laud, *S.P. Dom. Car. I.* 331, no. 71.

[3] *Works*, v. 108.

to have said to him as a boy, " remember Reading school " : but although Laud always thought of his birthplace with gratitude, his first attentions to it as Archbishop were somewhat arbitrary. In 1634, during his metropolitical visitation, he instructed Brent to make a particular enquiry into the spiritual health of Reading : and in 1636, by a characteristic infraction of corporate rights, he peremptorily required the Mayor and Corporation of the town to renounce their right of election and accept his nominee as schoolmaster, at the same time hinting that the stipend attached to that post was very small. The Corporation meekly obeyed, both admitting the nominee and undertaking to increase his stipend; and two years later Laud showed his continued interest by securing a new charter for the town.

Already, however, he had determined to enrich the town by a less impersonal gift. In January 1634 he recorded in his diary his intention " to do the town of Reading good for their poor : which may be compassed by God's blessing upon me, though my wealth be small. And I hope God will bless me in it, because it was His own motion in me. For this way never came into my thoughts (though I had much beaten them about it) till this night as I was at my prayers." He therefore entered his design " to settle a hospital of land in Reading of £100 in a new way ".[1]

If Laud was comparatively poor when he first moved to Lambeth, and made this resolution, by 1640 he was able to carry it into execution : and in March of that year he conveyed to the Corporation of Reading lands in Bray of the yearly value of £200, which he had bought from Sir John Blagrave of Southcote, Berkshire. During his lifetime, he reserved to himself the right to dispose of the rents as he pleased : but after his death the Corporation was directed to spend, two years out of every three, £120 a year to apprentice at Reading twelve poor boys, of whom ten were to be natives of Reading, one of Wokingham, where his father was born, and one of Bray, where the lands were situate. Every third year, the same sum was to be used to provide marriage-portions for six poor girls, of whom five were to be natives of Reading, and the sixth of Wokingham. Of the residue of the money, £50 a year was to go to the vicar of St. Lawrence's Church in Reading, £20 to the Reading schoolmaster, and the remaining £10 was to be set aside to defray the

[1] *Works*, iii. 220.

cost of a triennial visitation by the Warden of All Souls, the President of St. John's College, and the Vice-Chancellor of Oxford University. Later, this sum was found to be excessive for the purpose, and Laud agreed that £6 a year should be paid out of it to the town clerk. Soon afterwards, Laud bought lands in Warwickshire for £300, directing that the rents be used to apprentice poor children of Croydon : and in his will he stated that he had already made provision, probably of a similar nature, for Lambeth. By his will he further left £50 a year for the same purposes to Henley-on-Thames, Wokingham, Wallingford, Windsor, and Winchester.[1]

Shortly before fixing his benefaction for his native town, Laud was called upon by the Privy Council to deal with another Reading charity. This was Kendrick's charity, founded in 1624 by the will of a rich draper, who bequeathed £7500 to a variety of pious uses in the town. These included a workhouse, called " the Oracle ", and a stock of money from which small sums were to be lent to poor clothiers to further their trade. Later, however, the clothing-trade declined in Reading, and the richer merchants borrowed large sums from the stock in order to squeeze out of the market their poorer rivals for whom it was principally intended. On the complaint of the inhabitants, the case was referred to Laud, who advised that the stock be invested in land, and the annual revenues lent out in limited sums to small clothiers, the surplus being devoted to the binding of apprentices and the giving of marriage-portions, as in his own charity. This scheme was adopted, and the Archbishop thus retained for Reading the charity which would otherwise, according to the conditions imposed by the founder in case of mismanagement, have been transferred to Christ's Hospital.[2]

Thus in December 1639, although his own benefaction to Reading was not yet settled, Laud had already deserved the gratitude of his native town : and in view of the difficult political situation, he resolved to use this advantage in a characteristic way. Writing to the Mayor and Corporation, he requested the right to nominate a burgess for the coming parliament : and this request being " openly read and by all agreed and granted ", he nominated

[1] Cf. J. Bruce, *Archbishop Laud's Benefactions in Berkshire*, 1841 ; Charity Commission Report, xiii. 570 ; Laud, *Works*, iv. 445.

[2] *Ibid.* vii. 652.

the Solicitor-General, Sir Edward Herbert, whom Clarendon declared largely responsible, with Vane, for the premature dissolution of the assembly. Herbert was not entirely acceptable to the Corporation, — in fact, they voted against him by a majority of three to one — but as the Archbishop's nominee he was returned, together with Sir John Berkeley, nominated by Lord Holland as High Steward of the town. In fact, however, these nominations made no difference to the constitution of the Short Parliament: for both Herbert and Berkeley, being returned for boroughs in Wiltshire, resigned their Reading seats, which were filled by Sir Francis Knollys and his son.

Parliament assembled on April 13th, 1640, with appropriate pageantry. The bishops, it was particularly noticed, rode to Westminster on horseback, which was regarded as an innovation, although one critical observer remarked that the standard of apostolic horseflesh was not high, " many of them on bob-tailed horses, fitter for Mrs. Crayford in my opinion at Bridgehill than for an ecclesiastical baron's gravity and reverence there " ; and although the spectacle drew from the bystanders the exclamation of " the Church triumphant ! ", there was little reason to celebrate a clerical triumph.[1] Laud himself had indeed supported Strafford's motion for the calling of Parliament, but he had not looked forward to its assembly with the same confidence. In the interval he had studied the advice given to James I before the meeting of the Addled Parliament of 1614, which could hardly be regarded as a happy precedent, though it proved to be a true one ; and now, even if the members seemed conspicuous for the moderation of their behaviour, that was because they could afford to be moderate. The summoning of Parliament after so long a period of personal rule was in itself a victory for them, and they were resolved to concede nothing. Under the leadership of Pym, the Commons proceeded to enumerate all the grievances of the last eleven years, — ship-money, forest fines, coat-and-conduct money, ecclesiastical innovations, restrictions on trade, and " swarms of projecting canker-worms and caterpillars, the worst of the Egyptian plagues ". In ecclesiastical affairs, an attack was again made upon Cosin, again for denying

[1] *Oxinden Letters* (ed. D. Gardner), p. 162 ; Thomas May, *History of the Long Parliament*, p. 22.

the royal supremacy: and the Archbishop's secretary, William Dell, was brought to the Bar for misreporting Pym, and only escaped through the intervention of Hampden. Meanwhile in the Upper House, Laud's request that the session be adjourned for a week while the bishops were absent in Convocation was met by Lord Saye and Sele with the retort that the Lords could do their business well enough without the bishops: the validity of Roger Manwaring's elevation to a bishopric was called in question, and Laud did not conciliate the secular peers by declaring that even if Parliament deprived him, the King could restore him: and Bishop Hall was compelled to apologise at the Bar of the House for saying that Lord Saye and Sele "savoured of a Scottish Covenanter", — which was perfectly true. In the Tower, too, the irrepressible Bishop Williams was stirring again, secretly corresponding with John Hampden to secure his release. Hampden, however, was too wary to meddle in inter-episcopal scandals, and merely warned the Bishop that an early dissolution was likely, which would leave him worse off than before, should he attempt to secure his freedom by means of Parliament.[1]

As the full intentions of the parliament became clear, various counsels for dealing with it were submitted by the King's advisers. Strafford, fresh from the successful management of an Irish parliament, which had voted four subsidies with enthusiastic loyalty, was for bold action. He would divide Lords from Commons, and tempt the isolated Commons to grant a moderate supply by suggesting that the King might reward their devotion by a voluntary renunciation of some of his less popular rights. But Strafford's experience and success had been as a provincial governor: and when he returned from Ireland, it was soon seen that his methods were too elementary for a politically conscious people. The King followed his advice half-way, and then hesitated. Vane went down to the Commons and offered a hard and fast bargain — the withdrawal of ship-money in return for twelve subsidies, — by which the government would stand or fall. The appetite of the Commons was whetted. They demanded more than the withdrawal of ship-money; and the government, further frightened by the suggestion of Scottish negotiations which would have prevented a punitive expedition, had no alternative but a dissolution.

[1] Lambeth MS. 1030, pp. 105-8.

The decision was taken at a meeting of the Privy Council on May 5th. If anyone was individually responsible for the dissolution, it was, as Clarendon and Laud agreed, Sir Henry Vane, who had committed the government to a bargain which the Commons would not accept, and who now urged that further negotiations were useless, as Parliament would not grant a single penny. Strafford, who arrived late at the meeting, urged circumspection ; but only Holland and Northumberland gave their votes against a dissolution. Of the majority, Laud could claim to bear the least responsibility of all : for he arrived very late, having been misinformed as to the time of the meeting. Indeed, he had already renounced interest in the matter, and a few days earlier, when Hyde had called upon him in his garden to plead against a dissolution, he had replied, with resignation, that " for his own part, he was resolved to deliver no opinion ; but as he would not persuade the dissolution, which might be attended by consequences he could not foresee, so he had not so good an opinion of their affections to the King or the Church, as to persuade their longer sitting, if the King were inclined to dissolve them ".[1] It can hardly be doubted, however, that he was glad of the decision.

When the King returned to Whitehall after dissolving the Short Parliament, the Council met again to discuss the course which now remained. On this there could hardly be a doubt. Northumberland's opposition was unavailing, and Vane's plea for a defensive war only was repudiated by Strafford, who insisted that the only form of defence was attack. He promised Irish troops for an aggressive campaign, and declared with assurance that it would be over in a few months. The Archbishop supported him. There was, he said, no alternative. Every other method had been tried in vain, and now, by the law of God, the King might take the subsistence which was due to him, though by the law of man it had been denied. Cottington agreed, somewhat despondently : and the government decided once again to risk the chances of a short and successful war.

With this decision, as with the dissolution, Laud had no more intimate connexion than any other individual member of the Council. He had already renounced the initiative in matters of

[1] *Life*, p. 38.

policy to Strafford, whose lead he followed almost resignedly. Nevertheless, the unpopular policy of the government had by now become completely associated, in the mind of the public, with the Archbishop : and he was now held solely and personally responsible for every development. That policy, it seemed, had been all of a piece for eleven years, and it was unsatisfactory to associate its most recent manifestations with a Secretary of State who had held office only for a few months. The dissolution was also a logical consequence of Laud's former policy : and as Laud hated and feared parliaments on principle, while other politicians objected to them only on grounds of expediency, he was a better target for the popular indignation.

This indignation expressed itself immediately in a series of demonstrations against him. Libels were posted daily in the City. " So odious is he grown in the eyes of men ", ran one of them, " that we believe he stinketh in the nostrils of Almighty God " ; [1] and on the very morrow of the dissolution, a paper was exhibited calling on the London apprentices to join in hunting " William the Fox " for the breaking of Parliament. Three days later, a placard in the Exchange gave more precise directions. All lovers of liberty and the Commonwealth were invited to assemble in St. George's Fields in Southwark early on May 11th. The Council took precautionary measures, and sent the trained bands to the rendezvous, while Laud fortified his palace as best he could, and retired, by the King's command, to Whitehall. But the apprentices waited till the evening, and then, when the trained bands had withdrawn, marched, five or six hundred strong, preceded by a drum, to Lambeth. For two hours from midnight they besieged the Archbishop's palace, calling for Laud that they might tear him in pieces, and for three nights Laud remained at Whitehall, guarded by ordnance. Meanwhile two of the rioters were taken, and the savagery of their punishment showed the panic of the authorities. They were tried later in the month by a special commission, and one of them, who had acted as drummer, — a glover called Archer — was tortured on the rack before being executed, because it was thought that he could reveal information which he probably did not possess and certainly did not divulge. The other was a poor sailor, a boy of sixteen, one Thomas Bensted, who had been wounded by a

[1] Lambeth MS. 943, p. 717.

pistol-shot in the riot, and fell an easy victim. He was adjudged guilty of treason, and on May 23rd, two days after the execution of Archer, was hanged, drawn, and quartered. The Archbishop's enemies did not forget this savagery. A comparatively objective critic found himself more sympathetic towards " that poor fellow Thomas Bensted, whom he caused to be hanged, drawn, and quartered " than to any other of Laud's victims : and next year the Puritan pamphleteers depicted the Archbishop's peace at night in the Tower disturbed by the ghost of Thomas Bensted.[1]

After the Lambeth tumult, the Council sent the trained bands to guard the Archbishop's palace : but neither libellers nor rioters were greatly deterred. On May 15th the mob burst into the White Lion Prison in Southwark and released the prisoners : and ten days later the Venetian ambassador reported (though it was not in fact true) that Laud's house at Croydon had been sacked by the rabble.

Another with whom Laud found himself inconveniently associated in misfortune was the new papal Agent, Count Rossetti, who had recently succeeded Con. His house was also threatened with destruction, and he too took refuge elsewhere, lodging at the house of Marie de' Medici, which was also guarded by troops. Laud made every effort to dissociate himself from his popish fellow-sufferers, and Rossetti reported that on Whitsun-eve he even begged the King on his knees to persecute the Catholics as a political necessity. But his representations were in vain. The Queen was in childbed, — her youngest son, the Duke of Gloucester, was born on July 8th — and in these circumstances the King never refused her anything. All that Laud could do was to burn Roman Catholic books, and this impressed no one. Besides, there were political reasons for favouring the Catholics. A Spanish alliance against the Scots was being considered, and Strafford hoped for £300,000 of Spanish money to finance the war. The five commissioners for this alliance were Strafford, Northumberland, Cottington, Windebank, and Vane : and according to the French ambassador, Laud was to take a full part in all the negotiations : only such was his unpopularity that it was thought safer, for appearance's sake, to exclude his name.[2] The Archbishop's position during these critical days was not

[1] *Rome for Canterbury*, 1641 ; *Canterburie's Amazement*, 1641.

[2] Montreuil to Bellièvre, May 7/17th, 1640.

made any easier by the dangerous illness of Strafford, which many believed would be fatal, and which incapacitated him for business during the second half of May.

Meanwhile Convocation continued to sit, and the enemies of Laud found in its session and its activities another charge against the Archbishop, who in fact was not responsible for it. Summoned to meet at the same time as the Short Parliament, it had shown its loyalty, and drawn upon itself the censure of the parliament, by voting six subsidies, and its orthodoxy by drawing up a set of new canons which should give synodal authority to the ecclesiastical policy of the last decade. When the parliament was prematurely dissolved, the Convocation, according to the practice which had obtained since the Reformation, should also have been terminated : but neither were the canons yet completed, nor the Act for the subsidies drawn up, and the King, having missed twelve subsidies from the Commons, had no desire to lose six from the clergy. Therefore, when Laud applied for a writ to dissolve the Convocation, according to precedent, Charles replied that Convocation was to remain in session, as it had done on several occasions in the fifteenth century and before. Already aware of the general hatred with which he was regarded, Laud was apprehensive of increasing it by any action of doubtful legality, and expressed his surprise at this breach with tradition ; but the King said that he had applied to Lord Keeper Finch, and that Finch had assured him that it was quite constitutional. So Laud merely declared his dissatisfaction that the King should refer ecclesiastical matters to the Lord Keeper rather than to the Archbishop, and complied. Still, however, there were doubts. Some members of the Lower House of Convocation demurred, and again Laud applied to the King, demanding that panacea for all dubious actions, a guarantee of legality subscribed by the judges. This too was forthcoming : and with this assurance Laud continued the Convocation.[1]

Thus Laud cannot be charged with personal responsibility for the continuation of Convocation, or any illegality which may have been involved in it. The Convocation sat till May 29th, under the name of a synod, and proceeded to complete the work which it had begun. The six subsidies were incorporated in an

[1] *Works*, iii. 285.

Act, which described them (since subsidies required parliamentary confirmation) as a benevolence: and the canons, seventeen in number, were drawn up and presented for subscription. In form and content they were sufficiently moderate documents, expressing and explaining the doctrine of the Church of England as familiarised by the practice of recent years. The divine right of Kings was stated, the altar question discussed and determined, and the errors of Popery, Socinianism, and separatism equally declared intolerable. Their principal defect was not in their content at all, — for however unpopular that may have been, it was by now too familiar to provoke an outburst, — but in their publication. As the judicial decision which turned ship-money from an expedient into a right caused more discontent than the imposition itself, so these canons, which turned high-churchmanship from a policy into a principle, immediately drew attention to a state of affairs which had already persisted for several years, but which had not hitherto been so categorically formulated. Throughout his career, Laud trusted implicitly in the value of authoritative documents, whether they were royal instructions, judicial decisions, or ecclesiastical records: and he never understood that such declarations of principle, while they may win support if they coincide with the interests of those to whom they are addressed, like the Scottish Covenant or the Voluntary Association, will, if they are opposed to those interests, arouse far greater antipathy than a mere silent fulfilment of the policy which they embody.

In this particular instance Laud was doubly at fault; for not only were the canons themselves a formulation of objectionable doctrines, but they included yet another such formulation in the famous "Etcetera Oath", by which all in holy orders, "all masters of arts (the sons of noblemen only excepted), all bachelors and doctors in divinity, law, or physic, all that are licensed to practise physic, all registrars, actuaries, and proctors, all schoolmasters, all such as, being natives or naturalised, do come to be incorporated into the universities here, having taken a degree in any foreign university" were required to swear before November that they would do nothing to alter the established government of the Church by "archbishops, bishops, deans and archdeacons, etc." The meaning of the canon was fairly clear: but its legality was dubious — for the Commons maintained that the Convocation had no power to issue oaths binding upon laymen without parliamentary consent, — and its impolicy was indubitable. All the opponents of the government and the Church found in it something which they could unite to denounce, and all whose real objection was to nothing which needed to be implied in an "etc.", but to archbishops and bishops who were plainly enumerated in the text, exercised their fertile imaginations to discover the agents of Antichrist who might creep into the government of the English Church through the latitude of that careless abbreviation. Nevertheless, even here the responsibility was not the Archbishop's only. For the canons were presented, on their completion, to the King for his ratification, and in July were discussed at length at the Council Board, where Sir Henry Martin argued against them "with his utmost skill" for several days, before they were approved and published; so that, as Clarendon says, "whatsoever they were, the judges were at least as guilty of the first presumption in framing them, and the Lords of the Council in publishing and executing them, as the bishops, or the rest of the clergy, in either".[1]

The canons to which Sir Henry Marten at the Council table, and one or two canonists in Convocation, objected were those which concerned the ecclesiastical lawyers and their relations to the clergy: but another objection, which excited more scandal, was raised in Convocation by one of the bishops. This was Bishop Goodman of Gloucester, whose secret conversion to Popery was already known to Laud, and whose relations with the Archbishop, the government, and his diocese had been consistently uneasy. Now, when he found it impossible to dissociate himself in the public mind from the Romanist party at Court, and was even being reported as a convert himself, Laud secured from the King an explicit command to include in the canons an order against recusancy, and dilated in Convocation on the necessity of dealing firmly with Catholics. When a canon was thereupon framed requiring the clergy to use all the machinery at their disposal for the detection and punishment of Catholics, the conscience of Goodman was smitten, and he declared that he would rather be torn by wild horses than subscribe to it. Laud retorted that he must then be either a Papist or a Socinian or a sectary: but Goodman refused to give his reason, and challenged the legality of the

[1] Clarendon, *History of the Rebellion*, iii. 70.

sitting of Convocation after the dissolution of Parliament. The Archbishop declined to revert to that unwelcome topic, and required him to vote either for or against the canons. Goodman refused to do either, and Laud suspended him from his bishopric until, at the mediation of the Bishops of Exeter and Salisbury, he was persuaded to subscribe. Even then the King had him imprisoned in the Gatehouse for holding communication with the Court of Rome while a bishop in the Church of England, and he was not released till July, when the canons were brought up at the Council table, and he was again made to subscribe to them.[1] Next month he was writing to Laud, seeking once more to resign from his uncomfortable diocese.[2]

By the dissolution of the Parliament and the dubious legality of the canons, the government had committed itself to a war policy, and could seek no justification save in success. During the summer of 1640 this policy was tried for a second time, and again Laud had no part in politics except to wait for the result. More care was taken than in the previous year. New generals were chosen, and neither Holland nor Arundel was allowed to endanger the prospects of victory by incompetence or ill reputation. All the forces of the kingdom were put under the command of Northumberland: but the real director of the campaign was Strafford. The defence of the northern frontier was in the meanwhile entrusted to Lord Conway, a man who combined the advantages of a military reputation and a wide popularity, and who was a great friend of both Northumberland and Strafford. He was also supported enthusiastically by Laud, who, according to Clarendon, "had contracted an extraordinary opinion of this man, and took great delight in his company, he being well able to speak in the affairs of the Church, and taking care to be thought by him a very zealous defender of it, when they who knew him better knew he had no kind of sense of religion, and thought all was alike".

Conway kept Laud continually posted with the news from the north; but Laud was finding opposition nearer home than Newcastle. Wherever his bishops or officers attempted to enforce subscription to the Etcetera Oath, they were encountering stubborn refusal. Dr. Davenant from Salisbury, Sir John Lambe

[1] Laud, *Works*, iii. 287, 236.

[2] *Cal. S.P. Dom.*, 1640, p. 642.

from Northamptonshire, Cosin from Cambridge, wrote reporting opposition to the oath against which Puritan pamphlets were circulated, while in Kent the embarrassment of Dr. Duck was only ended by a practical joker who dispersed the gathering by cries of "A mad bull!"[1] On August 16th, when the Privy Council met to deal with the new situation in the north, where the Scots had taken the initiative and invaded Northumberland, the Archbishop asked the King for instructions about the treatment of those who refused to take the oath. The King told him to let it alone till October, when he would advise further on the question. Meanwhile applicants for ecclesiastical livings were to take it. By October the situation was worse, and the oath was suspended altogether until the next Convocation should decide on some course of action.[2]

Meanwhile the second Bishops' War fared worse than the first. While Strafford lay ill at York, the Scots routed Conway's force at Newburn on the Tyne and crossed into Durham. The English army, already ill-paid and mutinous, was now demoralised, as refugees poured into Yorkshire, and Archbishop Neile burnt his papers to save such incriminating documents from the hands of his enemies. On September 24th "a new convention, not heard of before, — that is, so old that it had not been practised in some hundreds of years", a Great Council of Peers, met at York to advise the King; and as most of its members were old enemies of Strafford, they had no hesitation in advising a parliament that should put an end to an administration which they hated. By the treaty of Ripon an armistice was concluded: but the Scots were allowed to remain in the country till an indemnity, which grew daily, was paid. And that indemnity could only come from a parliament.

From Lambeth Laud watched the northern debacle with helpless resignation. The departure of the King had been the signal for his adversaries to take courage again, and libels were posted in Covent Garden at the end of August calling on the apprentices to profit by the King's absence and murder the Archbishop, who was also reported to have taken refuge at the Queen's palace, and only to emerge with caution. Next month Laud was further distracted by the discovery of a great mare's

[1] Lambeth MS. 577, pp. 259-61; *Oxinden Letters*, p. 183.
[2] Laud, *Works*, vi. 584.

nest in Holland. Credulous Protestants were in the habit of detecting the machinations of the Pope and the Jesuits in every disturbance, and already congratulatory letters had been forged to prove that the whole Scottish business was nothing but a Jesuitical ramp. Now one Andreas ab Habernfeld presented himself to Sir William Boswell at the Hague with a circumstantial tale of a fantastic conspiracy against the King and the Archbishop, which has been regarded as the origin of the more famous Popish Plot of the next reign. According to Habernfeld, the details of the plot had been communicated to him by a former servant of Con, whose conscientious scruples had impelled him to turn King's evidence ; and he revealed how a vast scheme had been prepared, in which the most unlikely characters were involved, to raise civil war in Great Britain and create a situation there which the Jesuits would know how to turn to their profit. Sir Tobie Matthew, Wat Montague, the Earl of Arundel, Endymion Porter, and many others were declared to be the Pope's accomplices ; and the anonymous informant descended to the most minute particulars, as to the method of communication adopted by the conspirators, and the kind of death meditated for the Archbishop and the King, who was to be despatched by "an Indian nut stuffed with most sharp poison". Boswell communicated the whole affair to Laud, with instructions to reveal it only to the King, who was in York ; and the plot was taken sufficiently seriously for a committee of Lords to be summoned to deal with it. But the fertile imagination of its author overreached itself in some of the details, and between the scepticism of the committee and the pressure of the Troubles the conspiracy was soon forgotten. Nevertheless, it was dished up again in 1643 by Prynne to prove that the conspiracy was real and that Laud was one of its principal agents. As Laud was one of the principal victims marked out for assassination, this was difficult to prove ; but it was not beyond the resources of Prynne.

The treaty of Ripon, with its stipulation of a parliament, sounded the death-knell of the system of government which Laud and Strafford had sought to perpetuate. That form of government had proved unsuccessful over a short period of ten years, and the attempt to set it upon its feet again by a gambler's throw had failed. Now the result could only be a revolutionary change, and with the reversal of the old policy, as Strafford had forecast three years earlier, would come " the sacrificing those that have been the ministers therein ". Already on the first calling of the Council of Peers at York, Hamilton, who, with Laud and Strafford, had been the King's principal adviser since the Scottish troubles began, applied to his master for leave to go abroad, since " he well foresaw a storm, in which his shipwreck was most probable among others ". He added that he knew that Strafford and Laud were in the same danger, and that he had advised them to take the same course : " but ", he said, " the Earl was too great-hearted to fear, and he doubted the other was too bold to fly ".[1]

Hamilton's judgment, if Clarendon has correctly reported him, was true enough. Broken in health, but incapable of fear, Strafford could no longer hope to manage Parliament : but he was satisfied that nothing could be proved against him but faithful service, while he could turn the tables on his accusers by exposing their treasonable correspondence with the King's enemies. As for Laud, he had no such confidence. Indeed, he had no positive plan for the preservation of his person or his achievement. But none accused him of cowardice. Even during the first Bishops' War, when a woman was arrested for spreading reports that the Archbishop was to be abandoned to the Scots and had fled the country, she had added that she did not believe the latter part of the tale, for Laud would never flee. Now he awaited the assembly of a hostile parliament on November 3rd with complete resignation. The grateful borough of Reading would again have accepted his nominee as a burgess : but Laud declined to avail himself of their compliance. He was unwilling, he said, to sow dissension between the borough and the Commons : and he did not wish to involve his native town in his own present unpopularity.[2] Of this unpopularity he had but recently received a fresh manifestation. To avoid a repetition of the tumult at Lambeth in May, he had transferred the sessions of the Court of High Commission to St. Paul's : and there, on October 23rd, a crowd of some 2000, headed by one Quartermain, burst into the court and tore down all the benches, crying out that they would have no bishops and no High Commission. " I like not this preface to the parliament ", Laud wrote to Ussher, reporting the incident, and he appealed in vain to the Star Chamber to punish

[1] Clarendon, *History of the Rebellion*, ii. 104. [2] Laud, *Works*, vi. 587.

the offenders.[1] Other omens, too, presented themselves to his superstitious mind. A week before the opening of Parliament, he went into his study to examine a further collection of manuscripts which he was sending to Oxford, and found his portrait lying face downward on the floor. "I am almost every day threatened with my ruin in Parliament", he wrote, — for the auspicious season had again hatched a brood of libels: "God grant this be no omen"; and a well-meaning correspondent urged him to have the date of the assembly postponed if possible, since on November 3rd, 1529, that Parliament had met which had begun with the overthrow of Cardinal Wolsey, continued with the diminution of clerical power and privilege, and ended with the dissolution of religious foundations. An enthusiastic canon of St. Asaph, it is true, wrote to him at the same time extolling his many virtues in Hebrew, Chaldee, Syriac, Turkish, Arabic, Persian, Aethiopic, and Greek: but this was of little practical assistance.

[1] Laud, *Works*, iii. 237; vi. 586.

CHAPTER TWELVE

THE TOWER

"Though Justice against Fate complain,
And plead the antient rights in vain, —
But those do hold or break
As men are strong or weak."

MARVELL, "An Horatian Ode upon Cromwell's Return from Ireland".

WHEN Parliament met on November 3rd, Laud's career had already failed, as he himself knew, and the rest of his life is but an epilogue. Old and disillusioned, he had no stomach to prosecute a struggle which he had already virtually renounced, or to preserve his slender achievements from the powerful enemies now at last assembled. To the Lower House came country squires, merchants, and lawyers, conscious of their ascendancy, and determined to secure its recognition: in the Lords, the natural supporters of monarchy had been converted into its enemies by its contempt of their privileges; and in both there was a leaven of Puritanism which raised their ambitions into the higher region of ideals, and transmuted their interests into the more potent incentives of rights. Even those who were most favourably disposed towards the Archbishop were those whom, when in power, he had alienated or overlooked, and who, though they might defend his person, were little likely to fight for his achievements, — Selden, the champion of the law and the constitution: Roe, the neglected advocate of a Protestant foreign policy: Strangeways, who had been imprisoned for resisting the forced loan: Hyde, who was to lead the attack on the prerogative courts. Whatever divisions might subsequently appear in the Parliament now assembled, clearly all were agreed that the effective condemnation of Charles' past government, and the final removal of his advisers in it, were indispensable preliminaries; and the King, as he slid privately to Westminster by water, instead of the usual solemn procession, and the bishops, as they proceeded to Convocation protected by a guard of musketeers, showed that they were aware of it.

Against this hostile assembly, so formidably armed, what could the discredited ministers of the Government do? Could they justify their actions with any prospect of a sympathetic hearing? Even in the days of their success, their justifications had fallen upon deaf ears, and in failure they had even less chance of admittance. Could they manage Parliament by skilfully eliciting and manipulating the divergent interests which a common indignation at first concealed? But till that common indignation had been satisfied by some concession, those divergences could hardly be discovered: and the preliminary concession could only be the sacrifice of those ministers who might have played upon the divergences. And anyway, what bold or resourceful measures could be expected from a Privy Council divided and panic-stricken, every member less concerned to defend his past conduct than to secure his future safety? Unless they were conscious of having fought for a programme in which they believed, or of having faithfully served a master whom they trusted, there was little to inspire them to constancy: but what principles had dictated the policy of Finch and Windebank, what personal loyalty could be inspired by Charles I, till misfortune made him a martyr? Only for Strafford and Laud did the policy of the past years represent an ideal, even if imperfectly attained and ultimately defeated: and Strafford at least was prepared to defend it. After three days of rest, while he sought to repair his broken health at Wentworth Woodhouse, he rode south for London, too readily trusting the promises of the King, and prepared to forestall the attack on the Government by impeaching the parliamentary leaders for treasonable correspondence with the Scots.

Laud's mind, however, entertained no such bold projects. He had already half renounced the struggle in which he found his progress stayed, resigning the initiative in the Council to his more vigorous colleague: and although, during the last year, the burden of business had multiplied upon his shoulders, he had sought not to direct policy, but to execute it, not to advise, but to acquiesce, not to lay the foundations of a system of government and apply a system of law, but to put his house in order and perpetuate his charitable and academic foundations. Now, when his failure was openly manifested by the coming together of a parliament which could not, like its predecessor, easily be dismissed, he made no further attempt at resistance. He was not, like Strafford, a parliamentarian. Awkward in committees, unfamiliar with debate, he distrusted all deliberative assemblies: and by their long intermission he had neither learnt to manage them nor overcome his fear of them. So he was now prepared to capitulate rather than fight, believing, as he told his chaplain, that at the most he would only be removed from the King's counsels and confined to his diocese.

Hence, in these last five years, the interest in Laud's career shrinks together with his activity: for it was only his multifarious activities which had made him great. Now that his authority was stripped from him, and the basis of his power knocked from beneath him, he shrinks again to his personal dimensions, and becomes once more the uninteresting, unsympathetic, unsociable character of his early Oxford days, only rendered somewhat tragic by the loss of power, the knowledge of failure, and the imminence of revenge.

When Parliament met on November 3rd, one notable member was absent from the Upper House. This was Archbishop Neile, *felix opportunitate mortis*, the news of whose death had reached London on the previous day. His see, however, was not yet to be filled: for the Government, at so critical a time, could not afford to defy its enemies by a high-church, or surrender to them by a low-church appointment. Another archbishop who had died recently was Spottiswood, whose death had occurred in London almost a year ago. A trimmer to the last, ever loving the favour of the English Government rather more than he feared its policy, he had designated the objectionable Maxwell as his executor, and recommended him as his successor in the province of St. Andrews. Maxwell, however, was safe from the perils of another Scottish dignity. He was already designated for an Irish see, and, by the time which we have reached, was installed as Bishop of Killala and Achonry in time to be ejected by another rebellion.

In King Henry VII's chapel at Westminster Laud addressed the Convocation, and " in an eloquent but sad oration bemoaned the infelicities which he saw hanging over the Church, advising everyone there present to perform their duties, and not to be wanting to themselves or the cause of religion, as far forth as they were concerned in their several places". The chief infelicity at present overhanging the Church was the recollection of the unhappy canons promulgated at the last session, whose legality, already disputed in the country, would certainly be contested in the parliament: and in the lower house of Convocation one Warmister, clerk of the diocese of Worcester, proposed to his colleagues that they should forestall disaster by a timely and spontaneous condemnation of their own abortive offspring. This humiliation, however, was more than Convocation could stomach: and it preferred to wait and be accused.

It did not have to wait long: for Parliament, at a loss where to begin amid such a sea of abuses, was already striking out indiscriminately among them. Ecclesiastical innovations, unparliamentary exactions, dependent judges, and monopolist companies were being attacked in turn: Prynne, Burton, and Bastwick, their petitions for release granted, were returning in triumphal procession, feasted and fêted all the way to London, to hear their sentences reversed: and Bishop Williams, after long intrigues, resumed his place in the House of Lords, courting and courted by all the enemies of the Archbishop.

Meanwhile more urgent business required more definite measures. Under the direction of Pym, Parliament set to work methodically, dealing with its problems in order, and beginning with the most pressing. On November 10th a committee was formed to investigate the crimes of Strafford with a view to his impeachment: and next day, when Strafford had planned to forestall the blow by a counter-charge, Pym took the initiative, demanding and securing his impeachment on articles not yet formulated. On the same day the famous scene took place when Strafford, after kneeling at the Bar of the Upper House, was committed to Maxwell, gentleman usher of the Black Rod, and led away in his coach to custody before an astonished crowd, "all gazing, no man capping to him, before whom that morning the greatest in England would have stood discovered". A fortnight later he was transferred to the Tower, accused of "endeavouring to subvert the fundamental laws and government of the realms of England and Ireland, and instead thereof to introduce an arbitrary and tyrannical government against law".

All this time Laud did nothing. He had no plan, no intention, of anticipating the blow intended for him by any bold counter-stroke. He gave no initiative in Convocation. He did not speak in the Lords. He was busied with other, less political things. On November 6th he wrote to Oxford University, and, after lamenting the disturbances which distracted him from his work, presented to their safe keeping a further collection of classical and Oriental manuscripts. A week later he was arranging the details of his Reading benefaction, himself collecting the rents from his lands at Bray, and distributing them between his Reading charity and the Arabic lectureship. He also received a member of the Corporation of Reading, and gave his personal attention to the claims of individuals who wished to profit by his charity. Finally he turned to parliamentary business, and sought to divert the attack from the canons which he was no longer concerned to defend. On November 29th he wrote to Selden :

> Worthy Sir,
>
> I understand that the business about the late canons will be handled again in your House tomorrow. I shall never ask any unworthy thing of you ; but give me leave to say as follows. If we have erred in any point of legality unknown unto us, we shall be heartily sorry for it, and hope that error shall not be made a crime. We hear that ship-money is laid aside, as a thing which will die of itself; and I am glad it will have so quiet a death. May not these unfortunate canons be suffered to die as quietly, without blemishing the Church, which hath too many enemies both at home and abroad ? If this may be, I here promise you, I will presently humbly beseech His Majesty for a licence to review the canons and abrogate them : assuring myself that all my brethren will join with me to preserve the public peace, rather than that any act of ours shall be thought a public grievance. And upon my credit with you, I had moved for this licence at the very first sitting of this Parliament, but that both myself and others did fear the House of Commons would take offence at it (as they did at the last) and said we did it on purpose to prevent them . . .

It was the first occasion upon which Laud had ever admitted an error, or retired from a position which he had once taken up.

The canons, however, were not allowed to die quietly. Nor was ship-money, — both were too useful as sticks with which to beat the Government. But it was not their turn yet. On the day after Laud wrote to Selden, the question of the exemptions granted to Roman Catholics was considered, and Windebank was discovered to have been the principal agent in the business. Ten days later, Windebank forestalled the vengeance of the Commons by flight to France. On December 7th came the expected attack on ship-money and its chief defender, Lord Keeper Finch. Finch did not shirk the responsibility, and on December 21st he defended himself with ability before the Lower House. But the House was not interested in his arguments, and voted unanimously for his impeachment. That night Finch too sought safety in flight, and a ship of the Royal Navy conveyed him to his exile in the Hague. Meanwhile, on December 16th, the canons had come up for consideration. The attack was led by Francis Rous, the Cornish Puritan, who had assailed Arminian doctrines in the early parliaments of the reign: and although there were some who defended the canons, asserting the independence of Convocation within the limits set by statute, this argument was not allowed to prevail. For it was not primarily a constitutional question that was at issue, — in fact, in spite of many efforts, the canons were never declared unconstitutional, and at the Restoration the question of their validity was left undetermined. Parliament was fighting, not to uphold the sanctity of any established constitution, but to prevent the establishment, by uncontested precedents, of such a constitution as would have been a permanent legal barrier to its interests. So a resolution was ultimately accepted in which the power of Convocation to bind anyone by its documents without parliamentary assent, the canons which it had issued, and the benevolence which it had granted, were all condemned.

The exemptions granted to Papists had led to the attack on Windebank, and the question of ship-money to the impeachment of Finch, as the chief agents in those transactions: and now that the canons had been condemned it was asked whether here too there had not been "a principal solicitor". It was the signal for the attack on Laud. Sir John Hotham proposed that he be proceeded against for treason. Pym agreed: and Grimstone pointed out that there were other offences besides the formulation of objectionable canons of which Laud was guilty. "The Archbishop", he said, "was the root and ground of all our miseries", who had promoted to places of trust Strafford,

Windebank, and Wren, " and all the other wicked bishops now in England ". The Scottish commissioners, too, denounced him as an incendiary between the two kingdoms. On December 18th both parties began proceedings against him. The message of the House of Commons was taken up to the Lords by Denzil Holles, and Laud was formally impeached of high treason, on charges to be formulated later by a committee set up for the purpose.

The Archbishop spoke a few words in his defence, amid interruptions from the Presbyterian peers, and then withdrew and was summoned back to kneel at the Bar. Then he was delivered over to the custody of Maxwell, from whose house Strafford had but recently been removed to the Tower. He was permitted, however, to go in Maxwell's company to Lambeth first, to collect some books and papers necessary to his defence. " I stayed at Lambeth till the evening ", he entered in his diary, " to avoid the gazing of the people. I went to evening prayer in my chapel. The psalms of the day and chapter 50 of Isaiah gave me great comfort. God make me worthy of it and fit to receive it. As I went to my barge, hundreds of my poor neighbours stood there and prayed for my safety and return to my house : for which I bless God and them."

For ten weeks Laud remained at Maxwell's house, while the Commons proceeded methodically with their work, petitions against episcopacy came in from the counties, and the King, deprived of his chief advisers, and without a party in the Parliament, toyed with plans for the evasion of the conditions which would be imposed upon him. Apart from the speeches and libels continually directed against him, he suffered little from interference, and only fretted at the expense of his detention, — it cost him twenty nobles a day, and his total bill came to £466 : 13 : 4. This expense was increased by a fine of £500 imposed upon him for having ordered the imprisonment of Sir Robert Howard for adultery, an action which, he commented drily on writing up his troubles a year later, was regarded as " a most unjust and illegal punishment. Whereas the Parliament (to the great honour of their justice be it spoken) have kept me in prison now full thirteen months and upward, and have not so much as brought up a particular charge against me ; and how much longer they will keep me, God knows." His confinement, however, gave little trouble. His petition to be allowed liberty to take the air was granted with restrictions : and in January he heard that his patient and moderate behaviour since his committal had so predisposed some of the Lords in his favour that their original animosity against him had been considerably softened. Mrs. Maxwell, too, seems to have regarded him with indulgent condescension. During his confinement, says Heylin, " he gained so much on the good opinion of the gentlewoman of the house, that she reported him to some of her gossips to be one of the goodest men, and most pious souls, but withal one of the silliest fellows to hold talk with a lady that ever she met with in all her life ". No woman, whether it was Lady Scudamore, or the Queen, or Mrs. Maxwell, seems ever to have been greatly impressed by Laud.

On February 24th, 1641, he again occupied the attention of Parliament. On that day, while Strafford answered the charges against him in the Lords, the Commons unanimously voted the impeachment of the Archbishop on fourteen general charges. Like Strafford, he was accused of endeavouring " to subvert the fundamental laws of the kingdom ". He was said to have promoted books and sermons against parliaments and the law, to have reduced the judges to dependence upon the executive, to have sold justice, and to have promulgated illegal canons. In religion, he was charged with usurping " a papal and tyrannical power ", of seeking to introduce Popery, of preferring men of unsound doctrines and silencing and persecuting the " learned and orthodox ", and of holding secret communication with the Court of Rome. And he was declared to have stirred up war between England and Scotland and sought to evade punishment by " subverting the rights of Parliament and the ancient course of parliamentary proceedings ". Two days later these articles were carried up to the Lords by Pym, Maynard, and Hampden, and there introduced with an explanatory speech by Pym. Laud was then summoned to the Bar, and, having given a general answer to each of the charges, was ordered to the Tower. He begged that he might remain at Maxwell's house till after the week-end, in order to make his necessary preparations, and this was granted : but his former privilege of taking the air was revoked.

On Monday, March 1st, Laud made his journey to the Tower. He wished to go in the evening, for the sake of privacy, but as

Maxwell's duties required his attendance elsewhere in the evening, midday was chosen instead, it being hoped that the citizens would then be at dinner. There were still, however, sufficient numbers to make the journey an ordeal for the Archbishop. " All was well ", he recorded, " till I passed through Newgate Shambles and entered into Cheapside. There some one 'prentice first halloo'd out ; more and more followed the coach, the number still increasing as they went, till by that time I came to the Exchange the shouting was exceeding great. And so they followed me with clamour and revilings, even beyond barbarity itself, not giving over till the coach was entered in at the Tower gate. Mr. Maxwell, out of his love and care, was exceedingly troubled at it, but (I bless God for it) my patience was not moved. I looked upon a higher cause than the tongues of Shimei and his children."

So Laud and Strafford were both out of the way in the Tower, although strict orders were given to prevent their meeting. Meanwhile Laud's old adversary enjoyed his brief period of consideration. On the same day a Committee for Religion was set up in the Lords, consisting of ten bishops and twenty lay peers, under the chairmanship of Williams, who also presided over, and entertained with his customary magnificence, a sub-committee of divines upon which low-church bishops and respectable Presbyterians were alike represented. As an avowed enemy of the now discredited Archbishop, Williams had at last returned to the influential position from which he had been deposed fifteen years earlier. His imprisonment had prevented him from sharing the responsibility for the canons, and he was soon to succeed Neile as Archbishop of York. He was, says Heylin, " more honoured by the Lords and Commons than ever any of his order, his person looked upon as sacred, his words deemed as oracles. And he continued in this height till, having served their turn against the Archbishop, he began sensibly to decline, and grew at last to be generally the most hated man of all the hierarchy."

Once in the Tower, under a charge of high treason, Laud was left to himself, almost neglected. Libels continued to be published against him, and caricatures to be circulated : and reports that he had already been hanged were believed in the country ; but the immediate necessity of dealing with a more formidable character diverted the attention of the Parliament from him and his sufferings. "That which is the great *remora* to all matters", wrote the Scotsman Robert Baillie, "is the head of Strafford. As for poor Canterbury, he is so contemptible that all cast him by out of their thoughts, as a pendicle at the Lieutenant's ear."[1]

For seven weeks from March 22nd, the trial of Strafford in Westminster Hall focused the attention of all observers: but it is not necessary here to enter into the details of that dramatic scene. Against the charges of treason preferred against him, Strafford defended himself, in spite of his broken health, with brilliant dexterity. Though they elicited their pledged secrets from Privy Councillors, though they twisted Strafford's words till they meant the reverse of what he had said, and devised new interpretations of old statutes, his accusers found themselves unable to prove any of the articles against him, and Strafford, confident that no statute could condemn him, kept them continually at bay, now turning their own arguments against them, now dividing his adversaries by appealing to the judicial capacity of the Lords, or by reminding them of the dangers with which they were investing an office to which many of them aspired. But in the end it was in vain: for if his guilt could not condemn him, his bold and resourceful genius made him too dangerous to be acquitted, and the very methods by which the King sought to preserve his minister, by increasing the fears and suspicions of the Commons, made his death more certain. There was an army in Ireland which the King would not disband, and another in England, mutinous for lack of the pay which it saw diverted to satisfy the Scots. If Strafford were permitted to escape, what desperate stroke might he not effect with such instruments as these? The King's daughter was being married to William of Orange, and the price of her hand could only be conjectured. The King and Queen were both seeking privately to detach prominent members from the Opposition by promises of office and other favours; and plots for Strafford's delivery from the Tower were continually reported. As long as Strafford lived to profit by these conspiracies and use these resources, the terrified parliamentary leaders saw nothing but incalculable peril, and the very skill with which he defended his innocence determined them to hasten his condemnation. If their charges were refuted, if

[1] Baillie, *Letters and Journals*, i. 309.

law was insufficient to destroy him, they would appeal to other arguments. " Stone-dead hath no fellow ", said the Earl of Essex grimly. " We give law to hares and deer ", said Oliver St. John, " because they be beasts of chase : it was never accounted either cruelty or foul play to knock foxes and wolves on the head as they can be found, because they be beasts of prey." So the Commons dropped the impeachment and proceeded by bill of attainder, to make a law for Strafford's death since they could not find one for it, while the London crowds petitioned them to make haste, and besieged the doors to intimidate the reluctant Lords into acquiescence.

On May 1st, when the attainder had not yet received its final reading in the Lords, the King once again sought to save his minister, this time by direct appeal. Summoning the Commons to the Upper House, he declared that he could not in conscience find the Earl guilty and would not suffer him to die : and therefore he suggested that they should proceed against him for misdemeanours, and they would be satisfied : for he was determined never to employ his services again. It was a tactical error, suggesting as it did that the King would dictate the decisions of the court, and Strafford himself protested that he wished those words had never been spoken. Laud too heard them with misgiving. " Indeed ", he wrote, " to what end should the King come voluntarily to say this, and there, unless he would have bid by it, whatever came ? And it had been far more regal to reject the bill when it had been brought to him (his conscience standing so as His Majesty openly professed it did) than to make this honourable preface, and let the bill pass after."

Certainly the intervention was neither determined nor effective. A week later, hustled by the Commons, intimidated by the mob, suspicious of the King, the Lords passed the attainder : and on May 10th, with the rabble on one side threatening to pull down Whitehall and murder the Queen, and Bishop Williams on the other conjuring his conscientious scruples away, Charles yielded, and " with the same penful of ink " signed both the death warrant of his ablest minister and a bill perpetuating the present parliament.

On the following night, being Tuesday, Strafford sent for the Lieutenant of the Tower and asked for an interview with Laud ; but he was told that this was impossible without permission from Parliament. "You shall hear what passeth between us," he promised, "for it is not a time now either for him to plot heresy, or me to plot treason." Still, however, the Lieutenant insisted on his orders, and urged Strafford to apply to Parliament for leave. "No," he answered, "I have gotten my despatch from them, and will trouble them no more. I am now petitioning an higher court, where neither partiality can be expected, nor error feared." Instead, he sent a message through Archbishop Ussher, who had been in attendance upon him in the Tower, requesting Laud to give him his prayers that night, and to be at his window next morning, to give him his blessing on his way to the scaffold. This Laud promised to do.

Next morning, as Strafford passed underneath the Archbishop's lodgings, Laud was informed, and came to the window. "There the Earl, bowing himself to the ground, 'My Lord,' said he, 'your prayers and blessing.' The Archbishop lifted up his hands and bestowed both, but, overcome with grief, fell to the ground *in animi diliquio*. The Earl, proceeding a little farther, bowed the second time, saying, 'Farewell, my Lord: God protect your innocency'". Later, to excuse his weakness in fainting at the critical moment, Laud declared that he hoped that, when his own execution came, "the world should perceive he had been more sensible of the Lord Strafford's loss than of his own", — which, he added, would be reasonable, since Strafford had been "more serviceable to the Church (he would not mention the State) than either himself or any of all the churchmen had been".[1] And he gave his final judgment of Strafford as "the wisest, the stoutest, and every way the ablest subject that his nation has bred these many years. The only imperfections which he had that were known to me were his want of bodily health, and a carelessness, or rather roughness, not to oblige any: and his mishaps in this last action were, that he groaned under the public envy of the nobles, served a mild and gracious prince who knew not how to be, or be made, great, and trusted false, perfidious, and cowardly men in the northern employment, though he had many doubts put to him about it."[2]

With the death of Strafford, Laud might well look upon his

[1] *A Brief Relation of the Answers, etc., of the Earl of Strafford*, 1646, pp. 98-9.
[2] Laud, *Works*, iii. 443.

own life as over. For him, as he once wrote, to live was to be at work, and in the execution of his huge task he had had but one ally upon whose willingness, capacity, and thoroughness he could equally rely. Now that ally had been removed when he was most needed, and, at the same time, his own work was being attacked and undone, and no one sought effectively to defend it. As yet, indeed, the destructive legislation of the Parliament had not reached the pace which it was to acquire, but a bill for the exclusion of bishops from all secular employment was under consideration, and the temper of all parties in both Houses showed that whatever of the Church was left, it would not be the Church of Laud. On the day of Strafford's execution, Dr. Cornelius Burges was pressing upon Parliament the secularisation of deans' and chapters' lands. Already in February an act legalising enclosures had been read. Laud's agents were either in custody or threatened with it, while their former victims were encouraged to prefer charges against them. In May, Sir Edward Dering suddenly thrust his " root and branch " bill upon an unprepared house of Commons. And in July Laud's instruments, the prerogative courts, were declared illegal and abolished.

Without support among the new power-holders, deprived alike of his authority and the instruments through which he had exercised it, Laud was indeed an insignificant figure, and the Parliament, its hands already full, showed no anxiety to waste time on the difficult task of proving the charges against him. Considering his age, they may have hoped that his death in the Tower would relieve them of that necessity : or they may even have been prepared to connive at his escape. The latter, at least, was Laud's opinion. For about this time he was visited in the Tower by Edward Pococke, his lecturer in Arabic at Oxford, whom he had sent to the East to prosecute his studies and collect coins and manuscripts for him. On his way back to England, Pococke had had an interview in Paris with Grotius, and Grotius, remembering perhaps how he had once escaped from the castle of Louvestein in a crate of books, urged Pococke to recommend a like expedient to Laud. After receiving the Archbishop's thanks for his services, which could not now be requited as he had intended, Pococke gave Grotius' message; but the Archbishop would not hear of it. " I am obliged to my good friend Hugo Grotius ", he replied, " for the care he has thus expressed for my safety, but I can by no means be persuaded to comply with the counsel he hath given me. An escape indeed is feasible enough, — yea, 'tis, I believe, the very thing which my enemies desire: for every day an opportunity for it is presented to me, a passage being left free, in all likelihood for this purpose, that I should endeavour to take advantage of it. But they shall not be gratified by me in what they appear to long for; for I am now nearly seventy years old, and shall I now go about to prolong a miserable life by the trouble and shame of flying? And were I willing to be gone, whither should I fly? Should I go into France, or any other popish country, it would be to give some seeming ground to that charge of Popery they have endeavoured with so much industry and so little reason to fasten upon me. But if I should get into Holland, I should expose myself to the insults of those sectaries there to whom my character is odious, and have every Anabaptist come and pull me by the beard. No, I am resolved not to think of flight, but, continuing where I am, patiently to expect and bear what a good and wise Providence hath provided for me, of what kind soever it shall be." [1]

So Laud stayed in the Tower, a helpless spectator of the events which he had done so much to provoke. The Homeric struggle was accompanied, too, by a sort of running Batrachomyomachia in the contemporary Grub Street, where artisans and apprentices did battle for their rival divinities. Freedom of the Press having at last arrived, the Puritan pamphleteers made the most of their opportunities, and while the speeches of the parliamentary leaders were issued, authorised or unauthorised, almost as fast as they were spoken, squibs and broadsheets supplied the less literate with a commentary on the Archbishop's altered circumstances. Sometimes he was "Fortune's Tennis-Ball", tossed from power to prison: sometimes he was depicted in mourning, with the Pope and Jesuits, for the failure of their common designs: sometimes his solitary nights were disturbed by the appearance of appropriate ghosts, — now Cardinal Wolsey, his alleged prototype: now Strafford, his accomplice in guilt: now Thomas Bensted, his most recent victim. From the retirement of his Cumberland estates, Archy Armstrong issued his volume of anti-prelatical "Dreams": in his chambers at Lincoln's Inn, the rehabilitated Prynne resumed his familiar trade: and the

[1] Twells, *Life of Pococke*, p. 84.

antithetical causes of Faith and Works, Grace and Free-Will, Geneva and Canterbury, were disputed in the lusty style of Billingsgate by Henry Walker the ironmonger and John Taylor the literary bargee. On one occasion, however, the freedom of the Press was regarded as having degenerated into licence: for Henry Walker, seeking to secure a wider publicity for his *Terrible Outcry against the Loitering, Exalted Prelates*, assumed the pseudonym of William Prynne. An offence so nearly entrenching upon blasphemy could not be allowed to pass unnoticed, and Walker was committed to prison by the orders of Parliament.

To this paper warfare Laud was incapable of rising superior. His mind had always fussed over insignificant trifles, and every pamphlet that came before his notice infuriated him by its misrepresentations. After Strafford's death, he wrote, all the attacks of all the libellers were concentrated upon himself. "Libels and ballads against me were frequently spread through the city and sung up and down the streets: and (I thank God for it) they were as full of falsehood as gall. Besides, they made base pictures of me, putting me into a cage, and fastening me to a post by a chain at my shoulder, and the like. And divers of these libels made men sport in taverns and alehouses, where too many were as drunk with malice as with the liquor they sucked in. Against which my only comfort was that I was fallen but into the same case with the prophet David."

But it was not only in libels and cartoons that the opponents of Laud expressed their thirst for revenge. Parliament was besieged with innumerable petitions and complaints from all the classes which his multifarious activities had alienated. The tedious recriminations of the religious were swelled by the more determinate protests of printers ruined by the censorship, patrons deprived of their advowsons, foreign congregations forced to conformity, merchants stung by his rasping rebukes in the Star Chamber, ecclesiastical landlords indignant at his veto on profitable lease-making, and country squires, thwarted in their endeavours to improve agriculture and increase its profits by imitating their fathers and adding acre to acre at the expense of parson or people. Among the various petitioners against the fallen Archbishop had been the City of Oxford, which preferred against him the now almost meaningless charge of treason for issuing proclamations in his own name, as Chancellor of the

University, to regulate the market there. This was a charge which Laud easily refuted, producing the actual proclamations issued by his predecessors as precedents: but it determined him to resign the office which he was no longer capable of fulfilling, and for which he felt that another was gaping. Waiting therefore till the charges of the city had been finally disposed of, and till his Vice-chancellor, whom he would not hand over to an unsympathetic master, had completed his term of office, in June 1641 he obtained leave from the King, and wrote to the University conveying his resignation of the chancellorship. The reply of the University was submissive, and the usual adulatory superlatives were missing from it, — already, last November, an abstract of their more extravagant eulogies had been collected by Laud's enemies for use in case of need,[1] — but their regrets at the separation were sincere, and they recapitulated with gratitude the many benefits which they owed to his rule: "as long as your manuscripts, the spoils of the East, adorn our library: as long as the Arabic lecture, endowed by you, is occupied: as long as those ancient coins, defenders and witnesses of the past, are exhibited: as long as a sterner discipline, improved morals, and the statutes which are the measure of them, flourish: as long as the arts are studied, and letters are both honoured and honourable, your chancellorship will always be felt by the present and remembered by the future generation".

The severance of his long tie with the University, where alone his achievements were respected and his departure regretted, must have been a considerable personal loss for Laud: and his isolation, emphasised first by the execution of his strongest ally, then by the loss of his most treasured office, was illustrated in a more intimate way a few months later by the death of his favourite servant, whose long and faithful connexion with him he more than once commemorates, and always with affection. "On Thursday, September 23rd, 1641," he records, "Mr. Adam Torless, my ancient, loving, and faithful servant, and then my steward, after he had served me full forty and two years, died, to my great both loss and grief. For all my accounts since my commitment were in his hands, and had he not been a very honest and careful man, I must have suffered much more than I did. Yet I suffered enough, besides the loss of his person, who was now become almost the

[1] *Cal. S.P. Dom.*, 1640–41, p. 253.

only comfort of my affliction and my age. So true it is that afflictions seldom come single."

Early next month still further evidence of isolation was forthcoming. The death of Sir Henry Marten left the position of Judge of the Prerogative Court vacant. This Laud had designed for Dr. Duck, who, as chancellor of the diocese of London, had been a zealous instrument of orthodoxy when orthodoxy was fashionable. Now, however, he did not wish to derive his office too exclusively from his dependence on a fallen patron, and, thinking that he had the reversion settled, he did not put in an appearance to receive it. Thereupon Laud tore up the instrument by which he had bestowed it upon Duck, and gave it instead to another. Duck was indignant, and joined the petitioners against the Archbishop : but his petition was dismissed by the Lords, and his defection resulted in the failure which it deserved. " This was one of the basest and most ungrateful parts ", complained the Archbishop, " that ever any man played me." Another applicant for the same post was Sir John Lambe, who also displayed a certain cooling of his former ardour in the cause of the Church. Having once deserted his benefactor Williams to enter the more promising service of Laud, he was perfectly ready, now that Laud's fortunes in their turn were sinking, to look for a safer vessel : and, pretending that Laud had already promised him Marten's place, he professed his eagerness to leave an employment in which his zeal had made him odious. In abject terms he protested that all the charges now brought against him had been caused by the Archbishop, whom he had too devotedly served. " They say I have another great fault ", he moaned ; " I was most favoured by Your Grace, I lay at your house, I counselled you into all those great enormities you have committed, and you were directed and ruled by me, etc. But they know you not that say this, for you would be ruled by nobody, nor communicate yourself to any that I know, nor make yourself any party at Court, but stood upon yourself. It may be it was your fault rather." [1] So Lambe protested his innocence, — but of what use, he whined, was innocence now ? whither should he now go for safety ? Whither, indeed, but to the Prerogative Court, the very place for discretion and experience such as his. Thither, however, this time-serving official was not to go : but after being harassed

[1] *S.P. Dom. Car. I.* 484, no. 62.

by the victims of his former persecution, fled to Oxford to the inglorious safety of the royal Court.

On October 23rd another blow was struck at Laud when, at the instance of Bishop Williams, his jurisdiction was sequestered from him and entrusted to his inferior officials until such time as his trial should be over. It was further ordered that, before awarding any of the benefices at his disposal, he should submit the names of his candidates to the Lords for their approval. With this order, however, Williams had secured his last triumph over Laud: for although he was soon afterwards nominated Archbishop of York, already the "root and branch" party was growing to such strength in the Commons that it was no longer possible for one party among the bishops to rise at the expense of another: for the whole order was sinking together. Already thirteen of them were under impeachment for their part in the making of the condemned canons: and although Williams was safely uninvolved in their guilt, in December twelve bishops, including himself, absented themselves from the House of Lords through fear of violence from the mob, and, in a protest to the King, declared that all legislation passed in their absence was invalid. At once Lords and Commons united against them. The old impeachment was dropped and a new process begun: the twelve bishops were accused of the now familiar offence of endeavouring to subvert the fundamental laws of the kingdom and the very being of Parliament: and that night ten of them, including Williams, were in the Tower, and the other two, on account of their extreme age, committed to the milder custody of Maxwell. The fall of Williams was greatly relished by the pamphleteers and caricaturists, who likened him to a decoy-duck, only released from his captivity in order that he might return thither with a larger following: and one cartoon, which represented him with military uniform over his episcopal robes, even brought a few moments' merriment to Laud amid his troubles, —"whether out of his great love to wit, or some other self-satisfaction which he found therein", says Heylin, "is beyond my knowledge". The impartial critic, who may scrutinise Laud's whole career in vain for some vestigial symptom of a sense of humour, may be permitted to resolve the question which his chaplain has judiciously left in doubt.

For another two years Laud remained in prison, untried.

Lord Holland once suggested that, in view of his long confinement, his hearing might be despatched: but Parliament was in no hurry. It was too busy with more pressing matters, — removing bishops from the House of Lords, countering royal manœuvres, seeking to establish control over the militia, and finally abolishing episcopacy and conducting the war. So Laud was left to compile his apologia, which he hoped to see published in English and Latin to vindicate himself to the world, to settle the application of his charities, and to refute in writing the speeches of Lord Saye in the House of Lords. Meanwhile many indignities were put upon him, which solitude and a naturally querulous disposition magnified. His arms, kept for the defence of his palace, were confiscated. All the profits of his archbishopric were seized by ordinance. His young dun horse was taken away by warrant. An order from the Lords reduced his servants to two, although he petitioned successfully to retain a cook and a butler above this quota. His palace at Lambeth was taken over by the Parliament and converted into a prison, and the man who was set over it, and was sent to Laud to demand the keys, was his former libeller and victim, Alexander Leighton; and although his library and other possessions were secured to him by order of the Lords, it was not long before these too were seized and sold, Leighton first (according to Laud) helping himself to what he wanted. As for his library, — it went to another notorious Puritan, Hugh Peters, the fanatical prophet of Independency, whom the advent of better times had brought back from America to be Cromwell's chaplain. Already Peters had suggested, and the Commons had considered, sending the Archbishop, together with Wren, to New England: and the delicious irony of this suggestion was not wasted on the wits of Puritanism, who published a pamphlet purporting to be Laud's petition against such a sentence.

But the most frequent source of embarrassment to Laud was the order whereby he was required to submit to the House of Lords the names of any candidates whom he wished to present to the benefices at his disposal. This order was often interpreted by the Lords as a command to present their nominees, and Laud had no alternative but acquiescence. For a time he acquiesced: but as their demands grew more radical, he had recourse to the one means of evasion which he possessed. By declining altogether to present, he could allow the right of presentation to lapse to the King, who was more likely to favour his candidate than that of the Parliament. This method had already succeeded when the Lords refused to agree to the appointment of Sir Thomas Roe's chaplain, Mr. Newstead, — although Mr. Newstead got little profit out of his ultimate nomination, as he was at once driven out by his new parishioners, — but in February 1643 a second attempt to use the same method led to a crisis which precipitated Laud's trial.

The immediate cause of this crisis was provided by a private request that the Archbishop should appoint a certain Mr. Edward Corbet, of Merton College, to the living of Chartham in Kent. Now Chartham happened to be a rich living, and Corbet happened to be a personal enemy of Laud: and Laud announced categorically that he would never submit to such an indignity. At the same time his determination was reinforced by a letter from the King commanding him to give Chartham to a certain Mr. Reading, or, if otherwise required by Parliament, to refuse to present. In this way the right of presentation would lapse to the King, who would use it as he pleased. To the King's letter Laud replied that he would do as required: and to all the demands of Parliament, whether orders or, as they later became, ordinances, his answer was always the same: — he had already bestowed livings worth £800 a year at their dictation, and in this instance he was bound by a promise to the King. In May, since orders and ordinances had failed, Parliament proceeded by a more direct method. On the 23rd, Laud had petitioned the Lords for maintenance, pointing out that " he hath neither land, lease, nor money: that the small store of plate which he had is long since melted down for his necessary support and expenses, caused by his present troubles: that his rents and profits are sequestered, and now all his goods taken from him, and no maintenance at all allowed him, insomuch that, if some friends of his had not in compassion of his wants sent him some little supply, he had not been able to subsist to this present ". To this plea the reply of the Lords was plain and categorical. Maintenance, they said, and the presentation of Corbet to Chartham were a single question: and when his petition was referred to the Commons, it was rejected. Already, on one of Laud's previous refusals, the Upper House had ordered that a conference be held with the Commons " about expediting the trial of the said Archbishop, and to consider how the jurisdiction and disposing of livings may be sequestered out of his power and disposing ".

May 27th had been the date of Laud's last refusal to present Corbet to Chartham. Four days later he was roused at four o'clock in the morning by the arrival of a search-party with a warrant from the House of Commons to seize all the letters and papers of the prisoners in the Tower, ostensibly for the purpose of discovering the extent of delinquents' estates. To make the indignity more pointed, just as Leighton had been put in charge over Lambeth Palace, so the official authorised by a committee of both Houses to carry off Laud's papers was his old enemy William Prynne. Since his return from Mount Orgueuil and the reversal of his sentences of 1634 and 1637, Prynne had been busy pamphleteering in the seclusion of his chambers, and, apart from legal and political writings, *The Antipathy of the English Lordly Prelacy both to Regal Monarchy and Civil Unity*, condemning every bishop from St. Augustine of Canterbury to the present day, and *A New Discovery of the Prelate's Tyranny*, directed more exclusively against Laud, had swelled the corpus of his collected works. Now he emerged to play a more direct part in the final stage of the Archbishop's undoing.

Prynne arrived at the Tower with ten musketeers at his heels, and, disposing the others at strategic positions on the stairs, entered Laud's room accompanied by three of them, with muskets cocked. The Archbishop was still in bed, as were his servants, and Prynne at once set about rifling his pockets, while two of his servants rushed in, half dressed, to discover the matter. Laud demanded a sight of Prynne's warrant, which was produced, and then got up from bed, put on some of his clothes, and waited till the search should be over. This lasted till after nine o'clock, and then Prynne went away with twenty-one bundles of papers which Laud had prepared for his defence, the two letters from the King concerning Chartham and other benefices, the Scottish liturgy with the directions accompanying it, and the private diary which Laud had kept since his first entry into St. John's College as an undergraduate. When Prynne confiscated also his book of private devotions, the Archbishop begged him at least to leave him that : but it was in vain. Prynne, he complained, "must needs see what passed between God and me: a thing, I think, scarce ever offered to any Christian". Before making his departure, Prynne ransacked a trunk at the Archbishop's bedside, in which he found £40 in money, which he left, and a bundle of gloves, which he examined so curiously that Laud offered him a pair as a gift. This Prynne refused: but Laud assured him that "he might take them, and need fear no bribe, for he had already done me all the mischief he could, and I asked no favour from him. So he thanked me, took the gloves, bound up my papers, left two sentinels at my door, which were not dismissed till the next day noon, and went his way." Prynne was evidently much elated with his haul, and thought that he would soon have the necessary material to prove the charge of treason, long dormant for lack of evidence: for a few days later a Puritan preacher in the Tower declared "that Mr. Prynne had found a book in my pocket which would discover great things". The newly discovered material, however, did not quite come up to his expectations: for in August the Archbishop was told that his enemies were still baffled by lack of evidence. Thereupon Prynne had recourse to another argument. When Laud had visited Lambeth with Maxwell, after his committal by the House of Lords, Prynne declared that he had taken the opportunity to burn all his secret papers. This Laud denied. "Mr. Maxwell", he retorted, "was by command of the honourable House to be by me all the while: and he was not one minute from me, and knows I did not burn any one paper."[1] Another version of the story is given by Burnet, who states that, when his impeachment was brought to the Bar of the Lords, Laud sent Dr. Warner, Bishop of Rochester, with the keys of his closet and cabinets to destroy or secure all incriminating documents. For three hours, he says, Warner was busy at his task, until, upon Laud's committal to Maxwell, a messenger was sent to seal up his closet, from which all the most vital evidence had already been subtracted.[2] It is not easy to reconcile this story with Laud's own version: for if the Parliament's messenger had sealed up Laud's closet before the arrival of Laud and Maxwell, Laud would hardly have been permitted to ransack his study and take important papers away: while if Laud and Maxwell arrived first, the closet would hardly

[1] *Breviate of the Life of William Laud*, p. 24; Laud, *Works*, iii. 267.
[2] *History of his Own Time* (ed. Airy), i. 52.

have been worth sealing whether the Bishop of Rochester had been there or not. Nevertheless, Burnet's story is circumstantial, and explains how an original of Magna Carta came into his own possession from the son of Bishop Warner's executor. It was, of course, useful for Burnet to give such an explanation. For there were some who did not hesitate to suspect him of having acquired the relic by less unexceptionable methods, during his free researches among the public records.

The seizure of Laud's papers was quickly followed by the solution of the Chartham problem. On June 10th, an ordinance was passed finally depriving the Archbishop even of the limited control of his own patronage which he had hitherto exercised, and transferring it to his Vicar-General, Sir Nathaniel Brent, who, turned into a bitter enemy by Laud's discovery of his malpractices at Merton College, was now a reliable parliamentarian, and, in Wood's phrase, " ran altogether with the rebellious rout ".

Meanwhile Prynne and the committee which managed the evidence against him were at work. Ten new charges were gradually formulated, and the prosecution eventually based its case under three general headings : — an endeavour to subvert the fundamental laws and introduce arbitrary government, an endeavour to subvert the established religion and introduce popish superstition and idolatry, and an endeavour to subvert the rights of Parliament and the ancient course of parliamentary proceedings. Terrified by rumours of Catholic plots and alliances, Parliament was particularly sensitive on the second subject, and in August vain efforts were made to induce Sir Kenelm Digby to reveal the secret correspondence between Laud and Rome which was firmly believed to have existed. Soon afterwards, Prynne used his new material and his old imagination to inflame these suspicions, and produced, in August, *Rome's Masterpiece*, an attempt to connect the Archbishop with the imaginary popish plot " detected " by Andreas ab Habernfeld, in September *The Treachery and Disloyalty of Papists to their Sovereigns in Doctrine and Practice*, and in November *The Popish Royal Favourite*. Meanwhile Parliament had entered into military alliance with the Scots, and in September and October both Houses had accepted the Solemn League and Covenant, for whose consummation a more fitting sacrifice could hardly be offered up than the enemy alike of both kingdoms and their now common religion.

It was on October 24th that Laud received a copy of the ten additional charges, and knew that his trial was now not far off: but still it was a slow and dilatory business. His first appearance in the House of Lords was made on November 13th: but the unreadiness of both prosecution and defendant caused continual postponements: the impeachment was further deferred by another case in which Laud was required as a collateral defendant: and Prynne's time was also occupied by his prosecution of Nathaniel Fiennes for the surrender of Bristol to the royalists. The prosecution of the Archbishop had been entrusted to a committee, and one of the lawyers who was required to serve on it was Bulstrode Whitelocke: but Whitelocke declined to attend, protesting "that it was not fit for me to appear in it against one to whom I had been beholden for my education". This did not satisfy the chairman, who reported the refusal to the House. Whitelocke, however, defended himself to the Commons, declaring "that the Archbishop did me the favour to take a special care of my breeding in St. John's College in Oxford, and that it would be disingenuous and ungrateful for me to be personally instrumental to take away his life, who was so instrumental for the bettering of mine", and was discharged.[1] Others, however, were less scrupulous about past favours, — notably Sir Nathaniel Brent, who, though not a member of the committee, was particularly zealous as a witness against the Archbishop. Nevertheless, the composition of the committee was of little moment for all the proceedings were directed and animated by the tireless ingenuity and industry of one member of it, Prynne himself, who, it was alleged, kept a regular school of instruction to ensure that witnesses acted the parts which he had appointed for them. Laud, on the other hand, suffered from many inconveniences. His petitions for counsel, time, and a copy of the charges were granted; but the Committee of Sequestrations refused to allow him means out of his forfeited estate to fee his counsel, Glyn declaring that he could plead *in forma pauperis*: of the twenty-one bundles of papers which Prynne had removed, promising their return within three days, only three were ever restored, and the most Laud could obtain was permission to have the others copied at his own expense: and, in spite of several petitions, the prosecution would not distinguish between the charges of treason and those of mis-

[1] Whitelocke, *Memoirs*, p. 75.

demeanour. As, until the passage of the Trial of Treasons Act, defendants on charges of treason suffered from serious restrictions, which limited their evidence and discredited their witnesses, this was particularly disadvantageous, and the Archbishop's counsel declared plainly that he might as well have no counsel at all, unless the articles were distinguished.

On January 16th, 1644, Laud again appeared before the Lords: but again, being unprepared, he was allowed to return to the Tower. A week later he returned. The Thames was frozen over, and he was conveyed to Westminster in the Lieutenant of the Tower's coach, guarded by twelve warders with halberds, and followed by a derisive crowd. To all the charges he gave a single plea of "Not Guilty"; and to the thirteenth article, which concerned the Scottish wars, he pleaded the benefit of the Act of Oblivion since passed, — a plea which was construed by his accusers as an admission that he required it. After this, Prynne asked for more time, and on March 12th the trial began in earnest.

It is unnecessary to deal in detail with Laud's trial; for his whole life was objected against him. From the innumerable petitions sent in by the Archbishop's enemies and victims in every class, Prynne constructed a tedious series of charges which occupied him from March to the end of July: and to every charge Laud offered a patient and detailed reply. Of Prynne's malice there can be no doubt. That he tampered with witnesses was not doubted even by contemporaries — "The Archbishop is a stranger to me," one of them declared, "but Mr. Prynne's tampering about the witnesses is so palpable and foul that I cannot but pity him and cry shame of it"; [1] and that he tampered with evidence is proved by his editing of the Archbishop's diary. Nor was the tribunal before which the trial took place any less partial. The House of Lords was no longer the judicial assembly before which Strafford had pleaded. The bishops had long been excluded. The royalist peers had followed the King to Oxford at the outbreak of the war. And on the failure of the peace party in August 1643, still more had withdrawn from Westminster. By now, instead of the hundred odd peers, of all political parties, who had attended important sessions at the beginning of the Parliament, an average of only twelve to sixteen members was present: of those, too, who listened to Prynne's charges in the

[1] Laud, *Works*, iv. 51.

morning, few stayed to hear Laud's answers in the afternoon : and only the Speaker, Lord Grey of Wark, was present throughout the trial. In truth, people had lost all interest in Laud, his ideals, his past government, his present sufferings. " Canterbury every week is before the Lords for his trial ", Robert Baillie wrote to a friend in Scotland ; " but we have so much to do, and he is a person now so contemptible, that we take no notice of his progress." [1]

In addition to the vindictive hostility of his accusers, and the apathetic hostility of his judges, the very procedure adopted at the trial operated against the Archbishop. All morning, until two o'clock, the prosecution preferred the charges against him, and he was only given two hours in which to prepare his answers : after which one or more of the committee replied, and then, at about 7.30, the prisoner was rowed back to the Tower, " full of weariness, and with a shirt as wet to my back with sweat as the water could have made it, had I fallen in ". Nevertheless, even Prynne had to admit that he made " as full, as gallant, and as pretty a defence of so bad a case . . . as was possible for the wit of man to invent ", and the prosecution had to resort, as in Strafford's case, to a new interpretation of the law of treason. So Sergeant Wilde told Herne, one of Laud's counsel, " that all the misdemeanours, put together, do, by way of accumulating, make many grand treasons ". To which Herne replied, " I never understood before this time that two hundred couple of black rabbits would make a black horse ".

After the long trial was over, Laud asked the Lords for leave to make a general recapitulation of his whole defence, which was granted, and September 2nd fixed for its hearing. At the same time, he was informed that the House of Commons had agreed that he should enjoy the benefit of the Act of Oblivion which he had pleaded, so that the Scottish business was no longer to be charged against him. On September 2nd, therefore, when he set out once again for the House of Lords, the omens seemed to be in his favour. But whatever hopes he may have entertained were soon damped. " So soon as I came to the Bar ", he records, " I saw every Lord present with a new thin book in folio, in a blue coat." He had heard that very morning of William Prynne's latest literary venture, which was now printed by order of

[1] Baillie, *Letters and Journals*, ii. 139. [2] *State Trials*, iv. 599.

the House of Commons, and he knew that the thin blue folio was *A Breviate of the Life of William Laud, Archbishop of Canterbury*.

Laud had every reason to be "a little troubled" at the publication of this book. It was not only another document to swell the charge against him ; it was a cruel exposure of his most intimate life. For if ever he had revealed his inmost character, with all its pathetic weaknesses and limitations, it was in the private diary which, kept with such punctilious regularity, had been intended for no eyes but his own. Now, filched out of his pocket, it had been annotated and edited for an unsympathetic public by his most inveterate enemy. Nor was it a sufficient triumph for Prynne that he had been authorised to expose to the world all the private weaknesses of his great enemy, — the petty fears, the ridiculous obsessions, the minute observances, the insignificant omens, the superstitious dreams, to which he had attached such importance, — and to shed a revealing light upon Laud's early career, with its methods of insinuation and intrigue. With complete unscrupulousness, he had emended, glossed, and misinterpreted the text, in order to give a less favourable picture of its author. Any passage that might reflect credit on Laud was studiously omitted, and sentences were stopped short rather than permit the reader to reach their favourable conclusions. Where Laud had concealed his meaning by an abbreviation, Prynne had provided a damning explanation. The Latin passages were mistranslated to suit his purposes ; and where the text had been destroyed by fire, Prynne had supplied it from his own imagination. And sometimes he had enlivened the narrative by his own additional information, as when he informed the reader that Buckingham had made Laud "put off his gown and cassock, and dance before him like a hobgoblin, to make him merry". The extent of these textual emendations was not known till after Prynne's death, when Sheldon recovered the original diary, and even Heylin used the *Breviate* as an indisputable authority ; but even with Prynne's alterations, and even among Laud's enemies, there were some who drew from the *Breviate* a more favourable opinion of the author than of the editor. The Puritan Henry Robinson, who had already advocated religious toleration in a pamphlet on *Liberty of Conscience*, declared that Laud's diary showed "eminent signs of a moral, noble, pious mind, according to such weak principles as he had been bred up in (his own persecuting disposition disenabling him from being instructed better) ", and added, to the horror and indignation of Prynne, that he had been unable to detect any such piety or ingenuousness in the whole career of its editor.[1] To Laud, who despaired of the survival of the original to vindicate him, the publication was the culmination of Prynne's enormities. " For this Breviate of his," he wrote, " if God lend me life and strength to end this [history] first, I shall discover to the world the base and malicious slanders with which it is fraught."

Nevertheless, whatever the justice of it, there can be no doubt that Prynne's publication was a timely and effective piece of propaganda. The legal charges against Laud had been conspicuously unsuccessful. There was nothing in them that could be proved treason, and there was a great deal which could be shown to be malicious and unfounded. The expedient of cumulative treason had failed against Strafford, and could hardly succeed against Laud. Indeed, it is clear that Laud's real offence could not be defined in relation to the existing constitution : for it had consisted in demonstrating that the Reformation, since it had taken place without disturbing the ecclesiastical constitution otherwise than by the rejection of the papal supremacy, could be practically reversed with as little disturbance, provided the Roman authority was not restored. To make a legal charge against him, his enemies had had to pretend that he had envisaged such a restoration ; but this could not be proved. The offence, however, remained : and if it had been committed within the limits of the law, that only convinced the Puritans that a constitution capable of such different interpretations must be more exactly defined, and must be defined by their authority before it was defined by Laud's example. The difficulty of proving Laud to have broken the law did not remove the necessity of proving him guilty.

In this transition from legal to revolutionary methods, Prynne's *Breviate* played a useful part. Already the victory of Marston Moor in July, and the increasing influence in English politics of the Scots,[2] had driven the parliamentary party to adopt a more

[1] Quoted in Prynne, *A Fresh Discovery of some Prodigious New Wandering-blazing Stars*, 1645, p. 39. On Robinson see Firth, " An Anonymous Tract on Liberty of Conscience ", in *English Historical Review*, ix. 715.

[2] The influence of the Scots on Parliament's attitude towards Laud is emphasised by the author of *A Brief Relation of the Death and Sufferings of the . . . Archbishop of Canterbury* (Oxford, 1644), and by Hobbes (*Behemoth*, in *Works*, ed. Molesworth, vi. 254).

bellicose attitude: and now, when the impeachment of the Archbishop was foundering on the forms of law, Prynne had abandoned his legal formalities for a psychological appeal, and was representing the Archbishop as a self-confessed intriguer, now currying favour with the hated Buckingham, now plotting the extrusion of Williams and Abbot, now promoting the contemptible Windebank, now receiving offers of a cardinalate from Rome, now crowing over the elevation of Juxon, now shuddering at the prospect of a parliament; and lest these suggestive entries might be overlooked by the reader, who had learnt the advisability of skipping much of Prynne's literary productions, the words "Note this", in capital letters, were placed in the margin wherever a particularly damning entry occurred in the text. Everywhere the book excited great interest: nor could many readers, at such a time, review it with the impartiality of the Independent Henry Robinson. Besides the peers whom Laud saw with their copies in their hands, Puritans throughout the country explored with relish the dark secrets of their old enemy. A week later we learn of its reaction on Ralph Josselin, the Vicar of Olney in Bucks, a place afterwards to be made famous by the evangelical ministrations of John Newton. Josselin was a pious Puritan, who, having already reached the conclusion that he was predestined by God to eternal salvation, was continually finding corroborative evidence for this comfortable conviction, even in the most trivial incidents, as when a bee-sting on the nose did not prove fatal. The new book provided another such confirmation. "In a Breviate of Archbishop Laud's life", he recorded with complacency, "I find how the strings of his leg brake without any stepping awry. Lord, how many sad wrenches have I had in my walking, and yet Thou hast preserved me!"[1]

Thus, although the legal charge had broken down, and was effectively disposed of both by Laud, in his recapitulation, and by his counsel in the following month, his enemies did not relax their hostility. On October 22nd, his room in the Tower was again searched for incriminating documents, and, when that failed, appeal was made, as in Strafford's case, to the people. From the streets and the pulpits the death of the Archbishop was demanded, and petitions to the Parliament required the execution

[1] Ralph Josselin's Diary (Camden Soc., 1908), p. 18.

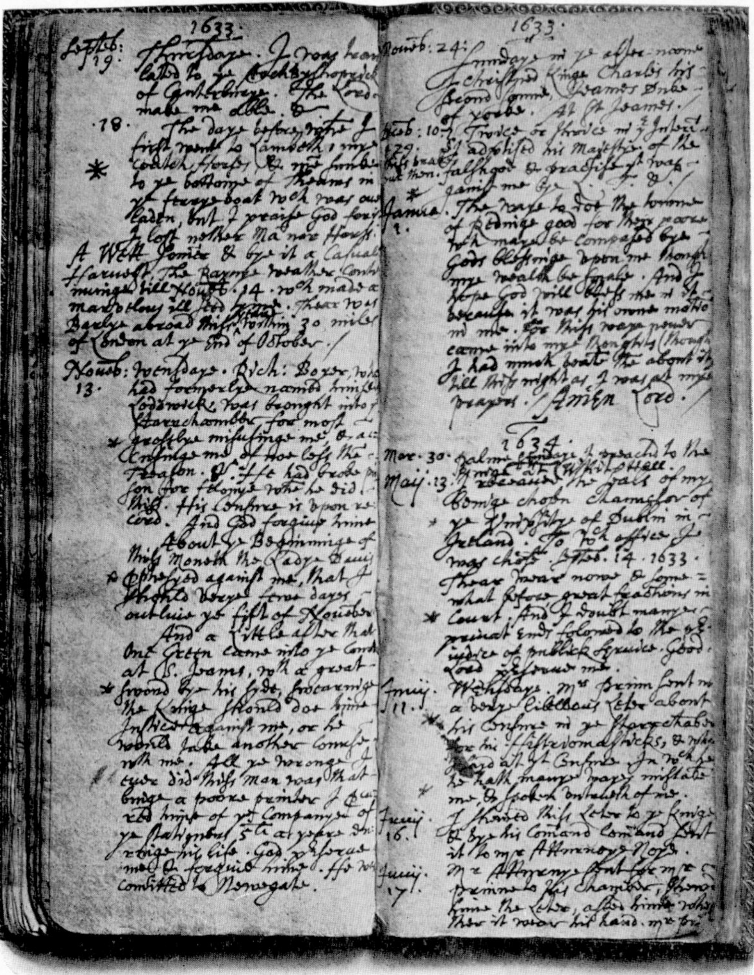

ARCHBISHOP LAUD'S DIARY

of both Laud and Wren. On November 2nd, Laud was summoned to appear before the Commons, and was acquainted with their intention to proceed by ordinance of attainder, unless he could satisfy them of his innocence. His arguments, produced on the 11th, were considered inadequate, and on the 16th the ordinance, passed by the Commons, was sent up to the Lords. There for a while it stuck: for the Lords, even in their attenuated condition, were still mindful of their judicial capacity, or at least of their dignity and independence, now the more valued since it was but a shadow. Next week, however, the intransigent spirit of the parliamentary party was shown by the humiliating conditions offered to the King at Uxbridge, which would have reduced the King to an agent of Parliament, and which excepted fifty-eight persons by name, of whom Laud was of course one, from the general amnesty. On the 28th, Strode threatened the Lords with mob-violence unless they hastened to pass the ordinance. Some show of resistance was made by the Upper House on receiving this message: but the Lords had already ceased to exercise independent authority, and their resistance was continued only long enough to show that they were still jealous of their dignity. As a method of yielding with decorum, they proposed a conference, which took place on January 2nd, 1645: and there the Commons disclaimed all intention of being bound by statute. If Laud was not guilty of treason by statute, they declared, he was guilty by common law: and in any case, he could be made guilty by ordinance. Two days later the Lords acquiesced, and the ordinance was passed.

Then Laud played his last, hopeless card. He produced the royal pardon which had been drawn up, nearly two years before, at the instance of Hyde, and sent to him when his trial was known to be imminent. It was rejected at once, — indeed, he could never have imagined otherwise, and had accepted it only as an ineffective testimonial that he was not forgotten by his master. Even his request to suffer death by the axe instead of by hanging, though supported by the Lords, was rejected without a division by the Commons. Ultimately, however, it was granted. His request to be attended on the scaffold by three clergymen of his own choice was also refused, and two reliable Puritan ministers were appointed by the Commons to accompany the Archbishop's chaplain.

On January 10th, Laud was led to the block on Tower Hill, — a scene upon whose details only professional hagiographers have any cause to linger. He preached his farewell sermon in the old, affected style of Lancelot Andrewes, with its subdivisions, its quotations, and its allusions: and then, after being subjected to some petulant theological heckling by the Irish Presbyterian, Sir John Clotworthy, he laid his head on the block, and the executioner removed it with the first blow. On his way to execution it had been observed that he maintained his usual high colour, so that some suspected him of using paint: but when his head was lifted up, white and lifeless, these suggestions were satisfactorily disposed of. His body was buried in the church of All Hallows, Barking, — a royalist clergyman, Thomas Fletcher, being discovered, who was willing to use the forbidden prayer-book for the ceremony.[1] After the Restoration, it was exhumed and reinterred in the chapel of St. John's College, Oxford.

When Laud went to the scaffold, he had already survived his authority by four years, and the will to exercise it by five. His agents were already scattered, his instruments destroyed. Bramhall, "the Irish Canterbury", had fled to France. Goffe, his agent for the Netherlands, had turned to Rome. His chaplain, Peter Heylin, and his casual amanuensis, John Berkenhead, had fled to Oxford to become the journalists of neo-royalism. Only Maxwell, at the peril of his life, clung to his post and his opinions, although not in the sphere where Laud had set him; and the fury of his fellow-countrymen pursued him when they had almost forgotten Laud. "Mr. Maxwell of Ross", wrote Baillie, just after Marston Moor, "has printed at Oxford so desperately malicious an invective against our assemblies and presbyteries, that, however I could hardly consent to the hanging of Canterbury himself, or of any Jesuit, yet I could give my sentence freely against that unhappy liar's life." [2] As for Laud's foundations, they fared no better. St. Paul's, whose restoration had begun with such pomp, remained half-built and neglected, while Laud was accused of extorting contributions for its repair, and Inigo Jones impeached for

[1] *Cal. S.P. Dom.*, 1663–4, p. 320.
[2] Baillie, *Letters and Journals*, ii. 208.

the demolition of St. Gregory's which it had entailed. It was to become the stable for Cromwell's horses, and the scaffolding was to be removed and sold to find pay for Cromwell's soldiers, before the building itself was destroyed by the Great Fire. Even the endowments of Laud's Arabic lectureship were seized, together with the rest of his estate, after his death, and it took two years before the intercession of Selden and Langbaine secured the restoration of Pococke to his position and his emoluments.

The reversal of Laud's policy, in so far as that policy had importance, was final, and only in the minds of pious ecclesiastics has it ever enjoyed a resurrection. Even when he seemed most successful, his success was partial and precarious wherever it was of significance, as was attested by his enemies; for they charged him with his failures as well as his success. Plurality and non-residence, said the Puritans, were characteristic vices of the Laudian clergy: but who had been more determined to end them than Laud? The poverty of the lower clergy was made a feature of his rule, and from his own diocese of Canterbury came repeated complaints of the reduced value of livings, which was charged to his account.[1] But in fact the improvement of the economic position of the poorer clergy was one of his most constant objectives, and he set himself, by punishment and persuasion, by the old legal forms and the new legal courts, to recover the impropriations that had been annexed by secular landlords. Where persuasion succeeded with Lord Scudamore and Lady Byron, a decree in the law courts and negotiation with the tithe-owners was used at Shrewsbury,[2] and elsewhere Laud's methods were more summary. When he increased the stipend of one poor minister, and Sir Arthur Haselrigg came and protested that it was a lay-fee in his possession, the Archbishop, he complained, replied "in a great rage" that "he hoped ere long not to leave so much as the name of a lay-fee in England".[3] When the forms and ceremonies and devotional paraphernalia of Laudian worship were revived at the Restoration, this more significant item of his policy, along with his opposition to enclosures and the rest of his social programme, was quietly dropped, and the instruments which might have enforced it were not revived. The Church

[1] See *Proceedings in Kent, 1640* (Camden Soc., 1861), *passim*.

[2] *S.P. Dom. Car. I.* 474, no. 43.

[3] *Cal. S.P. Dom.*, 1641–3, p. 547.

was readmitted only on condition that it dropped the policy which had made it a formidable social organ, and the continual friction, attested by continual petitions, between squires and parsons in the early seventeenth century, was followed by the halcyon agreement between the two, which followed the complete triumph of the one, in the eighteenth century. Nor was the political Church of Laud revived any more than the social. When Sheldon tacitly renounced the right of the clergy to tax themselves, he made it impossible for the Church to support the Government in a policy which the Parliament would not sanction. And Laud's political ambitions of "purifying" the administration by the advancement of clergymen to high office had little appeal to an administration which had a healthy distrust of clergymen and a sound appreciation of official perquisites. The precedent of Juxon was not to be followed in the juntos of Danby and Walpole: and the elevation of Bishop Robinson of Bristol as Lord Privy Seal in 1711 is interesting only as an engaging anachronism.

The posthumous history of Laud, in these circumstances, has been diverting. The epigoni of the Laudian divines, — the generation of their chaplains, who, after eighteen years spent an-hungering in the wilderness, were admitted again, in 1660, to the fleshpots of the Establishment, had learnt a useful lesson: and although they extolled the virtues and professed the opinions of their martyr, they were too discreet to imitate his example. Their attitude towards the Government and the governing classes was discreetly negative. Constrained to non-intervention, they preached non-resistance and practised non-criticism: and in the panegyrics which they offered to the memory of Laud, while dwelling with relish on those of his virtues which remained fashionable, — his orthodoxy, his loyalty, and his persecution of the less formidable sectaries, — they judiciously avoided emphasising those departments of his activity which lacked appeal to their new masters, the gentry and merchants of England. So for a generation Laud was the mascot of the restored Church: and then, when the Revolution, following so soon upon the case of the seven bishops, displayed the hollowness of its imagined strength, the Non-jurors carried him away with them into the wilderness.

In the eighteenth century he remained there: and Whigs and

Tories, sceptics and divines (as far as there was any difference between these various professions) were substantially agreed that he was not worth bringing out. Dr. Johnson, who professed such zeal for the Established Church and admitted a curious sentimentality in the matter of monasteries, read Laud's diary: but he forbore to make any comment upon its author;[1] and historians, whose duty compelled them not to appear ignorant of his existence, passed him over with perfunctory deprecation. Bolingbroke, in his *Letters on History*, dismissed him in a parenthesis as one "who had neither temper nor knowledge of the world enough to be entrusted with the government of a private college"; and Hume, while admitting that "his errors were the most excusable of all those which prevailed during that zealous period", ascribed his fall to lack of perspicacity on the part of his opponents, who failed to understand "that the very insignificancy of these ceremonies recommended them to the superstitious prelate, and made them appear the more peculiarly sacred and religious, that they could serve no other purpose in life".

From this comfortable backwater of benevolent contempt Laud was again brought out into the turmoil of partisan strife by the next century, which replaced the classical historiography of Hume by the political invective of Whig writers, and the fat slumbers of the eighteenth-century Church by the quaint foibles of the Oxford Movement. To the reputation of Laud the interpretation of the former school was damaging, that of the latter disastrous. For if the Whig historians introduced a new criterion into historical interpretation when they measured the politics of the seventeenth by the constitution of the early nineteenth century, it was at least an historical criterion: and if they insensibly judged the politics of Laud by political standards not admitted in his time, and to the old charge of imprudence added a new imputation of illegality, the new paladins of the Church,—men not unfamiliar with the intricacies of Byzantine theology,

[1] *i.e.* except his curious verdict in *The Vanity of Human Wishes*:

> Nor deem, when Learning her last prize bestows,
> The glitt'ring eminence exempt from foes;
> See, when the vulgar 'scapes, despis'd or aw'd,
> Rebellion's vengeful talons seize on Laud.
> From meaner minds, though smaller fines content
> The plunder'd palace or sequester'd rent,
> Mark'd out by dang'rous parts, he meets the shock,
> And fatal Learning leads him to the block.

nor unsympathetic with the remote fancies of the cloister — introduced theological canons into historical studies, and defended Laud against charges of violating the constitution and destroying intellectual liberty, by protesting that he had participated in the revelations of Keble and Pusey. That the Oxford Movement had its material causes, and that these causes bore some resemblance to the material causes of the Laudian counter-Reformation, no one, I think, would deny. Like the Caroline divines, the Tractarians viewed with horror the disposal by secular tribunals — parliaments and royal commissions — of ecclesiastical property. But while one was a social and practical, the other was a clerical and contemplative movement. To the Oxford Reformers the Church was not an organ of human society but a divine institution to be preserved from political changes in order that it might devote itself exclusively to spiritual things. If Laud represented Martha, Newman was Mary: while one sought to reverse the economic changes of the Reformation by the revival of a rich political Church, the other sought to escape from the aesthetic and intellectual accompaniments of the Industrial Revolution by piously wasting time in the innocent but uninformative pursuits of hagiography and martyrology. That one of the newly discovered saints and martyrs should have been Laud is pleasantly ironical: and there can be few prospects more entertaining to the profane historian than that of Anglo-Catholic divines threading their funambulatory course among sublime theological hypotheses, and claiming to follow in the wake of a restless, practical bureaucrat, "that little active wheel", as a hostile contemporary called Laud, "that set all the rest on work by his active motion".[1] Nevertheless, this is a prospect which frequently confronts us. We find the organiser of a lusty political Church, resolutely circumscribed by the limits and authority of the State, "historically" depicted by those to whom a Church is not a functional part of society at all, but the custodian of apocalyptic doctrines; and we are told that prosperous landlords and business men (a class not usually prone to thin-spun intellectual perplexities) rose in rebellion against him and voted his death in Parliament, because they were unable to endorse his metaphysical findings.

Thus Laud has had his defenders against the charges of Macaulay and Hallam: but these defenders have been clergymen,

[1] D'Ewes, *Journal* (ed. Notestein), p. 400.

who have confined their interest in their hero to those aspects of his career which they can understand, and have embedded him more deeply in the ecclesiastical forms in which they found him. He entertained the correct Catholic doctrine of the Mysteries: he enhanced the dignity of the Cloth, — these, in their eyes, constitute a sufficient claim to greatness. Martyrdom, too, lends its peculiar lustre, — for martyrs do not die, and martyrologies are not written, in vain. So his clerical eulogists feel themselves suffused with a glowing spiritual complacency as they record his lasting achievements, — the official retention of a Catholic mythology: the correct posture of the communion table: copes, mitres, and perfunctory genuflexions. "Laud saved the English Church", Canon Mozley wound up his panegyric. "That anyone of Catholic predilections can belong to the English Church is owing, so far as we can see, to Laud." To Laud himself, however, the survival of insignificant ceremonies at the expense of the policy which they represented would have appeared rather a mockery than an achievement.

Thus Laud failed: his failure was final: and the formal relics of his policy which are preserved in churches and pointed out by the religious as proof of his ultimate success are about as authentic, and as important, as the more tangible relics of other saints and martyrs. Our final judgment of his character, therefore, will not be determined by this illusory triumph, but by the difference between his aim and his achievement, which is more complex than either liberal propagandists or high-Anglican ecclesiastics are disposed to allow. Many writers have been tempted to digress from their immediate topic in order to dismiss Laud in an epigram: but between his grandiose design and its calamitous event the gulf is too vast for so delicate a bridge. What single definition can embrace his comprehensive social ideal and his narrow-minded application of it: his tolerant theology and his intolerant methods: his huge efforts and their tenuous results: the social justice which he advocated and the savage punishments which he inflicted? Yet the ideal and the practical, in Laud's policy, cannot be treated apart, for his ideal was only expressed in his practice — "Thorough" is not the motto of a doctrinaire — and his practice, though shaped by an ideal, was plainly inspired by his acute appreciation of actual conditions. A modern historian has described Laud as "the one second-rate Englishman who has exercised a wide influence upon the history of the world": [1] but even this judgment (occurring two pages after an account of Laud's essentially second-rate but widely influential patron Buckingham) is parsimonious of information as well as of language. For wherein does the quality of second-rateness consist? In comprehension or in execution? In method or design? If it is in failure to appreciate the aspirations of the time, what when there are two conflicting sets of aspirations? Laud was certainly more sensible than most of his contemporaries of one, and that the less articulate, set of aspirations; and although it proved to be the weaker cause which he interpreted and expressed, it would be dangerous to admit success as the criterion of value.

Laud achieved power at a revolutionary crisis, the end of a long revolutionary development: and if it is the quality of revolutionary genius to gather up and express in ideal form and relentless activity the inarticulate social discontents of an age, Laud may at first seem entitled to such a name. That the successful progress of the Reformation movement in the sixteenth century had led to wide, if inarticulate, reaction against its incidental dislocation in England cannot be denied. The old social framework had been broken to allow the emergence of a new class. A great estate of the realm had been so despoiled of its economic resources that it had lost its social and political influence. The Crown had become impoverished after the dissipation of its initial windfall, and was left, without the support of an intermediary estate, face to face with the new power-holders whom it had first raised up to be its instrument, and who now, enriched with spoils and elated by expansion, had become an independent political force. And those who had been unable to keep pace with the new movement, or to profit by it, had found themselves its victims. Against all these changes a reaction had set in, and in all these spheres voices were raised calling for some new framework to replace the old. Bacon advocated a strong administrative law: Andrewes a restored Church and doctrine: James I, in his preposterous way, an absolute monarchy. Since the emphasis of the time was upon ecclesiastical forms, and since the new movement had assumed a religious colouring, its opponents naturally appealed to, and idealised, the doctrines and ecclesiastical

[1] H. A. L. Fisher, *History of Europe*, ii. 650.

organisation against whose abuses only the reformers had claimed to rebel. Spelman deplored the sin of sacrilege: Francis Trigge protested in the words of Isaiah against the dispossession of Church and poor alike by acquisitive landlords: the Ferrars revived before a suspicious world the image of monastic piety. Voices from the country protested also against the unearned fortunes picked up at Court. And the poor, since they had no other way of advertising their grievances, rose in isolated, hopeless revolt against their new yoke, breaking down enclosures and killing the foreign engineers who deprived them of their old perquisites.

All these separate protests were gathered up in a single policy by Laud, and coloured over by the accepted varnish of an appropriate religious doctrine. Therein lies his greatness: and the determination with which he devoted his life to the realisation of this impersonal policy proves him to have been no mere idealist. But if his policy has in it the authentic lineaments of genius, his failure shows conspicuously the prodigious limitations which snatch from him the title which he can almost claim. It is not only in his methods, where they are so obvious, that these limitations appear, — his impatience in seeking to undo a revolution of a hundred by a reaction of a dozen years, his neglect to build up a party in court or country by admitting the claims of his potential allies, his preference for immediate repression over the slow process of education. His errors were more fundamental than this. He misjudged the material upon which he had to work, and whatever his methods it is unlikely that he could have made his work a permanent success.

First, he misjudged his own strength. Faced by a resolute opposition, he proclaimed a policy of direct attack before he had instruments wherewith to carry it out, and found himself betrayed by the apathy of those whose battle he believed himself to be fighting, — the King, the Court, and the clergy. Conspicuous among the backsliders were the clergy. Clergymen, in all ages, have been much the same, — that is, they have been men. They were no more enthusiastic participants in the Laudian counter-Reformation than they had been in Henry VIII's Reformation: and the only difference between the much-puffed "Caroline divines" and the much-derided eighteenth-century Latitudinarians was Laud. Laud harried and badgered them, sent them orders and instructions, visited them through his Vicar-General, bullied them through Wentworth, tempted them with preferment, threatened them with the High Commission. But it was not for such a life that they had entered the ministry of Christ, but to follow the example of their predecessors, — to attach themselves as chaplains to lords or bishops, to agree with their patrons and be recommended at Court, to preach before the King such opinions as he was known to approve, and ultimately to buy from him a bishopric by sacrificing part of its revenues, to appease their neighbours by titbits in the way of leases, and then to settle down in comfort to make what they could out of the rest. It took more than a decade of activity in Lambeth to eradicate the profitable habits of generations in the remote safety of Worcester and Gloucester.

If Laud misjudged his allies, he was equally deceived by his enemies; for in seeking to restore the old social framework, he took no account of the new forces which it was to enclose. Continually harking back to the days of Arundel and Morton, he sought to reimpose the order of society which he thought to have discovered there, and made insufficient allowance for the vast commercial and industrial expansion which had intervened. He failed to realise that the apparent harmony of those days was partly due to the very laxity of the Catholic system, which allowed the improving classes to evade its restrictions without appeal to a rival creed: and now, when those classes had already broken through the old coercive toils, and were intoxicated with success, increased in numbers, and fortified by a new dynamic faith, he interpreted the several cries of their victims and drew them together in a slogan for a frontal attack upon what proved to be a greatly superior force. Whether a Catholic system is compatible with an expanding commercial society, except as a deposit in its interstices, is questionable. When the yoke was light and formal, as in Venice, it was not broken because it could be ignored. But Laud's yoke was not light or formal. The claims which he represented were indeed justifiable claims: and the fact that he recognised them, and represented them, and asserted them, must be allowed to his credit, — for it attests his social consciousness and penetration. But they were the claims of a defeated party, which could only secure recognition through representation and negotiation, perhaps by propaganda, but not by direct authority. By leading that party again on the same ground upon which it had already been defeated, Laud led it to another, and this time a final overthrow.

APPENDIX

LAUD'S CORRESPONDENCE WITH LORD SCUDAMORE

(Chancery Masters' Documents, Duchess of Norfolk's Deeds, C. 115, box M, bundle 24, nos. 7758-7776 [1])

THE following series of letters, written by Laud to Viscount (then Sir John) Scudamore between 1622 and 1628, originally formed part of the Scudamore papers at Holme Lacy, where they were used by the Rev. Matthew Gibson, rector of the neighbouring parish of Door, in the compilation of his *View of the Churches of Door, Holme Lacy, and Hempsted*, published in 1727. The direct line of Lord Scudamore's family, however, became extinct in 1820, on the death of Frances, Duchess of Norfolk: and in the dispersal of the family papers, these and many other documents passed into Chancery, where they have since remained, uncatalogued. They were thus unknown to Bliss when he compiled his complete edition of Laud's works, and Bliss seems to have been equally ignorant of Gibson's book, which provided the only clue to their existence. It has therefore been thought worth while to publish them here in full. Laud's later letters to Scudamore (except for one letter published in Bliss' edition) do not appear to have survived: but three later letters from Scudamore to Laud (all printed in Gibson) are preserved, one in Chancery (Duchess of Norfolk's Deeds, C. 115, box M, bundle 12), and two in the British Museum (Add. MS. 11044, pp. 91 ff.). The latter MS. also contains Scudamore's correspondence with Grotius.

(1)

SIR,

I cannot recall wherein the answering of your letters denied secretly, or otherwise, the purport. This I am sure, I shall ever be glad to hear of you, and most when you bring good news, since it is only good which I must desire ever may befall you.

I find the next passage of your letter all in physic: and I care not how deep that were in, so you were out. What hath forced your body to this observance of it in your youth by this time you have learned

[1] No. 7764 appears to be missing.

to know, that you may the better observe: or else, if yet unknown, it is palpably worse, *et aliquid quod Natura sinistra perperit*. But upon your liver you cast the fault, and there I think it is. I shall be glad, when I come into those parts, to find both it and you stronger.

Now for yourself. Nothing can better please me than to keep that which you call your ill wont. For next to yourself, your letters are most welcome; and you cannot bestow your love where it is like to find more that is like itself. All my fear is, that the great charges which these times have put me to in my beginnings will keep me so low that I shall have no liberty from good husbandry to attend myself and my friends; but such as I have is yours. I pray remember my love and service to your grandfather and your lady, — almost all the acquaintance I have in those parts. So I leave you and them to the grace of God, and shall ever rest,

your assured loving friend,

GUIL. MENEVEN.

Durham House,
Feb. 12, 1621[-2]

I have herein sent you a bill of the preachers as they are designed for this Lent before the King.

(2)

WORTHY SIR

I had yesterday weeping weather, — it was fit I should not always brag of the fair. I got well to Gloucester before six, and might have been there sooner but that I had a greater mischance by the way than in all my journey beside. In the dirty bottom between Mr. Bridges his house and Ross, the careless man that led my sumpter went upon the side of a slippery bank, and overthrew my horse into a great slough. My horse had spoiled himself, if I had not caused one to lie upon his neck and keep him down till his girths were undone. One end of my sumpter was full of dirt, and I rid after in jealousy for my papers, lest they had drunk such water; but I found them dry, and care not for the rest.

I am now going to see my Lady Porter [1] and remember all respects to her from you and your lady, and so again to horse in hope of better fortune than yesterday I had. I could not send Mr. Staple empty-handed to you, having so many things for which to give you thanks: and thanks that are due are a debt which can never be paid too soon.

[1] Anne, Lady Porter, wife of Sir Arthur Porter of Lanthony, and mother of Lady Scudamore.

I can now neither be on horseback nor on foot, but I must thank you for both.

I have hitherto met no news on the way which is not known to you : so I have nothing left but to thank you for all my kind entertainment, which I shall ever profess was as full of respect as ever I found it of any friend : and desire you to remember me with like thanks to my lady, at whose service I shall ever be. My other adversary I may not forget, of whom I never deserved anything, but found much kindness for your sake. You may tell her that after my travel I found it was the left side on which I was beat. If my lady had had no more mercy on me than she, I had been beat on both sides. But to prevent more blows, I do, as conquered men use, yield myself to her commands if she have any charge to lay upon me. Thus I began at yourself, and am become a debtor to the whole house : which, with yourself, I leave to the grace of God, and shall ever labour to be found,

your assured loving friend,

GUIL. MENEVEN.

Gloucester,
Aug. 22, 1622

I would have Perrocke take my baillie's letters with him as well as mine, because he must call at Carmarthen. They are in Mr. Maunsell's hands.

(3)

SIR,

I am glad to hear of your health, and that God hath blessed you with a son to inherit your name first and your fortunes after. Nor is that which yourself observe the least degree in this blessing, the securing of them whom your often and dangerous sickness had made fearful. Yet notwithstanding, I hope the Tottering Wall which you mention shall stand long and safe, as it well may if you lay not too much weight upon it. And I hope you will remember, for your friends' sake as well as your own, that a wall that totters is not strong enough to be made a study wall. To God's grace and your own best moderation I leave you, being desirous that you should know I am leaving London and going to my benefice, not to return till about Michaelmas. And about that time we begin to hope again to see the Prince's Highness well in England. God grant it, and then I shall the more contentedly rest,

your very loving friend,

GUIL. MENEVEN.

Durham House,
Aug. 2, 1623

(4)

Sir,

I am very glad to hear of your health, and no less that you have your desires that you may be present to see the experience and source of a parliament: which God bless with peace and success to the good of the King and the good of this Church and Kingdom, to which I doubt not but you will readily put your best endeavours. I shall be glad of any occasion to see you, though I doubt at this time the business will so hamp both you and me that there will be but little time for free meeting, though I see you often. I hope when you come, and before too, you will remember that the spring draws on, and what a sick beginning you had of the last parliament. The weather is now as cold at least, and therefore I hope you will take care to fence yourself better against it. I thank your brother, he came very kindly to me that very day he came to town, and by them that went back with the horses you should have received this answer, but that I had not then leisure to write, and have not much now.

I pray remember my service to your lady. So I leave you and yours to the grace of God, and shall ever rest,

your very loving friend,

Guil. Meneven.

Durham House,
January 4, 1623[-4]

(5)

Worthy Sir,

I see by your letter that you have had no great joy of yourself since you left London. I do not remember any act made the last session that enjoins you to break so much sleep as it seems you have lost. If you have done it by commission (as it seems you have), I do not find anything in your sitting by day that should keep you waking at night.

I am glad to hear you are so well in the midst of such employment: and all I desire is you may continue so. So, I mean, for health: but for the employment as you like it.

I hope your lady will do well, though the tooth-ache hath been so much to her loss. God bless your second son, and her second hopes of security: but yourself especially, who are the best security both to her and hers.

Your mother's business I can be but sorry to hear of, and I presume the honour of that Table will conceive aright of you and your cause. It is hard it should come to this, considering what you have offered : but the best of it is, she will put you to all at once, and then I hope you will be free hereafter. I profess, if I did not find you full of dutiful respects to your mother, I should be one of the first that should take liberty to chide you. But unreasonable demands I cannot skill of.

I shall be glad at any time to see you : yet it will not be pleasing that this occasion should bring you to London before November. I am for the country so soon as the King is gone progress, and shall not have any constant abiding till Michaelmas.

I pray remember my love and service to yourself and your lady. Book it not too much, and all other businesses will help do themselves. Here is nothing but speech of the French match : but God knows what issue these great affairs will have. This only I can assure you of, the Lord Saye is made a Viscount. I have no skill in writing news : therefore I leave you to the old assurance, the grace of God, and so rest.

your very loving friend,

July 10, 1624 GUIL. MENEVEN.

(6)

SIR,

Your last letters I received on Saturday, but too late to send any answer by that day's carrier. Mr. Wellington, who brought them, fell ill by the way, which stayed them the longer. Other delay there was none, for he came to me with them before he went to his chamber.

When I read your letters I was very heartily sorry, and so am, to think of the heaviness which this late sad accident hath brought both upon yourself and your lady.[1] For yourself yet you do well to remember, and shall do better to practise, that which yourself expressed in your letters. And for my part, as I must ever wish and pray for my friends, that in cases of like nature their sorrow may be moderate, so did I never think that Christianity did teach any man to be senseless of such punishments when they come, or altogether fearless of their stroke, or in any degree careless of their prevention while it is possible. This I know, that the way to find out God's blessing in these punishments is patience ; but yet these greater and louder callings of God upon us do not put off the nature of punishment because they may contain some degree of mercy. I hope as you have been a remembrancer to yourself of David's case, so you will be mindful of his temper and of his prudence, and leave God to his mercy and his providence in that which is behind.

[1] The death of their infant son James, born 1623, died 1624. Twins born in 1621 had also both died.

For your lady, it does much trouble me to read the passion she has been in: and the best comfort that can be given her, under God, must come from yourself. And that, as it need not, so it cannot be prescribed unto you, but must be taken hold of as occasions present and offer themselves. Two things only I could wish were fitly represented unto your lady. The one is, that God did not take a son from her till he had given her another;[1] and the other, that if she give way to her sorrow to have a few more such fits as you describe caused by it, she may either make her end sudden or her life miserable. You see how far the sense of these things in my friends hath wrought upon me: and therefore, if I have preached to you in a letter, I hope you will remember 'tis my profession, and give me leave a little to express myself.

Now for the business. I sent presently to Sir William Paddy according as you directed, and his answer was that he had made all things ready, and that his apothecary had sent them away a week before: so that my hope is they were safely in your hand before your letters came to mine. I pray remember my love and service to your lady; and so, heartily wishing that I may hear a good settling of these sad and troublesome thoughts, I leave you to the grace of God, and shall ever rest,

your very loving friend,

Durham House, GUIL. MENEVEN.
November 19, 1624

(7)

SIR,

I am in your debt for two letters, but I did not answer that of last week partly for want of leisure and partly because I thought my late letters would by this draw another from you.

Your former letter is full of your devotion, for which, as I thank you, so I doubt not but you will be mindful to thank God. It will one day bring you more contentment than those things which to other men seem far more precious. That devotion makes you very bountiful to God, who, I make no question, will be as liberal to you and yours. The plate, therefore, which you desire should be made ready for the communion table in your parish church, I did presently bespeak upon the first of your letters, and I hope to have them ready to send to you

[1] James, Scudamore's fourth and eldest surviving son, was baptized on July 4th, 1624. He was educated at St. John's College, Oxford, no doubt on account of his father's connexion with Laud, and died before his father in 1668.

the next week, if the workman keep promise. But I shall restrain your purpose in part, and not make your flagons so large as you desire, the reason whereof I shall express when I send the plate. In the meantime I must desire you to think I will dispose of this business to the best so far as my judgment serves.

By your second letter I perceive you have read the book I sent you, and shall ever thank you for such love as you have ever showed me. But I see already in what page you have fixed an obstruction. I doubt it hath angered some, but I cannot help that and the cause too. But the cause I shall ever love, and their anger I hope I shall never fear.

I have received from your brother Mr. Barnaby Scudamore [1] an epistle. He took the pains to come see me at Westminster, and brought it with him. You may see his suit by the latter end. To Oxford he would fain go ; and if I did not misconceive him, he hoped that is your purpose, which he desires me to help forward. And surely if this epistle be all his own doing, you shall do well to send him, and the rather because he is grown tall and so less fit for schooling. This epistle I have sent you here enclosed. He thinks you have a purpose to send him to Magdalen College, and, if you be so resolved, I have nothing to say to that. Otherwise, I think Mr. Staple would be able to name you an honest and a careful tutor elsewhere.

Sir : to prevent your desires as much as I can, I have sent you word we are in a busy parliament, and yet we have sat six weeks and I cannot give you any account what we have done. But I am sorry to hear from you that your mother will come to no peace, and more than sorry that you should hear from me that our honourable friend the Duke is still followed in Parliament. There is nothing yet come to any issue. When it is, I shall impart so much as is fit my paper should know. In the meantime you shall do well to afford us your daily prayers : in which service I will owe you nothing. To God's grace I leave these great affairs and you, and so long as God gives life shall rest,

your very loving poor friend,

GUIL. MENEVEN.

March 18, [1625–6] [2]

I pray remember my service to your lady. I am much bound to you both that you would press me no further in Mr. Freemantle's suit. Since that time I hear the party is a most unworthy man, and that Freemantle cannot be ignorant of it.

[1] Later Sir Barnabas Scudamore, knighted for his defence of the royalist cause in Herefordshire.

[2] The date given in the MS. is March 18th, 1618 : but as Laud signs himself as Bishop of St. David's, and as there was no parliament sitting in 1618

(8)

SIR,

In haste. I was promised your plate ready yesterday, and the goldsmith hath kept word with me. When he brought them, I was not to them. If I had, I should not have received them, for they are exceedingly ill wrought. And though they were received in my absence, yet as they are I will never send them to you. These are therefore to let you know that I will this day return them to the goldsmith, and if the faults can be mended, you shall have them sent by the next carrier. If not, there is no remedy but you must stay till after Easter. The directions which I promised to send together with the plate must yet stay till it be sent. The price, at vi shillings per the oz., which is the lowest rate I can get, makes your plate rise to forty and seven pounds odd shillings, which money I will lay out: but I must desire you that it may be returned by some means or other at the beginning of Easter term, because I shall then be to pay in both tenths and subsidies to the King.

For the public business, we are yet no forwarder in Parliament than we were when we first sat down: and for my part I hold you a very happy man that you be not at this time a member of the House. I doubt much, if things go on a fortnight longer in the course they are now in, that all will be stark naught. So bad indeed that it is not fit for me to write what I think. Concerning my Lord Duke, I can write no otherwise than I did the last week: for the same spirit moves still, and with greater violence. We that are here in the tempest have need of your prayers, which I pray afford us. So I leave you to the grace of God, and shall ever rest,

your very loving friend,

GUIL. MENEVEN.

Westminster,

March 25, 1626

I pray remember my love and service to your lady.

this is plainly an error, presumably caused by dittography. The following letter, as well as the political references in this, prove that the correct date is as given above, when the second parliament of Charles I (of which Scudamore was not a member) had been in session for six weeks. By quoting the date, without giving the contexts which prove it to be wrong, Gibson gives the impression that Scudamore became acquainted with Laud before the latter had secured the favour of Buckingham or a bishopric: and it is presumably by following Gibson that H. G. Bull, in an otherwise excellent article in Hogg's *Herefordshire Pomona*, 1884, says that Scudamore came into contact with Laud at Oxford, and was intimate with him when he was President of St. John's.

(9)

Sir,

I am very glad to hear of your health, and that your lady is returned so well from the Bath : yet since I find by your letters that she is not perfectly recovered of all infirmities, I must continue in the judgment I was, which is that she must wash out the dreg of those passionate and sad thoughts which were the first cause of her indisposition, or the Bath without will do but little good. And so, I pray, remember my service to her.

For the bishopric of Bath, it rests in the King's thoughts as private as it did. But when I shall know what shall be done with it, you shall hear from myself with the soonest. And for your question, when you shall see me again at Holme Lacy if I leave Wales, it is not very hard to be answered out of your own letter. For you write that Wells is within a day's journey ; and if it be, then I hope you will keep your promise to come and see me, and it is not impossible but that I may find a starting time to see you and Holme Lacy. And though I shall not wish that any sickness may bring your lady to Bath, yet if that or any other good occasion make you step farther to Wells, I shall be glad to see you both there, if I get the place. If not, then you shall not need to think of moving from Holme Lacy, but as I pass by to St. David's you shall be sure to be troubled with me.

For your brother Mr. Barnaby, I should have been willing to have done the best I could for the disposing of him at Oxford, if I had not found that his resolutions were otherwise settled for Magdalen College : and I am still of opinion, considering that profiting in learning doth not depend upon the place, that it will not be ever fit to wrestle too much with his desires concerning it. I am sorry the occasion of your sister's sickness hath kept him from you (though I perceive he sent my letters before him), but when he comes I doubt not but you will find his inclination settled as I have told you.

For Parliament business, we are in as hot skirmishes as ever we were, and for my part I cannot look for any good end. The Earl of Arundel is come to the House, and so the question about privilege is ceased. The Duke put in his answer upon Thursday last, and in my judgment a very sufficient one. But the House of Commons have reserved a power to themselves to reply upon it. So when we shall have done, God knows. The Earl of Bristol is upon his charge, so upon Thursday last made a large speech to us (having entreated leave) at the Bar. It was such as showed great abilities in his person, but I doubt that first or last it cannot but do him harm. The reason why

I think so is not fit for letters. On Friday last the King sent a message to the House of Commons and a copy of the same letter to us. The scope is to hasten their answer for the subsidy and pass the bill in that House at last by the end of the next week, else he shall take all further delays for denial, and that this shall be the last message he will send them. What this will effect we shall soon see : but I for my part look for no good issue unless God show us more mercy than we or our courses merit. So, full of all troubles and troubled thoughts together, I leave you to God's grace and more contentment, and shall so rest,

your very loving friend,

GUIL. MENEVEN.

Saturday, June 10, 1626

(10)

SIR,

I made account to have been at Wells by this time : but that will not be, and I am so far from keeping my intended time that I am commanded by His Majesty to attend the whole progress, which will be very tedious, and how I shall be able to bear it, God knows : but, well or ill, it must be borne.

I should not have troubled you with letting you know thus much, but that peradventure you might have been to seek me, at the least by your letters, before Michaelmas Day, where I had not been to be found.

One particular only may be of consequence, if it come not too late. I remember Mr. Staple told me a desire he had to fall to the profession of the Civil and Canon Laws, and that he thought you would be willing to help him forward in that way. If he think of that course, I thought fit to signify to you that the Chancellor of Gloucester, Mr. Sutton, hath been shrewdly put to it at the High Commission, and it is thought he will not abide many more shocks. If Mr. Staple could get it, it would be a very good place for him, and near enough to you (unless you have hope of a nearest). If he meddle with it, I would wish him to provide himself this vacation that he may take his degree at the very beginning of Michaelmas Term, before the term begins at London. I pray let him know how I have troubled your Lordship thus much, partly because I have not leisure to write two letters, and partly that I might have some stuffing for this one.

I know not of any further business that I have with you, and I look not now to hear from you till Michaelmas ; till which time I shall return to my old courses and be a wanderer. I hope both you and your lady are in health, which I pray God continue. And so with my remembrance to you both, I wish you all happiness, and leaving you to the grace of God shall ever rest,

your very loving friend,

GUIL. BATHON. ET WELLEN.

Westminster,
July 14, 1626

(11)

SIR,

When your Lordship came to me, I was not in London. I had broken loose for some eight or ten days to take a country breath. If I had been in London, you should have had an answer sooner; but this, I hope, will be time enough, since your letters had nothing in them that required speedy answer, and I have as little worth the writing to fill mine.

Since I writ last, your sister Mrs. Meek was with me. Her business was to desire me to move my Lord of Buckingham to write his letters in her husband's behalf for a place then void about the Inner Temple. I was very loth to come to a business of this nature: yet, by her importunity and fear of her husband's going into Ireland for want of means, I was moved in pity to do against my judgment. But the place was suddenly gone, and both I and they prevented. If she and the friend that came with her had let me go my own way, I think I had come nearer the matter, if not obtained; but they would needs drive me their way, which went against my mind and their good. Afterwards I was importuned again to move my Lord to help him to a place about the Queen, upon the remove of the French:[1] but that was a business too big for me, and I durst not meddle. And I doubt they take it unkindly.

I have here at last sent you the landmark which you mention, by which you may know the old English Bible commonly called the Bishops' Bible from any other. I had purposed, as you may see by the spaces left, to have drawn more out of the body of the translation itself; but I have no leisure: and the last of these, touching the Epistles and the Gospels, would be sufficient alone.

I pray remember my love and service to your lady. I hope, as long as I hear nothing to the contrary, she hath recovered and retains confirmed health: which I heartily wish may continue to you both, with

[1] The Queen's French attendants were expelled at the beginning of August 1626.

all other blessings which may make you happy in this life and prepare you for a better. To God's grace I leave you, and shall ever rest,

your very loving friend,

Westminster, GUIL. BATHON. ET WELLEN.
August 26, 1626

I pray thank Mr. Staple for his letters.

(12)

SIR,

Your last letters told me that yourself and your lady were going towards Cornbury that very day. That made me delay answering your letter that week, and since that I have had little or no leisure. I hope by this time you have visited all friends you intended abroad, and are returning well and safe to your own home, which I shall be glad to hear. And I hope further that this journey and stirring in fresh air hath brought home your lady in better health than she went forth, and falsified all those prognostications which seemed to threaten relapse into her former indispositions. I am still of the same mind I was, that her own sadness and thoughts is the greatest cause of her bodily infirmity, and that one winter well mastered would do her more good than her physic.

For the landmarks (as you are pleased to call them), I have now found an opportunity to make them somewhat perfect upon an accident of meeting another book, and have here enclosed sent you a copy : so that now you may do what you please with the former. This is as perfect as I can make it.

I am sorry to hear that they of whom you have had so much care have made you such ill return ; but as I know little of that, so I dealt truly with you in relating what moved me to adventure that little which I did against my judgment. Since that time I have heard no more of them, which I am very glad of.

And now whereas you write that you are glad to see the same hand and a new name, I must thank you for it : [1] and I had no reason but at this time to do as I did, and fasten upon any indifferent thing to

[1] Gibson, quoting this sentence, deduces that it was through Scudamore's influence that Laud had been promoted to Bath and Wells. But if this were so, Laud would not have delayed his thanks till the third (at least) letter since his translation, nor would he expatiate, as he does here, on the unexpected disadvantages of the promotion. Laud had no need of an intermediary between himself and Buckingham, — the last letter shows that Scudamore's sister regarded him as more influential with the Duke than her brother. Plainly Laud is merely thanking Scudamore for his congratulations.

get out of Wales. But now, as God hath disposed of businesses, it is likely to prove my hindrance. For being so lately preferred, I know not how in modesty to be a present suitor again. But upon Monday morning last my lord the Bishop of Winchester [1] died, *et magnum illud Christiani orbis lumen exstinctum est*. This is likely to cause a great remove, and who shall succeed there, God knows. But that I shall not I know; — and believe it, for I write this seriously and, *rebus sic stantibus*, as you shall find it in the issue : I am at my wonted word and resolution, and let all things else waver and tumble as they will. One thing there is which I have many times feared, and do still, and yet I doubt it will fall upon me. I cannot trust my letters with it : but if it come, I will take my solemn leave of all contentment. But yet in that way or any other state I shall ever rest,

your very loving friend,

Westminster, GUIL. BATHON. ET WELLEN.

September ult, 1626

(13)

SIR,

I have read your letters of January 1st, and they were so full of kindness that I think you intended them for a new year's gift. I thank you heartily for them and your love, and had intended to send you this letter of thanks for your often and loving remembrances of me, though I had had no other occasion. But yesterday, January 12th, Mr. Staple came to me, and brought me a letter from you which requires more time to answer,[2] and finds me (as I am for the most part) with more business than time [less] to do it in. Notwithstanding, I will, God willing, dismiss him towards you by the end of this week that is coming in, with your business as well settled as I can. Yet I thought good to hold my former resolution and send you these letters before, that you may know that, though the weather and the ways be dangerous, yet Mr. Staple and your letters are safe come to me.

I heartily wish to yourself and your lady (to whom I pray let me be remembered) a very happy new year of this which is begun, and many like it. And I hope, now many of your careful businesses are settled, the rest of your life will be successful. So, wishing you all happiness, I leave you to the grace of God, and shall ever rest,

your very loving friend,

Westminster, GUIL. BATHON. ET WELLEN.

January 13, 1626[–7]

I have sent you a bill of these Lent services.

[1] Lancelot Andrewes. [2] This answer is given in the next letter.

(14)[1]

Worthy Sir,

I am full of Ash Wednesday and your business which waits upon it, for that your letters could not have taken me fuller of thoughts, or less able to entend your business, than I am at this present. I would not but you should attend the service of His Majesty in the loan,[2] and nourish that good opinion he hath of you. And for your chapman, you have no reason to make him jealous by a journey (as he may think) to survey the market. Sure I am, use, that eats all men, will not spare you if you keep between the teeth of it, which have ever been found to be grinders, and you do well to think betimes how to slip from them. The manner, you say, must be by sale of land: and your desire to part with some land hath thrust you into a scruple of conscience. For direction in this you call to me, so far as it is a matter of conscience. And though you know I trust not letters with anything of moment, yet, considering your occasions, I will dispense with my resolution, trust your messenger with my letters, and yourself with their contents.

If you find not all so clearly expressed as you desire, you must attribute it partly to the knots which are in the business, and partly to the little time I have to clear them. I am sorry so much of your estate is in impropriations, for it seems the sale you intend will not wholly quit your state of them. And your ancestors should have done well to have bought other land, though they had paid dearer for it. But this is now remediless, and 'tis a remedy which you look after, — indeed many remedies in one: a remedy against your debt: a remedy against use: a remedy against impropriations themselves, if they may be sold to remedy your state. To the business then.

1. Your first *quaere* is, whether the retaining of impropriations to your own use, being sold to your ancestors by King Henry VIII, with reservation of annual rent to his heirs and successors, be in you a sin.

To this: you know that all impropriations (except a little glebe) consist of tithes. So your doubt will be wholly upon this question, whether tithes be due to the priest, and him only, *jure divino*, by divine law, or by ecclesiastical constitution only. Neither my time nor my leisure will give me leave to dispute this question. But thus lies your doubt upon it. If tithes be due by divine law, and that law of God be indispensable by either Church or State (as, if it be moral law, it is), then, impropriations being tithes, no doubt can be made but you sin the sin of sacrilege by retaining them to your own use.

[1] A considerable part of this letter is either transcribed or paraphrased by Gibson.

[2] *i.e.* the forced loan, whose exaction Laud had supported (*vide sup.* p. 79).

Yea, but your ancestors bought them. True. But it was of him that had no right to sell, and they had as little to buy. For if one man will be so daring as to sell God's altar, yet his daring is no warrant for him to sell, or another to buy it.

Yea, but Henry VIII reserved an annual rent to his heirs (which is still paid). Be it so. Yet still if tithes be due by the moral law of God, he did but sell one part of the sin and reserve the other. Loth he was, it seems, to part with it all: and fain he would his heirs should inherit some little of it. The less the better. And I cannot but pray, for his successor's sake, that no canker be in that little. Yet you see his name is gone.[1]

Yea, but it was made lay-fee by an Act of Parliament. Well: if any man think an Act of Parliament is an absolution from sin against the moral law of God, he is much out of the way, and it will be a poor plea at another bar.

Yea, but the Pope and the Church of Rome had impropriated tithes to abbeys and monasteries and churches and colleges from the priest that served, before Henry VIII took them and sold them. 'Tis true. And let the Church of Rome answer that sin. Their fault cannot excuse another. And yet their sin was this much the less, because the tithes went to that which they then thought was the true service of God. But Henry VIII put them into lay hands and lay use. And what use most laymen put them to, I forbear to speak.

So I think this is clear: if tithes be due *jure divino morali*, which is the opinion of many great divines, you cannot hold impropriations to your own use without sin.

If tithes be due to the priest only by judicial or ceremonial law, as some are of opinion, at least for the quota, — *i.e.* the precise tenth part — yet if they hold that less than the tenth part (as the eleventh or twelfth part, etc.) may not be paid, the matter will be much about one. For if the divine moral law have not defined the quota at the tenth just, yet if it have settled that nothing under the tenth is sufficient, then it leaveth a liberty for any to give more, but warrants none to give less, or diminish that, or hold it when it is diminished.

If tithes be due only by ecclesiastical and civil laws, or either of them, then the Church and the State may alter the law upon just and good grounds. And that law once altered (as it was here upon the lay side, but whether the Church consented, or how far, I cannot tell), it may then be thought lawful for men to hold such tithes and impropriations as they have, buy more, or sell them, or do what they will upon a fair commerce.

[1] Henry, Prince of Wales, who would have succeeded as Henry IX, having died in 1612.

So, for your first doubt, a great part of it will lie upon your own conscience. For if in your conscience you be persuaded that tithes be due to the priest for his service by an indispensable moral law of God, you cannot hold them to your own use, nor sell them to another, without sin, and that sin against your conscience.

But if your conscience be persuaded that tithes are due only by Church or State law, then you are either truly or erroneously so persuaded. If truly, then, the Church and the State having first by another law expressed themselves (as here the State did, and involved the Church, but with what consent of hers I know not), then, supposing the Church's lawful consent, you may safely either keep or sell: and both without sin, because according to such law as is not sinful: and without any contradiction in your own conscience. If you be erroneously so persuaded, then you should not keep, nor sell: because you should have a better guide than an erring conscience.

Yet this you gain by the persuasion (if it be a persuasion indeed, and not assumed), that though you sin by following an erring conscience, yet you sin not against your conscience, and so commit no wilful sin, whether you keep impropriations or sell them. Now what you are persuaded in conscience concerning the right which the priesthood have to the tithe, that you must ask yourself and not me.

2. Your second *quaere*, whether the selling these impropriations free you from sin, though the money received from them be otherwise employed than upon the Church?

To this there is answer enough given in the former: for it rests upon the same foundation altogether. For if tithes be due by divine right, that is indispensable, then, as you have no right to hold them, so have you none to sell them and bestow the money upon other uses than the Church; nor can the sale free you from sin, because you sell that which by divine law is God's, not yours.

And the reason you give, that perhaps you may sell, though you cannot keep, because your ancestors bought them, is of no force. For you know, 'tis *caveat emptor*: 'tis the buyer that should consider what he buys, and of whom. And if they bought what they should not, you sell from the Church what they should not. And your conscience in this, as in the former, must be a great part of your own direction, though I cannot say it is fit you should follow it alone.

How you stand persuaded in conscience for the right of tithe, I know not. How I myself stand, I can easily tell, and upon what grounds too, had I time. But my opinion is not binding upon you. This then for the present necessity (of which I heartily wish you free) I wish you should consider.

First, since the lands were bought, and your state will not abide the giving of them back to their proper use, whether it were not better they were sold than kept, since you have a necessity to sell.

Secondly, when you have sold, and employed the money to the uses specified, which at this time lie both heavy and necessary upon you, whether you may not in time (God blessing you) by this sale better enable yourself to restore them, or some other as good as them, to the Church and service of God. If so, then they were better sold with a purpose (as God shall enable you) to restore all or some hereafter, that you should sell other land and leave your heir to inherit almost nothing but the sin of them.

If you were with me, I could say no more than this: Were your case mine, if I could not give my impropriations back, I would beg God's mercy and sell them, that I might be able to give. And when God had taken off my difficulty, and made me able, I would as readily give. And if I could not give all, yet some I would, and charge it upon my heir at my death to give either the rest, or such a proportion as I thought fit: and then bind him to charge his heir for the remainder, that your posterity may restore that to the Church which your ancestors consented to buy and take from it.

I pray fear not my exposing your conscientiousness to any man, — God bless you in the tenderness of it, and I hope He will. Your letters I have committed already to the safe custody of the fire, and sent you back your messenger in the same ignorance he came. And for this, if in any particular I fall short of your expectation, if you cannot lay it upon the shortness of the time, spare not to lay it upon my weakness, so withal you deny me not your prayers for increase of God's strength in me. In great haste I leave you to the grace of God, and rest,

your very loving friend,

GUIL. BATHON. ET WELLEN.

Westminster,
January 18, 1626 comp. Angl. [*i.e.* 1626–7]

(15)

SIR,

I have not yet seen your servant, but your letters I found ready for me at my house upon Tuesday last when I came from Court. I was very glad to see them, as having not now in a good space heard from you: but I was more glad a great deal to read them, since they went so cross to all those base and unworthy rumours which some idle people have taken up and spread.

I am very glad likewise to hear of your health, and heartily wish your lady enjoyed hers so well that she needed no help of my diocese the Bath. But since, as you write, she both needed and is gone, I wish unto her all the health and the happiness which may bless you both with contentment.

My Lord the Duke of Buckingham is not yet gone,[1] and I am glad you have helped to furnish him with horses; and I pray God heartily to bless him in the journey. You know I was never wont to trouble you with many news, and I presume you will now look for less from me, if less may be; and that, since I have no greater to lay upon you, will be a part of punishment for your uncharitable wish of my serving three apprenticeships in the troubles in which I am.

I must needs acknowledge I do desire a little to speak with you, as well as you seem to desire much to speak to me. The story of A. B. hath lost me in my own thoughts. And as I wondered to hear nothing of it out of Worcestershire (where I looked for information long since), so I wonder more to hear such an information from you, who I thought in that kind would not probably be acquainted with it. But I see rumours in all kinds fly, and thought (as I said) I could be contented to speak with you and know the reason how that Worcestershire report came to you with so great a change. Yet I am not in such haste but that I can stay till God send an opportunity for me to see you. In the meantime I have done with your letter as you desired; and with remembrance of my love to you, and my desire of all such happiness to you as you wish to yourself, I leave you to the grace of God, and shall ever rest,

your very loving friend,

Westminster, GUIL. BATHON. ET WELLEN.

May 24, 1627

(16)

SIR,

I am glad of any opportunity to hear from you, and your health is welcome to Court. Any occasion that gave me cause to hear from you must needs be welcome, though I confess nothing was at this time less expected.

The business you referred to, the bearer related: and by him I see how much he is bound to you, which I presume he will ever return with thanks and all fair carriage towards you. I refer you to him for my answer, both because there are some things which I would not write, and for that he hastes his return. Only I think your sum demanded is too dear, and I think he would have asked less, and made

[1] On the expedition to the Isle of Rhé.

more haste to part with it than he doth, if the great accident above had not happened.

I am called upon for haste that he may go part of his way tonight: and I shall not trouble him to carry, nor you to read, more lines than these few, which may tell you that I am in good health, though I have had much ado with a tedious journey, and there's worse behind. I wish you all happiness, and desire to be remembered to your lady, who, I hope, hath recovered good health at the Bath. In this bearer's haste I leave you to the grace of God, and shall ever rest,

your very loving poor friend,

GUIL. BATHON. ET WELLEN.

July 27, 1627

We have yet no certain news in court from my Lord Duke, but only that he is before the Isle of Rhé by Rochelle. I pray God bless him, and send him back with honour.

(17)

SIR,

May these find you in health and happiness. It seems you have had some great frights in the country, and I hope more than Milford itself. I heard no news of it before your letters came, but only once: and then no more than that some enemies had landed and burnt a little village I hope the hurt is not so much, though the fear was more.

His Majesty is not yet gone to Portsmouth, but goes on Monday or Wednesday at furthest, for aught yet appears. And the Lord Weston on Tuesday last was made Lord Treasurer, and the old Lord Treasurer President of the Council, and the old Lord President was Lord Privy Seal before. These things I presume you know, for I use not to write any news. The same day (being St. Swithin, and a fair day with us) I was translated to London: so you see it was a day of change both for clergy and lay. God make it happy: for I expect nothing but trouble and danger.

Other things are as your Lordship left them, save that I see all things made uncertain by the necessities of the time. How I shall comply with that, having always gone upon constant ways, I cannot tell. I pray remember my service to your lady, and, that done, in full wishes for your Lordship's happiness, I leave you and yours to the grace of God, and shall ever rest,

your very loving friend,

Westminster, GUIL. LONDON.

July 19, 1628

(18) [1]

Sir,

I received by your last letter the saddest news that ever I heard in my life.[2] Yet I must and do heartily thank you for writing so lovingly to me. For if you had not written as you did, I had been left to the wildness of the many reports which spread about the city. And I knew that your pen writ those letters from a heart full of sorrow for that great loss, and in special for the barbarous and damnable manner of it. I purpose not to write these either to declaim in his commendations, which so few would believe, or to express my grief, which as few would pity: but only to let Your Lordship know that though I have passed a great deal of heaviness, yet I have cause to expect more to come. And the benefit of this will be, that I shall for ever less esteem what the malice of the world can lay upon me. Under which, if any fall (as much is threatened), I thank you heartily for your second letter, that you will appear, what I have ever hoped, a friend in the time when friends fall off. And I hope you think I shall in my way be ready ever to serve your Lordship.

I crave pardon from you that I answered not your letters sooner. For to the first I was able to give no answer, my grief had so oppressed me: and the second, by Mr. Brown's absence out of town, came not to my hands till the carrier was gone. I was not with His Majesty since this execrable fact was committed till now he came to Windsor, but stayed in London to give the best comfort I could to the Lady Duchess, who, good lady, hath been in great extremity. Now the Court seems new to me, and I mean to turn over a new leaf in it for all those things that are changeable. For the rest, I must be the same I was, and patiently both expect and abide what God shall be pleased to lay upon me. To Whose gracious providence I leave you and myself, and shall ever rest,

your Lordship's very loving friend and servant,

Guil. London.

Windsor,
September 12, 1628

I pray remember my service to your lady.

[1] This letter is transcribed by Gibson.

[2] The Duke of Buckingham was assassinated on August 23rd, 1628.

INDEX

PRINTED IN GREAT BRITAIN
BY LOWE AND BRYDONE (PRINTERS) LIMITED, LONDON